INSIDERS' GUIDE®

INSIDERS' GUIDE® SERIES

INSIDERS' GUIDE®

NORTH CAROLINA'S CENTRAL COAST AND NEW BERN

FIFTEENTH EDITION

VINA HUTCHINSON FARMER AND TABBIE NANCE

Published and Marketed by:
By The Sea Publications, Inc.
P.O. Box 4368
Wilmington, NC 28406

Insiders' Guide®
Is an imprint of
The Globe Pequot Press

Fifteenth Edition
1st Printing

Printed in the United States
of America.

Publications from The Insiders' Guide® series are available at special discounts for bulk purchases for sales promotions, premiums or fundraisings. Special editions, including personalized covers, can be created in large quantities for special needs. For more Information, please write to:

By The Sea Publications
P.O. Box 4368
Wilmington, NC 28406
Or call (910) 763-8464

Cover Photo: Scott Taylor

“Sunrise Shrimper” by Bill Meserve
2006 Photo Competition Winner

Table of Contents

Thank you **to our Advertisers...**

...for another great year on the Crystal Coast!

NORTH CAROLINA'S CENTRAL COAST

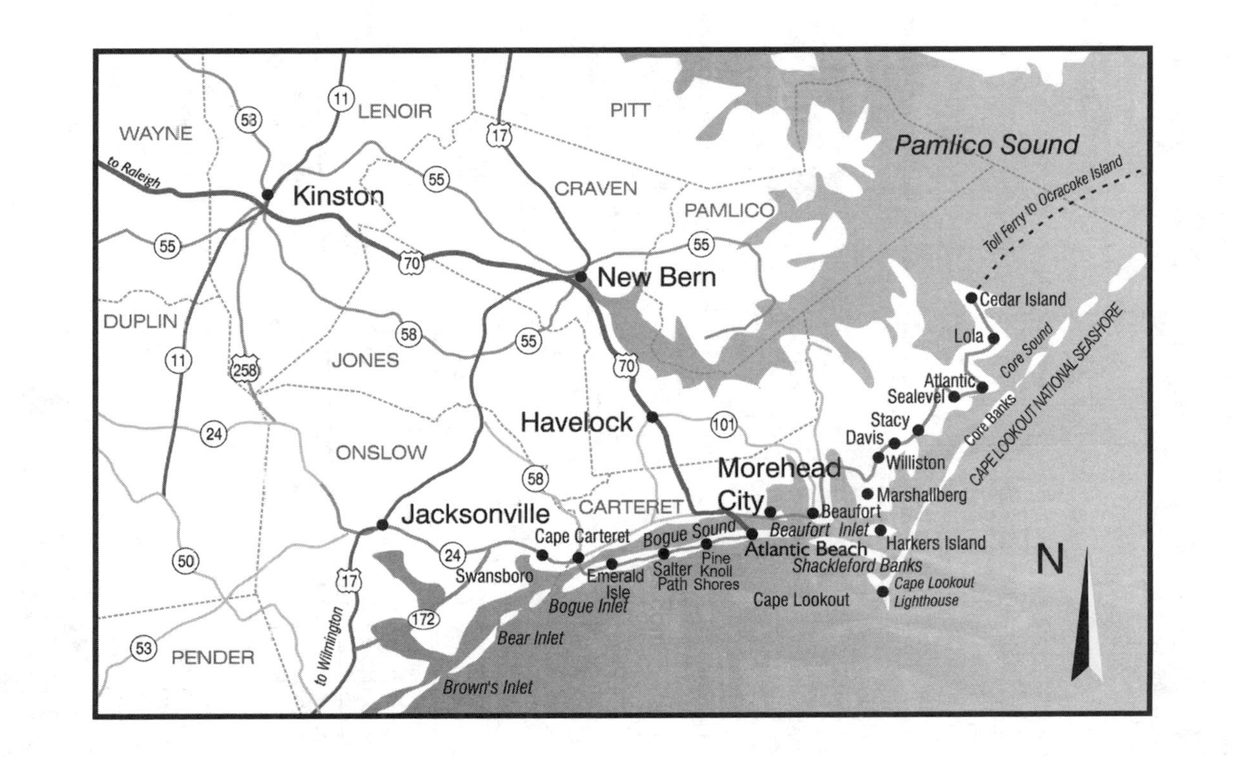

MOREHEAD CITY

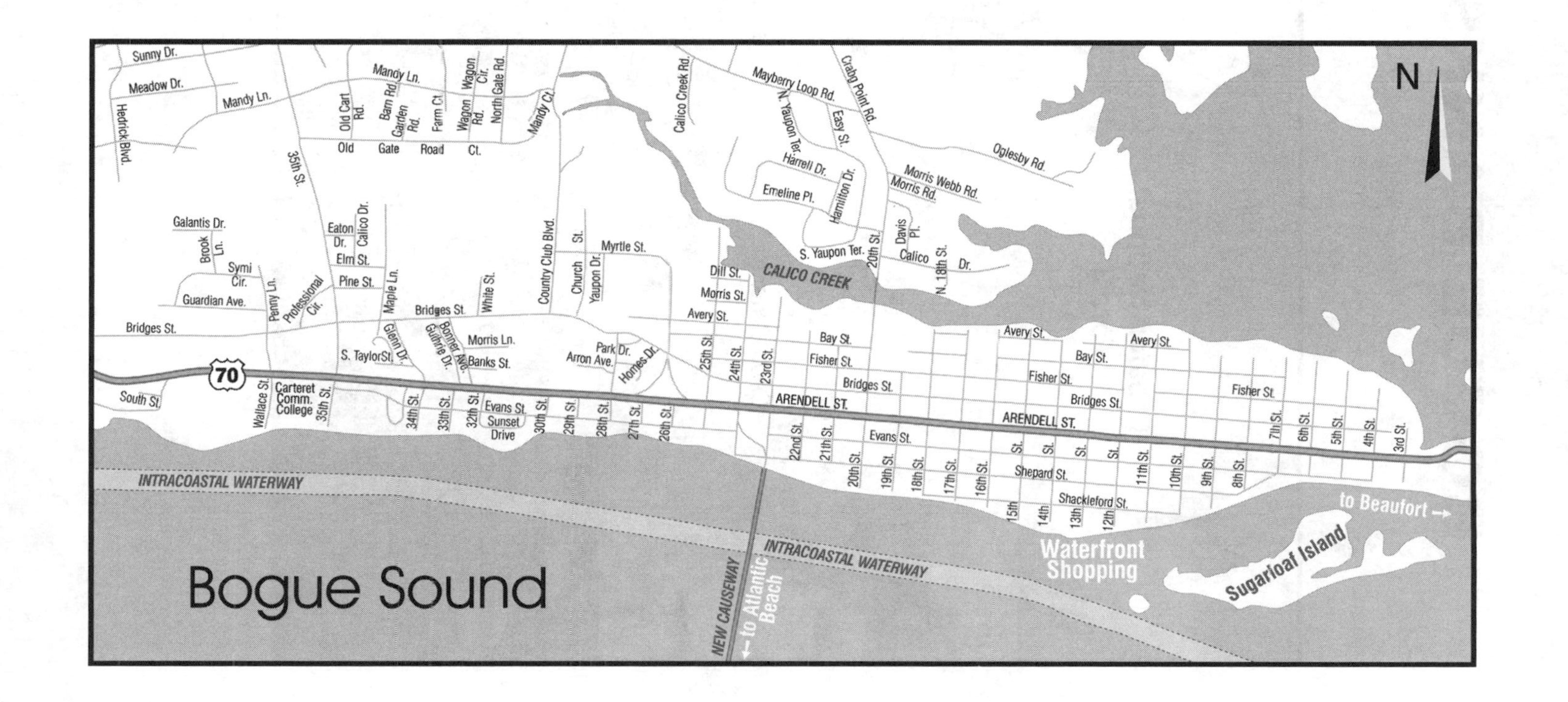

BOGUE BANKS

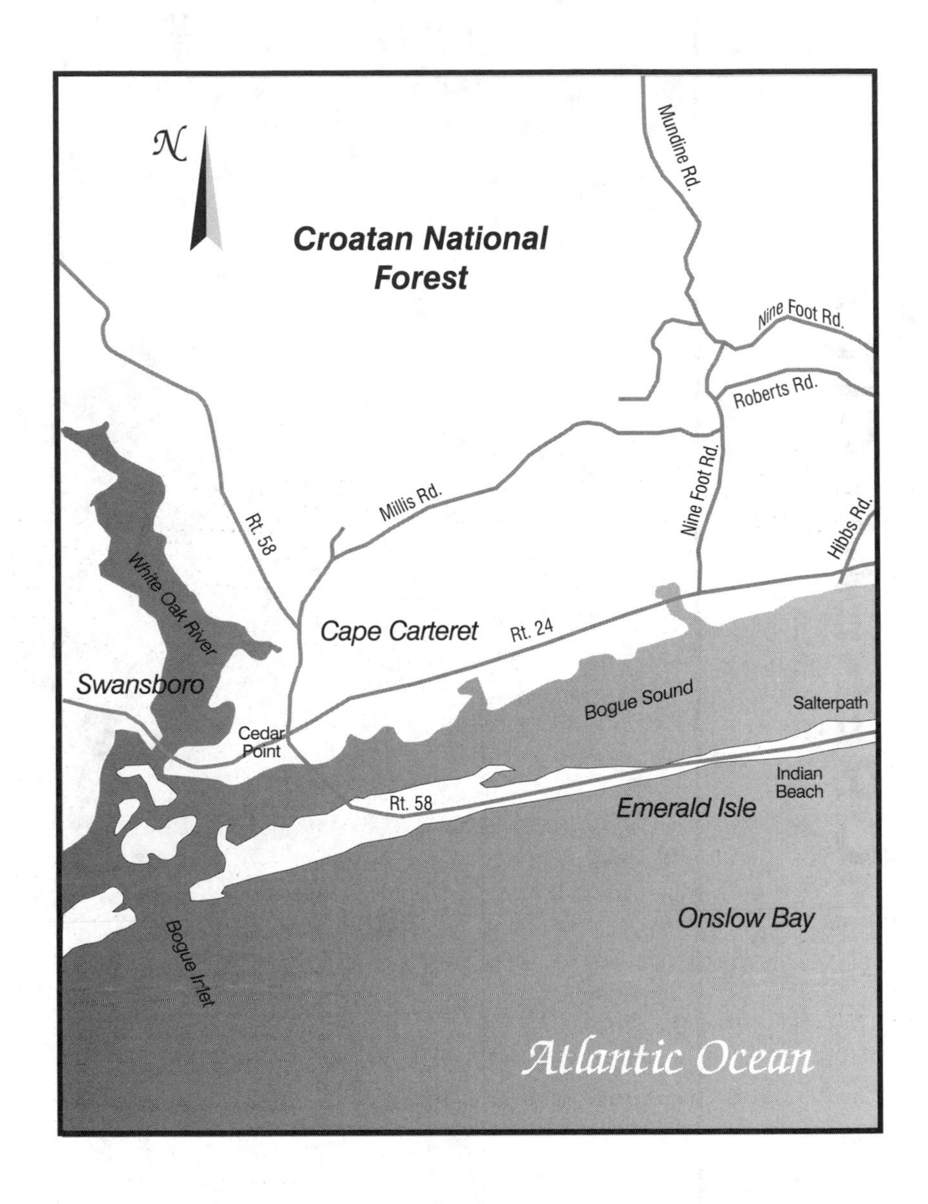
N
Croatan National Forest
Mundine Rd.
Nine Foot Rd.
Roberts Rd.
Nine Foot Rd.
Millis Rd.
Rt. 58
Hibbs Rd.
White Oak River
Cape Carteret
Rt. 24
Swansboro
Cedar Point
Bogue Sound
Salterpath
Indian Beach
Rt. 58
Emerald Isle
Onslow Bay
Bogue Inlet
Atlantic Ocean

BOGUE BANKS

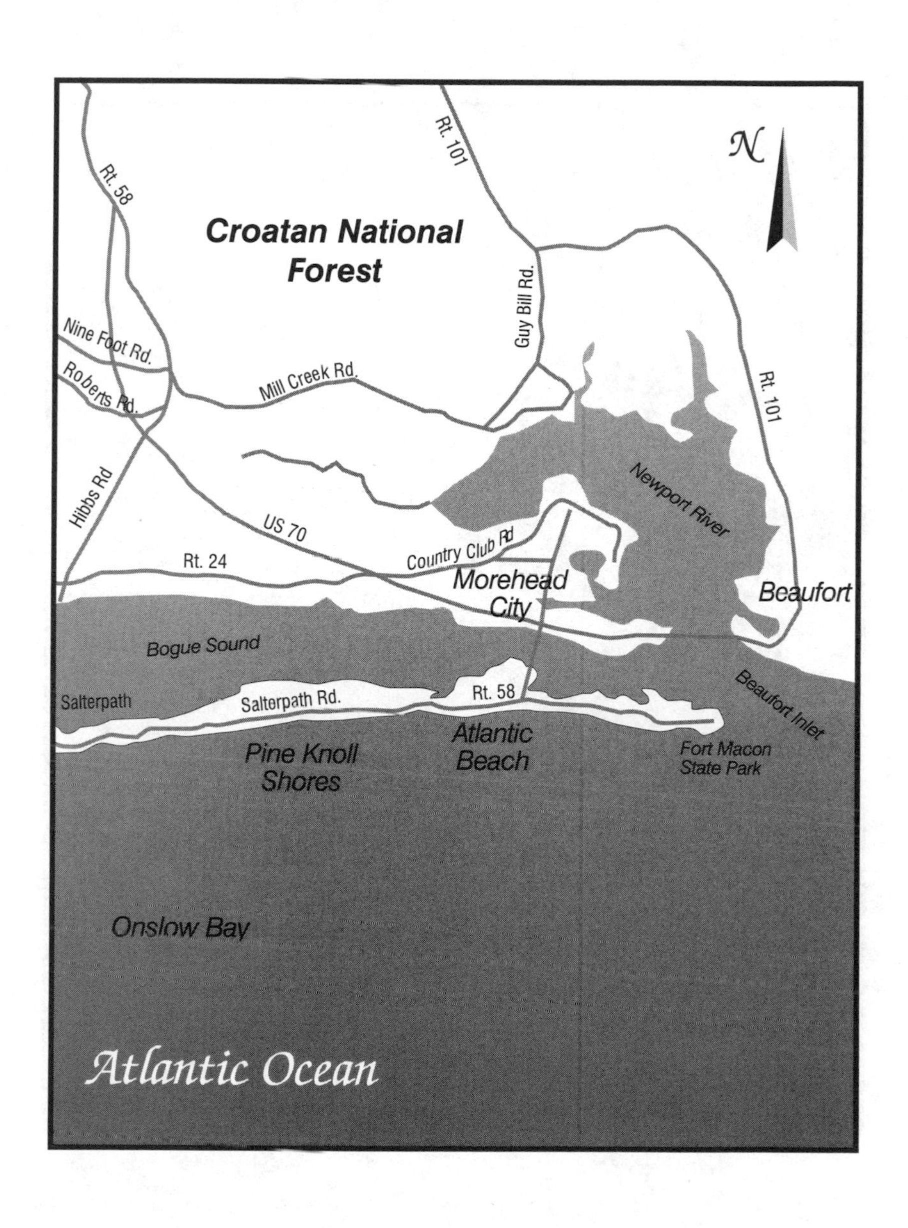

N
Rt. 101
Rt. 58
Croatan National Forest
Guy Bill Rd.
Nine Foot Rd.
Roberts Rd.
Mill Creek Rd.
Rt. 101
Newport River
Hibbs Rd
US 70
Country Club Rd
Rt. 24
Morehead City
Beaufort
Bogue Sound
Beaufort Inlet
Salterpath
Salterpath Rd.
Rt. 58
Atlantic Beach
Pine Knoll Shores
Fort Macon State Park
Onslow Bay
Atlantic Ocean

DOWNTOWN BEAUFORT

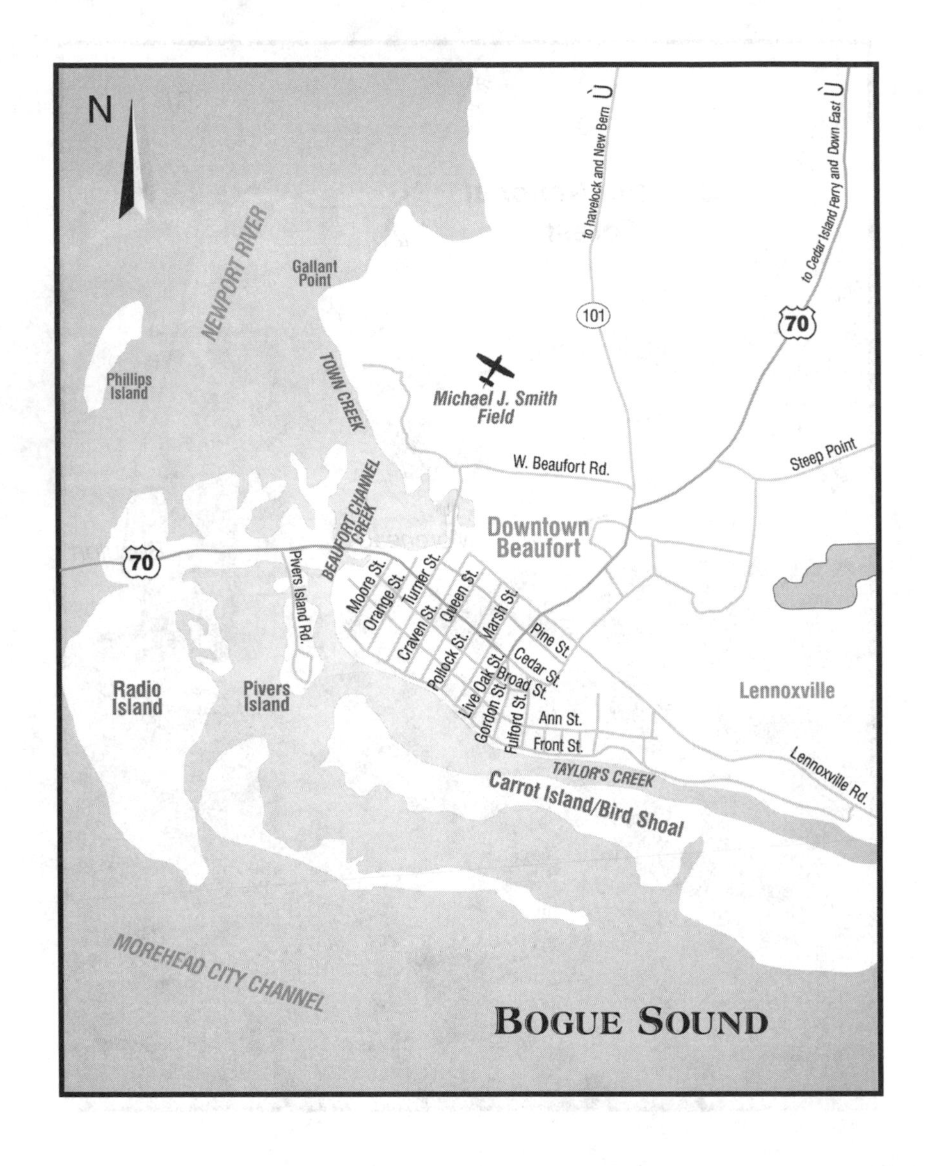

DOWN EAST

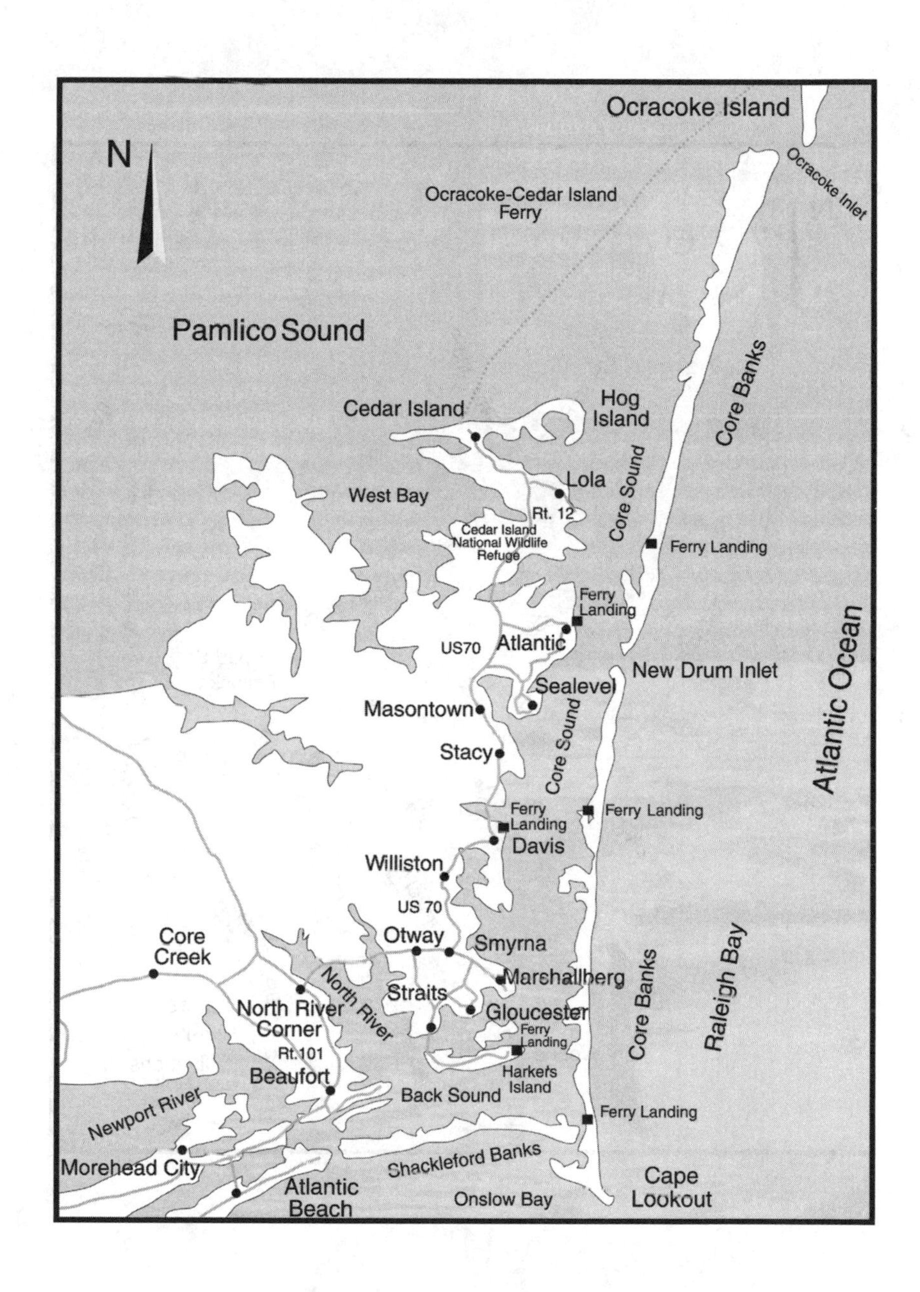

Ocracoke Island
N
Ocracoke Inlet
Ocracoke-Cedar Island
Ferry
Pamlico Sound
Core Banks
Cedar Island
Hog
Island
Lola
West Bay
Rt. 12
Core Sound
Cedar Island
National Wildlife
Refuge
Ferry Landing
Ferry
Landing
Atlantic Ocean
US70
Atlantic
New Drum Inlet
Sealevel
Masontown
Core Sound
Stacy
Ferry
Landing
Ferry Landing
Davis
Williston
US 70
Raleigh Bay
Core
Creek
Otway
Smyrna
Marshallberg
North River
Straits
Core Banks
North River
Corner
Gloucester
Ferry
Landing
Rt.101
Harkers
Island
Beaufort
Back Sound
Newport River
Ferry Landing
Morehead City
Shackleford Banks
Atlantic
Beach
Onslow Bay
Cape
Lookout

NEW BERN

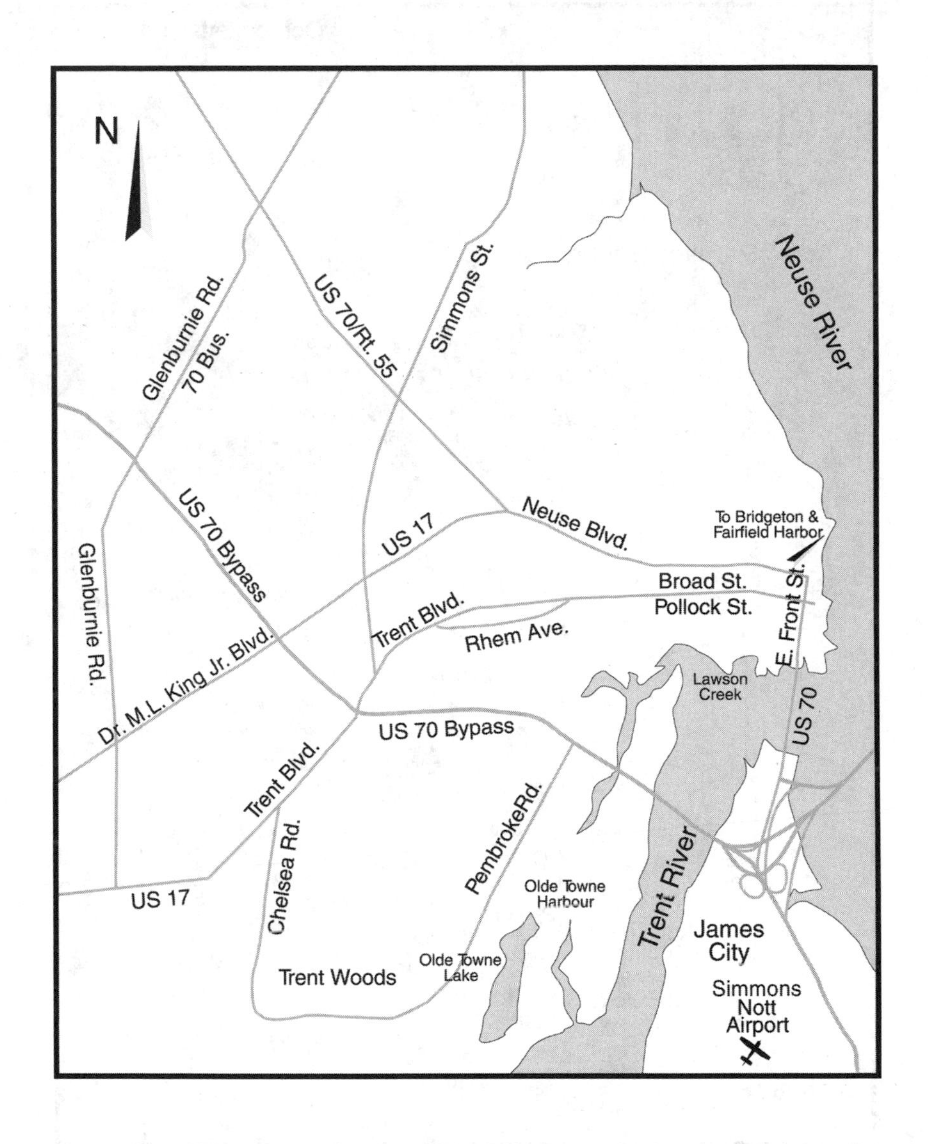

N
Neuse River
Simmons St.
US 70/Rt. 55
Glenburnie Rd.
70 Bus.
US 70 Bypass
Neuse Blvd.
To Bridgeton & Fairfield Harbor
US 17
Broad St.
Pollock St.
Glenburnie Rd.
Trent Blvd.
Rhem Ave.
E. Front St.
Dr. M.L. King Jr. Blvd.
Lawson Creek
US 70
US 70 Bypass
Trent Blvd.
Chelsea Rd.
PembrokeRd.
US 17
Olde Towne Harbour
Trent River
James City
Olde Towne Lake
Trent Woods
Simmons Nott Airport

NEW BERN HISTORIC DISTRICT

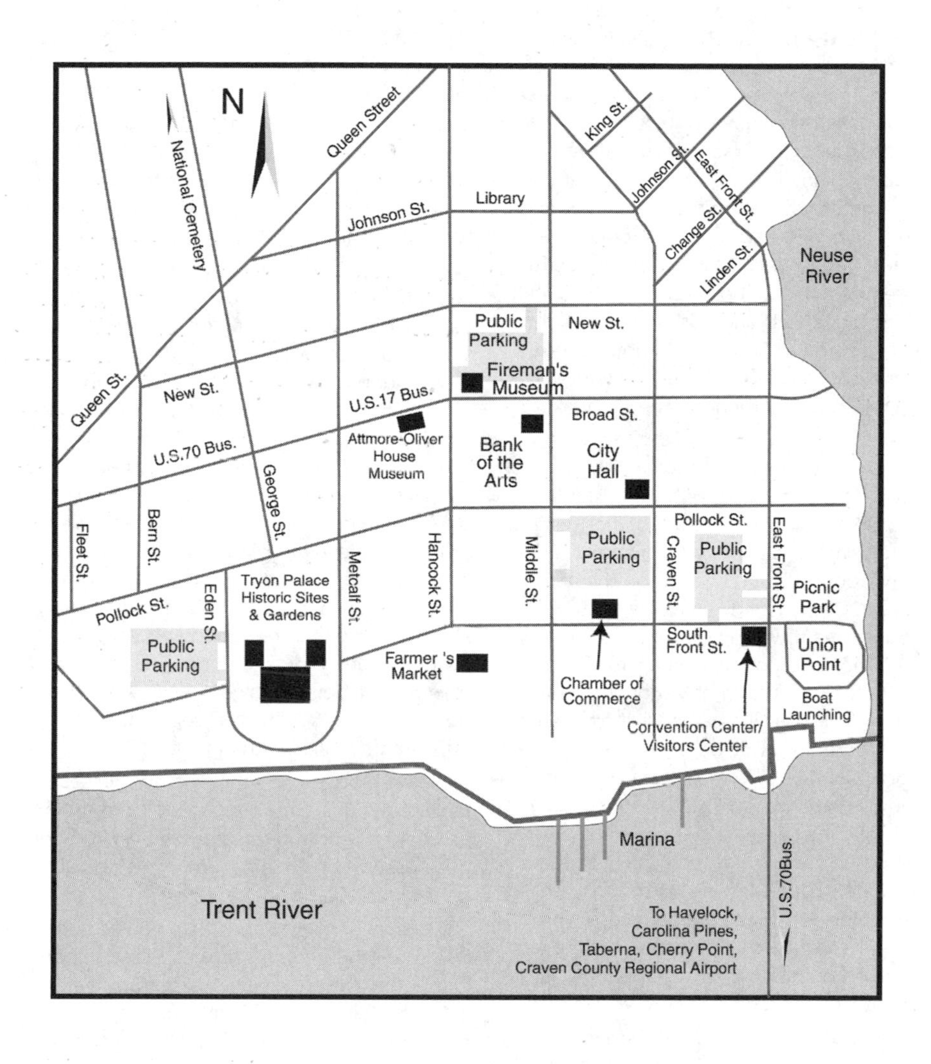

PREFACE

It's our pleasure to welcome you to the 15th edition of The Insiders' Guide® to North Carolina's Central Coast and New Bern. Our book will give you an Insider's knowledge of this beautiful coastal region. Use this guide like a road map and keep it handy. If you are a newcomer, you'll learn much by reading our Area Overview and Getting Around chapters. If you've been around awhile, you're sure to enjoy our short features (we call them Close-ups) and tips, and you might learn something you didn't know before. Share our invaluable guide with your visiting relatives and friends - they'll thank you for it.

We've divided this book into two major parts. The first part covers the beautiful Crystal Coast, which includes all of Carteret County and the town of Swansboro in Onslow County. Several years ago the name Crystal Coast was given to the Carteret County sea towns by the Carteret County Chamber of Commerce. Local folks hoped the name would attract visitors to the county's crystal waters and brilliant beaches — and it has. But we titled this book North Carolina's Central Coast because that name is more recognizable nationally, even though Crystal Coast is the preferred moniker of Insiders. The second major part of this book addresses the historic city of New Bern. Best known as the home of Tryon Palace, the city offers much to delight visitors and guests. It is Craven County's largest city, the second-oldest town in North Carolina and is rich with history.

Besides the Crystal Coast and New Bern, you'll also discover information about our neighboring city of Havelock, home to Marine Corps Air Station Cherry Point and the Naval Aviation Depot. Havelock is Craven County's second largest city and is continually growing. Following Havelock, we tell you about the riverside town of Oriental, the sailing capital of North Carolina. This charming village is quiet and slow-paced and just the place to help you forget your cares and focus on, well, perhaps nothing at all, except the beauty of Oriental. In the last section, we offer daytrip itineraries for a few favorite getaway spots such as Ocracoke Island, Wilmington and Belhaven.

We've packed this guide with chapters and sections that cover just about every topic you can imagine: Restaurants, Accommodations, Weekly and Long-Term Cottage Rentals, Shopping, Nightlife, Annual Events, Camping, Fishing, Boating and lots more. We tell you about where to have a picnic, go for a hike and play a round of golf; how to get a fishing report and a babysitter; and about places to launch and store your boat. For those of you who live here or plan to move here, we've written chapters on Schools and Child Care, Worship, Commerce and Industry, and Sports, Fitness and Parks. You'll find information about our neighborhoods and buying a home. For some of our readers, the best parts of this book are the sections on Kidstuff - indispensable information for parents of kids with bundles of energy.

Please be assured that the businesses featured in this book are chosen from the many as being the best in the area. We decide which businesses to include based on their quality, their uniqueness or their popularity.

Our general maps will help you see the overall picture. These should be used in conjunction with your regular road map. We also offer the following invaluable hints for getting around by car - U.S. Highway 70 takes on a different name in each town it passes through: Main Street in Havelock; Arendell Street in Morehead City; and Cedar and Live Oak streets in Beaufort. N.C. Highway 58 also takes on a new name in each of the beach towns it passes through: Fort Macon Road East or West in Atlantic Beach; Salter Path Road between

Atlantic Beach and Indian Beach; and Emerald Drive in Emerald Isle. Mile marker (MM) numbers are given to help you locate places along N.C. 58 on Bogue Banks.

From a map, the entire area might seem to be little more than a highway. However, North Carolina's Crystal Coast and New Bern have much to offer visitors and residents. If you are visiting, don't expect to see everything in one trip. If you have relocated to the area, we urge you to spend occasional weekends exploring the many treasures that surround you.

We've written about many, many of the wonderful sights, sounds and tastes of the Crystal Coast and its environs. We've done our best to ensure that all the information is accurate. And we are always eager to hear what our readers think so that future editions can accommodate your ideas and suggestions. Write to us in care of By The Sea Publications Inc., 3941 Market Street, Wilmington, NC 28403, or visit us online and make your comments there: www.insiders.com/crystalcoast. You can see this and many other Insiders' Guides online – in their entirety.

Our hope is that the coast's lure and its varied pleasures will satisfy you as much as they do us and other Insiders. We trust this book will guide you well and that you will enjoy exploring, revisiting or living along North Carolina's Crystal Coast and in New Bern.

ABOUT THE AUTHORS

Vina Hutchinson Farmer

Vina Hutchinson Farmer moved to the Carolina coast 17 years ago, wandering her way through several coastal and historic North Carolina towns before moving to New Bern in 1998. A native of Kentucky raised in West Virginia, she graduated from Marshall University (home of the Thundering Herd!) in 1988 with degrees in history and journalism. Vina is the Grants Coordinator for Tryon Palace Historic Sites & Gardens. She also serves as a freelance editor of the Historic New Bern Herald. In addition to her work on The Insiders' Guide® to the Central Coast and New Bern, Vina is the author of Images of America: New Bern and New Bern: Then & Now. Her books and her work with the Herald have been recognized with awards by the North Carolina Society of Historians. Vina is a member of the Leadership Craven Class of 2006 and her volunteer work includes serving as an ambassador for the New Bern Area Chamber of Commerce and on the New Bern Historical Society's Ghostwalk Committee. When not tackling yet another project in the renovation of her Ghent neighborhood home, she enjoys reading, writing personal essays and short fiction, and "blogging."

Tabbie Nance

Tabbie Nance was one of the original co-authors of the first Insiders' Guide® to North Carolina's Central Coast in 1991. She continued co-authoring the publication for five years — in the days before the online version. After a long break, she returned to the Insider's Guide three years ago. Tabbie holds an undergraduate degree in communications with a minor in human relations from High Point College (now University) and a master's degree in library studies from East Carolina University. She moved to Carteret County 22 years ago to work as a reporter/photographer for the local newspaper. A North Carolina native, she is now the Communications Director for the Carteret County Public School System and continues to freelance for a variety of publications. Tabbie is involved in various community volunteer activities, including the Cape Lookout Studies Program, Nelson Bay Challenge Sprint Triathlon and several other sports events. Her hobbies including training for and racing in triathlons (swimming, biking, running), cooking, quilting, and spending time outside especially in and on the water.

ACKNOWLEDGMENTS

Vina Hutchinson Farmer

My work on this book simply would not be possible without the encouragement I receive on a daily basis from family and friends. At the Insiders Guide, thanks to Jay, Susan, Molly and the rest of the Insiders gang who also work hard on making the Insiders Guide the best it can be.

I also express my appreciation, of course, to the many people in and around the Crystal Coast and New Bern, who through phone calls, personal visits, emails and faxes assisted with compiling the wonderful information you now hold in your hands. My hope is that you, dear reader, will not only find this information helpful but also come to love this area just as much I do.

I'd also like to offer my eternal and sincere thanks to four very special people who have always been super supportive of me, in moments of both triumph and darkness:

* James, your love and support are constant and dependable, and for that I am truly a lucky woman;

* Nick, may your bright outlook on life never dim, and may it inspire others as it has inspired me;

* Debbie Robinson of Oscoda, Michigan, growing up you were my big sister and my "little mother," and now I am fortunate to call you my best friend as well; and

* Alanna King of Jacksonville, thanks for always being there. Words are truly insufficient to convey how blessed I am to have you as my close and affectionate friend.

For this edition, I'd also like to thank Liz Senn, who helped me tremendously with working on this year's updates. Liz, I love your sunny smile and positive attitude and can't thank you enough for stepping in and helping me out. I'd also like to thank the New Bern Area Chamber of Commerce and my classmates in the Leadership Craven Class of 2006 for providing me with an in-depth, enriching and fun opportunity to learn more about the county — and 24 special people who choose to live, work and play here.

Tabbie Nance

It is my hope that readers will come to know and enjoy the coast of North Carolina as much as I do. After living here 22 years, I continue to discover new places and have new experiences. In 1984 I met Rodney Kemp, a Moreheader, who shared with me his contagious love for Carteret County through story-telling and his living. Rodney, I'll always be grateful to you for teaching me so much about this wonderful place. My thanks also go to Keith Rittmaster of the Cape Lookout Studies Program who continuously shows and teaches me new things about the coastal waters and islands.

My special thanks to Jay for creating this Insiders' Guide family; to Molly and Melissa for their patience; and to Matt for his direction. Thanks also to those who shared information about their businesses either in face-to-face meetings, over the phone, through email or fax.

Finally, my greatest love and appreciation are extended to my parents — Buddy and Tabbie Nance — who taught me by example to explore and be a lifelong learner — and to my sister, Miriam Lewis, and her family for always providing me with love and support in this venture and in all those I undertake.

GETTING HERE, GETTING AROUND

Miles of clean, sandy beaches, great waterways, abundant fresh seafood and historic and scenic vistas draw visitors from all over to the North Carolina Crystal Coast. These same attractions are what keeps residents here as well.

The Crystal Coast is at the southern end of the great barrier island chain called the Outer Banks. This narrow strip of land travels 81 miles of coastline, beaches, dunes and waterways down N.C. Highway 12 with connecting ferries. The Bogue Banks portion of the Crystal Coast is geographically unique. It sits on an east-west axis, allowing a sunrise and sunset view over the ocean and sun bathers to lie on the beach facing the ocean due south.

The Crystal Coast is about many things, especially water and water activities. In this area you'll see thousands of pleasure craft, sailboats in safe harbors, kayaks, the last of the menhaden fishing fleet, ocean-going research vessels, huge luxury yachts, tankers and container ships, and more than 6,000 commercial fishing boats, big and small, hauling in the catch.

About 95 percent of the visitors to the Crystal Coast arrive by car, although getting here by sea or air provides a beautiful journey.

LAND

The Crystal Coast is only a three-hour drive from the state capital of Raleigh, a straight shot on U.S. Highway 70, and only a couple of hours from Greenville, home of East Carolina University.

If you're coming to the area from the north or south, Interstate 95 or U.S. Highway 17 will take you to either U.S. Highway 70 and on to Morehead City or you can arrive on N.C. Highway 58, which leads straight to Emerald Isle. From the west, Interstate 40 will also take you to U.S. 70, which leads directly to Morehead City. From the east, the most picturesque journey into Carteret County, travelers must reserve space for the 2-hour ferry ride from Ocracoke Island to Cedar Island (see the ferry schedule in this chapter). At the ferry landing, N.C. Highway 12 continues a short distance to intersect with U.S. 70 W. near the community of Sea Level, the highway's point of origin. (Interestingly enough, U.S. 70's other terminus is in Los Angeles.) From here, it's an unforgettable ride through lowland fields of junkus and Spartina marsh grasses and Down East fishing villages to historic Beaufort and the Crystal Coast or on to Havelock and New Bern.

Between Morehead City and Emerald Isle or Swansboro, the main thoroughfare is N.C. Highway 24. This newly completed five-lane highway offers views of Bogue Sound as you cross its bridges at Broad Creek and Gales Creek. Make the sightseeing brief, because this is always a busy highway with commuter traffic, schools and neighborhood developments along the 25-mile stretch between U.S. 70 and N.C. 58.

On the island of Bogue Banks, N.C. 58 runs parallel to the beach for more than 22 miles, from Atlantic Beach west to Emerald Isle. Mile markers along the way make it easy to find things. Mile 1 (MM 1) begins at Fort Macon State Park on the east end of the island and the markers continue west, ending at the high-rise bridge in Emerald Isle leaving the island.

Bus and Taxi Service

Currently, there is no bus service to the county. Bus service is offered in Havelock.

Several cab and limousine companies service the area:

A-1 Yellow Cab, (252) 240-2700 or (252) 504-3680, takes passengers to Atlantic Beach, Beaufort, Morehead City, Down East and all airports and marinas.

Atlantic Beach Taxi, (252) 240-3555, serves all the towns between Atlantic Beach and Emerald Isle as well as Morehead City and regional airports.

Morehead City Yellow Cab Co., (252) 728-3483 or (252) 726-3125, offers service to Atlantic Beach, Beaufort, Morehead City, Newport, Down East and to all airports.

A Diamond Limousine Service, (252) 240-1680, offers service for local and long-distance trips.

Carolina Limousine and Shuttle Service (C.L.A.S.S.), (252) 637-RIDE (7433), offers chauffeur transportation to meet clients' needs.

N.C. Supershuttle, (252) 672-5050, makes two runs a day to Raleigh-Durham Airport (RDU).

Twilight Limousine Company, (252) 633-0027, is based in New Bern and features a H2 Hummer, 20-passenger super-stretch limo.

Car Rentals

This area has very few car rental establishments. More rental options exist in New Bern at Craven County Regional Airport. In Carteret County, Michael J. Smith Airport (Beaufort Airport) offers Enterprise rentals, (252) 728-1777, through Morehead City Enterprise Rent-A-Car. In Morehead City, Ford Rent-A-Car is operated by Morehead City Ford, 5557 U.S. Highway 70 W., (252) 247-2132; and Enterprise Rent-A-Car is located at 5317 U.S. Highway 70 W., (252) 240-0218.

AIR

Passenger airline service is available at several airports convenient to the Crystal Coast. You can reach New Bern by commercial carrier, or you can fly into New Bern or Beaufort by private plane. Flights directly to Carteret County are accommodated at the area's only airport in Beaufort.

Michael J. Smith Airport
N.C. Hwy. 101, Beaufort
(252) 728-2323, (252) 728-1928

The Crystal Coast's sole airport, located in Beaufort, offers only chartered or private aircraft service. A modern facility, it is the sixth busiest municipal airport in North Carolina. The Fixed Base Operator is Segrave Aviation, which handles all fueling, rentals, flight instruction, charters and sightseeing flights. The airport has pilot-controlled runway night lights, a localizer for 2.6, six different GPS approaches and a non-directional beacon (NDB) on runway 14. The airport is named for Capt. Michael J. Smith, a Beaufort native and pilot of the space shuttle Challenger, who perished with eight others when it exploded on takeoff.

Craven County Regional Airport
200 Terminal Dr., New Bern
(252) 638-8591

Craven County Regional Airport in New Bern is the nearest commercial service airport to Morehead City, Atlantic Beach, Beaufort and points Down East. This airport offers seven daily flights to Charlotte on USAirways Express. The general aviation side of the airport has a fixed-base operation, (252) 633-1400, offering full aviation services. It is equipped with GPS, ILS, pilot-controlled runway lights and a tower. Car rental agencies are based at the airport, and taxi services to Havelock and the Crystal Coast are wise to the arrival schedule for passengers' convenience.

Albert J. Ellis Airport
264 Albert J. Ellis Airport Rd., Richlands
(910) 324-1100

Commercial air service to the Crystal Coast is available from the Albert J. Ellis Airport, 20 miles northwest of Jacksonville off U.S. Highway 111 toward Richlands. It is the closest airport to Marine Corps Base Camp Lejeune in Jacksonville. The airport offers eight flights each day to Charlotte on USAirways. Car rental and taxi services are at the airport.

Raleigh-Durham International Airport
Aviation Pkwy., Morrisville, 10 miles from Raleigh and Durham just off I-40
(919) 840-2123

Raleigh-Durham (RDU) is the major international airport serving North Carolina from the Research Triangle Park area. RDU is a three-hour drive from the Crystal Coast. The airport is a major hub for domestic and international travelers and is served by all major domestic carriers, feeder carriers and by Air Canada. Commercial feeder service is available to Charlotte. Car rental services are at the airport.

SEA

Many visitors arrive via the Intracoastal Waterway (ICW), which provides access by water to the Crystal Coast via Morehead City, Beaufort, Swansboro and along Bogue Banks. To reach New Bern by water, slip into Pamlico Sound and head up the Neuse River. Beaufort is a favorite stop for boaters on the north-south ICW run in the spring and fall. Transient dockage at either the Beaufort Town Docks or Town Creek Marina is hospitable, and anchorage is plentiful in the town's harbor of refuge north of the Grayden Paul drawbridge or in the designated anchorage off the town's waterfront. A variety of docking points are available throughout the area for both overnight or long-term stays. See our chapter on Marinas for details.

Ferries

A number of state-owned and private ferries serve the Crystal Coast, offering visitors and residents an enjoyable transportation alternative via inland sounds and rivers.

Tourism is the Crystal Coast's No. 1 industry. It represents an estimated 20 percent of Carteret County's jobs and a $230 million annual income.

STATE FERRIES

The state ferries operate under the administration of the North Carolina Department of Transportation (NCDOT) and are large, seaworthy vessels. Three ferries connect Ocracoke Island with other parts of North Carolina. The Cedar Island-Ocracoke Toll Ferry is the state's most popular ferry and carries passengers and vehicles between the Crystal Coast and Ocracoke Island. This ferry is used by visitors coming to the Crystal Coast from the north and by those leaving the mainland to travel up the Outer Banks, as well as local visitors looking for a ideal daytrip. The Ocracoke-Hatteras Inlet Ferry connects Ocracoke with Hatteras Island and the northern Outer Banks at no cost. The Ocracoke-Swan Quarter Toll Ferry crosses the Pamlico Sound to connect Ocracoke Island with Swan Quarter. The Cherry Branch-Minnesott Ferry carries passengers and vehicles and is a good connection between the Crystal Coast and Oriental. Like the Ocracoke-Hatteras Ferry, this is a free trip and a great way to get a quick ride on one of North Carolina's ferries. The Hammocks Beach State Park Ferry transports passengers, but no cars, to Bear Island.

Regardless of the ferry you choose, you can almost always be sure of a safe crossing with plenty of time to look around. The ferries do not operate in rough weather, and all ferry schedules and tolls are subject to change without notice. For more information about state-owned ferry crossings, contact the N.C. Department of Transportation Ferry Division, (800) BY-FERRY. Reservations are always strongly suggested on those ferries that take reservations. No reservations are required if you are traveling as a pedestrian or with a bicycle. Following is a list of state-operated ferry schedules and fares.

Cedar Island–Ocracoke Toll Ferry

The Cedar Island-Ocracoke Ferry Service carries passengers and their vehicles between the Crystal Coast and Ocracoke Island. The Cedar Island terminal is about 45 miles east of Beaufort, but allow at least an hour and a half for the trip. Reservations must be claimed 30 minutes before departure time or they will be cancelled. Call the ferry terminals at Cedar Island, (252) 225-3551 or (800) 856-0343, or Ocracoke, (252) 928-3841 or (800) 345-1665, for reservations and to verify times.

2 hours crossing

Reservations Recommended at least one month in advance.

Summer Schedule

Mid-May through Late September

Depart Cedar Island	Depart Ocracoke
7:00am	7:00am
8:15am	---
9:30am	9:30am
---	10:00am
10:45am	Noon
Noon	*
1:00pm	---
1:45pm	---
3:00pm	3:00pm
---	4:30pm
6:00pm	6:00pm
8:30pm	8:30pm

Early April through Mid-May

Late September through early November

Depart Cedar Island	Depart Ocracoke
7:00am	7:00am
9:30am	9:30am
Noon	Noon
3:00pm	3:00pm
6:00pm	6:00pm
8:30pm	8:30pm

January 1 through Early April

Early November through Late March

7:00am	7:00am
10:00am	10:00am
1:00pm	1:00pm
4:00pm	4:00pm

* Additional departures Mid-May through Late-September

Fares (One Way):

Pedestrian, $1

Bicycle & Rider, $3

Motorcycles, $10

Vehicle and/or combination less than 20 feet, $15

Vehicle and/or combination 20 feet to 40 feet, $30

Vehicle and/or combination up to 65 feet, $45

Maximum length 65 feet; up to five axles

Ocracoke–Swan Quarter Toll Ferry

For departures from Ocracoke, call (252) 928-3841; from Swan Quarter, call (252) 926-1111

2 hours crossing - 28 car limit

Reservations Recommended

Summer Schedule

Mid-May 21 to Early September

Depart Ocracoke	Depart Swan Quarter
6:30am	7:00am*
12:30pm	9:30am
4:00pm	4:00pm

*Additional departures Memorial Day through Labor Day.

Winter schedule offers two crossings per day.

Fares are the same as those for the Cedar Island–Ocracoke Toll Ferry.

Cherry Branch–Minnesott Beach Free Ferry

The Cherry Branch–Minnesott Beach Ferry is essential for commuters from Oriental who must travel with their cars across the Neuse River to work in Havelock, at Cherry Point Marine Air Station and surrounding areas. On the Crystal Coast side, the Cherry Branch terminal is off N.C. Highway 101, about 5 miles south of Havelock. Signs along the highway give directions to the terminal. This ferry takes you to an interesting route for exploring Oriental to the north and is an especially nice route to Belhaven. This is a great short ride for anyone interested in just experiencing a ferry ride while on the Crystal Coast. This 20-minute free ride allows for great views of the impressive Neuse River as well as a chance to sit back and relax for a bit and watch the water and the sky.

20-minute crossing - 40 car limit

No Reservations Accepted - Free Ferry

Year-round Schedule

Depart Cherry Branch	Depart Minnesott Beach
Every 20 Minutes:	Every 20 Minutes
5:45am - 8:25am	5:45am - 8:25am
Every 30 Minutes	Every 30 Minutes
8:45am - 12:15pm	8:45am - 12:15pm
Every 20 Minutes	Every 20 Minutes
3:35pm - 5:55pm	3:35pm - 5:55pm
Every Hour	Every Hour
6:45pm - 12:45am	6:15pm - 12:15am

Saturday and Sunday morning ferries depart from Cherry Branch and Minnesott Beach every 30 minutes beginning at 5:45 AM.

Hammocks Beach State Park Ferry

The seasonal passenger ferry (no cars) at Hammocks Beach State Park provides transportation from the park headquarters terminal to Bear Island. The ferry terminal is off N.C. 24, 2 miles west of Swansboro at the end of State Road 1511. If you are visiting Bear Island between Memorial Day and Labor Day, get to the ferry landing early to avoid long lines. Pets are not allowed on the ferry, and alcoholic beverages are prohibited in the park (see our Attractions chapter). Call Hammocks Beach, (910) 326-4881, to verify times.

25-minute crossing - No vehicles

No Reservations Accepted

Memorial Day through Labor Day

The ferry runs daily. From the mainland, the ferry departs every hour on the half-hour from 9:30 AM to 5:30 PM. From Bear Island, the ferry departs every hour on the hour from 10 AM to 6 PM.

May and September

The ferry runs Wednesday through Sunday.

October through April

The ferry runs Friday through Sunday. A private water taxi service operates the ferry

Gulls and shorebirds pause in the shoreline on Bogue Banks.

photo: George Mitchell

November through March. Call the park for details.

Fares (round trip):

Adult, $5

Senior Citizens, 62 and older, $3

Children ages 6 to 12, $3

Children younger than 6, Free

Private Ferries

Privately owned vessels also stand ready to carry passengers to popular destinations along the Crystal Coast. Of course, you always have the option of hiring a luxurious sailboat complete with crew and catered meals or renting a small motorboat or kayak to do your own navigating. Whatever your choice, there is a lot to explore by water on the Crystal Coast.

Along with state-owned ferries and private charters, the National Park Service (NPS) offers contracts to what it refers to as "concessionaires." These folks, operating under NPS guidelines, carry passengers and/or vehicles to the uninhabited Cape Lookout National Seashore (see our Attractions chapter). The Seashore is a 56-mile stretch of barrier islands made up of North Core Banks, home of Portsmouth Village; South Core Banks, home of Cape Lookout Lighthouse; and Shackleford Banks, home to wild horses.

The NPS allows privately owned ferries to carry passengers and vehicles to North and South Core Banks and Portsmouth Village, where there is also a landing strip for small planes (see descriptions below). These small ferries operate out of the Down East communities of Davis and Atlantic and don't have all the extras you will find on the state ferries because of the depth of the water in which they operate. They do have medium-size, seaworthy vessels equipped to carry a handful of vehicles, a few passengers and some equipment. They normally operate from April to December, although schedules and fees vary. Most concessionaires require reservations, so it is best to call ahead for schedule information, to check current fares and to see if there is room aboard for you, and to also check weather conditions. Each concessionaire can provide information on cabins and camping (see the Accommodations and Camping chapters). Pets in pet carriers are allowed by most concessionaire ferry services and pets must be maintained at all times on the island with a 6-foot leash.

Morris Marina Kabin Kamps and Ferry Service Inc.
Morris Marina Rd., Atlantic
(252) 225-4261

From the Down East community of Atlantic, which is off N.C. 12, this ferry service transports passengers, vehicles and all-terrain vehicles to Portsmouth or to the south end of North Core Banks at Drum Inlet from March through early December. Trips run four times a day, and the time varies. Trips can also be run by request. Morris Marina's transportation cost is about $14 round trip per person and about $75 round trip for a standard sized vehicle 18 feet or smaller. The ferry can accommodate larger vehicles for an additional fee. Island transportation and delivery of supplies (ice, groceries, etc.) may be arranged. See our Accommodations chapter for cabin rental information.

Great Island Fishing Camps
(252) 225-4261

This ferry service serves South Core Banks and carries passengers, vehicles and all-terrain vehicles five times a day from late March through mid-December on a reservation basis. Fares are about $13 round trip for ages 12 and older, $6 for ages 5 to 11 and free for ages 4 and younger. The cost is about $65 round trip for a standard-size vehicle of 18 feet in length. The cabins are rustic and can be a great alternative when seeking a

Boats are a popular mode of transportation on the Crystal Coast.

photo: George Mitchell

little bit of respite from the hectic pace of today's world. For more information about the fishing camps, see our Accommodations chapter.

Mule Train Beach Tours
(252) 728-7827 (866) 230-BOAT (2628)

Once you are on the banks, catch the Mule Train for a memorable trip. One option is arrange to be dropped off for a specific amount of time and then picked up again, whether that be the same day or after a night of camping on the beach. Another option is to take a two-hour tour of the Cape. The tour offers riders a shaded and cushioned ride in the fresh air of the Cape. Narrators will share information as you visit Cape Lookout Lighthouse, pass loggerhead sea turtle nests, travel through the historic fishing village, pass the 1887 Lifesaving Station before arriving at Cape Point for some free time for shelling, swimming or soaking up the sun.

Other Ferries

A few other passenger ferries are permitted by the NPS to transport island hoppers to Cape Lookout, Shackleford Banks and the Rachel Carson Research Reserve — which is made up of such places as Carrot Island, Sand Dollar Island and Bird Shoals. Most of these ferries can also be hired for service to other areas or just for a cruise around the harbor. Reservations should be made in advance, and always call ahead to check the weather conditions. Charter and rental boats are available for getting around the area's waterways (see the Fishing, Boating and Watersports chapter).

Calico Jack's & Cape Lookout Ferry Service
Calico Jack's Inn & Marina, Harkers Island
(252) 728-3575

Passenger-only ferry service to the Cape Lookout Lighthouse is a 10-minute boat ride from Calico Jack's Marina. The ferry departs for the Cape or Shackleford Banks on demand for $10 per adult round trip, $6 per child. Campers with gear are ferried for $15 per adult and $12 per child. There is a $30 trip minimum, and there is a fee to park your vehicle in the departure area. Service begins in early March and ends in early December. Those who don't want to walk can take the land taxi, the Pony Express Shuttle available on Cape Lookout for fishermen and tourists. This shuttle can be arranged through Calico Jack's and is $15.

Ferry To Cape Lookout
Harkers Island Fishing Center, Harkers Island
(252) 728-3907

Barrier Island Transportation provides passenger ferry and water taxi service to Shackleford Banks and the Cape Lookout Lighthouse area. No vehicles are accommodated. Fares are $10 round trip per person, $6 for children 12 and younger, and $15 for overnight adult campers with gear and $12 for children campers. Group rates are offered. The ferry leaves at 45 minutes after the hour starting at 8:45 AM from the Harkers Island Fishing Center on Harkers Island. The ferry picks up on the hour until 5 PM. Service runs between Easter and Thanksgiving. Reservations are not required but are recommended for large groups.

Island Ferry Adventures
618 Front St., Beaufort
(252) 728-7555

Island Ferry Adventures offers ferry service to all the surrounding islands as well as water tours, dolphin watch tours and horse watch tours. The prices vary depending on the destination, but an example would be $14 for an adult and $6 for a child to Shackleford Banks. Weather permitting, the ferry leaves on demand at the top of each hour from 9 AM to 5 PM, depending on the season. Two boats run during the summer months to accommodate passengers, and this service can design a trip to meet your needs.

Local Yokel Ferry and Tours
516 Island Rd., Harkers Island
(252) 728-2759

The Local Yokel Ferry and Tours boasts some of the best deals on Harkers Island. The first ferry departs on demand daily, beginning at 8 AM, weather permitting. Earlier trips are available by reservation. After a 12-minute jaunt, travelers find themselves on Cape Lookout National Seashore; five minutes and they're at Shackleford Banks. Rates are $10 for adults and $6 for children 12 and younger. Group rates are available for 10 people or more. The company offers free parking on Harkers Island. Special tours and tickets for the Mule Train tour of the Cape Lookout area can be arranged here. Stay an hour, a day or bring a tent and stay the night.

Lookout Express
Front St., Beaufort
(252) 728-7827

This 149-passenger ferry, the largest in the area, takes passengers to Cape Lookout and Shackleford Banks. It offers half-day island excursions to Cape Lookout, sunset cruises and private charters. Once at the Cape, Lookout Express can arrange for transportation on the Mule Train — a truck and trailer service that can take you to the best shelling and fishing spots, and to quiet beaches. Just take what you need for a day at the beach and enjoy the ride and the day. The trip to the Cape is about one and a half hours and includes some narration about the area. The captain will also share a little history of the lighthouse and let you have a chance to walk around the lighthouse, take pictures and visit the keepers quarters before your return. This Cape trip is offered three times a day. Call for prices and to make reservations. (For more information, see the Mystery Tours in our Attractions chapter.)

Outer Banks Ferry Service
328 Front St., Beaufort
(252) 728-4129

Outer Banks Ferry Service operates year round seven days a week, offering transportation to the Rachel Carson Reserve and to Shackleford Banks, which part of the Cape Lookout National Seashore. The service runs on demand starting at 9 AM and offering its last pick up around 5 PM, depending on the season. Reservations should be made in advance. Costs range between $8 and $14 for adults and $4 to $6 for children, depending on your destination. Group rates are also offered. For those wishing to go it alone, this service rents house boats as well, and it shares the waterfront site with a kayak rental business.

Crystal Coast beaches face south rather than east from the southern point of Core Banks at Cape Lookout to the west end of Bogue Banks. This rare East Coast geography lets the sun rise and set on the ocean here, and the north wind calms the sea close to the beaches.

ONCE YOU'RE HERE

When you get to the Crystal Coast, you'll find that a car is almost essential. While several pages of America's colonial history were written here, there is still no public transportation service in the area, and a look at the map will show you that most communities are far enough apart to make a car the best way to get around.

There are some marked bike routes, but remember you're in a tourist area, and vehicle traffic is often heavy during the summer. Beaufort has a 6-mile marked bike route; a routing guide is available at the Safrit Historical Center, 138 Turner Street. Biking in residential developments on Bogue Banks and in Morehead City neighborhoods is safe and pleasant. The Atlantic Beach Causeway has biking and walking paths that link Atlantic Beach with Morehead City in relative

Getting there is half the fun on a ferry.

photo: George Mitchell

safety. The wide shoulders of N.C. 58 from Fort Macon State Park through Emerald Isle offer bikers an opportunity for riding with traffic-watching care. Also, the Town of Atlantic Beach continues to add more sidewalks for walkers and runners. A 26-mile bicycle touring route is marked in and around Swansboro.

U.S. Highway 70 is generally very easy to drive from New Bern through Havelock and on to Morehead City, Beaufort and Down East. From Beaufort east, however, U.S. 70 is a two-lane highway that winds through communities, marshes and between canals. An important detail to remember about U.S. 70 is that it has many names as it traverses Carteret County. In Morehead City, it's Arendell Street, the main street through town. It's also the Morehead-Beaufort Causeway. In Beaufort, it's called Cedar Street until it takes a left turn and becomes Live Oak Street. And by any name, it's always heavily trafficked in the Morehead City and Beaufort areas.

As you will find, there is much to see and do on the Crystal Coast. It's also a beautiful destination for doing nothing at all. Whatever you choose, you have an enviable exploration ahead of you.

Visitors Centers

Upon arrival in the Crystal Coast area, you can stop at the **Crystal Coast Tourism Authority** in Morehead City, 3409 Arendell Street, (252) 726-8148 or (800) SUNNY-NC (786-6962), next to the North Carolina Institute of Marine Sciences. In Cape Carteret the **Tourism Office** is on U.S. Highway 58 at the Cameron Langston Bridge to Emerald Isle, (252) 393-3100. These centers are full of informational brochures and local maps, including street maps. Friendly staff will answer your questions and help you find your way. The North Carolina Ferry Division welcomes Crystal Coast visitors at its center at the Cedar Island Ferry terminal.

AREA OVERVIEW

Travelers by the thousands feel an almost magnetic pull to our nation's shoreline and, like the gold rushers who settled the West, many choose to come and stay. Nowhere is this more apparent than in North Carolina's central coast, popularly known as the Crystal Coast for its sparkling, crystalline waters and miles of beaches and island sanctuaries.

You can see a dramatic sunrise on the ocean and watch egrets, gulls or white ibises lace through blue skies. You can see dolphins playfully break from inlet waters. As you stroll through towns in Carteret County, you hear mockingbirds call from surrounding live oaks. You can curl your toes in smooth beach sand and ease into evening as the sun sets in a copper disc. Away from the glare of bright city lights, you can gaze at a scatter of stars on a cloudless night.

A day can be as quiet or active as you desire. Each of the geographic areas — Bogue Banks, Beaufort, Morehead City, Swansboro, the Down East communities and western Carteret County — is different in its own special way.

The Crystal Coast is located in Carteret County, a place that is off the beaten path, and many say that fact alone is exactly what makes it so desirable. By car you must travel approximately 100 miles from Interstate 95 before you reach the county. The nearest major city is Raleigh, a three-hour car trip away. Historic New Bern is just 40 miles away. U.S. Highway 70, the main artery running through the county, is a direct corridor to Raleigh, so the drive isn't grueling.

Although not fast-paced, Carteret County is one of the fastest growing counties in the state but still with a year-round population of just 60,232. It contains 526 square miles and an ocean coastline of 81 miles, not to mention the miles of waterfront that stretch along Bogue and Core sounds and on the area's rivers and numerous bays, inlets and creeks.

The county is centrally situated on the North Carolina coast, perhaps the reason it was one of the first areas of the state explored and the third settled, giving it a rich history to blend with its natural beauty. To the north are the Pamlico Sound and the Outer Banks; to the south are the southern barrier islands, the city of Wilmington and the Cape Fear River.

Carteret County is at the confluence of the warm Gulf Stream waters from the south and cooler Labrador Current from the north. It provides a habitat for a widely varied mix of plants, a sanctuary for migrating birds and the northernmost point in the migration of exotic marine life such as the manatee. It is a place for visitors young and old to explore the wonder of a coast that on its brightest days is truly crystal.

Bogue Banks

Bogue Banks is the narrow barrier island that stretches below Morehead City, with its main highway N.C. 58 nearly parallel to N.C. Highway 24. One end is at Fort Macon in the town of Atlantic Beach in the east and the other is at Emerald Isle in the west. The body of water called Bogue Sound separates Bogue Banks from the mainland, and it's a paradise for boaters and anglers. The 30-mile-long island is connected to the mainland by two high-rise bridges, one at each end — one bridge from Morehead City to Atlantic Beach on the east end and the other bridge from Cape Carteret to Emerald Isle on the west end. Because the ocean and sound beaches attract visitors and summer residents, you will find many second homes, condominiums, hotels and summer rental cottages on the island.

Bogue Banks offers visitors a special treat. The island runs east to west and its Atlantic Ocean side faces due south, so visitors can watch the sun rise in the east over

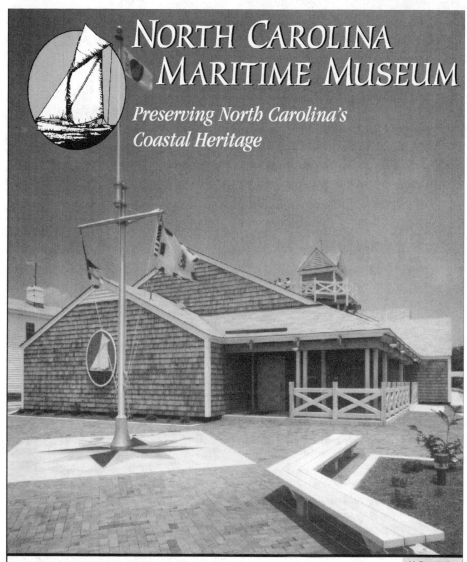

the ocean, travel across the sky, and set in the west over the ocean. This barrier island is also changing with each storm or hurricane as sand is shifted or eroded away.

N.C. Highway 58 extends the entire length of Bogue Banks. Along the way it is marked with green mile markers (MM). The MM series begins with mile 1 at the east end and continues along N.C. 58 to mile 21 on the west end. In this book we give the MM number as part of the address for places on Bogue Banks.

The majority of Bogue Banks' development, both commercial and residential, is along N.C. 58. A ride from one end to the other gives you an overview of the island communities. From several points along the road you can see both the sound and the ocean.

Bogue Banks embraces five townships that often seem to blend together. Atlantic Beach is at the far east end of the island and borders the town of Pine Knoll Shores. Indian Beach surrounds the small unincorporated community of Salter Path, and Emerald Isle is at the far west end of the island. Each town has its own personality, points of interest and governing body. Checking our maps will help you get an overall picture of how these towns combine into Bogue Banks.

As N.C. Highway 58 passes through the different communities, it often takes on a new name. In Atlantic Beach, it is called Fort Macon Road. East Fort Macon Road is the strip between the old fort and the main intersection in town. West Fort Macon Road is the strip between that intersection and the western edge of town. The longest stretch of the highway is called Salter Path Road, and it runs from Atlantic Beach through Pine Knoll Shores, Indian Beach and Salter Path. In Emerald Isle, the highway is called Emerald Drive. It really isn't as confusing as it sounds — N.C. 58 is just one road with several names that all spell scenery and coastline comforts.

ATLANTIC BEACH

Atlantic Beach is the oldest of the five towns on Bogue Banks. It was originally the site of a small pavilion built on the beach in 1887. The one-story building had a refreshment stand and stalls in the back for chang-

ing clothes. The popularity of surf-bathing was growing, and guests at the Atlantic Hotel in Morehead City were transported to the sound side of Atlantic Beach by sailboat. The guests then trekked across the island to the pavilion, which faced the ocean. Supplies were dragged over the sand dunes by ox cart.

In 1916 the original pavilion and 100 acres were bought by Von Bedsworth, and the 100-room Atlantic View Beach Hotel was built, a lone sentry on the now-populated strip of land. The hotel later burned, but by 1928 a group of county citizens had built a toll bridge from Morehead City to today's Atlantic Beach and had developed a beach resort with dining facilities, bathhouses and another pavilion. This complex would also perish to fire just a year later. A New York bank took possession of the property and built a new hotel, and Atlantic Beach slowly began to grow into the town it is today.

In 1936 the toll bridge was sold to the state and toll charges were dropped. In 1953 a drawbridge replaced the old bridge, and in the late 1980s, the drawbridge was replaced by the current Morehead City-Atlantic Beach four-lane, high-rise bridge. High-rise bridges play an important role along the Crystal Coast, allowing large vessels to easily maneuver the coastal waters. Past the North Carolina Port at Morehead City you will see tugs with barges, pleasure boats, long-line fishing boats and an occasional passenger cruise liner on the Intracoastal Waterway.

Today Atlantic Beach is home to about 3,500 year-round residents, although the population swells to a whopping 35,000 during the summer months. The center of town, known to locals as The Circle, is found at the southernmost end of the Atlantic Beach Causeway. The area continues to offer parking for a day at the beach and several souvenir shops, however major changes to this area are in the making. Plans are in the works for the construction of high rise condos, retail shops, restaurants, lodging and many other upscale improvements.

PINE KNOLL SHORES

Incorporated in 1973, Pine Knoll Shores starts at MM 4 and is the part of the island that has one of the most intriguing histories. In 1918 Alice Hoffman bought substantial acreage on Bogue Banks (known then as "Isle of the Pines"). She made her home here, off and on, until her death in 1953. The property was then inherited by her niece, wife of President Theodore Roosevelt Jr., and her four children. These Roosevelts envisioned Pine Knoll Shores as a planned community, sensitive to the delicate ecology of the maritime forest that surrounds it. Today, town officials stress the importance of protecting the environment and enforce regulations restricting the amount of acreage that can be cleared for development. As it was being built, early town planners worked hard to ensure that Pine Knoll Shores would be a residential community, and it has remained so.

The town's 1,700 year-round residents share their community with the North Carolina Aquarium at Pine Knoll Shores, one of the state's three aquariums. The aquarium offers educational exhibits, displays and a meeting area for civic and special interest groups.

Surrounding the aquarium is the Theodore Roosevelt Natural Area, a 265-acre maritime forest owned, maintained and protected by the state. It is one of the few remaining maritime forests on North Carolina's barrier islands. (See our Crystal Coast Attractions chapter for more about these sites.)

A historic marker stands at the corner of N.C. 58 and Roosevelt Boulevard (MM 7), noting the spot of the first landing of Europeans on the North Carolina coast. Giovanni da Verrazano, a Florentine navigator in the service of France, explored the state's coast from Cape Fear to Kitty Hawk in 1524. His voyage along the coast marked the first recorded European contact with what is now North Carolina.

INDIAN BEACH

As you leave Pine Knoll Shores and travel west on N.C. 58, you enter the resort and residential town of Indian Beach. It, too, was incorporated in 1973, and offers residents and visitors beautiful beaches for sunbathing, surf fishing and watersports. The region is home to condominiums, camping areas and restaurants, which you'll find profiled in various chapters within the Crystal Coast section. This town of about 100 residents surrounds the unincorporated community of Salter Path, creating an East Indian Beach and a West Indian Beach. So don't be surprised when you drive through Indian Beach, Salter Path and then Indian Beach again.

SALTER PATH

In the late 1890s the first families to settle in Salter Path came from Diamond City, which at the time was the largest community on Shackleford Banks, a 9-mile-long island that is now part of Cape Lookout National Seashore. Diamond City was a whaling community. A large hill in the center of town was used as a lookout, and when a whale was spotted, residents would jump into boats and row after it in hopes of harpooning the creature.

By 1897 approximately 500 people were living in Diamond City. The town was composed of several stores, a school, a post office and church buildings. Two hard storms in the late 1890s convinced many Diamond City residents that it was time to leave the island. They cut their houses into sections, tied them to skiffs and floated or sailed their dwellings across the water. Once at the new home site, the houses were reconstructed. Many residents of Diamond City settled on Harkers Island, in the Shackleford Street area of Morehead City or in Salter Path on Bogue Banks. Today, Shackleford Banks shows no sign that Diamond City ever existed. Buildings that weren't floated away were destroyed by subsequent storms, further endorsing the fact that the migrating families made the right decision.

Legend has it that the name Salter Path originated with Joshua Salter, a Broad Creek resident who often traveled by boat from the mainland to fish and hunt on Bogue Banks. Stories say he made a path from the sound side of the island, where he anchored his boat, to the oceanfront. Folks called the walkway Salter's Path, and like many things in Carteret County, the name just stuck.

Many locals credit the early residents of Salter Path with bringing shrimp into the culinary limelight. Early fishermen considered these delectable creatures a menace, and enjoyed instead such community fishing catches as the jumpin' mullet. But after local residents began to eat them, shrimp soon became a marketable and profitable commodity. Shrimping is now a lucrative industry

along the Crystal Coast, much to the joy of residents and visitors alike.

Salter Path sustained heavy damage during Hurricane Ophelia in September 2005, resulting in houses, restaurants, shops and other structures being destroyed. The clean-up and rebuilding continues to take place.

EMERALD ISLE

Stories say this end of the island was originally home to nomadic Native Americans and whalers. It is also says that about 15 families, perhaps from Diamond City, came here in 1893 and settled at Middletown, a small section of the island that is now part of Emerald Isle.

Other than those small groups, Emerald Isle was largely unsettled until the 1950s. Several years after Atlantic Beach was developed as a seashore resort, a Philadelphia man named Henry K. Fort bought the land that now makes up most of Emerald Isle along with 500 acres on the mainland, in what is now the town of Cape Carteret. Fort planned to link the island and his mainland property with a bridge and develop a large resort. When support for constructing the bridge could not be raised, he abandoned the project. Years later a ferry was created, and it carried motorists and pedestrians over to the Bogue Inlet beaches of modern-day Emerald Isle. The ferry landed near Bogue Inlet Pier, the first recreational spot at the island's west end.

Today, the Cameron Langston Bridge provides access from the mainland to Emerald Isle and the western end of Bogue Banks. It spans the Intracoastal Waterway, and from the top of the bridge there's a great view of the waterway and Bogue Banks.

Emerald Isle has a year-round population of more than 3,500 and a seasonal population of over 16,000. It is a thriving beach-vacation spot, with plenty to do for the entire family. The town's municipal complex and community center has large meeting rooms, a full basketball court and a gym (see our Sports, Fitness and Parks chapter). Several new housing sections have been developed west of the high-rise bridge, in the area surrounding the Coast Guard Station, and a few choice spots have become fairly exclusive gated communities.

Out of the eight types of sea turtles found in the Indian, Pacific and Atlantic oceans, the coast of North Carolina is home to five of these incredible marine animals: Leatherback, Atlantic Ridley, Green Turtle, Hawksbill and Loggerhead.

Beaufort

Many people find that crossing the drawbridge into Beaufort (pronounced BO-fort) is like taking a giant step back in time. Steeped in history, this well-restored colonial seaport village affords visitors a glimpse at what life in an early American fishing and port town may have been like. Not to be confused with the somewhat larger Beaufort, South Carolina, (pronounced BU-fort), Beaufort is still a town of only about 4,000 full-time residents, and fishing and fish processing still figure into its economy. With tree-lined streets and restored Victorian homes, Beaufort's historical diversity and Southern charm are evident as soon as you pull off U.S. Highway 70. This is a town that deserves more than a drive-through. Its Front Street faces Taylor's Creek with the Rachel Carson Estuarine Reserve, then Shackleford Banks, then the Atlantic Ocean straight ahead. With a walk of just a few short blocks, Beaufort starts to really share its quaint beauty. Residents and visitors alike enjoy a stroll along the wooden boardwalk, early or late, or down the quiet streets

CLOSE UP

The Revenge of Blackbeard

It may indeed be the revenge of Blackbeard to be the most remembered of all American pirates. That is probably why the finding of what is believed to be his flagship Queen Anne's Revenge is intriguing and has brought thousands of people to Beaufort and the Crystal Coast.

Probably uncovered by shifting underwater sands from the hurricanes of 1996, the wreckage is producing strong evidence that the ship found is, in fact, the notorious pirate's doomed vessel. Discovered in 1996 in 20 feet of water less than two miles off historic Fort Macon, the find includes a cannon, part of a blunderbuss and other 18th-century seafaring items that are on exhibit at the North Carolina Maritime Museum in Beaufort.

As far as American Colonial history is concerned, the Queen Anne's Revenge recovery is classified as a major 20th-century archaeological find. In some ways, probably more is known of Blackbeard's main ship than of the pirate himself, who despite any legendary portrayal, is not known to have killed a single person. But he captured many a ship in the years from 1716 to 1718 in his short pirate career that ended in November 1718 with Blackbeard's head hanging from the bowsprit of a British ship.

That Blackbeard lived in Bath, North Carolina, where he bought a house and filled it with lavish furnishings, is well documented. Governor Charles Eden granted Blackbeard and 20 of his men a pardon, and even attended Blackbeard's marriage to a 16-year-old. His bride did not know that she was Blackbeard's 14th wife.

Blackbeard's fierce countenance was a result of burning cannon fuses hanging from his wild beard and broad hat and a dozen pistol braces in his belts. This is probably the most recorded, and painted, image of the man. But history and legend often intertwine, and separating fact from fiction is not always easy. For example, you can pick up several biographies of Blackbeard, but where dialogue begins may be the end of fact and the beginning of fancy. Besides the Queen Anne's Revenge, Blackbeard also ran several pirate vessels, including the Revenge, The Royal James and the Adventure.

The search for what is dubbed the QAR has been actively pursued by a company called Intersal for a decade, and the diving is continuing. Intersal raised 15 cannons, three anchors used for vessels of at least 364 tons, shards from large lead-glazed storage containers, salt-glazed stoneware, large iron barrel hoops and a pewter dinner plate and platter with an identifying English maker's mark. They also recovered remains of bag shot, wads of lead shot of varying sizes imprinted with cloth fabric.

Among the most prized artifacts found was the bronze ship's bell. It bears the date 1709 and the inscription "IHS Maria," which state historians believe refers to Jesus and Mary. It is thought that the bell may have been looted from a victim ship. The bell, blunderbuss and other bronze items that are more easily preserved than iron or wood went on display at N.C. Maritime Museum in Beaufort in 1997.

Queen Anne's Revenge was launched in 1710 in England as a merchant ship commissioned the Concord. She carried 20 cannons and displaced around 300 tons. She had a short career in the service of England. In 1710 the French captured Concord and refit it as an armed transport ship renamed Concorde. She may have been involved in slave trade as she sailed routinely between Africa, South America and the Caribbean. Enter the man also known as Edward Teach of Bristol, England, who had left the service of privateer-turned-pirate Captain Benjamin Hornigold.

Teach took the Concorde out of the service of France in 1717, doubled her cache of cannons to 40 and renamed her Queen Anne's Revenge.

The days of piracy were numbered. The Caribbean and Colonial governments were souring on the common practice of privateering. It had been a lovely arrangement for a while to avoid duty payments to the Crown of England. Everyone profited. Privateers sold pirated merchandise to merchants who were able to make greater profits. But when cargoes that wealthy officialsand merchants had invested in were intercepted, that's when the privateers became criminals, or pirates.

Presumed literate, Blackbeard was a genius at marketing an image. A statuesque man, he wore a full black beard when beards weren't the style. His hair was long and he wore it thickly braided, probably like dreadlocks, at sea. For attacks, he braided his beard, which sprouted from just under his eyes. In his hair and beard, he laced fuse cords used to ignite cannons. They were treated in saltpeter and limewater to burn slowly when lighted. When he appeared on the deck of Queen Anne's Revenge to demand the surrender of a halted vessel. He had guns and knives strapped to him and was surrounded by smoke like a demon from Hell. So effective was the image that more than 45 ships are known to have surrendered to Blackbeard, as well as one city — Charleston, South Carolina — from which he demanded medicine to cure his crew of venereal disease. In fact, there are no recorded battles with ships of Blackbeard's fleet except for the battle at Ocracoke. Ships just surrendered.

where the smell of salty air puts a whiff of the past into quick moments of today.

Beaufort is the third-oldest town in North Carolina and was named for Englishman Henry Somerset, the Duke of Beaufort. The town was surveyed in 1713, nearly 20 years before George Washington's birth, and was incorporated in 1722. Beaufort is the geographic center of Carteret County and its county seat. The English influence is apparent in the architecture and, more noticeably, in the street names: Ann and Queen, for Queen Anne; Craven, for the Earl of Craven; Orange, for William, the Prince of Orange; Moore, for Col. Maurice Moore; and Pollock, for the Colonial governor at the time of the 1713 survey.

Beaufort offers a glimpse at a relatively unspoiled part of North Carolina's coastal history. The town takes great pride in its restored older structures. Much of that can be credited to the Beaufort Historical Association (BHA), which was organized in 1960 to celebrate the town's 250th anniversary. The association commemorates Beaufort's historic homes with special plaques, noting the original homeowner and the date in which the structure was built. To earn a plaque, a home must be at least 80 years old and have retained its historic and architectural integrity. The first home to be "plaqued" was the Duncan House, c. 1790, at 105 Front Street. Through the years the Beaufort Historical Association has moved several old structures — including an early American Courthouse, jail and apothecary that were threatened with demolition — to an area on Turner Street, which is now open to the public daily. For more information about the Beaufort Historic Site, see our Crystal Coast Attractions chapter.

Beaufort's designated historic district is between Gallant's Channel, which flows under the drawbridge, and the east side of Pollock Street and between Taylor's Creek and the south side of Broad Street. The one-block area of the county courthouse is also included in the historic district that includes many structures listed on the National Register of Historic Places.

Each historic house and site has its own story to tell; however, the house with the most lively history is the Hammock House of 1698, considered to be Beaufort's oldest standing house. It once stood so close to the waters of Taylor's Creek that visitors could tie a skiff, or flat-bottomed boat, to the front porch. Through years of storms and dredging the creek's shore and course have changed, and the house now stands one block back from the waterfront. At one time Hammock

House served as an "ordinary" (an inn), and Blackbeard, the fiercest of all pirates, was a regular guest. Legend has it that Blackbeard hung one of his wives from a live oak in the front yard, and neighbors say they can still hear her screams on moonlit nights. The house was later used as accommodations by the Union Army during the Civil War and is now privately owned.

The Old Burying Ground on Ann Street is one of Beaufort's most fascinating sites. Deeded to the town in 1731, the Old Burying Ground was declared full in 1825, and the N.C. General Assembly said no more burials would be allowed. The town was ordered to lay out a new graveyard, but the townspeople didn't support the act and continued to bury their loved ones in the Old Burying Ground until the early 1900s. The north corner of the graveyard is the oldest section of the cemetery, although many of the oldest graves don't carry a marker. The markers are fascinating. For a great self-guided tour, stop by the Beaufort Historical Association, 138 Turner Street, (252) 728-5225, for a map of the Old Burying Ground. If you can find a docent, be sure and ask about some of the graveyard's most interesting tales. BHA's volunteers are always eager to share a ghost story or two.

A few of the notables buried here are Capt. Josiah Pender, whose men took Fort Macon in 1861; James W. Hunt, who had the distinction of marrying, making his will and dying the same day; Esther Cooke, mother of Capt. James W. Cooke, who once commanded the ironclad Albemarle; the Dill child, buried in a glass-topped casket; the common grave of the Crissie Wright crew, who froze to death when the ship wrecked on Shackleford Banks in 1886; and the child who died aboard a ship and was brought to Beaufort in a keg of rum for burial — in the keg. People leave trinkets on the child's grave, along with money, jewelry and small toys — although no one seems to remember how the practice got started.

With the town's waterfront revitalization project in the late 1970s, Beaufort took a new direction. The renovation involved tearing down many old waterfront structures not considered salvageable and building the wooden boardwalk, docks and facilities that bring more sail boats and pleasure craft than the shad boats that once lined the creek. Some businesses were encouraged to stay while others opted to move into the downtown area. Soon word of the new old town spread, and it hasn't been the same since. What was once a coastal hideaway is now a favorite spot for visitors traveling by car or boat.

As you enter Beaufort from the west, you will cross the Grayden M. Paul Drawbridge. The bridge's namesake was a lively historian, best known for his songs, poems and tales about Beaufort and Carteret County. Drawbridges in coastal areas are becoming relics of the past as more and more towns are choosing to replace them with concrete high-rises. And that's the case for this old landmark. Because of increased traffic, discussions are ongoing about replacing the drawbridge in the next few years, and the issue has become a hot political ticket. Where to locate the bridge has been a sticking point, and people in Beaufort are divided between maintaining the drawbridge or building a new bridge to ease traffic snarls.

Even with all the town's history, there is still much development here. New structures continue to spring up right up to the edges of the Historic District, and new developments are under construction around town and in the town's surrounding areas. As more and more people discover Beaufort, the population continues to grow.

Beaufort is home to a number of attractions, not the least of which are the wonderful North Carolina Maritime Museum and Watercraft Center and the Rachel Carson Reserve, part of the North Carolina National Estuarine Research Reserve (see our Crystal Coast Attractions chapter for more information about both).

BEAUFORT'S NEARBY COMMUNITIES

Lennoxville is the community closest to Beaufort. It begins at the east end of Front Street in Beaufort and continues to the east end of Lennoxville Road where it cul-de-sacs beneath an awning of huge live oaks at a place ole' timers and true locals still call Black Cat. This is primarily an unincorporated residential area, with the exception of Beaufort Fisheries and Atlantic Veneer (see our Commerce and Industry chapter). Lennoxville

is surrounded by water: Taylor's Creek on the south and North River on the north with Core Sound and a perfect view of Cape Lookout Lighthouse. The lure of waterfront living has stimulated the development of a few small but very upscale subdivisions along Lennoxville's forested waterfront.

North River is a small community north of Beaufort on Merrimon Road. Baseball pitcher Brien Taylor put the community of North River on the map in 1991 when, as a senior at East Carteret High School, he signed a $1.55 million contract with the New York Yankees. An injury has prevented him from playing with the Yankees. A side street in this close-knit community is named for him.

Here's a riddle — the South River community actually lies to the north of the North River community. Named for the body of water at its banks, South River is a small traditional fishing and hunting community. Hurricane Isabel in 2003 flooded many of the homes, and the hardworking residents continue to elevate houses and repair damages. Some of the surrounding land is owned by recreational hunters and businesses, and several private airstrips are in the area. Many Native American artifacts and pottery pieces have been found in the South River area.

Open Grounds Farm lies in the South River area and extends east to community of Stacy. This 45,000 acre corporate farm includes 36,000 acres in crops - namely corn, soybeans and wheat. The remaining acreage is in forest.

To the west of South River lies the community of Merrimon. This rural area borders the Neuse River and Adams Creek, which is a stretch of the scenic Intracoastal Waterway. Homes in Merrimon were also flooded during Hurricane Isabel in 2003. The port town of Oriental is just across the Neuse River and is visible on most days and attainable via a free state-operated ferry.

In recent years a few neighborhood developments have sprung up around South River, Merrimon and the Intracoastal Waterway. Sportsman's Village, Sandy Point, Jonaquin's Landing and Indian Summer Estates offer waterfront and mainland lots.

i

When you're in doubt about directions, stop and ask a local. Chances are you'll meet a friendly person and learn a lot about the area.

Morehead City

With almost 8,000 residents, Morehead City is Carteret County's largest town. The town began with an early land prospector from Virginia named John Shackleford, for whom Shackleford Banks was named. In 1714 Shackleford saw a future for the area and purchased approximately 1,400 acres throughout Carteret County and Morehead City. The second land owner in the Morehead City area was David Shepard, who in 1723 purchased the land now known as Shepard's Point. Other notable early settlers include William Fisher, Silas Webb, Bridges Arendell and past N.C. Governor John Motley Morehead. All of these names can be seen on signposts around town today.

In 1852 the state decided to extend a railroad line to connect Raleigh with the coast, and several towns vied to be the end location, hoping to bring growth to their communities. For a while it was considered inevitable that the line would end in Beaufort. In 1857 William H. Arendell, John Motley Morehead and others formed the Shepard's Point Land Company, purchasing 1,000 acres at the western end of the Shepard's Point. Sixty home lots were created, the first of which were sold during a public auction on November 11, 1857.

In 1858 John Motley Morehead sang the praises of the infant town: "The City of Morehead is situated on a beautiful neck of land or dry plain, almost entirely surrounded by salt water; its climate salubrious; its sea breezes and sea bathing delightful; its drinking water good and its fine chalybeate spring, strongly impregnated with sulfur, will make it a pleasant watering place . . ."

The sale of the land was successful, and more importantly Gov. Morehead was successful in his bid for the railroad's destination and ultimately one of two state deep-water ports. Morehead City was incorporated in 1861. When the N.C. Legislature authorized the incorporation of the town, surveyors laid out the streets and named the primary ones after men who had been influential in the area's settlement — Fisher, Arendell, Bridges, Evans, Shackleford and Shepard.

Stop by the Crystal Coast Visitors Center, 3409 Arendell Street (U.S. Highway 70 E.), Morehead City, to pick up a free street map of Morehead, Beaufort, Swansboro, Atlantic Beach, Down East, Newport and many of the area's other towns.

The town was started just in time to be taken over by the Union forces when they attacked Fort Macon on April 26, 1862, thus ending for a time any significant development. Even after the end of the War Between the States, Morehead City struggled to regain its commercial life until the 1880s, when the shipping industry began to bring business to town, once again turning the area into a hub of activity. In the early 1880s a new Atlantic Hotel was built in Morehead City, replacing the old Atlantic Hotel that had been destroyed by a hurricane. The Atlantic Hotel had 233 rooms and claimed to have the largest ballroom in the South. It drew the cream of the state's society to the coast until it was destroyed by fire in 1933.

In 1911 the city began a road improvement program to keep up with the town's slow but steady growth. Better roads stimulated the growth of Crab Point, a part of the city east of Country Club Road and north of the 20th Street Bridge over Calico Creek. Morehead residents dubbed the area Crab Point because when tides came in crabs got trapped on the shoreline, making them an easy catch. In the early days Crab Point served as a port and had windmills for grinding grain and generating power for lumber companies. A private cemetery in the area has graves dating back to the early 1700s.

Today Morehead City is home to the North Carolina Seafood Festival (the state's second largest annual festival) and the Big Rock Marlin Tournament (see our Crystal Coast Annual Events chapter). The city continues to grow and strives to preserve its heritage as a fishing and port city. The most obvious recent improvements have occurred along the waterfront. Morehead City's leaders have provided a major face-lift to this charming section of town, resulting in wide sidewalks, new docks, bathroom facilities, art work, parks and a gazebo in City Park on Arendell Street. Waterfront restaurants, both new and old, and shops continue to bring visitors and deep-sea charter fishing boats line the dock to give them a day at sea. Some of the best places in Morehead City, however, are off the beaten path. You must cross Arendell Street, away from the waterfront, and walk down the side streets to Bridges Street, which parallels Arendell, to enjoy many fine old residences that have been refurbished. Some of these buildings have been turned into shops, bed and breakfast inns, art galleries and businesses. They are well worth turning a corner to find.

Swansboro

Swansboro is the only geographic area of our six described here that is not in Carteret County, but that's merely a technicality. Situated just across the county line in Onslow County, this water-oriented town sits on the Intracoastal Waterway along the mouth of the White Oak River, where the Atlantic Ocean is easily accessible through Bogue Inlet. Many fishing boats call Swansboro home, and residents keep sport-fishing boats at marinas in Swansboro. You can reach Swansboro by taking either N.C. 58 (from Bogue Banks) or N.C. 24 (from Morehead City). Recent road and bridge developments make Swansboro even easier to reach as you travel from Morehead City.

From its origins as the site of an Algonquian Indian village at the mouth of the White Oak River to its current status as the "Friendly City by the Sea," Swansboro is a lovely place to visit because of its mild climate and friendly citizens.

The town began about 1730, when Jonathan and Grace Green moved from Falmouth, Massachusetts, to the mouth of the White Oak River. With them, and owning half of their property, was Jonathan Green's brother, Isaac. They lived there about five years until Jonathan Green died at the early age of 35. His widow, Grace, married Theophilus Weeks, who had moved with his family from Falmouth to settle on Hadnot Creek a few miles up the White Oak River.

After their marriage, the Weeks moved into the Green family home on the Onslow County side of the White Oak River. Theophilus soon purchased all of Isaac Green's interest and became sole owner of the large plantation. Weeks first farmed, then opened a tavern and was appointed inspector of exports at the thriving port. In 1771 he started a town on that portion of his plantation called Weeks Wharf, selling 48 numbered lots recorded as being "in the plan of a town laid out by Theophilus Weeks," thus earning him the title of founder of the town.

Originally called Week's Point, the New-Town-upon-Bogue was established by law in 1783. The General Assembly named the town Swannsborough, in honor of Samuel Swann, former speaker of the N.C. House of Representatives and longtime Onslow County representative.

Swansboro (the later spelling of the town's name) was home to the famous Otway Burns. During the War of 1812, this native son became a privateer with his schooner, the Snapdragon. His participation during this "Second War of Independence" was acclaimed as an act of bravery and patriotism. After the war, he returned to the trade of ship building and was later appointed keeper of the lighthouse at Portsmouth, where he died in 1850. He is buried in Beaufort's Old Burying Ground.

Swansboro's port continued to prosper, mainly because nearby pine forests produced the lumber, tar, pitch and other naval items shipped through the port. Prosperity continued until the end of the Civil War. Then, gradually, the town came to support itself with farming and fishing.

One of the most enjoyable aspects of contemporary Swansboro is the historic downtown section built along the water's edge. Much of this area was heavily damaged by Hurricane Ophelia in September 2005 and is undergoing rebuilding. Here you will find specialty and antiques shops, restaurants and plenty of space to stroll and gaze at the water and pleasure boats. The town's historic commission supervises the restoration of many of the town's oldest structures. Several of these fine buildings now house businesses, while others remain private residences.

Down East

Down East is the local name for the land that stretches from the North River on the

Miles and miles of Atlantic Ocean beaches are waiting for you on the Crystal Coast.

photo: George Mitchell

east side of Beaufort to Cedar Island, which marks Carteret County's northeastern boundary. Here you'll find some of the most picturesque scenery in Carteret County — marshes, canals and undisturbed places filled with wildlife, particularly as you get closer to Cedar Island. The portion of U.S. 70 that runs through Down East is a N.C. Scenic Byway, so designated by the N.C. Department of Transportation because it offers incomparable scenery and a chance to observe something different from the fast traffic and commercial areas along major interstates. It is well worth your time to take U.S. 70 to Cedar Island, especially in autumn when the afternoon light is magical. At certain times of day, black needlerush seems to turn gold.

In the past, the livelihood of almost all Down East people depended on the water. Whether they made a living at commercial fishing, crabbing or boat building, people in this part of the county have a heritage tied to the water. The majority still rely on the water to make a living, however more and more residents are finding employment in Beaufort or Morehead City or at the Marine Corps Air Station Cherry Point in Havelock. The love for the water remains obvious, however, by the number of boats, fish houses and seafood businesses found in Down East villages.

The Down East area, particularly the towns of Marshallberg, Davis, Stacy, Sea Level and Cedar Island were hard hit by Hurricane Isabel in 2003 and again by Hurricane Ophelia in September 2005 and the residents are still trying to recover. Not only did the hurricanes put 2 to 5 feet of water in hundreds of homes, but also cars were flooded, commercial fishing equipment and businesses were destroyed, and local waters were closed to commercial fishing for months. The economic impact of these storms will remain with this area for years to come.

None of the towns in Down East is incorporated, so the area is governed by the county. Activities center on the schools, churches, volunteer fire and rescue squads, post offices and local stores. Most of these fishing communities, which were settled by watermen, lie along U.S. 70, the main road running through Down East. The history of Down East is rich and could fill volumes. We'll just give you a very brief taste and invite you to explore on your own.

After leaving Beaufort on U.S. 70, Bettie is the first Down East community you reach. It lies between the North River Bridge and Ward's Creek Bridge. The next community is Otway, named for famous Swansboro privateer Otway Burns.

As you turn off U.S. 70 onto Harkers Island Road, Straits is the community you see flanking the road to Harkers Island. The Straits is also the name of the body of water that lies between the community and the island. The spelling of Straits is shown on early maps as "Straights." Later cartographers probably noticed the name was not applicable to a water course and changed the spelling to Straits, meaning narrows. Years ago Straits was a farm community and a substantial amount of cotton was grown here. Straits United Methodist Church, c. 1778, was the first Methodist Church built east of Beaufort.

Originally called Craney Island, Harkers Island once was the home of a thriving band of Tuscarora Indians. By the turn of the 20th century, all that remained of the Native American settlement was a huge mound of sea shells on the island's east end, now called Shell Point. Folks say the Native Americans were attempting to build a shell walkway through the waters of Core Sound to Core Banks. Standing at Shell Point today, you can see the Cape Lookout Lighthouse and nearby islands.

In 1730 George Pollock sold the island to Ebenezer Harker of Boston. Harker moved to the island and later divided it among his three sons, using the divisions "eastard," "westard" and "center." These have remained unofficial dividers, at least for the natives of the island. The Harker heirs did not part with their land for years, so the island population remained sparse for some time. In 1895 fewer than 30 families lived there. The population grew when folks from the Shackleford Bank's community of Diamond City abandoned their town due to the devastation of hurricanes. Some loaded homes on boats and brought them to the safer ground of Harkers Island. With this new surge in population, schools, churches and businesses sprang up. Still, the island remained isolated until ferry operations began in 1926, with the ferry leaving from the island's west end and docking in the Down East community of Gloucester. A bridge to the island was built in 1941. Today, the island is home to the Core Sound Waterfowl Museum, the famous Core Sound Decoy Festival and the Cape Lookout National Park Visitor Center. See our Crystal Coast Attractions and Annual Events chapters for more information on these fascinating places and events.

As you leave Harkers Island and re-enter U.S. 70 headed east, Smyrna is the next Down East town. It was named in 1785 from a deed that conveyed 100 acres from Joseph Davis to Seth Williston. The land was on Smunar Creek, and the spelling was later changed to Smyrna.

Off U.S. 70 on Marshallberg Road is Marshallberg, originally named Deep Hole Point. This hamlet is built on a peninsula formed by Jarrett Bay and Core Sound. Folks say that clay was dug from the area and used to fill ramparts and cover easements at Fort Macon on Bogue Banks, leaving a large hole, thus the name. It was later renamed for Matt Marshall, who ran the mailboat from Beaufort.

In 1880 W. Q. A. Graham established Graham Academy at the head of Sleepy Creek in Marshallberg. The school prepared its students for college, and students who didn't live in town stayed in the school's dormitories. Monthly board was about $5.50 per student, and the school's attendance in 1892 was 126. The academy was destroyed by fire in 1910.

Between Marshallberg and Straits is the small community of Gloucester, so named in the early 1900s by Capt. Joseph Pigott for the Massachusetts town he loved. Back on U.S. 70 and a little way past Smyrna, you will find Williston, named for John Williston who was one of the area's first settlers. Williston has long been nicknamed "Beantown," though why is still a point of confusion. Some say it was because of the large quantities of beans grown in the community, and others say it was because residents had a reputation for loving to eat beans. The Williston United Methodist Church was built in 1883.

The village of Davis was settled by William T. Davis in the 1700s. People worked the water and the land to make a living. Farm crops, such as cotton and sweet potatoes, were taken by sailboat to Virginia to be sold or traded for flour, sugar and cloth. Davis residents were known as "Onion Eaters," either because of the number of green onions grown there or because Davis people simply liked onions. An Army camp was opened in Davis during World War II, and some of the old camp buildings remain along the water's edge.

Stacy is made up of two even smaller communities: Masontown and Piney Point. The post office was opened in 1885. Stacy Freewill Baptist Church is more than 100 years old.

Originally called Wit, Sea Level is still the fishing community it has always been. In 1706 the King of England granted Capt. John Nelson about 650 acres, with Nelson's Bay on the west and Core Sound on the east. That land is today's Sea Level. Sailors' Snug Harbor, the oldest charitable trust in America, opened a facility for retired Merchant Marines there in 1976. (The original facility of its type opened in 1833 on Staten Island.) The Snug Harbor center is now open to both men and women, offering a beautiful sanctuary in a picturesque forest. Taylor Extended Care Facility is a nursing home on Nelson's Bay. A satellite clinic of Carteret General Hospital operates alongside the nursing home.

U.S. 70 ends, or begins depending on how you look at it, in the township of Atlantic. This community was settled in the 1740s and was originally called Hunting Quarters. The first post office opened in 1880, and the name was changed to Atlantic. The community's nickname is Per, and old timers refer to their home as Per Atlantic. In the 1930s progress arrived in the form of paved roads. Today, Atlantic is home to two of the East Coast's largest seafood dealers, Luther Smith & Son Seafood Company and Clayton Fulcher Seafood Company as well as a 1,500-acre Marine Corps Outlying Landing Field.

From Atlantic, N.C. 12 takes travelers to Cedar Island, seemingly the end of the earth, where you'll find the North Carolina State ferry landing to Ocracoke Island and North Carolina's Outer Banks. Cedar Island was known by that name until two post offices were established in the early 1900s. Then the east end of the island became known as Lola and the west end as Roe, each with its own post office and school. In the 1960s, the two post offices closed and a new one was opened. The whole island became known as Cedar Island again, but locals still use the old names. Some homes on the island date back to the 1880s.

Newport/Western Carteret County

Newport is known as "the town with old-fashioned courtesy." When traveling from Carteret County to New Bern on U.S. 70, it is the first incorporated town through which you pass. The town continues to grow as Morehead City gets larger and as Marine Corps Air Station Cherry Point in Havelock expands.

Chartered in 1866, Newport was first supported by logging, farming and fishing. Today, many of its nearly 3,500 residents work at Cherry Point. Newport is home to a development park on U.S. 70 and the National Oceanic and Atmospheric Administration Weather Forecast Office that offers state-of-the-art weather tracking and forecasting. Operated as part of the National Weather Service, this facility houses a Doppler weather radar system with advanced weather capabilities and is well positioned to monitor the weather upsets that come where land meets ocean.

Newport has many quiet residential sections, an elementary school and a middle school, stores, a town hall and a public library. It is home to the popular Newport Pig Cooking Contest each April (see our Crystal Coast Annual Events chapter) and it boasts a strong volunteer fire department and rescue squad.

Northeast of Newport is the community of Mill Creek. This area continues to rely heavily on farming although many new homes are being built in the rural waterfront areas. Mill Creek can reached by driving through Newport or by approaching from N.C. 101 out of Beaufort.

Traveling west from Morehead City, N.C. 24 parallels Bogue Sound. The highway passes through several communities that dot this part of the county. Broad Creek is an old town, once made up almost exclusively of commercial fishermen and their families. Some of these fishermen came to the area as long ago as 100 years; others came from Diamond City on Shackleford Banks after the devastating hurricanes forced them to vacate. Today, there is a middle school and much new residential development in the unincorporated town.

Ocean was once a thriving village with one of the county's first post offices. Now it is the home of the North Carolina Coastal Federation (a nonprofit conservation group that offers exciting excursions into the county's marsh and forest habitats) as well as an elementary school, a high school and many new developments. As you leave the unincorporated town of Ocean, the next little town is Bogue. With almost 600 residents, it was only incorporated in a special election in September 1995 and now has a commissioner-mayor form of local government. The U.S. Marine Corps Auxiliary Landing Field is in Bogue.

At the junction of N.C. highways 24 and 58 lie two communities: Cedar Point, home to about 950, and Cape Carteret, where nearly 1,300 live. Cedar Point (not to be confused with the Down East community of Cedar Island) is the westernmost incorporated town in Carteret County and the westernmost point of the county. The town was established in 1713 but not incorporated until 1988.

Chartered in 1959, Cape Carteret is one of the few planned communities in the county. The late W. B. McLean, one of the developers of Emerald Isle, initiated the town's development. In laying out "Cape C," McLean donated land for a Presbyterian church, a Baptist church and White Oak Elementary School. The first homes were built on the Bogue Sound waterfront near the foot of what is now the B. Cameron Langston Bridge, the high-rise bridge built in 1971 to replace the ferry. The town grew slowly and today is complete with stores, a town hall, fire and rescue departments, a school and a new library and community college annex.

If you turn right at the traffic light at the intersection of N.C. highways 24 and 58, you will go northwest on N.C. 58 through the Croatan National Forest and through several old settlements including Peletier, incorporated in 1997 and home to about 500 residents, the Hadnot Creek community and Kuhn's Corner. Kuhn's Corner marks the intersection that leads to Stella, a once-thriving village with stores, mills, a good many farmhouses and even a couple of huge plantation houses. Traveling east on N.C. 58, you will cross the high-rise bridge that takes you to the beach town of Emerald Isle.

There is nothing better than a day at the beach.

photo: George Mitchell

SWAP SHOP
NOW
4 BIG HOURS
Buy, Sell, Trade, Give away
SATURDAYS
7 am to 11 am
BIG JOHN R
THE TALK STATION
107.3 FM
1240 AM

RESTAURANTS

Seafood is one of the Crystal Coast's grandest resources and pleasures. Local cultural history is frequently woven with recipes unique to our part of the world. Clam Chowder, Down East light rolls, stewed hard crabs, collards and dumplings are the tastes and smells that speak of home in Beaufort, Morehead City, Salter Path and Down East. Generations of Crystal Coast families and summer visitors were raised on the traditional seafood dishes of Morehead City's waterfront restaurants that, until the 1980s, fried just about everything but the cole slaw.

In the traditional waterfront restaurants, fried hush puppies are always served first, usually before the water glasses are on the table. Hush puppies are a local cuisine tradition as well as a standard of quality. They are made with cornmeal, flour, eggs and sugar. To create a unique taste, some folks add chopped onion, and others add sweet milk. Once blended, the mixture is dropped by the spoonful into hot fat and fried to a golden brown. Old-timers say the name derived from cooks who, while preparing meals, tossed bits of fried batter to quiet the dogs waiting for kitchen scraps.

Most natives were raised on conch and clam chowders, and even the newest eateries include these among their soups and appetizers. Local conch chowder is made with whelk, while traditional chowder is made with chopped seafood, water, butter, salt, pepper and diced potatoes. For a different flavor, some chefs might also add squash, onions and spices.

There's nothing like a traditional Down East clam bake, although you won't find eating like this on any restaurant menu. You can sometimes luck out and catch a school, church or fire department holding a fund-raising clambake. If that happens, drop your plans and head on over for great coastal food. It is said that the idea for the clambake came from the Native Americans, who taught early residents to cook clams, fish and corn in the steam of hot stones. Modern-day clambakes usually offer clams, chicken, sweet potatoes, white potatoes, onions, carrots, corn and sometimes a few shrimp. The items are usually steamed together in a net bag or cheesecloth and served with melted butter. This is not the time for table manners, so use your fingers!

Peelers, pickers, jimmies, white bellies, hens, steamers, paper shells or soft-shells -- no matter what you call them, they're still crabs. Learning the difference between the names and the stages of a crab's life is the hard part. Knowing when crabs are ready to shed and are marketable as soft-shells is important to the livelihood of many Crystal Coast crabbers. Understanding the process a crab goes through to become a soft-shell is an art as well as a science.

A peeler is a crab that will, if all goes well, become a soft crab within 72 hours. They are carefully handled and put in vats where they can go through this molting process. Jimmies are the large male crabs that measure 6 inches from upper shell tip to tip, and steamers or pickers are just regular crabs. The sure way to tell if a crab is a peeler is by the pinkish-red ring on the outer tip of the flipper or back fin. Those that complete the molting process are sold live or dressed. Many are packed with damp sea grass, refrigerated and shipped live to restaurants or seafood markets as far away as New York. Most are sold dressed, because live soft-shells are delicate to handle and have a life of only about three days. Insiders consider soft-shell crabs a delicacy, and favorite ways to prepare them include lightly frying them in batter or sauteeing them in butter and wine. There is nothing better, or stranger looking, than a soft-shell crab sandwich.

Shrimp burgers, another popular local seafood treat, are little more than fried shrimp on a hamburger bun with slaw and special sauce. Each restaurant has its own sauce, which is the secret to a great shrimp burger. Some places have come up with variations (oyster burgers, clam burgers), but it's all basically put together the same way. Oh, what a wonderful lunch a shrimp burger makes!

Collards are a traditional mainstay in the diet of most locals, especially those living Down East. A "mess" of collards cooking in the kitchen creates an unforgettable aroma that you either love or hate. These leafy green vegetables grow almost year round in this area. Most locals say the best way to cook them is with a streak-of-lean salt pork or some fatback added to the pot. Top it off with a few new red potatoes and some cornmeal dumplings, an eastern North Carolina specialty made by shaping cornmeal, water and salt into small patties. Drop the dumplings into the collard pot for about 15 minutes - and then you'll have some really good eating!

Within the past few years, somewhat more sophisticated culinary talent has begun to flourish in our haven of fabulous seafood. On the Beaufort and Morehead City waterfront, new gourmet restaurants reflect the demand of increasingly upscale appetites. Openings around Morehead and in Beaufort, new menus and redecorated restaurants from Atlantic Beach to Emerald Isle tell us that our tastes are changing. Our dining choices certainly are.

Great numbers of fast-food and chain restaurants are as convenient on the Crystal Coast as they are in every corner of the civilized world. Most of these establishments are concentrated on U.S. Highway 70, the main artery through Carteret County. This guide does not review chain restaurants, under the assumption that you are already familiar with their fare. However, we do have a section at the end of this chapter on fast food; we write about some of the local eateries where good, quick food is not to be missed if you have a yen for great burgers, coffee, bagels, pizza and deli fare.

Planning and Pricing

When planning your lunch or dinner outing, we recommend you call ahead to verify the information offered in our restaurant profiles and to check the hours or seating availability. While we intend to reflect each restaurant as accurately as possible, menu modifications do occur. Some area restaurants close during slow winter months, and some that remain open may limit menu items to ensure freshness.

The serving of mixed drinks in North Carolina is regulated by the Alcohol Beverage Control Board. Restaurants designated as having "all ABC permits" can sell mixed drinks in addition to wine and beer. In Carteret County, restaurants and lounges serve mixed drinks in all the incorporated communities expect the town of Newport, which restricts the serving of alcoholic beverages to wine and beer. Mixed drinks are not served in Down East establishments or in any other unincorporated area except the Bogue Banks community of Salter Path. Unless we state otherwise, the restaurants described here have all ABC permits.

Many area restaurants also offer special discounts to early diners (particularly in the winter), and many have discounts for senior citizens and specially priced children's dinner menus.

Because of the large number of restaurants on the Crystal Coast and the limited space in this chapter, we refer you only to restaurants that continue to be favorites. There certainly are many more restaurants to choose from - check the local phone book and newspaper advertisements for other suggestions.

Restaurants are arranged alphabetically according to their location. We have given the mile marker (MM) number for those on N.C. Highway 58 on Bogue Banks to help you find them more easily. Most of the dinner

Bogue Sound melons, both cantaloupes and watermelons, are renowned for their sweetness and are sold at roadside markets on N.C. Highway 24 by late June.

establishments listed honor all major credit cards and take reservations.

PRICE CODE

This price code will give you a general idea of the cost of dinner for two. Because entrees come in a wide range of prices, the code we used reflects an average cost of entrees, not the most expensive item or the least expensive item. For restaurants that do not serve dinner, the price code reflects the cost of lunch fare. Price code averages do not include appetizers, drinks, desserts, gratuity or the state's sales tax.

$	Less than $20
$$	$20 to $30
$$$	$31 to $40
$$$$	More than $40

Bogue Banks

ATLANTIC BEACH

Amos Mosquito's Swampside Cafe $$
MM 2, 703 N.C. Hwy. 58, Atlantic Beach
(252) 247-6222

Amos Mosquito's is designed to feel like nighttime on Shackleford Banks, with a "swampy" theme. Owners Hallock Howard, executive chef, and Sandy Howard, general manager, offer patrons reasonably priced dinners, simply presented and a treat to the palate. The kitchen strives for consistency in taste and the use of fresh, in-season vegetables and seafood. A typical dinner special is roasted whole red snapper for two accompanied by a trio of Thai dipping sauces. Other favorites include brown-sugar–glazed meatloaf served with homemade macaroni and cheese; an 8-ounce shoulder filet with lobster, provolone smashed potatoes and homemade Worcestershire sauce; fresh fish prepared a number of ways and the chef's incomparable crab cakes. Children are welcome at Amos Mosquito's. A particular treat for them are s'mores, those old-fashioned chocolate, marshmallow and graham cracker concoctions. They are served tableside in braziers so the kids can get involved in assembling them. (The staff cleans up the marshmallow mess.) Grown-ups generally prefer the melt-in-your-mouth homemade cheesecake and crème brulee. The cafe is open seven days (with brunch on Sunday) during the season. Winter hours are shorter, so call first. Amos' has a spacious patio for al fresco dining with a water view. The restaurant is a half-mile east of the Atlantic Beach stoplight.

Fresh vegetables and flowers are great pickings at roadside farm markets or at the Curb Market on summer Saturday mornings at 12th and Evans streets in Morehead City.

Caffeine Cuisine $
Waterfront on The Circle, Atlantic Beach
(252) 726-7200

Enjoy a specialty coffee and pastry at the oceanfront cafe located in the Utopia building. Either sit outside on the deck or on the upstairs balcony overlooking the ocean. You can chose whether to enjoy coffee, hot and cold blended drinks, iced teas and snacks inside in the living room setting or at the tables outside overlooking the boardwalk and the Atlantic Ocean. Inside you will find Internet access, game boards and a reading area. Caffeine Cuisine serves lunch in the summers and features a variety of sandwiches and more.

Channel Marker Restaurant & Lounge $$$
Atlantic Beach Cswy., Atlantic Beach
(252) 247-2344

Channel Marker specializes in grilled fish and Black Angus beef. Overlooking Bogue Sound, the restaurant offers waterfront dining during dinner hours and has all ABC permits. House specialties include prime rib, grilled fish, land and sea combinations, seafood platters, steak-and-shrimp kebabs and broiled lobster tails. A grilled or broiled fish special is offered each night, and the chef also prepares cold-plate entrees, grilled chicken breasts and stuffed flounder. Desserts include a large variety of homemade cheesecakes and creme brulee. Channel Marker's Double Fudge Espresso Cake won best in show at the 2005 Chocolate Festival. The dock in front of the restaurant is available for those arriving by boat, and the adjoining lounge (see our Nightlife chapter) has all permits and a large selection of liquor, wines and beers. The restaurant can accommodate banquets of up to 100. The restaurant and lounge are open every day, year round, for dinner in-season. Lunch is served Saturday and Sunday.

Crab's Claw Restaurant **$$**
201 W. Atlantic Blvd., Atlantic Beach
(252) 726-8222

The Crab's Claw is an oceanfront fine dining experience located in the heart of Atlantic Beach on the Boardwalk. The restaurant was established in 1997 and was recently featured in Southern Living magazine. The owners are both chefs and have a passion for the palate-pleasing experience. The chef prepares dishes with tender, loving care. Appetizers include such creations as Harkers Island littleneck clams, crab cakes and crab dip. Entrees include such treats as blackened tuna, grilled salmon, Cajun shrimp and chicken, crab cakes, steak and lobster, conch fritters and steamer pots. Patrons can enjoy a panoramic view of the Atlantic Ocean from the oceanfront decks and a full-service steam bar. Outside dining is available in season, so you can see the spectacular view, listen to the sound of waves and smell the aroma of salty ocean air. Crab's Claw offers catering for beach weddings, family reunions and other occasions. Call for off-season hours.

El Zarape **$-$$**
204 Atlantic Beach Cswy., Atlantic Beach
(252) 727-9410

El Zarape offers tasty Mexican food at affordable prices. From enchiladas and tacos to shrimp burritos and an array of house specialties, El Zarape brings the taste of Mexico to the old South. A local favorite is a wonderful tuna dish. Just don't fill up on the freshly cooked tortilla chips and salsa that arrive first, and remember to save room for dessert. El Zarape restaurants are also located in Morehead City and Beaufort.

Loughry's Landing Restaurant **$$-$$$**
Atlantic Beach Cswy., Atlantic Beach
(252) 808-3663

Loughry's Landing has a loyal following and it is no wonder. Joe and Donna Loughry have been serving fine foods on the Crystal Coast for 15 years. Loughry's Landing offers great food, outstanding service and a sunset restaurant view that has been voted as one of the top in the area. This is the place to go to enjoy seafood, steaks, chicken, pasta dishes and more. And the steamers are popular -- whether it is crab legs, lobster, shrimp or oysters, you'll find them fresh here. And the true Key West Key Lime Pie is a favorite. Loughry's Landing has all ABC permits and an extensive beer and wine selection. It's open for dinner at 5 PM every day in the summer; winter hours vary so call ahead.

Shades by the Sea Restaurant **$-$$$**
Sheraton Atlantic Beach Oceanfront Hotel, MM 4.5,
N.C. Hwy. 58, Atlantic Beach
(252) 222-4019, (252) 240-1155

Overlooking the ocean in Atlantic Beach, Shades by the Sea is located in the Sheraton Hotel. Guests can enjoy breakfast, lunch and dinner in this relaxing restaurant. A full menu breakfast is served, as well as an outstanding breakfast buffet in the summer. The lunch menu revolves around unique, upscale sandwiches and salads, and has something to please everyone. Dinner entrees focus on seafood, steaks and salads. The Friday and Saturday night buffet is a hit - prime rib and seafood plus all the extras. Shades by the Sea is open every day of the week.

Watermark Restaurant **$$$**
Atlantic Station Shopping Ctr.,
MM 3, N.C. Hwy. 58, Atlantic Beach
(252) 240-2811

Insiders looking for a great piece of beef go to the Watermark. Open for dinner only, Watermark specializes in grilled certified Black Angus cuts, including rib eye, New York strip and filet mignon. Entrees are accompanied by potato or wild rice, salad and grilled bread. Fresh seafood is offered grilled, fried, baked or panned in butter. Friday and Saturday nights, prime rib is offered any way your palate desires. With such good food, this restaurant is a very popular spot. However, it's also small, so call first for reservations. Watermark is open for dinner seven days a week.

White Swan Barbecue & Fried Chicken **$**
MM 4.5, N.C. Hwy. 58, Atlantic Beach
(252) 726-9607

White Swan serves eastern North Carolina barbecue and Southern fried chicken. Whether you want to eat at the restaurant or get takeout for a boat trip or picnic, this is the perfect place. The White Swan has been in business since 1949, and the Atlantic Beach restaurant opened two years ago. It offers all the great sides the original restaurant is known for -- slaw, seasoned green beans, boiled potatoes, potato salad, hush puppies and banana pudding. Don't forget the homemade Brunswick stew made from a family recipe. The White Swan can also cater your event for up to 2,000 people. The White Swan is open every day in the summer - call for winter hours.

PINE KNOLL SHORES

Clamdigger **$$**
Clamdigger Inn, MM 8.5, N.C. Hwy. 58, Pine Knoll Shores
(252) 247-4155, ext. 7

Open for breakfast, lunch and dinner, the Clamdigger is a favorite of locals as well as visitors. You'll find fluffy omelets for breakfast and delicious sandwiches for lunch; try the soft-shell crab, a shrimp scampi melt, roast beef or a classic club. Dinner entrées include steaks and all kinds of seafood. There is a special every evening - oysters on Monday, rib eye steak on Tuesday, three-way seafood combination on Wednesday, shrimp on Thursday, flounder on Friday, chicken parmesan on Saturday, and steak and shrimp on Sunday. Locals have the schedule memorized, and many enjoy the advantage of the take-out service. The Clamdigger opens at 6:30 AM every day.

INDIAN BEACH/SALTER PATH

Carlton's **$$$**
MM 11, N.C. Hwy. 58, Salter Path
(252) 808-3404

If you're looking for fine dining at the beach, head to Carlton's. This new, upscale restaurant offers delectable lunches and dinners. Dinner entrees include filets, duck, steaks and local seafood. One of their specialties is an exceptional Maryland jumbo lump crab cake that's sure to become a favorite. The chocolate pudding cake and cheesecakes are Insiders' favorites. The atmosphere at Carlton's is elegant yet casual. These mouth-watering meals are not to be missed.

Frank and Clara's Restaurant & Lounge **$$**
MM 11.5, N.C. Hwy. 58, Salter Path
(252) 247-2788

Next to the Salter Path Post Office, Frank and Clara's serves a variety of dinner choices that include fried or broiled seafood and steaks. Insider favorites are jumbo shrimp stuffed with crabmeat, char-grilled rib eyes or filet mignons, and flounder stuffed with your choice of crab and shrimp or scallops and oysters. Cheese and crackers are on the table to enjoy while you make your selections. Dinner entrées come with either a salad topped with homemade dressings or a cup of clam chowder or she crab soup; a choice of potato, rice or cole slaw; and hush puppies or rolls. Special entrees are available for

senior citizens and children. If there is a wait, the upstairs lounge is a comfortable spot for a refreshment. Frank and Clara's is open year-round but open only on Friday and Saturday nights during the winter. Reservations are recommended.

EMERALD ISLE

Bushwackers Restaurant **$$$**
100 Bogue Inlet Dr., Emerald Isle
(252) 354-6300

Bushwackers, at Bogue Inlet Pier, is known for its fun wait staff, spectacular oceanfront view and adventurous decor. It is a favorite dinner spot for fresh seafood prepared in a variety of ways, including grilled, blackened, broiled and steamed, all served with a nice variety of fresh vegetables. There are also steaks and inventive pastas and ribs. The appetizer menu is extensive, including gator bites and calamari. We love the blooming onion and the stuffed clams. Entrees feature fresh seafood, chicken, char-grilled Angus steaks, prime rib and more. Bushwackers has all ABC permits, serves beer and has an expanding wine selection. The island adventure opens for dinner every night during the season, and winter hours vary.

Celloes **$$-$$$**
Emerald Plantation Shopping Ctr., MM 19, N.C. Hwy. 58, Emerald Isle
(252) 354-4050

You can enjoy breakfast, lunch or dinner at Celloes and always be treated well. A full breakfast begins at 6 AM, served every during the summer (check on the winter schedule). The lunch menu is filled with creative sandwiches on unique breads, shrimp burgers, soups and salads. For dinner, guests can enjoy quality steaks and seafood as well as a good selection of other entrees. Call ahead and find out about the nightly special. Celloes has all ABC permits and a good selection of wines and beers.

RuckerJohn's **$$$**
Emerald Plantation Shopping Ctr., MM 19.5, N.C. Hwy. 58, Emerald Isle
(252) 354-2413

Bring the whole family to RuckerJohn's to enjoy great food in a casual, contemporary atmosphere filled with plants and handsome woodwork. Dinner entrées, prepared to order, include fresh seafood, pasta, barbecue shrimp, beef ribs, steaks, chicken and pork chops. Favorite appetizers include fried calamari, hot crab dip and chicken wings. For lunch, try the grilled Cajun chicken salad, the spinach salad with hot bacon-honey mustard dressing, any of the juicy burgers or a creative sandwich. A recent addition to the menu is RJ's 12-inch grilled pizza in four distinct flavor combinations -- spinach, barbecue chicken, seafood or the classic cheese pizza.

In the warmer months, have lunch on the sunny outdoor patio. Be sure to save room for fresh homemade cakes and cheesecakes for dessert. The lounge (see our Nightlife chapter) is a cozy gathering place enjoyed by the local population, especially on winter nights when there's a crackling fire in the fireplace. RuckerJohn's is open for lunch and dinner every day.

Tortugas **$$**
140 Fairview Dr., Emerald Isle
(252) 354-9397
www.tortugas.net

"The Jewel of Emerald Isle." Those are the words a restaurant reviewer used to describe Tortugas. This restaurant is a favorite and has diners coming back again and again. From appetizers to desserts, this is a true upscale casual dining experience and the first of its kind in Emerald Isle. Tortugas provides a lush Caribbean atmosphere that compliments the eclectic-fusion menu. Insiders recommend the appetizers of Thai tiger shrimp and baked crème de crab. Then you are on your own for the difficult decisions - gourmet pizza, pasta or another specialty. Try the Certified Black Angus steaks, Ahi tuna, pork tenderloin, center-cut filet mignon, crab cakes or the daily fresh catch. Whatever you select, be assured it will be delicious and creatively prepared. Compliment your meal with a selection from the extensive wine list and a sinful dessert. The crème brulee is a house specialty and is fabulous. Tortugas is open year-round for dinner at 5 PM and accepts reservations. A buffet brunch is offered on Easter and Mother's Day, with made-to-order waffles and Eggs Tortugas. Tortugas offers catering for any type of party or event on or off-premise. The restaurant can accommodate 80.

Beaufort

Aqua Restaurant **$$-$$$**
114 Middle Ln., Beaufort
(252) 728-7777

Small plates, big wines. Aqua Restaurant is inspired by Spanish tapas fare, and this exciting restaurant features a wonderful array of tastes. Here you will truly enjoy savory tastes in "just right" portions. The menu changes frequently and always offers the freshest ingredients served in the most creative ways. Start your meal with a delicious Caesar salad, fried sesame chicken over arugula or possibly fried goat's cheese over organic greens. For your next course, try a coconut grilled tiger shrimp kebob or jumbo lump crabmeat gratinee with Asiago cream, spinach and toasted crostini. And for dessert why not end it all with bananas foster, cappuccino mousse or their sinful creme brulee? Aqua offers an extensive wine list and has all ABC permits. Also try Aqua's food and wine paring menus. Monthly, the chef pairs four courses from the menu with four half-glasses of wine to give you the ultimate food and wine pairing experience. Aqua is nestled behind Clawson's Restaurant and is open Tuesday through Saturday for dinner. Aqua is quickly becoming a favorite of locals and visitors to the area, so reservations are suggested.

Beaufort Grocery Co. **$$$**
117 Queen St., Beaufort
(252) 728-3899

At Beaufort Grocery Co. everything served is exquisite, and the service is professional and friendly. Favorite lunch choices might include the Joshua Tree (seasonal greens, cucumber, mushrooms, onions, cashew butter, or the smoked Gouda and vinaigrette rolled in Lavosh). Dinner starts with such appetizers as pizza with pesto and three cheeses, fabulous Carolina crab cakes, or assorted Mediterranean dips and spreads (hummus and olive tapenade in phyllo cups with harissa and toasted pita points). Diners may choose entrees of fresh seafood, choice steaks, free-range chicken, veal and lamb. Each is served with a salad, fresh vegetables and delicious breads baked daily. Insiders suggest the Grilled Pork Chop stuffed with Fresh Mozzarella, roasted tomatoes and Pesto on roasted potatoes, broccolini and Marsala Demi Glace. Top your meal off with pecan pie or any other dessert, because they are all made on the premises and they're all delicious. Beaufort Grocery Co. offers Sunday Brunch, a take-out menu and a full delicatessen with meats, cheeses, homemade salads and breads. Private catered dining facilities are next door at 115 Queen Street. The restaurant has all ABC permits and closes in January and Tuesdays between Labor Day and Memorial Day. Otherwise, it's full speed ahead. Dinner reservations are recommended.

Blue Moon Bistro **$$$**
119 Queen St., Beaufort
(252) 728-5800

Blue Moon Bistro offers fine dining in a casual atmosphere in historic Beaufort. Dinners are prepared from scratch daily and vary depending on the season and the chef's preparation for the day. You'll always find the best fish, shellfish, chicken and steaks around town. To start your meal, enjoy Blue Moon's mixed green salad with seasonal garnish. Appetizers might include lamb chops, pork potstickers with tamari-ginger dipping sauce, or seared sea scallops on enoki/oyster mushrooms in a mustard-miso sauce. Entrees change often and could feature Angus ribeye, veal tenderloin with Yukon Gold mashed potatoes, or seared Atlantic salmon. Guests can also enjoy outstanding soups and a variety of salads. Room for dessert? While the Blue Moon dessert list changes, past favorites have included cheesecake, crème brulee or fluffy pound cake with fruit. Blue Moon is open for dinner Monday through Saturday in season, and winter hours vary. Reservations are recommended.

Boardwalk Cafe **$-$$**
510 Front St., Beaufort
(252) 728-0933

Boardwalk Cafe is a wonderful little place to have great food in a relaxed atmosphere while learning about the area's history and enjoying the waterfront view. Open at 7 AM, breakfast offerings include waffles, eggs, pancakes, bacon, sausage and more. Lunch is served through 3 PM and features sandwiches, seafood, creative hot dogs and hamburgers - including great seafood burgers - and salads. The Soda Fountain serves dinner in the summer with a menu of beef, fish, pastas, salads and homemade soups. An Insider favorite is the creamy clam chowder. Whether you dine inside overlooking the water or outside on the boardwalk, you will enjoy it all. Open every day during the summer, Broadwalk Cafe has a nice selection of beers and wines, and offers espresso, lattes and cappuccinos all day long.

Clawson's 1905 Restaurant **$$**
425 Front St., Beaufort
(252) 728-2133

Clawson's 1905 is a favorite destination of Insiders and visitors to the area throughout the day and throughout the year. An architectural focal point in the middle of downtown, Clawson's 1905 is housed in what was Clawson's General Store back in the early 1900s. Clawson's has lots of options - step up for a cup of joe at the Fishtowne Java coffee bar; shop the general store shelves for a T-shirt or other Clawson's-branded merchandise; proceed to the living room and catch up with the world according to CNN; move on to the rear for the best beer selection in town; or be seated upstairs or down for lunch or dinner.

Lunch favorites include a long list of sandwiches and burgers and the Dirigible - a hearty baked potato stuffed with seafood, vegetables and meats. Appetizers are wonderful and include seared tuna, seafood creations and more. Dinner always offers fresh seafood prepared with style, zesty ribs, steaks, chicken and pasta. Whether for lunch or dinner, Clawson's Seafood Bisque is really extraordinary and is, singularly, worth a trip to Beaufort. Private banquet facilities are available, and Down East FolkArts Society concerts are performed here in the off season. Clawson's is open daily for lunch and dinner. After Labor Day, it rests on Sundays until summer. Clawson's gets crowded during the summer months, so reservations are suggested. No matter - it's worth the wait.

FRONT STREET GRILL
at STILLWATER
HISTORIC BEAUFORT
WATERFRONT BISTRO
INSIDE & OUTSIDE DINING
Lunch, Dinner & Sunday Brunch
252-728-4956
300 FRONT STREET • BEAUFORT, NC 28516

Finz Grill in Beaufort **$$$**
330 Front St., Beaufort
(252) 728-7459

Finz is the perfect place to relax, enjoy good food and visit with friends in a casual atmosphere. Guests may arrive by water or land and are seated inside or on the back porch over Taylor's Creek. The lunch and dinner menus offer sandwiches, burgers, soups (try the wonderful gumbo or black bean) and fresh baskets of fried fish. You'll also find crab cakes, and oyster and shrimp burgers. Dinner focuses on seafood, especially fresh shrimp and scallops and fish that can be grilled, blackened or fried. Specialties include crab cakes, soft shell crabs, hot crab dip, spiced triggerfish and Mediterranean fajitas. Steaks and pasta dishes and chef's features are also options. Finz has great homemade desserts, all ABC permits and serves lunch and dinner every day. Call for winter hours.

Front Street Grill at Stillwater **$$$**
300 Front St., Beaufort
(252) 728-4956
www.frontstreetgrillatstillwater.com

Front Street Grill at Stillwater is considered one of the premiere restaurants on the North Carolina coast. The warm yellow dining room with its large picture windows overlooking the water is the perfect setting to showcase their New World cuisine. The menu features a wide array of signature dishes from the brother and sister team of Chefs Bryan and Tracey Carithers. These dishes have been developed from their love of the Outer Banks and the Caribbean. Starters include favorites such as Crispy Calamari with ginger aioli, Crab Spring Rolls with plum sauce, Baked Oysters and Goat Cheese salad. Favorite dinner entrees include Sugarcane Rum Glazed Yellowfin Tuna, Lump Crab Cakes, Sesame Sweet Chili Shrimp, and prime choice meats. The lunch menu offers guests large salads, soups, sandwiches and daily seafood specials. All breads and desserts are baked in house. The restaurant's location on the Historic Beaufort Waterfront offers spectacular views. The interior of Stillwater is warm and casually elegant, enhanced by crisp white linens and fresh flowers. Just outside the bar area are waterfront decks filled with large market umbrellas, illuminated by hurricane lanterns in the evening. A new feature for 2006 is an outdoor bar area called the Rum Bar, which is perfect for an evening relaxing at the water's edge. The restaurant is a perennial winner of the prestigious Wine Spectator Award of Excellence. The restaurant has all ABC permits and serves lunch, dinner and a Sunday brunch that is not to be missed. Reservations are highly recommended for dinner, however walk-in guests are welcome.

Net House Restaurant **$$**
133 Turner St., Beaufort
(252) 728-2002

If you ask where to go for seafood, many Beaufort residents will send you to the Net House. Just across the street from the Beaufort Historic Site, the Net House specializes in steamed shellfish and broiled and lightly battered fried seafood. Guests enjoy an atmosphere of weathered pine and nautical antiques at this family-owned eatery. Try the Down East clam chowder, she-crab soup or creamy seafood bisque as a dinner appetizer. Dinner focuses on fresh seafood. Local favorites include the fried, over-stuffed soft-shell crab and the broiled grouper Dijon. The Net House is also known for its famous Key lime pie. No reservations are taken, but folks start lining up early. Hours vary according to season, so call ahead.

No Name Pizza and Subs $
408 Live Oak St., Beaufort
(252) 728-4978, (252) 728-4982

This is as good as it gets for pizza in Beaufort, according to our own personal survey. No Name is also a great place for subs (everything from meatball to vegetarian), burgers and spaghetti with meatballs. The Greek salad is loaded with feta cheese and served with a loaf of garlic bread. No Name serves pasta dishes, Greek dishes, sandwiches and chicken. The baklava is wonderful. The menu is the same for lunch and dinner, but dinner specials are announced daily. You may purchase beer and wine to accompany your meal. You'll leave satisfied, knowing like you got your money's worth. No Name offers dine-in or drive-through service and is open seven days.

Ribeyes Steakhouse $$
509 Front St., Beaufort
(252) 728-6105

Ribeyes is quickly becoming a destination in Beaufort. Located on Front Street, the steakhouse offers customers choice Omaha brand grain-fed beef, boneless chicken breasts and grilled shrimp along with a wonderful salad bar. Entrees also come with a choice of a baked potato or a sweet potato. Mike Lavoy personally takes your order and ensures the meat is cooked to order. With all ABC permits, Ribeyes offers nightly drink specials, and has a large relaxing sofa-filled bar area. A take-out service is available, as is the use of The Angus Room, which accommodates up to 36 people for special occasions. The restaurant opens for dinner every night of the week.

Royal James Cafe $
117 Turner St., Beaufort
(252) 728-4573

The Royal James Cafe is the oldest continually existing business in Beaufort's historic district and has a color of its own that keeps people coming and its name in conversation from Canada to the Caribbean. It offers a simple line of quality fast food including shrimp burgers, steamed shrimp and Down East clam chowder. The signature sandwich is a 90/10 lean double cheeseburger with secret chili sauce. With an early '50s Formica, wood and neon look, this cafe and pool room has been favorably mentioned in editorial publications including the Chicago Tribute, the Atlanta Constitution-Journal, the News & Observer and Southern Living. It draws an interesting mix of locals and tourists, families and singles, and has hours from 9 AM until last call every day except Sunday, when it is open from noon to 7 PM.

The Sandbar Restaurant **$$$**
232 W. Beaufort Rd., Beaufort
(252) 504-SAND(7263)
www.thesandbar.org
www.clairitastikibar.com

A quiet, out-of-the-way spot, The Sandbar Restaurant at Town Creek Marina offers sensational dining and spectacular views seven days a week. With a commanding view of the Intracoastal Waterway and Beaufort/Morehead causeway bridge, The Sandbar's beautifully appointed dining room allows you to watch vessels navigating the channel against spectacular sunsets and the harbor skyline. On warm evenings you can dine on the covered veranda. After dinner, step out to the Caribbean-inspired Clairita's Tiki Bar, where you'll find a complete menu of domestic and exotic drink selections. On weekends, you can party to your heart's content under the stars as popular live bands entertain Town Creek guests. The Sandbar offers a sumptuous selection of lunch, dinner and Saturday and Sunday brunch fare. The lunch menu includes such favorites as homemade breads; daily pasta, salad, fish and other specialties; and big, juicy burgers. Dinner options include palate-teasing appetizers; fresh wahoo; crab-stuffed lobster topped with garlic and herb cream sauce; sesame-seared yellow-fin tuna served rare, with pickled ginger, wasabi drizzle, soy dipping sauce and seaweed salad; and five chef specials every evening. And, you'll want to say yes to dessert with such tempting delights as Molten Chocolate Lava Cake and Perfect Cheesecake. Visit The Sandbar and enjoy Chef Donatello Giannini's new menu for the year.

Sharpies Grill & Bar **$$$-$$$$**
521 Front St., Beaufort
(252) 838-0101
www.sharpiesgrill.com

Sharpies Grill & Bar on the waterfront is a wonderful addition to the Beaufort restaurant scene. This has quickly become an Insiders favorite for many reasons -- the great atmosphere, the creative dishes and the friendly service. Sharpies offers fine dining in a wonderful setting. The restaurant redefines coastal dining by constantly creating a new, limited menu using fresh ingredients, fresh local seafood, certified black Angus beef, homemade pastas, an outstanding meat and poultry selection, and incredible desserts. Call ahead and see what creations are on tap for the night. You might find grilled prawns with applewood smoked bacon, tomatoes and spinach over polenta or a braised mushroom ravioli with light cream and fresh chives. Sharpies' full bar is the perfect place to meet friends, enjoy specialty drinks and an unusual selection of wines chosen from small domestic and international wineries. Sharpies is a very popular dinner spot, so reservations are recommended.

The Spouter Inn **$$$**
218 Front St., Beaufort
(252) 728-5190

A sign with a whale spouting (thus the "Spouter Inn") marks the Front Street entrance to this intimate dining establishment, which is over the water and offers a panoramic view of Beaufort Inlet and Taylor's Creek. The Spouter Inn Restaurant offers fresh local seafood, just off the boat. The lunch menu offers a unique selection of sandwiches, soups, salads and pastas. Sunday Brunch specials include seafood omelets, quiche, eggs benedict, and eggs Orleans.

Dinner is as enticing with plenty of seafood. The sesame seared tuna with a soy glaze, wasabi aioli, and pickled ginger is a favorite, but the maple-bourbon BBQ ribs are tempting as well. Fresh-baked breads and desserts are prepared in the restaurant's new bakery. The Spouter Inn has a waterfront deck; you can come by land or sea as docking is available. Dinner reservations are recommended. The restaurant is open daily during the summer months. Call for hours during the off-season.

Morehead City

AJ's Seafood Restaurant **$$-$$$**
2806 Arendell St., Morehead City
(252) 247-3119

AJ's offers a variety of fresh seafood prepared to order, along with outstanding steaks. Chefs Albert Cowan and Joseph Sharp bring years experience to AJ's. The restaurant specializes in fried, broiled and blackened seafood, served with a Carteret County flair. Favorites include broiled flounder stuffed with crabmeat, fried chicken fillets and grilled-to-order steaks. Don't forget about the wonderful homemade desserts – lemon and apple pie are two favorites. AJ's is open for lunch and dinner Monday through Saturday.

A Taste of Italy **$$**
4466 Arendell St., Morehead City
(252) 222-0166

A Taste of Italy offers a real treat – authentic Italian food and continental cuisine right here on the Crystal Coast. Dinner is served with homemade pasta and breads. While there's a variety of options on the menu, folks come back time and time again for the veal you can cut with a fork. On- and off-premise catering is offered for 10 to 400 people. The restaurant is open at for dinner Monday through Saturday.

Bistro By The Sea **$$$**
4031 Arendell St., Morehead City
(252) 247-2777

Bistro By The Sea, or as locals call it, The Bistro, is a favorite for both food and hospitality. Regulars love the friendly service, excellent cuisine and distinctive presentations at The Bistro. Enjoy wonderful dinner entrees prepared using fresh vegetables, seafood and tasty cuts of beef. Seafood entrees vary nightly according to freshness and availability. In addition to seafood specialties, locals recommend the char-grilled filet mignon or prime rib, liver in orange liqueur or stir-fried chicken with rice and won tons. We also like the pasta creations, such as cappellini with pesto, vegetables and scallops. The Bistro now also offers sushi and Japanese bento boxes. Sandwiches are available, as are tempting desserts. Bistro By The Sea is open for dinner Tuesday through Sunday and takes January off. Reservations may be made for parties of six or more.

CC Ralwiggies **$-$$**
3710 Arendell St., Morehead City
(252) 240-8646

CC Ralwiggies is the place to go for a feel-good, and good for you, lunch. Described as a Vegetarian Playground, this is the place to go for healthy foods. Guests can enjoy a 50-plus item salad bar filled with fresh healthy veggies and more, plus with wonderful homemade soups, which vary daily. Fresh breads, a potato bar, and fresh fruit and soy milk smoothies are also offered. Chef Toni Oberci and her staff also offer a full to-go service with salad platters, hot soups, salad by the pound and platters for events of all types, and they can cater any occasion. Everything prepared is MSG free because, as the menu states – "You are what you eat. Be great"!

El Zarape **$-$$**
4138 Arendell St., Morehead City
(252) 808-2233

El Zarape offers tasty Mexican food at affordable prices. From enchiladas and tacos to shrimp burritos and an array of house specialties, El Zarape brings the taste of Mexico to the old South. A local favorite is a wonderful tuna dish. Just don't fill up on the freshly cooked tortilla chips and salsa that arrive first, and remember to save room for dessert. El Zarape restaurants are also located in Atlantic Beach, Beaufort and Emerald Isle.

Finz Grill of Morehead **$$$**
105 S. Seventh St., Morehead City
(252) 726-5502

Finz has two locations – one in Beaufort and one in Morehead City. With a outside

deck and live music on the weekends, Finz Grill of Morehead is the perfect place to relax, enjoy good food and visit with friends in a casual atmosphere. A full breakfast is served and the lunch and dinner menus offer sandwiches, burgers, salads, cheesesteaks, soups (try the wonderful gumbo or she crab) and fresh baskets of fried fish as well as entrees including seafood grilled, blackened or fried, salads and more. Specialties include items from the chef's features menu and crab cakes. Steaks and pasta dishes are also wonderful. Finz is proud of offering seafood caught by local fishermen. Finz has great desserts, all ABC permits and serves breakfast, lunch and dinner every day. Call for winter hours.

Floyd's 1921 Restaurant & Bar **$$-$$$**
400 Bridges St., Morehead City
(252) 727-1921

Floyd's 1921 opened in 2005 to rave reviews and in just one year has created a following of its own. Well-known local Chef Floyd Olmstead opened this restaurant in the 1920s-era, two-story house that once was home to Nikola's Italian Restaurant, and this will be a place not to miss. The restaurant serves lunch, dinner and Sunday brunch. The lunch menu offers creative salads, sandwiches and "old southern fixins " like high cotton crab cakes, fried chicken, low country meatloaf, and shrimp and grits. Insider favorites are the grouper po-boy sandwich, and the fried oysters and mango spinach salad. Dinner sandwiches and salads are offered, along with an wonderful entree selection ranging from long time favorites for country styled ribs and ribeye steaks to roasted rack of lamb and seafood. Try Floyd's creation of shrimp and tasso-ham gravy served over skillet corn bread, or drunken shrimp sauteed with orange segments, molasses, jerk seasoning and spiced rum. Homemade salad dressings and desserts complete an unforgettable experience.

Hooters of Morehead City **$$**
5050 U.S. Hwy. 70, Morehead City
(252) 727-1803

Hooters has opened a restaurant here on the coast. Like the others in this chain, the restaurant specializes in clams, wings, shrimp, oyster roasts and is staffed by the "nearly famous Hooters girls."

Kabuto - Japanese Steakhouse & Sushi Bar **$$**
U.S. Hwy. 70, Morehead City
(252) 222-3111

Kabuto has restaurants throughout the state, offering Japanese dishes and a full sushi menu. This restaurant opens for dinner every day of the week to greet guest with a wonderful selection of freshly prepared soups, salads, creative entrees and sushi.

Private party facilities and gift certificates are available. Reservations are accepted.

Kountry Kitchen **$-$$**
Brandywine Crossing, 5380 U.S. Hwy. 70, Morehead City
(252) 240-0046

Kountry Kitchen offers full breakfast, lunch and dinner menus and is sure to please with new dishes as well as long-time favorites. Kick off the day with a breakfast of eggs, grits, waffles, hot cakes and meats. They even serve sausage gravy and fried bologna. The lunch/dinner menu is available starting at 11 AM. Enjoy burgers, subs, steaks and seafood, or try one of the outstanding daily specials. The special might be baked ham, pork chops or a Friday favorite of a fish sandwich and chowder. Kountry Kitchen opens at 6 AM each morning and remains open until 8 PM Monday through Wednesday, until 9 PM Thursday through Saturday and until 3 PM on Sunday.

Mickey's Eatery & Pub **$-$$**
U.S. Hwy. 70, Morehead City
(252) 726-0250

Mickey's serves up a great breakfast, lunch and dinner so stop by anytime and enjoy the food and the company. A full breakfast is a treat here – especially the pancakes. Lunch features such things as soups, salads, sandwiches, chicken dishes and great reuben sandwich. Dinners offer a variety of seafood, pastas, steaks and a great Jamaican jerk chicken. For dessert try the cheesecake or the Key lime pie or both. Mickey's serves beer and wine, and is open every day during the summer. They start serving breakfast at 6 or 7 AM, depending on the season.

Mrs. Culpepper's Crab Cafe **$**
5370 U.S. Hwy. 70, Morehead City
(252) 240-1960

Mrs. Culpepper's Crab Cafe offers wonderful Thai cuisine and fresh seafood in a relaxed diner-type atmosphere. For lunch or dinner, enjoy crab cakes, oysters, shrimp, soft crabs or scallops. You'll also find such creations as pork with ginger, spicy beef with basil, Pad Thai, and oysters with bean sprouts. A favorite is the sampler where you select two or three items served with jasmine rice and a spring roll. Mrs. Culpepper's also offers retail sales of the uncooked crab cakes that made this place famous. You can also take home fresh shrimp, soft shell and hard crabs, and shrimp or pork spring rolls. The cafe is open for lunch Tuesday through Saturday, and for dinner Tuesday and Thursday through Saturday.

Mrs. Willis' Restaurant **$$**
3114 Bridges St., Morehead City
(252) 726-3741

Mrs. Willis and her family have been serving home-cooked meals since 1949. The restaurant actually began in the home of "Ma" Willis as a barbecue and chicken take-out place specializing in mini-lemon pies.

Customers ate right in the kitchen. In 1956 the restaurant moved into the garage, which is the front of today's restaurant, and additions have been made through the years. The restaurant is a favorite of locals and visitors who want a meal made from family recipes without going to the trouble themselves. Specialties include fresh pork barbecue, local seafood and char-grilled steaks. We recommend the clam chowder for starters and then the prime rib -- for the money, it's one of the best around. Other entrees include the seafood combination plate, chicken livers, pork chops, hamburger steak, stuffed flounder, rib eye, frog legs, grilled fish, chicken and roast beef. The platter of fried fish is excellent, light and crispy. Mrs. Willis' offers specials every day and night and accommodates groups of any size. Lunch is served Sunday through Friday and dinner is served seven days a week. The restaurant is open year round.

On A Roll Gourmet Deli **$**
907 Arendell St., Morehead City
(252) 726-5101

On A Roll starts the day early - at 6 AM - serving breakfast and lunch every day. Breakfast is also served all day on Saturday and Sunday. Breakfast entrees include the favorites of eggs, ham, toast and grits. Enjoy hotcakes, corned beef hash and buttermilk pancakes. Lunches include sandwiches, wraps and more. Try an Italian hoagie with prosciutto, capicola and provolone cheese, or a Jewish hoagie with corned beef, salami, cole slaw and Russian dressing. Favorites include reubens, burgers, liverwurst and onions, and gyros. You'll also find Greek and Caesar salads, cold tuna and chicken salad plates, and corned beef specials. On A Roll also offers a full catering service.

Sanitary Fish Market & Restaurant **$$**
501 Evans St., Morehead City
(252) 247-3111

Sanitary has been a landmark on the Morehead City waterfront for more than 60 years. In 1938, Ted Garner and Tony Seamon, both now deceased, opened a waterfront seafood market in a building rented for $5.50 per week with the agreement that no beer or wine would be sold and that the premises would be kept clean and neat. The name Sanitary Fish Market was chosen by the partners to project their compliance. When 12 stools were set up at the counter, the first seafood restaurant on the city's waterfront was in business. Today, Ted Garner Jr. operates the family-oriented business. Customers find old favorite menu items along with many new additions, all ordered by number. Best known for fresh seafood served broiled, steamed, grilled or fried, the Sanitary also offers steaks, poultry, pork and pasta entrees. Lunch always includes a good selection of vegetables and attracts lots of locals. Sanitary Fish Market, next to the restaurant, sells fresh local seafood for those who prefer to cook it themselves. The Sanitary now offers a good selection of beer and wine, and lunch and dinner are served every day of the week, but the restaurant closes the Sunday after Thanksgiving and reopens the first Friday in February.

Shepard's Point **$$$**
913 Arendell St., Morehead City
(252) 727-0815

Shepard's Point is an uptown steakhouse with a plethora of seafood and a bar specializing in martini cocktails and infused vodkas that are second to none. Friday is Happy Hour with free appetizers in the bar until 7 PM. Other daily specials are offered throughout the week. An exposed cellar offers a glimpse of extensive wine selections from around the world, and you can view the chefs in the open kitchen preparing your meal. Diners can choose traditional appetizers or such innovative ones as Shrimp Wontons or Fried Oysters on Gilled Artichoke with Tasso Hollandaise. All breads are baked from scratch daily. Fresh local seafood is the specialty of the house, plus there is a wide range of other steaks and chops. Tuna steak is on the menu regularly along with Braided Flounder, Shrimp and Scallops. Patrons receive a small salad and an array of sides, such as a loaded baked potato, three-cheese macaroni or asparagus with hollandaise included with their entree. Desserts at The Point are works of art: Flaming Baked Alaska, Mango Crème Brulee or Chocolate Chiao Cake with Anise Anglaise. Look to The Point to be open for Sunday Brunch this summer. Private dining rooms are available for up to 90 people. Smoking is permitted in the bar only, where fine cigars are sold. Shepard's Point is an offshoot from Beaufort Grocery Co. Reservations are recommended. Dinner starts at 5:30 PM and Sunday Brunch is at 11 AM. It's closed Tuesdays.

Trateotu Fine Dining **$$-$$$**
506 Arendell St., Morehead City
(252) 240-3380

Trateotu offers fine dining and is called "the restaurant at the end of the universe." Chef Donny Gilliam offers a creative Mediterranean cuisine that's sure to please. Guests will enjoy many pastas, vegetables and fresh local fish. A hand-written menu is prepared each day to ensure the freshness of all meals, and you will not find anything frozen here. The restaurant opens at 6 PM Monday through Saturday, offering nightly specials and often music. Catering is also available.

Windansea **$$$ - $$$$**
708 Evans St., Morehead City
(252) 247-3000

Windansea opened its doors on the Morehead City waterfront in January 1997 and has been busy ever since. The restaurant provides the feel of an open kitchen, and a featured addition is a wood-fired oven that produces homemade breads as well as specialty pizzas and the restaurant's signature wood-fired, brick-baked grouper. With an emphasis on seafood, the seasonal menu is supplemented with a series of daily specials featuring fish fresh from local boats, served with a changing series of accompaniments. Locally grown vegetables are a spring and summer staple at Windansea. The menu is changed with the seasons, but one will always find a Chipotle-Dusted Rib Eye or Teriyaki-Glazed Pork Tenderloin available. Crab cakes, scallops and grouper are also menu regulars. Dinner is served nightly except Monday from May through October. From November through April the restaurant is open Wednesday through Sunday. Seating is limited, and reservations are recommended. Windansea also provides take-out meals and full-service catering.

Newport

Yesterday's Retro **$**
254 Chatham St., Newport
(252) 223-2796

Yesterday's Retro will take you back to another place and time. This "blast from the past" has it all -- the best cheeseburger around, hot and cold sandwiches, dinner plates, salads, floats, shakes, sundaes and malts. This family-owned and operated business is open 11 AM to 9 PM Monday through Saturday, and from 11 AM to 3 PM Sunday.

Swansboro

Capt. Charlie's Restaurant **$$$**
328 N.C. Hwy. 24 at Front St., Swansboro
(910) 326-4303

Capt. Charlie's Restaurant specializes in fresh seafood, prime rib and steaks. The

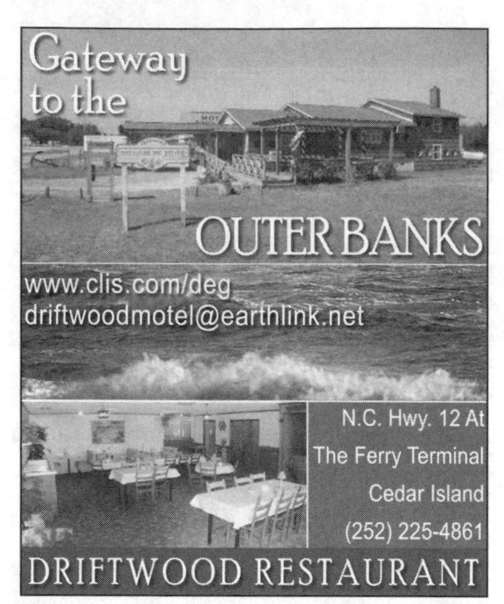

traditional menu offers lots of fried seafood, although there are plenty of other choices. Try the stuffed flounder or broiled shrimp and scallops. The steaks have an enormous following too. The desserts here vary but if the white chocolate raspberry cheesecake is on the menu order it. Well-prepared foods served in ample amounts bring people back to Capt. Charlie's again and again. Have a drink in the lounge while you wait for your table. Capt. Charlie's has all ABC permits and is open for dinner seven days a week in the summer and every day but Monday in the off season.

Gourmet Cafe **$$$**
99 Church St., Swansboro
(910) 326-7114

Gourmet Cafe offers a delightfully diverse menu for lunch and dinner in a brightly appointed locale overlooking the water. Lunch offers a pleasing selection of salads, sandwiches and fried seafood, to name a few of the options. Dinner presents a tantalizing variety of appetizers, with the crab dip being the favorite. Entrees focus on fresh seafood, steaks, pastas, lamb and pork. Try the wonderful rib eye or a dish featuring crab meat. One of the specialties is the homemade bread; the other is the dessert selection of homemade cheesecakes. A meal in the relaxed atmosphere of the Gourmet Cafe makes your visit to Swansboro truly memorable. The restaurant is open all year.

Yana's Ye Olde Drugstore Restaurant **$**
119 Front St., Swansboro
(910) 326-5501

Just about everybody in Swansboro eats at Yana's at some time during the week. Whether it's the food or the nostalgic '50s music that attracts you, once you've been, you'll come back again and again. Yana's opens every day at 7 AM for breakfast and serves lunch through 3 or 4 PM. Breakfast specialties are cooked to order and served all day. Enjoy a traditional breakfast of eggs and ham, French toast or waffles. Lunch can include a variety of sandwiches, salads or soups, but the Bradburger, a hamburger with egg, cheese, bacon, lettuce and tomato, is worth a sample. You'll also want to enjoy the fresh chicken or tuna salad. And the desserts? See for yourself! Try the milk shakes. Yana's serves breakfast and lunch daily.

Down East

Captain's Choice Restaurant **$-$$**
977 Island Rd., Harkers Island
(252) 728-7122

Open for lunch and dinner, Captain's Choice offers a good menu selection and lots of Island atmosphere. There is always a lunch special and plenty of meats, seafood and vegetables, along with chowders and salads. Dinner is a seafood and steak event, all prepared to order. A huge seafood buffet is offered each Friday and Saturday evening. Captain's Choice is open every day of the week, but does not serve dinner on Mondays.

Driftwood Restaurant **$$**
N.C. Hwy. 12 at the ferry terminal,
Cedar Island
(252) 225-4861
www.clis.com/deg/

On the banks of Pamlico Sound, the Driftwood includes a motel, restaurant, campground and gift shop, but locals refer to all those things at the complex by simply saying "at the Driftwood." The restaurant is known far and wide for the weekend prime rib special. Other entrees feature all types of seafood, prepared any way you like, including fresh crabmeat, shrimp salad, five seafood combination plates and soft-shell crabs. You'll also enjoy chicken, barbecue, pasta and vegetarian dishes and a children's menu. A

There are easier ways to dine on fresh seafood along the Crystal Coast.

photo: George Mitchell

full salad bar is offered, and the homemade lemon meringue pie is wonderful. Lunch is offered in the summer months. Beer and wine are available, or you can bring your own alcoholic beverage. The restaurant is beside the Cedar Island-Ocracoke ferry terminal. The Driftwood Restaurant closes in late January and reopens in the spring. For information about the motel, see our Accommodations chapter; for information about the campground, see our Camping chapter.

Western Carteret County

Mazzella's Italian Restaurant **$$**
1206 N.C. Hwy. 58, Cape Carteret
(252) 393-8787

Mazzella's is an authentic Italian restaurant located about 2 miles north of Cape Carteret. The family-owned and operated business provides only the finest Italian cuisine and keeps diners coming back again and again. A number of Italian entrees are made with fresh pastas, homemade sauces and seafood. Sandwiches and pizzas are also offered. The restaurant is open for dinner year round except Sunday and Monday.

Really Great Fast Food

Yes indeed, the Crystal Coast does have some really delicious fast food, much of which is homemade and unbeatable in value and taste. We would be remiss if we did not tell you about some of the best establishments -- places where you can get a good, quick bite for breakfast, lunch and sometimes dinner. Many are family owned and have stood the tests of time and taste. Our choices are listed in alphabetical order.

Big Oak Drive-In **$**
MM 10.5, N.C. Hwy. 58, Salter Path
(252) 247-2588

Turn on the blinker and pull in here. Big Oak has the best shrimp burger on the Crystal Coast. Other restaurants may serve a good shrimp burger, but Big Oak serves a great one. They've been at it for 27 years in Salter Path, where the locals remember when shrimp were first harvested commercially.

Other goodies you'll want to sample are chicken and barbecue sandwiches, burgers, hot dogs, pizza and BLTs. Big Oak has plates of barbecue, fried chicken and shrimp as well as mighty good French fries, onion rings and slaw. Pizza is served Friday and Saturday nights. But it's that shrimp burger that will keep you coming back!

The Coffee Affair **$**
2302-G Arendell St., Morehead City
(252) 247-6020

The Coffee Affair is a favorite hang-out in Morehead City that has been offering customers a home away from home for several years. You'll find all your favorite coffees and teas on hand as well as fresh sandwiches, pastries, muffins and more. Come in and enjoy a fresh brew, a bite to eat, a visit with friends and check your email -- all in one stop. Coffee Affair opens at 6:30 AM Monday through Saturday and at 7:30 AM Sunday. Closing time varies from 9 to 11 PM.

El's Drive-In **$**
3600 Arendell St., Morehead City
(252) 726-3002

El's has been a Carteret County tradition since 1959. This is an old-fashioned drive-in, which means you are waited on by a carhop and sit in your vehicle and eat. El's has great burgers, hot dogs, fries and milk shakes. The Superburger, assembled with mustard, onion, slaw and chili, is a Carteret County favorite. Try a shrimp or oyster burger, a BLT, a fish or steak sandwich, a shrimp or oyster tray, or fried chicken. This is a much-enjoyed lunch and dinner spot for locals, so go early to get a parking place. And don't forget to lob a French fry or two out the window to the waiting sea gulls. El's is open from 10:30 AM to around 10:30 PM or midnight every day.

New York Deli **$**
Causeway Shopping Ctr., Causeway Rd., Atlantic Beach
(252) 726-0111

This is the place for authentic deli food. We recommend the South Philadelphia cheesesteak -- heck, order two cheesesteaks and we'll join you. The deli serves overstuffed sandwiches, subs, chili dogs, homemade soups, salads and pasta. There's also a new Italian Market with olive oils, roasted peppers, pastas and olives. The Deli also offers some nightly specials on certain nights of the week - like a Pasta Night and a Seafood Night - so call ahead to find out what is fresh from the oven. The Deli has a good selection of imported beers and wines. Deli meats and cheeses are available for you to take home and create your own feast. New York Deli offers take-out or eat-in service in an attractive cafe atmosphere, catering, party trays, gift baskets and homemade bagels for sale. During the summer, New York Deli is open for breakfast and lunch Tuesday through Sunday, and open for dinner Thursday, Friday and Saturday.

Sea Side Galley **$**
Island Rd., Harkers Island
(252) 728-6171

Sea Side Galley offers a variety of foods for eating in or taking out. Enjoy seafood, burgers, subs, pizza and more. The Galley is the first building on the left once you cross the drawbridge on to Harkers Island.

Tracks in the sand tell a story of who has been there before you.

photo: George Mitchell

NIGHTLIFE

Nightlife comes in a variety of forms on the Crystal Coast and varies from person to person. Most visitors have a full day of outdoor activities and are happy with quiet evening activities, like a drink after dinner and a stroll on the beach or waterfront. Still, the Crystal Coast offers a few spots where you can kick up your heels and enjoy a night of fun. City dwellers must keep in mind that things are done on a much smaller scale in these parts, so you won't find the large dance clubs offered in a more metropolitan area or larger beach city. You will, however, find a nightlife that welcomes visitors and is quick to accommodate most musical tastes.

Many of the local nightspots offer you a choice of staying inside or enjoying a water view in an outdoor lounge. For those who prefer to be outdoors, which our area's mild climate allows most of the year, there are harbor cruises, the beach and deck bars. Besides the many waterfront bars, several local boats offer sunset trips or dinner cruises. Check our Attractions chapter for more information about entertainment cruises.

Shag dancing to beach music is popular here, and many clubs cater to people who enjoy this pastime. The shag is a type of dance that was probably a derivative of the beach bop, although it is smoother and done to rhythm and blues or North Carolina's own beach music. The dance is basically an eight-step, alternate-step that has a definite rhythm and distinct appearance. A few local beach clubs and a few Parks and Recreation departments offer shag lessons for those wanting to learn.

i *The gulls that follow the Cedar Island Ferry always expect a handout. They'll almost eat from your hand. Ferry officials ask that you feed them only from the back of the ferry.*

Here we have listed the spots that cater primarily to nightlife seekers. Some of these close or are only open a few nights each week during the winter so calling ahead is always a good idea in the off-season. If the business is on Bogue Banks, we have used the mile marker (MM) number for easy location. Bear in mind that many restaurants are considered nightspots because they feature live entertainment on weekends during the season or have a bar, so check our Restaurants chapter for more information on those as well. The local newspaper or any one of the weekly vacation guides might also help you in selecting a nightspot. If we mention ABC permits, it means that the establishment can legally sell liquor in addition to beer and wine. ABC stands for Alcohol Beverage Control, the state agency that regulates the sale of liquor in North Carolina.

At the end of this chapter we have supplied information about movie theaters and a list of ABC stores in the area.

Bogue Banks

ATLANTIC BEACH

When locals think of beach nightlife, they think of Atlantic Beach. It's home to a number of nightspots, but the town retains a family atmosphere and surely doesn't have the night scene other beach-front towns along the East Coast have. Nightspots have come and gone during the years, although there are a number of reputable places that have stood the test of time and continue to offer quality entertainment. There are others, but we'll only tell you about the ones we feel comfortable recommending. New places often open each spring, others close in the fall. If you spot a business we haven't listed, there may be several reasons for its omission -- it may not be one we would recommend to a friend; it may have just opened in the spring; or we may have unintentionally overlooked it.

Beach Tavern (BT)
MM 2.5, N.C. Hwy. 58, Atlantic Beach
(252) 247-4466

BT is open year round and offers an informal, fun place to hang out. Originally known as the Beach Tavern, BT has been around since 1972 and continues to attract a diverse group of people who aren't looking for anything fancy. Lots of folks are glad BT allows kids in from 11 AM to 9 PM, and you'll often see families enjoying meals here. You can play pool, darts, Foosball, NTN trivia and pinball, listen to the jukebox and watch sports on a wide-screen TV. The grill serves sandwiches, burgers, hot dogs and good pizza. BT has all ABC permits and is open until 2 AM seven days a week, year round.

Channel Marker
Atlantic Beach Cswy., Atlantic Beach
(252) 247-2344

The Channel Marker is a mainstay in the summer nightlife of the county and has been for 24 years. This is a waterfront spot that has definitely gained a positive reputation with visitors and locals. You'll find great food, a fun waterfront bar with an atrium lounge, and a beautiful deck overlooking Bogue Sound. There's even dock space available for folks who prefer to boat up for their dinner reservations. The bar has all ABC permits, a great selection of beers and wines, and is a favorite nightspot for people of all ages.

Memories Beach and Shag Club
MM 1.5, 128 E. Fort Macon Rd.,
Atlantic Beach
(252) 240-7424

There's been much fuss during the years about where shag dancing actually began -- was it Myrtle Beach, South Carolina, or right here in Atlantic Beach? The folks at Memories Beach and Shag Club don't spend too much time pondering things of the past, however, they're just glad to keep the spirit alive. During the spring and summer, this is one hopping joint, with shaggers coming from far and wide to participate in an array of weekend contests and events. Dance lessons are offered year round and lessons are offered on the beginner, intermediate and advanced level. Winter months find Memories open a few nights a week and on weekends. Be sure to call ahead for a schedule and for special events information.

PINE KNOLL SHORES

Cutty Sark Lounge
Clamdigger Inn, MM 8, N.C. Hwy. 58,
Pine Knoll Shores
(252) 247-4155

For a great spot overlooking a calming pool, check out this lounge at the Clamdigger Inn. Cutty Sark opens on weekdays at 5 PM and on weekends at noon. The lounge often features special DJ nights and has all ABC permits. Call for the schedule.

INDIAN BEACH/SALTER PATH

Frank and Clara's Restaurant & Lounge
MM 11, N.C. Hwy. 58, Indian Beach
(252) 247-2788

The lounge is upstairs over the restaurant and gets in full swing in the summer, offering a DJ playing a variety of music from beach and shag to country and rock. It opens at 5 PM every day during the season. In the winter, the lounge is open on Fridays and Saturdays. Call for the entertainment schedule.

EMERALD ISLE

RuckerJohns Restaurant and More
Emerald Plantation Shopping Center,
MM 19.5, N.C. Hwy. 58
(252) 354-2413

This upbeat nightspot is very popular with the younger and middle-age sets. You'll find a nice bar separated from the dining area with an extensive selection of draft beer and wines by the glass and all ABC permits. In the summer RuckerJohns often offers entertainment on the outdoor patio, and that's a great place to relax, visit with friends or meet new ones.

Beaufort

Back Street Pub
124 Middle Ln., Beaufort
(252) 728-7108

This laid-back place is in an alley behind Clawson's Restaurant, but don't let that stop you from checking it out. Regulars simply call it Back Street, and this small, nothing-fancy, popular spot is usually standing room only on the weekends. A little outdoor alley garden offers some respite from the crowds. Beer, wine and wine coolers are served at the huge

wooden bar. Upstairs is a "sailors' library" where folks can bring a book to swap or to read. Back Street Pub has live music year-round; call for details on performers. Winter visitors will find a cozy fire and a pot of soup.

The Dock House
500 Front St., Beaufort
(252) 728-4506

There's something special about The Dock House. This waterfront bar fronts Taylor's Creek and has long been a favorite of locals and Crystal Coast visitors alike. Space is limited inside, but the large upstairs and downstairs deck and boardwalk provide plenty of room for all the visitors during the summer. Live entertainment is offered outside in the summer and inside in the winters. The Dock House has all ABC permits, a good selection of pub food and live entertainment on tap during the season.

Front Street Grill at Stillwater
300 Front St., Beaufort
(252) 728-4956
www.frontstreetgrillatstillwater.com

The Rum Bar at Front Street Grill is an exciting new addition to the restaurant and to the nightlife scene in Beaufort. The restaurant's location on the Historic Beaufort Waterfront offers guests spectacular views of Beaufort Inlet, Carrot Island and evening sunsets. And the Rum Bar - a wonderful outdoor bar area - is perfect for an evening relaxing at the water's edge. This is the perfect place to enjoy selections from an extensive rum list, cocktails, wine, beer and light foods outside. The restaurant has all ABC permits and

For some, nightlife is as simple as enjoying a sunset over the water.

photo: George Mitchell

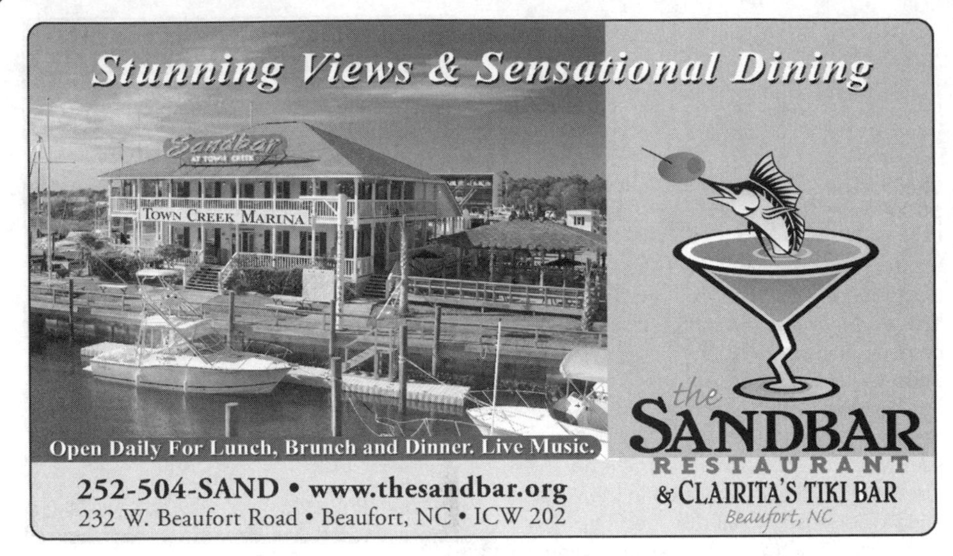

serves lunch, dinner and a Sunday brunch that is not to be missed.

Royal James Cafe
117 Turner St., Beaufort
(252) 728-4573

Royal James Cafe, named for one of Blackbeard's ships, is the oldest continually existing business in Beaufort's historic district and has a local flavor all its own that keeps people coming and its name in conversation from Canada to the Caribbean. With an early '50s Formica, wood and neon look, this cafe and pool room has been favorably mentioned in editorial publications including the Chicago Tribute, the Atlanta Constitution-Journal, the News and Observer and Southern Living. It draws an interesting mix of locals and tourists, families and singles, and has hours from 9 AM until last call every day except Sunday when it is open from noon to 7 PM. In addition to the Brunswick Anniversary and Century edition regulation pool tables, you'll find an Internet connected juke box, video games and a flat-screen TV tuned to sports, weather or breaking news.

The Sandbar Restaurant and Tiki Bar
232 W. Beaufort Rd., Beaufort
(252) 504-SAND (7263)
www.thesandbar.org
www.clairitastikibar.com

The Sandbar Restaurant at Town Creek Marina offers sensational dining and spectacular views seven days a week. With a commanding view of the Intracoastal Waterway and Beaufort/Morehead causeway bridge, The Sandbar features a beautifully appointed dining room, which allows guests to watch vessels navigating the channel against spectacular sunsets and the sparking harbor skyline. On warm evenings you can dine on the covered veranda sipping drinks and be lulled by the nautical breezes. After dinner, step out to the Caribbean-inspired Clairita's Tiki Bar, where you'll find a complete menu of domestic and exotic drink selections. On weekends, you can party to your heart's content under the stars as popular live bands entertain Town Creek guests.

Morehead City

Crystal Coast Jamboree
1311 Arendell St., Morehead City
(252) 726-1501, (866) 580-7469

Billed as the "Hottest Ticket At The Beach" this live variety show is filled with family entertainment. The Jamboree cast offers a new show for 2006, featuring two-hours of high energy that blends country, oldies, dancing, comedy and event a little "Orange Blossom Special". But don't think there is only one show offered here. The Jamboree brings in top nationally known recording artists throughout the year, and puts on a wonderful Christmas show. Last year more than 90 shows were performed and more will likely be scheduled this year. Early reservations are suggested because many of the shows sell out. The Jamboree is quickly becoming a destination for visitors and bus tour groups.

Midnight Rodeo
5386 U.S. Hwy. 70 W, Morehead City
(252) 222-0111

This Western nightclub and saloon is a hit in the area and regularly brings in nationally known performers. The club offers live performances, as well as karaoke nights and dance lessons and a full-time DJ. The general store offers munchies and western wear, and there are three pool tables, a large dance floor, an outside patio and two bars -- one downstairs and one upstairs. Midnight Rodeo has all ABC permits and offers a variety of beer and wine. The club is open to members, and there is a cover charge for guests, a charge that varies depending on the evening's entertainment.

Raps Grill & Bar
715 Arendell St., Morehead City
(252) 240-1213

Set in a casual atmosphere, Raps is a favorite gathering place among locals year round. The roomy bar is often packed during the summer months, but it should definitely be included on your schedule of things to do. The downstairs bar area surrounds a huge oak bar and has tables and plenty of floor space. Raps has all ABC permits and offers a large selection of beers and wines. There are televisions at the bar and two big-screen TVs for watching games. This is the area's hotspot for watching the Super Bowl and other major sporting events. Upstairs are two levels of dining.

Tours

Some want to see the Crystal Coast by day, some want to see it by night. Below are a few of the area tours that also offer a bit of nightlife. More information about these tours and others are offered in the Attractions chapter.

TourBeaufort.Com
Beaufort
(252) 342-0715

TourBeaufort.Com offers several types of tours for visitors and residents of all ages.

The Beaufort Ghost Walk takes guests on a evening stroll through town, with stops at Blackbeard's Hammock House and the Old Burying Ground. This tour group also offers a Wild Horse and Shelling Safari, a Legend of Blackbeard Tour and a great Kid's Island Adventure. Reservations are needed for the tours, which vary in price and point of origin.

Diamond City
Big Rock Landing, 405 Evans St., Morehead City
(252) 728-7827, (866) 230-BOAT
www.mysteryboattours.com

This is Carteret County's only floating nightclub. The Diamond City, docked on Morehead City's waterfront next to Big Rock Landing, is available for special charters, wedding cruises, corporate meetings and fun tours. The Diamond City's night club cruise leaves Friday and Saturday evenings at 9:30 PM for a special party cruise. Call for the schedule. Onboard the 246-passenger vessel you'll find a captain and crew prepared to make your voyage fun and enjoyable. The evening dinner cruise from 7 to 9 PM, including fine dining and dancing. The "floating party cruise" is designed for the young and young at heart. With all ABC permits, state-of-the-art sound system and either a DJ or live entertainment the Diamond City is the place to be to party. Folks age 18 and older are invited aboard for for the late-night party cruise for $10 per person. Reservations are required, and they offer free soft drinks and coffee to designated drivers. Also check out the Diamond City's sister vessels, Mystery and the Lookout Express, which are both docked in Beaufort.

Lookout Cruises
Beaufort Waterfront
(252) 504-SAIL

Steve Bishop captains the Lookout, a 45-foot catamaran that can hold 42 passengers. He offers a relaxing 90-minute sunset cruise and in the past the rate has been $25 per adult and $15 per child. Complimentary beverages are served. It is always best to call ahead to book a cruise on this popular vessel.

Mystery Tours
The Mystery Tour Boat Lookout Express
Front St., Beaufort
(252) 728-2527, (866) 230-BOAT
www.mysteryboattours.com

Docked in Taylor's Creek, the 65-foot, double-decked Mystery tour boat offers cruises along area waterways. Complete with a covered cabin, snack bar and a resident pirate who delights all the passengers, especially the kids, the boat provides visitors with a view of Beaufort's historic homes, island ponies, salt marshes, bird rookeries, Morehead City State Port, Fort Macon, Shackleford Banks and other islands along the Intracoastal Waterway. Tours last one and a half hours and are conducted daily at 2, 4:30 and 7 PM from April through October.

The Mystery also offers half-day fishing trips from 8 AM to noon. The boat is available for special-occasion charters such as birthdays, weddings and anniversaries. Special-interest trips can be arranged for birders, shell collectors and other groups. Educational trips for school groups are also a specialty.

Sunset cruises combine two trips into one. Guests can enjoy a fully narrated trip along the Historic Beaufort Waterfront, and then enjoy a high speed ride out to view Cape Lookout Lighthouse and watch the sunset on the Atlantic Ocean.

The Lookout Express is operated by Mystery Tours and is the world's largest speedboat. This 73-foot, 149-passenger, 1,800-horsepower ferry boat takes passengers to Cape Lookout and offers sunset cruises and private charters. The Lookout Express operates from April to October, and those interested are invited to call for reservations and prices.

Outer Banks Sail and Kayak
612 Atlantic Beach Cswy., Atlantic Beach
(252) 247-6300
www.obsk.com

Sit back and relax on the Siriuslee as Captain Lee Sutton sails the waters of Taylor's Creek at sunset. During the popular dinner cruise, you'll enjoy the Beaufort waterfront at sunset, followed up with a run over to the Morehead City waterfront for dinner at the Key West Seafood Restaurant. Capt. Sutton and his crew invite you to call play at OBSK -- just call for reservations and then come prepared to have fun.

Movie Theaters

The area's movie theaters listed here offer discounts for seniors and children. They also run matinees at reduced prices, but check to make sure which days because off-season matinees are usually restricted to weekends. Movie listings are printed in the Carteret News-Times, published every Wednesday, Friday and Sunday.

Atlantic Station Cinema 4, MM 3, at the west end of the Atlantic Station shopping center in Atlantic Beach, (252) 247-7016

Emerald Plantation Cinema 4, MM 20, in the Emerald Plantation Shopping Center, Emerald Isle, (252) 354-5012

Plaza Cinema One, Two and Three, Morehead Plaza Shopping Center, Bridges Street in Morehead City, (252) 726-2081

Liquor Laws and ABC Stores

Though you can buy beer and wine at food stores, you must purchase liquor in Alcohol Beverage Control (ABC) package stores. Local ABC stores are open Monday through Saturday. There are seven local ABC stores.

Beaufort ABC Store, just north of the U.S. 70/Live Oak Street intersection

Morehead City ABC Store, K-Mart Shopping Center, 4915-G Arendell St., U.S. 70

Atlantic Beach ABC Store, MM 2.5 on N.C. 58

Emerald Isle ABC Store, MM 20 on N.C. 58, in the Emerald Plantation Shopping Center

Cape Carteret ABC Store, N.C. 24 beside the police department

Newport ABC Store, just east of the U.S. 70/Howard Boulevard intersection beside Subway

Swansboro ABC Store, N.C. 24 on west side of Swansboro

HOTELS AND MOTELS

The Crystal Coast is a diverse resort area with a wide variety of accommodations. There are many attractive lodging choices, some rich with history and all full of our special Southern hospitality. Choose from luxurious oceanfront or sound-side hotels and resorts, family-style motels and efficiency suites. Folks looking for something off the beaten path will find even more options in our chapters on Bed and Breakfast Inns, Camping and Weekly and Long-Term Vacation Rentals.

On the beach, as in most resort areas, rates vary according to the season and the lodging's proximity to water. If, for economy's sake, you are considering a location away from the water, you may want to ask about access either to the ocean or to the sound and inquire as to whether or not it is within walking distance.

The Crystal Coast is becoming a year-round resort town. We recommend you make reservations in advance no matter what time of year you plan on visiting. During the early spring and late-fall shoulder seasons and in the winter, however, many establishments offer attractive weekend getaways, golf packages and special rates. The area is a popular site for meetings, conventions and fishing excursions throughout the year, and many facilities offer meeting rooms and convention services. The Crystal Coast Civic Center (see our Attractions chapter) in Morehead City accommodates sizeable shows and gatherings with hotels and other lodgings conveniently nearby.

Each lodging establishment has a different deposit and refund policy. While some require a deposit equal to one night's stay in advance, others will simply hold your reservation on your credit card. Often a 24-hour notice is sufficient for a full refund, but some require as much as a three-day notice. Because of the area's popularity, extending your stay can be difficult but not impossible. Some places require up to 72-hours notice for extensions past your originally scheduled departure date.

In cases of emergency, we also recommend that you inquire into a hotel's hurricane or emergency policy. Sometimes, hurricane evacuations can mean an abrupt end to a vacation. Most area resorts have policies in place to make refunds available under these conditions, but be sure to ask what that policy is before you pay.

Many of the area's lodgings offer nonsmoking rooms by request. The pet policy is the proprietor's option. Most do not allow pets in rooms, although some lodgings do make provisions for them. If your pet will be traveling with you it is best to ask before making reservations.

This guide doesn't attempt to list all the accommodations available on the Crystal Coast. Rather, we've provided a sampling of some of our favorites. For more information about lodging and weekend availability, contact the Carteret County Tourism Development Authority, P.O. Box 1406, Morehead City, NC 28557, (800) SUNNY NC or (252) 726-8148. The Tourism Authority operates visitors centers at 3409 Arendell Street (U.S. Highway 70) in Morehead City and on N.C. Highway 58, just north of the Cameron Langston Bridge to Emerald Isle.

PRICE CODE

For the purpose of comparing prices, we have placed each accommodation in a price category based on the average rate for a double-occupancy room per night during the summer season. There is often a wide range of rates offered at all accommodations based on amenities offered. As we have averaged the rate range, you may expect to find rooms at higher and lower prices when you call for reservations. Winter rates can be substantially lower, and holiday rates always higher. Rates shown do not include state and local taxes. Amenities and rates are subject to

change. It's best to verify information important to you, including credit cards accepted, when making your reservations.

$	$70 and less
$$	$71 to $90
$$$	$91 to $125
$$$$	More than $125

Bogue Banks

All the accommodations we would recommend on the beach are just too numerous to list. In this section we offer a sample range of accommodations from full-service resorts to family and angler favorites with fewer frills. We also suggest you contact condominium developments (see the Crystal Coast Weekly and Long-Term Cottage Rentals chapter) because most offer attractive vacation rates.

ATLANTIC BEACH

Budget Inn **$$-$$$**
MM 2, N.C. Hwy. 58, Atlantic Beach
(252) 726-3780, (800) 636-3780

This clean, comfortable motel was remodeled last year and offers family and commercial rates by the day, week or month. All the 37 standard rooms have HBO, telephones, microwaves, refrigerators and access to the pool. The motel is an easy two-block walk from the ocean and is close to restaurants, shopping areas and the main beach amusement circle.

Caribbe Inn **$-$$**
MM 1.5, N.C. Hwy. 58, Atlantic Beach
(252) 726-0051
www.caribbe-inn.com

This clean, cozy, family-owned and operated inn, located on an access channel to Bogue Sound, is an inviting setting for fami-

lies, fishermen and scuba divers. The friendly hospitality at Caribbe Inn is punctuated by its colorful aquatic decor. Each room is painted in splashy colors with different fish murals and Caribbean designs. All of the rooms have telephones, refrigerators, microwaves and cable TV with HBO. Studio efficiencies with full kitchens as well as some pet-friendly rooms are also available. Guests are welcome to use the complimentary boat slips, picnic areas with grills, dock with a fish-cleaning station and a freezer to store their catches of the day. Caribbe Inn is just a short walk to the ocean and within easy walking distance of restaurants, fishing piers, shopping, shag clubs and entertainment. Golf and fishing packages are available. Darrel and Trish Lawrence look forward to making your visit an enjoyable one.

Oceanana Family Resort
Motel and Pier **$-$$$**
MM 1.5 , N.C. Hwy. 58, Atlantic Beach
(252) 726-4111
www.oceanana.com

This comfortable motel on the ocean provides lots of extras. Long a favorite of families with children, the Oceanana offers a pool, a children's play area and equipment, a fishing pier, picnic tables and grills, free poolside breakfasts in the summer season, beach chairs, and poolside and beach services. Guests choose from 109 rooms – standard rooms, oceanfront rooms or two-room efficiencies; all have refrigerators. The accommodations here are clean and comfortable. The Oceanana closes for the season in mid-November and re-opens in early April.

Sheraton Atlantic Beach
Oceanfront Hotel **$$$$**
MP 4.5, N.C. Hwy. 58, Atlantic Beach
(252) 240-1155, (800) 624-8875
www.sheratonatlanticbeach.com

Sheraton is a full-service beachfront resort hotel. All 200 ocean-view rooms and suites were renovated for the 2004 season. New carpet, bedding, bedspreads and drapes have been added, and all bathrooms have new tile, wall vinyl, vanities and fixtures. Rooms include a coffee maker, refrigerator, hair dryer, iron and ironing board, two phone lines, wireless Internet connections and a private balcony. Suites with one bedroom, a living room and a whirlpool tub are available. Guestrooms now have Sheraton Sweet-Sleeper beds. The staff will arrange anything from same-day dry cleaning to golf and tennis. A summertime children's activities director offers a full schedule of daytime fun. Fine dining is available in the resort's restaurant, and in season an oceanfront grill serves casual fare and beverages. The resort has its own fishing pier for anglers. Catering and full banquet services are available for small or large meetings. Guests enjoy the indoor and outdoor pools, plus a whirlpool and fitness room.

Show Boat Motel **$$-$$$**
Atlantic Beach Cswy., Atlantic Beach
(252) 726-6163, (800) SHO-BOAT

With easy access to Bogue Sound, this familiar motel with a stern paddlewheel offers lodging at affordable rates. Guests can fish from the motel dock, complete with a fish-cleaning table, or take a dip in the povol. All 42 rooms have refrigerators, and guests can enjoy picnic areas, grills and continental breakfasts. The motel offers family, corporate and AARP rates and is open all year. The Show Boat is generally closed during the winter months.

PINE KNOLL SHORES

AmeriSuites **$$$**
MM 5, N.C. Hwy. 58, Pine Knoll Shores
(252) 247-5118, (800) 747-8483

This four-story hotel has 111 suites, each featuring a sleeper sofa and two double beds or one king-size bed. Every suite offers a microwave, refrigerator, coffee maker, wet bar and work desk consisting of a data port, two phone lines, modems and voice mail. AmeriSuites overlooks Bogue Banks Country Club Golf Course and is directly across the highway from the ocean. Guests may enjoy the beach via an ocean access walkway. A luxurious, complimentary breakfast featuring English muffins, bagels, Danish pastries, sausage, yogurt, fresh fruit and waffles is served every day. Guests can enjoy the heated outdoor swimming pool, a well-equipped fitness center and laundry facilities on site. Be sure to ask about the special golf packages. And if you need a meeting room, several are available, each with the amenities necessary for conducting successful business meetings. Pets are welcome.

Atlantis Lodge **$$$-$$$$**
MM 5, N.C. Hwy. 58, Pine Knoll Shores
(252) 726-5168, (800) 682-7057
www.atlantislodge.com

Set among beautiful live oaks on the oceanside, Atlantis Lodge was among the first hotels built on Bogue Banks. Many of the guests at the Atlantis consider it their "second home" and return year after year. Most units are arranged as suites, offering efficiency kitchens and dining, living and

sleeping areas. All have patios or decks facing the surf, cable TV and other expected amenities. Recreation areas, equipment, golf packages and complimentary beach furniture and beach services are extended to guests. The outdoor pool is a quiet place for sunning and swimming, and the third-floor lounge has an adjoining library. Unlike most hotels, the Atlantis makes provisions for pets. The lodge proudly sponsors two popular sand-sculpture contests -- the Mile of Hope in early May for children with cancer and a competition in August that benefits the Outer Banks Wildlife Shelter. See our Annual Events chapter for details.

Seahawk Motor Lodge **$$$**
MM 4.5, N.C. Hwy. 58, Pine Knoll Shores
(252) 726-4146, (800) 682-6898
www.ncbeach-motel.com

This comfortable lodge offers 38 oceanfront rooms with balconies or patios. Each room has a phone, cable TV and refrigerator. Connecting double rooms, a two-bedroom cottage and two three-bedroom, three-bath villas are also available. A pool is situated in the middle of a large, grassy lawn facing the ocean. Guests are offered bicycles and grills. Many guests enjoy relaxing in the hammocks and swings on the oceanfront lawn.

Windjammer Inn **$$$**
MM 4.5, N.C. Hwy. 58., Pine Knoll Shores
(252) 247-7123, (800) 233-6466
www.windjammerinn.com

All of the 46 rooms at the attractive Windjammer Inn are oversized and oceanfront with private balconies, refrigerators, microwave ovens, cable TVs and two telephones. The glass-enclosed elevator is an unexpected surprise and offers a great view of Bogue Sound. Guests enjoy the oceanfront pool, private beach area with beach services and complimentary coffee each morning. There is a two-night minimum during summer weekends and a three-night minimum on holiday weekends. We recommend you get one of the Jacuzzi rooms overlooking the ocean or relax in the outside hot tub by the pool.

SALTER PATH

Oak Grove Motel **$**
MM 10.5, N.C. Hwy. 58, Salter Path
(252) 247-3533

We're impressed by this motel because it's so tidy, and, in the shade of live oaks, it always looks cool, even on the hottest days. It has one- and two-story stone-sided units

i

The deep roots of sea oats help anchor the sand dunes. The plant is protected by law, so don't even think of harvesting a few, even if they're dead.

with 10 standard double-bed rooms and 13 kitchenettes all with porch rockers for enjoying the shade. This motel is a family facility and has lots of repeat business. Two-night minimums are required on summer weekends, and a three-night minimum is required during major holidays.

William and Garland Motel **$**
MM 10.5, N.C. Hwy. 58, Salter Path
(252) 247-3733

This small, family-owned motel has eight rooms and three mobile units. Nine are efficiencies, and two provide only simple sleeping accommodations. Each room has a refrigerator and microwave. Don't expect anything fancy, but do expect a family atmosphere and clean, comfortable surroundings. Peggy and William Smith are wonderful hosts. Guests have ocean access via a nature trail walkway (about 200 yards) and access to the 20-acre Salter Path Dunes Natural Area, perfect for swimming, fishing, walking, sunning and picnicking. This is the place to go to really get away, because the rooms have no phones. There is generally a two-night minimum stay in the summer.

i *To catch the Cedar Island Ferry to Ocracoke Island with your vehicle, you must be in line half an hour before departure time or your reservation will be cancelled. No exceptions!*

EMERALD ISLE/CAPE CARTERET/ CEDAR POINT

Best Western Silver Creek Inn **$$-$$$**
801 Cedar Point Blvd. (N.C. Hwy. 24), Cedar Point
(252) 393-9015, (877) 459-1448
www.bestwesternsilvercreekinn.com

Best Western Silver Creek Inn is located in Cedar Point, just minutes from the beaches, golf courses, Historic Swansboro and Hammocks Beach State Park. The inn offers 65 rooms, including suites and whirlpool rooms. Each room offers guests a refrigerator, microwave, coffee maker, iron and iron board, hair dryer and free high-speed Internet access. Guests can also enjoy an outdoor pool, an exercise facility and free continental breakfast. Silver Creek Inn can accommodate meetings of groups from two to 50, and specializes in assisting with wedding planning, family gatherings and business meetings. Golf packages are also available.

Islander Motor Inn **$$-$$$**
Islander Dr., Emerald Isle
(252) 354-3464, (800) 354-3464

Islander is on the ocean in Emerald Isle, and although the majority of the 81 rooms do not directly face the water, most offer a wonderful east-west view of the sea and beach. The two-story brick motel offers easy beach access, a pool and a nice lawn area. Guest rooms have refrigerators, two double beds, microwaves and cable television.

Parkerton Inn **$**
N.C. Hwy. 58 N., Cape Carteret
(252) 393-9000, (800) 393-9909

Parkerton Inn is on the mainland just north of the intersection of N.C. Highways 58 and 24. With 45 rooms, the inn offers several room arrangements, including kitchenette efficiencies and rooms equipped for the handicapped. Standard rooms have two queen-size beds and two executive suites offer king-size beds. The outdoor pool is a popular spot. Golf packages are offered. Every room features a microwave and a refrigerator. Free coffee is available in the lobby.

Beaufort

Most of Beaufort's accommodations are bed and breakfast inns. See our Bed and Breakfast Inns chapter for options other than those listed here.

Beaufort Inn **$$$**
101 Ann St., Beaufort
(252) 728-2600

This inn is in the ideal location for lodging in historic Beaufort. Located on Gallant's Channel at the end of Ann Street, it offers rooms with a water view and rooms overlooking the town's historic district. Some rooms have refrigerators and microwaves, and there is an outdoor hot tub for guests to enjoy. Guests are treated to Katie's special breakfast pie as part of the morning meal. The inn offers guests use of bicycles for riding along the streets of Beaufort and along the waterfront. Boat slips are available.

Inlet Inn **$$$**
601 Front St., Beaufort
(252) 728-3600, (800) 554-5466
www.inlet-inn.com

The 36-room Inlet Inn opened in 1985 in the same block of Front Street occupied by the original Inlet Inn of the 19th century, which brought guests from across the state to bask in the Beaufort sun. Today's inn, of similar design, is directly on the waterfront and offers harbor-front rooms on the first and second floor. These rooms have a king-size bed and sofa. Third-floor rooms overlooking the water offer two queen beds and a wonderful window seat for viewing

Beaufort Inlet, the waterfront and beyond. Nestled in the heart of the historic district, many rooms open onto private porches and offer bars, refrigerators with ice makers and built-in hair dryers. Six of the first floor rooms offer cozy fireplaces, and all rooms provide dial-up Internet access. A continental breakfast, served in the rooms, consists of muffins, bagels and juice. Coffeemakers are provided in each room. A courtyard garden, the rooftop Widow's Walk Lounge and an on-site meeting room are also available for guests' use year round.

Morehead City

Buccaneer Inn **$$-$$$**
2806 Arendell St., Morehead City
(252) 726-3115, (800) 682-4982

The Buccaneer Inn has 91 attractive rooms. The majority of the rooms have standard double beds, though some have king-size beds. Guests are offered complimentary hot breakfasts, newspapers, free local calls and cable TV, and rooms feature refrigerators and microwaves. Meeting and banquet facilities are available. Special packages include golf, diving and fishing. The inn is beside Morehead Plaza and is a short driving distance from Atlantic Beach. The Anchor Inn Restaurant and Lounge (see our Restaurants chapter) is beside the motel.

Comfort Inn **$$**
3100 Arendell St., Morehead City
(252) 247-3434, (800) 422-5404
www.moreheadhotels.com

Comfort Inn, like others in the national hotel chain, offers reliably comfortable rooms with either one king or two double beds, a pool and complimentary deluxe continental breakfast served each morning in the guest lounge. Convenient to the Crystal Coast Civic Center and all beach and historic attractions, Comfort Inn has 101 guest rooms to accommodate any gathering. Local phone calls are free, fax service is available, and each room has cable TV and a hair dryer and coffeemaker. Some are equipped with microwaves and refrigerators. Golf packages are available, and there are special rates for fishing and diving. Restaurants are within walking distance. The inn neighbors the Morehead Plaza. Corporate, AARP and AAA discounts are offered.

Econo Lodge Crystal Coast **$$**
3410 Bridges St., Morehead City
(252) 247-2940, (800) 533-7556

The Econo Lodge is two blocks from the Crystal Coast Civic Center and one block from Carteret General Hospital. It offers 56 rooms at reasonable rates and is within easy driving distance of the beaches. The majority of the rooms are furnished with two double beds and a few have king-sized beds. Amenities include cable TV, free local calls and complimentary continental breakfast. Some rooms feature refrigerators. Special value

---

i

The local Marine Mammal Strandings Network telephone number is (252) 728-8762. It is not in the local directory and could be important if you encounter an out-of-place dolphin or whale.

---

packages for golfing and diving are offered. Restaurants are close by, and there is plenty of parking for cars and boat trailers.

Hampton Inn **$$**
4035 Arendell St., Morehead City
(252) 240-2300, (800) 467-9375
www.hamptoninn.com/hi/moreheadcity/

Hampton Inn, overlooking Bogue Sound, offers beautiful views of the Intracoastal Waterway and the island of Bogue Banks. The inn's 119 guest rooms are decorated in fresh aquatic colors with a choice of two doubles or a king-size bed. Two-room suites have a separate living area. Guests enjoy an outside pool and deck area, free continental breakfasts served in the sun room, free accommodations for children and an exercise room. Meeting rooms, plenty of parking and attractive golf, tennis and fishing packages are available. Restaurants and shopping areas are nearby.

Down East

There are a few motels in the Down East area, and we've listed them here. Many people also enjoy the kind of island getaway that is a real back-to-basics experience, so we've also told you about accommodations available on Core Banks (Cape Lookout National Seashore). For information about Down East campgrounds, see our Camping chapter.

Morris Marina Kabin Kamps
North Core Banks **$**
1000 Morris Marina Rd., Atlantic
(252) 225-4261

Twenty rustic cabins that vary in size to accommodate from six to 12 people may be rented by the day on North Core Banks (Cape Lookout National Seashore). The price indicated here is a per-person rate based on a full cabin. "Rustic" means bunk beds, gas cooking stoves, solar power electricity, a sink and a toilet. Although water is potable, most visitors bring their own. Pack as you would for a camping trip, and you'll be most comfortable. Long a guarded secret of anglers, this cabin settlement is also the choice getaway for shell-seekers in the spring and bird-watchers in the fall. Ferries run from the town of Atlantic to the cabins several times each day, except from December through mid-March. Making reservations well in advance is recommended. If you take your four-wheel-drive vehicle over on the ferry, you can drive the 22 miles of beach on this island. See our Getting Here, Getting Around chapter for more information on the ferry.

Great Island Cabins
South Core Banks $
Davis
(252) 225-4261

Twenty-five rustic cabins are available on South Core Banks at Cape Lookout National Seashore. These cabins are arranged to accommodate 4, 6, 8 or 12 people and are rented on a per-night basis. The cabins are rustic and include several beds with mattresses, a gas stove with an oven, potable water, sinks, toilets and showers. There is no electricity in these cabins so this is the perfect way to enjoy the natural beauty of the Banks. There are hookups for generators, if you bring your own. Bring everything else you'll need, including cooking utensils and linens. A caretaker is available on a limited schedule to deliver basic supplies such as ice. The ferries providing transportation to these cabins operate from the Down East community of Davis. These cabins are very popular, so plan ahead and reserve early. The camp is closed from December through mid-March. See our Getting Here, Getting Around chapter for more information.

Driftwood Motel $
N.C. Hwy. 12 at the ferry terminal,
Cedar Island
(252) 225-4861
www.clis.com/deg/

Surrounded by beautiful beaches, the Driftwood is the perfect place to escape day-to-day stress and live the island life. Remodeled last winter, this 37-room motel is located by the Cedar Island-Ocracoke Ferry Terminal. Rooms offer either two double beds or one king-sized bed, and all rooms have cable television with HBO. The fact that there are no phones in the rooms makes the Driftwood the perfect escape. Bring your beach chair, your kayak or your boat and enjoy all the island has to offer. Pets are accommodated at the Driftwood. The motel also has a restaurant known for fresh local seafood and prime rib (call ahead for hours), a gift shop and a campground (see our Camping chapter). The motel is open year-round. A continental breakfast is served.

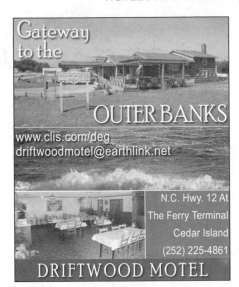

Calico Jack's Motel and Ferry Service $
Island Rd., Harkers Island
(252) 728-3575

During spring, summer and fall, this 24-room motel offers comfortable rooms and efficiencies with two double beds. Restaurants are nearby. The motel shares the property with a full marina that offers a ramp, gas, supplies, refreshments and a complete tackle shop. Cape Lookout Ferry Service is also on the property to offer visitors water-taxi service to Cape Lookout and other places. Four-wheel drive trucks are stored on the Outer Banks to accommodate guests who want to explore. Calico Jack's staff can make charter boat arrangements for guests as well.

BED AND BREAKFAST INNS

Bed and breakfast-style hospitality is available on the Crystal Coast for folks who prefer a slower pace, a personal touch and a relaxed atmosphere. Bed and breakfast lodging can be the ideal retreat for those seeking a quiet, stress-free vacation. Room arrangements and breakfast specialties vary at each inn. Most do not have facilities for young children or pets, and smoking, if allowed at all, is often restricted to certain areas.

Nearly all lodgings in Beaufort are historic bed and breakfast inns. They offer charming surroundings, memorable views and warm hospitality, and most are within walking distance of the historic district, the waterfront boardwalk, shopping, restaurants and the North Carolina Maritime Museum.

The inns described here (we list them in alphabetical order) offer a range of prices based on amenities of each room or suite of rooms.

PRICE CODE

The price codes reflect an average figure for double occupancy in the peak season from April through October. As always, it's best to verify the information that is important to you - including acceptable forms of payment - when making your reservations.

$	Less than $100
$$	$101 to $125
$$$	$126 to $150
$$$$	More than $150

Beaufort

Captain's Quarters Bed & Biscuit **$$**
315 Ann St., Beaufort
(252) 728-7711, (800) 659-7111

This two-story, white home with its luxurious wraparound porch offers the quiet elegance of a Victorian summer at the shore. You'll find Ms. Ruby, Capt. Dick Collins and their daughter Polly to be delightful hosts. The three upstairs bedrooms feature private powder rooms and baths. House traditions include Ms. Ruby's fresh "riz" biscuits, continental breakfasts and complimentary beverages to welcome the sunset each evening. The Collins family will gladly help you with area information and dinner reservations as well as provide you with the use of a computer, modem and fax machine. The Captain's Quarters has been rated "Excellent" by the North Carolina Bed & Breakfast Association. Payment by personal check is preferred.

The Cedars by the Sea **$$$**
305 Front St., Beaufort
(252) 728-7036
www.cedarsinn.com

At the corner of Front and Orange streets, the two stately homes that make up The Cedars are surrounded by gardens whose summer flowers color each lovely guest unit and the inn's dining room. Each house - circa 1768 and 1851 - is beautifully restored and furnished with period pieces. Owners Linda and Sam Dark extend their hospitality to every detail. There are 11 rooms and suites, all with private baths. Some rooms have fireplaces and separate sitting rooms, the honeymoon cottage has a whirlpool, and high-speed wireless Internet service is provided throughout the inn. In the spring, incomparable lace-cap hydrangeas in the front garden are a feast for the eye and soul. A complimentary full breakfast is served in the dining room every morning. Other amenities are a wine bar and free bicycles. The Cedars is a nonsmoking inn and welcomes children age 10 and older. It is an ideal spot for parties and corporate retreats. It's closed Thanksgiving, Christmas and New Year's, and pets are not allowed. The Cedar's was nominated for Best Small Inn in North America by Condé Nast Johansens.

Carteret County Home Bed & Breakfast $$
299 N.C. Hwy. 101, Beaufort
(252) 728-4611

Located on N.C. Highway 101, a half-mile north of the intersection of U.S. Highway 70 E., the Carteret County Home Bed & Breakfast is just minutes from Beaufort's famed historic district. Known as the County Home, it is one of the town's most interesting buildings and is listed on the National Register of Historic Places. Built in 1913–14, before the days of Social Security and welfare, it was operated by Carteret County for 29 years as a house for the area's "poor, aged and infirm." The building's architectural and cultural interest kept it safe from demolition until it was bought by Terry and Nan O'Pray for restoration into a bed and breakfast. Because of the building's simple yet classic design, don't expect the stereotypical Victorian home most imagine for a bed and breakfast. Instead, you'll find ten private, individually decorated efficiency suites complete with comfortable, charming decor. Its location and backyard pavilion on two acres make it an ideal getaway for weddings, family reunions or special weekends. Tell your family and friends you're going to the poorhouse. Then come enjoy the "grumpy hosts, lumpy beds, bad food, and nasty cat, and really spoiled dog." Kids and pets are welcome at the Carteret County Home Bed & Breakfast.

Cousins Bed and Breakfast $$
305 Turner St., Beaufort
(252) 728-3917

Cousins Bed and Breakfast in downtown Beaufort, known for a sumptuous breakfast, is also the only bed and breakfast that allows you to do a little shopping in your nightgown. Martha and Elmo Barnes offer two air-conditioned rooms with private baths, furnished with an island motif. Located in the Historic District, Cousins resides in the Jarvis-Brown House, circa 1820, and is right across from the historic Carteret County Courthouse.

Cousins' tariff covers an incomparable, full, sit-down breakfast prepared by Elmo, who is a master chef and has published his own cookbooks. Whether you're a guest or not, make sure you visit their shop right there, Martha's Collection of Spices & Gifts, which is full of wonderful items for yourself or to take home as a gift. (See our Shopping chapter for more information.)

Delamar Inn Bed and Breakfast $$
217 Turner St., Beaufort
(252) 728-4300, (800) 349-5823
www.delamarinn.com

The Delamar Inn in Beaufort's Historic District was voted in Arrington's Bed and Breakfast Journal as one of the Top 10 B&Bs in the South. The inn is maintained in the restored Gibble-Delamar House, circa 1866. Hosts Mary and F. J. Hurst offer guests four rooms with private baths. Guests are welcomed year round at the Delamar, which is beginning its 18th year. Mornings begin with a breakfast of quiche, breads, jams, cereals, fresh fruit, coffee and your favorite teas and juices.

From the inn's Turner Street location, it is only a short walk to the Historic Restoration site, downtown shops and waterfront. The hosts are happy to help guests arrange for boat rides to the Cape Lookout Lighthouse or a kayak paddle up "The Cut." A special treat is relaxing in the living room with its fireplace, amid the collection of fine old books, some dating to the early 1800s. Mary is also an artist, and a guest may find her in the studio working on her limited-edition etchings.

Inlet Inn & Conference Center **$$$**
601 Front St., Beaufort
(252) 728-3600, (800) 554-5466
www.inlet-inn.com

The 36-room Inlet Inn opened in 1985 in the same block of Front Street occupied by the original Inlet Inn of the 19th century, which brought guests from across the state to bask in the Beaufort sun. Today's inn, of similar design, offers harbor-front rooms on the first and second floor with a king size bed and sofa. Third-floor rooms overlooking the water offer two queen beds and a wonderful window seat for viewing Beaufort Inlet, the waterfront and beyond. Many rooms open onto private porches and offer bars, refrigerators with ice makers and built-in hair dryers. Six of the first floor rooms offer cozy fireplaces, and all rooms provide Internet access. A continental breakfast, served in the rooms, consists of muffins, bagels and juice. Coffeemakers are provided in each room. A courtyard garden, the rooftop Widow's Walk Lounge and an on-site meeting room are also available for guests' use year round.

The Langdon House **$$$-$$$$**
135 Craven St., Beaufort
(252) 728-5499
www.langdonhouse.com

The innkeepers and restorers of the Langdon House (circa 1733), Jimm and Lizzet Prest, extend the hospitality of good friends and provide all the extras that give their guests a personalized experience of Beaufort. Each of the four guest rooms has a queen-size bed and a private bath and is furnished with antiques in keeping with the old Colonial/Federal home. The latest renovation is their "Master Guest Room" with an extra large whirlpool bath for two and tandem shower with a Grohe Aquatower as well as other surprises. Go there to relax; sleeping late is considered a compliment to the innkeepers. The hallmark of the Prests' hospitality is a full breakfast, served until 11 AM. A hearty helping of fresh fruit is followed by one of the house specialties, such as stuffed French toast, Belgian waffles or Lizzet's Mexican cuisine, if your appetite is adventuresome. With a word in advance, the Prests are happy to cater to special diets and preferences. Credit cards are not accepted, but personal checks are just fine. Bring a change of clothes and a good attitude, and they'll take care of the rest.

Pecan Tree Inn **$$-$$$**
116 Queen St., Beaufort
(252) 728-6733, (800)728-7871
www.pecantree.com

This 1860s, two-story Victorian home, complete with gingerbread trim, is a charming bed and breakfast with seven guest rooms. Each spacious room with private bath has a distinctive character. Two romantic suites have king-size canopied beds and Jacuzzis. A stay at the inn includes an expanded continental breakfast served in the dining room or on the inviting wraparound front porch. You will enjoy fresh-baked homemade muffins, cakes and breads, fruit, cereal and fresh roasted coffee. Hosts Allison and Dave DuBuisson are glad to assist with daytrip plans, dinner reservations or flowers. Beach chairs and bicycles are available. Allison and Dave encourage simple relaxation on the cool porches overlooking the inn's expansive herb and flower garden. All rooms have cable TV and wireless high-speed Internet service.

Down East

Otway House Bed & Breakfast **$-$$**
368 U.S. Hwy. 70, Otway
(252) 728-5636
www.otwayhouse.com

Innkeeper Janice Mines offers visitors a truly restful retreat. Located on six acres in the Down East community of Otway, this B&B features four private rooms each with a private bath and antique and reproduction furniture. Guests enjoy a full breakfast of coffee, tea, juices, pancakes, eggs and meats, as well as other treats Janice whips up. Otway House features trails for walking and exploring, launching areas for kayaks, and a wonderful porch surrounded by mature pecan trees. Janice is also a breeder for AKC Labrador retrievers, and she offers guests use of an indoor/outdoor kennel facility for their dogs. This is a relaxing, quiet place to stay that is convenient to Beaufort, the beaches, Cape Lookout National Seashore and the Down East communities.

Hosts at all bed and breakfast accommodations routinely reserve adventures and activities for their guests, such as kayaking, Gulf Stream fishing, sailing, golf or tennis.

Cape Carteret/ Emerald Isle

Emerald Isle Inn Bed and Breakfast **$$$**
502 Ocean Dr., Emerald Isle
(252) 354-3222

Elaine and Jim Normile accommodate their island guests in four suites: two suites are apartments rented by day or week, the other two suites come without kitchen accommodations and can also be rented by day or week. Each suite has a private entrance and a private bath. There are also televisions, VCRs and movie libraries in each suite. Guests enjoy views of the ocean and sound from porches with comfortable swings. Beach accesses are nearby, and beach chairs and umbrellas are available for guest use. A full breakfast is served each morning in the dining room.

Harborlight Guest House **$$$$**
332 Live Oak Dr., Cape Carteret
(252) 393-6868, (800) 624-VIEW (8439)
www.harborlightnc.com

With six luxury suites, the Harborlight Guest House is situated on a spectacular peninsula on Bogue Sound just off N.C. Highway 24 near Emerald Isle. This three-story inn offers high-end bed and breakfast accommodations in what once served as a restaurant for the ferry service. The inn is graced with spectacular views of 530 feet

of shoreline and sits in a quiet area close to beaches, Hammocks Beach State Park and all the amenities of the Crystal Coast. Rocking chairs on the decks are perfect spots to read a good book or just enjoy the wildlife along the waterfront. Suites offer the luxury of fireplaces and whirlpools and the incredible water views that make Harborlight so special. Handicapped-accessible accommodations on the ground level are fully equipped with all necessities. The hospitality of owners Debbie Mugno and Bob Pickens includes a gourmet breakfast served privately in-suite or deck-side daily. Open year round, the inn offers its 20-person capacity conference room for seminars and other group gatherings. Harborlight Guest House has been featured in Southern Living magazine as one of the five outstanding bed and breakfast inns in North Carolina. It has also been named among the "Top Undiscovered Inns in America."

WEEKLY AND LONG-TERM VACATION RENTALS

The Crystal Coast is the perfect place to vacation. If this is your first visit, you are about to discover why so many people return year after year. There are about 10,000 beds for rent on the Crystal Coast, according to the Tourism Development Authority (TDA), (252) 726-8148 or (800) SUNNY-NC. Vacation rental options range from small fishing units near the sound, ocean or fishing pier -- perfect if you spend all your time fishing -- to plush condominiums and seaside homes with an array of amenities. All you need to do is make a few simple decisions, starting with when you wish to visit the coast.

The Rate Season

Rental rates change according to the season, and that's sometimes confusing. To add to the confusion, not all rental agencies on the Crystal Coast use the same season schedule. It's always best to check with each rental company for specific season/rate changes.

Most rental agencies on the east end of Bogue Banks and in other areas of Carteret County base rental rates on two seasons: in-season (Memorial Day through Labor Day) and off-season (any other time). On the west end of the island many rental agencies charge rent based on a four-season schedule: May through mid-June and mid-August through September are mid season; mid-June through mid-August is prime season; September through November and March through April are shoulder season; December through February is off-season or winter. Prime season is the most expensive time to rent a vacation accommodation.

Vacation rentals can vary from $300 to more than $3,000 a week. You may find rates as much as 20 to 25 percent less in the shoulder season and off-season (after Labor Day and during the winter months) than in-season (Memorial Day through Labor Day). For that reason, many people prefer to vacation during the beautiful weather of the shoulder season -- April and May and September through November. Decide what you need and call a rental agency listed in the following pages or another listed in the phone directory to see what is offered. The Tourism Development Bureau is also a good source of general information. It is located in the Crystal Coast Visitor Center at 3409 Arendell Street in Morehead City.

The base rental rate is not the complete cost of renting a vacation place, so ask questions. Agencies add a cleaning fee to every rental, which can range from $35 to $100. There are also taxes. North Carolina's sales tax is 7 percent and Carteret County's occupancy tax is 5 percent, so the total tax on your rental bill is 12 percent. In addition, you will have to provide a security deposit (the amount varies with the rental company), which will be refunded provided nothing is damaged.

Locations and Types of Accommodations

Rental agencies can help you find the perfect place, whether it's the casual angler's cottage, family accommodations within walking distance of the beach, or the oceanfront condo with all the amenities of home and more. Rental costs vary with the type of accommodation and the location. Always check rental brochures or with an agent about the location. This is very important if you are planning to walk to the beach. Carrying chairs, coolers and an umbrella while watching out for your children can make a short trip seem a lot longer if you are several rows back from the water. Of course, generally speaking, the farther away from the water, the less expensive the rental rate.

At the beach, location is everything and an understanding of location descriptions can make all the difference in your family's vacation. Imagine a small strip of land, one

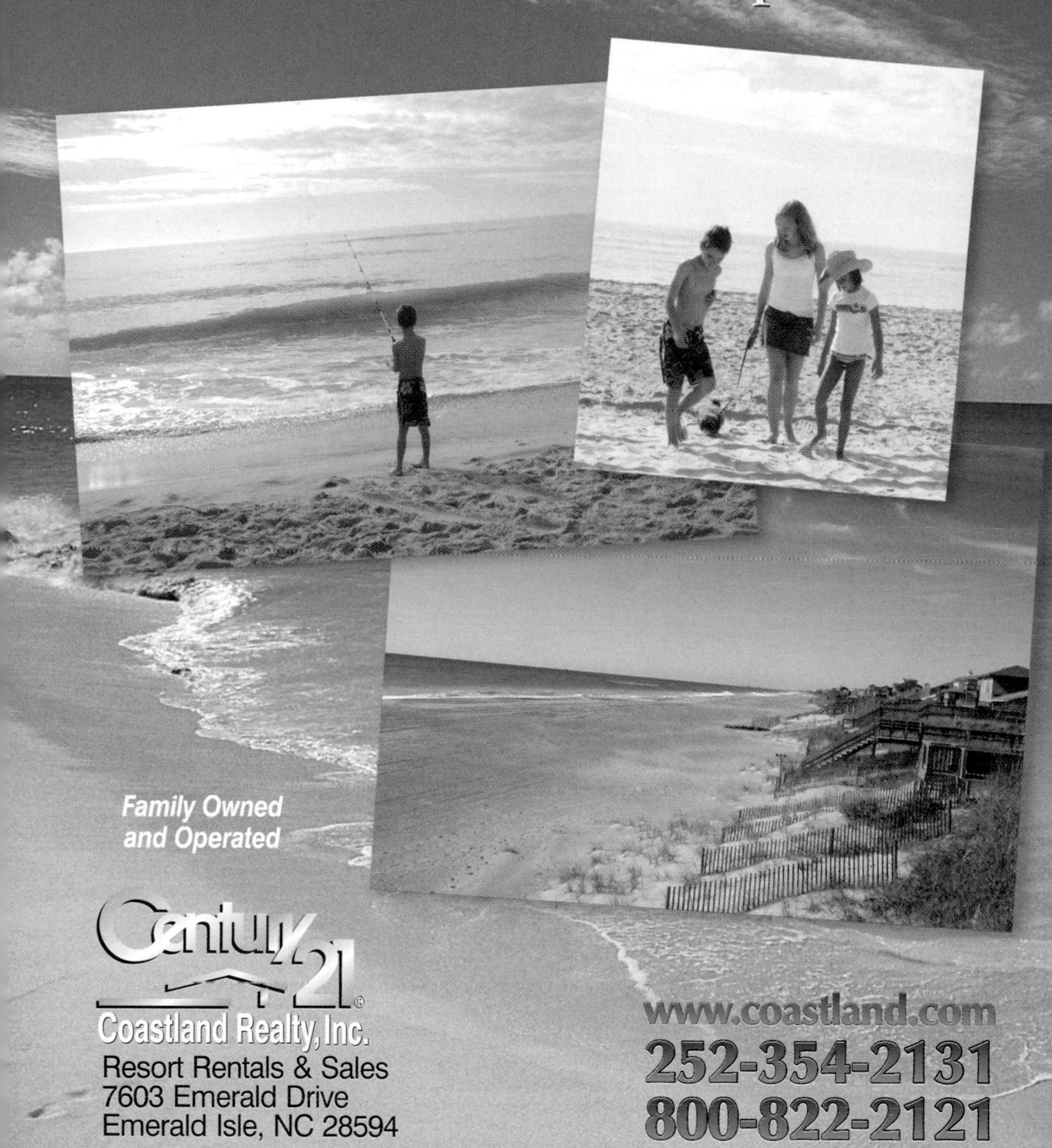

Knowing The Beach
is our business.
Helping you find your place
at the beach is our pleasure.
Family Owned
and Operated
Century 21
Coastland Realty, Inc.
Resort Rentals & Sales
7603 Emerald Drive
Emerald Isle, NC 28594
www.coastland.com
252-354-2131
800-822-2121
Call for a FREE COLOR BROCHURE today
Online Booking Available! www.coastland.com

side facing the sound, the other side facing the open ocean. That makes it easier when deciding what sort of accommodations work best from you. When speaking in terms of accommodation location, oceanfront means facing the ocean with no physical barrier, road or property lines between you and the beach. Oceanside means you can walk to the beach without crossing a major road, but there might be other rows of houses between your cottage and the ocean. Soundfront means the cottage fronts the sound and you have easy access to the water. Soundside means you are on the sound side of the road and in walking distance of the sound. Often, soundside cottages and developments offer guests access to the ocean and beach by means of a walking path.

Pets

If you plan to bring a pet with you on vacation, tell the rental agent. Some places allow them and charge an additional fee; most places don't allow pets at all. For a listing of accommodations that do allow pets, see our Insiders Guide website (www.insiders.com/crystalcoast/main-rentals.htm) and click on the Pet Friendly Accommodations link under Premier Companies. Boarding kennels are available in the area. Check the Yellow Pages for options.

Furnishings and Equipment Rentals

If you are renting an apartment or condo, it will likely be fully furnished. Most rental brochures list the furnishings (small appliances, TVs, VCRs, stereos, toasters, microwaves, etc.) and other items that are provided, such as beach chairs and umbrellas, hammocks and grills. You might only need to bring your sheets and towels, or you can rent those from your booking agency. If not, there are a few independent agencies that rent linens along with other extras, such as baby furniture and folding beds. (See Rental Services at the end of this chapter.) In many units, a telephone is available for local calls and credit card or collect long-distance calls. Some do not have phones, so if that's important, check ahead.

Length of Stay

Most vacation homes and condos are rented on a weekly basis, particularly in the summer. If you would like just a few days at the beach, check with an agency and see what can be arranged for a two- or three-day rental. Everything is more flexible in the off-season. Each rental unit is governed by rules and regulations spelled out in rental brochures and contracts.

Other Tips

Renting vacation accommodations is a business, so approach it that way. Be sure to read the rental agreement carefully and ask questions if there is anything you don't understand. By getting all your questions answered, you can often reduce the number of items you bring and make it an enjoyable vacation for everyone. If you are a smoker, check to see if smoking is permitted. If you are planning a house party, let the agent know in advance. If large parties are prohibited and you ignore this rule, you could be evicted and lose your money.

Most visitors who arrange rentals on the Crystal Coast are family-oriented people who prefer a quiet, relaxed beach vacation. Bearing that in mind, most vacation rental companies do not rent to large party groups, such as fraternities, sororities and prom and graduation celebrators; these prohibitions are spelled out in the rental agreements.

Rental companies are usually happy to take messages and mail for you. Be sure to let the folks at home know the name and street address of the unit where you will be staying and the mailing address and phone number of the rental company.

Rental Companies

The Crystal Coast offers numerous cottages and condos to choose from, but you need to shop early because many places are booked early in the year. One of the smartest things you can do is send for the rental companies' brochures or check their websites. Either through a brochure or a website, you

can see the available cottages and condos and that can help you make your choice. Up-to-date brochures and websites are a wealth of information, not only about individual rates and policies, but also about area attractions and special events. Generally, agencies will include a checklist of items you should bring with you for vacation, tell you some things you shouldn't do (like not picking sea oats or scrambling about on the sand dunes), and advise you of overall weather conditions. All of them clearly spell out the rates and policies of the rental company. Additionally, many agencies are now using online reservations.

Here we have listed a few of the many Crystal Coast companies that handle rentals. We have alphabetically arranged these companies for your convenience. To receive brochures, call the agencies at the numbers listed.

ATLANTIC BEACH

Atlantic Beach Realty, Inc.
Causeway Shopping Ctr.
Atlantic Beach Cswy., Atlantic Beach
(252) 240-7368, (800) 786-7368
www.atlanticbeachrealty.net

Atlantic Beach Realty is a full-service real estate firm, handling condominiums and cottage rentals of all types, with a special focus on properties in Atlantic Beach and Pine Knoll Shores. Owners Charles and Mary Duane Hale are longtime residents of the area and have extensive knowledge of properties on the Crystal Coast. With a primary office in Atlantic Beach, the firm also offers offices at Dunescape Villas and at Island Beach & Racquet Club.

Atlantic Beach Villas
Peppertree, 715 W. Fort Macon Rd.,
Atlantic Beach
(252) 247-5841, (800) 438-6493

Atlantic Beach Villas offers one, two and three-bedroom villas with all the extras. Each unit has a full kitchen and at least one deck. A private boardwalk leads guests from their villa to the wide beach and the Atlantic Ocean. On site, guests can enjoy an indoor and an outdoor pool, a laundry facility, a beauty salon/day spa, a recreation room, a children's playground and pool, grills and picnic areas and a basketball court.

Atlantic Sun Properties
205 Atlantic Beach Cswy., Atlantic Beach
(252) 808-2SUN, (252) 622-9571
www.atlanticsunproperties.com

You're on island time! That's the slogan of Atlantic Sun Properties, where the staff is just waiting to help make your perfect vacation memory happen. Atlantic Sun Properties strives to offer the best of the beach. Each rental cottage, condo and duplex managed by this firm has its own unique offerings, and there is one sure to fit your vacation desires. Let the staff of Atlantic Sun Properties make your vacation unforgettable.

Beach Vacation Properties
1904 E. Fort Macon Rd., Atlantic Beach
(252) 247-2636, (800) 334-2667
www.beachvacationproperties.com

Whether it is seasonal short-term rentals or off-season long-term rentals, Beach Vacation Properties can find just the right cottage or condominium to suit your needs. This company also handles sales and the timeshare inventory at A Place at the Beach, and offers property management services. No matter the size of housing you need, or the length of your stay, the staff at Beach Vacation Properties can help.

Bluewater GMAC Real Estate
311 C Atlantic Beach Cswy., Atlantic Beach
(252) 726-3105, (866) 467-3105
www.bluewatergmac.com

Bluewater GMAC Rentals has two offices (the other is in Emerald Isle) and offers ocean rentals on Bogue Banks from Atlantic Beach to Emerald Isle. With more than 700 vacation rentals, 250 monthly off-season rentals and 200 annual rentals, there is something for everyone. Many of the rentals allow pets. Bluewater's website offers interior and exterior color photos, descriptions, online booking, rates and last-minute specials. This company is also a full-service real estate company and the developer of Bluewater Cove on the White Oak River.

Cannon & Gruber, REALTORS
509 Atlantic Beach Cswy., Atlantic Beach
(252) 726-6600, (800) 317-2866

Cannon & Gruber has a number of cottages and beautiful oceanfront condos for rent on Bogue Banks. From Indian Beach to Atlantic Beach and across the bridge along the water in Morehead City, Cannon & Gruber is eager to help vacationers find a perfect site.

North Carolina bans grilling on the decks and balconies of condos. In Carteret County, strong prevailing winds make grilling near cottages a dangerous activity—so check with your rental agent to find out where you can use your grill.

Coldwell Banker Spectrum Properties
515 Atlantic Beach Cswy., Atlantic Beach
(252) 247-7610, (800) 334-6390
www.spectrumproperties.com

Spectrum Properties offers the finest selection of vacation rental properties on the Crystal Coast and is unsurpassed in customer service. Choose from oceanfront, oceanside and soundfront homes, duplexes and condominiums of all sizes and prices. Spectrum also offers a wide variety of properties for rental on a long-term basis. Call Spectrum's rental specialists or log onto their website to discuss and/or view great rental properties. Online booking is also available.

Gull Isle Realty
Atlantic Beach Cswy., Atlantic Beach
(252) 726-7679, (252) 726-0427,
(800) 682-6866

Gull Isle handles 200-plus long-term rentals on Bogue Banks and in Beaufort, Morehead City and Newport. It is also a full-service sales and appraisal company.

Ocean Resorts Condo Rentals
2111 N.C. Hwy. 58 (W. Fort Macon Rd.), Atlantic Beach
(252) 247-3600, (800) 682-3702
www.atlanticbeachrealty.net

This agency handles vacation rentals for the condos and villas of Dunescape Villas and Island Beach & Racquet Club, with on-site offices at both locations. Choose from accommodations with views of the ocean, sound, pools or beautifully landscaped courtyards.

Realty World First Coast Realty
407 Atlantic Beach Cswy., Ste. 1, Atlantic Beach
(252) 247-5151, (800) 972-8899
www.ncbeach-vacation.com

The features of this agency include seasonal rentals of all types --beach cottages and condominiums, oceanfront to soundside -- in a variety of price ranges. Realty World First Coast Realty offers rentals on Bogue Banks from Atlantic Beach to Emerald Isle and on the mainland in Morehead City, Beaufort and Newport. This company also offers cottages and condos perfect for a memorable coastal wedding, reception or romantic honeymoon, and has the resources to accommodate an entire wedding party. The company also has offices in Beaufort, Emerald Isle and Morehead City.

SurfSide Realty
204 Sandpiper Drive, Newport
(252) 726-0950
www.surfsidevacationrentals.com

SurfSide Realty handles rentals at Atlantic Beach's Sea Spray and South Winds. These two condominium properties are beside Fort Macon State Park, offering miles of beachfront for relaxing and recreation. SurfSide specializes in family rentals and making sure all the renters needs are met.

Whispering Sands Realty
212 N.C. Hwy. 58, Atlantic Beach
(252) 247-3429, (800) 682-7019

This agency offers many desirable Bogue Banks cottages and condominiums. Condo listings include A Place at the Beach III, Southwinds, Sea Spray, The Breakers and many others.

INDIAN BEACH / PINE KNOLL SHORES

The Ocean Club
1700 N.C. Hwy. 58 (Salter Path Rd.), Salter Path
(252) 247-2035, (888) 237-2035

The Ocean Club offers an idyllic vacation experience for families or couples, and it's also the perfect setting for retreats, corporate executive meetings and seminars. All the villas are fully furnished. Enjoy The Ocean Club year round with an outdoor heated pool and spa. Guests can also enjoy sound access, small boating and an all inclusive spa and wellness center.

Sunny Shores
520 N.C. Hwy. 58, Pine Knoll Shores
(252) 247-2665, (800) 624-8978
www.sunny-shores.com

Sunny Shores handles many vacation rentals of condos and cottages in Atlantic Beach as well as Beacon's Reach in Pine Knoll Shores. The full-service agency has a variety of offerings lodgings, both large and small, in all price ranges, and offers a property management service. Contact Debra for information about long-term rentals in the Morehead City area as well.

Whaler Inn Beach Club
323 N.C. Hwy. 58, Pine Knoll Shores
(252) 247-4169, (800) 525-1768

Attractive oceanfront one- and two-bedroom condominiums and efficiencies are the feature here. Completely furnished, the condo units offer fully equipped kitchens. Each unit offers a washer/dryer and a full kitchen. Owners have full access to the ocean beaches in front of the club as well as to the club's heated pool and Jacuzzi. Ownership also allows those living or visiting nearby to continue to use the facility for parking, beach access, showers, swimming, game room and other amenities. Whaler Inn is part of Interval International, allowing owners access to more than 11,000 resorts worldwide.

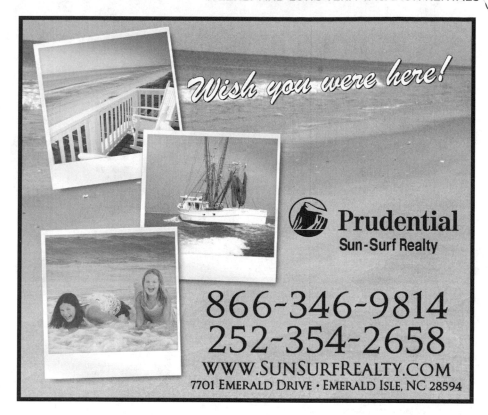

Windward Dunes
N.C. Hwy. 58, Indian Beach
(252) 247-7545, (800) 659-7545

Windward Dunes is an eight-story condo development in Indian Beach that includes 50 units, with 25 of those units available for rental. All units are oceanfront with one- or two-bedrooms. The facility offers an elevator, indoor and outdoor pools and tennis courts.

EMERALD ISLE

Bluewater GMAC Real Estate
200 Mangrove Dr., Emerald Isle
(252) 354-2323, (888) 258-9287
www.bluewatergmac.com

Bluewater GMAC Rentals has two offices (the other is in Atlantic Beach) and offers ocean rentals on Bogue Banks from Atlantic Beach to Emerald Isle. With more than 700 vacation rentals, 250 monthly off-season rentals and 200 annual rentals, there is something for everyone. Many allow pets. Bluewater's website offers interior and exterior color photos, descriptions, online booking, rates and last-minute specials. This company is also a full-service real estate company and the developer of Bluewater Cove on the White Oak River.

CENTURY 21 Coastland Realty Inc.
7603 Emerald Dr., Emerald Isle
(252) 354-2060, (800) 822-2121
www.coastland.com

CENTURY 21 Coastland Realty has been in business for more than 25 years, and the owners and staff take pleasure in serving vacationers. They offer more than 200 properties for short or long-term rental. Call their friendly staff to find that perfect family vacation getaway or check the website for availability and online booking.

Emerald Isle Realty
7501 Emerald Dr., Emerald Isle
(252) 354-4060, (800) 304-4060
www.emeraldislerealty.com

Emerald Isle Realty offers vacation rentals of all types along beautiful Bogue Banks. From 10-bedroom luxury oceanfront homes to cozy soundfront cottages to condos, this firm can arrange your perfect vacation rental. Representatives can also arrange for all the services you might also need, from organizing a special event to finding that perfect boogie board. This family-owned and operated company also offers sales, long-term and short-term rentals, and property management services.

Prudential Sun-Surf Realty
7701 Emerald Dr., Emerald Isle
(252) 354-2658, (866) 662-4704
www.SunSurfRealty.com

Offering more than 300 cottages and condos, Prudential Sun-Surf Realty rents property in Emerald Isle, Indian Beach, Salter Path and Pine Knoll Shores. The knowledgeable staff can help you find the perfect vacation property that suits your needs. The company's reservation line is staffed 24 hours a day. On-line reservations are accepted using Visa or Mastercard. Call for a free full-color brochure.

Shorewood Real Estate Inc.
7703 Emerald Dr., Emerald Isle
(252) 354-7858, (888) 557-0172
www.shorewoodrealestate.com

Shorewood Real Estate is a family-owned business that specializes in vacation rentals, property management and real estate sales. Celebrating its 10th year of service to property owners and guests of the Crystal Coast, the owners and staff of Shorewood Real Estate pride themselves on the delivery of exceptional customer service, professionalism and courtesy. With a wide selection of vacation rentals with amenities such as private pools, hot tubs and game rooms, you are sure to find a property to met your vacation rental needs.

Spinnaker's Reach Realty, Inc.
9918 M. B. Davis Ct., Emerald Isle
(252) 354-5555, (800) 245-7746
www.spinnakersreach.com

Spinnaker's rents luxury single-family and duplex houses in the gated community of Spinnaker's Reach subdivision in Emerald Isle, off Coast Guard Road. The firm also handles

Recycling is easy and popular along the Crystal Coast. Most towns offer curb-side pickup of recyclable items. Residents outside town limits can call the county office, (252) 728-8450, for directions to the closest drop-off point.

rentals in Dolphin Ridge (another gated community), The Point and Sea Watch. Many of the offerings are oceanfront or ocean-view, and many have private pools and elevators. Each rental comes with the amenities offered in the community.

Beaufort

Beaufort offers no condominiums to vacationers, but some rental apartments and houses are available. Typically, rentals are advertised with local agents. To find a rental in Beaufort, contact the agents we list here, check The Carteret County News-Times or ask an Insider.

Beaufort Realty
325 Front St., Beaufort
(252) 728-5462, (800) 548-2961
www.beaufortrealtync.com
www.vacationbeaufort.com

Beaufort Realty offers annual and vacation rentals in historic Beaufort. The company offers many unique and historic homes in the historic district and on the waterfront for your enjoyment. It also specializes in residential and commercial property in the Beaufort historic district and often has some desirable historic properties for sale. Agents also handle sales in Down East, Morehead City and on the beach.

Eddy Myers Real Estate
131 Middle Ln., Beaufort
(252) 728-5013, (888) 211-2203
www.eddymyers.com

Eddy Myers Real Estate handles a number of vacation rental properties and can surely find the one just right for you. These listings are in the Beaufort historic district, in the surrounding area of town, on Radio Island and in the Down East community of Harkers Island.

Down East

A drive Down East, particularly to Harkers Island and Cedar Island, will turn up several nice rental cottages/houses. Many of these are not handled by a real estate agency; they simply have the owner's name and a phone number posted out front. Most rentals are booked year after year by the

Wading in the surf is a delight for all ages.

photo: George Mitchell

same people, so we suggest you find the one you are interested in and make arrangements early.

The Down East area offers a slower pace for vacationers. Don't look for a vacation that's full of brightly lit stores, bustling hotels or wild night spots. Instead, expect a step back in time to when things worked at a much slower pace. Plan on relaxing, spending time on the water, dining on some of the freshest seafood around and taking ferry rides to nearby Cape Lookout National Seashore.

Mason's Vacation Rentals
104 Tils Landing, Harkers Island
(252)728-5870

One of the only vacation rental agencies located on Harkers Island, Mason's offers fully equipped two-bedroom mobile homes, with linens and paper products provided. Pets are welcome. The site is located close to the public boat ramp and ferry services. There is a two-day minimum, and guests get one night free with a week-long stay. Come stay a while with these folks and relax. Larry and Sandy Mason will be happy to see you.

Rose's Vacation Rentals
293 Bayview Dr., Harkers Island
(252) 728-2868

There are five mobile units/cabins at Rose's, each hand-decorated and furnished by the proprietors. Prices are reasonable, although rates vary depending on the size of the unit and length of stay. Margaret Ann Rose, who manages the business, is flexible about check-in and departure times and can offer a wealth of information about nearby attractions. During the busy seasons there is a two-night minimum stay on the larger units. Restaurants and passenger ferries are nearby. Overnight docking and a ramp for smaller, shallow draft vessels is available.

Timeshares

Several developments on the Crystal Coast are set up for timesharing. Billed as a way to have a lifetime of affordable vacations, timeshares allow you to actually purchase a block of time, usually one or more weeks, for a specific unit. Each year, the time you purchased is yours at that unit. If your plans should change, most of the companies will allow you to exchange your week on the Crystal Coast for another location around the nation or the world -- depending on their company's real estate holdings. Check on this before you purchase.

Before you arrange to buy into a timeshare condo, make sure you understand all the arrangements -- including the maintenance fee. Once you pay off the note, you receive the deed to your week in your specific unit. Some organizations do put restrictions on resale, even after you own the time in that unit, so check on that before you put your name on the dotted line.

The unit will be completely furnished, down to the linens, dishes and pans, so you just stop by the supermarket and unload your stuff, and you're set for the duration. Each of the timeshare facilities listed here is loaded with amenities, and each one is different.

If you are seriously considering buying into a timeshare property, give the resort a call and arrange a tour. For a list of companies that sell timeshares visit the timeshare part of our real estate chapter.

Beach Vacation Properties
1904 E. Fort Macon Rd., Atlantic Beach
(252) 247-2636, (800) 334-2667
www.beachvacationproperties.com

There are 98 units in the timeshare inventory and 202 units in the rental inventory at A Place at the Beach. Designed as one-, two- and three-bedroom units, each provides all the luxuries of home and then some. Every unit is fully furnished, and linens, towels and a fully equipped kitchen are provided. A laundry facility is on site. Additionally, the two- and three-bedroom units feature washers and dryers. A Place at the Beach has an indoor heated pool and outdoor pool with a waterslide.

Whaler Inn Beach Club
323 N.C. Hwy. 58, Pine Knoll Shores
(252) 247-4169, (800) 525-1768

Attractive oceanfront one- and two-bedroom condominiums and efficiencies are the feature here. Completely furnished, the condo units offer fully equipped kitchens. Each unit offers a washer/dryer and a full kitchen. Owners have full access to the ocean beaches in front of the club as well as to the club's heated pool and Jacuzzi. Ownership also allows those living or visiting nearby to continue to use the facility for parking, beach access, showers, swimming, game room and other amenities. Whaler Inn is part of Interval International, allowing owners access to more than 11,000 resorts worldwide.

Rental Services

Instead of hauling so many extras (baby cribs, beach chairs, blankets, towels, linens, etc.) to your rental house, consider renting items from one of the rental service companies listed here. It saves packing, unpacking and cleanup time, giving you more time for fun.

Beach Wheels Bike Rentals
607 Atlantic Beach Cswy., Atlantic Beach
(252) 240-BIKE, (800) 504-2450
www.deannahullrealty.com

Offering "different spokes for different folks," Beach Wheels Bike Rentals provides one of the best and largest selections of bikes on the island. Beach Wheels offers beach cruisers, adult bikes, children's bikes, tag-a-longs, adult trikes, tandems and more. In its fourth year of business, this company provides friendly and convenient service with a free delivery and pick-up service anywhere on the Crystal Coast. Call ahead, reserve your wheels and when you arrive your bikes will be waiting.

Bogue Banks Beach Gear & Linen Rentals
Bell Cove Village, Emerald Isle
(252) 354-4404, (866) 593-GEAR (4327)
www.boguebanksbeachgear.com

From their brightly colored beach umbrellas and beach bikes to their custom beach towels and luxurious linen sets, Bogue Banks Beach Gear & Linens has all your rental needs covered. This company offers a wide selection of beach and baby equipment rentals and offers free delivery along the Crystal Coast. Daily beach chair and umbrella rentals are available at the Emerald Isle Eastern and Western Public Beach Accesses. This family owned and operated business has offered quality rental items and friendly customer service for eight years. Whether it is a crib, high chair, grill or other item, let Bogue Banks Beach Gear & Linen Rental handle it for you. Open year-round, seven days a week, the business accepts VISA/MC.

Island Essentials
208 Bogue Inlet Dr., Emerald Isle
(252) 354-8887, (888) 398-8887

Island Essentials can make your vacation much easier. Just let them take care of all of your vacation rental needs. From bed and bath linen rental packages to custom beach chairs and umbrellas, they have one of the largest selections on the Crystal Coast. The business offers vacationers convenient free delivery and pickup from vacation homes. From beach bikes to grills, cribs, high chairs and much more, they have it all. This business is open throughout the year.

USA Island Rental
134 Fairview Dr., Emerald Isle
(252) 354-8839, (800) 590-1711

USA specializes in items for vacationers. Cottage renters can get rollaway beds, cribs, high chairs, bicycles, beach chairs and umbrellas and other basic beach equipment. The company also offers delivery and pickup of items.

CAMPING

For Insiders who enjoy camping, the Crystal Coast is almost heaven. The area offers excellent camping opportunities, from rent-a-space RV sites with all the conveniences of home to tent camping with no conveniences at all.

Camping along the coast is popular almost year round because of the mild local climate. Summer campers may need to create shade with tarps or overhangs to protect themselves from the hot sun. Campers will find beach camping a little different from mainland camping. You will probably need longer tent stakes to hold things down in the sandy soil. Netting is almost a must, except in the dead of winter, to protect against the late-afternoon and early morning mosquitoes and no-see-ums, those barely visible flying insects that only make themselves known when they bite. A roaring fire and a good insect repellent also help. If you aren't fond of plastering yourself with pesticides, try mixing Avon's Skin-So-Soft with water and spraying it on. This mixture will fend off most insects, and it smells good too.

Primitive camping is available at Cape Lookout National Seashore, Bear Island and in the Croatan National Forest (see our Attractions chapter for more about the National Forest). To really get away from it all, try camping in those areas that are only accessible by boat or ferry. There are no designated camping sites on Cape Lookout National Seashore, but camping is allowed everywhere except on a small amount of well-marked, privately owned land. Bear Island has quiet, secluded campsites. Croatan National Forest, which includes land in Carteret and Craven counties, offers two options. You can stay in one of the planned campgrounds or pitch a tent anywhere on National Forest land that isn't marked for private use.

Overnight fees vary and usually depend on the location (whether oceanfront or off the beaten path) and the facilities offered. Almost all the commercial campgrounds charge extra for more than two people at one site. Reservations are suggested. Full hookups typically include water, sewer and electricity. There is no charge to camp at Cape Lookout National Seashore or at some sites in Croatan National Forest.

Most piers along Bogue Banks also rent RV and tent spaces (see our Fishing, Boating and Watersports chapter).

Bogue Banks

Holiday Trav-L-Park Resort
MM 21, N.C. Hwy. 58, Emerald Isle
(252) 354-2250

Located on the oceanside of N.C. Hwy. 58 at the intersection with Coast Guard Road, Holiday Trav-L-Park offers 375 sites with full hookups along with a host of amenities: cable TV, laundry and shower facilities, an outdoor swimming pool, a recreation room, bicycle and go-cart rentals, a playground and more. The park is also home of the Emerald Isle Wine Market and is within walking distance of grocery stores, a movie theater, golf, shops and restaurants. Reservations are required at Holiday Trav-L-Park; nightly fees range from $25 to $70 for two people ($5 for each additional person), depending on location and season. Pets are welcome to stay for an additional $5 per night. Spaces can be rented on an annual basis as well. The park is closed from December through February.

Western Carteret County

Goose Creek Resort
350 Red Barn Rd., directly off N.C. Hwy. 24, 12 miles east of Swansboro
(252) 393-2628

Goose Creek Resort offers 600 RV sites, with full 30- and 50-amp hookups, for family camping on Bogue Sound. There are two boat ramps, a pool, a waterslide, a game room, a climate-controlled bathhouse,

a camp store, tent sites, a 250-foot fishing pier, basketball, crabbing and a dump station. Goose Creek has an amphitheater for dancing and offers church services on Easter. In addition to the regular RV sites, the resort has 90 extra-wide units that accommodate park model RVs. Open year round, Goose Creek's overnight rates range from $35 to $45 for two adults and kids younger than 12; extra adults are charged $3 per person. Water- and power-accessible tent sites cost $30 per night. The resort has accommodations for camping clubs for up to 50 units. It also offers special long-term rates and on-site boat and RV storage. Leashed pets are allowed.

Oyster Point Campground
8 miles off Mill Creek Rd., Newport
(252) 638-5628

Oyster Point, a primitive campground with 20 sites, can be found by making a right turn off Mill Creek Road on to Forest Road 181. Amenities are few but include drinking water, restrooms, picnic tables and grills. Campsites are $8 per day. The gate to the campground is locked each night from 10 PM to 8 AM, but a host is available to unlock the gate in case of emergencies. Nearby attractions include hiking on the Neusiok Trail, swimming and fishing.

Waters Edge RV Park
N.C. Hwy. 24, Newport, 4.5 miles from Morehead City
(252) 247-0494

This peaceful, secluded campground on the banks of Bogue Sound is open year round and offers 72 large sites with full hookups. Folks with tents, campers and RVs can rent a space for $25 to $30 per night per family. Waters Edge amenities include a climate-controlled bathhouse, a 200-foot fishing pier and a meeting room for clubs or family gatherings. Ask about seasonal and monthly rentals; they are a bargain for those who can get to the Crystal Coast often.

i

When camping, keep in mind that wild animals, such as skunks and raccoons, are common in this area but are normally cautious and will stay away from humans and their pets. If a wild animal persists in approaching your campsite, particularly during daylight hours, report this to your campground host or the local animal control facility at (252) 728-8595. Do not feed or attempt to pick up wild animals.

Waterway RV Park
850 Cedar Point Blvd. (N.C. Hwy. 24), Cedar Point
(252) 393-8715

This 28-acre park is situated on the Intracoastal Waterway between Cape Carteret and Swansboro. Waterway RV Park offers 350 RV sites with full hook-ups, and cable TV is available. Open year-round, Waterway RV Park features volleyball and basketball courts, a game room, laundry and shower facilities, two boat ramps, a playground and a swimming pool. Shopping and restaurants are located nearby. Rates are $25 per night for two adults; pay for six nights and the seventh night is free. Children younger than 10 stay free. Monthly rates also are available.

Whispering Pines Campground
N.C. Hwy. 24, 8 miles west of Morehead City
(252) 726-4902

Situated close to Bogue Sound, Whispering Pines has 130 full-hookup sites, a 70-foot swimming pool, a clubhouse with a kitchen, a freshwater pond and fishing. The camp store and the park are open all year. Whispering Pines offers a 10 percent discount to Good Sam and AARP members. Daily rates for travel trailers and mobile homes range from $28 to $35. The fee for tents is $26 per night. On-site and off-site storage are available for boats and campers. Mail and phone message services are offered.

Swansboro

Bear Island
1572 Hammock's Beach Rd., west of Swansboro Ranger Station
(910) 326-4881

Access to Bear Island is provided by ferry from Hammock's Beach State Park (see our Attractions and Getting Around chapters) or by private boat. Tickets are required for everyone riding the ferry, and the fee is $5 for adults and $3 for seniors and children

Down East life revolves around the water.

photo: George Mitchell

ages 6 to 12. Free ferry tickets are available to children younger than age 6. The 3.5-mile island offers primitive camping at designated spots for $9 minimum per night ($12 maximum). For groups, the fee is $1 per person, with a limit of 12 campers at each of the three available group sites. The sites don't have water, sewer or electric hookups, although restrooms and showers are available. These facilities are not available from November through March. Campers must register with the park office on the mainland before going over to Bear Island, and groups only should make reservations in advance. Campsites for boaters are also offered, but some sites are tricky to get to because of shallow water. Campers traveling by ferry are advised to travel light because it is close to a half-mile walk from the ferry landing to some sites. Those interested in camping on Bear Island should be aware that alcoholic beverages, open campfires and public nudity are not allowed; for cooking, they should bring a grill or camp stove. Although pets are allowed on the island, they are not allowed on the ferry so you can only get them there by personal boat. Owners also are required to clean up after their pets and keep them on leashes of six feet or less at all times.

Down East

Cedar Creek Campground and Marina
111 Canal Dr., Sea Level
(252) 225-9571

Owners Catherine and Jerry Nelson cater to family camping with easy access to Core Sound and Drum Inlet. Open April 1 through November 30, the campground offers its guests such amenities as a swimming pool, flush toilets, hot-water showers, a dump station, boating, fishing, horseshoes and basketball. There are 35 sites with full hookups, 18 with only electrical and water, and 20 tent sites. Nightly rental for two adults is $25 for complete hookup and $17 without hookup. Extra guests are charged $2 per person. Leashed pets are permitted. Cedar Creek also offers an RV storage area and gives a 10 percent discount to Good Sam and AAA members.

Coastal Riverside Campground
216 Clark Ln., Otway
(252) 728-5155

Open April through December, Coastal Riverside Campground, located on a finger creek of the North River, features 54 RV sites with full hook-ups and 25 additional sites for tents. Campground amenities include laundry facilities, showers, a boat ramp and pier, and cable hookups. Reservations are required, and nightly fees are $20 for two people (plus $2 for each additional person) for a full hook-up site; $15 for a site without hook-ups.

Driftwood Campground
N.C. Hwy. 12, Cedar Island
(252) 225-4861
www.clis.com/deg/

This 65-site, waterfront campground sits next to the Cedar Island-Ocracoke ferry terminal. Overnight fees are $18 with full hookup, $16 for water and electricity only and $14 for a tent site. A bathhouse and dump station are available. Swimmers and sunbathers will enjoy the camp's sandy beach on Pamlico Sound. Kiteboarding, kayaking and surf fishing are very popular. The campground is open year-round, although water service is not available December 15 through March 1. It is part of the Driftwood complex, which includes a motel, restaurant and gift shop. Driftwood's restaurant is well known for its great food. Call for the restaurant hours. (See our Restaurants and Accommodations chapters for more information.)

Core Banks

Cape Lookout National Seashore
131 Charles St., Harkers Island
(252) 728-2250

Cape Lookout National Seashore (see our Attractions chapter), which has four barrier islands and spans 56 miles of remote coastline from Ocracoke Inlet to Beaufort Inlet, offers waterfront camping at its best -- and plenty of privacy. You might see a ranger and a few anglers around the cabins or folks around the lighthouse keepers quarters, but otherwise you are on your own. Imagine sitting around the fire at dusk, listening to the sound of waves and watching the sweeping light of the Cape Lookout Lighthouse, with water as far as you can see in either direction. This camping area has no developed campsites and no bathhouses (the lighthouse has a toilet and there is a composting toilet near the beach). Because there are no facilities available -- not even trash cans -- campers must bring in everything they need, including water, and must take their garbage with them when they leave.

While there are no fees charged to camp at Cape Lookout, park officials request that campers register either at park headquarters on Harkers Island, the keepers quarters at the lighthouse or with a park ranger. Campers are not allowed to camp near the lighthouse or the restrooms.

There also are two cabin complexes maintained by private concessionaires and overseen by the National Park Service. They vary greatly in their amenities, although most have cooking facilities, flush toilets and hot showers (see our Hotels and Motels chapter).

So how do you get to this wonderland? By boat or ferry. Ferry service is provided by two concessionaires permitted by the National Park Service (see our Getting Around chapter) and numerous privately operated ferry services permitted by the National Park Service. Four-wheel drive vehicles are permitted in some areas (and the ferry services may charge an extra fee to transport them to the island). As in all national parks, some restrictions apply, so talk to a ranger before scheduling your trip or ask that a brochure detailing camping requirements and restrictions be mailed to you.

Croatan National Forest

Croatan National Forest
Ranger Station: 141 E. Fisher Ave., New Bern, approx. 25 miles north of Morehead City off U.S. Hwy. 70
(252) 638-5628

Croatan National Forest is made up of 157,000 acres spread between Morehead City and New Bern. Recreational areas are available for a day's outing or for overnight camping. The forest's planned campsites include Cedar Point, Neuse River (Flanners Beach) and Fishers Landing, where you will find drinking water, bathhouse facilities and picnic areas. Primitive camping is permitted all year, and campfires are usually permitted (check with the ranger office during the dry season). For more information on the Croatan National Forest, see our Crystal Coast Attractions chapter or the New Bern Camping chapter.

Cedar Point Campground
Croatan National Forest, Cape Carteret
(252) 638-5628

On the White Oak River a mile north of Cape Carteret (follow the signs from N.C. 58), this campground is a good stopover if you want to experience coastal marsh and maritime forest in their truest forms. At Cedar Point, lovers of the outdoors can enjoy many activities -- camping, picnicking, fishing, boating and hiking. The site offers 40 camping units with electrical hookups, a bathhouse with flush toilets and warm showers, drinking water and a shallow boat ramp. A fee of $12 per night for non-electrical sites, and $17 for electrical, is charged for camping, and Cedar Point is open year-round. The Cedar Point Tideland Trail, an interpretive nature trail at this location, offers a 0.6-mile short loop that crosses the salt marsh and its edges, and a 1.3-mile loop that skirts the edge of the White Oak River and is popular with birders.

SHOPPING

Many Crystal Coast visitors enjoy the shopping as much as the beach. While the area does not have a large shopping mall, it does have a variety of individually owned stores, boutiques and specialty shops. You are sure to find a little of everything -- from a rare antique vase to a one-of-a-kind designer gown to unique nautical carvings to the perfect bathing suit. Initially, a newcomer or visitor may find it difficult to locate what he or she needs. While there are a Wal-Mart and a Kmart, there are no major all-inclusive large shopping centers or malls. But their absence is exactly what makes shopping fun around here. And besides, lots of shops and stores do exist. There are mini-malls, shopping neighborhoods and several good-size shopping centers with some of the major chain stores people are used to. This combination affords you plenty of places to find what you need and want.

Since the Crystal Coast is considered a resort area, you'll find dozens of shops that cater to the beachgoer or surfer. Whether you're looking for a beach souvenir, a gift for someone back home, the perfect-fitting swimsuit, a special T-shirt or a beach wrap, you'll find it here. If you need clothing or equipment for your favorite summer sport, you will find many brands of outdoor clothes and sports equipment to chose from -- everything from tennis togs and golf apparel to surfboards and kayaks. Be aware, however, that many area shops close or shorten their hours during the winter, so call first to make sure the store you want to visit is open.

We have designed this section to give you a brief look at some of the retail businesses in each Crystal Coast community. Antiques shops are listed separately at the end of this chapter. With such an array to chose from, we can't mention every shop that warrants your attention, so be sure to explore on your own. Except for a few rare cases, shops tend to be clumped together, so take your time to browse to walk through retail areas, like the waterfronts in Swansboro, Beaufort and Morehead City, to visit the individual shops and enjoy the treasures they behold. If you're in need of help, other Insiders will be delighted to share information with you.

Bogue Banks

Most Bogue Banks' shopping is focused on the active lifestyle of both resident and visiting beachgoers. Shops offer swimwear, watersports accessories, casual wear, seashells and souvenirs. There are also some great specialty shops that shouldn't be missed.

We offer a sampling of some of the shops you'll find on Bogue Banks, beginning in Atlantic Beach and wandering west to Emerald Isle. We have given the mile marker (MM) number for the shops on N.C. Highway 58 (the main road on the island). When winter business is slow, Bogue Banks shopkeepers often close early and limit the days they stay open, so call before you head out.

You'll find that the huge, specialty stores of Wings and Pacific have found their way to Bogue Banks. These stores are so obvious that you can't possibly miss them, and inside you'll find beachwear, sunglasses, souvenirs, clothing and novelty items. Wings has two stores in Atlantic Beach and Pacific has a store in Atlantic Beach and one in Emerald Isle.

ATLANTIC BEACH

Marsh's Surf Shop
Atlantic Beach Cswy., Atlantic Beach
(252) 726-9046

This shop carries everything from quality dresses and shorts to T-shirts and jackets for men, women and children. There are plenty of beach items too: sunglasses, surfboards, swimsuits and all types of accessories. Marsh's carries a wonderful selection of leather clogs and active footwear. It's open seven days a week.

Capt. Stacy Fishing Center - Gift Shop
416 Atlantic Beach Cswy., Atlantic Beach
(252) 247-7501, (800) 533-9417
www.captstacy.com

Located right on the dock, this gift shop has many unique and unexpected items. You will find jewelry, gifts and flags, many with nautical or beach themes. The shop offers etched glass, crystal and a variety of holiday decorations, as well as T-shirts, casual clothing for men and women, beach bags and hats. The shop is open year-round, although winter hours are limited.

Bert's Surf Shop
MM 2, N.C. Hwy. 58, Atlantic Beach
(252) 726-1730

With three beach locations, Bert's is a Crystal Coast landmark. It changes with the season, but it's like an old friend you can continue to visit year after year. Bert's stocks swimwear, active wear, foot gear, beach T-shirts, sunglasses and a large variety of sports equipment, including surfboards and skateboards. You'll also find some infant and toddler clothing and a youth department. There is a large selection of women's name-brand swimwear and men's sportswear by Rusty, Quicksilver and Billabong. You can buy skate shoes here too. It's open seven days a week. Call for winter hours.

Hi-Lites
MM 2, N.C. Hwy. 58, Atlantic Beach
(252) 726-3496

Hi-Lites specializes in discounted clothing in juniors, misses and plus sizes with an emphasis on sporty separates. You'll also find swimsuits, belts, earrings, bags and hats and a full line of clothing suitable for the office. The store is open daily year round.

Sandi's Beachwear
MM 2.5, N.C. Hwy. 58, Atlantic Beach
(252) 726-4812

Sandi's offers a wide selection of women's specialty swimwear. Shoppers can find the right suit for every size and taste: sizes 4 to 24, long torso, special cup sizes, maternity and mastectomy. Brand-name casual and cruise wear include Athena, Anne Cole, Liz Claiborne and Anne Klein. Separates make it easy for all body types to find the perfect suit. Shoes and accessories, cover-ups and sarongs are also offered. Sandi's is open seven days a week in season. Call for winter hours.

Atlantic Beach Surf Shop
MM 2.5, N.C. Hwy. 58, Atlantic Beach
(252) 726-9382

This is where you'll find quality beachwear and upscale casual clothes, plus some great clothing to wear to the office. Footwear, sunglasses, surfboards, T-shirts, sandals and all the accessories are for sale. Pick up a cool sticker for the kids or a chunk of wax for your surfboard. And check out the extensive juniors items. Atlantic Beach Surf Shop has it all. The store is open daily year round.

Boater's World/Outer Banks Outfitters Marine Center
Atlantic Station Shopping Ctr., MM 3, N.C. Hwy. 58, Atlantic Beach
(252) 240-0055

Boater's World and Outer Banks Outfitters have joined forces to bring serious anglers just about everything they could want. Along with all manner of marine electronics, this store carries fishing tackle, lures, compasses and GPS, an enormous collection of rods and reels, outdoor clothing, shoes and much more. Be sure to ask about gift certificates.

Beach Book Mart
Atlantic Station Shopping Ctr., MM 3, N.C. Hwy. 58, Atlantic Beach
(252) 240-5655

Beach Book Mart is the perfect place to pick up reading materials. This discount bookstore offers all types of books, best sellers and magazines. Check out the store's extensive selection of youth and children's books; your preteens and teens will enjoy a gripping adventure (or romance, maybe) to read while soaking up the rays and keeping one eye on the beach scene. There are lots of cookbooks and books of local interest -- all at reduced prices. The store is open daily.

Kites Unlimited
Atlantic Station Shopping Ctr., MM 3, N.C. Hwy. 58, Atlantic Beach
(252) 247-7011

Flying a kite on the beach is a joy unsurpassed. In Carteret County, Kites Unlimited is where you go to find a special kite (and then grin from ear to ear as you get it aloft). The store has hundreds of wind-borne treasures in designs and sizes for all ability levels, including single line and steerable kites. Besides quality kites, take a look at the windsocks, flags, unique games and puzzles. Kites Unlimited is the business that sponsors kite-flying at 10 AM each Sunday at Fort Macon State Park; see our Crystal Coast Attractions chapter. The store is open daily.

Coastal Crafts Plus
Atlantic Station Shopping Ctr., MM 3, N.C. Hwy. 58, Atlantic Beach
(252) 247-7210

Coastal Crafts Plus features the work of many crafters, including pottery, jewelry, paintings and woodcrafts. You'll find a large selection of attractive and reasonably priced remembrances of your Crystal Coast vacation. Insiders shop here for gifts, T-shirts, yarn, nautical items and craft supplies. Coastal Crafters is open daily year round.

EMERALD ISLE

Fran's Beachwear
MM 19, N.C. Hwy. 58, Emerald Isle
(252) 354-3151

Fran's Beachwear carries an excellent selection of swimwear sure to fit every body type and need, including tummy control suits. Patrons will also find sporty and dressy separates and a wide range of shoes, bags, jewelry and accessories. Fran's Beachwear is open seven days a week from the middle of February through the end of October. Fran's celebrated its 30th year in business last year and has a loyal client base.

Fran's Gift Shop
MM 19, N.C. Hwy. 58, Emerald Isle
(252) 354-6712

Next to Fran's Beachwear is Fran's Gift Shop, a longtime favorite for locals and visitors. Inside you'll find different and unique gifts and collectibles. Fran's also has a creative selection of home decor -- including rugs and pillows -- in every style imaginable. Whether it is a nautical theme or traditional, Fran's has it. The shop is open seven days a week from the middle of February through the end of December.

Bert's Surf Shop
MM 19, N.C. Hwy. 58, Emerald Isle
(252) 354-6282
Across from Bogue Inlet Pier
(252) 354-2441

Bert's was Emerald Isle's first surf shop and now has two stores in Emerald Isle and one in Atlantic Beach. The stores stock just about everything you need for a fun time at the beach. You can always find a good choice of casual clothes, sunglasses, hats, beach T-shirts and bathing suits plus shells and jewelry. Bert's is open seven days a week.

Tom Togs Outlet
Emerald Plantation Shopping Ctr., MM 20, N.C. Hwy. 58, Emerald Isle
(252) 354-7140

This store sells a large selection of famous-name clothing at value prices. You will find scores of cotton shorts, T-shirts and tops plus pants, sundresses, hats and outfits for kids. New stock comes in every week. The majority of clothing is for women. The clothing is casual, and you'll also find Flax clothing items here. Be sure to check Tom Togs before you pay full price elsewhere; shopping here is a smart way to save vacation dollars. The store is open daily.

J. R. Dunn Jewelers
Emerald Plantation Shopping Ctr., MM 20, N.C. Hwy. 58, Emerald Isle
(252) 354-5074

Dunn's features distinctive jewelry for women, men and children, along with many nautical creations. The store will repair and remount your jewelry and watches and gift wrap your purchases. The staff is knowledgeable and very helpful, especially for those of us who can't quite figure out what to select for that special someone. J. R. Dunn also has a shop in Morehead City in the Cypress Bay Plaza on U.S. Highway 70.

Emerald Isle Books & Toys
Emerald Plantation Shopping Ctr., MM 20, N.C. Hwy. 58, Emerald Isle
(252) 354-5323

This place is all you'll ever want or need in a bookstore. It has hundreds of books and magazines for all ages, an extensive collection of regional and travel books, and local interest books. Of course, the store has all the best sellers in paperback and hard cover. Plenty of kids' toys from the strictly fun to the educational are available. Visitors will also find bath items, including Primal Elements gels and soaps, Upper Canada products, Burt's Bees creams and scrubs and Mad Gabs massage oils. Emerald Isle Books is open seven days a week, all year.

Carteret Country Store
Emerald Plantation Shopping Ctr., MM 20, N.C. Hwy. 58, Emerald Isle
(252) 354-3800

The Country Store is a complete souvenir and gift shop where you will find the perfect thing for yourself or for family and friends. The store sells nautical and rare gifts, baskets, windsocks, flags, cards, clocks and frames. The staff is friendly and courteous and more than willing to help you select just what you need. The store is open daily year round.

Planet Wear
Emerald Plantation Shopping Ctr., MM 20, N.C. Hwy. 58, Emerald Isle
(252) 354-7262

This is a popular store that specializes in tie dye and import clothing, candles, jewelry, rock and roll collectables, hemp accessories and more. You'll find beads, incense, stickers and a large selection of Grateful Dead items. Planet Wear is open every day.

Beaufort

The specialty shops in Beaufort are sure to suit anyone's taste. Although there are others, most shops are along or near the downtown waterfront, making it easy to stroll along the scenic Front Street and spend a day visiting the town's shops. Only a few of Beaufort's shops close in the winter. The town's many attractions -- the waterfront, the Maritime Museum, historic sites and pubs -- provide respite for those who find themselves in Beaufort with a born shopper. We couldn't possibly list all the shops, so we encourage you to explore on your own. We start with shops on Turner Street because Turner is a key access street to Beaufort's historic downtown and the waterfront. Next we cover the places on Front Street, which faces the water and offers a nice view of Carrot Island. Then we take you to a few places off Front Street yet still in the historic district, and finally to a few great shopping spots just outside Beaufort's downtown district.

Parking is at a premium during the summer season. Clearly marked, free parking places are plentiful in downtown Beaufort, but you may have to hunt for an empty one. Don't worry, though; all downtown Beaufort shops and restaurants are within the same couple of blocks, and walking around Beaufort is an activity you'll enjoy. The First Baptist Church of Beaufort kindly allows free parking (except during worship hours on Sunday) in its spacious lot on Turner Street.

BEAUFORT HISTORIC DISTRICT

Turner Street

The Old Beaufort Shop
Beaufort Historic Site, 130 Turner St., Beaufort
(252) 728-5225

Housed within the Safrit Historical Center, this gift shop is operated by the Beaufort Historical Association. Its proceeds help finance the association's educational and restoration programs. Many of the items for sale cannot be found elsewhere because they are made by BHA volunteers. Insiders shop here for artwork by locals, handmade dolls and books on local history. In summer the shop sells cuttings propagated by the BHA Herb Society. These are usually quite a bargain and are selected for their ability to thrive in our coastal environment. You can shop here Monday through Saturday all year.

Front Street

When you come to the corner of Turner and Front streets, you'll see Somerset Square, a broad, two-story building with white porch railings. It is home to a number of shops and affords a pretty view of the water. Most of Beaufort's stores are within walking distance once you park. A public parking lot sits next door and street parking is available but limited during the summer months.

Beaufort Trading Company
Somerset Square, 400 Front St., Beaufort
(252) 504-3209
www.beauforttradingcompany.com

Beaufort Trading Company says it "has your family covered," and that is true. In its fifth year on the Beaufort waterfront, Beaufort Trading Company has quite a following of regular customers. Inside you'll find quality Beaufort T-shirts, sweatshirts, hats and caps that fit infants to adults. Kevin and Doris Carlin offer Life is Good and Seadog T-shirts and caps, along with Teva and Columbia sandals and sportswear. Visitors to the store will also find kites, sunglasses and leashes, wind chimes, and beach cover-ups.

The Rocking Chair Book Store
Somerset Square, Front St., Beaufort
(252) 728-2671

The Rocking Chair offers a wide variety of books. Be sure to check the selection of regional books, sailing and marine books, cookbooks, children's books, best sellers, classics, new and used books, hard-covers and paperbacks. The store proudly offers a selection of books by North Carolina writers too. This staff is full of information and they will order any book for you. The store is open daily year round.

The Fudge Factory
Somerset Square, 400 Front St., Beaufort
(252) 728-6202, (800) 551-8066

You guessed it: This store makes fudge -- creamy, sinful fudge in many flavors from natural ingredients on marble-top tables right before your eyes. You can buy it by the slice or the pound, to eat or ship anywhere. The Fudge Factory is open daily.

Handscapes Gallery
410 Front St., Beaufort
(252) 728-6805
www.handscapesgallery.com

Handscapes is an Insiders' favorite and is the perfect place to find unusual gifts and treasures. The gallery specializes in works by North Carolinians as well as artists and craftspeople from all over the country. Owner Alison Brooks fills the shop with pottery, jewelry, prints, paintings, glass and metal craft items. More than 180 artists are represented and it is a joy to see the fine workmanship offered. Handscapes Gallery was voted by Niche Magazine as one of the top 100 retail-

ers of American crafts in 2003 and 2004. The store is open year round, seven days a week. Call for winter hours.

Island Traders
421 Front St., Beaufort
(252) 504-3000

Island Traders is a name-brand and catalog clothing outlet, carrying ladies, men's and juniors items at 40 to 70 percent off regular retail prices. You'll also find deck shoes, nautical flag license plates, nautical belts and stickers, along with Beaufort print sweatshirts and tees, hats, belts and beach bags. The store is open every day, year round, with extended summer hours.

Fabricate Apparel
431 Front St., Beaufort
(252) 728-7950

Fabricate specializes in clothes of cool, comfortable natural fibers. The shop offers trendy, expressive clothes for women and men. You'll find jewelry, belts, bags, hats, scarves and shoes along with quality T-shirts and sweatshirts that feature Beaufort scenes. Fabricate is open 10 AM to 5 PM (winter), 10 AM to 6 PM (summer), and Sundays 1 to 5 PM from March through December.

Ibis
432 Front St., Beaufort
(252) 728-7220

Next to Fabricate, Barbara Pearl's shop, Ibis, features upscale women's clothing such as Eileen Fisher and Sigrid Olsen, along with hats by Kaminiski and Eric Javits. If the name Ibis doesn't intrigue you, the store window will surely lure you inside for a look around. The store is open Monday through Saturday year round.

Scuttlebutt
433 Front St., Beaufort
(252) 728-7765

Scuttlebutt specializes in "nautical books and bounty." You'll find an outstanding, high-quality selection of books, clocks, music, games, toys, models and galleyware, along with a selection of casual clothing and hats. This is a great store to visit and explore -- check out the maps and charts. The store is open daily year round.

Stamper's Jewelers
435 Front St., Beaufort
(252) 728-4967

Stamper's Jewelers has a full line of jewelry and excellent engraving and repair services. It's a great shop for brides and grooms. You can find diamond bridal jewelry and gifts for the attendants. Stamper's also offers popular sterling silver jewelry and name-brand watches. The skilled craftsmen at this store can engrave trophies. Stamper's is a cut above with its jewelry, watch and clock repair. It's open Monday through Saturday.

Taylor's Big Mug Coffee Cafe
437 Front St., Beaufort
(252) 728-0707

Taylor's Big Mug offers 100 percent fair trade coffee along with ciders and great espresso drinks. Enjoy a casual cup of joe and a snack at a cafe table or kick back on the sofas. You'll also find bagged coffee to take and enjoy at home or give as a gift. Wireless Internet access is available here, and there are live performances some days and nights. Taylor's Big Mug is open every day at 7 AM and closing time varies.

The General Store
515 Front St., Beaufort
(252) 728-7707

A novelty in Beaufort, The General Store is a favorite with locals and visitors alike. For great ice cream or a few more souvenirs, stop by and find all kinds of memorabilia.

From hats, T-shirts and shells to saltwater taffy and jewelry, this store has something for everyone. Kids like this place because their spending money goes a long way. You're sure to see a few kids sitting on the bench on the store's front stoop, licking away at a dripping ice cream cone on a warm summer's day. For boaters, food and other staples are available, as are laundry facilities. The store is conveniently located directly across from the town dock and is open Monday through Saturday.

Down East Gallery
519 Front St., Beaufort
(252) 728-4410

It couldn't even be considered a true tour of Beaufort without a stop in the Down East Gallery. Local artist Alan Cheek displays his work here. Alan's artwork will serve as a lovely reminder of your time spent in the enchanting seaport of Beaufort. Down East Gallery will custom-frame anything you wish. The gallery is closed Monday during the winter; otherwise it is open daily.

Bell's Drug Store
Front St., corner of Turner St., Beaufort
(252) 728-3810

Bell's Drug Store has been serving Beaufort and its visitors since 1918 and continues the same friendly, professional service today. Along with drugstore items, Bell's has fountain drinks, personal-care items, gifts, cards and a nice collection of glass collectables. Bell's is open Monday through Saturday.

N.C. Maritime Museum Store
315 Front St., Beaufort
(252) 728-7317
www.ncmm-friends.org

The Maritime Museum Store is where you should buy a memento of your visit to the museum. Excellent books abound: books about maritime habitats, sea creatures, North Carolina cuisine, seashore plants and much more. Look for subjects you or your kids have always wanted to know about but never got around to researching. Many of the titles are short, to-the-point and well illustrated. You'll also find outstanding, reasonably priced posters and pictures, plus kids' toys and greeting cards. Boaters will be interested in NOAA navigation charts, topo maps and related publications on navigation, boatbuilding and ship-model building. The store is open seven days a week all year.

Just off Front Street

Coastal Community Market
606 Broad St., Beaufort
(252) 728-2844

Coastal Community Market offers patrons organic foods and natural products. Here you will find gourmet, Oriental and Indian foods. The store also offers products for people with food allergies, and has wheat-free or sugar-free items for special dietary needs. You'll find bulk food items, 25 different cheeses, farm fresh eggs, locally made breads and granola, and hundreds of items for your pantry.

Harbor Specialties
127 Middle Ln., Beaufort
(252) 838-0059

Harbor Specialties offers a variety of "nautical but nice" items, including Dubarry deck shoes, Tilley hats and ships models. This shop features Vera Bradley handbags, and offers custom embroidery. You'll also find insulated glassware ideal for the boater, clocks and barometers. For a unique shopping experience, stop by this shop on Middle Lane.

In The Spirit
125 Craven St., Beaufort
(252) 728-4968

In The Spirit, located in a beautiful old house, is a floral and gift shop. You'll find fresh and silk flowers for all occasions, exclusive gifts, unusual and distinctive Christmas decorations, wreaths and swags, centerpieces, gift baskets and much more. Let In The Spirit handle your wedding or special event or your decorating needs.

Scott Taylor Photography Gallery and Studio
214 Pollock St., Beaufort
(252) 728-0900
www.scotttaylorphoto.com

At Scott Taylor's Photography Gallery and Studio you are sure to find that unique image of Beaufort or the surrounding coastal areas. Scott is well known for his scenic photography, and also for exclusive, yet reasonable engagement, wedding and event photography. He specializes in color, black and white, or split toned images. If you are

Everyone will find something that pleases them while shopping on the Crystal Coast.

courtesy of Tryon Palace Historical Sites & Gardens

looking for a very special gift, let Scott create a family beach portrait that will be treasured for a lifetime. Scott's book titled Coastal Waters - Images of North Carolina is available in the gallery and is the perfect way to remember your trip to the coast or the perfect gift.

Beyond Beaufort's Historic District

Holland's Shoes
Beaufort Square Shopping Ctr., U.S. Hwy. 70, Beaufort
(252) 728-4355

Holland's slogan says it all -- "from high heels to steel toes for the men, women and children." Holland's carries an excellent selection of shoes for the entire family with great prices to match. You'll find brand names, including Reebok, Rockport, Sperry and Birkenstock, along with handbags, socks, laces and shoe-cleaning items. You'll also find a nice selection of women's clothing and accessories. The store is open daily year round.

Gaskill's Hardware
U.S. Hwy. 70 and Lennoxville Rd., Beaufort
(252) 728-3757

Gaskill's Hardware is the store that has everything. It is one of those unique places that make living in or visiting Beaufort the special treat that it is. The full-service hardware store houses everything you'll need for your home and garden, for your animals and your hunting. You'll find paintball supplies along side chainsaws, feed, seeds and plants. Old-fashioned service rules at Gaskill's. Whether you need a simple wood screw, a new garden hose, a decorative pot or a screen for your window, the attendants are quick to help as soon as you come in the door. They'll walk you through the store and make it easy to find everything you need. The store carries Carhartt clothing, Georgia Boot and much more.

Morehead City

Morehead City offers the largest selection of shops on the Crystal Coast. Shopping opportunities are spread from one end of the city to the other and range from clothing boutiques and craft shops to bookstores and marine hardware suppliers. We describe a few of the shops in the city and have arranged them by area. As you read this section of our Shopping chapter, note that Arendell Street, Morehead City's main thoroughfare, is divided by a railroad track that runs from Third Street to the intersection of Arendell and Bridges streets, a distance of about 32 blocks.

MOREHEAD CITY WATERFRONT

Morehead's waterfront shopping section has benefited significantly from revitalization.

Sidewalks, trees, benches, parks and gazebos invite visitors to take a stroll or sit a spell, but the shops will entice you to come inside. Facing Bogue Sound, most waterfront shopping runs along Evans and Shepard streets. Plenty of free parking is available, but it can be hard to find an empty space in the height of the summer. When that's the case, park on Bridges Street, which parallels Arendell Street at this point, and walk across Arendell to the waterfront. Everything is close together, so even if you can't find a parking place on the waterfront, you won't have to walk very far.

Waterfront Junction
412 Evans St., Morehead City
(252) 726-6283

Waterfront Junction is the place to stop for craft supplies, needlework, prints, crewel, embroidery and nautical gifts. The shop is well-known for its custom framing and its large and diverse stock of ready-made frames. You'll also find nautical themed items - from coasters to lamps to wall decor. The children's book section features Dover Books, and the gift selection and greeting card section are wonderful. Shop at Waterfront Junction Monday through Saturday.

Dee Gee's Gifts & Books
508 Evans St., Morehead City
(252) 726-3314, (800) DEE-GEES
www.deegees.com

Dee Gee's Gifts and Books is a tradition on the waterfront and continues to offer a huge selection of books, gifts for all occasions, cards and novelties. Dee Gee's features special sections of local and regional books, children's educational books, toys and games and nautical charts. The staff will be happy to special-order any book. Often Dee Gee's has book-signing parties for local authors or for authors who have written about the area. Dee Gee's carries an excellent selection of decorative pieces for the home and garden. Visitors and locals shop here for special-occasion gift giving, knowing that the just-right serving platter, vase or outdoor fountain will be found here. Anything you select can be gift-wrapped and shipped to your home or to the lucky recipient. As an added bonus, Dee Gee's has a monthly contest to see just how far the store's original newsprint bags can travel. Heading to China or Bermuda or the Grand Canyon this summer? Take a Dee Gee's bag and send them a picture of you with it. You may be the winner of a $20 gift certificate. The store is open daily, and telephone orders are welcomed. Dee Gee's is a BookSense Store, part of a national affiliation of independent bookstores. They sell BookSense Gift Certificates, which can be used in more than 1,200 stores in all 50 states.

Windward Gallery
508 Evans St., Morehead City
(252) 726-6393

Windward offers oils, acrylics and pastels by acclaimed local artist Alexander Kaszas and many others. Some beautiful selections of jewelry, pottery, glass and copper yard ornaments are available too. The gallery is open Monday through Saturday, and often on Sunday during on holiday weekends.

Arts & Things
704 Evans St., Morehead City
(252) 240-1979

Arts & Things is on the beautiful Morehead City waterfront. Owners Porter and Lou Wilson offer the Crystal Coast's finest selection of art supplies and gallery treasures that you don't want to miss. It is the place to find the newest and most unique art in Eastern North Carolina. From local art to international artists, Arts & Things offers art for every taste. Paintings, prints, stone and wood sculptures, stained glass, pottery and art glass can be the perfect accent pieces for any home. A stroll through this relaxing gallery will inspire art collectors and casual art admirers. Bring a favorite painting or print and have it expertly framed on site. Lou and Porter have over 25 years of framing experience, and you'll be thrilled with their work. For beginner and seasoned artists alike, Arts & Things is completely stocked with fine art supplies and a selection of paper, brushes, paints, pastels, throwing clay, clayboards, easels and drawing supplies. You will probably also take home some new materials to try out just for the fun of it. A variety of art classes

are also offered. Any trip to Arts & Things will brighten your day or palette.

Carolina Artist Studio Gallery Inc.
800 Evans St., northwest corner of Eighth St., Morehead City
(252) 726-7550

If you are at all interested in original, imaginative paintings, pottery and photographs, you truly cannot pass up CASG. Several years ago, five artists banded together to form this nonprofit artists' cooperative, and the gallery on Evans is the testament to their success in creating a highly visual and satisfying experience. And a feast awaits. Approximately 30 North Carolina artists show their work here. Sun-filled gallery rooms contain original watercolors, oils, acrylics and pastels; hand-painted stoneware; pen-and-ink drawings and prints; and glazed pottery pieces. You can purchase the artwork (every piece is for sale at reasonable prices), or simply relax, contemplate the art and just hang out. The cooperative has strong ties to the community. Members teach art classes, encourage art students to visit and sponsor special programs. Classes include beading, watercolor and oil painting, among others. Visit Carolina Artist Studio Gallery Monday through Saturday year round. Parking is in front of the gallery.

DOWNTOWN MOREHEAD CITY

As you leave Morehead's waterfront and drive west (toward Newport) on Arendell Street, several shops between 5th and 12th streets are well worth visiting. Although there is free street parking in front of these stores, you may have to park on a side street or take advantage of a new public parking lot created in the center of the downtown area.

Crystal Coast Crafters
513-A Arendell St., Morehead City
(252) 726-3492

Don and Ellie Zurek, proprietors of Crystal Coast Crafters, will teach you how to make any of the craft items displayed in their store: stained glass, shell craft, lamps and shades and holiday decorations. There are also classes in painting. Don and Ellie specialize in stained-glass repair and restoration. The Zureks also carry a large selection of art and craft supplies. The store is open Monday through Saturday.

City News
514 Arendell St., Morehead City
(252) 726-6320

Folks who keep up with world happenings can choose from an endless number of magazines and many major newspapers at City News. If you want a copy of the Sunday New York Times, you will find it here, along with an assortment of local, regional and national newspapers. Greeting cards are available, as are bestsellers and books about local lore. You will also find maps, cold drinks and books for kids. The store is open seven days a week, all year round.

Tim Green Photography
(252) 726-8074

Tim Green specializes in wedding photography, family portraits and special-occasion photography. His wedding services range from engagement packages to bridal packages to wedding day packages. Tim specializes in studio and beach photography. He offers a wide range of photography services including school, sports, prom and senior pictures.

Sew It Seams
905 Arendell St., Morehead City
(252) 247-2114

At Sew It Seams you can buy sewing patterns and notions, fabrics and books and choose from a large collection of buttons. But the emphasis here is on quilting. The store offers quilting classes with experienced teachers ready to show you how to create your own quilts, whether by machine or by hand. If you're not interested in quilting your own top piece, Sew it Seams has new machinery and can handle the job for you. The store has 2,000 types of fabric. Sew It Seams is open Tuesday through Saturday.

Parson's General Store
808 Arendell St., Morehead City
(252) 726-8188

Located in an old Victorian home, Parson's is a great place to stop because it has an extensive collection of gifts, local crafts, home accessories, seasonal decorations and sweets. The shop also offers Hershey's ice cream. It is open all year, seven days a week.

Ginny Gordon's Gifts And Gadgets
1011 Arendell St., Morehead City
(252) 726-6661

Ginny Gordon's shop carries a great collection of cookware, cookbooks from near and far, every cooking utensil imaginable plus gadgets you can't do without. You might also find a cooking class, and you'll always find good advice about kitchen gadgets, and she will demonstrate the workings of anything in the store. Ginny Gordon's Gifts and Gadgets is open all year, Tuesday through Saturday.

AROUND MOREHEAD CITY

As you leave the waterfront and downtown sections of Morehead City and continue driving west on Arendell Street (toward Newport and Havelock), you will encounter a number of small shopping centers. We have listed some of them here, enterprises that are in or just outside the city's limits but not clustered in any single area. The street addresses should make them easy to find.

Bell Photography
Morehead City
(252) 247-1058

Established in 1956, Bell Photography has been meeting and exceeding the photography needs of locals and visitors to the area for years. Owner David Bell now carries on the quality of tradition started by his father, the late Gene Bell. He offers a mixture of photography styles including contemporary, storybook and journalistic. Whether indoor or outdoor, David strives to keep the rates affordable and to ensure the pictures reflect the beauty of your special day.

Captain Jim's Seafood
4665 Arendell St., Morehead City
(252) 726-3454

Captain Jim's Seafood is a fresh seafood market. Their motto says it all: "If it swims, we've got it." You'll find fresh shrimp, mahi mahi, tuna, wahoo, triggerfish, scallops and much more. Captain Jim's is one of the cleanest seafood markets in the county. Need help with your purchase? They'll pack coolers for free. The market has volume discounts, and wholesale is available. You'll know you're in the right place for seafood -- the knowledgeable staff offers 109 combined years of seafood experience. Captain Jim's is open seven days a week in season.

Budding Artists Ltd.
Morehead Plaza Unit 8, Morehead City
(252) 247-5111

This gallery takes pride in showcasing local and regional artists. It emphasizes whimsical artwork and features Brian Andreas' delightful Storypeople (rendered in drawings, books and furniture). You won't be able to resist the prints, watercolors, sculpture, photographs and other three-dimensional art pieces at Budding Artists. If you have in mind a print that isn't in the gallery, ask to see the art catalogs; they will be glad to order for you. The shop provides complete framing services, and stylish gift wrap is available for anything you purchase. Shop at Budding Artists Monday through Saturday year round.

Coastal Image Photography
Morehead City
(252) 726-7488
www.coastalimagephoto.com

Carolyn Temple is a true professional and can prepare a photography package just right for your special day. She has the only lush garden outdoor studio area in eastern North Carolina and will schedule location photos at the beach at no extra charge. Just let her know what you would like, and Carolyn can prepare the perfect wedding package for you and your wedding party.

Teacher's Pet and A Sea of Learning
2410 Arendell St., Morehead City
(252) 240-2515

These shops (under the same roof) are two of the most wonderful places in the area. Whether you are a teacher, a parent or learning yourself, you are sure to enjoy the stores. Teacher's Pet focuses on all types of learning aids -- everything from charts and artwork to books and equipment. A Sea of Learning features educational games and toys for children of all ages. The store offers Thomas the Tank Engine trains, themed birthday party supplies and other building supplies for kids. Teacher's Pet also offers tutoring. Certified teachers are available to tutor one-on-one in the store after school hours and on Saturday; call for fees. Shop here seven days a week.

The Golden Gull
Pelletier Harbor Shops, 4426 Arendell St., Morehead City
(252) 726-2333

Since 1975 Golden Gull has made sure women in Carteret County are handsomely outfitted in the latest casual wear, sportswear, dresses and after-five ensembles. The store carries a full line of accessories to complement the clothes. Golden Gull now also has a Merle Norman cosmetics studio on the premises. The shop is open Monday through Saturday.

Lynette's Two
Pelletier Harbor Shops, 4426 Arendell St., Morehead City
(252) 726-3733

Lynette's carries distinctive fashions for women. The shop offers lovely sportswear, jewelry, handbags and all the right accessories. It is open Monday through Saturday.

Knowledge of Christ Books & Gifts
Pelletier Harbor Shops, 4428 Arendell St., Morehead City
(252) 726-7370

This store is filled with books, gifts, stained glass, collectibles, dolls, prints and paintings. You will also find Bibles for adults and children. Shop here Monday through Saturday.

EJW Outdoors
4667 Arendell St., Suite B, Morehead City
(252) 247-4725

EJW's has been in business for more than 50 years and recently expanded its extensive inventory with a move to its new location. EJW's continues to offer all types of outdoor gear -- from Columbia and Carhartt clothing and accessories to fishing and hunting gear. The store also sells bikes and services fishing equipment and bikes.

The Party Place
4667 Arendell St., Suite A, Morehead City
(252) 247-4725

The Party Place offers everything you need to have a party -- large or small, wild or intimate. Whether it is paper products, guest favors or decorations, this store has it all.

The Intimate Bridal and Formal Wear
5370 Brandywine Crossing, Morehead City
(252) 808-2221

Let The Intimate make planning your wedding an enjoyable and fun experience. The professional at this shop offer an elegant, friendly atmosphere and will work to ensure you look your best for whatever the occasion happens to be. As a full-service bridal shop, The Intimate offers a tremendous selection of bridal gowns, bridesmaid dresses starting at $99, prom dresses and social occasion dresses from sizes 2 to 30. There is something to fit every budget, as well as tuxedo rentals and sales. Free groom and ring bearer specials are available. The Intimate is experienced in accommodating large volume tuxedo rentals and out-of-town wedding parties, and ensures the perfect fit. This shop offers elegance and style for the bride to be and her wedding party. Whether it is that special dress or just the right tuxedo, the friendly staff here can take care of your every need and offer professional advice on clothing, color schemes and sizes. Immediate delivery is available on certain styles, and The Intimate also offers wedding gown preservation. The Intimate also has a store at 230 Middle Street, New Bern, (252) 638-1220.

West Marine
4950 Arendell St., Morehead City
(252) 240-2909

This is a true hardware store for the boating crowd. It has everything you need for power and sailboats, with well-marked aisles and friendly, helpful salespeople. West Marine stocks safety and repair equipment, fishing gear, boat electronics, ropes, log books and many other items. It has a good selection of nautical books and charts too. About one-quarter of the store is devoted to men's and women's outdoor clothing, including Topsider shoes. The store is open daily.

The Book Shop
Parkway Shopping Ctr., 4915 Arendell St., Morehead City
(252) 240-1163

This bookstore offers a wide selection of new and used paperback, hard-bound and children's books at discounted prices. Any new book not in the store can be ordered and delivered promptly. One side of the shop carries used books, where you will find loads of value-priced novels, cookbooks, history, kids' stories and former bestsellers in both paperback and hardcover. You can trade your used books for the store's used books too. The Book Shop is open seven days a week.

Tal-Y-Bont Interiors, Ltd.
5113-C U.S. Hwy. 70 W., Morehead City
(252) 726-6872

Tal-Y-Bont Interiors is a full-line furniture and interior design store. The 20,000-square-foot showroom contains a wide variety of contemporary and traditional styles, including wicker and rattan furniture. The store will special order items for you, but it carries a large inventory for immediate delivery, which is especially convenient if you are furnishing a Crystal Coast vacation home or your permanent residence. Besides furniture, Tal-Y-Bont provides window treatments, bedspreads, wallpaper and a large list of accessories to complete your design scheme. And don't hesitate to call upon the talents of Tal-Y-Bont's professional design staff. They will help you make decisions for your entire home or just the finishing touches. The store is closed on Sunday.

J. R. Dunn Jewelers
Cypress Bay Plaza, Morehead City
(252) 726-8700

Dunn's features distinctive jewelry for women, men and children, along with many nautical creations. The store will repair and remount your jewelry and watches and gift wrap your purchases. The staff is knowledgeable and very helpful, especially for those of us who can't quite figure out what to select for that special someone. J. R. Dunn also has a shop in Emerald Isle.

General Nutrition Center
Cypress Bay Plaza, U.S. Hwy. 70 W., Morehead City
(252) 808-3900

GNC is staffed with friendly people who are knowledgeable about the store's products and who are glad to help you with your selections. This store is filled the store with thousands of products designed to promote good health. At GNC you will find vitamins and supplements of every type, a wide variety of herbs, items specially for kids, topical books, healthy snack foods and a fully stocked weight-reduction section. The store also has shampoos, scrubs and skin care products. It is open seven days a week.

Fred's Beds
5360 U.S. Hwy. 70 W., Morehead City
(252) 726-3888

Fred's Beds is a full-line bedroom furniture company that is sure to have just what you need and want for the bedrooms in your home. The store carries quality furniture from Timeless, Sensa, Simmons, Tempur-pedic, Spring Air and Kingsdown. You'll find complete bedroom groups -- beds, night stands, mirrors, chests and dressers. Fred's Beds has the East Coast's largest selection of futons and has a large selection of day beds and water beds. With delivery and set up offered, this is the place to go for anything in the way of comfortable bedding.

Bill's Pet Shop
5370-A Brandywine Crossing, U.S. Hwy. 70, Morehead City
(252) 240-1116

This is your complete pet store, no matter what you need. Bill's Pet Shop sells pets of all types -- dogs, cats, birds, ferrets and some reptiles --- along with all the supplies and products you need to care for your best friend. This is truly a one-stop, full-service pet shop. You'll find pet crates, cages, leashes, medications and more. Bill's also has a complete tropical and saltwater aquarium section with professional staff ready to guide you in the proper set up and care of your tanks. There are sister stores in Havelock and New Bern.

Priscilla's Crystal Coast Wines
5370-K Brandywine Crossing, U.S. Hwy. 70, Morehead City
(252) 240-3234
www.crystalcoastwines.com

This shop has wines for every day enjoyment or for a special occasion. Priscilla offers a wide selection and she can recommend just the right wines to accompany your meals or to be featured at your parties. The shop offers gift baskets, gourmet foods, wine tastings and classes. A new section of the store is called The Barn Yard and offers quality dirt cheap wines sure to please.

The traditional ways of making a living are still alive and well on the Crystal Coast.

photo: George Mitchell

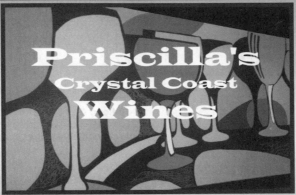

Wolf Spirit
5370-C Brandywine Crossing, U.S. Hwy. 70, Morehead City
(252) 247-WOLF (-9653)

Wolf Spirit offers patrons a fine selection of quality Native American items. You'll find pottery, prints, sun catchers, artifacts, feature work, cradle boards, peace pipes, jewelry and throws, as well as maps, symbols and post cards. The shop also offers Kachinas and dance dolls. For those who enjoy creating their own art, Wolf Spirit features a craft area offering beads, features and leather.

Churchill's Cigars, Tobacco and Gifts
5087 U.S. Hwy. 70 W., Morehead City
(252) 727-1993

When looking for a special gift, don't look over Churchill's, a favorite store of new fathers as well as connoisseurs with a taste for a fine cigar. You'll find an array of gift ideas and perhaps even something for yourself -- smoker or nonsmoker.

Window & Wall Interior Decor
4130 Arendell St., Morehead City
(252) 726-9027

Window & Wall Interior Decor specializes in custom window treatments. The designer-owner has more than 20 years experience in home decor, and the store offers a wide selection of fabrics and wall coverings. They carry a complete line of plantation shutters, Hunter Douglas shadings and blinds, plus custom-made valances and draperies. They also offer custom upholstery, slipcovers and bed coverings. The showroom is well stocked, and there is no charge for the "shop at home" service.

Swansboro

Shops in Swansboro are basically in two areas - along the river on Front Street and its adjoining side streets, and along N.C. 24. We suggest you take some time to walk along the White Oak River, shop a bit, enjoy lunch at one of the restaurants and relax in Bicentennial Park.

Russell's Olde Tyme Shoppe
116 Front St., Swansboro
(910) 326-3790

At Russell's you'll find country crafts, costume jewelry, handcrafted clothing, pottery, furniture, baskets, silk and dried flowers, along with kitchen and cooking utensils. Owner Maxine Russell also offers a wide variety of hand-painted items -- from photo albums to glass to wooden items. Each purchase in the store is placed in a hand-painted shopping bag, a gift in itself. The store is open daily.

Through the Looking Glass
101 Church St., Swansboro
(910) 326-3128

When you purchase a gift at Through the Looking Glass, you can be certain it will delight the recipient. This store has an excellent selection of home and garden accessories, fragrances, jewelry, tableware, candles, wines and children's gifts. The Christmas items are extensive and include decorations, nativity scenes, dishes and more. Look for the specialized children's clothing. Need a bouquet of silk or fresh flowers for that special someone? Through the Looking Glass will design an arrangement sure to reflect your feelings. You can shop here daily, but call for winter hours.

The Mercantile
131 Front St., Swansboro
(910) 326-7216

Shops at the Mercantile Building houses two stores well worth your stop. Silver Fish Book Co. has everything you need to make a day on the beach complete -- the perfect book. You'll find books for all ages and interests, from cookbooks and bestsellers to local authors and historical sketches. You'll also find unique gifts of all types.

Vilinda's is the place to shop for comfortable and stylish resort and casual clothes You'll find a wide selection of cotton, linen and jersey knits plus sweatshirts, T-shirts and cardigans that feature Swansboro scenes. Jewelry, hats and sandals are also available. The shop is open seven days a week, year round.

Down East

Only a few shops can be found Down East, but each is uncommon and well worth the trip. Because hours vary, we suggest you call ahead. As you drive through the Down East area, you will find numerous homes with signs out front welcoming you to stop and consider buying model boats, decoys, crafts and more.

Core Sound Waterfowl Museum Gift Shop
1785 Island Rd., Harkers Island
(252) 728-1500

Located at the end of Harkers Island Road by the Cape Lookout National Seashore Visitor Center, the Core Sound Waterfowl Museum is something you do not want to miss. Look for signs to guide your way. The museum gift shop is filled with Down East gifts, most of which have waterfowl and environmental themes. Decoys are abundant, as are wildlife art, books, cards, house flags, windsocks, T-shirts, birdhouses, bird feeders and much more. The shop also features decoy and local history exhibits. The gift store is open daily. (For more information about the museum, see our Attractions chapter.)

Capt. Henry's Gift Store
1341 Island Rd., Harkers Island
(252) 728-7316

This is a treasure trove of Down East decoys. Well-known local carver Wayne Davis owns Capt. Henry's and often his works are offered along with nautical sundries, pottery, prints and jewelry. Shoppers will be charmed by the baskets, bird houses and wind chimes. Capt. Henry's is open for business Monday through Saturday, with winter hours varying.

East'ard Variety Store
Harkers Island Dr., Harkers Island
(252) 728-7149

East'ard Variety is the place to go Down East for whatever you need. The place carries almost everything -- nuts, bolts, screws, gasoline, bread, milk, beer, plumbing supplies, video rentals, paint, scoop ice cream, sundaes and just about any item you'll need for a local fishing trip. You'll find hardware, electrical and automotive supplies and rain gear. Need a screen door repaired? An extra key made? Your chainsaw sharpened? How about a hot dog or dip ice cream? Go to East'ard's. It's open seven days a week all year.

Nature's Corner
U.S. Hwy. 70, Smyrna Corner
(252) 729-1800

Nature's Corner is a unique shop that is well worth the drive no matter where you live. The shop specializes in natural gifts and has a nice selection of plants to attract butterflies and hummingbirds. You'll also find carnivorous plants and complete water garden supplies here, along with unusual lawn and garden accessories.

Edgewater Gardens
U.S. Hwy. 70, Smyrna
(252) 729-1842

Edgewater Gardens is a full-service lawn and garden center. This business is located Down East, but is worth the drive.

Sea Side Stop-N-Shop
Island Rd., Harkers Island
(252) 728-5533

Sea Side Stop-N-Shop offers a variety of services. Whether you need fuel for your car or boat or convenience store items, this is a great place to stop. You'll also find a gift shop that offers unique nautical items, baby gifts, seasonal items, candles and more. At the other end of the building, Sea Side Galley offers pizzas, burgers, subs, seafood and more to eat in or take out.

Western Carteret County

Most communities in the western part of the county have a convenience/gas store, a beauty salon and tanning booth, or maybe a craft and flower shop. In addition to the selected stores we describe here, two roadside stands deserve mention – Winberry Farm Produce, on N.C. Highway 24 in Cedar Point, and Smith's Produce in Ocean, also on N.C. Highway 24. Both offer seasonal local vegetables, Bogue Sound watermelons and cantaloupes. They are usually open for business during the growing seasons of spring, summer and early fall.

Carolina Home and Garden
N.C. Hwy. 24, Bogue
(252) 393-9004

Carolina Home and Garden offers a variety of trees, shrubs and plants along with hardware, gardening items and lawn-care supplies at reasonable prices. Carolina Home is open daily most of the year; it is closed on Sunday in the winter.

Redfearn's Nursery
N.C. Hwy. 24, Cedar Point
(252) 393-8243

Redfearn's offers landscaping services and sells potted plants, planters, garden seeds, fertilizers, herbicides and pesticides. The nursery is open daily, except in the winter when it closes on Sunday.

Antiques Shops

Antiques shops are plentiful along the Crystal Coast. We highlight a few in this section, beginning with Beaufort and Morehead City and ending with several in the western part of the county. We definitely recommend a day or two of antiques-shop exploration throughout Carteret County.

BEAUFORT

The Marketplace Antiques and Collectibles
131 Turner St., Beaufort
(252) 728-2325

The Marketplace displays the wares of 16 dealers from far and near. It's a must-stop shop for browsers and collectors, with lots of the stuff that you used to find in your grandmother's house. Loads of figurines, old woodworking and garden tools, ancient magazines and books, Depression glass, china tableware, old lithographs (some framed, some not) wooden chests and Coke memorabilia are just some of the things you'll find here. The Marketplace is open seven days a week.

Beaufort Antiques
126 Turner St., Beaufort
(252) 504-3838

This shop offers antiques and collectibles from the owner's family, estate pieces from New Orleans and Beaufort, as well as quality reproductions. Shoppers will also find folk art. The store is an authorized Fenton Glass and Franz Potter dealer. It's open daily during the summer season; call for winter hours.

MOREHEAD CITY

Olde Towne Antiques
1308 Arendell St., Morehead City
(252) 247-7478

Olde Towne Antiques offers an excellent selection of old coins and medals, but there's so much more as well. You can browse through old silver pieces (plate and sterling), china, glass work, dolls, local art, period furniture and handmade decoys. Old prints and picture frames are also available. Shop at Old Towne seven days a week.

Seaport Antique Market
509 Arendell St., Morehead City
(252) 726-6606

Seaport Antiques is a treat for the senses. Here you'll find the wares of many vendors, giving you an opportunity to see more than one collector's items at a time. You'll find furniture, books, glassware, knickknacks, jewelry and even some household accessories. Keep coming back. The vendors rotate the offerings in their spaces regularly. Seaport is open daily.

SWANSBORO

Swansboro Antique Center
448 Cedar Point Blvd., Cedar Point
(252) 393-6003

This rambling building shows the wares of more than 25 dealers in an attractive space. You'll find kitchen collections, decoys, hunting and fishing equipment, furniture, quilts, paintings, toys, books, old radios and cameras, political memorabilia, clothing, tobacco products, old medical items and original stained glass. For the inveterate collector, this place shouldn't be missed. Shop here every day of the week except Monday year round.

ATTRACTIONS

Ocean-related activities and coastal parks are much of what make the Crystal Coast so attractive to tourists and so protected by residents. Natural attractions, such as Cape Lookout National Seashore, Fort Macon State Park, Hammocks Beach State Park, Theodore Roosevelt Natural Area, Rachel Carson Estuarine Research Reserve, Croatan National Forest and Cedar Island National Wildlife Refuge, offer a wide variety of pristine beaches, maritime forests and waterways to enjoy and explore.

This chapter highlights the many attractions of the Crystal Coast - the unique cultural and natural history of the area, natural attractions, the lighthouse and museums - that enhance the tourists' visits and residents' lives. Some folks come particularly for festivals and events that we discuss in detail in our Annual Events chapter. Other things we Insiders think are particularly attractive about living here, such as parks, we've described in the Sports, Fitness and Parks chapter. For more attractions the whole family will enjoy, see our Kidstuff chapter.

General Attractions

BOGUE BANKS

North Carolina Aquarium at Pine Knoll Shores
MM 7, N.C. Hwy. 58, Pine Knoll Shores
(252) 247-4003
www.ncaquariums.com

Experience the thrill of exploring sunken ships - without getting wet - at the new North Carolina Aquarium at Pine Knoll Shores. Three shipwreck exhibits recreate the adventure of recreational diving off the North Carolina coast.

Visitors also can feel the spray from a mountain waterfall, hold a crab, touch a stingray, see big sharks and watch river otters play. The aquarium, near Atlantic Beach, is one of three operated by the state on the North Carolina coast that draw hundreds of thousands of visitors each year. The others are at Fort Fisher and Roanoke Island.

The aquarium recently reopened after a $25 million expansion that tripled its size to 93,000 square feet. The new theme, "From North Carolina's Mountains to the Sea" takes visitors on an unforgettable aquatic journey from the state's grand peaks to the open Atlantic, much as a raindrop makes its way to the ocean.

Five galleries - Mountain, Piedmont, Coastal Plain, Tidal Waters and Ocean - and more than 2,500 animals depict these aquatic zones.

The 306,000-gallon Living Shipwreck, with a 70-foot replica of a sunken, coral-encrusted World War II German submarine, is the centerpiece display. Around it glide fierce-looking sand tiger sharks up to 8 feet in length, along with stingrays, barracudas, schools of fishes and many other creatures that typically congregate around shipwrecks. A 63-foot window offers superb views, and divers in the exhibit chat with visitors through underwater microphones.

The 50,000-gallon Queen Anne's Revenge duplicates the scene of an 18th century shipwreck in Beaufort Inlet. The wreckage, discovered in 1996, is thought to be from a pirate ship once commanded by the infamous Blackbeard. In this realistic representation, nurse sharks, sea turtles, cobia, bluefish, drum and other animals circle replicas of half-buried cannons and other artifacts.

The shipwrecks are among nearly 40 new, innovative exhibits. A favorite stop is the River Otter exhibit, where Neuse and Pungo, two playful North American river otters, swim and frolic in their Piedmont habitat.

Two touch pools allow personal contact with stingrays, whelks, horseshoe crabs and other creatures. Other favorites include the Jellyfish, Octopus, Seahorses and Lionfish displays. Diving demonstrations, live-animal

BIGGER.
THE NEW
NORTH CAROLINA
AQUARIUM
at Pine Knoll Shores
252-247-4003
www.ncaquariums.com

programs and animal feedings are among the daily activities.

The aquarium offers summer camps for children in grades 2-9 and many programs, activities and field trips for all ages. Ocean-going collecting cruises, Newport River excursions, snorkeling classes, canoe trips, crabbing and clamming classes, surfing lessons, interpretive beach walks and forays to remote barrier islands are a few of the choices.

These special programs require advance registration and most have a small fee. The aquarium also has wonderful settings, a catering kitchen and various rental options for meetings, ceremonies, parties and presentations. The expansion also brought a new and expanded gift shop and snack bar.

The aquarium is open 9 AM to 5 PM daily. Hours are extended to 9 PM Thursdays in July for Family Night. The Aquarium is closed Thanksgiving, Christmas and New Year's.

Admission is $8 adults, $7 age 62 and over; $6 ages 6 to 17. Children 5 and younger, registered North Carolina school groups and members of the North Carolina Aquarium Society are admitted free. Admission is free on Veteran's Day and Martin Luther King Jr.'s Birthday. Admission fees are the same at all three North Carolina Aquariums, and go into a special fund for improvements at all the facilities.

Membership in the North Carolina Aquarium Society entitles participants free admission to each of the state's three aquariums and to more than 150 other aquariums and zoos across the country, along with other benefits.

BEAUFORT

Beaufort Historic Site
100 Block of Turner St., Beaufort
(252) 728-5225, (800) 575-SITE
www.beaufortthistoricsite.org

People come from far and wide to see the Beaufort Historic Site, a 2-acre area with seven beautifully restored buildings in the center of town. Cared for by the Beaufort Historical Association, the site annually hosts nearly 60,000 visitors, who tour the buildings and participate in the tours, classes, workshops and historical re-enactments scheduled throughout the year. This site, along with the Beaufort waterfront, is what makes this little seaport so special and appealing.

Before you begin to look around, go to the Robert W. and Elva Faison Safrit Historical Center at 130 Turner Street. The center welcomes and orients visitors to the historic site with free exhibits, video presentations and demonstrations. If you decide to take any of the tours that charge a fee, the Historical Center is where you pay and meet the tour guide. The Old Beaufort Museum Gift Shop is also here (see our Shopping chapter) as well as loads of information about the town of Beaufort and other not-to-be-missed attractions. The center is open Monday through Saturday 9:30 AM to 5 PM March through November and 10 AM to 4 PM December through February. After a visit to the Safrit Historical Center, we guarantee you'll want to spend a few more days in town.

Preservation efforts have kept Old Beaufort much as it was when the town was incorporated in 1723. Most of the restored buildings you see were moved to the historic site from other locations in town. These moves were necessitated in many cases by property owners who were ready to tear down an old structure to build a new one. So visitors can get the most out of their tour, BHA has restored and preserved the buildings as authentically as possible. The collections and furnishings help interpret a particular period in the building's history. Guided walking tours of the buildings (we describe some of them here) are conducted four times a day Monday

through Saturday year round for $6 per adult and $4 for children.

Josiah Bell House is the large yellow house with side gardens that is often photographed to represent the site. Built between 1790 and the early 1800s and purchased by Josiah Bell in 1825, its interior reflects the opulent Victorian era.

Samuel Leffers Cottage, c.1778, was once the schoolmaster's house. It is furnished in a primitive style and features a distinctive Beaufort-type roof line.

The John C. Manson House, c. 1825, was the first building purchased by the Beaufort Historical Association in the 1960s. Located on its original site, this Federal Period home is an excellent study in the decorative arts complete with an authentic faux finished interior.

The Carteret County Courthouse of 1796 has been completely restored to its original condition. It is the only 18th-century framed courthouse of its size in North Carolina that has been restored or is in a condition which would allow restoration. The courthouse serves as an invaluable educational tool, according to BHA staff, helping show the transformation of the legal system in North Carolina. The authentic preservation project won several local, state and national awards.

Old County Jail, c.1829, has two cells and jail keeper's quarters, which were in use until 1954. There is a museum room in one of the cells.

The Apothecary Shop and Doctor's Office, c.1859, features a fascinating collection of medical instruments and memorabilia from the county's early doctors and dentists.

R. Rustell House, c.1732, is home to the Mattie King Davis Art Gallery. In its time, the building was a typical Beaufort cottage and was owned by prominent early citizen Richard Rustell Jr. The gallery operates year round and represents more than 100 local and regional artists.

After touring the historic site, hop on the vintage English double-decker bus for a terrific narrated tour of Beaufort's historic district (an area much larger than the historic site). The tour comes complete with stories about town residents who colored local history. Bus tours depart the historic site on Monday, Wednesday, Friday and Saturday, April through October. Bus tour fees are $6 for adults and $4 for kids. Reservations must be made for group tours.

Don't miss the Old Burying Ground, the cemetery on Ann Street, which dates from 1731. BHA gives narrated tours of the grounds Tuesday, Wednesday and Thursday (fees are $6 for adults and $4 for children), June through September. Group tours can also be arranged year round. Or take the tour on your own, using a map available at the Safrit Historical Center. See our Close-up for more information on the Old Burying Ground.

In addition to these activities, the Beaufort Historical Association conducts the fabulous annual Beaufort Old Homes Tour and Antiques Show during the last full weekend in June (see our Annual Events chapter). Activities include tours of private and association-owned homes and gardens, musical performances, more than 40 antique dealers from all over the east coast, military re-enactments and more.

In case you decide you just can't leave, you may volunteer for a multitude of involvements in coastal history at the Beaufort Historic Site (see our Volunteer Opportunities chapter). The Beaufort Historical Association is a nonprofit organization dedicated to research, education and the preservation of Carteret County's significant history. Memberships are welcomed.

North Carolina Maritime Museum
315 Front St., Beaufort
(252) 728-7317
www.ncmm-friends.org

The North Carolina Maritime Museum's mission is to preserve and interpret all aspects of the state's rich maritime heritage through educational exhibits, programs and field trips. Now led by Dr. David Nateman, its exhibits and programming focus on North Carolina's maritime history and coastal natural history.

The museum is located at 315 Front Street in Beaufort in an area immediately adjacent to shops, restaurants and the boardwalk along Taylors Creek. The 18,000-square-foot building is constructed of wood, and some of its design features resemble those of the early life-saving stations that were prevalent along the Carolina coast starting in the late nineteenth century. Public areas, in addition to the exhibit hall, include an auditorium, reference library and the Museum Store.

In the Harvey W. Smith Watercraft Center, located directly across the street, visitors can watch boat restoration and construction from a platform above the boat shop floor. In the John S. MacCormack Model Shop, builders construct scale models of a variety of vessels. Classes in boat-building skills are offered for novices and experienced woodworkers alike. Topics include lofting, boatbuilding carpentry, boat modeling for children, diesel maintenance, plane making and others. Class size is limited, and all tools and materials are provided. Classes are generally offered on the weekends.

Museum exhibits include Coastal Marine Life, North Carolina's Working Watercraft, U.S. Lifesaving Service and Commercial Fishing. Displayed are a typical 1950s outboard motor shop and outboards, ship models, fossil and shell collections, an observation bell, coastal plant and animal life exhibits, indigenous watercraft and more. The museum's library is available for reading and research.

A permanent exhibit in the museum lobby features Blackbeard and Queen Anne's Revenge. Included in this display are artifacts, ballast stones and implements such as tacks with decorative heads and a whetstone, which was used to sharpen weapons and knives. There are bones (pig), shards and ceramic fragments of utilitarian containers, and parts of instruments such as dividers and a surveyor's chain. Additionally, there are small arms hardware, pewter platters and cannon balls.

The museum's education staff has provided environmental education programs for the public since 1975. Coastal habitats are highlighted in trips to barrier island beaches, maritime forests, salt marshes and tidal flats. In addition there are trawling trips aboard a research vessel, bird-watching, fossil hunts and kayaking trips. All museum trips and programs are guided and presented by natural science curators with many years of experience in the field.

Both the Rachel Carson Estuarine Research Reserve and the N.C. Maritime Museum schedule guided tours focused on specific ecological environments of the Crystal Coast. Quarterly calendars are available at each facility for making trip plans. All trips require reservations.

The Cape Lookout Studies Program offers learning opportunities on the coastal waters and islands near Beaufort. Managed by the N.C. Maritime Museum, the program utilizes the museum field station on Cape Lookout National Seashore, 10 miles southeast of Beaufort. The field station was formerly a Coast Guard Station, which was built in 1917 and decommissioned in June 1983. A wide variety of programs and field study opportunities are available for individuals or small groups through scheduled museum calendar programs. Educational, environmental or other special interest groups can custom design a program for workshops, retreats or conferences.

The museum's annual programs and field trips attract all ages, all interests, all year. The Wooden Boat Show held the first Saturday in May features wooden boats of all kinds, races, workshops and demonstrations for the enjoyment of everyone who appreciates wooden boats. The Junior Sailing Program is a basic-through-intermediate sailing program open to children ages 8 and older. Boat-related program offerings also include Adult Learn to Sail, Beaufort Oars, Sea Scouts, kayaking and Traditional Boat Handling. The Summer Science School for Children offers individual classes and hands-on field trips for students entering first through tenth grades (see our Kidstuff chapter).

Membership as a Friend of the Museum brings the newsletter, The Waterline, the museum's quarterly Calendar of Activities, special invitations and discounts in the Museum Store. This nonprofit support organization has been vital to the museum's growth, including the acquisition of 36 acres in the Gallants Channel area, just north of the Beaufort drawbridge. The Gallants Channel site houses a repository for artifacts recovered from the shipwreck presumed to be that of Queen Anne's Revenge, Blackbeard's flagship that was discovered near Beaufort Inlet in November of 1996. (For more about Blackbeard, see our Close-up in the Area Overview chapter.)

The museum will serve as host for The Tall Ships as part of the Pepsi America's Sail

2006. The ships are scheduled to be docked in Beaufort June 30 to July 5, 2006, and the excitement is already building.

Museum and the Watercraft Center hours are Monday through Friday 9 AM to 5 PM, Saturday 10 AM to 5 PM and Sunday 1 to 5 PM. No admission fee is charged.

Be sure to take time to visit the Museum Store, (252) 728-7317. It's the best place to find a special book on natural or maritime history or a navigation chart or topographical map. For more information, see our Shopping chapter.

MOREHEAD CITY

Crystal Coast Civic Center
3505 Arendell St., Morehead City
(252) 247-3883
www.crystalcoastcivicctr.com

On the campus of Carteret Community College overlooking Bogue Sound, the Crystal Coast Civic Center is a multiple-use facility with 18,000-square-feet of flexible space. The civic center can accommodate groups from 10 to 1,000. Each year the Crystal Coast Civic Center hosts a variety of events, some being major attractions to the resort area. Exhibitions and trade shows, banquets, fundraisers, weddings and reunions are frequent throughout the year. Events such as the Big Rock Blue Marlin Tournament awards dinner, the Ducks Unlimited Banquet and the Coastal Home & Garden Show are annual favorites. The center also hosts the opening ceremonies luncheon during the North Carolina Seafood Festival weekend. Many private businesses and families schedule use of the Crystal Coast Civic Center for events involving a large and small groups of people. Accommodations include a full-service catering kitchen, state of the art public address system, high speed internet, portable stage and a 5,600-square-foot outdoor plaza overlooking the beautiful waters of the Intracoastal Waterway. Call the Civic Center to book your event.

The History Place
1008 Arendell St., Morehead City
(252) 247-7533

Everything old is new again at The History Place. This is a 12,000-square-foot facility that houses the museum gallery, the Jack Spencer Goodwin Research Library, a classroom, the Les A. Ewen Auditorium, the Museum Store and offices. The Tea Clipper, a delightful tea shop and cafe operated by Elaine Gross, is also located in the building.

The History Place houses an extensive collection of textiles, period clothing and furniture, military memorabilia, glassware and artwork, all representing Carteret County. The library has more than 7,000 books and publications and an extensive picture file documenting the history of Carteret County. The genealogy materials and the Civil War history collections are especially notable. Special exhibits are displayed throughout the year, and year-round programs, seminars and musical events keep Carteret County history fresh.

The History Place is open Tuesday through Saturday 10 AM to 4 PM. The museum is open free of charge to the public, but donations are always welcome. Special guided tours for schools are free, and there is a $2 per person charge for adult guided tours.

Volunteers are needed to assist with a variety of responsibilities. Please see our Volunteer Opportunities chapter for more information.

NEWPORT

Outer Banks Wildlife Shelter (OWLS)
100 Wildlife Way, Newport
(252) 240-1200

This indispensable wildlife hospital is located on N.C. Highway 24, 5 miles west of U.S. Highway 70. Look for a residential building with a pond and bridge in the front yard. OWLS has become a much-depended-on agency along the Crystal Coast for assistance with wounded wildlife. This nonprofit group cares for more than 1,000 injured or sick birds, mammals and reptiles annually through the efforts of volunteers and licensed rehabilitators. Individuals finding injured or sick wildlife are asked to call and then deliver the animal to OWLS. Tours on Tuesdays, Thursdays and Saturdays at 2 PM include a look at the hospital, orphan nurseries and the permanent resident hawks, owls, opossum, vultures and falcons. Groups are asked to call ahead to schedule a tour. The fee is $2.50 per person; children 2 and younger get in free. The facility also offers a nature trail open during daylight hours. Check in at the clinic to register for a self-guided tour of the trail. Wildlife programs, featuring a live bird or mammal, are available to school groups. There is also a gift shop, a wildlife reference library, hiking trails and free teacher materials. The sanctuary operates Monday through Saturday from 9 AM to 5 PM, and hours vary in the off season.

DOWN EAST

Core Sound Waterfowl Museum
1785 Island Rd., Harkers Island
(252) 728-1500

Nestled at the "end of the road" on Harkers Island, the Core Sound Waterfowl Museum was established in 1992 and is funded entirely by its own 2,500+ members. Each December the museum hosts the Core Sound Waterfowl Weekend (see our Annual Events chapter), based at the new Core Sound Waterfowl Museum on Harkers Island. The weekend celebrates the entire community with preview events ranging from wild-game feasts to boat-building demonstrations, community church services and children's activities along with the mid-Atlantic region's finest carvers, artists and writers. This event has grown to encompass the entire island, beginning with the decoy show at the elementary school and now expanding to include food sales and bazaars at churches, fund-raising for Scouts and community groups, and an Island Holiday Decorating Contest on Friday night.

For more than a decade the Waterfowl Museum has been a clearinghouse for heritage, traditions and history of the Down East communities of Carteret County -- a virtual hub for heritage tourism. Local exhibits and programs focusing on local heritage are offered year round, and the museum houses the area's finest collection of carvings and waterfowl art. The museum archives oral histories and artifacts from the Down East communities. Museum staff offers programs for school groups, bus tours, church trips and others. Call to schedule a tour and plan for a real "Down East" experience with local carvers, boat builders, storytellers and musicians.

Construction on the museum's 22,000-square-foot facility began in 1999 and the nearly completed building opened to the public in 2003. Work must still be done on

the interior of the west side of the building, however the majority of the building is in full use. Willow Pond, the 4-acre freshwater centerpiece of the museum's environmental education program, is being restored with financial efforts of Ducks Unlimited, the Conservation Fund, N.C. Wildlife Commission and the N.C. Wildlife Habitat Foundation with assistance from the National Park Service and volunteer labor from across the region.

There is no admission charge to enjoy the Core Sound Waterfowl Museum. Hours are Monday through Saturday 10 AM to 5 PM and Sunday 2 to 5 PM. The Museum is closed Easter Sunday, Thanksgiving Day and for three days at Christmas. Membership categories start at $25 for individuals, and benefits vary based on the amount of contribution.

Tours

Seeing the area is what all visitors want to do. And the area offers a number of ways to do that - by foot, by boat or by bus. Walking tours are offered by a few businesses and are also offered by such groups as the Beaufort Historic Site. The site also offers double-decker bus tours of Historic Beaufort. While the major of tours offered in the area are by water, we start off the list with a business that offers all types of tours.

TourBeaufort.Com
Beaufort
(252) 342-0715

TourBeaufort.Com offers all types of tours for visitors and residents of all ages. The Beaufort Ghost Walk takes guests on a evening stroll through town, with stops at Blackbeard's Hammock House and the Old Burying Ground. There are also ecology and sunset sailing, kayak tours, airplane tours and flying boat tours. Some tours take clients to nearby Carrot Island and others take guests to Cape Lookout Lighthouse. Reservations are needed for the tours, which vary in price and in point of origination.

Diamond City
Big Rock Landing, 405 Evans St., Morehead City
(252) 728-7827, (866) 230-BOAT
www.mysteryboattours.com

Docked on Morehead City's waterfront next to Big Rock Landing, the Diamond City is owned and operated by Mystery Tours and offers tours of the area. While it's available for special charters, wedding cruises, corporate meetings and fun tours, the Diamond City's nighttime offerings have gained it an

The Crystal Coast's most popular attraction is the beach.

photo: George Mitchell

CLOSE UP

Beaufort's Old Burying Ground

As the members of the Beaufort Historical Association are fond of saying, history lives in Beaufort-by-the-Sea. North Carolina's third oldest town has the ability to take high school history lessons and turn them into something as vivid as a fantasy thriller. Beaufort's Old Burying Ground has the tangible keys to the imagination that can keep that history fresh. From the little girl buried in a rum barrel to the soldier buried standing up, the graveyard is alive with stories.

The town of Beaufort was surveyed in 1713 and incorporated in 1723. The Old Burying Ground was deeded to the town in 1731 by Nathaniel Taylor. According to historical records, the first burials on the site were in 1711 and were marked with wood. Only a handful of the wooden markers remain, but the marble and stone grave markers that were later used have survived the passage of time remarkably well. Listed on the National Register of Historic Places, nearly 600 gravestones remain today.

Nestled on Ann Street -- named for England's Queen Anne -- the Old Burying Ground is a feast for the senses. Ancient live oaks offer an eerie shade, cooling the cemetery even on the warmest of days. Sunlight filters through the protective branches, creating a peaceful, almost surreal, atmosphere. A natural sandy path beckons visitors through the iron gates and leads them on a winding trail. The Burying Ground is located close to the Beaufort Historic Site and is guarded by churches on three sides: Ann Street United Methodist Church, circa 1854, First Baptist Church, circa 1854, and Purvis Chapel A.M.E. Zion Church, circa 1820.

The cemetery's layout is haphazard, with graves placed with little rhyme or reason. But that's only one of the things that makes a trip to the site so awe-inspiring. Visitors are invited to meander through the deep recesses of the site to catch a glimpse of all of the stones. Small ones are tucked away in nooks and crannies, while others are large and centrally located, demanding attention. The condition of the stones varies greatly. Some are broken and chipped, while others have begun to lean in the soft North Carolina sand. Others yet are as imposing as they must have been on the day they were erected. Regardless of their condition, all of the markers speak volumes of what life must have been like for this sleepy seaport village in days of yesteryear. Here you can hear the whispered voices of Colonial life, war and the life on the sea.

And amid the whispers and the inscriptions on the stones, stories start to emerge that paint a picture of the past. It's here that visitors will find the grave of Nathan Fuller, an ensign with the Carteret County Militia during the Revolutionary War. Records show that Fuller sailed from Beaufort to Barbados, England and the West Indies, returning home with supplies. According to the newly published book Beaufort's Old Burying Ground, in 1779 Fuller owned "100

Beaufort's Old Burying Ground is a fascinating attraction.

credit: Amanda Dagnino

acres, two Negroes, 15 cattle, half a lot and 920 pound." In 1784, however, he owned 400 acres and in 1785 he was elected to serve in the North Carolina House. Fuller's home still stands today on Front Street, where most people know it as the Cedars Bed and Breakfast.

Interestingly, Fuller's grave isn't far from the resting place of Josiah Fisher Bell, who served as an agent in the Confederate Secret Service. It is said that Bell, whose home still stands on the Beaufort Historic Site, made arrangements for Confederate troops to enter Carteret County, travel to Cape Lookout, and blow up the two lighthouses.

The Old Burying Ground is indeed a place where people have been laid to rest, but it's also a place where history comes to life. Guests can pick up a map at the Beaufort Historic Site and guide themselves through the graveyard. Guided tours of the Old Burying Ground run from June through September on Tuesday, Wednesday and Thursday at 2:30 PM. Tickets are $6 for adults and $4 for children. Group tours are offered year round. It is best to call for availability.

entry in our Nightlife chapter. Friday and Saturday at 9:30 PM it leaves the dock for a special party cruise. Call for the schedule and enjoy this ride. This is Carteret County's only floating nightclub, but that's not all. Onboard the 246-passenger vessel you'll find a captain and crew trained to make your voyage fun and enjoyable. Reservations can be made for a two-and-a-half-hour "ultimate" tour, leaving at noon. You'll see horses, dolphins, historic Beaufort, Fort Macon, the Outer Banks and more. Lunch is included. The Diamond City also offers daily dolphin watches and Sunday brunch with the dolphins. Evening cruisers

From the air, you can see that barrier islands like Bogue Banks are nothing more than skinny strips of sand.

photo: George Mitchell

Phillips Island is in the Newport River just north of the N.C. State Port in Morehead City. From the high-rise bridge passing by the port, it is the most visible of several local islands leased by the National Audubon Society for the protection of nesting colonial waterbirds. A brick chimney on the island is all that remains of a defunct fish-processing facility.

enjoy dinner from 7 to 9 PM, including fine dining and dancing. Then, for the young and young at heart, a party cruise is offered. The vessel has all ABC permits, a state-of-the-art sound system and either a DJ or live entertainment. Folks age 21 and older are invited aboard for $10 per person. Also check out the Diamond City's sister vessels, Mystery and the Lookout Express, which are both docked in Beaufort.

Good Fortune
Beaufort Town Docks, Front St., Beaufort
(252) 247-3860, (252) 241-6866 cell

If you are fascinated by coastal ecology or want to know more about the subject, arrange to sail with Capt. Ron White, a marine biologist and owner of the 42-foot sailboat Good Fortune. This custom-built craft accommodates six and is available for full-day and two-hour sojourns, educational trips, group and corporate charters, and evening sails. Capt. Ron will also take you snorkeling and provide the gear and can provide sailing instruction on the Good Fortune or on two smaller vessels. Sunset excursions conclude with complimentary wine. Whether you want a two-and-a-half hour trip or think you can go all day, trips are priced to accommodate. Trip fees vary depending on length -- a day-long trip is $100 and includes lunch prepared aboard or $90 without lunch; a six-hour trip is $75 without lunch; and a half-day trip (4.5 hours) is $55 a half-day without lunch. Enjoy a wonderful sunset (2.5 hours) sail for $45 with complimentary beverages. Capt. Ron offers a dolphin sail for $40 for adults and $25 for children younger than 12. All trips have a four-passenger minimum, and lunches are $15 per person. All shore trips (4.5, 6 and 8 hour trips) include snorkel gear and kayaks. You'll find Capt. Ron at the docks from April through October. If you want a cruise during the other months of the year, just give him a call.

Island Ferry Adventures
610 Front St., Beaufort
(252) 728-7555

From April through the end of October, the ferry leaves on demand from 9 AM to 5 PM for Shackleford Banks, Carrot Island, Sand Dollar Island and Bird Shoals. Tours and dolphin or horse watches are available during the summer. Two boats run during the summer months to accommodate passengers. This ferry service does not operate in the winter.

Lookout Cruises
Beaufort Waterfront
(252) 504-SAIL

Steve Bishop captains the Lookout, a 45-foot catamaran that can hold 42 passengers. The vessel operates on a regular schedule from May 1 through October 31, and is available year round for special charters such as parties, birthdays and anniversaries. The regularly scheduled early morning, two-hour dolphin watch is very popular with children and their families; the trip is a smooth ride up the Newport River and costs $20 for adults and $15 for kids.

If you want to swim, snorkel and look for shells, try the six-hour trip to Cape Lookout. This trip leaves the dock at noon and offers lunch catered by the Beaufort Grocery Co. (see our Restaurants chapter), snacks, fresh fruit, shell bags and complimentary beverages as part of this cruise. The fee is $55 for adults and $40 for kids younger than 12. A romantic, relaxing, 90-minute sunset cruise is also available for $25, and if you want to take your children on this nighttime trip, they will be charged $15 each. Complimentary beverages are served. It is always best to call ahead to book a cruise on this popular vessel.

Mystery Tours
The Mystery Tour Boat
Front St., Beaufort
(252) 728-7827
Lookout Express
(866) 230-BOAT
www.mysteryboattours.com

Docked in Taylor's Creek, the 65-foot, double-decked Mystery tour boat offers cruises along area waterways. Complete with a covered cabin, snack bar and a resident pirate who delights all the passengers, especially the kids, the boat provides visitors with a view of Beaufort's historic homes, island ponies, salt marshes, bird rookeries, Morehead City State Port, Fort Macon, Shackleford Banks and other islands along the Intracoastal Waterway. Tours last one and a half hours and are conducted daily at 2, 4:30 and 7 PM from April through October. The Mystery also offers half-day fishing trips from 8 AM to noon. The boat is available for special-occasion charters such as birthdays, weddings and anniversaries. Special-interest trips can be arranged for bird watchers, shell collectors and other groups. Educational trips for school groups are also a specialty. The Lookout Express is operated by Mystery Tours. This 73-foot, 149-passenger, 1,800-horsepower ferry boat takes passengers to Cape Lookout and offers sunset cruises and private charters. The Lookout Express operates from April to October, and those interested are invited to call for reservations and prices.

Outer Banks Sail and Kayak
612 Atlantic Beach Cswy., Atlantic Beach
(252) 247-6300
www.obsk.com

Sit back and relax on the Siriuslee as Captain Lee Sutton sails the waters of Taylor's Creek on a half-day trip, introduces you to the thrill of sailing offshore at Cape Lookout on a full-day trip, and cruises the Beaufort waterfront at sunset. During the popular dinner cruise, you'll enjoy the Beaufort waterfront at sunset, followed up with a run over to the Morehead City waterfront for dinner at the Key West Seafood Restaurant. Capt. Sutton and his crew invite you to call play at OBSK -- just call for reservations and then come prepared to have fun.

Ecology Tours

North Carolina Coastal Federation Events and Programs
3609 N.C. Hwy. 24, Ocean
(252) 393-8185

The North Carolina Coastal Federation (NCCF) is the state's largest non-profit organization working to restore and protect the coast. NCCF headquarters is located in Ocean between Morehead City and Swansboro and is open Monday through Friday from 8:30 AM to 5 PM. The headquarters includes NCCF's main offices, information displays, a nature gift shop, the Daland Nature Library, the Weber Seashell Exhibit, the ShoreKeeper Learning Center and a nature trail.

The Nature Library houses more than 800 nature and coastal titles suitable for all ages, as well as videos and periodicals. Area guests are welcome to browse in the library, and NCCF members can check out books for up to three weeks. More than 300 North Carolina and Atlantic coast seashells are on exhibit at the headquarters as part of the Weber Seashell collection. A printed guide is available. The Nature Shop features environmental and coastal books for readers of all ages, as well as coastal puzzles, games and educational gifts.

Visit NCCF's two Nature Trails in Carteret County, which are open to the public every day during daylight hours. The Patsy Pond Nature Trail in the Croatan National Forest is located directly across from NCCF headquarters in Ocean and features a longleaf pine forest with spectacular shallow ponds. Visit a globally endangered maritime forest and NCCF's oyster sanctuary while hiking the Hoop Pole Creek Nature Trail located in Atlantic Beach off N.C. Highway 58 next to the Atlantic Station Shopping Mall. Maps are available at the trailheads.

NCCF'S Coastkeepers conduct educational programs throughout the season, including Beach Walks and fishing trips at Cape Lookout National Seashore. To learn more about any of these programs, call the NCCF at (252) 393-8185, visit www.nccoast.org or go by the NCCF headquarters on Highway 24.

Pelican Guided Ecology Tours
Morehead City Waterfront, Morehead City
(252) 504-2447

If you really want to get to know the Crystal Coast, you must explore it from the water with a knowledgeable guide. And Pelican Guided Ecology Tours is just the one to call. The Pelican is captained by Paul Dunn, an easy-going man with more than 25 years experience fishing and boating in the area waters. Once aboard the 23-foot boat, you will be off for a memorable journey -- just be ready to get some hands-on experience! This is a tour that will have you in and out of the boat using seines, dip nets and throw nets to catch and study live specimens. You'll stop on islands and beaches to look for seashells, sand dollars, driftwood and more. Capt. Paul will show you how to use a clam rake and, hopefully, you'll end up with some bounty for your supper. Along the way, expect to see bottle-nosed dolphin, sea turtles, nesting osprey, waterfowl of all types, the ponies of Carrot Island and Shackleford Banks as well as the Cape Lookout Lighthouse and more. Capt. Dunn enjoys many repeat customers, and they continue to recommend Pelican Guided Ecology Tours to others. The Pelican can accommodate up to six individuals, and each trip is planned to meet your individual interests. Capt. Paul's fee is $300 for up to six people. The typical trip is six hours of easy going, unrushed fun and education. This is a great way to take a close look at the sounds, marshes, barrier islands and beaches that are only accessible by boat. Trips are by reservation only.

State and National Parks

The Crystal Coast is fortunate to have national, state and local parks scattered from one border to the other. Here, we offer a look at national and state parks. Local parks are described in our Sports, Fitness and Parks chapter. Our coastal parks will fascinate you with historic interest and natural beauty, so get out there and enjoy them.

Fort Macon State Park
N.C. Hwy. 58 N, Atlantic Beach
(252) 726-3775

Fort Macon State Park highlights Fort Macon, one of the most complete forts of the Civil War era in the United States. It is totally intact, covering about five acres on the tip of Bogue Banks, where it was located to protect the channel and Beaufort Harbor from attacks by sea.

"Structurally, it is in great shape," says Park Superintendent Jody Merritt. "We finished in 2003 a four-year restoration and renovation. It is first rate compared to any fort in the nation."

Fort Macon, once an active military stronghold, is now a state park, and a very popular one at that.

Photo: George Mitchell

The park also offers Fort Macon Beach and is one of the most visited state parks in North Carolina. With an estimated 1.3 million people a year, it is by far the most visited site of any attraction on the Crystal Coast.

Walking on the wide path to the fort, a visitor comes to the huge wall and moat, 24 feet deep, that was intended to be flooded with seawater as another obstacle to attackers. Crossing the moat bridge, a visitor is drawn back into the reality of what life was like in such forts. Huge cannon emplacements still surmount the ramparts, and two mortars stand out amid the interior, which also vaulted ceiling casemate rooms where the garrison lived. Re-enactments are held in April, July and September.

The critical defense location had been considered before, with Fort Dobbs, named for Governor Arthur Dobbs, begun in 1756 but never completed. In 1808 and 1809 Fort Hampton, a small masonry fort, was built to guard the inlet. Hampton was abandoned shortly after the War of 1812 and by 1825 had been swept into the inlet.

Fort Macon was designed by Brig. Gen. Simon Bernard and built by the U.S. Army Corps of Engineers between 1826 and 1834 at a cost of $463,790. The fort was named for Nathaniel Macon, who was speaker of the House of Representatives and a U.S. Senator from North Carolina. The five-sided structure was constructed of brick and stone with outer walls 4.5 feet thick. The fort was deactivated after 1877 and then regarrisoned by state troops in 1898 for the Spanish-American War. It was abandoned again in 1903, was not used in World War I and was offered for sale in 1923. An Act of Congress in 1924 gave the fort and the surrounding land to the state of North Carolina to be used as a public park. The park, which is more than 400 acres, opened in 1936 and was North Carolina's first functioning state park.

At the outbreak of World War II, the Army leased the park from the state and, once again, manned the fort to protect a number of important nearby facilities. In 1946, the fort was returned to the state, and the park reopened the following year.

Today, Fort Macon State Park offers the best of two worlds -- beautiful, easily accessible beaches for recreation and a historic fort for exploration. Visitors enjoy the sandy beaches, a seaside bathhouse and restrooms, a refreshment stand, designated fishing and swimming areas and picnic facilities with outdoor grills. The park is full of wildlife, including herons, egrets, pelicans, warblers, sparrows and other animals.

The fort itself is a wonderful place to explore with a self-guided tour map or with a tour guide. Restored rooms and a bookstore offer exhibits to acquaint you with the fort and its history. The fort and museum are open daily year round. Fort tours are guided through late fall. Reenactments of fort activities are scheduled periodically from spring to fall. Talks on the Civil War and natural history are conducted year round. The fort is open daily from 9 AM to 5:30 PM. Admission is free.

Theodore Roosevelt Natural Area
MM 7, Roosevelt Dr., Pine Knoll Shores
(252) 726-3775

This little gem of woods surrounds the North Carolina Aquarium on Roosevelt Drive in Pine Knoll Shores, and borders N.C. Highway 58 as it winds through Bogue Banks. Maintained by the aquarium staff and North Carolina State Parks, the 300 acres have extensive maritime forests and freshwater ponds. The land was donated to the state by the family of President Theodore Roosevelt. The forest attracts naturalists, birders and photographers. There are two trails through the natural area: the Alice G. Hoffman Trail, accessed through the aquarium, and the Theodore Roosevelt Trail, beginning outside the aquarium at the southern end of the parking area.

The soundside trails are good places to see land birds. The saltmarsh overlook areas on the aquarium's Salt Marsh Safari boardwalk leading to the Alice G. Hoffman Trail can be good areas for wading birds and migratory waterfowl sightings, depending on the time of year; however, marshes along this section of Bogue Banks are not extensive, so shore and waterbird sightings can be spotty.

Rachel Carson Component of the North Carolina National Estuarine Research Reserve
135 Duke Marine Lab Rd., Beaufort
(252) 728-2170

Just across Taylor's Creek from the Beaufort waterfront is a series of islands that make up the Rachel Carson Component of the North Carolina National Estuarine Research Reserve. Most locals refer to the entire chain of islands as Bird Shoal or Carrot Island, the names the islands were known by before the state acquired the land.

These islands are roughly 3.5 miles long and have an interesting history. Through the years, the land was privately owned by individuals or groups. In 1977, when the owner of 178.5 acres announced plans to divide the land and sell it in tracts, locals formed The Beaufort Land Conservancy Council and began collecting money and support for preserving the island chain. They sought the aid of the Nature Conservancy, a national nonprofit organization dedicated to the protection of natural areas, and together with the Duke University Marine Laboratory, the groups raised $250,000 from individuals and businesses for the purchase of the islands. Now the state of North Carolina manages the island reserve.

In the late 1960s Congress recognized the need to protect coastal resources from pollution and the pressures of development. In particular danger were the nation's estuaries, those valuable, fragile areas where rivers meet the sea. So the National Estuarine Research Reserve was established. Now administered by the North Carolina Division of Coastal Management, the reserves are sites for walking, exploring and learning about the natural and human processes that affect the coast.

Estuaries are composed of the bays, sounds, inlets and sloughs along the coast and are among the most biologically productive systems on earth. More than two-thirds of the fish and shellfish commercially harvested in coastal waters spend part or all of their lives in estuaries. The economy of many coastal areas depends heavily on the health of these environments. North Carolina is fortunate to have four protected sites: Zeke's Island, Currituck Banks, Masonboro Island and the Rachel Carson site. Other sites in the N.C. Coastal Reserve Program are Kitty Hawk Woods, Emily and Richardson Preyer Buckridge, Buxton Woods, Permuda Island, Bald Head Woods and Bird Island.

The Beaufort site is named in honor of the famed scientist and author Rachel Carson, who conducted research on the islands in the late 1930s and, through her research and writing, made people aware of the importance of coastal ecosystems. The reserve is an incomparably beautiful, unspoiled stretch of salt marshes, tidal flats, eelgrass beds, sand flats and artificially created dredge-spoil islands.

Feral horses live on the reserve. They are descended from domesticated horses taken to the islands to graze. Today they roam the sandy expanse, living in small bands called harems, each consisting of one stallion, several mares and the year's foals. Bachelor males roam the island alone or in pairs. These are either older stallions who have lost their harem to a younger, stronger male or young stallions who have not yet challenged the dominant males.

The Rachel Carson site is a favorite spot for beach combing, swimming, sunbathing and clamming, but camping is not allowed and dogs are required by the county to be on a leash. Visitors are encouraged to leave everything - the animals, plants and research equipment - undisturbed. Education coordinators and specially trained volunteers conduct tours of the reserve during the warm months and assorted program tours are offered free to the public each Tuesday through Thursday from June 1 through September 2. Tours leave by boat from the Pivers Island location. Call for tour days and times and for making a reservation. School groups are also welcome to arrange for special tours throughout the year.

A self-guided trail brochure is available at the Reserve Education office, the N.C. Maritime Museum, or ferry service offices. Kayaks are available for rent along the Beaufort waterfront, and many people make a day of paddling around the island. An information sign about the reserve is displayed on Front Street in Beaufort across from the Inlet Inn.

Hammocks Beach State Park
1572 Hammocks Beach Rd., Swansboro
(910) 326-4881

Venture to Hammocks Beach State Park on Bear Island and be rewarded with one of the most beautiful and unspoiled beaches in the area. The park consists of a barrier island off the southernmost point of Bogue Banks and a small area off N.C. 24 just south of the residential area of Swansboro, where the visitors center and ferry landing are located. Watch for state directional signs. The island is accessible only by boat or ferry (see our Getting Here, Getting Around chapter), and camping is allowed (see our Camping chapter). There is a small fee for the ferry to Bear Island, which operates from April through October. Contact the visitors center for the ferry schedule and rates. Ranger programs are conducted for visitors.

Loggerhead turtles come ashore at Bear Island at night during nesting season to make nests above the tide line. Explorers can observe marine life in tidal creeks and mudflats.

Outdoor showers, restrooms and drinking water are available to visitors. Go prepared to shade yourself and take along refreshments. It is a half-mile walk from the ferry landing to the ocean beach. Pack light with day packs and beach supplies, since wagons and carts are not allowed on the ferry boats. Whether you spend an hour or the whole day, the trip is always worthwhile.

Cape Lookout National Seashore Headquarters, 131 Charles St., Harkers Island (252) 728-2250

Cape Lookout National Seashore is one of America's few remaining undeveloped coastal barrier island systems. It encompasses about 28,500 acres of islands, most of which run roughly parallel to the eastern shores of Carteret County (see our Down East map in the front of this book). The system is bounded on the north by Ocracoke Inlet and on the south by Beaufort Inlet. Four islands make up the 56-mile seashore: North Core Banks, also known as Portsmouth Island; Middle Core Banks, South Core Banks (including Cape Lookout); and Shackleford Banks. While each of the islands is distinctive in history and characteristics, all four are remote and virtually unspoiled by the hands of man. Congress authorized Cape Lookout National Seashore to be included in the National Park System in 1966. The National Park Service (NPS) maintains authority over the seashore. Stopping first at Park Headquarters on Harkers Island is a good idea before you take off for the islands. The attractive visitor center, open seven days a week from 9 AM to 5 PM except for December 25th and January 1st, provides a wealth of information to visitors. Of particular interest is the video that gives information about barrier islands and their special characteristics. Park rangers and volunteers can answer questions about transportation (only by boat), camping, kayaking and more.

You cannot access the seashore from the Park Service Headquarters because the NPS does not provide a ferry service. However, several private ferries operate from Harkers Island, Beaufort, Morehead City, Davis, Atlantic and Ocracoke. For some of the islands' sites, limited ground transportation can be arranged with the ferry operator prior to departure, as can accommodations. For more information, see the Ferries section of our Getting Here, Getting Around chapter and our Accommodations chapter.

Bear in mind when planning a visit to any of the islands, that they really are undeveloped. No amenities, drinking water, fast-food concessions, or places to buy beach umbrellas or suntan lotion are available. Whatever you need for your trip, you must bring with you; and when you leave, you must take everything out with you. See our chapter on Camping for more details.

The seashore's pristine ocean beaches are an incomparable escape for surfcasters, sunbathers, surfers, snorkelers and shell collectors. Other recreational pursuits in the park include picnicking, primitive camping, migratory waterfowl watching and hunting. The area is noted for its natural resources. Birds and animals are the only permanent residents. The endangered loggerhead sea turtles nest on the beaches each summer and seldom nest any farther north. The park is an internationally recognized bird habitat area. Raccoons, rabbits, nutria, a variety of insects, snakes and lizards are also among the park's permanent residents. Ghost crabs, mole crabs and coquina clams populate the beaches.

The Cape Lookout Lighthouse, two miles from the southern tip of South Core Banks, is still an active aid to navigation. The first lighthouse was built on Core Banks in 1811-12 and was painted with red and white stripes. But the current lighthouse, completed in 1859, wears a distinctive black and white diamond pattern.

Visitors are welcome in the restored lighthouse keepers' quarters, which houses a small natural history collection, sales

Walking on or fishing from a pier is a great way to spend an afternoon or evening.

photo: George Mitchell

area that carries books, souvenirs and water. Orientation and information are also provided. Other associated structures are also preserved near the lighthouse where there are shelters for picnicking, a swimming beach and a boardwalk that leads from the lighthouse area, over the dunes, to the ocean beach. The lighthouse itself accepts visitors only four times a year on special anniversaries. Anyone really wishing to see the coast from up top should be sure to check for climb and reservation dates on the seashore's website at www.nps.gov/calo. Climbing the tower is by reservation only.

At the northernmost end of Core Banks at Ocracoke Inlet is Portsmouth Village. The village was established in 1753 to serve as the main port of entry to several coastal communities. Named for Portsmouth, England, the port village was busy with "lightering" incoming vessels, an unloading and reloading process that allowed vessels to pass through the shallow Ocracoke Inlet. During its heyday in the 1860s, the village had a population of 600. After Hatteras Inlet opened, the village became less important in its port services. From 1894 to 1934, the population of Portsmouth centered around the lifesaving station. After a severe hurricane in 1933, the village population declined, and by the early 1970s, no year-round residents remained.

Today, Portsmouth village looks much like it did in the early 1900s, although it took quite a blow from Hurricane Isabel in 2003. The remaining homes, cemeteries, church and pathways are still used by former residents and their descendants. A reunion occurs every other year in Portsmouth Village. Structures that are not under historic leasing are maintained by the Park Service. Portsmouth Village was placed on the National Register of Historic Places in 1979.

Looking east from Fort Macon, Shackleford Banks is the island across Beaufort Inlet. It stretches nine miles east to Cape Lookout (South Core Banks) and is bordered by the Atlantic Ocean on the south and Back Sound on the north. The island's sound side has long been a favorite weekend destination for residents escaping the peopled mainland beaches. The rock jetty is a favorite spot for anglers. Shackleford Banks officially became part of Cape Lookout National Seashore on the first day of 1986. Until then, the island was dotted with cabins or camps that former banks' residents and their descendants used as getaway shelters. The acquisition of Shackleford Banks meant removing the structures and the livestock that had been left to roam the island. Before 1986, the island was home to hardy herds of wild cattle, sheep, goats, pigs and horses. Only the horses remain today. These famous horses have roamed free for centuries. The exact route of the ancestors of these small, hardy horses to this barrier island is unknown, but genetic research shows evidence of Spanish ancestry in the herd. More than 100 horses roam the island, having divided themselves into harems (one or sometimes two stallions, some unrelated mares, and their foals) and bachelor bands (males without harems). These groups of horses find their own food on the island; they are sometimes found in the maritime forest, but mostly graze in the marshes, swales and dunes. Fresh water is available in numerous pools and digs along the length of the island. The horses are managed in as much of a hands-off manner as possible, though roundups still occur in order to remove some horses for adoption to the public or introduction into other wild herds. The horses are co-managed by the National Park Service and the Foundation for Shackleford Horses, Inc., an organization formed to protect them on the island. Visitors should remember that they are wild animals and, for your safety and their well-being, the horses should not be approached.

Shackleford Banks was named for John Shackleford, who purchased the land (which became the island) in 1723. Permanent residents once populated communities on Shackleford. New England whaling vessels visited the area as early as 1726. By 1880, six crews of 18 men from Diamond City were whaling off the banks' shores. The whalers were a hardy people and included the Davis, Moore, Guthrie, Royal and Rose families -- names still common in Carteret County. Whaling was the backbone industry of this island. Local merchants sold the oil as lamp and lubricating oil or used it to make soap. Whale bone was valuable in making corset stays, ribs for umbrellas and other items. They sold the rest of the whale to be used as fertilizer.

The largest community on Shackleford was Diamond City, at the east end of the island. By 1897, about 500 people populated this community, which included church buildings, stores and a school. The population grew in the 1850s because of a boom in the whaling industry.

East of Diamond City, across what is now Barden's Inlet, was the U.S. Lighthouse Service Station. West of Diamond City was Bell's Island, a settlement known for bountiful persimmon trees. The western part of Shackleford Banks was known as Wade's Shore. Two hurricanes that closely followed each other in 1896 and 1899 convinced most island inhabitants to move to the mainland. Many moved their homes by boat to Harkers Island or to the Promised Land section of Morehead City. Others resettled in the Bogue Banks community of Salter Path.

Cedar Island National Wildlife Refuge
879 Lola Rd., Cedar Island
(252) 225-2511

This 14,480-acre wildlife refuge on the southern end of Cedar Island is administered by Mattamuskeet National Wildlife Refuge, (252) 926-4021, and provides areas for hiking, bird-watching, launching boats, picnicking and duck hunting. There is a refuge employee on duty, and, while ranger services are not available, the employee can answer questions about the refuge from the Cedar Island number.

Waterfowl abundant during the year are mallards, black ducks, redheads, pintails and green-winged teals. Other wildlife at home in the refuge are raccoons, whitetail deer, black bears, woodpeckers and river otters. In the spring and fall, this is a delightful picnicking and bird-watching destination. The Cedar Island Wildlife Refuge was formed in 1964 under the Migratory Bird Act to provide a sanctuary for migratory birds.

The access is well-marked on Cedar Island. Turn on Lola Road and follow it to the refuge office. One boat ramp is at the end of Lola Road and another is at the base of the Monroe Gaskill Memorial high-rise bridge.

Fort Macon's renovations and the N.C. Aquarium's $3.4 million make-over are complete. Both bring big changes that make these attractions even better tourist destinations.

Croatan National Forest
141 E. Fisher Ave., New Bern
(252) 638-5628

Located between New Bern and Emerald Isle, the Croatan National Forest is made up of 161,000 acres and features coastal and inland swamp habitats. The Croatan Forest is home to the largest collection of carnivorous plants in any National Forest and it is near the northern range limit of the American alligator. It also has an amazing collection of bugs. Much of the forest is characterized as swampy with thick underbrush. It is perhaps not a forest suited for everyone, but it is very attractive to area fishermen and hunters, and is popular for its hiking trails, boat launches, campgrounds and day-use areas.

The forest actually spreads in a triangle between Morehead City, Cape Carteret and New Bern. Forest headquarters are on Fisher Avenue, approximately 9 miles east of New Bern off U.S. Highway 70. Well-placed road signs make the office easy to find. Because the Croatan is so expansive and undeveloped, it is best to pick up a forest map from the headquarters if you plan to explore extensively. For short day trips or hiking excursions, site brochures are sufficient.

The name Croatan comes from the Algonquian Indians' name for "Council Town," which was once located in the area. Because of the forest's coastal location, you'll find many unusual features here. Some of the components of the ecosystem are pocosin, longleaf and loblolly pine, bottomland and upland hardwoods.

Sprinkled throughout the Croatan are 40 miles of streams and 4,300 acres of wild lakes, some fairly large, such as Great Lake, Catfish Lake and Long Lake. Miles of unpaved roads lace through the woodland, providing easy, if at times roundabout, access to its wilderness.

The forest offers excellent hiking, swimming, boating, camping, picnicking, hunting and fresh- and saltwater fishing. Boat access

The surf is fun for all ages.

photo: George Mitchell

is provided at several locations. Rangers advise that lake fishing is generally poor because of the acidity of the water. All fishing, hunting and trapping activities are regulated by the N.C. Wildlife Resources Commission. A kids' fishing day is generally held in July and specific information is available by calling the Ranger Station. The forest has several camping sites (see our Camping chapter) that are open throughout the year. Primitive camping is permitted all year, and sites are plentiful. Some areas of the forest close seasonally, and fees can vary, so call headquarters for current rates and availability.

As with all national forests, the Croatan's natural resources are actively managed to provide goods and services for the public. Pine timber is harvested and replanted each year, and wildlife habitat for a wide range of animals is maintained on thousands of acres. Endangered and sensitive animal and plant species are protected. The red-cockaded woodpecker is among the endangered animals that find safety here. More common animals are the southern bald eagle, alligators, squirrels, otters, white-tailed deer, black bears, snakes and wild turkeys.

The area is known for its beautiful wildflowers, including five types of insectivorous plants, a combination rarely seen elsewhere. Among the insectivorous plants are pitcher plants, round-leaved sundew, butterworts, Venus's-flytraps and bladderworts, all of which die if removed from their natural habitat; it is against the law to disturb them. Pamphlets about the wildflowers and insect-eating plants are available at the forest headquarters.

Summer fires, whether spontaneous in nature or controlled for forest nurturing, are common and as a result, few public education programs are offered during typical tourist season. The insect-eating plants that proliferate in pocosin habitats are actually fire dependent, another reason not to try to take them home. After a good burning, they're well-nurtured and hungry for bugs. Nature is stranger than fiction.

The forest features several trails ranging in length from 1.4 miles to 20 miles. Call the office for trail maps, canoe rental locations and other information.

KIDSTUFF

Beaches, sand and surf are definitely the main attractions of the Crystal Coast for children, however some parents find that their children seek activities beyond the wind and waves. Not to worry - Carteret County is home to a wide variety of options for families.

Set out for fun at one of the amusement areas, learn about colonial times, zip down a water slide, take the helm of a bumper boat, putt a round of mini-golf, take a spin in a go-cart or attend a camp.

Carteret County has some of the best summer camps around. If you're interested in how the seashore environment works or want to learn how to sail a boat, make sure you check out the North Carolina Maritime Museum's Summer Science School or Junior Sailing Program. The courses are short, so they won't take up your whole vacation.

Many of the sites for adventures that follow are also described in other chapters and, for further details, we have referred you to them. And, as always, if you seek other ideas, look in other areas of this book or just ask an Insider kid.

Amusements

Carteret Lanes
U.S. Hwy. 70 W., Morehead City
(252) 247-4481

Everyone in the family can enjoy knocking down a few pins at Carteret Lanes. It's bowling in a family atmosphere with an arcade and snack bar available. Of course, leagues and competitions bring out the matching shirts, but the unpolished amateurs also have lots of fun. Carteret Lanes is open year round and has gutter guards that make even the youngest members of the family all-star bowlers. Or the video games and snacks can liven up things for the kids while the grownups bowl daily from 9 AM to 10 PM. It is best to call ahead to make sure lanes are available.

Golfin' Dolphin
N.C. Hwy. 24, Cape Carteret
(252) 393-8131

This expansive family entertainment complex, off N.C. 24 in Cape Carteret, is where athletes of all ages and stages can hone their competitive edge. The complex includes a 50-tee driving range, baseball and softball batting cages and an 18-hole miniature golf course. While the bigger kids are sharpening their skills, the little ones enjoy the bumper boats with water spray attachments and go-carts. The Golfin' Dolphin also has a snack bar. A party room is available for private birthday parties and celebrations. The complex is open from March through Labor Day daily from 9 AM until 11 PM, and the complex does stay open part of the off-season so call for hours.

Playland & Lighthouse Golf
MM 20.5, 204 Islander Dr., Emerald Isle
(252) 354-6616

Playland in Emerald Isle has eight super-fast water slides and all sorts of rides for toddlers and youngsters, including bumper cars, bumper boats and slick and grand prix tracks. Adjoining Playland is the Water Boggan, (252) 354-2609, and Lighthouse Golf, (252) 354-2811, an 18-hole miniature golf course. Playland also has a snack bar and a picnic area to keep the kids completely happy and give the adults a break. Playland is open daily during the summer months. Admission to the park is free, but you must purchase tickets for each ride.

Professor Hacker's Lost Treasure Golf and Raceway
MM 10.5, N.C. Hwy. 58, Salter Path
(252) 247-3024

How about a ride on a mining train through caves, ancient ruins and under waterfalls to begin the adventure? The family will enjoy an active day at this Salter Path park. You'll love the go-cart ride over bridges and banked curves. You can splash in bumper boats, play games in a high-tech arcade and putt 18 fabulous holes of miniature golf. Ice cream may be purchased. A picnic area can be used for parties, and group rates are offered. Tickets for each activity are sold separately.

Sportsworld
U.S. Hwy. 70 W., Morehead City
(252) 247-4444

Skating is what it is all about at Sportsworld. Whether on regular roller skates or on inline skates this is a popular place for the younger-than-driving-age set. Sportsworld is well-maintained and super-vised with all the right music and activity changes on the skating floor. A snack bar with arcade games is a comfortable vantage for viewing the skating without actually having to relearn the sport. There are also batting cages on site. Sportsworld is open year round, and offers after-school programs. Skating sessions are scheduled throughout the day and cost range from $3 to $5.50. Skate rental is $1 for regular, $2.50 for inline skates. Call for hours and activities.

Go Fishing

North Carolina Seafood Festival All Kids' Pier Fishing Classic
(252) 726-NCSF (6273)
www.ncseafoodfestival.org

During the first weekend in October, this tournament offers young anglers a chance to fish in Atlantic Beach as part of the N.C. Seafood Festival. Prizes are awarded for the largest of any kind of fish caught, and each angler goes home with a prize.

Hot To Shop

A Sea Of Learning/Teacher's Pet
2410 Arendell St., Morehead City
(252) 240-2732

This is the greatest place for games and videos and for things to build, cuddle, paint, put together, discover and, OK, learn. Age-appropriate educational toys run the gamut here, from silly to serious. It's a delightful place to take a kid or to shop for a birthday present surprise. The shop also houses edu-cational materials for teachers and conducts workshops in the use of materials. That's

because it's the enterprise of a couple of former teachers.

Lots To Learn

Junior Sailing Program
N.C. Maritime Museum, 315 Front St., Beau-fort
(252) 728-7317
www.ncmm-friends.org

The Junior Sailing Program is a basic and intermediate sailing program open to children ages 8 and older each summer. The program uses the fun of sailing and the competition of racing to teach rigging, sailing, seamanship, navigational skills and maritime traditions and history to young sailors. Instructors are certi-fied by the U.S. Sailing Association as Small Boat Sailing Instructors and are certified by the American Red Cross in First Aid and CPR. These programs fill quickly, and students are accepted on a first-come, first-served basis. Call the N.C. Maritime Museum for class schedules and fee information.

i

Take a field guide to seashells on your beach trips so you can answer "What's this?" each time the kids find a shell. The Discovery Cart of common beach finds at the N.C. Maritime Museum will remind them of all they've learned.

Kids love walking along the local harbor-fronts and looking at the boats.

photo: George Mitchell

Library Storytime
Carteret County Public Libraries
(252) 728-2050

Summertime means storytime at the Carteret County Public Libraries. At the Beaufort branch, tots 18 months to 3 years old can enjoy storytelling at 10 AM on Fridays; preschoolers 3 to 5 can settle into some great storytelling on Wednesdays at 10 AM; and Rambling Around The World is offered to those 6 and older Thursdays at 4 PM

In the summer, the county libraries offer special programs for young people. Contact the individual libraries for details:

Beaufort -- (252) 728-2050

Bogue Banks -- (252) 247-4660

Western Carteret -- (252) 393-6500

Newport -- (252) 223-5108

Storytime is often offered in the children's section at the Webb Memorial Library, 812 Evans Street in Morehead City, although it isn't affiliated with the county library system. Groups should call ahead to arrange for storytime sessions. Call (252) 726-3012 for details.

Summer Science School for Children
N.C. Maritime Museum, 315 Front St., Beaufort
(252) 728-7317
www.ncmm-friends.org

The Summer Science School for Children is a program offered to entering 1st through 10th graders in a variety of subjects. Hosted by the North Carolina Maritime Museum (see our Attractions chapter), the school offers classes each week from mid-June to early August. Small class size of 8 to 12 students, hands-on activities and field trips combine to make this program a unique educational experience. Call the museum for schedules, applications and fees.

N.C. Aquarium at Pine Knoll Shores
MM 7, N.C. Hwy. 58, Pine Knoll Shores
(252) 247-4004
www.ncaquariums.com

The North Carolina Aquarium at Pine Knoll Shores recently reopened after a $25 million expansion, and educators have designed a number of fun and innovative programs and special activities just for youngsters. The hour-long "Sea Squirts"

CLOSE UP

The Feral Horses of Carrot Island

One of those rare gifts of history and circumstance that Beaufort takes great pride in is the feral horses that roam over the inside barrier islands now known as the Rachel Carson Estuarine Reserve. You can see these "ponies" that have never seen a saddle most any day while riding or walking down Front Street along the Beaufort waterfront. They range over the small islands across Taylor's Creek, 100 to 200 yards away from the bustling waterfront.

The horses that now call the Reserve home are descended from domesticated horses taken to the islands to graze years and years ago. Today they roam the sandy expanse, living in small bands called harems. Each harem consists of one stallion, several mares and the year's foals. Bachelor males roam the island alone or in pairs. These bachelors are either older stallions who have lost their harem to younger, stronger males or stallions who have not yet challenged the dominant males.

For a time in recent years there was a battle over removing the Beaufort horses, with claims made by some officials that they were an "exotic" species and would ruin the islands. The efforts of Beaufort and area legislators won out, and now the horses are protected. For decades, people in Beaufort have kept a watchful eye on them, even taking forage over to the islands in bitter winters.

The islands that make up what is now the reserve are Town Marsh, Bird Shoal, Carrot Island and Horse Island, though folks debate where one leaves off and another begins, depending on the tides. But the tides do not bother the horses, which now number about 40; they will simply swim from one to another when necessary.

The horses are compact and naturally small, usually less than 14 hands high, and their rugged appearance is a result of living in the wild. The people who work for the estuarine reserve do not feed the ponies because to do so would affect their status as wild animals. The horses must find food and water on their own. Food comes in the form of various salt-marsh grasses that grow on the tidal flats and low dunes. Drinking water comes from temporary freshwater pools. When they have to, the horses sniff out rainwater that's trapped beneath the soil and use their hooves to dig down until they reach the fresh water.

The mainland is not the only vantage point from which to enjoy the feral horses. The best opportunity to come upon one or more of these animals is on the reserve itself. Fortunately for us, quick trips to the Rachel Carson site are available from several ferry services in Beaufort. While walking about these pristine islands that seem untouched by civilization, you may look up to see a few ponies watching you from just a few yards away, wondering what you are doing there.

For more about the Rachel Carson Component of the North Carolina Estuarine Research Reserve and nature walks of the islands, see our Attractions chapter.

program introduces kids to marine life and is offered most months of the year. The classes feature live animals, crafts, storytelling and videos. Older kids can enjoy the similar "Sea Wizards" during the warm months. For children in grades 2 to 7, the Aquarium also offers week-long summer day camps that are filled with hands-on, feet-wet, field-trip experiences that get youngsters out and about in sounds and marshes. A summer surfing camp has been designed for beginning surfers in grades 8 and 9. Aquarium programs vary with the seasons, and special activity programs require advance registration and fees. To find out what's going on, call the aquarium or see the website for the complete calendar.

Other Good Stuff

Boys & Girls Club of Coastal Carolina, Inc.
601 Mulberry St., Beaufort
(252) 504-2465
3300 Bridges St., Morehead City
(252) 222-3007

The Boys & Girls Club operates a club in Beaufort and a club in Morehead City. The Beaufort Club was the first in the county, opening in 1997 in the former Queen Street School. That facility has seen some renovation since that time, and the membership has grown. It started a trend of community involvement that spread to Morehead City. At the club students spend afternoon hours with directed programs of sports and interesting, interactive, positive goings-on. There is also a homework time. Club activities for kids from ages 6 to 18 are available on weekdays from 3 to 7 PM. Summer and holidays bring about expanded hours.

Morehead City Parks and Recreation
1600 Fisher St., Morehead City
(252) 726-5083

This department offers a lot of sports programs for children designed to not only teach them the fundamentals of the games but also the value of team participation and sportsmanship. Team sports include T-ball, basketball, girls softball and coach-pitch baseball. In addition to sports, the department hosts a number of fun activities for children and adults. Many programs are free, but those with fees are reasonable and well-worth the cost for the enrichment they provide. Both city residents and nonresidents are welcome to participate in the department's programs. The department also sponsors the North Carolina Seafood Festival 8K Twin Bridges Road Race that takes place the first weekend of October in conjunction with the Seafood Festival.

Shellby's Kids Club
Beach Vacation Properties,
1904 E. Fort Macon Rd.,
Atlantic Beach
(252) 247-2636, (800) 334-2667
www.beachvacationproperties.com

Kids ages 5 to 12 who vacation at A Place At The Beach, Sea Spray or Sands Villa Resort in Atlantic Beach and rent through Beach Vacation Properties can register at a special kids' desk while their parents check in at the regular desk. Kids get an identification wristband so they won't get lost, a free gift and access to many fun activities of the kids' club. Between mid-June and mid-August, club activities are scheduled Monday through

Canoeing is a great way to explore the area waterways.

photo: George Mitchell

For a great daytrip from the Crystal Coast, take the kids to New Bern's Tryon Palace to learn about history.

courtesy of Tryon Palace Historical Sites & Gardens

Friday at the resort pool and water slide, on the beach or on field trips and boat rides to exciting places along the coast. Everyday resort activities include fun stuff like pool games, tie dyeing, arts and crafts, kite flying, treasure hunts and lots of things parents don't want to do.

Outside Fun

Diamond City Cruises
Big Rock Landing, 405 Evans St., Morehead City
(252) 728-7827, (866) 230-BOAT
www.mysteryboattours.com

What kid wouldn't want to hunt treasure on the coast. Diamond City Cruises offers a Treasure Hunt for children, complete with an authentic pirate. Children and their families are taken to an island and given maps. Then the hunt begins with the pirate at the lead. Everyone finds a treasure chest filled with goods. After the hunt, you can enjoy the beach for about an hour before heading back to port. Treasure hunters are urged to take their own picnics and swimsuits and beach gear.

Kites Unlimited
Atlantic Station Shopping Center, MM 3, N.C. Hwy. 58, Atlantic Beach
(252) 247-7011

Kites Unlimited sponsors kite-flying events at Fort Macon State Park, and everyone is invited to join. Sundays at 10 AM bring a kite because you'll want to try the things you see after the demonstrations. For truly competitive kite fliers, the Carolina Kite Fest at A Place at the Beach Resort in October is also sponsored by Kites Unlimited (see our Annual Events chapter).

Sea Of Dreams
Shevans Park, 16th and Evans Sts., Morehead City
(252) 726-5083

This imaginative public playground, designed with input from the kids who are now enjoying it, was constructed by nearly 200 residents of Carteret County in May 1997. Walk through the entry towers and encounter a maze that sends kids ages 3 and younger in one direction and the older ones in another. Inside, there are slides, swings, ladders, spring bridges, a balance beam, a boat, a race car and so much more that it keeps the parking area full every day. Kids younger than 10 must have an adult with them. Groups of 10 kids or more may reserve time to use the playground.

Camps

The Crystal Coast serves as the location for a variety of camps, from day camps to month-long summer camps to family camps available for group use year round. And nearby, at the mouth of the Neuse River, are some of the most prestigious summer camps in the eastern United States for youth campers. Costs vary depending on the summer camp programs chosen. Call for program descriptions and prices.

Camp Albemarle
156 Albemarle Dr., Newport
(252) 726-4848

This Presbyterian camp in a beautiful setting on Bogue Sound operates year round and is open to the public. Summer camp sessions are divided into age groups, with weeks dedicated to campers from 2nd through 12th grades. There is also a two-night, three-day mini camp for 1st through 4th graders. Activities include swimming in the pool and sound, basketball, sailing and canoeing, along with other traditional camp activities.

Camp Sea Gull and Camp Seafarer
Sea Gull, 218 Sea Gull Landing, Arapahoe
(252) 249-1111
Seafarer, 2744 Seafarer Rd., Arapahoe
(252) 249-1212

Camp Sea Gull for boys and Camp Seafarer for girls are on the Neuse River in Arapahoe, about 27 miles north of Morehead City and about 25 miles east of New Bern by car. The camps share an outpost and docks on the Morehead City waterfront. Camp Seafarer for girls opened in 1961, and Camp Sea Gull for boys has been in operation since 1948. Both are owned and operated by the Capital Area YMCA.

Sea Gull and Seafarer feature a nationally recognized seamanship program, including sailing, watersports and ocean excursions from the Morehead City waterfront outpost. Seafarer offers horsemanship, and both camps offer archery, golf, tennis, soccer and group camping. Specialty camps are also offered, such as scuba and golf. The camps conduct environmental education programs that serve schools throughout the state and offer facilities for corporate training and conferences. During the summer, the camps offer weekend and one-week family programs. There are also two-week and three-to-four-week camps for youth. Fall and spring camping programs for families and for kids -- both weekend and weeklong -- are also available. Contact the camps for details.

Summer Day Camps

Morehead City Parks and Recreation Day Camp
1600 Fisher St., Morehead City
(252) 726-5083

Youth from across the county can take part in this Morehead City Day Camp. It is open to any child from preschool and school age and offers a variety of activities -- field trips, arts and crafts, swimming, skating, music, drama and sports games. Campers are divided into different age groups and supervised by a trained staff. The camp operates from 8 AM to 5 PM, and campers bring their own lunch. The camp offers an incredibly reasonable price for both city residents and nonresidents.

i

Knowledgeable mothers pack powdered meat tenderizer in their beach bags to soothe almost any kind of sting a kid may encounter on the beach.

Sound To Sea Day Camp
Trinity Center, N.C. Hwy. 58, Pine Knoll Shores
(252) 247-5600

If you're a kid and expect to spend a week or two in Pine Knoll Shores this summer, ask your parents to arrange for you to spend a week at Trinity Conference Center's environmental education day camp. You'll get great hands-on exposure to five coastal habitats: the sound, marsh, pond, maritime forest and ocean dunes. You'll learn about the creatures living in each environment, play interesting games, wade in the ocean, make crafts and learn about coastal cultures starting with Native Americans. From 9 AM to 4 PM, you'll be with other kids your age, from rising 1st graders to rising 6th graders, who are fun to play and learn with. Campers bring their own lunches. You'll have plenty to say about the fun activities you participated in, and your teachers will think you're quite bright when you get back to school. Registration for this popular camp opens in mid-February.

N.C. Aquarium at Pine Knoll Shores
MM 7, N.C. Hwy. 58, Pine Knoll Shores
(252) 247-4004
www.ncaquariums.com

The new Aquarium has added several new summer day camps to its schedule, now that the $25 million renovation is complete. Camps lasting five days include Aquatic Adventures for grades 2 and 3; Coastal Explorers for grades 4 and 5 and Sea Scholars for grades 6 and 7. A three-day Surfing Camp is offered for eighth-grade and ninth-grade campers. All the camps are filled with hands-on, feet-wet learning adventures for participants. The camps have a fee, and advance registration is required. They are offered at different times throughout the summer, so check the calendar for more information.

WEDDING PLANNING

Long walks on the beach, sunsets over the water, and private, uncrowded beaches. Those all spell romance, and they all happen here on the Crystal Coast. Many people come here to date and end up returning to marry.

Whether the wedding is inside or outside, the beach often plays a part - either in the pre-event parties, the ceremony, the reception or the honeymoon. Plus, members of the wedding party enjoy the great location before and after the big day.

Wedding Show

Crystal Coast Bridal Fair
Crystal Coast Civic Center, Morehead City
(252) 247-3883

An annual Bridal Fair takes place each year in early January at the Crystal Coast Civic Center, and it is an event the bride-to-be must attend. Take the groom, the mother, the future mother-in-law and any others involved in the planning. Booths are set up by planners, DJs, photographers, officiants, honeymoon travel agents and other vendors. You can sample creations by catering companies and wedding cake bakers, plus a fabulous fashion show highlights wedding gowns, dresses for the mother of the bride and groom, bridesmaids and flower girl dresses.

Marriage Licenses

A North Carolina marriage license is a must. You may get the license in any county, but you must turn it into the Register of Deeds in the county where the wedding takes place. This is very helpful for out-of-town couples coming to the beach area to be married, because they can get their license at home (if they live in North Carolina) and bring it with them.

Courthouses are open Monday through Friday but are closed on holidays; hours vary, so phone ahead (Register of Deeds offices are listed below). Both parties must be present. Take with you three forms of identification - certified birth certificate, Social Security card and valid driver's license or DMV picture card ID. If a person has been divorced, the divorce decree must be recorded and in some instances, you'll be required to show a copy of the divorce decree itself. No blood test, physical exam or waiting period is necessary to obtain a marriage license, which costs $50 to $60 and is payable by cash only.

The license is valid for 60 days after being issued. Obviously, bring your marriage license to the wedding. Two witnesses must sign the license following the ceremony. The person who performs the ceremony is responsible for getting the license back to the Register of Deeds in the county in which you were married within 10 days. After you're married, the officiant or magistrate will issue you a marriage certificate.

Wedding Locations/ Reception Facilities

The decision of where to hold the wedding ceremony and all the other special events surrounding the day is complicated. There are so many choices on the Crystal Coast. Should it be inside a church, on the beach or in a private garden or home? Before you go much further, set the day and start calling places to see if that location is available on that day.

A list of churches can be found in the Yellow Pages of the local phone book. Also see our Worship chapter. Churches often have rules about their use of their facilities for weddings, such as charging non-members a set fee or only allowing approved pastors to conduct the ceremony in the church.

Other popular wedding locations include area hotels and resorts, parks, beaches and historic grounds. Several of the top wedding locations on the Crystal Coast are listed below.

Fort Macon State Park, east end of Atlantic Beach, (252) 726-3775

N.C. Aquarium at Pine Knoll Shores, five miles west of Atlantic Beach, (252) 247-4003

Beaufort Historic Grounds, 100 Block of Turner Street, Beaufort, (252) 728-5225

Cape Lookout National Seashore, (reachable by ferry or boat only), (252) 728-2250

Crystal Coast Civic Center, 3505 Arendell Street, Morehead City, (252) 247-3883

Diamond City, Morehead City Waterfront, (866) 230-BOAT

Core Sound Waterfowl Museum, Harkers Island, (252) 728-1500

Caterers

The area offers many fine caterers. Several operate independently, and the services of others are offered through hotels in the area. If you are planning your rehearsal dinner, wedding or reception to take place in an area hotel, check with the events coordinator before you continue planning. The management of many hotels require the use of in-house caterers. We have provided a list of several independent caterers recommended by Insiders.

Catering by Marcella
(252) 925-1799

When you hire Marcella to plan or cater your event, you need not worry again. Marcella and her staff will ensure every detail meets your standards. She specializes in weddings, receptions, rehearsal dinners and cocktail parties. Whether it is a sit-down dinner, a carving board or gourmet smorgasbord, Marcella can plan and handle your special affair.

Crab's Claw
201 W. Atlantic Blvd., Atlantic Beach
(252) 726-8222

The Crab's Claw offers catering for beach weddings, rehearsal dinners, family reunions and other occasions – offering a variety of catering packages. Enjoy your occasion at the restaurant, at the site of your choosing or on a boat. Offering oceanfront fine dining in the heart of Atlantic Beach, the restaurant's location allows patrons to enjoy a panoramic view of the Atlantic Ocean. Dine inside or outside on the deck. The restaurant was recently featured in Southern Living magazine and specializes in unique seafood creations.

Front Street Grill at Stillwater
300 Front St., Beaufort
(252) 728-4956
www.frontstreetgrillatstillwater.com

Front Street Grill at Stillwater offers catering, specializing in wedding receptions, rehearsal dinners, anniversaries and corporate parties. The restaurant's private dining room is available for groups of 20 to 40 guests, and 70 to 90 guests can be accommodated in the main dining room. If your plans call for outdoor dining, Stillwater can accommodate you on the waterfront decks. The decks and restaurant offer sweeping views of Taylors Creek, Carrot Island, Beaufort Inlet and sunsets over the water, and the new outdoor bar is the perfect place to relax. You'll find innovative menu items paired with special wines that make private dining at Stillwater a special event for everyone.

Roland's Barbecue
Cedar St., Beaufort
(252) 728-1953

Roland's is certainly not a fancy catering service, however you can be assured of a great casual meal. Let Roland cater a fun pig pickin' rehearsal dinner on your deck or a clam bake on the beach. This business offers everything -- pork barbecue (whole hog or chopped), fried chicken, baked beans, slaw, hush puppies, tea, lemonade. When Roland's rolls in, everything is provided down to the utensils, napkins and plates.

Sharpies Grill & Bar
521 Front St., Beaufort
(252) 838-0101
www.sharpiesgrill.com

Sharpies is the perfect location for your wedding events. From engagement parties to rehearsal dinners to receptions, this Beaufort waterfront restaurant can provide the perfect setting. Select from the private dining room, the entire restaurant or a romantic tent outside in the historic district. A full catering menu and beverage services are available. Let the friendly and professional staff at Sharpies arrange all the details, including the invitations, flowers, photography, music, salon treatments and area tours.

Tortugas Restaurant
140 Fairview Dr., Emerald Isle
(252) 354-9397
www.tortugas.net

For a special event of any size, let Tortugas of Emerald Isle cater at their restaurant or at your site. They offer a full array of event management skills for rehearsal dinners, wedding receptions, engagement parties, corporate functions, or any other social event of any size. They can manage any size catering event off-premises, as well as cater to 80 people at their own facility.

Wedding Registries

Wedding-gift registry is available in several local stores. You can register at major chain stores or at local jewelry stores. See our Shopping chapter for more about these stores.

Belk, U.S. Hwy. 70, Cypress Bay Plaza, Morehead City, (252) 726-5121

Core Sound Waterfowl Museum, 1785 Island Road, Harkers Island, (252) 728-1500

Dee Gee's, 508 Evans Street, Morehead City, (252) 726-3314, (800) DEE GEES, www.deegees.com

Lowes Home Improvement, 5219 U.S. Hwy. 70, Morehead City, (252) 727-5011

Stamper's Jewelers, 35 Front Street, Beaufort, (252) 728-4967

Wal-Mart, 300 N.C. Highway 24, Morehead City, (252) 247-0511

Wedding Planners and Officiants

While many couples opt to have a clergy person perform their wedding ceremony, others seek alternatives. There is often confusion about whether a boat captain can legally marry someone. For the record, this is not true. In North Carolina you must be married by an ordained minister or a magistrate. We have listed a few professional event planners as well as nondenominational ministers for hire.

Dee Gee's Gifts & Books
508 Evans St., Morehead City
(252) 726-3314, (800) DEE-GEES
www.deegees.com

Dee Gee's Gifts and Books is a great first stop for wedding planners. There you will find all types of assistance and ideas. There are plenty of wedding planning books for the do-it-yourselfer or someone who just needs a few more ideas. Brides can also register at Dee Gee's for all such things as table top dinner ware, serving pieces and art work. Dee Gee's offers a full line of custom wedding and shower invitations and the paper napkins and plates that can personalize any event. Also, you'll find a wonderful selection of unique gifts for all occasions, and a huge selection of books, cards and novelties. Dee Gee's features special sections of local and regional books, children's educational books, toys and games and nautical charts. The staff will be happy to special-order any book. The store is open daily, and telephone orders are welcomed. Dee Gee's is a BookSense Store, part of a national affiliation of independent bookstores. They sell BookSense Gift Certificates, which can be used in more than 1,200 stores in all 50 states.

Front Street Grill at Stillwater
300 Front St., Beaufort
(252) 728-4956
www.frontstreetgrillatstillwater.com

Front Street Grill at Stillwater can help plan that special event. This waterfront restaurant specializes in wedding receptions, rehearsal dinners, anniversaries and corporate parties. The restaurant's private dining room is available for groups of 20 to 40 guests, and 70 to 90 guests can be accommodated in the main dining room. If your plans call for outdoor dining, Stillwater can accommodate you on the waterfront decks. The decks and restaurant offer sweeping views of Taylors Creek, Carrot Island, Beaufort Inlet and sunsets over the water, and the new outdoor bar is the perfect place to relax. You'll find innovative menu items paired with special wines that make private dining at Stillwater a special event for everyone.

Emerald Isle Realty
Emerald Isle
(252) 354-3315, (800) 849-3315
www.emeraldislerealty.com

Emerald Isle Realty offers a large selection of vacation homes and now also offers complete wedding planning and special-event coordination for family celebrations and corporate meetings. Whatever your special occasion, the expert events staff here will manage everything -- from weddings to family reunions to business retreats. Arrangements and coordination include family and guest accommodations, ceremony and reception locations, catering and dinner parties, including Eastern North Carolina pig pickins', crab roasts and clam bakes, plus flowers, photographers, music and entertainment.

Sharpies Grill & Bar
521 Front St., Beaufort
(252) 838-0101
www.sharpiesgrill.com

The friendly and professional staff at Sharpies will arrange all your wedding details, including the invitations, flowers, photography, music, salon treatments and area tours. Sharpies is the perfect location for your wedding events. From engagement parties to rehearsal dinners to receptions, this Beaufort waterfront restaurant can provide the perfect setting. A full catering menu and beverage services are available.

TourBeaufort.Com
Beaufort
(252) 342-0715

TourBeaufort.Com offers a variety of walking and exploring tours. The company also offers a Do It Yourself Wedding Guide for $24.95 for those planning to marry in the area. Designed to save you the countless hours of leg work and endless phone calls, the Guide offers lists of wedding locations and rain locations, pastors/preachers, photographers, caterers, DJs and musicians and videographers/photographers. You'll also find equipment rental companies, marriage

From a formal church wedding to a barefoot-on-the-beach ceremony, weddings are special on the Crystal Coast.

photo: Scott Taylor

licensing requirements and locations, tux rental and dress shops, limousine companies and rehearsal and reception arrangement information.

Florists

Whether it be a wedding filled with flowers or just a few simple, elegant arrangements, there are florists in the area that can professionally handle any request.

Designs by Ernest
820 Live Oak St., Beaufort
(252) 728-7022

Let Ernest Chiles handle all the details for your special occasion. He can provide unique floral designs and superior personal service for any event -- whether a wedding, a home party or a business occasion.

Floral Creations
727 Arendell St., Morehead City
(252) 222-0660

The arrangements created here are breathtaking. For unique wedding arrangements or traditional arrangements with a flair, arrange an appointment with the staff at Floral Creations.

K.D.'s Florist
1622 Live Oak St., Beaufort
(252) 728-4852

K.D.'s is a local tradition. This friendly staff of locals can create just the right arrangement to express your feelings on your special day.

Sandy's Flower Shoppe
4702 Arendell St., Morehead City
(252) 247-3323

Sandy and her staff of professionals can work with your plans -- no matter how large or small.

Through The Looking Glass
101 Church St., Swansboro
(910) 326-3128

Arrangements from Through The Looking Glass are sure to reflect your feelings. They offer fresh and silk arrangements of all types.

Bridal Shops and Formal Wear

Finding the perfect wedding dress, bridesmaids' dresses or tuxedoes is important, and local shops can provide you with a wide selection sure to fit.

The Black Tie
5270-B U.S. Hwy. 70, Morehead City
(252) 240-2900

Located in the same space as Paula's Beach Day Spa and Tanning Studio, this business offers tuxedo rentals for the gentlemen in the wedding party. The company offers attire for men age three years and up.

The Intimate Bridal and Formal Wear
5370 Brandywine Crossing, Morehead City
(252) 808-2221

Let The Intimate make planning your wedding an enjoyable and fun experience. The professional at this shop offer an elegant, friendly atmosphere and will work to ensure you look your best for whatever the occasion happens to be. As a full-service bridal shop, The Intimate offers a tremendous selection of bridal gowns, bridesmaid dresses starting at $99, prom dresses and social occasion dresses from sizes 2 to 30. There is something to fit every budget, as well as tuxedo rentals and sales. Free groom and ring bearer specials are available. The Intimate is experienced in accommodating large volume tuxedo rentals and out-of-town wedding parties, and ensures the perfect fit. This shop offers elegance and style for the bride to be and her wedding party. Whether it is that special dress or just the right tuxedo, the friendly staff here can take care of your every need and offer professional advice on clothing, color schemes and sizes. Immediate delivery is available on certain styles, and The Intimate also offers wedding gown preservation. The Intimate also has a store at 230 Middle Street, New Bern, (252) 638-1220.

Music

If music is what you want, contact a professional service and let them line up the tunes to suit your wedding theme.

John Drake - DJ and MC
Morehead City
(252) 223-5717 or (252) 422-4355

John Drake specializes in providing music for all types of events, large or small. With more than 1,000 CDs, John can create the perfect party theme for you -- whether it be Big Band, Top 40, Classic, Country, Jimmy Buffett, beach music or something in between. John also provides wedding consultation and can handle all the details of your wedding, from location to catering to decorations.

Alan Hilbert
Morehead City
(252) 726-8365

Alan provides DJ services and has a wide selection of music to allow you to create the mood for your special occasion. He can provide just the right music for your wedding ceremony, your reception or your special event for any age groups.

Photography

Pictures of your special day are important, so hiring a photographer you can trust is important. Line up a professional photographer well in advance.

Bell Photography
Morehead City
(252) 247-1058

Established in 1956, Bell Photography has been meeting and exceeding the photography needs of locals and visitors to the area for years. Owner David Bell now carries on the quality of tradition started by his father, the late Gene Bell. He offers a mixture of photography styles including contemporary, storybook and journalistic. Whether indoor or outdoor, David strives to keep the rates affordable and to ensure the pictures reflect the beauty of your special day.

Coastal Image Photography
Morehead City
(252) 726-7488
www.coastalimagephoto.com

Carolyn Temple is a true professional and can prepare a photography package just right for your special day. She has the only lush garden outdoor studio area in eastern North Carolina and will schedule location photos at the beach at no extra charge. Just let her know what you would like, and Carolyn can prepare the perfect wedding package for you and your wedding party.

Deja Vu Multi-Media Productions
(252) 646-3307

Jason Campobasso offers a variety of wedding video packages for your selection. He specializes in live audio and video production as well as post production work, and he works with many local bands. Jason can tape events of all types, adding music and sound to make the creation complete. Also, he can run the sound during your event. Whether inside or out, Jason can ensure your wedding video is complete.

Tim Green Photography
(252) 726-8074

Tim Green specializes in wedding photography, family portraits and special-occasion photography. His wedding services range from engagement packages to bridal packages to wedding day packages. Tim specializes in studio and beach photography. He offers a wide range of photography services including school, sports, prom and senior pictures.

Photographic Services By George Mitchell
(910) 326-4425 or (910)382-3644
www.carolina-photo.com

George Mitchell has extensive experience in capturing your special event on film. He provides professional services for all types of events -- from weddings and portraits shots to commercial and advertising shots. Whether you are interested in color or black and white, indoor scenes or outdoor, one shot or a complete package, he can create a treasure for you to enjoy for years to come.

Masterworks Video Productions
(252) 223-0525

Bryan Sibley has more than 20 years experience and can capture your special day in a meaningful way. He offers a variety of wedding video packages for your selection and can easily record inside or outside. Bryan will make sure your wedding video is special and will bring you joy for years.

Sunrise Sunset Digital Images
(252) 393-3284

Owner Constance Soule is a photographer, graphic artist and webmistress. She specializes in wedding, beach and portfolio photography. She also offers pet photography so put a bow tie on Fluffy and include her in the wedding pictures.

Scott Taylor Photography Gallery and Studio
214 Pollock St., Beaufort
(252) 728-0900
www.scotttaylorphoto.com

For exclusive, yet reasonable engagement, wedding and event photography, contact the area's premier wedding photographer -- Scott Taylor. He specializes in color, black and white, or split toned images sure to fit the image of the wedding and reflect the couple's wishes. Whether he is taking a bridal portrait in his studio/gallery or photographing the wedding party on the beach or traveling to a church or boat wedding, Scott works to capture the candid, intimate images you will treasure for a lifetime. He handles large and small weddings, and offers a new flush-mount magazine-style wedding album in addition to the traditional albums. Scott always commits the time needed to ensure a high level of personal attention is given to each bridal couple at the event and in preparing their photographs afterward.

Transportation

Arranging for your wedding party and for the bride and groom to arrive in style simply tops off the day. There are several services in the area that can help you set up just the right way to arrive.

All Stretched Out Limousine Service
(252) 728-4188

With all amenities, this service is sure to please your wedding party. This company provides full limousine service in Carteret County as well as the surrounding counties.

Diamond Limousine Service
(252) 240-1680

Diamond Limousine offers vehicles with all amenities -- CD stereos, TV and DVD players, VCR players, full bar and more. This company has been in business since 1995.

Presidential Limousine Service and Class Limousine Service
(252) 726-8109

Presidential Limousine offers fully equipped limousines driven by friendly staff. The company offers regular, super stretch and SUV super-stretch vehicles as well as vans and sedans. This company also offers antique wedding cars to make that special day even more unique.

Rental Equipment

Why buy things to use only one day, when you can rent quality equipment?

Bogue Banks Beach Gear & Linens
Bell Cove Village, Emerald Isle
(252) 354-4404, (866) 593-GEAR (4327)
www.boguebanksbeachgear.com

Bogue Banks Beach Gear & Linens offers traditional vacation rental items as well as special items perfect for your wedding or your beach wedding or special event. You'll find a custom array of colorful beach umbrellas and matching chairs. The service also offers linen packages or cottage, beach and baby equipment rentals, grills and much more. It's open year-round, seven days a week.

Country-Aire Rental - Party Store
5459 U.S. Hwy.70 W, Morehead City
(252) 247-0117
1253 S. Glenburnie Rd., New Bern
(252) 638-6000
206 Brynn Marr Plaza, Jacksonville
(910) 353-8589
779 W. Corbett Ave., Swansboro
(910) 326-8588

Leave your planning and your equipment needs to the professionals at Country-Aire Rental. The company has four Special Events stores that offer everything your party or special event could ever need -- from tents of all sizes to tables and chairs to wedding and catering supplies. If you need linens, candelabras or flower stands, contact Country-Aire. An event planner at each of the locations can make sure the day goes just as you wish. The company also offers delivery, setup and takedown services.

Printers

When it comes to printing invitations for your wedding events, there are a number of reputable printers in the area. They offer a selection of invitations to choose from or they can work with you to create one especially for you.

Coastal Press, Inc., 502 Arendell Street, Morehead City (252) 726-1549

Eastern Offset Printing Co., 410 W. Fort Macon Road, Atlantic Beach, (252) 247-6791

DAY SPAS AND SALONS

Relaxation and reducing stress is something we all want. The Crystal Coast offers residents and visitors plenty of places to relax. There are several salons and spas waiting to give you that special peaceful feeling. All you have to find is the time. Information about healthcare, massage therapy, physical therapy, acupuncture and alternative healthcare can be found the Crystal Coast's Healthcare chapter.

Day Spas

For a real treat, spend the day or part of the day having the works at a local spa.

Oasis Day Spa Salon
5380-E Brandywine Crossing, U.S. Hwy. 70 W, Morehead City
(252) 726-2600
www.oasisdayspasalon.com

Oasis Day Spa is just the place to send a special friend or loved one, or yourself, to be pampered. This spa offers a variety of massage therapy techniques -- from deep tissue and hot stone to trigger point and Swedish. Enjoy a therapy soak in a whirlpool tub before your massage. Oasis also offers facials, body waxing, manicures and pedicures, as well as makeup application using Grafton cosmetics. The spa's hair salon provides clients with cuts, coloring and styling, and specializes in wedding or special event hair styling. Spa packages can be designed to meet your special needs and range from one and a half hours to seven hours of luxury.

Paula's Beach Day Spa & Tanning Studio
5270-C U.S. Hwy. 70, Morehead City
(252) 222-5750

Paula's Beach Day Spa offers a variety of salon services. Guests can enjoy complete hair care and design by one of seven creative hair dressers and an assistant. Nail and pedicure technicians are on staff, and the studio offers a complete tuxedo rental department. The studio offers tanning beds (further information is provided in the Tanning Salon section of this chapter). There are three different spa packages offered, and services can include hair, nail and pedicure care, and massages. "Queen for a Day" packages make great gifts.

Spa By The Sea
Carteret Village Shopping Center, 4644 Arendell St., Morehead City
(252) 247-9727

Spa By The Sea is a complete spa, designed to pamper and provide quality care and enjoyment. The spa offers full and express manicures and pedicures, body waxing and makeovers. Massage therapy and body treatment are specialties of this spa, which offers Swedish, trigger point, deep tissue, myofascial release and reflexology. The complete services also include facials, microdermabrasion and exfoliating treatments for all skin types. Air-brush tanning is also offered (see the Tanning Salon section of this chapter). Spa packages at Spa By The Sea are the perfect gifts for the bride-to-be and her wedding party, an unforgettable anniversary gift or the ultimate "no reason at all" gift for someone like yourself.

Hair Salons

For that special occasion, or simply to get a new look, visit one of the many area hair salons and let the professionals take over. Most salons also offer nail care as well.

121 Craven St. Salon
121 Craven St., Beaufort
(252) 838-0007

This salon has quickly become the salon of local salons. Jack Best and a staff of four hair artists offer a full hair salon and facial waxing services. Among the services clients can receive are consultations, cuts, colors

and styles. This salon also specializes in color correction.

Paula's Beach Day Spa & Tanning Studio
5270-C U.S. Hwy. 70, Morehead City
(252) 222-5750

This is a complete hair-care salon with seven hair dressers and an assistant on staff. They also provide complete nail-care services. More information is in the Day Spa section of this chapter.

Strandz Salon
5053 Executive Dr., Morehead City
(252) 808-2887

Strandz Salon offers complete hair care and has designers on staff to create that perfect look. The salon also offers waxing services and tanning.

Total Concept Salon Ltd.
4426 Arendell St., Morehead City
(252) 247-5464

This well-established salon offers complete hair care, including cuts, styling, color and more. The salon also provides body-waxing services, facials and microdermabrasion treatments.

Skin-Care Specialists and Cosmetic Consultants

Crystal Coast residents and visitors enjoy the area so much because of the opportunities to be in the great outdoors. However, the exposure to the sun, salt air, wind and water can leave skin feeling dry and damaged. Sunscreen is a must, but for more skin-care help and for make-up consultations, there are several professionals in the area. Skin care is also addressed through facials, microdermabrasions and exfoliating treatments at several of the spas listed in this chapter.

Oasis Day Spa Salon
5380-E Brandywine Crossing,
U.S. Hwy. 70 W., Morehead City
(252) 726-2600
www.oasisdayspasalon.com

Oasis Day Spa offers make up application using Grafton cosmetics. More information about Oasis is provided in the Day Spa section of this chapter.

A dip in a tidal pool is always relaxing.

photo: George Mitchell

Belk
Cypress Bay Plaza,
U.S. Hwy. 70, Morehead City
(252) 726-5121

A number of consultants at Belk provide tips on cosmetics application and selection. Belk's cosmetic lines include Clinique, Estee Lauder and Lancome.

Tanning Salons

While most Insiders know the dangers of overexposure to the sun's harmful rays, there are some who long for a tanned look year round. For them, area tanning salons offer those services.

Paula's Beach Day Spa & Tanning Studio
5270-C U.S. Hwy. 70, Morehead City
(252) 222-5750

Paula's Beach offers 13 tanning units, including the Cyber Dome. There is also a unit that allows clients to stand up while tanning. Paula's Beach is also a full-service salon offering hair and nail care as well as massage therapy.

Spa By The Sea
Carteret Village Shopping Center,
4644 Arendell St., Morehead City
(252) 247-9727

Spa By The Sea is a complete spa that also offers air-brush tanning to clients.

Strandz Salon
5053 Executive Dr., Morehead City
(252) 808-2887

Strandz Salon offers tanning services as well as complete hair care and waxing services.

Get your body beach ready at a local spa.

photo: George Mitchell

THE ARTS

The arts are alive and well along the Crystal Coast. Beaufort and Morehead City combined have earned a mention in John Villani's book The 100 Best Small Art Towns in America, and more and more people choose to journey to the area for its myriad galleries and art shows. Art often imitates life on the coast, and much of the local art reflects the relationship of coastal people with the sea.

Many artists find the pace of coastal living conducive to developing their talents and move here for that reason. It's not unusual to meet people who were professionals in other locations now earning a living painting, writing or making pottery on the Crystal Coast. The vibrant community of coastal artists is involved in an eclectic array of artistic productions. Arts organizations, especially the Arts Council of Carteret County, actively support artists' endeavors and welcome new members and volunteers.

In this chapter you'll find a sampling of the arts groups and galleries in the area. If there is no address for a group, we have listed the name and phone number of a person to contact. Another great source of arts information is Arts Alive (see our Media chapter). Arts Alive is published monthly from March through December and the months of January and February are combined. This free regional publication showcases the arts in Carteret, Onslow, Craven and Pamlico counties, and can be found in local news stands. If there's something specific you're interested in finding, just ask one of the local artists.

Arts Organizations

Arts Council of Carteret County
812 Evans St., Morehead City
(252) 726-9156

This nonprofit organization, partially funded by the North Carolina Arts Council, is housed in the historic Webb Memorial Library and Civic Center, a privately owned public library in the heart of Morehead City. The Arts Council works as a distributing agent, funding arts events and education, promoting arts organizations, assisting artists seeking grants and sponsoring a variety of workshops, lectures and classes. Every February it sponsors the Art From The Heart exhibition, which involves artists from three surrounding counties (see our Annual Events chapter). The council also sponsors workshops and performances that are announced throughout the year.

The addition of programs conducted or assisted by the Arts Council since 1976 has resulted in a community arts concept that embraces drama, literature, dance, music, traditional crafts, the visual arts and the family. Summer art camps are often offered for youth. Volunteer assistance and membership support keep the programs of this organization active and growing. Now without a full-time director or county funding, the Arts Council needs volunteers more than ever.

Carteret County Arts and Crafts Coalition
(252) 726-3354

What began in the late 1970s as a small group of professionally oriented artists seeking an outlet for their work has grown into a juried, professional art group of almost 70 members. The coalition conducts four major shows each year -- on Memorial Day weekend, the Fourth of July weekend, Labor Day weekend and a four-week Christmas gallery show before the Thanksgiving holidays. New members are welcome, and jurying of new work takes place twice each year.

Core Sound Decoy Carver's Guild
Guild Building, Harkers Island
(252) 838-8818

Born from an idea of seven decoy carvers at a birthday party in 1987, the Core Sound Carvers Guild now has a membership of more than 400 active decoy carvers, collectors, breeders, taxidermists and waterfowl artists

in more than 25 states. The Core Sound Decoy Festival (see our Annual Events chapter) in December and Core Sound Waterfowl Museum (see our Attractions chapter) on Harkers Island is an outgrowth of the efforts of the Decoy Carvers Guild. The guild welcomes new members and meets each month on the third Tuesday at 7:30 PM in its new headquarters on Harkers Island Road in Straits. Guild members offer carving classes for adults and other classes for children.

Crystal Coast Quilter's Guild
Beaufort
(252) 728-2672

This energetic group of quilters meets each month on the third Thursday to exchange ideas and learn from presenters. The guild is made up of members who enjoy quilting by traditional and modern methods, including hand piecing, machine quilting and fabric dying. Along with the monthly meetings, workshops take place throughout the year with nationally known quilters and designers. Guild members make and donate children's quilts to the local domestic violence shelter and help with other charitable projects. Each May the guild hosts a Quilt Show in Morehead City.

Down East FolkArts Society
Beaufort
(252) 504-2787

Folk music comes from the heart and soul of any locale, and its listeners are sometimes travelers with an ear cant to the sea. Between September and June, each month brings a concert to the Crystal Coast for the Folk Concert and Dance Series. Organized and sponsored by the Down East FolkArts Society, concerts and contradances most often take place at Clawson's 1905 on Front Street in Beaufort, the Duke University Marine Lab auditorium on Pivers Island and at the Trent River Coffee Company in New Bern. Larger venue events take place at other locations throughout the area. In addition, the Down East FolkArts Society sponsors workshops, classes, large concerts, an overnight dance retreat and school and community outreach programs. Call for membership information, to be placed on the mailing list and for concert schedules. All events are open to the public.

Dance

The Arts Council of Carteret County brings professional talent in dance, drama and music to the area through a variety of grants and its own budget. Visiting artists hold concerts as well as instructional programs in the public schools in conjunction with these public performances. Such concert and instructional programs have featured African dance, jazz, dance and contra dancing.

Private dance studios on the Crystal Coast offer classes in ballet, tap and modern dance for everyone from toddlers to adults, and local recreation centers often offer dance-exercise line-dancing classes for all ages. Students perform recitals and often participate in area festivals, group functions and parades. Dance organizations are also active in community events.

Carolina Strut Performing Arts Centre
303 N. 35th St., Morehead City
(252) 726-0431

This studio offers classes for adults and children in tap, ballet, pointe, modern, lyrical and jazz styles, as well as tumbling and music lessons. The studio offers a Wiggles class for children as young as 2 years old and continues classes through adults.

Company Tap
1390 Lennoxville Rd., Beaufort
(252) 728-7704

This Beaufort studio opened two years ago and is now very popular. The studio offers tap, ballet, modern dance, jazz, tumbling, point and gymnatics, as well as summer and after-school programs for all ages from toddler to teen. A special tot tumbling class provides instruction for children as young as 18 months and their accompanying adults. Traditional programs are offered from September through early June, and special camps and programs are offered during the summer months. These camps include cheerleading, dance, gymnastics, drama and even an arts camp.

Dance Arts Studio
123 Bonner Ave., Morehead City
(252) 726-1720

Dance Arts Studio offers tap, ballet, pointe, modern dance, jazz and African dance instruction in classes for ages 3 through adult. Special classes are offered for adult beginners.

Gulls and Buoys Square Dance Club
of Carteret County
John and Phyllis Stone
(252) 247-0306

The Square Dance Club meets each Friday at the First Presbyterian Church in Morehead City. The club is actively seeking new members, so don't be shy. If you don't know how to square dance, the club is more than happy to give you lessons, and John promises you can be dancing after two or three lessons. Professional square dance callers come to the county for these Friday events. Visitors are always welcome at the 7:30 to 10 PM monthly swings as well.

Music

The Crystal Coast is home to several choral groups that perform often and occasionally audition new prospects. We are fortunate to host an extraordinary concert series, a wonderful music festival weekend in the spring, and active jazz and folk art music societies that promote, in concerts and education, America's most innovative music styles.

American Music Festival
(252) 728-4488
www.americanmusicfestival.org

The American Music Festival is an exquisite chamber music series featuring five concerts performed from September through May. The year 2006 will mark the concert series' 15th season. The series is supported by subscription ticket purchase, donations and donor sponsorships, and by a volunteer board of directors. Donations to the fund further promote music with an educational outreach program that takes the gifted musicians into area schools. Past concerts included world-class performances by musicians of Duke University's Ciompi Quartet, the New Century Sax Quartet and the Cassatt String Quartet as well as series favorites

such as pianist Barbara McKenzie and the Carolina Piano Trio. Series subscriptions for five concerts cost $80. Individual performance tickets cost $20 for adults and $10 for students and military. Performance locations include The History Place in Morehead City and the NC Maritime Museum in Beaufort.

Beaufort By-The-Sea Music Festival
(252) 728-0707

Beaufort's Music Festival takes place in April of each year. The event has four or five stages featuring a variety of music with something to suit everyone's tastes, regardless of their age. The event is free, and town merchants join in the fun with special offers. The concerts are performed in downtown Beaufort so it's a walking weekend with some dancing in the street. See our Annual Events chapter for more about this event.

The Coastal Jazz Society
(252) 728-2594
www.coastaljazz.org

Founded in 1992, The Coastal Jazz Society is a non-profit group with a mission of promoting the understanding and appreciation of jazz. The group also puts a special emphasis on jazz education for all ages. Membership to the society is open to anyone who likes to listen to or play jazz, and the membership is made up of local year-round residents as well as regular visitors to the area or second-home owners in the county.

Crystal Coast Choral Society
Marilyn Zmoda
(252) 247-5929

The Crystal Coast Choral Society is made up of members from across several counties and is under the direction of Finley Woolston. The group meets for weekly rehearsals each Tuesday evening in Swansboro and welcomes new members. This chorus offers local concerts and often travels to perform.

Carteret Chorale
Laurence Stith
(252) 726-6193

This group of 40 talented vocalists from Morehead City, Newport and Beaufort has performed together for 20 years, creating a chorale known widely for its top-notch performances. The chorale performs benefit concerts regularly in Carteret County and has taken its talent to Williamsburg, Carnegie Hall, the National Cathedral, Yugoslavia and Russia. Director Laurence Stith, retired professional pianist, vocalist and educator, is also a composer, and the group often performs his original music. "Have tux, will travel," say the members, who pay their own travel expenses and provide their stage wardrobes for performances.

North Carolina Symphony
- Carteret County Chapter
(919) 733-2750

The North Carolina Symphony is a full-time, professional orchestra of 64 members presented statewide with the highest artistic standards to enrich, entertain and educate the people of North Carolina. The Carteret County Chapter of the North Carolina Symphony sells tickets and raises funds to bring the state's symphony to the area for an annual Holiday Pops concert held in conjunction with the Festival of Trees. Additionally, the Symphony performs an education concert each year for elementary school students.

Writers' Organization

Carteret Writers
Jere Geurin
(252) 222-5722

This active group of professional and aspiring writers gathers at 11:30 AM sharp on the second Tuesday of each month at Captain Bill's Restaurant in Morehead City. Meetings include lunch, friendly conversation about the art of writing, and a scheduled speaker to further inspire the writers. The May meeting is an evening awards program, and meetings are not held during the summer months of June, July and August. The group often conducts special workshops, seminars and contests, which are open to everyone. The door is always open to new members and to those simply curious about crafting their writing skills with the support and camaraderie of fellow scribes.

Public Art Exhibits

On the Crystal Coast, art exhibits can be enjoyed in a number of public places -- from museums and libraries to waterfronts and post offices. The N.C. Maritime Museum,

315 Front Street, Beaufort, (252) 728-7317, exhibits work of state and local artists. These works complement the museum's maritime focus. Monthly exhibits are shown at Carteret General Hospital, 3500 Arendell Street, Morehead City, (252) 247-1616, sponsored by the Arts for the Hospital committee. The History Place, 1008 Arendell Street, Morehead City, (252) 247-7533, features works of various local artists. The Carteret County Public Library branches in Beaufort, Pine Knoll Shores and Newport sponsor artists in displays that change monthly, and often include the work of adults and students.

Carteret Community College, 3505 Arendell Street, Morehead City, (252) 222-6000, displays the work of students in the college library. The Upstairs Gallery at the college also features work by students and other local and regional artists.

The Morehead City Waterfront and Downtown area is now home to a Fish Walk. Local artists have created a number of two to three foot columns that feature fish of various types.

Four beautifully restored murals depicting local scenes may be admired in the Beaufort Post Office on Front Street. Russian-born artist Simka Simkovitch painted these oil-on-canvas paintings in 1940. He was engaged by then-postmaster W. H. Taylor and paid $1,900 for his work. Simkovitch's fee was funded by the Fine Arts Program, a federal project that provided work for artists during the Great Depression. The large oils, ranging from 10 to 12 feet, show the Cape Lookout Lighthouse, the Orville B. mail boat, the wreck of the Crissie Wright, and a stunning scene of Canada geese. All were recently restored by conservator Elizabeth Speight of Philadelphia.

On Harkers Island, the Core Sound Waterfowl Museum, (252) 728-1500, exhibits the best of hand-carved decoys and wildlife art.

Art Lessons

Carteret Community College and the Arts Council continuously offer art lessons and classes to residents and visitors. Additionally, many of the art galleries listed below offer art lessons and workshops on various types of art -- from watercolor and drawing to pottery and stained glass. The Core Sound Decoy Carvers Guild, listed above in Art Organizations, also offers carving lessons for adults and children.

Continuing Education Department
Carteret Community College, 3505 Arendell St., Morehead City
(252) 222-6200

The Continuing Education Department at Carteret Community College offers courses in various arts techniques each semester. There often is no tuition charge for county residents age 65 or older. Fees for younger folks are nominal. Call for more information.

Arts Council of Carteret County
812 Evans St., Morehead City
(252) 726-9156

Workshops and classes are offered throughout the year to artists and budding artists of all ages. From painting to pottery to sketching, the Arts Council continues to support and coordinate the area's art scene. Recent developments include Art Marketing and Business seminars and a highly popular writers' workshop.

Art Galleries

The number of galleries in Carteret County continues to increase. Much to our satisfaction, many of our local artists have decided to dedicate their lives to the business of art, showcasing not only their own work but also the work of others. What follows is merely a sampling of some of the area's tried-and-true galleries. As you tour the area, we promise you'll find a treasure chest of other galleries to visit too.

BEAUFORT

Beaufort Fine Art
121 Turner St., Beaufort
(252) 728-4955

This gallery offers an outstanding collection of works by North Carolina and regional artists. Works include paintings and sculptures.

Down East Gallery
519 Front St., Beaufort
(252) 728-4410

This gallery represents the paintings and prints of local artist and Beaufort resident Alan Cheek along with a few pieces by other area artists. Framing services are also available.

Handscapes Gallery
410 Front St., Beaufort
(252) 728-6805
www.handscapesgallery.com

Handscapes is an Insiders' favorite and is the perfect place to find unusual gifts and treasures. The gallery specializes in works by North Carolininas as well as artists and craftspeople from all over the country. Owner Alison Brooks fills the shop with pottery, jewelry, prints, paintings, glass and metal craft items. More than 180 artists are represented and it is a joy to see the fine workmanship offered. Handscapes Gallery was voted by Niche Magazine as one of the top 100 retailers of American crafts in 2003 and 2004. The store is open year round, seven days a week. Call for winter hours.

Mattie King Davis Art Gallery
Beaufort Historic Site,
100 block of Turner St., Beaufort
(252) 728-5225

Carteret County's oldest art gallery sells the varied works of more than 100 local and regional artists. Paintings, basketry, glass, wood, pottery and textiles are represented. A different artist is featured every 60 days, and a reception is held to unveil the work and meet the artist. The gallery is a great place to not only see some outstanding artwork but also to receive an introduction to the Beaufort Historic Site.

Scott Taylor Photography Gallery and Studio
214 Pollock St., Beaufort
(252) 728-0900
www.scotttaylorphoto.com

At Scott Taylor's Photography Gallery and Studio you are sure to find that unique image of Beaufort or the surrounding coastal areas. Scott is well known for his scenic photography, and also for exclusive, yet reasonable engagement, wedding and event photography. He specializes in color, black and white, or split toned images. Let Scott create a family beach portrait that will be treasured for a lifetime. Scott's book titled "Coastal Waters - Images of North Carolina" is available in the gallery and is the perfect way to remember your trip to the coast.

True Colors Gallery
129 Middle Ln., Beaufort
(252) 728-5000

This gallery features original works, prints and contemporary crafts, along with creative custom framing. Works include metal sculptures, oils, art glass, carvings, raku, watercolors and more.

MOREHEAD CITY

Arts & Things
704 Evans St., Morehead City
(252) 240-1979

Arts & Things on the Morehead City waterfront has something for all art enthusiasts. With a very knowledgeable and helpful staff, this gallery offers a diverse and large collection of original art, and limited edition and open edition prints. Arts & Things also features art glass, pottery, shorebird carvings and stained glass. They offer framing, art supplies and workshops in a variety of media.

Bridges Street Pottery
1910 Bridges St., Morehead City
(252) 808-2818

Once a church, now a gallery and working potters' studio, Bridges Street Pottery displays and sells functional and decorative raku, porcelain and stoneware pottery made by local artists. Artists also create art tile for residential and commercial use. Potter Scott Haines, an instructor at Carteret Community College, teaches private lessons here.

Budding Artists Ltd.
Morehead Plaza,
3000 Arendell St., Morehead City
(252) 247-5111

For bright colors, movement and a flair for fun, Budding Artists is the place to go. The gallery features original artwork in a variety of media by North Carolina and regional artists. The gallery specializes in open and limited edition prints and has a large selection for special orders. Whether it is acrylics, oils, watercolors or pottery, this gallery has quality items you are sure to enjoy. The gallery offers custom framing and has a gift and bridal registry.

Carolina Artists Studio Gallery, Inc.
800 Evans St., Morehead City
(252) 726-7550

With approximately 30 participating artists, this is a non-profit co-op gallery operated by the artists. Members' work is displayed, and active works in progress are visible. Members offer classes and workshops in watercolor, pastel, clay, collage and oriental brush painting. The gallery is open Monday through Saturday 10 AM to 4 PM and on summer Sundays from 1 to 5 PM. Visitors are welcome to special art openings.

Carteret Contemporary Art
1106 Arendell St., Morehead City
(252) 726-4071

This gallery shows an extraordinary selection of paintings and sculpture by regional, national and local artists in frequently changing exhibits. It's open Monday through Saturday 10 AM to 4 PM.

Gallerie E!
Chelsea Place, 5270 U.S. Hwy. 70, Morehead City
(252) 247-5557

This gallery sells a variety of artwork and art supplies and offers classes. The exhibits change frequently and feature works by many local and regional artists.

Studio 101
101 Lockhart St., Morehead City
(252) 726-8950

This working art gallery represents local artist Bett Davis. Works in glass, metal, jewelry, acrylics and watercolors, mixed-media collage, serigraphs and limited-edition prints are exhibited and sold. Lockhart Street is off Arendell Street between Auto Zone and Wendy's.

Windward Gallery
508-C Evans St., Morehead City
(252) 726-6393

This waterfront gallery represents the paintings of local artist Alexander Kaszas as well as other artists in varied mediums. Art restoration and framing are also offered. Call ahead for hours.

ANNUAL EVENTS

Traditions, history and community are very important on the Crystal Coast, and many events take place each year to celebrate these very things. From the American Music Festival concert series each winter and the famous Newport Pig Cooking Contest each April to the numerous kayak events and the Core Sound Decoy Festival in December, you'll find that Carteret County events are excellent ways to enjoy yourself and learn a little about the area.

The area's traditional festivals, even the N.C. Seafood Festival (the second largest festival in North Carolina), have the sense of warmth often only found at family reunions. In the midst of what may appear to be a public gathering of random strangers, hugs and greetings are likely to break out anywhere.

Fold in with the crowd and feel right at home. The simple pleasures of just being on the Crystal Coast provide a full plate, but including any of the following events in your plans expands a sample taste of the area into a real feast. Nearby communities host great events as well. Check our New Bern Annual Events chapter and the Havelock and Oriental chapters for more events.

January

Penguin Plunge
Main Beach, Atlantic Beach

The 2006 Penguin Plunge marked the third year friends gathered to dip into the ocean on New Year's Day, and 79 people took part in the event. Mark your calendar to join in the fun on January 1, 2007, at 1 PM. Plungers are asked to donate $5 to help with a local charity. Organized by Tabbie Nance and Miriam Sutton, the plunge offers fun seekers a way to get a fresh, a real fresh, start to the new year.

American Music Festival
Assorted venues in Morehead City and Beaufort
P.O. Box 1099, Beaufort, NC 28516
www.americanmusicfestival.org

This chamber music series has brought extraordinary concerts to the Crystal Coast since 1990. Each year, five or six concert performances are scheduled from October through April. The location of each concert is different, but all are in the Beaufort-Morehead City area. Series subscriptions for the concerts are $80 for adults and $40 for students. Individual tickets are $20 per show for adults and $10 for full-time students and active-duty military.

Bridal Fair
Crystal Coast Civic Center,
3505 Arendell St., Morehead City
(252) 728-247-3883

An annual Bridal Fair takes place each year in early January at the Crystal Coast Civic Center, and it is an event the bride-to-be must attend. Take the groom, the mother, the future mother-in-law and any others involved in the planning. Booths are set up by planners, DJs, photographers, officiants, honeymoon travel agents and more. You can sample creations by catering companies and wedding cake bakers, plus see a fabulous fashion show highlighting wedding gowns, dresses for the mothers of the bride and groom, bridesmaids and flower girl dresses, and much more.

February

Art From the Heart
Location varies each year, Morehead City
(252) 726-9156

This two-week exhibition and sale of original, innovative and traditional works

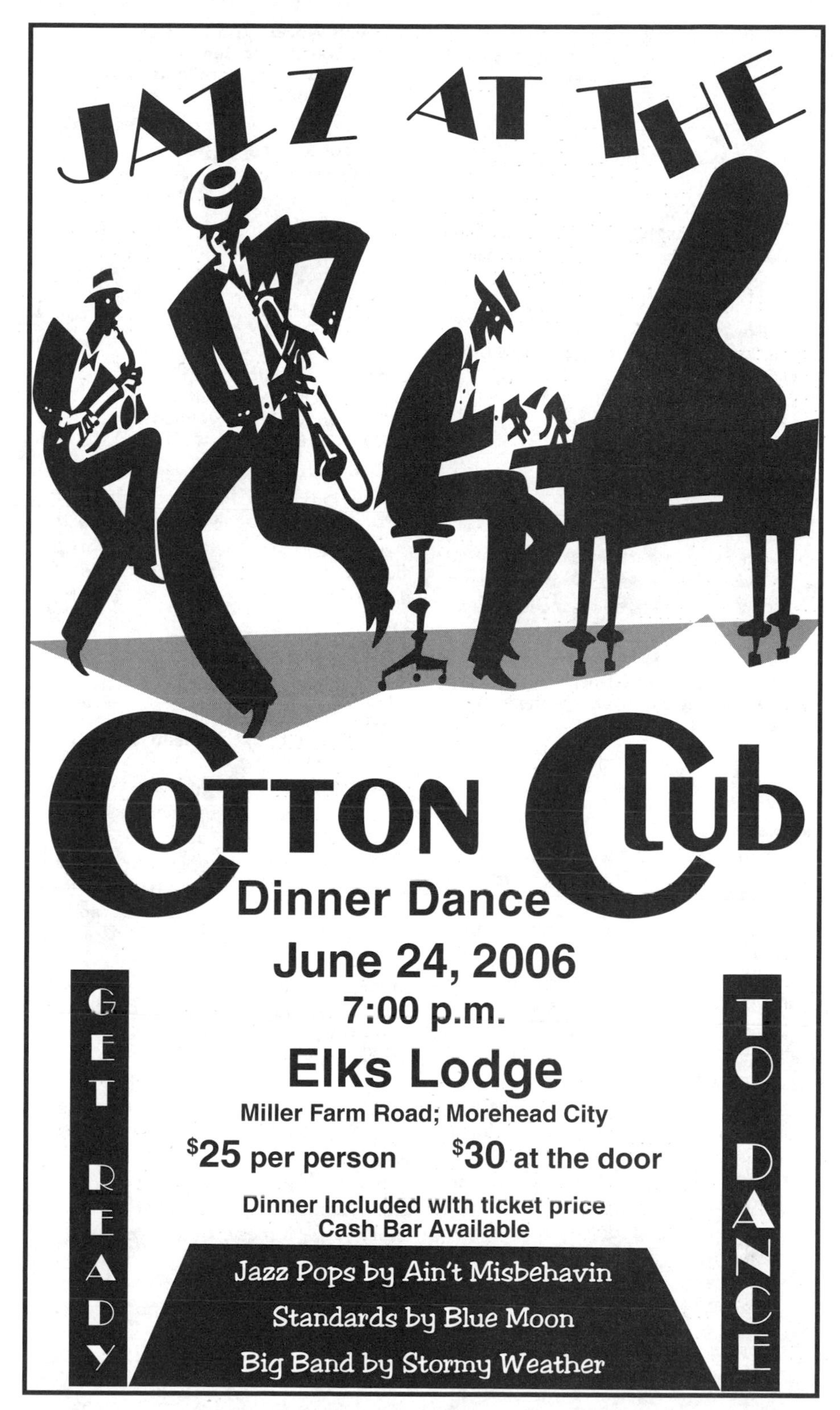
JAZZ AT THE
COTTON CLUB
Dinner Dance
June 24, 2006
7:00 p.m.
Elks Lodge
Miller Farm Road; Morehead City
$25 per person
$30 at the door
Dinner Included with ticket price
Cash Bar Available
Jazz Pops by Ain't Misbehavin
Standards by Blue Moon
Big Band by Stormy Weather
GET READY
TO DANCE

by selected area artists occurs each year in mid-February. The Arts Council of Carteret County organizes and funds this fine-arts event. Combined with an annual exhibit of work by area schoolchildren, this exhibition is a great opportunity for art lovers to view (and buy) original drawings, paintings, photographs, lithographs, sculpture and pottery pieces. Proceeds benefit the Arts Council and provide scholarships to Children's Art Camp. Admission is free.

Empty Bowls
Crystal Coast Civic Center, Morehead City
(252) 504-2203

This annual event raises money to feed the hungry and is very popular. Carteret Community College, local potters, high school students, art classes and area restaurants team up for this event in an effort to raise money for area soup kitchens and food banks. For $12, guests receive a handcrafted soup bowl and some delicious soup. Tickets are sold in advance at various locations and at the Civic Center.

Carolina Chocolate Festival
Crystal Coast Civic Center, Morehead City
(877) 848-4976

Chocolate lovers should mark their calendars for early February and make their way to the Crystal Coast for the annual Carolina Chocolate Festival. Started in 2003, the event has continued to grow each year. Taking place at the Crystal Coast Civic Center in early February of each year, the event offers visitors an opportunity to enjoy exhibit booths with chocolate demonstrations from professional chefs and to support local nonprofit groups selling tasty treats. The festival has expanded to three days and includes Gala Dinner Friday Night to benefit the Boys & Girls Club, and a Champagne and Truffles party Saturday afternoon. Saturday night will feature a bluegrass concert and storytelling by Fish House Liar Rodney Kemp. A Chocolate Sunday brunch to benefit PAWS of Carteret will also take place. The festival offers fondue, a hands-free pudding eating contest for children, music, and a baking contest. There is also a supervised place for kids to play. Admission supports local charities and is $8 for adults, $2 for children 5 to 12 years of age and free for children younger than 5.

Women's World Expo
Crystal Coast Civic Center,
3505 Arendell St., Morehead City
(252) 247-3883

Women's World Expo focuses on all aspects of a woman's life. The show features booths and demonstrations on health, well-being, fashion, careers and more. Fashion shows as well as seminars on women's issues shows take place during the expo.

March

Coastal Home Show
Crystal Coast Civic Center,
3505 Arendell St., Morehead City
(252) 247-3883

This annual trade show in early March assembles the services, wares and expertise of local businesses that focus on aspects of building, landscaping and decorating. Gather ideas, good advice and the right products for do-it-yourself projects or shop for professional services during the Friday-through-Sunday show.

Fun Fest
Crystal Coast Civic Center,
3505 Arendell St., Morehead City
(252) 247-3883
www.ncseafoodfestival.org

Fun Fest is an annual fund-raising event of the North Carolina Seafood Festival (NCSF). This Saturday night event features food, music and lots of fun. The NCSF takes place the first weekend in October and is a wonderful coastal event.

St. Patrick's Day Festival
Emerald Plantation Shopping Center,
8700 N.C. Hwy. 58, Emerald Isle
(252) 354-6350

Winter hibernation is halted by this mid-March event, held on the Saturday closest to St. Patrick's Day at Emerald Plantation Shopping Center. A great day full of fun and games for the entire family, the event includes corned beef and cabbage, traditional beverages and music. Green is plentiful when it comes to attire and decorations. Sponsored by the Emerald Isle Parks and Recreation Department, the festival supports local craftspeople and civic organizations. It's free and loads of fun for the entire family.

Swansboro Oyster Roast
Swansboro Rotary Civic Center,
1104 Main St. Ext., Swansboro
(910) 326-6175
www.swansbororotary.com

This is an event not to be missed if you enjoy oysters or a pig-pickin'. And while you are enjoying all the food and having fun, you are helping the community. The event funds scholarships awarded each year by the civic organization. From Swansboro through Emerald Isle and beyond, the population turns out for all-you-can-eat oysters, flounder, clam chowder, hot dogs or a pig-pickin' with traditional slaw and hush-puppy trimmings. The event usually happens around St. Patrick's Day. Tickets generally range between $30 and $35, with a discount for advance sales. The event takes place from 5 to 8 PM.

April

Newport Pig Cooking Contest
Newport Park, Howard Blvd., Newport
(252) 223-PIGS

The annual Newport Pig Cooking Contest is one of the largest whole-hog, pig-cooking competitions in the state. This huge barbecue competition comes with the first Friday, Saturday and Sunday in April and draws folks from all along the Eastern seaboard for the best barbecue on earth. The event kicks off with a hometown-type parade down Howard Boulevard, and then the teams begin the serious cooking. You'll find great food, baked goods, live entertainment, rides and children's activities. Delicious Down East barbecue goes on sale around 11 AM on Saturday, as soon as judging has been completed. Drive-up service is even available for folks who want a great lunch but don't want to wade through the crowds. The event benefits numerous civic organizations. The winning cooks go on to the state championship.

Woman's Fair
Crystal Coast Civic Center,
3505 Arendell St., Morehead City
(252) 247-3883

Woman's Fair is a trade show that focuses on women's lives. The show features booths and demonstrations on health, well-being, fashion, careers and more. Fashion shows and seminars take place during the expo.

Publick Day
Beaufort Historic Site,
100 block Turner St., Beaufort
(252) 728-5225

On a Saturday in mid-April, this annual event features a Colonial-style flea market with the outdoor sale of varied merchandise and crafts, along with entertainment, mock trials and exhibits. The day recalls Colonial excitement generated by the arrival of the circuit court judge to Beaufort. Proceeds benefit the preservation of historic structures through the Beaufort Historical Association. Admission is free, but expect to have your pocketbook tempted by the array of crafts and goodies available. Hours are from 9 AM to 4 PM.

Portsmouth Island Homecoming
(252) 728-2250

This annual heritage event is at the Portsmouth Historic District in Cape Lookout National Seashore, just south of Ocracoke Inlet. Access is only by boat. The event provides a unique look at early island life. Friends and descendants of island residents get together for an old-fashioned church homecoming and dinner on the grounds. Call for details.

Beaufort By-the-Sea Music Festival
(252) 728-0707

Music flows along Taylor's Creek and through downtown Beaufort each April during the Music Festival. The festival features four or five stages set up throughout town, featuring a variety of music with something sure to suit the ears of all ages. The festival is free, and the whole town gets in on the act.

Emerald Isle Homes Tour & Art Show
Western Carteret Public Library,
Cape Carteret
(252) 354-3691

The Emerald Isle Homes Tour and Art Show, in its ninth year in 2006, is sponsored by the Friends of the Western Carteret Public Library on Taylor Notion Road, where the tour begins. The event takes place on the fourth Saturday in April. Tour hours are 10 AM until 4 PM and hostesses at each home welcome visitors. Tickets can be purchased at the library and the Tourism Center on N.C. Highway 58 and are generally about $15. Tickets come with a map to the homes and gardens found in Emerald Isle and Cape

Carteret. The art show features works by local artists and takes place in the Clubhouse at Land's Inn. Money raised goes toward new book purchases at the library. Books are also on sale.

Fort Macon Civil War Reenactment
Fort Macon State Park, Atlantic Beach
(252)726-3775

This July event features Civil War period activities performed throughout the day by members of the 1st NC Volunteers. Similar events take place in April and September. Talks on flags, uniforms and Civil War dress are held, as well as musket firings and drills. The event is free.

Lookout Spring Road Race
Sports Center, 701 N. 35th St., Morehead City
(252) 726-7070

This annual family fun and fitness road race in Morehead City is sponsored by the Lookout Rotary Club and takes place on the last Saturday of April. The road race begins and ends at the Sports Center, and participants can run a 10K, 5K or 1 mile, or take part in the baby jogger race. Proceeds from the event benefit local charities and civic organizations. There is an entry fee, and families get a price break. Prizes are awarded.

Easter Egg Hunt
Beaufort Historic Site,
100 block Turner St., Beaufort
(252) 728-5225

On Easter weekend, the Beaufort Historic Site is the perfect setting for a traditional Easter egg hunt for the younger members of the family up to age 7. It's a bring-your-own-basket event heaped with small-town warmth and charm. Arrive by 11 AM. Admission is free. Everyone is welcome.

Easter Sunrise Services

The dawning of Easter morning is celebrated in services at several locations across the county, many on the waterfront or beach. The Carteret County News-Times lists service locations and times the week before Easter.

May

Nelson Bay Challenge-Sprint Triathlon
Sea Level

The annual Nelson Bay Challenge Sprint Triathlon includes a 750-meter swim in Nelson Bay, a 20K bike ride and a 5K run the first Saturday of May and is sanctioned by the USA Triathlon. Proceeds from the race, raised by entry fees and sponsors, benefit the Sea Level Rescue Squad, where the event begins at noon. The $45 entry fee (register online at active.com) includes a pasta dinner the night before the race and a clam bake after the race.

Wooden Boat Show
N.C. Maritime Museum, 315 Front St., Beaufort
(252) 728-7317
www.ncmm-friends.org

The Wooden Boat Show of the North Carolina Maritime Museum in Beaufort was the first and is the largest gathering of wooden watercraft in the Southeast. This fascinating event takes place the first Saturday in May. This is not a commercial show. Instead it is a full day of scheduled demonstrations, talks and races that attract people who share an interest in the art, craftsmanship and history of wooden boats. Enthusiasts race radio-controlled boats in the pool on the Maritime Museum patio, and the public is given an opportunity to sail in traditional North Carolina boats. This show has something fun for all ages. Admission is free.

Carteret Numismatic Coin Show
Crystal Coast Civic Center,
3505 Arendell St., Morehead City
(252) 247-3883

Coins collectors from near and far travel to this annual event to view, sell, swap and trade coins of all types. This show is hosted by the local Numismatic Coin Club and is a popular event.

"YOU ASKED FOR IT, YOU GOT IT"
Swansboro Rotary Memorial Day tournament will have ONLY ONE DAY of King Fishing
$25,000 GUARANTEED CASH
1ST PLACE KING MACKEREL
26th Annual
SWANSBORO
ROTARY
King Mackerel Blue Water
TOURNAMENT
May 26th-28th, 2006

SCHEDULE OF EVENTS

REGISTRATION
Friday, May 26, 2006 » 12:00pm - 9:00pm
at the Swansboro Rotary Civic Center

CAPTAIN'S MEETING
Friday, May 26, 2006 » 6:30pm - Bluewater Captain's Meeting
Friday, May 26, 2006 » 7:00pm - King Mackerel Captain's Meeting.

FISHING DAYS
Saturday & Sunday, May 27-28, 2006 - Bluewater Fishing
Saturday, May 27, 2006 - King Fishing

COOKOUTS
Friday, May 26, 2006 » 5:00pm - BBQ Dinner for Participants & Guests
at Swansboro Rotary Civic Center. Extra Tickets $5.00 Each.

Sunday, May 28, 2006 » 5:00pm - Fish Fry for Participants and Guests
at Swansboro Rotary Civic Center. Extra Tickets $5.00 Each.

AWARDS CEREMONY
Sunday, May 28, 2006 » 7:30pm - Lots of CASH & Merchandise

FOR COMPLETE TOURNAMENT INFORMATION:

call: 910•326•FISH
(3474)

visit us at:
www.swansbororotary.com

Crystal Coast Quilt Show
Crystal Coast Civic Center,
3505 Arendell St., Morehead City
(252) 247-3883

Quilts, quilts, quilts and all things to do with quilts and quilting are what you will find at this annual event. Sponsored by the Crystal Coast Quilt Guild, the event is held in mid-May. Each year the talented members of the guild make a quilt to be raffled off at the show, as well as exhibit their creations in a judged show. Vendors offering quilting and sewing supplies and materials.

Swansboro Rotary King Mackerel/
Blue Water Fishing Tournament
Swansboro
(910) 326-3474, 326-6175
www.swansbororotary.com

This annual fishing competition, held at the end of May, has a variety of categories and is sponsored by the Swansboro Rotary Club. Traditionally, some big surprises have been reeled in, including billfish in the huge range. Proceeds from the tournament fund the Meals-On-Wheels program in Swansboro, a variety of youth and school projects and the Rotary's scholarship program. Participants pay category fees to compete in the tournament.

Morehead City Home & Garden Tour
Morehead City
(252) 808-0440

This annual event held in late May is sponsored by the Downtown Morehead City Revitalization Association and focuses on a particular neighborhood, so it can truly be a relaxing stroll. Tickets are generally around $12 in advance, $15 on tour day and are available at The History Place and the Revitalization office. Call for details.

Carteret County Arts and Crafts Coalition Spring Show
Beaufort Historic Site,
100 block Turner St., Beaufort
(252) 726-3354

This outdoor exhibition and sale of arts and crafts by juried coalition members is held during Memorial Day weekend, Saturday from 10 AM to 5 PM and Sunday 1 to 5 PM. Demonstrations, food and music enhance the festive atmosphere, and quality is tops. According to organizers, the show grows each year and the art options continue to evolve. Admission is free.

June

Big Rock Blue Marlin Tournament
Various locations
(252) 247-3575
www.thebigrock.com

Big Rock -- one hardly needs to say more. This is one of the oldest and largest sport-fishing tournaments in the country. It involves great events, parties and daily public weigh-ins on the Morehead City waterfront during a week in mid-June, and it all benefits charities and nonprofit organizations. Of course, the tournament winners benefit from a handsome monetary reward. The purse in 2005 totaled $1.4 million; participants pay category entry fees that begin at about $2,500.

Big Rock Blue Marlin Festivities
Crystal Coast Civic Center, 3505 Arendell St., Morehead City
(252) 247-3883
www.thebigrock.com

The Big Rock Blue Marlin Festivities center around the huge fishing tournament and include a Captain's Party, Wednesday Wahoo and the awards banquet.

Beaufort Old Homes and Gardens Tour
Beaufort Historic Site,
100 block Turner St., Beaufort
(252) 728-5225, (800) 575-SITE

The Old Homes and Garden Tour has become a favorite of visitors from around the world. During the last full weekend in June, the tour opens some of the county's oldest private homes and buildings for narrated tours on Friday and Saturday. New restorations and those in progress keep the tour fresh. You'll see the Beaufort Historic Site, Beaufort Fisheries, Living History demonstrations, the Old Burying Ground and eight delightful gardens. Visitors can also enjoy an antique car show and militia encampment. Advance tour tickets are $16; tickets are $20 on tour days. Children age 12 and younger get in for half price and a combo ticket for the Antiques Show and Sale (see next entry)

is available. This fund-raising activity benefits the Beaufort Historical Association.

Antiques Show and Sale
Crystal Coast Civic Center,
3505 Arendell St., Morehead City
(252) 728-5225, (800) 575-SITE

Held in conjunction with the Beaufort Old Homes and Gardens Tour each June, this show features more than 40 dealers. Enjoy the Gourmet Tea Room with sandwiches, dessert and beverages. Tickets cost $5 and are good Friday through Sunday of Old Homes and Gardens Tour weekend. A combo ticket for the tour and show/sale is offered.

July

Independence Day Celebrations
Various locations

Fourth of July fireworks and festivities take place throughout the Crystal Coast. Morehead City and Atlantic Beach regularly have evening fireworks, and Beaufort has a great "small-town" morning parade along the waterfront that is followed by a community picnic. Consult the local papers for times and festive locations before the weekend, or call the Crystal Coast Visitor Center, (252) 726-8148. Fireworks also light up the Swansboro waterfront every Fourth of July.

Carteret County Arts and Crafts Coalition Summer Show
Beaufort Historic Site,
100 block Turner St., Beaufort
(252) 726-3354

This outdoor exhibition and sale of arts and crafts is usually held on the Fourth of July weekend. With the Tall Ships coming to Beaufort in 2006, the event will be moved but not date has been selected for this show of art by juried coalition members. Demonstrations, food and music enhance the festive atmosphere. The show grows each year, and the artistic options continue to evolve. Admission is free of charge.

Fort Macon Civil War Reenactment
Fort Macon State Park, Atlantic Beach
(252)726-3775

This July event features Civil War period activities performed throughout the day from 10 AM to 4 PM by members of the 1st NC Volunteers. Similar events take place in April and September. Talks on flags, uniforms and Civil War dress are held, as well as musket firings and drills. The event is free.

Concert at the Fort
Fort Macon State Park, Atlantic Beach
(252) 726-3775

One of the many outreach projects of the Friends of Fort Macon is a summer concert series with free admission. There are generally eight concerts spread from June through August, each beginning at 7 PM.

Jazz Festival
New Bern Riverfront Convention Center, New Bern
(252) 247-3883, (252) 726-7081
www.coastaljazz.org

Sponsored by the Coastal Jazz Society, Hot Jazz on the Riverfront in 2006 features Chuchito Valdes. With influences of Caribbean rhythms and jazz, Chuchito creates an exciting and energetic blend of spicy music that drives audiences wild. The event takes place in late July and tickets in the past have been $25. Call for details or check the website for information.

Historic Beaufort Road Race
Front St., Downtown Beaufort
(252) 222-6359

This popular road race takes place on the third Saturday in July and is now in its 27th year. The morning event includes a certified 10K run, a certified 5K run and walk, and a 1-mile run and walk. There are also 10K and 5K wheelchair events and a 5K baby-jogger race. All the events start and end on the Beaufort waterfront. Set for the third Saturday in July each year, the race is organized by Beaufort Ole Towne Rotary to benefit area youth and community projects. The race generally attracts more than 750 entries. There is an entry fee, and families get a price break. Prizes are awarded.

Buddy Pelletier Longboard Memorial Contest
Atlantic Beach
(252) 726-2314

This annual contest takes place in late July at the Oceana Pier on Atlantic Beach. Each year it attracts a growing number of amateur and professional surfers from the East Coast and various countries, including

former and current East Coast, and world champions. The contest is held by the Buddy Pelletier Surfing Foundation, an organization that sponsors fellowships and renders humanitarian aid to members of the East Coast surfing community. The contest offers beginning surfers the chance to get in the water with some of the best the world has to offer while raising funds to help fellow surfers.

August

Outer Banks Wildlife Shelter Sand Castle Contest
On the beach at Atlantis Lodge,
123 N.C. Hwy. 58, Pine Knoll Shores
(252) 240-1200

Held on the first Saturday in August to help support the efforts of the Outer Banks Wildlife Shelter, this sand-castle building competition brings out the best and the brightest in Carteret County and beyond. What began as one energetic family's pastime at a reunion now draws some serious competition for adults and children. The creations are spectacular every year, and it's well worth the trip. The competing sand-sculpting teams raise contributions to benefit the Outer Banks Wildlife Shelter.

Emerald Isle Dog Days Celebration & Triathlon
Emerald Isle
(252) 354-6350

This Emerald Isle Parks and Recreation event is sponsored by the Emerald Isle Business Association. The celebration includes beach music and all types of entertainment. The event kicks off with a sprint triathlon that has competitors taking a swim in the ocean, biking on Highway 58 and running a short neighborhood course. Contact Alicia Sanderson for details or to register.

September

Carteret County Arts and Crafts Coalition Fall Show
Beaufort Historic Site,
100 block Turner St., Beaufort
(252) 726-3354

This organization of fine artists and craftspeople gathers for an outdoor show and sale of excellent quality original arts and crafts on Labor Day weekend. Open from 10 AM to 5 PM Saturday and 1 to 5 PM Sunday, this promises treasures from the best of area craftsmen and artists. Food and music add to the festive atmosphere. Admission is free.

Atlantic Beach King Mackerel Tournament
Sea Water Marina, Atlantic Beach Cswy., Atlantic Beach
(252) 247-2334
www.abkmt.com

This tournament, celebrating its 28th year in 2006, is one of the nation's largest all-cash king mackerel fishing competition events. The September tournament, held the 7th through 9th in 2006, benefits the Atlantic Beach Volunteer Fire Department and the Carteret County Sportfishing Association's Artificial Reef Fund. Registration and all events are at Atlantic Station Shopping Center, with weigh-ins at Sea Water Marina.

Fort Macon Civil War Reenactment
Fort Macon State Park, Atlantic Beach
(252)726-3775

This September event features Civil War-period activities performed throughout the day by members of the 1st NC Volunteers. Similar events also take place in April and July. Talks on flags, uniforms and Civil War dress are held, as are musket firings and drills. The event is free.

Bald Headed Men of America's Convention
Bald Headquarters, 102 Bald Dr., Morehead City
(252) 726-1855, (252) 726-1004

There are no bad hair days during this annual event that takes place in Morehead City. The gathering of this international hair-free group includes a weekend of self-help workshops, testimonials, golf games, picnics, contests for the most kissable head and other activities. Held the second weekend in September, the event has literally put Carteret County on the map, bringing national media attention to the area. The organization was founded by Morehead City's John Capps.

NC Big Sweep
NC Cooperative Extension Service
(252) 222-6352

NC Big Sweep is a statewide effort to clean trash from waterways, beaches and roadsides. The annual event involves many volunteers and takes place in late September or early October. Locally the event is coordinated through the North Carolina Cooperative Extension Service.

October

North Carolina Seafood Festival
Morehead City Waterfront
(252) 726-6273
www.ncseafoodfestival.org

The N.C. Seafood Festival takes place the first weekend in October on the Morehead City waterfront. The 2005 event drew about 175,000 people for this three-day major outdoor annual festival. The second largest festival in North Carolina, its highlights are an endless variety of seafood prepared in a multitude of ways, street dances, concerts (including at least one big-name musician), crafts, educational exhibits, programs and a fair with rides and games. The festivities are spread from the North Carolina State Port to Ninth Street. Parking is available at the port and in the downtown area, and shuttles get festival-goers to the fun. Festival headquarters and a gift shop are located at 907B Arendell Street in Morehead City, and a staff works all year planning and conducting festival-focused activities, like the photographic and art contests that pick poster art for promoting the event and the scholarship golfing extravaganza. Admission is free.

Mullet Festival
Downtown Swansboro
(910) 326-1174

This is the area's oldest festival, started about 55 years ago to celebrate the completion of the new bridge over the White Oak River in Swansboro. The first festival was so fun that it's been celebrated ever since with a parade, a street carnival, arts and crafts and, oh yeah, bountiful mullet and seafood. Held the second Saturday in October, the event boasts of mullet fried, smoked and stewed -- mullet any way you could want it -- and it benefits local civic organizations. This is also a road race for local runners. Admission is free.

Surf Fishing Tournament
Atlantic Beach
(252) 726-6350, (800) 622-6278

The Carteret County Chamber of Commerce and the Town of Atlantic Beach host this fun family event in mid-September. More than 80 anglers vie for prizes, and awards are given on a point system and also for the largest fish in each species. Events include a casting contest.

Carolina Kite Fest
A Place At The Beach,
1904 E. Fort Macon Rd., Atlantic Beach
(252) 247-2636

On this late-October weekend, the sky fills with kite demonstrations, competitions and night kite flying, which absolutely boggles the mind. Imagine the kites you flew as a kid and then add to that every type of kite known to man. That's what you'll find October in Atlantic Beach. It's a spectacle to behold. Participants arrive from across the country. The event is held in late October. Kites Unlimited in Atlantic Station, (252) 247-7011, and Beach Vacation Properties sponsor the annual event. Admission is free.

November

Mill Creek Oyster Festival
Mill Creek Volunteer Fire Dept.,
2370 Mill Creek Rd. (S.R. 1156), Mill Creek
(252) 247-4777

Here's another all-day feed and family event not to be missed. The annual oyster roast in early November is an all-you-can-eat feast for one reasonable charge, usually around $12 (determined by the market price). The early November festival also features other kinds of seafood and includes music and crafts.

Annual Antique-A-Thon
The History Place, Morehead City
(252) 247-7533 ext 101

The annual Antique-A-Thon is scheduled for early November at The History Place in downtown Morehead City. The event gathers experts to assist those with questions about antiques they bring to this event.

Ducks Unlimited Banquet
Crystal Coast Civic Center,
3505 Arendell St., Morehead City
(252) 247-3883

The annual fund-raising benefit for the preservation of waterfowl habitat is eagerly anticipated each year. Ticket price includes membership, a wonderful dinner and an evening at the Crystal Coast Civic Center with more than 400 people committed to waterfowl habitat preservation. There are also live and silent auctions.

Candlelight Art Tour
Galleries in Morehead City and Beaufort
(252) 726-9156

Each November the Arts Council of Carteret County organizes a weekend Candlelight Art Tour. The first day focuses on art galleries in Morehead City and the second day highlights galleries in Beaufort. Art enthusiasts can enjoy an afternoon of touring galleries, enjoying refreshments and watching arts demonstrations at no charge. Maps of gallery locations are available at local businesses and from the Arts Council of Carteret County, 801 Arendell Street, Morehead City. The tour is free.

Jumble Sale
Beaufort Historic Site,
100 block Turner St., Beaufort
(252) 728-5225, (800) 575-SITE

The Beaufort Historic Site turns into a community market with art, handmade crafts, holiday gifts, pre-loved treasures, antiques, clothing, food and much more. Admission is free.

Community Thanksgiving Feast
Beaufort Historic Site,
100 block Turner St., Beaufort
(252) 728-5225, (800) 575-SITE

From 11:30 AM to 1:30 PM on the Sunday before Thanksgiving, a traditional Thanksgiving feast is served at the Beaufort Historic Site. Beaufort restaurants contribute the feast fixings, and the community gathers together in thanks. Proceeds from this ticketed event benefit preservation efforts of the Beaufort Historical Association. A limited number of tickets are sold at the Beaufort Historic Site and usually sell out before the day of the event. Dinners are available for takeout or can be enjoyed in the warmth of the heated tent.

Carteret County Arts and Crafts Coalition Holiday Show
Morehead City
(252) 726-3354

This three-week show and sale of original juried artwork by members of the Carteret County Arts and Crafts Coalition opens each year in alternating locations. Local artists combine their work to create the show for Christmas shopping opportunities and, because of the outstanding works, it is truly and event not to be missed.

December

Christmas Flotillas
Morehead City and Beaufort waterfronts
(252) 728-5806
Swansboro waterfront
(910) 326-7222

On the Crystal Coast, Santa arrives by boat. Evening parades of decorated and lighted boats bring him in to kick off the Christmas season celebration on the coast. On a Saturday in November, late in the morning, Santa arrives at the downtown Beaufort docks, where spectators are waiting to greet him. From then until mid-December, Santa stays busy in his Seaside Santa Workshop on the boardwalk. On both the Morehead City and Beaufort waterfronts at sunset in early December, families gather to ring in the season as the brightly decorated boats slowly drift by in the Crystal Coast Christmas flotilla.

Core Sound Decoy Festival
Harkers Island Elementary School and various locations, Harkers Island
(252) 838-8818

The Core Sound Decoy Festival is a coastal tradition. Held the first full weekend in December on Harkers Island, this two-day festival includes competitions in carving and painting decoys, exhibits and sales of old and new decoys, a loon-calling contest, a children's painting contest and other special competitions. There are additional fun activities for children, educational exhibits and an auction. The festival benefits the Core Sound Decoy Carver's Guild and Harkers Island Elementary School and is the area's largest off-season event.

Waterfowl Weekend
Core Sound Waterfowl Museum, Harkers Island
(252) 728-1500

The Core Sound Waterfowl Museum opens its doors the first weekend in December and offers a slate full of traditional down-home fun. Educational exhibits, competitions, retriever demonstrations, arts and crafts and food can be found at the museum's Shell Point headquarters, near the very end of Island Road on Harkers Island. A Hunting and Fishing Expo is held in conjunction with the festivities at the museum. There are many other special events -- such as a special dessert supper -- associated with this weekend, so call the museum for the latest information.

Festival of Trees
Morehead City
(252) 247-1390

Sponsored in early December by the Friends of Hospice of Carteret County for the benefit of those receiving Hospice services, the annual Festival of Trees features a display of more than 60 decorated trees, a gala preview party and Santa. Local choral groups, school groups and musicians entertain throughout the five-day event.

Coastal Carolina Christmas Walk
Beaufort Historic Site, 100 block Turner St., Beaufort
(252) 728-5225, (800) 575-SITE

In early December historic bed and breakfast inns and buildings in and around the Beaufort Historic Site are decorated for Christmas in traditional styles and open their doors to the public during this annual holiday tradition. The afternoon event generally takes place from 2 to 4:30 PM and offer tours with entertainment and refreshments. The event is free to the public. There is a fee to ride the double-decker bus or to purchase raffle tickets to benefit preservation of historic structures through the Beaufort Historical Association.

FISHING, BOATING, WATERSPORTS AND BEACH ACCESS

The Crystal Coast is the perfect place for water-related activities. Surfers searching for ocean waves, windsurfers and water-skiers looking for calm sound waters, and anglers hoping for something in between will find exactly what they want along the Carteret County coastline. A wonderful bonus for all water enthusiasts is the generally mild climate, which allows folks to participate in their favorite sports nearly all year.

In this chapter we offer a look at fishing, boating, equipment rentals and places where you can access our beautiful beaches. For businesses and beach access areas on Bogue Banks, we have given the mile marker (MM) to help you find them.

Fishing

The Crystal Coast hosts numerous fishing tournaments. The Swansboro Rotary Club hosts its King Mackerel/Blue Water Fishing Tournament in May, and one of the nation's largest king mackerel tournaments, the Atlantic Beach King Mackerel Tournament, is held in September. The Big Rock Blue Marlin Tournament, one of the largest and oldest blue marlin tournaments, is held each June. For details and dates, see our Annual Events chapter.

Federal government studies report that your chances of catching fish in North Carolina waters are unsurpassed along the entire East Coast. Of the 21 recorded catches of Atlantic blue marlin in excess of 1,000 pounds, five have been caught off the North Carolina coast. In fact, a 1,002-pounder is on display in the parking lot behind the Crystal Coast Visitors Center in Morehead City.

Seasoned anglers know a secret: Year-round fishing is a reality here. Ten miles east of Morehead City and Atlantic Beach is Cape Lookout, where saltwater anglers have access to miles and miles of inshore fishing from the sounds, bays, rivers and creeks that define the natural wonderland of our coastal county. Cape Lookout also affords inlets that are passages to ocean waters and deep-sea fishing. Weather permitting, local fishing is soul satisfying in the spring, summer, fall or winter. Consult the Sportfishing Guide in this chapter to find out which months are best for catching particular fish species.

Whether you surf fish from the barrier island beaches, dangle your line from one of the piers dotting the coastline or charter a private boat or head boat, you're sure to have the time of your life. Sport anglers are not required to obtain a fishing license. However, to make sure your fishing experience is fun and legal, before you fish contact the N.C. Division of Marine Fisheries, (252) 726-7021, for a list of size and catch limits and harvest restrictions.

If you desire a remote fishing experience, try vacationing at the fishing camps out on the banks. You'll find more information about these hideaways in our Accommodations chapter.

FISHING SCHOOL

Most anglers come to the Crystal Coast equipped with fishing skills and knowledge, but a growing number of people want to know more about fishing in area waters or want to improve their chances of hooking the big one. The N.C. Aquarium in Pine Knoll Shores, (252) 247-4003, conducts a surf fishing workshop every fall during the second weekend in October. It's taught by experienced fishing guides and is designed for novice surf fishermen, but all anglers are welcome.

FISHING REPORTS

What's biting when and where is as important to avid anglers as the world news is to the rest of us. Information about catches is available at most bait and tackle shops, marinas, piers or charter boat rental offices. To

get the inside track on where to fish, read the Carteret County News-Times. Every Friday it publishes "On the Line," a column by fishing writer Capt. Jerry Dilsaver.

FISHING GEAR

Now that you've boned up on how to fish, it's time to get your gear. Local tackle shops not only have the fishing stuff you'll need, but they also offer bits of advice about what fish are biting and where. We've listed just a few of the many good shops in the area.

Freeman's Bait & Tackle
Atlantic Beach Cswy., Atlantic Beach
(252) 726-2607

Freeman's is easy to find -- just look for the big sign that says "Fish Tales Told Here." This complete saltwater tackle shop sells rods, reels, bait, clothing and other supplies, and offers a repair and cleaning service. Freeman's has been in business for more than 35 years and knows the ins and outs of fishing along the Crystal Coast. Have a question? Just ask. But remember, you may hear a fish tale or two along the way.

EJW Outdoors
4667 Arendell St., Morehead City
(252) 247-4725

EJW's has been in business for more than 50 years and recently expanded its extensive inventory with a move to its new location. EJW's continues to offer gear for a variety of sports, including hunting, biking, paintball and archery. Fishing, however, is its primary focus, and you can find an assortment of rods and reels along with all kinds of bait and clothing. The store also services fishing equipment and bikes.

Harkers Island Tackle Co.
989 Island Rd., Harkers Island
(252) 728-3016

Harkers Island Tackle Co. is a complete saltwater outfitter. Whether you intend to go inshore or offshore saltwater fishing, Harkers Island Tackle Co. has all the equipment you need. They stock Shimano and Penn reels and rods by St. Croix, Crowder, Star and Shimano. It also carries a complete selection of Columbia sportswear.

K&V One Stop Shop
K&V Plaza, 307 Mangrove Dr., Emerald Isle
(252) 354-7100

K&V One Stop Shop is a convenience store and gas station as well as a bait and tackle shop. At this year-round shop anglers will find groceries, all kinds of bait, crabbing supplies and tackle boxes. Also for sale are rods and reels and rain gear for those dedicated to fishing no matter what the weather. K&V also can hook you up with a charter boat.

FISHING PIERS

Fishing and crabbing from piers is a favorite pastime along the Crystal Coast. While hurricanes in recent years have wreaked havoc on several favorite spots, there are still a few piers open for business. Fishing piers are popular spots during the spring, summer and fall. The piers listed here are commercial enterprises and charge a fee, usually between $4 and $8, for a day/night of fishing. Take along your kids or anyone who has never fished -- it's fun!

Oceanana Fishing Pier
MM 1, N.C. Hwy. 58, Atlantic Beach
(252) 726-4111, (252) 726-0863
www.oceanana.com

This lighted pier is part of the Oceanana Family Resort Motel, but you don't have to be a motel patron to fish from it. Fishing passes are the lowest cost on the Crystal Coast, and motel guests fish for free in the off-season. Catering to families, the Oceanana has a large, oceanfront, grassy recreation space with lots of playground equipment situated so that parents can relax while the kids play. The Oceanana also rents rods and reels and has an arcade, a tackle and snack shop, and plenty of parking. The pier's grill offers delicious breakfast and lunch menus for all beachgoers.

i

In Crystal Coast waters, the best fish to catch in the surf are striped bass, bluefish, summer flounder (also known as fluke), weakfish, speckled trout, red drum, kingfish, croaker, spot, pompano and Spanish mackerel. (Source: Surf Fishing–Catching Fish from the Beach, by Joe Malat.)

Bogue Inlet Fishing Pier
MM 19, N.C. Hwy. 58, Emerald Isle
(252) 354-2919

This 1,000-foot lighted pier is a popular spot for anglers and beachgoers. Parking in the large lot is free weekdays and $5 on Saturday and Sunday; from there access to the ocean beach is a short walk through the lot and down some wooden stairs. People who want to fish may do so from the pier all day at rates starting at $7. Bathrooms, a place to clean your catch, tackle, bait and a snack bar are on the premises.

Head, Charter and Tour Boats

Fortunate anglers can fish from their own boats, but lacking your own (or a friend's) you can choose from the dozens of commercial rentals and charters. One good way to enjoy a day of inexpensive fishing is on a head boat. These large vessels take as many as 50 people out into the Gulf Stream for a day's worth of deep-sea fishing. The name came about because you pay by the head, or per person, for the trip. You don't hire the entire boat, just a spot on the deck. The crew provides the rods, reels and bait; you just take your personal belongings, such as a cooler of drinks and snacks, seasickness prevention, weather gear and sun protection.

Charter boats are smaller vessels hired by a private party of four to six individuals. A typical half-day excursion will take you bottom fishing offshore where grouper, red snapper, triggerfish and grunts are plentiful. A whole day of deep-sea fishing involves motoring some 40 miles offshore to the Gulf Stream. Chartering a boat to troll the Gulf Stream is what you want if you hope to catch tuna, wahoo, dolphin, marlin and sailfish. Be advised, though, that boat charters are expensive -- daily fees range from $500 to $1,200 or more for a full party. If you don't have a complete group, a charter captain may be able to hook you up with another half-party willing to share the expenses of chartering the boat.

Most head and charter boats operate year round, with less frequent trips in the dead of winter. For more information about head and charter boats, we recommend you walk along the Morehead City and Beaufort waterfronts, check out the marinas on the Atlantic Beach Causeway or talk with other anglers. Outer Banks Sail and Kayak, 612 Atlantic Beach Causeway, (252) 247-6300, offers charter services, as well as sailboat and kayak rentals.

More than 70 licensed charter boats and head boats operate year-round on the Crystal Coast so we can't list them all here. Our descriptions are representative samples of the vessels available for hire.

Capt. Stacy Fishing Center
Atlantic Beach Cswy., Atlantic Beach
(252) 247-7501, (800) 533-9417
www.captstacy.com

Capt. Stacy's fleet consists of more than 14 vessels, including everything from 35-foot sport-fishing boats to a 65-foot head boat and an 83-foot head boat. The head boats offer half- and full-day trips along with a 24-hour trip. The fleet's charter boats can be hired for half- and full-day trips year-round. The Capt. Stacy Center also offers private cruises for weddings and other parties.

Carolina Princess
Sixth St., Morehead City
(252) 726-5479, (800) 682-3456

Owner-Captain WooWoo Harker is one of the area's best-known captains. Since 1952 the 95-foot head boat Carolina Princess has offered a variety of ways to enjoy the area and the Gulf Stream. Full-day and 18-hour fishing trips are available year round, and half-day trips are offered Monday, Wednesday and Friday in the summer. Also available are affordable stand-up sport-fishing cruises for up to 12 anglers hoping to land big game such as tuna, dolphin, wahoo and marlin. The Carolina Princess can accommodate 100 people. Group fishing trips, parties, receptions and weddings can also be arranged.

Coastal Ecology Sails
Beaufort Docks, Beaufort
(252) 247-3860

Capt. Ron White of the Good Fortune, a 41-foot center-cockpit ketch with red sails, and his trusty first mate, Lt. Willis, take passengers on custom sailing tours that may include dolphin watching, beach exploration, lighthouse visiting, snorkeling, shelling, wild horse watching and, of course, sailing. With 26 years experience, Capt. White can customize a package, for up to six people maximum, that will make your visit to the Crystal Coast a truly memorable one.

Continental Shelf
711 Shepard St., Morehead City
(252) 726-7454, (800) 775-7450

The Continental Shelf is a 100-foot head boat that goes out on half-day and full-day fishing trips in season, with half-day trips are offered on Tuesdays and Thursdays. Other trips available include 15-, 18- and 24-hour trips. The boat docks on the Morehead City waterfront beside Discovery Diving. The Continental Shelf is available for private charter groups, fishing, evening cruising or daytime sightseeing.

Mystery Tours
410 Front St., Beaufort
(252) 728-7827, (866) 230-BOAT
www.mysteryboattours.com

Enjoy inland bay fishing aboard the Mystery. The trip includes your rod, reel, bait, tackle and ice. Mates onboard help bait hooks and remove fish. So it couldn't be easier to try your hand at catching flounder, blues, croaker and sharks. The Mystery will have you to your first fishing spot within 15 minutes of leaving the dock. There is also an onboard snack bar with light snacks, cold drinks and hot coffee. Call to book a trip.

Nancy Lee Fishing Center
N.C. Hwy. 24 E., Swansboro
(252) 354-3474, (910) 326-4304

Three miles from Emerald Isle, Nancy Lee Fishing Center offers five-hour headboat fishing charters for adults and children as well as five-, eight- and 11-hour private charters that consist of bottom fishing and trolling. All of Capt. Lee Manning's vessels are Coast Guard inspected and equipped with the latest safety and electronics gear. Private dolphin-watch cruises are also available.

Boating

MOTOR/SAILBOAT RENTALS AND SAILING INSTRUCTION

There's nothing finer on a bright, breezy sunny day than taking to the water in a boat, particularly a sailboat. You'll often hear sailing enthusiasts quote, oddly enough, The Wind in the Willows: "There is nothing -- absolute NOTHING -- half so much worth doing as simply messing-about in boats." Watersports Rentals, with locations at MM 11, Salter Path, (252) 240-4FUN and at MM 12, Indian Beach, (252) 247-7303, features sailboats for rent and sailing instruction. Kids ages 8 and older who want to learn how to sail should check out the North Carolina Maritime Museum's summertime Junior Sailing Program, (252) 728-7317.

Causeway Marina
Atlantic Beach Cswy., Atlantic Beach
(252) 726-6977

Causeway does not charter, but it does rent do-it-yourself, outboard-driven Carolina skiffs and pontoons. Local navigation information and charts are furnished with each boat. Reservations are recommended at this popular spot.

Outer Banks Sail and Kayak
612 Atlantic Beach Cswy., Atlantic Beach
(252) 247-6300
www.obsk.com

If you've ever wanted to learn how to sail, now is the chance with Outer Banks Sail and Kayak's great instructional programs geared toward sailors of all skill levels. Set up your personalized class schedule, either by yourself or with a group, with one of the US Sailing certified instructors. After completion of your class, you can then rent a boat by the hour, half day or full day to test your newly learned skills on the water. Kayak rentals and tours also are available. The children's program is designed to introduce youngsters to the wonderful world of sailing and kayaking during half and full-day programs.

If you're not in the mood to captain the boat yourself, sit back and relax on the Siriuslee as Captain Lee Sutton sails the waters of Taylor's Creek on a half-day trip, introduces you to the thrill of sailing offshore at Cape Lookout on a full-day trip, and cruises the Beaufort waterfront at sunset. During the popular dinner cruise, you'll enjoy the Beaufort waterfront at sunset, followed up with a run over to the Morehead City waterfront for dinner at the Key West Seafood Restaurant.

Capt. Sutton and his crew invite you to call play at OBSK -- just call for reservations and then come prepared to have fun.

KAYAKING

With hundreds of miles of inland and coastal waterways, kayaking along the Crystal Coast gains in popularity yearly. As interest in kayaking grows, so do the number of businesses offering rentals and tours. Unlike the wild, crashing rides through roiling river waters, kayaking along the coast is a peaceful, safe way to explore the naturally shallow waters of our abundant inlets, creeks and estuaries, which are home to an incredibly rich diversity of wildlife.

Outer Banks Sail and Kayak
612 Atlantic Beach Cswy., Atlantic Beach
(252) 247-6300
www.obsk.com

In addition to sailboats, Outer Banks Sail and Kayak also rents kayaks and offers kayaking tours. Full and half day trips will introduce you to beautiful waterways along Bogue Sound, Brandt Marsh or Hoophole Creek, among other locations. Experience is not necessary; reservations are recommended. The children's program also introduces children to kayaking during half and full-day programs.

WaterSports Rentals I
MM 12, N.C. Hwy. 58, Indian Beach
(252) 247-7303

WaterSports Rentals II
MM 11, N.C. Hwy. 58, Salter Path
(252) 240-4FUN

WaterSports Rentals offers personal watercraft, kayaks, paddle boats and sailboats for rentals. The experienced staff also is willing to provide lessons and guidance to beginners and others. If you are looking for something a little less active and a little more fun, consider embarking on a banana boat ride or renting a paddle boat. Both locations also sell gifts, jewelry and clothing. The Indian Beach location invites landlubbers to enjoy the sand and surf and watch not just the action but also the spectacular sunsets from its 180-foot pier and observation deck, also

To get the inside track on where to fish, read the Carteret County News-Times. Every Friday it publishes "On the Line," a column by fishing writer Capt. Jerry Dilsaver.

known as the Dolphin Deck Tiki Bar. Water lovers will find hot showers and changing rooms on the premises, as well as a selection of beer, soda, snacks and sandwiches.

Core Sound Kayaks and Touring Co./Cape Lookout Outfitters
Harkers Island Rd., 3.7 mi. off U.S. Hwy. 70
(252) 728-2330

Kayakers now have easy access to the beautiful waters Down East, thanks to Core Sound Kayaks and Touring Company and Cape Lookout Outfitters. Here you can rent a kayak from Core Sound native Capt. Dennis Chadwick and his wife, Robin, plus find some basic instruction and gain some Insider knowledge on the most picturesque areas for a day of paddling. Go at it alone or let the Chadwicks give you a tour through to local destinations such as Cape Lookout Lighthouse. Kayaks are rented by the half-day and full day. Drinks and snacks are available on-site. Core Sound is an authorized dealer of Wilderness Systems Kayaks. Capt. Chadwick also offers birding and sight-seeing tours around Harkers Island, Cape Lookout, Shackleford Banks, and the Rachel Carson estuary for groups up to six abroad his Harkers Island–built flared bow wooden skiff.

DolphinMoonKayak
(252) 808-7485

DolphinMoonKayak specializes in individual and small group touring and instruction to assist in your exploration of the pristine Crystal Coast region. This is the one to contact to learn about the history, environment and geology of the coast as you glide past the shorebirds, horses, dolphins and sea turtles that inhabit this barrier island region. Local touring favorites include trips to Rachel Carson Estuary, Cape Lookout, Beaufort waterfront, Shackleford Banks, Core Banks and Hammock's Beach. Half day, full day and extended trips are available and custom trips can be designed just for you.

BOAT RAMPS

Catering to water lovers is something the Crystal Coast does best, and you'll find a variety of boat ramps in Carteret County to get you on your way. Whether you've rented a boat or have your own, you'll need to know where you can launch it. Private ramps are in every part of the Crystal Coast, and most marinas and campgrounds have boat ramps. For a list of the free town- or county-maintained ramps see our Crystal Coast Marinas chapter or call the marina closest to you and, chances are, you won't have to drive far to put your boat in the water.

Watersports

PERSONAL WATERCRAFT RENTAL

The popularity of one-person (or sometimes two- or three-person) watercraft is growing quickly, and shops renting Jet Skis and Waverunners are keeping up with that popularity. Some local townships have placed regulations on the use of such watercraft, so be sure to ask your rental or service agent about current rules before hitting the water for a day of fun. WaterSports Rentals, MM 12, Indian Beach, (252) 247-7303, offers personal watercraft rentals and lessons as well as scenic guided tours.

SCUBA DIVING AND SNORKELING

The Crystal Coast has been named one of the ten best diving locales in North America by several popular dive magazines. And with the number of shipwrecks located off Carteret County's coastline, wreck diving is growing in popularity. Local businesses are quick to keep up with demand, and new dive shops are a common sight. Diving is an all-year activity thanks to the Gulf Stream's warm waters, which are about 40 miles offshore. In summer, water temperatures average in the 80s, with visibility of 75 feet to as much as 150 feet. The best dive months are June through September, when most tropical fish are present. Since 1994, readers of Scuba Diving magazine have consistently ranked North Carolina as one of the Best Diving Destinations in North America. It's also been recognized by Scuba Diving readers as the top spot for Wreck Diving and Big Animal Life Diving.

Olympus Dive Center
713 Shepard St., Morehead City
(252) 726-9432

In business since 1976, Olympus is operated by the Purifoy family. With two custom dive boats, it is a full-service shop offering

Early risers are sure to catch their limit.

photo: George Mitchell

full- and half-day dive charters, equipment rental and instruction. The shop is also a Nitrox facility. Beginners can take National Association of Underwater Instructors (NAUI) and Professional Association of Diving Instructors (PADI) entry-level courses. For the advanced diver, the center offers specialty certifications such as night diving and wreck diving. Equipment rentals and sales, charters and instruction are available for everyone from the novice to the serious diver. Olympus also has some interesting dive artifacts on display, and it's worth a trip to check these out.

Discovery Diving Company
414 Orange St., Beaufort
(252) 728-2265

When you're ready to learn, Discovery can teach you to scuba dive or snorkel. On the water on Orange Street, the company offers Professional Association of Diving Instructors (PADI) Open Water Diver training. Discovery has an in-house repair shop and rents and sells just about everything you need for diving: tanks, regulators, masks, fins, snorkels and wet suits. The company arranges and conducts dive trips to fascinating sites: submerged submarines, ocean liners, tankers, freighters and armed trawlers. If you're not part of a group, Discovery will set you up with other interested divers.

WINDSURFING

To many, windsurfing is the thrill of thrills, and wave sailors are discovering that the Crystal Coast is a nearly perfect place for the watersport they can't seem to get enough of. Everything windsurfers need -- mild temperatures, miles of open water and windy conditions -- is right here on the Crystal Coast. Island Rigs, MM 12, Indian Beach, (252) 247-7787, offers windsurfing lessons and basic equipment rentals during the summer.

Insiders know the shallow, protected waters of Bogue Sound are ideal for the neophyte windsurfer, while the more exposed areas, such as Beaufort, Bogue, Shackleford and Drum inlets, offer exciting challenges for experienced sailors. Comfortable water temperatures, provided by the Gulf Stream, and steady winds year round add to the attraction of windsurfing in our area.

PARASAILING

Beaufort Inlet Watersports
Front Street, Beaufort
(252) 728-7607

You've seen the Crystal Coast by land, now see it from a unique perspective -- by air in a parasail! Based on the Beaufort waterfront directly across from the Inlet Inn, Beaufort Inlet Watersports offers parasailing trips that will give you spectacular aerial views of Fort Macon, Shackleford Banks, Carrot Island,

Cape Lookout Lighthouse, Morehead City, Beaufort, marine life and the wild ponies from two choices of height. No experience, skills or gear are necessary -- Beaufort Inlet Watersports provides adults and children ages 3 and up everything they need. Up to six passengers can be accommodated on each trip, and two at a time are launched from the boat. Because you are launched from and returned directly to the boat, you don't even need a bathing suit to enjoy parasailing the Crystal Coast. It's so easy, that's why owner Daryl Austin and his crew have adopted the motto, "Bathing suits not required". Other unique activities offered by Beaufort Inlet Watersports include water tubing and rentals of single and tandem clear-bottom and solid kayaks.

SKIING

We're talking water-skiing here. Most surf shops carry water skis and will provide you with information on where to ski. Favorite water-skiing spots are Bogue Sound west of the Atlantic Beach high-rise bridge, the waters of Back Sound between Beaufort and Shackleford, and Core Creek north of Beaufort. These areas are typically free from no-wake zones and are wide enough to allow for skier safety.

SURFING

Surfing is and always has been very popular along the North Carolina coast. There are plenty of places to catch the swell on the Crystal Coast. Any of our surf shops can provide information about wave conditions and surf contests, and local surfers along the Atlantic Beach oceanfront are great sources of information. Most local outfits also rent surfboards and body boards. Listed below are some of the surf shops that can fulfill your needs.

Action Surf Shop, 5116 U.S. Highway 70 W., Morehead City, (252) 240-1818

Bert's Surf Shop, MM 2, N.C. Hwy. 58, Atlantic Beach, (252) 726-1730; MM 19, N.C. Hwy. 58, Emerald Isle, (252) 354-6282; and across from the Bogue Inlet Pier at 300 Islander Drive, (252) 354-2441

Marsh's Surf Shop, 615 Atlantic Beach Causeway, Atlantic Beach, (252) 726-9046

Hot Wax Surf Shop, 200 Mallard Drive, Emerald Isle, (252) 354-6466

SWIMMING

You can swim just about anywhere along the Crystal Coast, with the exception of a few posted areas. But even the most skilled pool swimmer may have difficulty dealing with ocean waves and undertows, so be careful and never swim alone.

Riptides and undertows are very common along the North Carolina shoreline. If you find yourself being pulled by frightening currents, the most important thing to do is to stay calm. If you are caught in a riptide, relax and let it carry you toward the sea. Eventu-

It looks like the bite is on!

photo: George Mitchell

A good way to get to know the Crystal Coast is to escape to Shackleford Banks and explore on your own. Take your own boat or catch one of the passenger ferries described in our Getting Around chapter.

ally it will dissipate. Swim parallel to the shore to get out of the riptide, and then swim toward the shore.

Be aware that only a handful of beaches employ lifeguards. Areas along Bogue Banks, such as the Atlantic Beach Circle area and Fort Macon State Park, post lifeguards during the summer season. Swimming is not allowed around Fort Macon's rock jetties or on the inlet side.

There are no public pools on the Crystal Coast, only those at hotels, condominiums, private communities and fitness centers. (Read our chapter on Sports, Fitness and Parks to learn more about fitness center swimming pools.)

Beach Access

If you want to swim, walk or run, surf fish, collect shells or sunbathe, how do you get onto our marvelous Crystal Coast beaches? As is true in many coastal areas, getting onto the beach can be confusing. It can be difficult to tell where the private property ends and public access begins. Parking can also be difficult at times. Towns along Bogue Banks, including Indian Beach, Pine Knoll Shores and Emerald Isle, are currently working on making the beach more accessible to visitors and locals. Until then, Insiders know where to go. In this section we list many of the spots that will take you directly to the ocean or sound. We also tell you which places have parking and bathroom facilities and are disabled accessible.

Public Beach Access areas are marked with signs that feature blue letters and a sea gull flying in an orange circle. These signs are not large, so keep your eyes open for them. For the Bogue Banks areas we cite the mile marker (MM) and we begin with one of the area's most popular public beach playgrounds, the access at The Circle. Then we work from east to west (from Fort Macon to Emerald Isle). Some access areas have gates that are opened at first light and closed at dusk; others allow driving on the beach with certain restrictions.

ATLANTIC BEACH

When you crest the Atlantic Beach bridge you know you've reached the beach at last. Beautiful Bogue Sound spreads out before you, busy with boats and the beckoning spray of their wakes. The all-embracing horizon, whether sun- or cloud-filled, promises ocean waves and sandy beaches. As you descend the bridge, you can detect the colorful beach structures that characterize The Circle. At the intersection of Atlantic Beach Causeway and N.C. 58, The Circle is directly in front of you. Three big flags -- American, State of North Carolina and Atlantic Beach -- wave in greeting.

Traffic signs on The Circle advise vehicles to bear right on West Drive. A half-block down this street is the West Atlantic Boulevard Regional Access. (The Town of Atlantic Beach keeps parking meters around The Circle during the vacation season. The meters are removed near Labor Day and replaced the week before Easter, so parking is free in the fall and winter.) There are bike racks, bathrooms, a bathhouse with outdoor showers, drinking fountains, faucets for cleaning fish and a covered gazebo should you wish to stay out of the sun. The beach is easily reached by a wooden ramp, suitable for disabled persons.

Vehicular access to the ocean is just off The Circle, at the south end of Raleigh Avenue. Atlantic Beach closes the beach to vehicles between Good Friday and Labor Day.

Fort Macon State Park, at the eastern tip of Bogue Banks, offers miles and miles of sandy ocean beaches on which to roam, swim and sunbathe. The park has two popular access areas. The one at the west end, before you pass by the park office, is a Regional Public Beach Access area (look for the inconspicuous Bath House sign on the right side of N.C. 58 as you approach the fort). These popular family beaches are disabled accessible and feature a large bathhouse, outdoor showers, a seasonal refreshment stand, picnic shelters, outdoor grills and ample parking. Here you can indulge in all the beach activities you wish.

The other Fort Macon beach access is a sandy track leading from the southwestern corner of the parking lot that serves visitors to the fort. This pathway takes you over the dunes to a wide stretch of beach facing Bogue Inlet. Visitors cannot swim, wade or surf at this access, but walking, observing shore and sea life and basking in the sunshine are permitted. The only restroom is at the entrance to the fort. (For more information about Fort Macon State Park, see the Crystal Coast Attractions chapter.)

The Les and Sally Moore Public Beach Access at MM 1offers toilet facilities, outdoor showers, a covered gazebo and a boardwalk over the dunes to the beach. It is equipped for the disabled and offers parking for about 50 cars. Once on the beach, the young and not-so-young will find swings at the foot of the primary dunes.

Farther west on Salter Path Road near MM 4, the Sheraton Atlantic Beach Oceanfront Hotel maintains a parking lot. The Sheraton charges a fee for all-day parking during the season; otherwise, this public access is available to pedestrians only. Look for the access sign on the east side of the lot.

PINE KNOLL SHORES

Pine Knoll Shores has worked hard over the past few years to provide more public beach access points throughout the town. Two of the town's largest public access points are located at Memorial Park, MM 6, with 40 parking spaces, an overlook deck and a picnic table and adjacent to the Iron Steamer, MM 7, featuring parking spaces for about 60 cars and a restroom.

Parking only is available at these access points: 10 spaces near the Royal Pavilion, MM 5; 25 spots along the western boundary of the Ramada Inn near MM 8; and 20 slots underneath the water tower at the Indian Beach/Pine Knoll Shores town boundary, right past MM 9.

SALTER PATH

Carteret County maintains the Salter Path Regional Public Beach Access, MM 10 off Salter Path Road. It's a 22-acre park with paved parking for 75 cars, a boardwalk over the dunes to the ocean, a picnic area, bathrooms and outdoor showers. It is equipped for disabled persons. Needless to say, this is a very popular spot and is usually full from dawn to dusk.

INDIAN BEACH

The western portion of Indian Beach has one access at MM 11 off Salter Path Road; it is the only off-road-vehicle location in the middle of the island. Turn on S.R. 1192. The sandy access is at the end of that road. You'll find angled parking spaces on one side of the road that leads to the ramp.

Other access areas include the Sea Isle Plantation Access, located in wooded area just east of MM 10, with 10 spaces; the Ocean Club Access, at the border of Salter Path Campground and Ocean Club Townhouses right past MM 11, with 10 slots; and the old Indian Beach Pier Access at MM 12 with 10 spots.

EMERALD ISLE

Emerald Isle features quite a few public beach access points, many of them handicapped-accessible. Beach wheelchairs for physically challenged individuals are available for check out from Emerald Isle Fire Station #1 from 8 AM to 5 PM seven days a week. Be aware that parking at many of the access points may be limited or non-existent. We've listed a few of the largest ones that offer public parking.

Third Street Ocean Access, located just west of the Indian Beach line near MM 12, offers parking for 10 cars, an overlook picnic area and a ramp that goes over the dunes to the beach.

The Eastern Ocean Regional Access is located at 2700 Emerald Drive between Pier Point and Ocean Reef Condominiums. The parking lot can accommodate 245 cars, and daytrippers will appreciate the picnic gazebo, outdoor showers, bathrooms and drink machines.

The Western Ocean Regional Access is located just over the B. Cameron Langston Bridge near the Islander Motor Inn at 299 Islander Drive. This access area features sand volleyball courts, restrooms, outdoor showers and parking for 250 cars.

Emerald Isle Parks and Recreation loans out four beach wheelchairs for disabled persons. The wheelchairs have great big tires for negotiating the sandy beaches, and they break down to fit into a car trunk. You can

borrow one for a day for free; pick them up at the Emerald Isle Fire Department on N.C. 58. Pick up after 8 AM and return by 8 PM. A driver's license is required to borrow a wheelchair. Handicapped access points include Randy's Way Access at 9519 Ocean Drive and Wyndtree Access at 10535 Wyndtree Drive; both feature a single handicapped parking space.

BEAUFORT

The Newport River Park is on the east side of the Beaufort-Morehead City high-rise bridge, off the causeway on U.S. 70. It has a pier, sandy beach, picnic area, bathhouse and launching ramp sufficient for small sailboats. This is a popular spot for fishing. The park entrance is directly across from Radio Island.

Radio Island, off the causeway on U.S. 70, is the largest island between the Beaufort-Morehead City high-rise bridge and the drawbridge into Beaufort. It is home to a variety of businesses -- marinas, boat builders and a fuel terminal. The beach access is a favorite spot for locals because it fronts Beaufort Channel and affords an impressive view of Beaufort and the surrounding islands. Swimmers are advised to stay close to shore when swimming due to dangerous currents in the deeper water. Portable toilets are provided, grills and picnic tables are available, and there's plenty of parking.

HARKERS ISLAND

Located on the southeast side of the Harkers Island drawbridge, this beach access point offers 20 parking spaces but no facilities.

MARINAS

North Carolina has the largest area of inland waters on the East Coast. The Outer Banks enclose several large inland sounds: Currituck, Albemarle, Pamlico, Core and Bogue, which are laced together north to south by 265 miles of the Intracoastal Waterway (ICW). This liquid highway of inland waters makes the numerous coastal resorts and historical points of interest easily accessible by boat.

Of Carteret County's total 1,063 square miles, 531 miles are water. The bountiful brine giving definition to the Crystal Coast challenges the greater portion of the populace and most annual visitors to see the area by water. The weather lures pleasure boaters and sailors almost year round. Even in the coldest months, you'll find a few days that are too pretty to stay ashore.

Because many boaters enjoy the shallow, protected waters along the Crystal Coast, numerous marinas are available to serve the fleet of water traffic. There are more than 35 marinas, most on or just off the ICW. And, via the ICW, boaters can sojourn to nearby Oriental (see our chapter on Oriental) and New Bern, where a number of marinas serve power and sailing vessels. See the Marinas section of our New Bern On the Water chapter for those marina listings.

Crystal Coast marinas have varying water depths, services, amenities, transient accommodations and proximity to sights and services. Many condominium developments and campgrounds provide private docks for their owners and renters. Here we list many of the Crystal Coast's marinas. Please call to inquire whether a marina offers the specific services you'll need.

For you boaters who don't leave home without your craft trailing behind, we've also given the locations of public launch ramps. There is no launch fee at these locations. At most of the marinas we've listed, launch ramps are available. In general, marinas charge a small fee for use and to leave your vehicle and trailer while your boat is in the water.

Marinas

BOGUE BANKS

Anchorage Marina
517 E. Fort Macon Rd., Atlantic Beach
(252) 726-4423

Anchorage Marina is convenient for anglers and pleasure boaters. It has 130 slips, rented on an annual basis, for boats up to 60 feet, a launch ramp, and gas and diesel fuel. Anchorage Marina also is located within walking distance of motels and restaurants.

Atlantic Beach Causeway Marina
300 Atlantic Beach Cswy., Atlantic Beach
(252) 726-6977

On the causeway in Atlantic Beach, Causeway Marina has 13 wet slips, repairs, supplies and gas or diesel fuels. It is the authorized sales and service dealer for Suzuki outboards and Carolina Skiff.

Island Harbor Marina
510 W. Marina Dr., Emerald Isle
(252) 354-3106

With channel access off the ICW, Island Harbor Marina has 150 wet slips for boats up to 50 feet, three launch ramps, a ships store, gas and diesel fuel, fenced storage for boats on trailers and boat rentals.

Sea Water Marina
400 Atlantic Beach Cswy., Atlantic Beach
(252) 726-1637

A favorite of sport-fishing boats, Sea Water Marina on the Atlantic Beach Causeway has 25 wet slips, on-site gas and diesel fuel stations and a complete ships store.

Capt. Stacy Fishing Center
410 Atlantic Beach Cswy., Atlantic Beach
(252) 247-7501, (800) 533-9417
www.captstacy.com

Known for its charter boats and deep-sea fishing trips led by highly experienced and respected captains, Capt. Stacy Fishing Center also has 15 permanent slips with deep-water access. Diesel fuel and electrical services are available, and a gift, tackle and bait shop are located on-site. For more information about Capt. Stacy Fishing Center, see our Fishing, Boating, Watersports & Beach Access chapter.

Triple S Marina Village
1511 E. Fort Macon Rd., Atlantic Beach
(252) 247-4833

Near Fort Macon State Park, Triple S Marina Village has 65 slips often used by weekend anglers. Camper spaces and a launch ramp are on site, and gasoline is also available. Restaurants are nearby.

BEAUFORT

Boaters who arrive in Beaufort via the ICW may drop anchor in Taylor's Creek in the designated anchorage on the south side of the channel. A number of moorings are privately owned, and boaters are asked to respect waterway courtesies of space and anchorage. There is no charge for anchoring and no limit for length of stay. A public dinghy dock and restrooms are available. The dockmaster at the Dock House is available to answer questions. Town Creek on the north side of Beaufort is also a designated anchorage with dinghy landing.

Airport Marina
294 W. Beaufort Rd., Beaufort
(252) 728-2010

At the north end of Turner Street on South Creek, Airport Marina has 17 wet slips, a launch ramp and restrooms. Boaters also can purchase snacks, cold sodas and beer, ice and fishing tackle.

Beaufort Gas Dock
330 Front St., Beaufort
(252) 728-4129

Services offered at this dock include gas and diesel fueling, 30/50-amp electric service for transient yachts, three spaces for overnight dockage, and a convenience store. Other amenities feature parasailing adventures, a restaurant and ferry service to Cape Lookout and the Rachel Carson Reserve. Houseboats and kayaks also are available for rent.

Beaufort Docks
500 Front St., Beaufort
(252) 728-2503

Probably the most frequented marina by transient boaters visiting the Crystal Coast, Beaufort Docks has 100 slips and gas and diesel fueling services. It accommodates boats up to 250 feet. Right on the boardwalk in downtown Beaufort, the marina is convenient to restaurants and lodging, and it offers a courtesy car to use for supply runs.

Morehead Sports Marina
202 Radio Island Rd., Beaufort
(252) 726-5676

On the Morehead-Beaufort Causeway, this marina has 20 wet slips, dry storage on racks, a launch ramp and gasoline. It also sells and services outboard engines.

Radio Island Marina
156 Radio Island Rd., Beaufort
(252) 726-3773

Radio Island Marina, located on the Morehead City-Beaufort Causeway, has 25 wet slips, lift-out dry storage and gasoline. It offers repairs and sells boat and fishing supplies.

Sea Gate Marina
729 Sea Gate Dr., Beaufort
(252) 728-4126

Off N.C. Highway 101, 1 mile north of Core Creek Bridge on the ICW, Sea Gate is a development with a 72-slip marina used for both residents and non-residents. An additional 25 slips are currently in the works. Gas and diesel fuels and a launch ramp are also available, as are 24-hour laundry facilities, a boaters' lounge, a small ships store and showers.

Town Creek Marina and Yacht Sales
232 W. Beaufort Rd., Beaufort
(252) 728-6111

Just north of the Beaufort drawbridge, Town Creek offers many services, including a complete boat yard with a 50-ton lift, 88 wet slips with floating docks, transient dockage for boats up to 140 feet, dry storage and gas and diesel fuels.

MOREHEAD CITY

Coral Bay Marina
4531 Arendell St., Morehead City
(252) 247-4231

On Pelletier Creek, Coral Bay Marina offers 20 slips for boats up to 50 feet and dry-storage services for boats of 30 feet and less. Slips are rented by the month. Gasoline, diesel fuel and engine repair services are available.

Harbor Master
4408 Central Dr., Morehead City
(252) 726-2541

On Pelletier Creek, Harbor Master has 30 slips rented by the year. It offers haul-out and dry storage in a working boat yard, which includes a propeller shop. Harbor Master also offers hurricane haul-out services.

Morehead City Yacht Basin
208 Arendell St., Morehead City
(252) 726-6862

Famous in Carteret County as the spot where Ernest Hemingway once docked his boat, the Yacht Basin, as it's known around town, is just off Calico Creek north of the Morehead City high-rise bridge. Seventy slips are available for monthly and transient dockage for boats up to 150 feet. Gas and diesel fuels are on site. Internet service is available for customers, as are laundry facilities, showers, a ships store and an observation deck. Sea Tow is located on the premises.

Morehead Gulf Docks
608 Evans St., Morehead City
(252) 726-5461

This dock offers gas and diesel fueling, 30/50-amp electric service, and four spaces accommodating boats up to 120 feet. It is within walking distance to a ships store, a gift shop and several restaurants.

Portside Marina
209 Arendell St., Morehead City
(252) 726-7678

Dry stack and out-of water storage are available at Portside Marina, located between the North Carolina State Port and the Morehead City waterfront. Gasoline, diesel, 15 slips and repair services are offered. Boaters will also find showers, laundry services, cable television hook-ups and 30/50/100-amp power.

70 West Marina
4401 Arendell St., Morehead City
(252) 726-5171

Visible as you drive through Morehead City, this marina on Pelletier Creek is centrally located with easy access to a variety of shops and restaurants. 70 West Marina offers dry storage for 350 boats and is a dealer for the sale and repair of Mercury, Volvo and Yamaha outboards.

A sport-fishing boat makes its way to the Gulf Stream.

photo: Scott Taylor

WESTERN CARTERET/SWANSBORO MARINAS

Almost every home or business on the White Oak River or Bogue Sound has a dock, boat ramp or both. But the commercial docks, particularly the ones big enough and with channels dredged deep enough to accommodate a very large motor or sailing yacht, are few.

Casper's Marina
301 S. Water St., Swansboro
(910) 326-4462

Conveniently located on the Intracoastal Waterway in Swansboro, Casper's has 150 slips for dry storage of boats 30 feet or less, and 180 feet of open dock for transient boaters. Haul-out repairs, gas and diesel fuel also are available.

Dudley's Marina Inc.
N.C. Hwy. 24 E., Cedar Point
(252) 393-2204

North of Swansboro off the ICW, Dudley's is a working boat yard and marina with 25 slips, overnight dockage at the fuel dock, repair services and gas and diesel fuels. It services Mercruiser, Mercury and Volvo Penta marine engines.

Swansboro Yacht Basin
N.C. Hwy. 24, Cedar Point
(252) 393-2416

Off the ICW north of Swansboro, Swansboro Yacht Basin offers 90 feet of dockage. No fuel or other services are offered, but three terrific restaurants, including The Flying Bridge, are located on site.

DOWN EAST

Calico Jack's Inn & Marina
1698 Island Rd., Harkers Island
(252) 728-3575

Calico Jack's offers 50 slips by the month or night, a launch ramp, a supply store and a motel. Slips accommodate boats up to 30 feet.

Harkers Island Fishing Center
1002 Island Rd., Harkers Island
(252) 728-3907

A full-service marina with 70 slips for boats of 30 feet or less, Harkers Island Fishing Center has a launch ramp, repair services, a lift for dry storage, a supply store, and gas and diesel fuel service. Efficiency motel rooms, rental cottages and ferry service to Cape Lookout also are available.

Morris Marina
1000 Morris Marina Rd., Atlantic
(252) 225-4261

You can launch your boat and store it in or out of the water at Morris Marina in Atlantic. The marina has a grill and fishing supply store on site and ferry service to its fish camps on Core Banks.

Boat Sales and Service

For boat and motor sales and service, one of these businesses should be able to help. In the previous discussion of marinas, we've mentioned the authorized dealers and repair services if they are on site at the marina. Other dealers of boats and motors are listed below.

Jones Brothers Marine
5136 U.S. Hwy. 70 W., Morehead City
(252) 726-8404

This Yamaha dealership is also headquarters for the Jones Brothers Bateau, Cape Fisherman and Southport Boats.

Morehead Marine Inc.
4971 Arendell St., Morehead City
(252) 247-6667

This is an authorized sales and service dealer for Evinrude, Yamaha and Mercury outboards as well as Parker and Grady White boats.

Public Boat Ramps

The Crystal Coast has many boat ramps, large and small, public and private. Below is a short list of just a few of the state-maintained public ramps. Because most ramps don't have names, we've listed them alphabetically according to location. You won't have to pay a fee to launch your boat at any of these ramps.

MOREHEAD CITY

Municipal Park, behind the Crystal Coast Visitor Center at 3409 Arendell Street (U.S. 70), has several launching areas and lots of parking. While swimming is not allowed, a shady picnic area with grills and tables offers a nice resting spot to enjoy a view of the sound. The park is just east of Carteret Community College.

A boat ramp at 10th and Shepard Streets in Morehead City serves as the nearest launch location to Sugarloaf Island, the undeveloped island across from the city waterfront. The launch ramp accommodates boats 16 feet or less and parking is available. Locals say Sugarloaf Island "is a nice place to get away from it all while being close to everything."

BEAUFORT

Curtis A. Perry Park is a public ramp with four launching areas into Taylor's Creek. The park is at the east end of Front Street near the tennis courts.

Two ramps and docks, as well as a fishing pier and comfort station, are offered at the Town Creek Water Access at Turner Street and West Beaufort Road. These are maintained by Carteret County Parks and Recreation Department.

The Grayden Paul Jaycee Town Park, on Front Street at the south end of Pollock Street, provides a short, wide pier. Boats may be launched from a soft-sand area and docked on the west side of the pier. Diagonal parking is available on Front Street.

DOWN EAST

The Salters Creek Wildlife Ramp is available on the east side of the high-rise bridge on U.S. Hwy. 70 just before you get to the Down East community of Sea Level.

Access to the Oyster Creek Wildlife Ramp at the Oyster Creek Bridge just northeast of Davis is also available from US Highway 70.

HARKERS ISLAND

At the Cape Lookout National Seashore Picnic grounds, there is a small sand beach adequate for launching canoes and kayaks. Let the park rangers in the Visitor Center know that you're going out on a trip.

A public launch ramp is located on the Straits at the north side of the Harkers Island bridge. Another small launch site with a parking area is at the western end of Harkers Island at Fisherman's Inn fish camp. Fees are charged for overnight parking.

CEDAR ISLAND

A ramp is beyond the Cedar Island National Wildlife Refuge office on Lola Road at the south end of the island.

The refuge also maintains a ramp on the west side of (and almost below) the high-rise bridge, on N.C. 12, just west of the island.

CEDAR POINT

A ramp maintained by the N.C. Wildlife Commission is on the south side of N.C. Highway 24 between Cape Carteret and Swansboro.

The Cedar Island National Wildlife Refuge maintains a boat ramp on the west side of the high-rise bridge (on N.C. 12) that crosses Thorofare Bay.

Boating Emergency Numbers

Coast Guard Information, (252) 247-4598

Search/Rescue Emergencies, (252) 247-4544, (252) 247-4545

Swansboro Lifeboat Station, Emerald Isle, (252) 354-2719 - emergencies; (252) 354-2462 - non-emergencies

Boating is a way of life in the waterfront towns along the Crystal Coast.

photo: George Mitchell

SPORTS, FITNESS AND PARKS

North Carolina's Crystal Coast has plenty to offer in the way of sports -- in and out of the water. Insiders will find there's something about the weather along North Carolina's coast that makes people want to spend as much time as possible outdoors. Whether it's walking on the beach, running, basketball, beach volleyball, boating bicycling, wind surfing or kayaking, the year-round mild climate and wonderful coastal scenery make any activity more fun. If the weather just won't cooperate or you need some equipment, you can visit one of the local fitness centers.

Here, we offer a brief introduction to some of the area's most popular sports and, in most cases, give you a contact. Watersports, such as wind-surfing, kayaking and sailing, are described in our Fishing, Boating and Watersports chapter. At this chapter's end, we list some of the county and city parks on the Crystal Coast. Information about state and national parks is given in our Attractions chapter.

Sports

Like most areas, the Crystal Coast has its share of sports enthusiasts who participate in their favorite events casually or as part of an organized team. Here we have listed popular sports and how to contact someone in the know.

BASEBALL AND LITTLE LEAGUE

Teams for children and adults are sponsored by the Carteret County Parks and Recreation Department, (252) 808-3301.

Watching the Kinston Indians, a minor-league professional baseball team, play is always exciting. The 2004 Carolina League Champs are based in nearby Kinston and provide great family entertainment. Games are played on week nights and weekends during the season in a newly renovated park with all the extras. Kinston is less than a two-hour drive from Morehead City. For ticket information and a game schedule, call (252) 527-9111 or (800) 334-5467.

BASKETBALL

Most of the Crystal Coast parks have basketball courts, as do a few of the area fitness centers. The Carteret County Parks and Recreation Department, (252) 808-3301, sponsors a basketball league.

BICYCLING

As far as Insiders are concerned, the beach (during low tide) is an outstanding place to ride your off-road bike. Consult our chapter on Fishing, Boating and Watersports to find out where and how you can access the beaches. For road, racing or fat-tire bikes, Salter Path Road (N.C. Highway 58) is fun for cycling, especially since the state has smoothed and resurfaced the shoulders, which serve as a small bike path. Most bike riders will agree the state does not seem to understand the need for adequate bike lanes, so Salter Path Road is about as good as it gets in this area. Emerald Isle's Coast Guard Road has a bike path. For an intimate look at beautiful Beaufort, try the Beaufort Bicycle Route, a 6-mile cruising loop around town. Pick up your route map at the Safrit Visitors Center at the Beaufort Historic Site on Turner Street.

The Swansboro Bicentennial Bicycle Trail is 25 miles of good biking that begins in historic Swansboro. The loop trail crosses the White Oak River to Cape Carteret, winds through the Croatan National Forest, crosses the river again and returns to Swansboro.

North Carolina's Bicycle Program offers a color map showing bicycle enthusiasts where to cycle on the Outer Banks. Three loop and two linear bicycle routes are highlighted and include portions of the mainland as well as the barrier islands. Contact the Bicycle Program, N.C. Department of Transportation, P.O. Box 25201, Raleigh, NC 27611, (919) 733-2804.

BOWLING

Carteret Lanes
U.S. Hwy. 70, 1 mile west of Morehead City
(252) 247-4481

Carteret Lanes is equipped with 24 lanes, pool tables, video games and a snack bar. You'll also find a pro shop where you can buy bowling balls and shoes as well as get any of your bowling gear serviced. Carteret Lanes always has special summer teen programs as well as senior citizens specials throughout the year. Call to find out what's doing this summer. Carteret Lanes rents bowling shoes, and you may bring your own ball or use one of theirs.

FITNESS CENTERS

Morehead City

Gold's Gym
Cypress Bay Plaza, U.S. Hwy. 70, Morehead City
(252) 247-4653

Gold's Gym is part of a nationwide franchise gym and has been flexing its muscles in the fitness community since opening three years ago. The gym offers unlimited mutual use of its facilities for those with annual or bi-annual memberships and a travel exchange program for other Gold's Gyms across the country. Memberships vary in price and can be arranged by the week or month. Guest visits are $10, or just $5 when accompanied by a member. Equipment includes Life Fitness, Hammer Strength and a wide variety of cardiovascular equipment and world-class group exercise programs, including body pump and body flow, as well as a wide variety of free weights. There is free child care for ages 1 to 11, tanning facilities and a pro shop with apparel, supplements and smoothies. Gym hours are Monday through Thursday from 5 AM to 10 PM, Friday from 5 AM to 8 PM, Saturday from 8 AM to 5 PM and Sunday from 9 AM to 5 PM.

Lady of America
3000 Arendell St., Morehead City
(252) 247-6398

Lady of America is a full-service fitness center and spa that provides specialized workouts and weight loss solutions for women. The center focuses full attention on women's individual needs and goals. Boasting to be the "club that knows your name", Lady of America believes your success is their success and that fitness is their most important product. Members are offered a full schedule of free fitness classes on a patented "floating" aerobics floor that reduces impact to the joints by up to 80 percent. Life Fitness Cardio equipment and uniquely designed female-sized strength equipment is offered, along with personal training, tanning and sauna spa facilities, free childcare and more. Membership rates vary from $19.95 to $59.95 per month depending on the length of the agreement. The center offers a special rate for women in one family, and non-residents memberships are available for $5 per day/$20 per week/$50 per month or $120 for three months. Lady of America is open Monday through Friday 6 AM to 7:30 PM and on Saturday from 8 AM to noon.

Morehead City Community Center
1600 Fisher St., Morehead City
(252) 726-5083

This is a popular place with many city residents and guests. Members have use of the fully equipped weight room, loaded with free weights and machines, a gym with a full-size basketball court and a game room with pool and Ping-Pong tables. The center also offers floor aerobic classes and yoga classes. Managed by the city's Parks and Recreation Department, this facility is likely the area's most affordable fitness center. Individual rates are $30 for city residents and $40 for non-residents. Family rates are $40 and $70. If you are interested in a day pass to only use portions of the gym, the costs vary from $2 to $5. The gym operates Monday through Friday from 8 AM to 8 PM and Saturday from 1 to 6 PM. It is closed Sunday.

Sports Center
701 N. 35th St., Morehead City
(252) 726-7070

The largest fitness center in Carteret County, Sports Center takes a holistic approach to family fitness. The center is newly renovated and is now nicer than ever. The knowledgeable staff offers members and guests a fully equipped weight room, Nautilus and fitness equipment, racquetball courts, an indoor walking/running track and classes of all kinds, including karate, and water and floor aerobics. The Sports Center also has a tanning salon, stair climbers, treadmills, spinning and an Olympic-sized outdoor pool with surrounding picnic tables. For relaxing, you'll find saunas, a whirlpool, a steam room and massage therapists. The indoor swimming pool with lap lanes is also used for swimming lessons and water aerobics will again be offered once the renovations are completed, and a second-floor lounge offers a space to relax. The basketball/volleyball court is large and well lit. The center has a vitamin store and pro shop, a snack bar and child-care services. Daily and weekly rates are available, as is a short-term six-month membership. The center is open Monday through Thursday from 5 AM to 10 PM, Friday from 5 AM to 9 PM, Saturday from 8 AM to 6 PM and Sunday from 1 to 6 PM.

Beaufort

Curves for Women
1726 Live Oak St., Beaufort
(252) 728-1444
4219 Arendell St., Morehead City
(252) 247-5239

Curves for Women is part of a nationwide franchise, although each gym is locally owned and operated. Join one Curves and you can get a travel pass to use at any Curves in the country or aboard. Workouts are based on circuit training, and all equipment is hydraulic to be easy on your joints. Individuals rotate from upper body workout equipment to lower body workout equipment with recovery/spring board stations in between. The workouts are done based on time and are fast moving. Membership is $29 per month plus a one-time sign-up fee.

Eastern Athletic Club
105 Professional Park Dr., Beaufort
(252) 728-1700

This fitness club offers a full line of Nautilus workout equipment, a free-style weight room with quick-change collars, treadmills, EB Power Ride bikes and much more. The gym offers a variety of classes including water and floor aerobics, spin classes, yoga, body pump and more. It also includes a 25-foot, heated junior Olympic swimming pool, a steam room, tanning beds and a large, tiled hot tub spa. Memberships include an enrollment fee and then $45 per month for a single person, $50 for a couple, and $60 for a family. There are student discounts as well. Club hours are Monday through Friday 5:30 AM to 9 PM, Saturday from 8 AM to 5 PM and Sunday from 1 to 6 PM. These hours are reduced somewhat in the summer.

Bogue Banks

Emerald Isle Parks & Recreation Community Center
7506 Emerald Dr., Emerald Isle
(252) 354-6350

The center is open to residents and nonresidents, offering a full-size gym for indoor tennis, basketball, volleyball and soccer. Classes vary and often include aerobics -- both step and step-free -- classes, karate, Pilates and yoga. The facility also features a weight room, a game room with Ping-Pong and card tables, restrooms with showers and a fully equipped kitchen. Space for meetings and parties is available. Outside you will find tennis courts, a basketball court and a children's play area. Rates are $5 per day or $20 for a week of fun. Annual memberships are also available. The center's hours are Monday through Friday 8 AM to 9 PM and Saturday 9 AM to 4 PM. The center is closed on Sunday.

Western Carteret County

Cape Carteret Aquatics and Wellness Center
300 Taylor Notion Rd., Cape Carteret
(252) 393-1000

Open seven days a week, this full-service wellness center takes its summer visitors into account. The club offers an indoor 25-yard competition heated pool, hot tub and steam room, an indoor basketball court, and a fully equipped weight room. Classes of all varieties, including Pilates mat and reformer sessions as well as water and floor aerobics offer members a variety of workout choices. Licensed professionals ensure that quality guidance and instruction is given to members. Day passes are available for $12 per day or $100 for 15 visits. The center is open Monday through Friday from 5:30 AM to 9

Use a fishing reel to hold your kite string. Some say that's cheating, but a reel sure makes it a breeze to bring a high-flying kite back to earth.

Windsurfing is the best way to experience the power of the waves and the wind.

photo: George Mitchell

PM, Saturday from 8 AM to 4 PM and Sunday from 1 to 6 PM.

FLYING

Michael J. Smith Airport
N.C. Hwy. 101, Beaufort
(252) 728-2323, (252) 728-1928

The Crystal Coast's sole airport, located in Beaufort, offers only chartered or private aircraft service. A modern facility, it is the sixth busiest municipal airport in North Carolina. Here you can arrange the services of private planes for trips or sightseeing or you can line up private flying lessons. The airport is named in memory of Capt. Michael J. Smith, a Beaufort native who served as pilot of space shuttle Challenger, which exploded January 28, 1986. Navy Capt. Smith learned to fly at this airfield. More complete details of the airport are in the Getting Around chapter.

GOLF

Golf can be played on the Crystal Coast practically 365 days a year. Golfers who know the area know it is one of the best golf bargains around. Information about golf courses in the area is provided in the Golf chapter.

GYMNASTICS

Cedar Point Gymnastics Training Center, Inc.
135 Sherwood Ave., Cedar Point
(252) 393-6441

Cedar Point Gymnastics is open year round and provides classes for those interested in gymnastics and cheerleading. The gym was started in 1996 by Marti Feagle, a self-described "professional gymnastics mom," who grew weary of driving her daughter throughout the area for gymnastics lessons and competitions. The center offers a complete girls and boys gymnastics program for ages 2 and older. Training is provided by certified coaches, who can provide instruction for beginners through very advanced. Fees start at $32 a month and vary depending on the program and the number of hours. The center is open for classes Monday through Friday. The club also is available for birthday parties with a reservation.

HORSEBACK RIDING

Acha's Stable
1341 Nine Mile Rd., Newport
(252) 223-4478

Acha's is a family business that provides lessons and offers boarding and stall rentals by the month for horse owners. The stable is just west of Morehead City.

By The Sea Farms
380 Pigott Rd., Gloucester
(252) 729-1756
www.bytheseafarms.com

By The Sea Farms is a breeding farm of some of the rarest breeds of horses. The farm focuses on producing high-quality Andalusian and Azteca horses in conformation class as well as for multi-disciplines. These horses are perfect for dressage, three-day eventing, driving, jumping, reining or even cow work. This small business offers a family, yet professional touch to horse training and ownership. By the Sea Farms offers horses for sale or lease as well as breeding. This farm is home to Ladino TG, a dark bay Andalusian stallion who stands at stud on the farm. He produces blacks, bays and chestnuts foals. You can learn more by visiting the farm's website or visiting the farm itself.

Cedar Island Stables
120 Driftwood Dr., Cedar Island
(252) 225-1885

Cheryl McMahon, owner and operator of Cedar Island Stables, calls this "the most beautiful place to ride on the planet". Cedar Island Stables offers the best beach rides on well-trained horses that provide an up-close look at the beautiful landscapes and seascapes of Cedar Island. One-hour rides with a guide cost $40 per person and cross the beautiful 1,000-foot river to the next island. Shorter rides and pony rides may be possible. Anyone older than age of 3 without fear of horses is welcome. Rides are scheduled throughout the afternoon, and morning rides may be possible. Call ahead and make reservations for this wonderful experience. Cedar Island Stables is open year-round.

Beaufort's waterfront is a popular early morning walking and running spot, with many folks arriving by 5:30 AM to enjoy the peace and quiet while exercising.

Zeigler's Stables
Off Howard Blvd. (across from the ballpark), Newport
(252) 223-5110

The stable offers riding lessons, boarding and a tack shop. Week-long summer riding camps teach children and adults how to ride and care for horses.

HUNTING

Guide services have long been a popular means for duck and goose hunters to experience new locales. Using knowledgeable guides cuts down on your chances of spending time in the wrong spot.

Adams Creek Gun Sports
6240 Adams Creek Rd., Havelock
(252) 447-6808

Open to the public, Adams Creek Gun Sports provides knowledgeable and friendly guides for duck hunting, deer hunting and inshore fishing. This is a family owned and operated business, and June and Rusty Bryan and Julie Brown can certainly lead you to the best hunting spots. They also have a full-station sporting clay course and five-stand available by appointment. Accommodations are offered in an 1870 country farmhouse lodge overlooking Adams Creek, a part of the Intracoastal Waterway. The Bryans maintain impoundments, natural woodland ponds, and marsh and floating blinds. Shooting instructors are available for beginners or those people eager to enhance their skills. Hunting parties are welcome, and the lodge is always open for business meetings, parties and weddings. Call for an appointment. Be aware that reservations are a must and that the Bryans book months in advance.

KARATE

Karate lessons are often offered by the Morehead Recreation Department, (252) 726-5083, and also at several of the local fitness centers (see the Fitness Centers section previously in this chapter).

Lewis Tae Kwon Do Center & Lil' Dragons Tae Kwon Do
4444 Arendell St., Morehead City
(252) 808-2400

This business has a reputation for providing quality instruction and for students placing high in competitions. Owned and operated by Russell Lewis, the center offers instruction for beginners through advanced for ages 5, teens and adults.

KITE FLYING

Kite flying is popular along the Crystal Coast beaches. Fort Macon State Park, on the eastern end of Bogue Banks, is the most popular location for everyone to fly kites. Every Sunday morning it is the most popular place in the county to fly, with folks meeting there at 9 AM in the summer and 10 AM in the winter to fly kites. Fort Macon Beach is also the site for the annual Carolina Kite Festival, which takes place on the last weekend in October that is not Halloween. The Festival is sponsored by Kites Unlimited, (252) 247-7011.

RUNNING/WALKING

Running and walking are favorite forms of exercise along the Crystal Coast. Because of mild year-round temperatures, one seldom has to miss a day of exercise and outdoor enjoyment. The Beaufort and Morehead City waterfronts and the beaches continue to be the most favored running and walking spots, and they are heavily traveled by early morning and evening exercisers. Those runners who like to test their skills or run with a group can participate in the races described below. Most of them include walks too.

Lookout Rotary Spring Road Race
Morehead City
(252) 726-7070

This race kicks off the local race season and takes place on the last Saturday morning in April with a flat 10K, 5K and 1-mile run/walk beginning and ending at the Sports Center, N. 35th Street in Morehead City. The race is sponsored by the Lookout Rotary Club of Morehead City. For more information, call the Sports Center at the number above.

Beach Run Series
Atlantic Beach
(252) 808-3301

This series of seven runs sponsored by the Carteret County Parks and Recreation Department begins in the spring. This low-key weekday series attracts lots of local runners and walkers for evening runs. The 1-mile run/walk, 5K and 10K are on the beach and begin and end at the beach access area at The Circle in Atlantic Beach. Dates vary depending on the tides.

Historic Beaufort Road Race
Beaufort
(252) 222-6359

Sponsored by Beaufort Ole Towne Rotary Club, this is the area's most popular race and it always takes place on the third Saturday of July. Participants are promised a scenic course that is "hot, flat and fast." Hundreds turn out to tackle the 1-mile run/walk, or the certified 5K run/walk and 10K courses. This is such a popular race, families from across the country plan their vacations around this event. Race proceeds fund youth scholarships and programs and many community needs.

Twin Bridges Race
Beaufort to Atlantic Beach
(252) 726-6273

You have few choices with the Twin Bridges Race. You either run the 8K or stay on the porch. Because there aren't any hills on the coast, the race directors throw in two high-rise bridges. The race, slated for the first Saturday in October, is the kick off for Saturday's events at the N.C. Seafood Festival on the Morehead City waterfront. The race begins at the drawbridge in Beaufort and ends on the Atlantic Beach Causeway.

SKATING

Sports World
U.S. Hwy. 70 W, Morehead City
(252) 247-4444

The Sports World skating rink is for all ages. It offers a variety of rates depending on the time of day, ranging from $3 to $4, and

$5.50 for evening skating. The center offers special programs for after school, including transportation, as well as Saturday morning programs. Parents get to skate free with children at some events. Skate rental is $1 for regular skates and $2.50 for inline skates.

SOCCER

There's a lot of action on the soccer fields across the area for children and adults. Carteret County Parks and Recreation Department, (252) 808-3301, sponsors leagues for younger players and for women and men. Rotary Park and Soccer Complex opened in the fall of 2004 and features lighted soccer fields and many extras. Information about that park is listed below in the Parks section.

SOFTBALL

The Carteret County Parks and Recreation Department sponsors a men's and women's softball league each year. The teams are usually sponsored by local businesses and are very competitive. Call (252) 808-3301 for information.

TENNIS

Tennis is another one of those not-so-well-known Crystal Coast treasures. The Crystal Coast has really good places to play tennis, just not many of them. As with golf, you can play tennis almost all year round. (Some parks that aren't mentioned in this section have tennis courts too. See the Parks section at the end of this chapter.)

Bogue Banks Country Club
N.C. Hwy. 58, Mile Marker 5 at Oakleaf Dr., Pine Knoll Shores
(252) 726-1034

This semi-private club features four beautifully maintained clay courts along with its picturesque 18-hole golf course. The island setting includes rolling sand dunes, tall pines and majestic oaks. Non-members are welcome, and memberships are available. Tennis courts can be rented daily from 9 AM to 5 PM with a lapse mid-day when the courts are watered and dried. Fees are $8 per visit. Mike See, a certified USTA pro, has both adult and junior leagues that are open to anyone interested in joining. Group and private lessons are offered, and you will find a well-stocked tennis pro shop that carries professional-quality rackets and a full line of clothing. The club sponsors a Golden Years and Platinum Years Tournament around Memorial Day, junior novice tennis, league play, and the Big Sisters/Little Sisters tennis tournament.

TRIATHLON

Nelson Bay Challenge Sprint Triathlon
Sea Level

This popular sprint triathlon takes place in Sea Level (a small town Down East) at noon on the first Saturday in May each year. The event includes a 750-meter swim in the protected waters of Nelson Bay, a 20K bike ride and a 5K run. For many, the race is a warm-up for the triathlon season ahead. This race offers spectators easy viewing of the transition area and a great post-race clambake. Money raised benefits the Sea Level Rescue Squad and local youth programs. The race is held in memory of long-time Nelson Bay Triathlon director James Davis. Known for his humor and his dedication to community projects, James died in a triathlon in June 2003. For more information, visit www.nelsonbaytriathlon.com.

VOLLEYBALL

Beach volleyball is catching on. Tournament nets are on the main beach at The Circle in Atlantic Beach, and there is usually plenty of action there. For information about beach volleyball tournaments, call the Atlantic Beach Town Hall, (252) 726-2121. An indoor volleyball league is sponsored by the Carteret County Parks and Recreation Department, (252) 808-3301.

Parks

COUNTY PARKS

The Carteret County parks system offers visitors and residents more than 150 acres of open space for recreational enjoyment. An oft-forgotten treasure, the system of parks, ball fields, beach accesses and three fishing piers (Straits, Town Creek Water Access and Newport High Rise) are managed by the county's Parks and Recreation Department.

The parks and ball fields offer picnic areas and parking access. Here we describe what's available in the way of amenities for each of these facilities. (Beach accesses and fishing piers are detailed in our Fishing, Boat-

ing, Watersports and Beach Accss chapter. National and state parks are detailed in our Attractions chapter.) Along with maintaining the parks, the county also offers a rich variety of programs, from summer camps to recreational teams, Senior Games to Special Olympics. Call the Parks and Recreation Department, (252) 808-3301, for the latest schedule.

Eastern Park
1 mile east of Smyrna on U.S. 70

This 30-acre facility has lighted adult and youth fields, basketball courts, lighted tennis courts, lighted multi-purpose fields, a playground, horseshoe pits, beach volleyball courts and a walking trail. Visitors to the park will also find a picnic area, restrooms and a large parking area.

Harkers Island Beach Access
Southeast side of drawbridge on Harkers Island

This area offers parking space and water/beach access. No facilities are offered and there are no lifeguards. Swim at your own risk.

Manley Gaskill Field
Next to Harkers Island Elementary School

The facilities available are one large lighted ballpark, one youth ball field, a concession stand and a storage shed.

Leon Mann Jr. Enrichment Center
3820 Galantis Dr., Morehead City

This county facility offers fitness facilities for seniors, including a fully equipped kitchen, physical fitness rooms with showers and lockers, a game room, three classrooms (one with microwave, stove/oven and refrigerator), a health room, a general purpose room, two all-purpose rooms and a library. Outdoor facilities include shuffleboard courts, patio areas and horseshoe pits.

Mariners Park
Off U.S. Hwy. 70 in Sea Level across from the hospital

This park consists of 20 acres, including lighted adult and youth athletic fields, tennis courts, a basketball court, a playground and restrooms.

Marshallberg Picnic Area
Marshallberg Rd. at the Harbor

These picnic shelters are situated overlooking the water and provide a beautiful water view for visitors.

Newport Ball Field
Next to the Newport Elementary School

This park has two ball fields and a storage shed.

Newport River Park
East of the Beaufort-Morehead City High Rise Bridge, between Beaufort and Morehead City

The park's 4 acres encompass an island of sand, a sunning area, picnic tables, a short fishing pier and a boat ramp sufficient for launching small sailboats. The entrance is directly across from the entrance to Radio Island.

Radio Island Water Access
Southeast Radio Island (U.S. Hwy. 70 Causeway)

This facility offers a place for wading and swimming, picnic tables, grills and a restroom with outside showers. There is a dangerous current in deeper water -- swimmers are urged to stay close to shore. There are no lifeguards on duty.

Salter Path Beach Access
N.C. Hwy. 58, Salter Path

This facility provides 64 parking spaces, a comfort station, dressing rooms, outdoor showers, a 465-foot boardwalk and a picnic area.

Salter Path Park
Ballpark Dr. in Salter Path

This area provides a ball field, playground, basketball court, parking lot, and picnic shelter.

---

i

The bicycle is legally considered a vehicle in North Carolina. Traffic laws require bicyclists to ride on the right-hand side in the same direction as other traffic; obey all traffic signs and signals; and equip the bicycle with a front lamp and a rear reflector.

Dolphins Are a Wonderful Sight

Catching a glimpse of bottlenose dolphins traveling, feeding, resting or socializing along the Crystal Coast is a wonderful treat, and not so rare. From the beaches, bridges and riverbanks, locals and visitors alike can often see dolphins. If you are boating, dolphins can be seen in most waterways.

There is a difference between dolphins and porpoises, and many people get them confused. What you will see in this area are dolphins. Porpoises do not generally venture into North Carolina waters. The only porpoise species that has been spotted near the East Coast is the harbor porpoise and it typically ranges from Virginia to Canada.

Bottlenose dolphins are long and streamlined, with a distinct pointed beak and a prominent dorsal fin that curves toward the tail. They are bigger than their porpoise cousins, with adults generally ranging in length from 8 to 10 feet (males are slightly larger than females) and weighing between 500 to 800 pounds. Dolphins' teeth are sharp and shaped like cones. These aquatic creatures are cetaceans, the taxonomic order of marine mammals that includes all the great whales, dolphins and porpoises. Dolphins are also members of the suborder odontocetes, meaning toothed whales. More than 40 species of toothed whales live in the waters of the earth -- and most of them are found in relatively shallow, temperate coastal waters.

Bottlenose dolphins are a species of toothed whale. It's not unusual to spot them in groups of about a dozen, fairly close to shore. They usually have light-colored bellies and dark backs -- colors that help them blend in with their surroundings. These graceful creatures are powerful swimmers and often frolic in the bow waves of boats or surf on large waves.

Bottlenose dolphins along the East Coast of the United States are severely and negatively impacted by human activities. After a die-off that killed up to half of the population, the National Marine Fisheries Service in 1993 listed them as depleted under the Marine Mammal Protection Act. Dolphins have washed ashore dead with evidence of having been struck by boats, entangled in fishing nets, and with foreign material (human trash) in their stomachs. Yet little basic information that is critical for their conservation is known, such as reproductive rates, residency and migration patterns, and habitat needs.

That information is being gathered by a small group of dedicated professionals. Keith Rittmaster, Natural Science Curator at the North Carolina Maritime Museum, directs a program that identifies local dolphins and records their movements, associations and reproduction information. The process used is called photo-identification and involves the use of photographs of the scars and notches that dolphins acquire on their dorsal fins to recognize and verify resights of known individuals. Rittmaster, along with his wife, Victoria Thayer, have been studying the bottlenose dolphins in this area since 1985. Individually identified dolphins that they first photographed in 1985 are still seen regularly in the waters around Beaufort. They have also matched dolphins identified in Beaufort with photographs from study sites as far south as central Florida, as far north as New Jersey and many sites in between. This collaboration is critical to the study, and researchers from the Virginia Marine Science Museum, National Marine Fisheries Service, Duke Marine Lab, Nags Head Dolphin Watch and UNC-Wilmington all share photographs and data.

In addition to studying the live, free-swimming dolphins, Rittmaster is authorized under the Marine Mammal Protection Act to respond to strandings of whales and dolphins as part of the Marine Mammal Stranding Network. Examining carcasses of beached dolphins has shown him many negative effects of human interactions. Dolphins tangled in fishing nets and lines die trapped in the debris. Dolphins are also sliced by boat propellers and ingest litter that can often be lethal.

People have fed wild dolphins, and Rittmaster cites reports of people even giving the dolphins Twinkies, sunglasses or whatever is in the boat with them when they run out of fish. Lens caps, fishing hooks and other litter have been found inside of dead dolphin stomachs. Dolphins are wild animals, and if they get used to coming to people, it can create danger to the animals as well as to humans. Some wild dolphins have come to expect the handouts, and have been known to become aggressive and bite. It is against federal law to feed or harass wild dolphins, punishable by imprisonment and/or fines.

To raise money to help protect and increase understanding of dolphin behavior and human impact on them along the North Carolina coast, the N.C. General Assembly approved the sale of a $30 special license plate with all revenues going to support the education, conservation and research programs of the N.C. Maritime Museum. For more information about the research program or the license plates, call (252) 504-2452.

One more thing -- the "dolphin" on a restaurant menu or for sale in a fish market is not the marine mammal. Instead it is the dolphin fish that is commercially fished in local waters. Insiders usually call that fish by its Hawaiian name -- mahi mahi.

Dolphins are very playful creatures.

credit: Kieth Rittmaster, North Carolina Maritime Museum

South River Park
S.R. 1318, near Merrimon

This area provides a playground, parking spaces, a basketball court, a picnic shelter/comfort station and restrooms.

Town Creek Water Access
Behind Airport at Turner St. and W. Beaufort Rd., Beaufort

This facility has two floating docks, a fishing pier, two boat ramps and a comfort station.

Western Park
Cedar Point, off N.C. Hwy. 58, a quarter-mile northwest of the intersection of N.C. Hwys. 24 and 58, on S.R. 1113

This park's 34 acres include lighted adult and youth fields, a lighted multipurpose field, restrooms, playgrounds, a basketball court, lighted tennis courts and a picnic shelter. The park also includes a community center featuring two small classrooms, one large meeting room and a kitchen.

MUNICIPAL AND CITY PARKS

Bogue Banks

The island has a few parks and the majority of those focus on access to the beach. For descriptions of the beach access areas, see our Fishing, Boating and Watersports chapter.

Emerald Isle

Emerald Isle Parks and Recreation Department, (252) 354-6350, maintains several public parks and continues to increase the number and quality of these facilities. To learn about the numerous beach access areas in Emerald Isle, see our Fishing, Boating and Watersports chapter.

Blue Heron Park & Tennis Courts
MM 19, Emerald Isle

Located behind the Emerald Isle Town Hall, this park features two tennis courts, a basketball court, a picnic shelter and a children's playground. Use of the tennis courts require reservations, which must be made in person by the picnic shelter, and there is a fee of $2 per person for use of the tennis courts.

Emerald Isle Woods
Coast Guard Rd., Emerald Isle

Located along Coast Guard Road, this sound-side, 41-acre park features walking trails and sound access. Additional amenities are in the planning stages for this lovely park.

Merchant's Park
MM 19.5, Emerald Isle

Merchant's Park, is on the south side of Emerald Drive at MP 19 and offers parking, picnic tables, a shelter and restroom facilities

Beaufort

Grayden Paul Jaycee Park
Front St. at the south end of Pollock St., Beaufort

This pretty little park offers a grassy picnic spot, a gazebo, a dock and a swimming area. The park was named for the late Grayden Paul and it is maintained by the local Rotary Club.

Beach volleyball is increasing in popularity, and the Atlantic Beach waterfront is the place to watch or join the action.

Freedom Park
S.R. 1412 off Lennoxville Rd. in Beaufort

This 15-acre tract is surrounded by woods and is a popular place for all types of activities. It has lighted regulation adult and youth fields, a play lot, basketball courts, a picnic shelter and restrooms.

Curtis A. Perry Park
East end of Front St. adjacent to the boat ramp, Beaufort

You'll find a basketball court, two lighted tennis courts, restroom facilities, a dock and a waterfront picnic areas complete with grills. The park was built around the four boat ramps provided by the N.C. Wildlife Service and named in memory of the town's former public works director.

Morehead City

Morehead City Parks and Recreation Department, (252) 726-5083, oversees the city's parks and the Morehead City Community Center at 1600 Fisher Street. (The center also houses the department's offices.) Directly behind the community center are two multi-purpose sports fields used primarily for softball and baseball. Each of the city parks offers different amenities. The department also offers aerobics, dance and karate classes, dog-obedience classes and youth sports programs. For the latest information about what's going on, call Parks and Recreation at the number above.

City Park
1000 Block, Arendell St., Morehead City

This is a shady city park with playground equipment and a few picnic tables. Additional parking has recently been added, making City Park a great place to stop for lunch, or play time, while cruising the Morehead City waterfront shops. This park is equipped with a large gazebo and bathroom facilities. Reservations for large groups and shelter use is required. There is a $25 charge for residents to use the gazebo.

Jaycee Park
On the water at the south end of 9th St., Morehead City

This is the site of the city's Summer in the Park concert series hosted by the Parks and Recreation Department on Saturday evenings during the summer months. You'll find parking, picnic tables, a gazebo, swings and a short pier at this park.

Municipal Park
Arendell St., behind the Crystal Coast Visitors Center, Morehead City

Visitors will find plenty of parking, picnic areas and a boat ramp. The park borders Bogue Sound, just west of the Atlantic Beach high-rise bridge. You'll like this park: It's an attractive place to eat lunch and watch the boats and sea birds. Restroom facilities are available in the Visitors Center.

Piney Park
2900 block of Bridges St., east of Morehead Plaza, Morehead City

This tiny green park spot offers a quiet respite to anyone who feels like getting outdoors. You'll find pine-tree shade and picnic tables.

Shevans Park
1600 Block, Evans St., Morehead City

Shevans Park has four tennis courts, two of which of lighted, and shelters with picnic tables. It has a large, impressive children's maze, completed in 1997 by volunteers, called Sea of Dreams. Based on the kids' ideas, the playground's basic theme is a castle. At the front of this unusual play place are two towers and a walk-through maze. Children ages 3 and younger go one way; older children go in another direction. Inside, kids can play on cable ladders, spring bridges, a balance beam suspended from chains, a boat, a race car, rings, musical chimes, a wooden-horse ride, a pirate's ship and a playhouse complete with a toy stove and kitchen. This community project was financed by private donations of cash and materials and built by volunteers. To share in the magic that brought this park together, one must only read the names etched in each board and piece of equipment. People who donated their time and effort to the project will forever be remembered by having their names mentioned in some part of the park. There is a $25 fee to reserve the large shelter at the park. There is no fee to reserve the small shelter, however a reservation is required.

Swinson Park
1 mile west of Morehead City on Country Club Rd., next to Morehead City Primary School

This 34-acre park is a popular spot for sports and family outings. Visitors will find lighted and unlighted adult and youth athletic fields, lighted tennis courts, basketball courts, play lots, a picnic shelter and a comfort station.

Rotary Park - Soccer Complex
Off 20th St. and Mayberry Loop, Morehead City

This 15-acre park and soccer complex opened in the fall 2004 and is a wonderful addition to the city's park system. It was paid for with a combination of federal and state grant money and support from county Rotary Clubs and other community organizations. The site features three regulation, lighted soccer fields that are often converted to make seven fields for play by younger athletes. The park features two picnic shelters, two lighted basketball courts and two restroom facilities. A 6/10-mile walking trail around the perimeter of the park features a boardwalk through the woods and later will tie into the city's sidewalk system.

Swansboro

Bicentennial Park
At the base of the bridge into Swansboro on N.C. Hwy. 24

The park was dedicated in 1985 and contains a life-size statue of Otway Burns, Swansboro's favorite privateer from the War of 1812, and a memorial to Theophilus Weeks, founder of the town. It's the perfect place to fish from the sea wall, play, or simply sit and enjoy the beauty of the White Oak River.

GOLF

From the beach to the driving range, eastern North Carolina's temperate climate makes it an ideal location for all sorts of outdoor activities, including golf. The Crystal Coast has a variety of scenic and challenging courses awaiting golf enthusiasts, and most of the area's exceptional club courses are open to the public. Courses are busy year round, and many Insiders consider fall the most favorable time to play. However, golf can be played here practically 365 days a year, if you wish. It's best to call ahead to reserve tee times, especially on weekends. Golfers who know the Crystal Coast know it is one of the best golf bargains around. Several local hotels offer golf packages that include accommodations, meals, guaranteed starting times, greens fees and a few extras; call the businesses listed in our Accommodations chapter and ask about special incentives for golfers.

Where possible, local courses take full advantage of the area's natural beauty. Many greens and tees offer glorious views of waters and wildlife, so the intrepid golfer gets a chance to experience a little something extra as the game unfolds. Several of the courses listed have recently completed multi-million dollar makeovers that bring them into the new millennium in championship form.

The courses we recommend will bring you many enjoyable rounds of golf. All fees are for 18 holes of play unless noted otherwise, and be sure to ask about seasonal rates since these may vary from course to course. We've also listed a local driving range.

Courses

Brandywine Bay Golf and Country Club
N.C. Hwy. 24 and U.S. Hwy. 70,
Morehead City
(252) 247-2541
www.brandywinegolf.com

West of Morehead City, this 18-hole, par 71 championship course was ranked as the area's best by Golf Digest in 1995. A very popular course, it is set in dense woods laced with streams and ponds. Indeed, water and woods are part of the play for every hole. Designed by Bruce Devlin and Bob Von Hagge, Brandywine plays 6609 yards from the championship tees, 6150 from the regular tees, 5390 yards from the gold, and 5192 yards from the women's. Improvements recently have been made to greens and fairways, and the installation of cart paths is ongoing.

Golfers will find a pro shop, a snack bar, putting greens and a chipping area with practice bunkers. Greens fees (including carts) are $47 in season and $37 off season. Walkers may play for $30 in season and $20 off season, but Insiders recommend that you call ahead for time limitations. June through September golfers can take advantage of the twilight special, 18 holes of golf plus a cart for $30 after 2 PM. A junior program and group rates also are available.

The Country Club of the Crystal Coast
152 Oakleaf Dr., at MM 5, N.C. Hwy. 58,
Pine Knoll Shores
(252) 726-1034

This 18-hole course is the only golf course on the island of Bogue Banks. Nestled among the sand dunes and maritime forests of Pine Knoll Shores, the course has four holes that overlook Bogue Sound. Beautiful water oaks, lofty pines and abundant wildlife enhance the appeal of this course. The course is par 71 from the blue and white tees, and par 72 from the reds, measuring 6,039 yards from the blue tees, 5,686 yards from the white tees, and 5,036 from the red tees. In-season, rates are $54 for 18 holes before 2 PM and $38 after 2 PM. Off-season rates are $40 for 18 holes before 1 PM, and $32 after 1 PM. All rounds include the use of a cart. Tee times are required seven days a week and may be made one week in advance. Golfers will also find fully stocked pro shop and clay tennis courts on the club grounds. A new clubhouse and lounge are currently under construction and will open in late 2006.

Carolina Pines Golf and Country Club
390 Carolina Pines Blvd., Havelock
(252) 444-1000

On the scenic Neuse River just west of Havelock and about ten miles east of New Bern, this challenging 18-hole, par 72 course is everything the golfer could want. The course features elevated greens, bermudagrass fairways, abundant sand traps and ample water that rewards the accurate shotmaker on seven of 18 holes. Tim Dupre, the club pro, will arrange lessons for those who are interested. Golfers will also find a pro shop, a driving range, target greens and a clubhouse with a lounge and patio that overlooks freshwater lakes and the golf links. Fees are $28 weekdays and $33 weekends, including cart. Carolina Pines is directly off U.S. Highway 70; look for the signs. The Flounder Jubilee, held the first weekend in June, is the course's big event tournament.

The Links at Plantation Harbor
1885 Adams Creek Rd., Havelock
(252) 444-4653

The Links is a USGA-regulation size, 18-hole, par 72 course with a total of 6000 yards from the championship tees. Golfers play on a combination of continuous single and double fairways, with nine holes returning to the clubhouse. The course's topography is basically level, but a few major slope changes take advantage of the natural ridges and valleys that enhance the beauty of the pine and hardwood roughs. Surrounding many greens are bunkers composed of moderately packed loose sand, 4 to 5 inches deep. Several ponds, lakes and canals offer additional challenges to players.

The Links is open year round, seven days a week, from sun up to sun down. The club has a pro shop, a clubhouse, a snack bar and a large practice putting green and driving range. Tee areas are well-marked with signs that note yardage and describe each hole. Fees to play 18 holes, including cart, are $25 on weekdays and $28 on weekends and holidays year round. On Wednesday, folks can play for $18. If you choose, you may walk the course for $15 during the week and $18 on Saturday and Sunday. Call for tee times.

Rock Creek Golf & Country Club
308 Country Club Blvd., Jacksonville
(910) 324-5151

Rock Creek is convenient to Emerald Isle, New Bern, Jacksonville, Topsail Island and even Wilmington. This 18-hole, 7102 yard, Jerry Turner & Assoc.-designed par 72 features numerous water dangers and pine tree-lined fairways with lush Bermuda carpeting. Onslow County's first planned recreational

A variety of challenging courses await golf enthusiasts on the Crystal Coast.

photo: George Mitchell

community, the facility truly caters to its golf-crazy residents. After a hot round of summer golf, the bar and Mulligan's Steakhouse await your arrival. The pro shop is open at 7 AM for all the early birds, and lessons and clinics are available for every level of golfer. PGA Pro Rick Morton calls Rock Creek his home, and you'll be tempted to do the same.

Silver Creek Golf Club
N.C. Hwy. 58 N., Cape Carteret
(252) 393-8058, (800) 393-6605

On N.C. 58 just north of Cape Carteret, the Silver Creek Golf Club is a 7005-yard, par 72 championship course, renovated with Tif Eagle greens and beautiful fairways and tees. Designed for championship play by Gene Hamm, Silver Creek is the longest course in Carteret County, and it is known for the gusty winds that challenge golfers year round. Year-round rates are $35 to $55, depending on season, and include the use of a cart. Walk-ins are allowed year-round after 1 PM; fees range from $25 to $40 depending on the season. Call in advance for tee times. Special twilight rates are available from late May to mid-September.

The Southern-style clubhouse and snack bar has a wide porch overlooking the course. The pro shop carries a good selection of merchandise, and a pool and tennis courts are available as well as a practice green and driving range for pre-game warm up. A large bucket of balls costs $3.

Crystal Palms Par Three
and Hawaiian Thunder Mini-Golf
N.C. Hwy. 58 N., Cape Carteret
(252) 393-1020

Next door to the Silver Creek Golf Club, the club's newest additions are the Crystal Palms 18-hole, par 3 course and the Hawaiian Thunder, an 18-hole mini-golf course. Both are lighted in-season and enable the whole family to enjoy the game of golf together.

Star Hill Golf Club
202 Club House Dr., Cape Carteret
(252) 393-8111, (800) 845-8214

Star Hill offers 27 holes in a wooded, hilly setting. Opened in 1965, it recently underwent a $4 million redesign by R. T. Birney and is now one of the area's finest championship courses, measuring more than 9000 yards. At the junction of N.C. Highways 24 and 58 between the Intracoastal Waterway and the Croatan National Forest, Star Hill offers the Sands (3194), the Pines (3212) and the Lakes (3212).

Star Hill's rate structure is $65 for 18 holes in season, $42 off season. Reserved tee times are recommended throughout the year. Star Hill also offers three-play and 10-play passes. While the three-play pass is offered for in-season use only, the 10-play pass is good year-round. Junior and active duty military discounts also are available.

Patrons will find a pro shop offering rental clubs, a full line of clothes and accessories and professional equipment. Other amenities include a Cayman driving range, a total short-game practice area, and a swimming pool. The attractive, casual-atmosphere Champions Room lounge is open daily, as is the Sandbar Grill, which offers breakfast and lunch daily. Those arriving by air will enjoy the use of Star Hill's private airstrip.

Driving Range

Golfin' Dolphin
N.C. Hwy. 24, Cape Carteret
(252) 393-8131

This business offers fun for serious golfers -- and for their companions who would rather do something else. People who want to practice their golf swing can use the 250-yard driving range. Buckets of balls cost $5 for 60 balls, $7 for 85 balls and $12 for 215 balls. Not-so-serious grown ups and kids will get a charge out of the 18-hole mini-golf course (with elevations up to 22 feet), batting cage, go-cart track, KidzKarts ride and bumper boats. The batting cage is for softball and baseball, and the go-cart track and bumper boats are a great way to give vent to the competitive spirit in all of us. Golfin' Dolphin is behind Hardee's in Cape Carteret and is open from 9 AM to 11 PM every day during the summer. Fall hours through December are 10 AM to 5 PM. Winter hours vary.

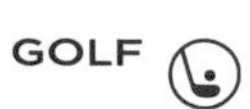

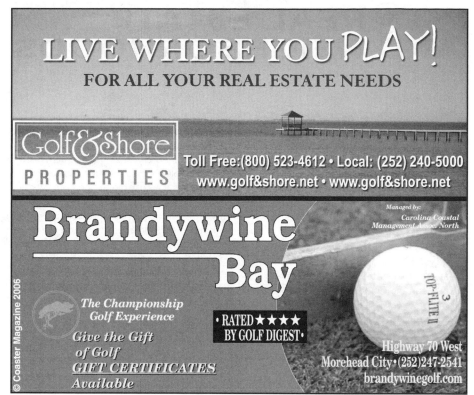

REAL ESTATE AND NEIGHBORHOODS

The Crystal Coast has always been a great place to live and it continues to be discovered by more and more people. If you are looking to join those seeking to call this area home, or "second home", this chapter is just for you. It is specifically designed to assist you in searching for an existing home or property in the area.

In this chapter we introduce you first to the neighborhoods that make up the expansive Crystal Coast area and then to some of the area's real estate companies. Our lists are by no means complete, but they will serve to familiarize you with the area and help you locate neighborhoods, businesses and services. The realty firms recommended here are listed in the area of their home office and then alphabetically. These are not the only fine and reputable firms in the area, but we simply couldn't list them all. We revise this book annually, and we welcome your comments concerning additions or omissions in the next edition.

Before we start with neighborhoods, we should point out that an invaluable source of free information for anyone interested in purchasing property is HOMES Magazine of the Crystal Coast. This free monthly guide, published in cooperation with NC Coast Communications and the Carteret County Association of Realtors, contains descriptions of all the residential and commercial property in Carteret County. The guide also lists e-mail and homepage addresses for many of the individual Realtors. You can pick up a free copy at supermarkets, drug stores, restaurants and hundreds of local commercial establishments.

We begin our review of the area by looking at beach neighborhoods. When we talk about the beach we are referring to the island of Bogue Banks, which encompasses the townships of Atlantic Beach, Pine Knoll Shores, Indian Beach, Salter Path and Emerald Isle. From there we move to historic Beaufort, then to the central town of Morehead City, westward to Swansboro and finally to the Down East reaches of Carteret County.

Like everywhere else, homes on the Crystal Coast vary tremendously in price, and location is everything. Here, good locations are determined by proximity to water, historic districts, golf courses and upscale subdivisions. While it's possible to find comfortable inland living quarters in the $90,000 to $100,000 range, you can also spend a million or more for a large, plush home on the waterfront or in an exclusive waterfront neighborhood with a slip for your boat. Significant development has taken place away from the water recently, and a wide range of housing is available.

There is no specific relocation service on the Crystal Coast; however, rest assured that most real estate agents will go to great lengths to ensure that your move is smooth. After all, they are in the business of sharing with newcomers what we Insiders have already learned – this is a great place to be! The Chamber of Commerce, (252) 726-6350, can also provide you with some information about the area.

A note on zoning: If the property you are considering is not in an incorporated city or subdivision, ask your real estate agent or the county planning office what uses are permitted in that area. Large portions of Carteret County are not zoned and may permit certain uses you have not considered – for your lot as well as your neighbor's. As with all major purchases, ask questions so you'll know before you commit.

As more and more people discover the Central Coast, real estate prices continue to increase. The average inland neighborhood home currently sells for around $200,000 to $300,000. If you are seeking a waterfront home in the area, expect to pay between $1 and $1.5 million. Waterfront lots on Bogue Banks and in Beaufort can sell for $1 million.

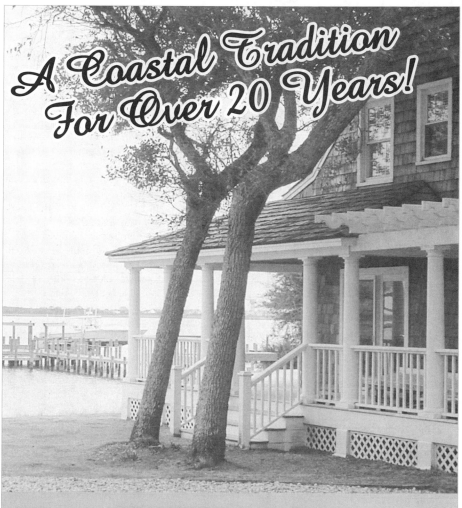

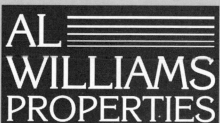

NEIGHBORHOODS

Bogue Banks: The Beaches

Like most beach resort areas, the Crystal Coast has a number of condominium developments. We mention a few here; however, for a more complete list of what is available, check with a real estate agent. Also, for information on timeshares, check our Crystal Coast Weekly and Long-Term Cottage Rentals chapter.

Many newcomers move to the Crystal Coast for one reason: to live by the water. Atlantic Beach, Pine Knoll Shores, Indian Beach and Salter Path often have existing homes on the market. However, new construction has been a constant during the last several years, leaving an array of newer homes, condominiums and townhouses. Keep in mind that homes in this part of the county generally have a water view, a fact that increases the price of the property tremendously.

If searching for a summer or vacation home at the beach, note that most of the condominium complexes have rental units managed by area realty companies. Not sure which site fits you best? Spend a week or a weekend there and see if the site is what you had in mind.

ATLANTIC BEACH

With a remaining hint of a nostalgic air about it, Atlantic Beach is seeing its 1950s beach houses change to modern structures. There are still plenty throwback-to-the-1950s rambling beach houses and small cottages nudged right up next to ponderous two-story clapboards on narrow streets running parallel to the ocean. Atlantic Beach continues to be primarily made up of "local" residents -- people who have lived here most of their lives and wouldn't dream of living anywhere else. The demographics at this end of Bogue Banks are slightly different. Expect a younger crowd at Atlantic Beach instead of the large concentration of retirees found at other beach locations. Families in their 30s and 40s are commonplace, probably because of the small, affordable, near-beach cottages that allowed these couples to purchase their home at a reasonable price in years past.

Today, change is happening on Atlantic Beach. Atlantic Beach is making great strides to revitalize itself. The Circle, a once popular family amusement area, is being renovated and plans are well under way for major developments and improvements to the area. Condos, restaurants and shops will soon fill the area that once was home to a ferris wheel, go cart tracks and amusement arcades.

Private homes, vacation rentals and mobile homes are mixed throughout this small oceanfront town, and over the years building has extended several blocks back from the water to N.C. Highway 58 (Salter Path Road). Most of the dwellings in Atlantic Beach are within walking distance of the ocean or sound, and the majority of new homes are concentrated on the eastern end of the island, along Fort Macon Road.

Here, too, are a number of condominium and townhouse developments, such as Seaspray, A Place At the Beach, Southwinds, Sands Villa Resort, Island Quay and others. There are only a handful of new subdivisions in Atlantic Beach because nearly all the residential property has been developed. Most of the homes are re-sales, and prices vary greatly.

By far Atlantic Beach's most colorful development is Sea Dreams, MM 1.5. Built on a high dune with views of the ocean and sound, this small development offers bright cheery homes and a clubhouse, playground and pool.

PINE KNOLL SHORES

Pine Knoll Shores is truly a planned community, and the original developers deserve credit for their farsightedness. Built in a maritime forest, the town has done an admirable job of trying to lessen the impact on the natural environment. Drive through town and you will see what we mean. Trees are everywhere. Restrictive covenants require a complete survey on each lot of all trees larger than a 3-inch circumference. Before you can get a permit to build, you have to prove you will save as many trees as possible and disturb the land as little as possible. The process can be tedious, but the result is worth it, as most all residents will agree.

Pine Knoll Shores is nearly 90 percent developed, but both large and small homes come on the market fairly regularly. Home sites and homes vary in price, depending on proximity to the ocean, the sound, the many canals or the 18-hole golf course located in town. Within the central portion of the town, many homes are built on canals, with the option of private docks. Homes on the ocean or sound can be very pricey. While new development in Pine Knoll Shores is rare, here are a few of the largest, established communities. This is merely a sampling, and a drive down N.C. 58 will offer the best look at the real estate Pine Knoll Shores and other beach communities has to offer.

Bogue Shores Club and Beachwalk at Pine Knoll Shores are townhouse and condominium developments between MM 6 and 7 on N.C. 58. All are on the ocean and in nice maritime forest settings. Design features include courtyards, sun porches, gourmet kitchens, private balconies and other upscale luxuries.

The McGinnis Point subdivision is a Bogue Sound community, with homes on, near or removed from the water. As with all property on Bogue Banks, prices for single-family homes vary widely, depending on location.

Beacon's Reach, MP 8 through 9, is a large village-type development in a maritime forest on land once owned by the Roosevelt family. It includes both multi-family and single-family dwellings. Each village is carefully planned, and residents have access to lighted tennis courts, swimming pools, a marina and parks on the ocean and the sound. Meticulously landscaped, the villages include Ocean Grove, with three- and four-bedroom units; Westport, with one-, two- and three-bedroom units and both sound-front and freshwater lagoon-front units; the Breakers, with oceanfront condominiums; Fiddlers' Walk with sound-side condominium units; and Maritime West, with oceanfront units.

SALTER PATH/INDIAN BEACH

Many of the longtime residents in these two small communities are descended from fishermen, and some still make their living on the water. You'll find a variety of homes here. Some homes are low, rambling structures, nestled under windswept live oaks bent from prevailing winds. Others are mobile homes, while others are large, new homes. Hurricane Ophelia in the fall of 2005 damaged many homes and businesses in these two communities.

The town of Indian Beach has seen the development of an upscale residential community: Sea Isle Plantation. Sea Isle is probably one of the priciest areas on the island. At MP 10, Sea Isle offers home sites and custom-built residences on both sides of Salter Path Road, and on Bogue Sound and the ocean.

The Summerwinds condominium complex is a large, oceanfront complex offering spacious living quarters. Recreational

facilities include an indoor, heated swimming pool, a whirlpool, saunas, exercise rooms, a spa and racquetball courts. Outside are three oceanfront pools with sun decks and a boardwalk.

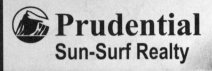

Kiawa (kee-wah) is another Indian Beach sound-front community, off N.C. 58 between the towns of Atlantic Beach and Emerald Isle. Water-view and sound-front building lots are being offered at a starting price of $48,000. Individual sound-front docks are available. Sea Ridge Townhomes in Indian Beach offers oceanfront and ocean-view two-bedroom townhouses.

Indian Beach's newest development is The Ocean Club. Billed as a luxury family resort and conference center, The Ocean Club offers condominium homes in a beautifully landscaped environment. Each mid-rise building has 12 condominium homes with elevator service. The site has an oceanfront pool, picnic areas, an exercise room, spa and more amenities.

EMERALD ISLE

The western end of Emerald Isle is family-oriented with a growing number of permanent year-round residents. Originally, the only access to the western end of the island was by boat and, later, ferry. It wasn't until the 1970s that the B. Cameron Langston high-rise bridge opened the area to tourists and newcomers. Emerald Isle is now one of the fastest-growing areas of the county. Sections along Coast Guard Road, off N.C. 58, have seen an astounding amount of development in recent years.

You'll find many of the town's recently built residences quite impressive. Homes and cottages come in all styles, but most are multi-storied with wide porches and decks, so residents can take advantage of the beach view and sea breezes. Although some developers have bulldozed dunes and cleared much of the natural vegetation, others have left stands of maritime forest. There are a number of condominium and town-home

developments as well, such as Pebble Beach, Queen's Court and Sound of the Sea.

Lands End is an exclusive gated residential community on Coast Guard Road off N.C. 58 near the Point in Emerald Isle. Ownership includes use of a spacious clubhouse, a pool, four lighted tennis courts, stocked freshwater lakes and a lighted boardwalk to the beach. All roads are private, and utilities are underground.

Emerald Plantation is a sound-side subdivision that extends from N.C. 58 to Bogue Sound. A mixed-use development with single-family homes, townhouses and patio homes, amenities include a clubhouse, a pool, a boat ramp, tennis courts and a security gate. The Wyndtree subdivision is a large tract near Emerald Isle Point that has restrictive covenants for house sizes but offers a wide diversity of sites from oceanfront to ocean view.

The Point on Coast Guard Road off N.C. 58 at the westward tip of the island is one of the most established areas and has a wonderfully wide beach.

Deerhorn Dunes, Sea Dunes and Ocean Oaks are three well-planned subdivisions that are almost indistinguishable from one another. On Coast Guard Road off N.C. 58, all are relatively new and were built around the same time. They are made up primarily of single-family homes, nicely landscaped on spacious lots.

Cape Emerald off N.C. 58 on the sound-side of Coast Guard Road is a subdivision of primarily permanent residents. Amenities include a clubhouse, a heated pool and spa and two tennis courts. It has a security entrance and a community sewage system. Emerald Landing, Royall Oaks, Dolphin Ridge and Pointe Bogue are beautifully landscaped developments that offer peace and privacy in a verdant, spacious, wooded setting. Lots vary from 75-feet wide to 30-feet wide on ocean- and road-fronts. Interior lots also vary in size due to efforts to preserve the area's wetlands. Emerald Landing, Pointe Bogue and Royall Oaks have soundfront sites, and Dolphin Ridge has oceanfront building sites.

Also off Coast Guard Road is Spinnaker's Reach, an area described as a "sound to sea community." This development is tucked into the maritime forest and features a community pool, guarded entrance and a sound-side pier and nature trail. Single-family dwellings and oceanfront duplexes are being constructed.

White Oak Crossing, aptly named by its location on the White Oak River, is a residential community. This planned community offers a state-of-the- art tennis facility and a boat ramp for homeowners.

Beaufort

Everything in Beaufort revolves around this historic district or the water -- sometimes both. The town's geographic design lends itself to small residential areas built around roads and water. The older and more established neighborhoods and developments are in the historic area. Most new development is east of Beaufort along U.S. Highway 70 or north along N.C. Highway 101. This small port town is a haven for boaters and is a hub of activity during the summer months. Many of its historic homes have been restored as residences or bed and breakfast inns. Its lovely waterfront is a natural setting for music and socializing at outdoor cafes. The town's many shops, restaurants and tourist attractions give Front Street a festive air. Runners, strollers, walkers and bike riders flow constantly along the main Front Street thoroughfare, and the Historic District can easily be covered on foot.

As of spring 2006, Beaufort is currently under a moratorium on new construction, whether a new structure or an addition. This is based on a special order from the state that prohibits any new sewer connections until the town has repaired and replaced sewer lines.

Beaufort's Historic District is the oldest residential area in town, covering about 15 square blocks. Homes here date back to the 1700s, and exterior characteristics are governed by guidelines of the Beaufort Historic Preservation Commission. Charged with assuring the integrity of the area, the commission reviews all proposals for exterior changes such as paint color, siding, window treatments, redesign and other building changes.

Businesses and signage in the historic district are also regulated. The historic commission was not formed until the 1980s, so you will see a few things that would not meet their standards today but were "grandfathered" in. Property prices vary greatly in the historic district, depending on distance from the water, size and age of the house or building and its condition.

Beaufort homes outside the historic district also carry a variety of price tags, again depending on the distance from the water as well as size, age and condition. Deerfield Shores, Gibb's Landing, Howland Rock and Sea Gate are examples of water access subdivisions north of the downtown area. The Oaks at Beaufort and Taylor's Creek are newer developments on the east end of the Beaufort waterfront, and Graystone Landing is a build-to-suit development along N.C. 101. An 11-house development off Taylor's Creek called 1612 Front Street is designed in the "Old Beaufort Style" with sidewalks, deep front porches, 10-foot ceilings and heart-pine floors. Turner's Creek Plantation, on Steep Point Road off U.S. 70, is within the city limits of Beaufort.

Deerfield Shores, north of Beaufort off N.C. 101, is an attractive area on the Newport River and Intracoastal Waterway. Central to the development is the Carolina Marlin Club, a private boating (sail and motor) club complete with a 73-slip marina, a clubhouse and a swimming pool. Slip owners own the marina and clubhouse, which is also used by the Morehead-Beaufort Yacht Club. While a handful of lots are still on the market, re-sale homes in Deerfield are just beginning to pop up.

Gibb's Landing is a small subdivision on North River, reached by following U.S. 70 east of downtown Beaufort and turning right on Steep Point Road. Subdivision amenities include a community dock, pool and gazebo.

Howland Rock is a small subdivision that offers residents such amenities as a boat ramp, docks, recreational area and a homeowners association. The entrance road is on U.S. 70, just across from the Food Lion grocery store. Most of the homes were custom-built with attention to detail.

Jones Village is in the Beaufort town limits and is one of the area's oldest subdivisions. There are several entrances from Live Oak Street (U.S. 70) to the subdivision, which wraps around behind Jones Village Shopping Center. The development is a quiet, well-settled area that seems to attract a pleasant mix of people.

Tiffany Woods is a newer development about 4 miles east of Beaufort on U.S. 70. Several cul-de-sacs extend from the lighted main road, giving the neighborhood a feeling of privacy. This is one of the nicer new neighborhoods in the area. Sea Gate is a waterside resort community 7 miles from Beaufort on N.C. 101 at Core Creek. The development is on the Intracoastal Waterway with a deep-water marina, a ships' store, gas and diesel fuel, a clubhouse, a playground, a swimming pool,

tennis courts, a boat ramp and a security entrance.

Construction of The Oaks at Beaufort began in 1997. This development on Lennoxville Road offers a real community feeling and seeks to replicate the look and feel of old Beaufort, particularly the front porches and alley-accessed garages. Although it's not in the historic district, a short footpath provides homeowners quick access to Front Street and then an easy mile and a half walk to downtown Beaufort. The 42-lot, single-family subdivision offers eight basic home styles, each with many interior and exterior variations.

At the east end of Lennoxville Road is the pricey new development of Taylor's Creek. This waterfront community consists of only a few homes, and residents also have use of a pool and boat docks.

Graystone Landing is located about 3 miles up N.C. 101 from Beaufort. This neighborhood offers about 60 building lots. A few waterfront lots are available, although the majority are wooded interior lots in quiet surroundings. The houses in Graystone are custom-built and vary in style and price.

Other relatively new neighborhoods are Old Beaufort Village, Palmetto Place and The Courtyard East. The Village and Palmetto Place offer single-family homes and Courtyard East offers garden-style condos. The development fills Professional Drive, off of U.S. 70 East on the outskirts of Beaufort. Residents can easily walk to stores and the post office.

North Harbor and Heron Woods are located off U.S. 70 about three miles east of Beaufort. North Harbor offers mostly cleared lots, while Heron Woods features partially wooded lots. Phase I of Heron Woods has only a few lots remaining, and Phase II is now open.

Beaufort town commissioners have given the green light to the developers of the North River Club, a development that will be built over the next 20 years on a 629-acre tract between Highway 70 and Highway 101 north of Beaufort. Over that period of time, about 1,500 residential units will be constructed. Phase I will start this year and will include approximately 200 units on the southern most end of the tract. A 200-acre golf course will be included in the project.

Eastman Creek Landing is one of the area's newest developments and it is still under construction north of Beaufort between N.C. 101 and the Intracoastal Waterway. This neighborhood offers a clubhouse, pool, docks and boat slips.

Stanton Landing is a gated waterfront community on the Intracoastal Waterway. Located north of Beaufort on Highway 101, the subdivision offers two-thirds-acre lots, some with deep-water docks, and all owners can enjoy the clubhouse, pool and docks.

Sandy Point on the north shore of Carteret County along the Intracoastal Waterway is a Weyerhaeuser community that prides itself on its white sandy beaches. Amenities include a beachfront gazebo, a boardwalk, large recreation areas, underground utilities and paved streets. Sandy Point's 79 wooded home sites range in size from 1.4 to 10.9 acres.

Olde Towne Yacht Club is situated on Radio Island, between Beaufort and Morehead City. With condo units arranged in high rise buildings, owners have outstanding views of the surrounding waterways, islands and Cape Lookout National Seashore. Units feature 9-foot ceilings and the yacht club offers owners a gated entry, waterslide swimming pool, hot tub and fitness facilities. The marina features deep water boat slips, floating and fixed docks.

Morehead City

Morehead City is the area's largest city, and it has the most neighborhoods. Most early communities began at the water's edge because that's where the work was. Today people continue to live by the water, but not so much for the work as for the beauty of the views and the breeze. The city's earliest inhabitants lived near what is now the N.C. State Port, bounded by Bogue Sound, the Newport River and Calico Creek. As the area filled up, homes were built farther west.

Morehead City's downtown is seeing many improvements and an active Revitalization Committee is hard at work. Between Arendell Street and Bogue Sound, from about Ninth to 14th streets, is a neighborhood of small, wood-sided homes known as the Promise Land. Some of these houses were moved to the mainland on sailing skiffs at the turn of the last century when severe storms almost destroyed the once-flourishing fishing village of Diamond City on Shackleford Banks. Homes were dragged out of the water and rolled on logs to their new foundation. As the story goes, one spectator commented on the sight, "It looks like the Children of Israel coming to the Promise Land." The name stuck. There is now a promise of good appreciation in real estate as this area is very desirable for second-home buyers who love its location and charm.

Several condominium projects are on the drawing boards for the Downtown Morehead City area. One project is planned at the east end of Bridges Street, at the edge of the marina. Another project, a proposed nine-story condominium building, is being planned for the 900 block of Shepard Street.

More and more developments are popping up along the outskirts of town, many in the direction of Crab Point via N. 20th Street, Country Club Road and Barbour Road. Once an isolated farm community, Crab Point is one of Morehead City's oldest subdivisions and also the site of many newer developments, so prices vary greatly. Clustered within each development are houses with a broad range of prices, mainly because of the high prices demanded by houses on the water.

Joslyn Trace is a peaceful subdivision on N. 20th Street at the junction of Country Club Road. Homes here are both one and two stories. Creek Pointe and Mandy Farms are two neighborhoods just off Country Club Road.

South Shores is an established waterfront community off Country Club Road on the Newport River. It offers members of its homeowners association lighted streets, curbs and gutters, a swimming pool and tennis courts. Across Country Club Road is Brookewoods subdivision, a neighborhood with lots of friendly families.

Country Club Road is a main thoroughfare along the north side of Morehead City. West Carteret High School is at the western end, and the Morehead City Country Club is toward the eastern end. In between are mostly long-settled neighborhoods, although a few new developments have gone up in recent years. In most areas the lovely old trees have been left in place, and most homes are suitable for retirees or young families. An equal number are huge and obviously expensive.

Country Club East is a development across from and fronting the golf course. Two- and three-story homes are the norm. Prices vary, depending on the size, features and distance from the golf course.

River Heights lies to the east of the country club and is one of the older suburbs. Homes here are rarely on the market, and when they are, they are sold relatively quickly at affordable prices.

Hedrick Estates on the west side of Country Club Road features nice one-and two-story homes with well-landscaped yards. Adjacent to Hedrick Estates is Westhaven Village, made up of one- and two-story homes on large wooded lots.

West-Car Meadows off Country Club Boulevard is a well-established, affordable development, backed by Swinson Park and close to Morehead City Primary School, the high school and shopping areas. This is a good location for young families with children. Northwoods is a nice development off Country Club Road, with single-family and two-story dwellings on large tree-covered lots.

Justin's Corner is an attractive community of starter or retirement homes on Mandy Lane, just off 35th Street, south of the Sports Center. These houses are 1,200 to 1,700 square feet, with attached garages, fully equipped kitchens and no interior steps to climb. All Justin's Corner homes have three bedrooms and two bathrooms and several different exterior styles from which to choose. Every yard is graded, seeded and landscaped with shrubs, and lots are smaller than average size for less maintenance.

Blair Point is a waterfront development located at the eastern end of Country Club Road. This subdivision has building lots situated on an artificial pond, Dill's Creek, and on the Newport River. The development has sidewalks, pedestrian bridges, lighted-curbed streets and private docks. A wide price range is found here, depending on proximity to water and water depth, which for some lots is 5 to 6 feet at low tide.

In the same area is Olde Farm Island, a very unique small island connected to the

Crystal Coast neighborhoods are close to the shoreline.

photo: George Mitchell

mainland by a bridge through scenic wetlands.

Just west of Blair Point is Blair Farm. This large development is tucked away by Blair Pointe off of Country Club Road. Blair Farm offers something for everyone in unique neighborhoods - single family homes, patio homes and large homes - depending on what Blair Farm neighborhood you choose. A few building sites are still available, with one last section yet to be offered. Amenities include a clubhouse, a community swimming pool, a playground and tennis courts. More new areas are being developed.

Greengate is a nicely developed residential neighborhood in Morehead contiguous to Mayberry Loop Road. Greengate offers eight floor plans and two-, three- and four-bedroom, energy-efficient homes.

Bonham Heights, Mansfield Park and Mitchell Village are older, spacious, well-established neighborhoods along Bogue Sound off U.S. 70. Homes vary from modest bungalows to two-and three-story residences. Most residents have lived in these areas for a number of years; however, homes do occasionally go on the market. Many waterfront homes have water access at their back doors. It's worth a drive through these areas to see what is available.

The Landings at Mitchell Village is a townhome project offerings two and three bedroom units, each with a garage. Single-story and two-floor models are featured.

The Bluffs is a condominium development at the end of Mansfield Parkway, overlooking Bogue Sound. Units are individually owned townhouses or condominiums, most with a sound view.

Morehead City's selection of neighborhoods is quite good. There are many areas available in a variety of price ranges. As they say, there's something for everyone - if you're willing to search. Or contact a local real estate agent and let them find something that fits you needs and budget. But don't wait too long to decide - inventory is low and the number of buyers is high.

Western Carteret County

As the county's population increases, development in the western part of Carteret County continues. This area has some long-established neighborhoods, but many new ones are springing up along N.C. Highway 24 between Morehead City and Cape Carteret and along U.S. 70 between Morehead City and Havelock.

Spooner's Creek and Spooner's Creek East are long-standing neighborhoods built around the marina at the mouth of Spooner's Creek and along Bogue Sound. The area features large homes, many with their own private docks. Spooner's Creek South is a new development in the area, offering many lots with boat slips.

Brandywine Bay is an exclusive planned subdivision, stretching from Bogue Sound to U.S. 70. Begun in 1972, the project was built around the Earle Webb estate. The Webb Mansion, an impressive brick structure surrounded by majestic live oaks high on a bluff overlooking Bogue Sound, burned to the ground many years ago, although a replica private residence remains the centerpiece of Brandywine. The waterfront portion of Brandywine Bay consists of a noncommercial marina with a community boat ramp surrounded by residential building lots. Marina slips are individually owned. Three townhouse projects surround the harbor with homes attractively placed, creating the image of a village. There are single-family residences, and lots available on either side of the townhouses and harbor. The project continues across N.C. 24, where it surrounds a beautiful 18-hole championship golf course. Some homes were built in the 1970s, and there is usually a nice selection of re-sales. Brandywine North is the subdivision's newest neighborhood.

Village Green at Brandywine Bay offers duplex style homes arranged with two units per building. There you will find one- and two-story units. Bay Colony is between N.C. 24 and Bogue Sound and offers a pier and a pool.

The Village at Camp Morehead by the Sea is on the site of the former Camp Morehead between N.C. 24 and Bogue Sound. This waterfront development offers residents a clubhouse, pier, tennis and basketball courts and swimming pool.

Gull Harbor, Soundview, Ho-Ho Village and Barnesfield are all established developments along Bogue Sound on N.C. 24. While some homes are quite large and elaborate, others are moderate in size and style. Many have deep-water docks. Somerset Plantation is off N.C. 24 and features a swimming pool, tennis courts, a boat ramp, a residential day dock, boat slips and a secured entrance.

In the Broad and Gales Creek areas are Bluewater Banks, Fox Lair and Rollingwood Acres. These are subdivisions close to Broad Creek Middle School. Bluewater Banks is a soundfront development, and Rollingwood Acres is on Broad Creek. Home prices vary greatly, depending on location and water access. Fox Lair is a non-waterfront development.

Farther up N.C. 24, toward Swansboro, are Pearson subdivision, Bogue Sound Yacht Club, Blue Heron Bay and Hickory Shores. Again, some of these developments are longer settled than others. Homes vary from spacious and elaborate to small and practical. In Cedar Point, at the intersection of N.C. 58 and N.C. 24, is Magen's Bay. This is a residential, soundfront area with a minimum lot size of 20,000 square feet. Magen's Bay features private-gate entry, a pool and a bathhouse, tennis courts, deeded water access and a 100-foot pier to Bogue Sound.

Four miles east of Cape Carteret is Cedar Key. Nestled along Bogue Sound, this development offers beautiful views of Carolina sunsets. Water access is available, and a pier, park and picnic areas are open for residents.

Bluewater Cove is a relatively new subdivision located off N.C. 58 on West Fire Tower Road. Located across from Silver Creek Golf Course, the 65 lot subdivision offers residents water access, a pool and clubhouse, and a boat ramp and day dock.

Swansboro

Historic Swansboro offers a variety of housing opportunities, including historic houses near the business district, mobile homes on the outskirts of town and charming new homes on unbelievably beautiful lots overlooking the water. Swansboro attracts those seeking to relocate to a quiet, coastal

area, and the waterfront offers outstanding restaurants and shops of all types.

In the town itself, there are basically three types of homes. In the oldest part of town are the historic homes, some rehabilitated and restored and others in need of attention.

Around the fringes of the business district and extending several blocks in all directions are houses that were built about 50 years ago. They, like the older homes, are a mix of beautifully restored and maintained residences, with some that would be on the market as fixer-uppers. Closer to the city limits are homes built within the past 25 or 30 years. Most are still in good condition but not particularly distinctive in design.

In recent years, new developments have been opening, bringing a totally new look to Swansboro's housing picture. The River Reach development is perhaps the most dramatic change in Swansboro's real estate market and is almost fully settled, although re-sales are now found on occasion.

The Villages at Swansboro is a new development on Mount Pleasant Road, and it is especially for seniors over 55 years of age. This single-family, one-story condominium community is set in a park-like area. Exterior home and yard maintenance are taken care of so seniors can live a care-free life.

Plantation Estates is a waterfront subdivision on the White Oak River. Hurst Harbour is an exclusive subdivision near the ferry landing at Hammocks Beach State Park. Oyster Bay offers moderately priced homes and lots and is being settled by the area's young professionals. Walnut Landing was designed for more economical residences.

Port West Townhouses are beside Swansboro Primary School and are made up of 13 buildings with four units each. Most units are rentals; however, some are owner occupied. The townhouses feature one, two or three bedrooms.

Swann Harbour is a waterfront condominium development off N.C. 24 on the White Oak River offering one- and two-story homes with two or three bedrooms. There are three floor plans available ranging from 1,300 to 1,700 square feet. Many units face the river, which is accessible by a boardwalk; other units face Swansboro town park. Community amenities include a swimming pool, a boat-landing gazebo and a dock.

Pirates Cove is a townhome subdivision with a pool and clubhouse environment. These properties are being purchased for investment or by people looking for low-maintenance housing centrally located in Swansboro.

Deer Run is also another town subdivision with more than 60 homes. Re-sales for these properties are excellent.

Down East

Traditionally, the Down East communities themselves make up the neighborhoods. The communities string along U.S. 70 and the waterfronts and revolve around the churches or the volunteer fire/rescue departments. You should keep in mind that Down East living isn't for everyone. Newcomers must be ready to forfeit the conveniences of town living and be able to entertain themselves with the simple pleasures of day-to-day life. If you are ready to make those trade-offs, you may have found your little piece of paradise.

Many of the county's traditional fishermen and boat builders live Down East, an area along U.S. 70 that merges into N.C. 12 and extends from Bettie to Cedar Island. As you cross the many Down East bridges, it is not unusual to see clammers hip-deep in the water. Boat sheds are more common than garages, and the whir of saws and smell of wood chips are sure signs of boat builders. Fishing and shrimp boats ply the waters year round, and egrets, herons, ospreys and other shorebirds live in the marshes and wetlands along the highway.

Like many people who hold on to land settled by their ancestors and who look to Mother Nature for their livelihoods, the people who make up these communities are reserved and self-sufficient. They are fiercely independent and expect others to be the same. But in times of trouble or crisis, you will find none more kind or gracious than those living in the little fishing villages that make up Down East.

As more people move to Carteret County, its eastern sector has seen the development of a few subdivisions outside the small communities. Homes and acreage are becoming increasingly available and, although prices vary widely, they are going up -- especially properties situated on the many creeks, inlets, bays, marshes and rivers that are the beauty of Down East. But if you want to get away from it all, for now this is the place to do it.

None of the Down East area is zoned, and therefore the area falls under Carteret County jurisdiction. And therein lies a problem. Down East residents, both natives and new comers to the beautiful area, do not want new high-density development approved. Concerned this development would change the quiet way of life and would harm the areas fragile environment, citizens have rallied to petition County Commissioners to put a moratorium on construction in the Down East area while the county's Land Use Plan can be revisited.

There are a number of neighborhoods and subdivisions in the Down East area.

Harbor Point in Straits has two sections and was established several years ago. With home sites are on a secluded peninsula, the development offers a park area and boat ramp and is completely sold out. Resales are infrequent.

Midden's Creek is a waterfront community about 15 minutes east of Beaufort in the Down East town of Smyrna. Waterfront lots offer direct boat access to Cape Lookout and Drum Inlet by way of Core Sound. These lots are in excess of one acre and each has a septic permit.

Ward's Creek Plantation and Tranquility Estates are both in Otway. Ward's Creek offers waterfront, water-view and water-access lots, and Tranquility Estates is a waterfront and interior lot subdivision on Ward's Creek. Jade Point is a developing waterfront community located off Crow Hill Road in Otway.

There are a few developments on Harkers Island, including Harkers Point and Harkers Village. These two areas are sold out, and if a lot resale does open up it goes quickly. West Bay is a new development on Harkers Island and was sold out even before the permit and approval process was finalized.

Because of current regulations and coastal development requirements, land suitable for development is sparse in the Down East portion of Carteret County. This is a treasured area that many people seek to call home so land is in great demand. Land prices vary greatly depending upon location, view, elevation and amenities.

REAL ESTATE COMPANIES

Atlantic Beach

Atlantic Beach Realty Inc.
Causeway Shopping Ctr.,
Atlantic Beach Cswy., Atlantic Beach
(252) 240-7368, (800) 786-7368
www.atlanticbeachrealty.net

Owners Charles and Mary Duane Hale are longtime residents of the area and have extensive knowledge of properties on the Crystal Coast. Atlantic Beach Realty is a full-service real estate firm, handling condominiums and cottage rentals of all types. With a primary office in Atlantic Beach, the firm also offers an office at Dunescape Villas and another at Island Beach & Racquet Club.

Beach Vacation Properties
1904 E. Fort Macon Rd.,
Atlantic Beach
(252) 247-2636, (800) 334-2667
www.beachvacationproperties.com

Whether it is seasonal short-term rentals or off-season long-term rentals, Beach Vacation Properties can find just the right cottage or condominium to suit your needs. This company also handles sales and offers property management services. No matter the size of housing you need, or the length of

your stay, the staff at Beach Vacation Properties can help.

Bluewater GMAC Real Estate
311 C Atlantic Beach Causeway, Atlantic Beach
(252) 726-3105, (866) 467-3105
www.bluewatergmac.com

Let the six agents at Bluewater GMAC Real Estate handle all your needs, whether you are selling or buying property. This company handles residential and commercial listings, as well as second home purchases. The company also offers long and short term rentals, and provides professional management services to owners.

Cannon & Gruber, REALTORS
509 Atlantic Beach Cswy., Atlantic Beach
(252) 726-6600, (800) 317-2866

Formed in 1995, Cannon & Gruber offers many enviable listings not often on the market. This firm offers residential listings, with beach and soundfront condominiums as a specialty. They also handle commercial properties and property management. Contact them for a listing of properties that are currently available.

Coldwell Banker Spectrum Properties
515 Atlantic Beach Cswy., Atlantic Beach
(252) 247-7600, (800) 237-7380
www.spectrumproperties.com

This Coldwell Banker firm is a full-service agency in Atlantic Beach. The Realtors specialize in properties throughout Carteret County. Agents handle condominiums, homes and home sites as well as long-term and seasonal rentals and professional property management services.

Gull Isle Realty
611 Atlantic Beach Cswy., Atlantic Beach
(252) 726-0427, (800) 682-6866

In business since 1971, Gull Isle Realty handles appraisals as well as the sales of condominiums, homes, building lots and investment properties on Bogue Banks and the mainland. Gull Isle Realty also handles a number of long-term rentals. The firm has a state-certified appraiser. Call owner-broker David Waller for any real estate need.

Deanna Hull Realty
607 Atlantic Beach Cswy., Atlantic Beach
(252) 240-0273, (800) 477-4180
www.deannahullrealty.com

Owner Deanna Hull is a native of Carteret County and has 22 years experience in the real estate business. This agency handles all types of properties for buyers and sellers here on the Crystal Coast. She also handles timeshare re-sales with no up-front fee. Whether buying or selling, stop by and visit for an honest professional approach. Located in the "big yellow building" right on the Atlantic Beach Causeway.

Kivett's Happy House Realty
613 Atlantic Beach Cswy., Atlantic Beach
(252) 342-4444
www.happyhouserealty.com

Kivett's Happy House Realty handles properties throughout Carteret County, including the mainland and Bogue Banks. The company specializes in residential homes and sells them for 3.9 percent. They offer their customers the use of a moving truck for local moves, and you can view a special video on the company's website.

Realty World First Coast Realty
407 Atlantic Beach Cswy., Ste. 1, Atlantic Beach
(252) 247-0077, (800) 849-4801
www.nc-coast.com

This full-service agency in Atlantic Beach provides an extensive inventory of homes, condominiums and building lots. Knowledgeable agents match new homeowners with affordable property in the right locations. The office has a good reputation for its property-management program and its vacation and annual rental department, (252) 247-5151, (800) 972-8899. This company also offers cottages and condos perfect for a coastal wedding, reception or romantic honeymoon.

Alan Shelor Real Estate
407 Atlantic Beach Cswy., Ste. 3, Atlantic Beach
(252) 247-7700, (800) 849-2767

This company offers properties all over the Crystal Coast and has been in business for more than 25 years. Alan Shelor is the exclusive agent for the Coral Bay Ridge subdivision in Atlantic Beach. Nine Realtors are on staff to help clients find just the right residential, resort or commercial property.

Smith & Weil Premier Properties
201 W. Fort Macon Rd., Atlantic Beach
(252) 727-5656, (877) 333-4466

Sally Smith and Louis Weil have formed a new comprehensive real estate company that carries the slogan The Star Team - Coastal Property Specialists. This firm offers properties of all types -- from first and second homes and investment properties to new construction and commercial. They handle properties throughout Carteret County and also specialize in waterfront properties, acreage and new construction.

Sound 'n' Sea Real Estate Inc.
205 Atlantic Beach Cswy., Atlantic Beach
(252) 726-1239

Owned and managed by Ellen and Demus Thompson, Sound 'n' Sea Real Estate specializes in the sale of homes and condos on the island and mainland. The Thompson firm is the oldest continuously owned and operated full-service real estate business in the Atlantic Beach–Pine Knoll Shores area.

SurfSide Realty, Inc.
204 Sandpiper Dr., Newport
(252) 726-0950
www.surfsidevacationrentals.com

SurfSide Realty focuses on finding just the right property for the client. Whether that is an island home, a house on the mainland, a vacation place, or a condo, this mother-daughter team can find just the place. Both are brokers and licensed Realtors, and act as an agent for buyers or sellers. SurfSide also handles rentals.

Whispering Sands Realty
212 N.C. Hwy. 58, Atlantic Beach
(252) 247-3429, (800) 682-7019

This agency offers sales of resort residential properties and condo re-sales on Bogue Banks, as well as handles residential sales throughout the county. It also provides property management services and offer rentals of many desirable Bogue Banks cottages and condominiums.

Al Williams Properties
407 Atlantic Beach Cswy, Ste .5B, Atlantic Beach
(252) 726-8800, (800) 849-1888
www.alwilliamsproperties.com

The company slogan states Al Williams Properties has been a "coastal tradition" for more than 20 years. Agents offer a strong knowledge base of the local area. Listings often include exclusive condominium properties and waterfront homes on the beach and in Morehead City as well as building lots and acreage. Al Williams' Realtors are available to show you any of them, and this firm offers property management services.

Pine Knoll Shores/ Indian Beach

First Commercial Properties
1700 N.C. Hwy. 58 (Salter Path Rd.), Salter Path
(252) 247-2035, (888) 237-2035

First Commericial Properties offers development acreage, building lots, investment properties and private residences throughout Bogue Banks, Newport, Morehead City and the surrounding area. This firm's market niche is commercial ventures. In business for over 20 years, it has solid expertise in handling commercial transactions and consulting with small businesses. The company is also the exclusive agent for The Ocean Club Resort, a world-class resort on Bogue Banks.

Pine Knoll Shores Realty
320 Salter Path Rd., Pine Knoll Shores
(252) 727-5000

Share your real estate dreams with these professional and let them go to work. Pine Knoll Shores Realty specializes in properties on Bogue Banks, as well as handles listings throughout the county. Whether you are interested in a primary home, a second home, a condo or a lot, they can find just the right property. The company has eight brokers that hold the designations of ABR, CRS, GRI, RRS and SRES.

Sunny Shores
N.C. Hwy. 58 (520 Salter Path Rd.), Pine Knoll Shores
(252) 247-7347, (800) 624-8978, (800) 626-3113
www.sunny-shores.com

Sunny Shores is a full-service company operated by experienced Realtors. The company offers sales, vacation rentals and property management, along with maintenance and cleaning services. Sunny Shores' specialty is meeting unique rental requirements. For rental information, call (800) 626-3113. The office is across from the Clamdigger Inn.

Emerald Isle

Angelfish Properties
7601 Emerald Dr., Emerald Isle
(252) 354-8984
www.angelfishproperties.com

Angelfish Properties is a full-service agency that specializes in oceanfront, waterfront and investment properties. While their main focus is on Emerald Isle, Swansboro and Cape Carteret, Brian Peele and his five agents can locate just the property you are seeking anywhere in the surrounding area as well. This knowledgeable and friendly agency handles the sale of homes, lots and condos as well as commercial properties.

Bluewater GMAC Real Estate
200 Mangrove Dr., Emerald Isle
(252) 354-2128, (888) 354-2128
www.bluewatergmac.com

While this is the main office, this firm also has offices in Atlantic Beach and Cape

Carteret. Let this full-service real estate firm assist you with your dream of owning coastal real estate, whether it be a quaint cottage, an elegant oceanfront home, a carefree condo or an undeveloped home site. The Bluewater GMAC sales team offers friendly, knowledgeable and professional Realtors. The staff can also show you the wisdom of vacation ownership by renting to others as an easy way to help pay for your beach property. The office is open every day.

Century 21 Coastland Realty Inc.
7603 Emerald Dr., Emerald Isle
(252) 354-2131, (800) 822-2121
www.coastland.com

This full-service company has been in business since 1981 and was the first realty franchise on the beach. The company offers many completed homes, both new and previously owned, in some of Emerald Isle's most exclusive locations. It also sells building lots, constructions in progress, and acreage. Condominium re-sales and pre-construction sales are their specialties. The agency has a vacation and long-term rental department as well.

Emerald Isle Realty
7501 Emerald Dr., Emerald Isle
(252) 354-4060, (800) 304-4060
www.emeraldislerealty.com

Emerald Isle Realty is a family owned and operated company offering sales, vacation rentals and property management services. This firm's knowledgeable and professional sales staff can help you make the correct decision whether you're buying for pleasure or investment or selling. The team specializes in resort sales on Bogue Banks as well as residential and commercial listings on the island and on the mainland. The company also offers short and long term rentals, as well as vacation rentals.

Prudential Sun-Surf Realty
7701 Emerald Dr., Emerald Isle
(252) 354-2958, (866) 662-4704
www.sunsurfrealty.com

Prudential Sun-Surf's slogan "Come For A Week ... Stay For A Lifetime" says it all. The company offers more than 300 condominiums and homes, and you can book your vacation online or by calling toll-free for a brochure. Then let their experienced, professional sales staff help you make your place at

the beach a reality. Prudential Sun-Surf offers vacation buying sales packets, buyer agency representation and property management services.

Realty World First Coast Realty
7413 Emerald Dr., Emerald Isle
(252) 354-3070, (800) 682-3423
www.nc-coast.com

This full-service agency provides an extensive inventory of homes, condominiums and building lots throughout Emerald Isle and the surrounding Cape Carteret areas. Knowledgeable agents match new homeowners with affordable property in the right locations. They also handle commercial properties and can act as agent for buyer or seller. The office has a good reputation for its property-management program and for its vacation and annual rental department, (252) 354-3928.

Shorewood Real Estate Inc.
7703 Emerald Dr., Emerald Isle
(252) 354-7858, (888) 557-0172
www.shorewoodrealestate.net

A full-service, family-owned business, Shorewood Real Estate specializes in real estate sales, property management and vacation rentals. Celebrating its 10th year of service to property owners and guests to the Crystal Coast, the owners and staff of Shorewood Real Estate pride themselves on the delivery of exceptional customer service, professionalism and courtesy. Whether your interests are in real estate as an investment, a second home or as a primary residence, our sales team is ready to assist you in your purchase.

Spinnaker's Reach Realty, Inc.
9918 M. B. Davis Ct., Emerald Isle
(252) 354-5555, (800) 245-7746
www.spinnakersreach.com

The agents at Spinnaker's sell properties in Spinnaker's Reach, an Emerald Isle community with ocean- and soundfront, waterview and interior lots and homes, as well as across the county. The firm specializes in helping clients choose property, consult with the in-house designer, decide on a blueprint, select a builder and find an interior designer. Let the representatives at this firm act as your agent or broker.

Watson-Matthews Real Estate
9102 Coast Guard Rd., Emerald Isle
(252) 354-2872

This business has been active since 1979 with sales of condominiums, single-family dwellings and investment and commercial property. Watson-Matthews offers homes and lots in prestigious Lands End, Cape Emerald and other Emerald Isle developments as well as along Bogue Banks and on the mainland. The firm can also assist you with pre-construction packages.

Beaufort

Beaufort Realty
325 Front St., Beaufort
(252) 728-5462, (800) 548-2961
www.beaufortrealtync.com,
www.vacationbeaufort.com

This company specializes in residential and commercial property in the Beaufort historic district and it often has some desirable historic properties for sale. Beaufort Realty also handles sales in Down East, Morehead City and on the beach. The company is one of the few firms that offers annual and vacation rentals in historic Beaufort.

Century 21 Down East Realty
415 Front St., Beaufort
(252) 728-5274, (800) 849-5795

Century 21 Down East Realty specializes in Down East and Beaufort properties. It also handles property in Morehead City and is affiliated with the Newsom-Ball Century 21 office in Morehead City. The firm handles residential and commercial sales as well as

Heading off into the sunset.

photo: George Mitchell

appraisals. It is Beaufort's oldest full-service real estate company.

Copeland Real Estate
220 Front St., Beaufort
(252) 504-3334, (866) 803-0073

Copeland Real Estate offers quality services to clients seeking investment property, a first home, a second home or a place to retire. The firm's four agents also handle commercial properties and can act as buyer or seller agents.

Core Sound Realty
2622 U.S. Hwy. 70 E., Beaufort
(252) 728-1602, (800) 211-8202

Core Sound Realty handles all types of real estate -- residential, commercial, acreage and lots -- all over the county. It specializes in waterfront, water-view and water access properties in Beaufort and Down East and acts as agent for buyers and sellers.

The Holland Group Real Estate
113 Turner St., Beaufort
(252) 504-2400, (888) 879-7790

Owned by hard-working owner/agent Jeanette Holland, this agency is a quickly growing company that handles property throughout the county. Whether it is a first home, a second home, a retirement home or an investment property, this company has six agents who can act for the seller or buyer. The company also offers commercial real estate and property management services.

Eddy Myers Real Estate
131 Middle Ln., Beaufort
(252) 728-1310, (800) 321-9240
www.eddymyers.com

Eddy Myers Real Estate specializes in a selection of waterfront and water-view properties in historic Downtown Beaufort and in surrounding areas of the North Carolina Central Coast. They can help with waterfront estates, historic or commercial properties, condos, beach homes, vacation cottages or year-round residences.

North River Realty
412 Front St., Beaufort
(252) 728-6455

North River Realty is a full-service real estate company specializing in coastal golf, waterfront and other resort and boating-oriented properties. The firm and its agents can act as agent for buyer or seller and work hard to find just the right property to meet your needs and wishes. North River Realty is also the exclusive broker for North River Club, a 620-acre community being developed on the east side of Beaufort. Just five minutes from the historic district, North River Club will feature an 18-hole world-class golf course designed by Bob Moore of JMP Golf Designs. The community will also feature a complete swimming and tennis center. Call Sharon Barnes at North River Realty for all the details.

Realty World First Coast Realty
400 Front St., Ste. 12, Beaufort
(252) 728-4991, (800) 849-4801
www.nc-coast.com

This full-service agency offers an extensive inventory of homes, condominiums and building lots. Knowledgeable agents match new homeowners with affordable property in the right locations. The office has a good reputation for its property-management program and has associated offices in Atlantic Beach, Emerald Isle, Morehead City and Salter Path.

Down East

Many of the real estate agencies throughout the county handle property in the Down East area, which is east of Beaufort. There are only a few real estate companies with offices actually in the Down East area.

Eastern Gateway Realty
535 U.S. Hwy. 70, Bettie
(252) 728-7790, (800) 205-5765

For more than 20 years owner Mary Hill has served the real estate needs of Down East. Her expertise in Down East properties is well-known and highly regarded throughout the county. Eastern Gateway Realty specializes in residential houses, lots and acreage, including an enviable number of waterfront listings. The firm also offers long-term rentals in the Down East area. Mary and her five agents are all Down East local people who know the area extremely well.

Golden-Lew Realty
383 U.S. Hwy. 70 E., Otway
(252) 728-3974, (800) 366-0691

Owner-broker Catherine Golden has handled sales of residential, commercial and waterfront properties for 20 years. Golden-Lew serves Down East, Beaufort, Morehead City, Newport and western Carteret County.

Sea Level Real Estate
500 U.S. Hwy. 70, Otway
(252) 504-7177, (877) 835-9034
www.sealevelrealty.com

Sea Level Real Estate is proud to serve the real estate needs of both sellers and buyers. This company takes pride providing each client with outstanding service. Members of the Sea Level Real Estate team reside in the communities of "The Original Down East" and are knowledgeable of the area's rich heritage. Whether looking for a first home, a retirement dream or anything in between, this team can help.

Morehead City

Century 21 Newsom-Ball Realty
4644 Arendell St., Morehead City
(252) 240-2100, (800) 849-5794

Ken Newsom owns both the Morehead City business and the Century 21 office in Beaufort. Between the two offices there are 15 sales associates all with well-rounded knowledge of the area. The company offers complete services, emphasizing the sale of homes, businesses and acreage throughout the county. Century 21 also provides appraisals and commercial leasing services.

Chalk & Gibbs Realty
1006 Arendell St., Morehead City
(252) 726-3167, (800) 849-3167

In operation since 1925, this agency handles real estate across the Crystal Coast, including sales of single-family dwellings, townhouses and condos, building lots and acreage. They also offer property management, annual rental services and certified appraisals. They also have a complete insurance branch.

Gena Gilbert Real Estate
4219-H Arendell St., Morehead City
(252) 240-0259, (877) 240-0259

Gena started her successful career in real estate by being named Carteret County Realtor of the Year her very first year in business. This firm handles mostly residential listings of homes and condos, as well as investment properties. She specializes in waterfront property, working as a seller's agent and a buyer's agent.

Golf & Shore Properties
Brandywine Bay,
U.S. Hwy. 70, Morehead City
(252) 240-5000, (800) 523-4612
www.golfandshore.net

Golf & Shore Properties specializes in properties in Brandywine Bay. The company also represents properties throughout the county, and the experienced agents can help you select lots, single-family homes and town homes. The office is right inside the U.S. 70 gate to Brandywine.

Home Finders Robinson and Associates
304 N. 35th St., Morehead City
(252) 240-7653, (877) 849-0234

Alan and Sharon Robinson own and operate this family business with the help of an additional agent. Alan Robinson has been in the real estate business since 1979, and his wife joined him in 1988. The company handles single-family homes from Morehead City to Newport plus lots and acreage. It also offers property management services and works with several builders.

Kivett's Happy House Realty
1205 Arendell St., Morehead City
(252) 342-4444
www.happyhouserealty.com

Kivett's Happy House Realty handles properties throughout Carteret County and in Havelock. The company specializes in residential homes, lots and acreage as well as some commercial properties. They offer customers the use of their moving truck for local moves.

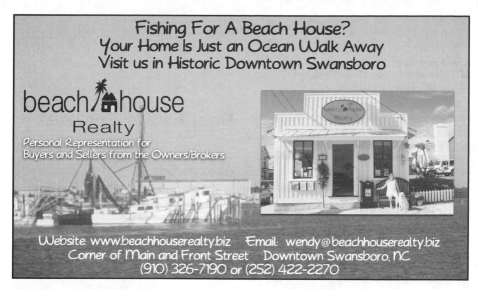

Putnam Real Estate Company
3800 Arendell St., Morehead City
(252) 726-2826

Putnam Real Estate is a full-service agency that specializes in the sale of new and established homes and commercial properties throughout the county as well as building lots and constructions-in-progress. The company, in business since 1972, offers full appraisal services, property management and long-term rentals.

Realty One - Tom Saunders Real Estate Company
100 N. 28th St., Morehead City
(252) 247-7444, (800) 587-2549

This company offers a great variety, from homes in some of the area's most exclusive residential districts to fixer-uppers with investment potential. It offers lots, acreage and commercial properties and specializes in waterfront and residential properties, and a few long-term rentals. The firm can provide appraisals, property management and relocation services.

Realty World First Coast Realty
4747 Arendell St., Morehead City
(252) 222-4747
www.nc-coast.com

This full-service agency offers an extensive inventory of homes, condominiums and building lots. Knowledgeable agents match new homeowners with affordable property in the right locations. The office has a good reputation for its property-management program and has associated offices in Atlantic Beach, Beaufort, Emerald Isle and Morehead City.

Linda Rike Real Estate
1410 Arendell St., Morehead City
(252) 247-6922, (800) 240-6922

Linda Rike has been providing real estate services in the county for 20 years. With that experience, this firm knows the county well and handles new construction, re-sales, condominiums, homes and lots. The company specializes in waterfront and second homes, resort and recreational properties and retirement relocations. It also offers a few long-term rentals.

Western Carteret and Swansboro

Beach House Realty
107 Main St., Swansboro
(910) 326-7190
www.beachhouserealty.com

Beach House Realty specializes in waterfront and waterview homes, with an emphasize on first homes, second homes or investment properties. The principles/brokers offer personable representation for buyers and sellers. With offices in Historic Swansboro, this friendly hard working team of professionals handles properties from the White Oak River to Cedar Island. The firm is a member of the Onslow County and the Carteret County MLS.

Bluewater Cove
201 Bluewater Cove, Cape Carteret
(252) 393-2128

Affiliated with Bluewater GMAC Real Estate, Bluewater Cove is an on-site broker service exclusively handling sales in Bluewater Cove and construction by Bluewater Builders. Bluewater Cove has a total of 65 lots; however; only a handful remain. This upscale neighborhood offers residents a clubhouse, boat ramp, day dock, boat storage and easy access to the Intracoastal Waterway.

Bluewater GMAC Real Estate
415 McLean Dr., Cape Carteret
(252) 393-2111, (800) 752-3543
www.bluewatergmac.com

With offices in Emerald Isle and Cape Carteret, this full-service real estate firm can assist you with your dream of owning coastal real estate, whether it be a quaint cottage, an elegant oceanfront home, a carefree condo or an undeveloped home site. The Bluewater GMAC sales team offers friendly, knowledgeable and professional Realtors ready to assist you. The staff can also show you the wisdom of vacation ownership by renting to others as an easy way to help pay for your beach property. The office is open every day.

Century 21 Waterway Realty
406 Corbett Ave. (N.C. Hwy. 24), Swansboro
(910) 326-4152, (877) 326-4152

This agency, one of the oldest in Swansboro, sells building lots, new homes and re-sales in the Swansboro/Cape Carteret/Emerald Isle area. Most of the company's agents are longtime residents of the area. The company also handles commercial properties, lots and acreage along the White Oak River and the Intracoastal Waterway, and long-term rentals.

Timeshare Sales

Deanna Hull Realty
607 Atlantic Beach Cswy., Atlantic Beach
(252) 240-0273, (800) 477-4180
www.deannahullrealty.com

Serving timeshare owners and buyers since 1984, Deanna Hull Realty specializes in Atlantic Beach oceanfront resort property, handles re-sales with no up-front fee, and works to save buyers on closeout inventory and re-sales. Whether buying or selling, contact Deanna for an honest, no-pressure approach. Timeshare rentals are also available.

Real Estate Services

Progress Energy Carolinas, Inc.
(800) 452-2777

Progress Energy has headquarters in Raleigh and is a company that was once known as Carolina Power & Light (CP&L). The customer service number is (800) 452-2777, and the number to report outages is (800) 419-6356. All required city and county inspections must be completed prior to connecting your permanent electric service. An electrical inspection is required for newly constructed homes or manufactured homes. Since electricity is billed after it is used, Progress Energy may require a security deposit before completing your application for service. If a deposit is required, the company will contact you either by e-mail or phone to provide additional instructions.

Carteret-Craven Electric Membership Cooperative
1300 N.C. Hwy. 24 W., Newport
(252) 247-3107

Providing electrical service to much of western Carteret County, this member-owned corporation has more than 30,000 members. It services all residents of Bogue Banks except those living in Atlantic Beach; all residents in Cape Carteret, Cedar Point and along N.C. Highway 58 to Maysville; residents along N.C. 24 from the Swansboro line to Gull Harbor and down Nine Foot Road and Lake Road to Havelock; residents along U.S. 70 from Morehead City to the old residential district in Newport; and Morehead City residents in some areas of Country Club and Crab Point. The Cooperative also provides service to portions of Havelock and small areas in Jones and Onslow counties. A deposit may be required when making an application, or a letter of good credit from another utility company may waive that deposit requirement.

Harkers Island Electric Membership
849 Island Rd., Harkers Island
(252) 728-3769

Harkers Island Electric Membership provides reliable electricity to residential property owners and businesses on Harkers Island. This is an electric distribution cooperative owned by the people it serves, with a board of elected officers. The co-op was formed in 1939 and continues to provide electric utility service on the island.

Kinetico Advanced Water Systems of Central and Coastal Carolina
5633 U.S. Hwy. 70, Newport
(252) 223-4444, (800) 865 1208

Kinetico provides residents of Carteret County with an important commodity: treated water. Much of the county's water comes from private wells, and much of the local well water contains iron and calcium. Kinetico sells water treatment equipment that continuously delivers high-quality drinking water with a 90 percent removal rate of all chemicals. Product designs include nonelectric twin tanks for 24-hour protection and a system that lets you know when it is time to change filters. All of Kinetico's water softeners, purification and filter systems, and drinking water systems have the longest factory warranties and the highest independent certifications available.

Sprint
(252) 633-9011

While many people may recognize Sprint as a long-distance carrier, in these parts it's also the local telephone company. Depending on your previous record, you may be asked to pay a deposit before service is initiated. The deposit usually is refunded after a year. Connection can take three or four working days, longer if there has not been telephone connection at that address before.

Apartments

The apartment complexes along the Crystal Coast offer a nice selection for renters. This coastal area is not filled with a large number of apartment complexes like other beach areas, so once the nicest ones are filled, there is a often a slow turnover rate. Area real estate companies often manage rental properties for the owners, and rentals are also listed in the classified section of the Carteret County News-Times. We have listed a few of the larger apartment complexes for you below.

Beaufort Town Apartments I & II
201 Glenda Dr., Beaufort
(252) 728-2940

Located about two miles from the waterfront, Beaufort Town Apartments offers two bedroom, one and half bath units and two bedroom, two and half bath units. Residents can enjoy a pool and a small playground area. The complex allows children, and cats and small dogs are allowed with a separate deposit.

Country Club Apartments
4600 Country Club Rd., Morehead City
(252) 726-2389

Country Club Apartments are centrally located in Morehead City and feature many trees on the property and a nice playground. Here you will find one, two and three bedroom apartments. Children are welcome, and pets are permitted with some stipulations regarding size, number and fees.

Kings Mill Apartments
1200 Daughters Dr., Newport
(252) 223-6311

Kings Mill offers affordable housing to individuals 55 years of age or older. One and two bedroom apartments are offered in this new complex, and there is an earning limit for residents.

Orlandah Court Apartments
3115 Bridges St., Morehead City
(252) 247-3688

Orlandah Court Apartments feature 32 units ranging from one bedroom to two bedroom. This quiet complex allows children but not pets.

RETIREMENT

Retirees love the Crystal Coast. It doesn't snow all winter, it's not excessively hot all summer, golf and gardening are great nearly year round, the fishing is fantastic, and the people are charming. Adding to the attraction are the relatively inexpensive property costs, compared with other popular retirement areas. Because of the large bang for the retirement buck, the Crystal Coast enjoys a fast-growing population of highly educated, well-traveled and active retired citizens.

As the number of older residents increases, the county and its various towns develop more activities directed toward suiting the needs and interests of the senior set. With the variety of sports, hobbies, volunteer opportunities and entertainment available, most retirees stay as busy as they want to be.

Housing requirements can change quickly during the retirement years. Townhouse and condominium developments are perfect for retirees who also decide to retire from house and lawn maintenance. All real estate companies can guide you toward more simplified living arrangements in beautiful locations. See the Crystal Coast Neighborhoods and Real Estate chapter for a complete discussion of housing alternatives available.

Housing exclusively for older citizens on the Crystal Coast is available in a variety of settings, from federally subsidized accommodations for the elderly and disabled on fixed incomes to exclusive retirement complexes where you buy the unit and pay a monthly maintenance fee that includes taxes, meals, laundry and around-the-clock security service. In addition, there are nursing homes, rest homes and family-care centers for those who need extra attention. If you need information about any or all of the nursing-care facilities in the Crystal Coast area, call the Department of Social Services at (252) 728-3181. If you are shopping for a nursing-care facility, be sure to make several visits to the places you are considering so you can make the very best choice.

Services and Organizations

Area Agency on Aging (AAA)
Eastern Carolina Council
233 Middle St., New Bern
(252) 638-3185

Based in New Bern but serving the elderly throughout eastern North Carolina, this agency helps adults 55 years or older maintain and improve their quality of life by addressing their needs and concerns. Programs include adult day care, care management, disaster preparedness and assistance, family caregiver support program, information and referral, in-home aid, transportation, and more. New programs are always in development; call for more information. See our New Bern Retirement chapter for more information about this agency.

Help-At-Home
1202 S. Glenburnie Rd., New Bern
(252) 672-9300, (866) 672-3100

Providing in-home care 24 hours a day, seven days a week, Help-At-Home allows seniors throughout eastern North Carolina who need just a little bit of "help at home" to stay in their homes and enjoy their independence. This service matches caregivers to senior clients and provides services such as meal planning and preparation, light housekeeping, medication reminders and bill paying assistance, bathing safety monitoring, errand running, and local transportation.

Leon Mann Jr. Enrichment Center for Senior Services
3820 Galantis Dr., Morehead City
(252) 808-4066

The Leon Mann Jr. Enrichment Center for Senior Services, open weekdays from 8 AM to 5 PM, offers programs and services for Crystal Coast seniors older than 55. The center is fully disabled-accessible, bright, modern and well-designed and includes large meeting rooms, classrooms, a library, a game room and a health center.

Classes, trips, workshops and entertainment events include lively lessons in line dancing, exercise, billiards, table tennis, club meetings and the like. Facilities are also used for a variety of community activities including the Foster Grandparents program and other community services. Hot lunches are available for qualifying seniors age 60 and older, but arrangements need to be made at the center. A representative from New Bern's Social Security office is available at the center on Wednesdays from 8:30 AM to 2:30 PM; no appointment is necessary.

Meals On Wheels
Meals Coordinator
(252) 726-4654

Area Meals-On-Wheels programs provide home delivery of hot meals, usually one a day, five days a week. The program is designed to help the elderly, shut-ins, those recuperating from surgery, and disabled persons. Some systems require full payment for meals, some seek contributions, and others operate entirely on donations. Churches in Carteret County coordinate the programs and its volunteers.

Senior Pharmacy Program
502 Middle St., New Bern
(252) 638-3657

The Senior Pharmacy Program assists eligible seniors, ages 60 and over in Craven, Jones, Pamlico and Carteret counties, with costs for prescription medications. An outreach of Catholic Social Ministries, it helps pay for prescriptions that treat chronic diseases such as cancer, high blood pressure, heart disease, diabetes, glaucoma, acid reflux, arthritis and clinical depression. Post-hospitalization medications may be covered on a limited basis. Sites for the monthly distribution of vouchers, to be used toward the prescription costs, are generally at area senior centers. Call ahead for an appointment. The program's mailing address is P.O. Box 826, New Bern, NC 28563.

i

There's no need to drive all the way to New Bern to visit the Social Security office. A representative from the office is available at the Leon Mann Jr. Enrichment Center for Senior Services on Wednesdays from 8:30 AM to 2:30 PM; no appointment is necessary.

Senior Games
Carteret County Parks and Recreation Dept.
801 Arendell St., Ste. 8, Morehead City
(252) 808-3301

Carteret County has a year-round Senior Games program designed to keep residents age 55 and older healthy, active and involved. Local games are held each May, and a year-round program leads up to the annual state Senior Games held in Raleigh in September. Competitions include tennis, golf, swimming, biking, table tennis, horseshoes, croquet, track, billiards, bowling and more. Get the picture? It's active. Games also include Silver Arts competition in painting, sculpture, writing, heritage crafts, instrumental and vocal music. Local winners compete in the state Senior Games during the fall and can advance to the nationals. The Senior Games committee sponsors workshops to prepare prospective athletes or artists. Registration is required to participate.

Housing Options and Facilities

Somerset Court of Newport
3020 Market St., Newport
(252) 223-2600, (800) 948-4333

Somerset Court offers 16 beautifully furnished two-bedroom apartments, each accommodating four residents who are able to live independently with some assistance. Assistance includes three nutritious meals a day (with special diet considerations) served in the dining room, laundry, housekeeping services, medication monitoring and administering, scheduled transportation and a variety of social, recreational and educational opportunities. The community-within-a-community complex is designed around an exterior courtyard with a gazebo-style bandstand for special performances and events and a village green for community gatherings. Each apartment has a courtyard patio. Monthly

The AARP offers a low-cost driver safety program for motorists, primarily for ages 50 and older. The course reviews the basic rules of the road, offers tips for avoiding traffic violations that older drivers are more likely to do, and covers defensive driving techniques. For local class information, call Charles Peckham at (252) 444-3983.

rental includes all services, and an enthusiastic staff is available at all times.

Ekklesia I and Ekklesia II
405 Barbour Rd., Morehead City
(252) 726-0076

Ekklesia I and II is a HUD-subsidized retirement complex in a quiet part of town off Barbour Road. About two blocks from Morehead Plaza Shopping Center, Ekklesia I and II includes 94 one-bedroom units and six two-bedroom units, all arranged in clusters around the community center, which houses laundry facilities, a mail room and a large meeting room with a kitchen. The offices of the site manager and activities director are also in the community center. Regular activities include monthly birthday parties, holiday parties, bingo, club meetings and such special events as an annual bake sale. A service coordinator also is available to help residents find community programs that may be of assistance to them.

Harborview Towers
812 Shepard St., Morehead City
(252) 726-0453

Locally owned and operated, Harborview Towers is in a downtown residential neighborhood on the Morehead City waterfront overlooking Bogue Sound. The modern 10-story, 50-apartment complex is adjacent to Harborview Health Care Center, a skilled-nursing and intermediate care facility for 122 patients. Residents purchase lifetime rights, with deeds of trust, to live in the Towers' efficiency apartments and one- and two-bedroom units. A monthly fee includes maintenance, housekeeping, laundry, emergency and scheduled transportation, one meal a day in the dining room, property taxes, and all utilities except telephone, Internet access and cable. All but the smallest units have balconies providing views of either Newport River or Bogue Sound. There is outdoor parking, with some covered parking on the building's ground floor. The facility has an activities director and full-time security.

Snug Harbor on Nelson Bay
272 U.S. Hwy. 70 E., Sea Level
(252) 225-4411, (800) 257-5456

Originally built for retired Merchant Marines and operated by one of oldest charitable trusts in the country, the retirement community of Snug Harbor offers rich maritime history and the picturesque surroundings of Nelson Bay . Snug Harbor is the only retirement community in Carteret and Craven Counties to offer three levels of care: independent living, assisted living and skilled nursing care. Private accommodations, including suites for couples, are available. Fine cuisine is prepared and served three times a day in the elegant dining room. Medical care and a full-scale activity calendar ensure that residents can stay as healthy and active as possible. Overnight accommodations are available for visiting family members.

Taylor Extended Care Facility
U.S. Hwy. 70 E., Sea Level
(252) 225-4611

Formerly Sea Level Extended Care, this former hospital was renamed in 1998 in honor of the four brothers who donated it to the county: Daniel, William, Alfred and Leslie Taylor. Opened in 1953, Taylor Extended Care is a 104-bed, long-term care facility offering skilled nursing care as well as custodial care for the aged. A primary-care clinic and pharmacy are located on the premises.

North Carolina Senior Care is a state program which provides prescription drug assistance and insulin to low income residents age 65 and older who have been diagnosed with heart disease, chronic lung disease or diabetes and are not eligible for Medicaid or other third party prescription drug benefits. For information, call (866) 226-1388.

Family-Care Centers

Family-care centers provide a homelike atmosphere for those who need some care but can basically live independently. Residents must be ambulatory and perform some light-housekeeping duties. They usually have kitchen privileges. Residents generally live in semiprivate bedrooms with a shared bath, have meals together and use the living room or other facilities jointly with other residents. There is a resident supervisor who does the heavy housework and cooking and, in general, looks after the residents. Transportation for medical attention, worship and shopping is provided. Medicine is under lock and key and is dispensed by the supervisor according to the doctors' directions.

Crystal Coast Family Care Home
107 Graham Ln., Beaufort
(252) 728-4422

In a quiet, rural setting off N.C. Highway 101, Crystal Coast Family Care Home offers private rooms with shared baths and common-use living areas for 12 residents. Each of the two homes in the facility has a live-in supervisor to prepare meals, dispense medicines or give any needed attention 24 hours a day. Meals are served family-style. Planned activities include cookouts, transportation, worship and shopping. The Crystal Coast Family Care Center for ambulatory and semi-ambulatory residents has been operating since 1991.

Veterans' Groups

Because of the proximity of several military bases and military hospitals, Carteret County is home to many veterans. The more than 9,700 veterans living on the Crystal Coast make up nearly one-fifth of the permanent population. There are numerous veterans' organizations in the area, and all welcome new members. The Veterans' Service Office at 613 Cedar Street in Beaufort, (252) 728-8440, offers problem-solving services to veterans. The Carteret County Veterans Council, (252) 393-6178, is the coordinating body for member veterans' organizations of Carteret County. The council sponsors the Morehead City Veterans Day Parade and Carteret County Memorial Day Ceremony and promotes exhibits and issues relevant to veterans.

The Morehead City VA Outpatient Clinic, (252) 240-2349, operated by the Durham VA Medical Center, is located at 5420 U.S. 70 W. The clinic, which is open Monday through Friday, provides primary care, mental health, immunization and blood-drawing services by appointment to VA-enrolled patients in Carteret, Craven, Jones and Pamlico counties. Walk-in and emergency services are not available.

Other veterans' organizations in the area are:

American Legion Post 46, 1881 N. 20th Street, Morehead City, (252) 726-5427

Military Order of the Purple Heart Chapter 639, (252) 808-3766

Veterans of Foreign Wars Post 2401, 107 Earl Avenue, Beaufort, (252) 728-4390

Veterans of Foreign Wars Post 9960, VFW Road (off N.C. Highway 58), Swansboro/Cape Carteret, (252) 393-8053

Veterans of Foreign Wars Post 8986, 1316 Hibbs Road, Newport, (252) 726-8806

Vietnam Veterans of America Chapter 749, (252) 393-6178

SCHOOLS AND CHILD CARE

Educational opportunities in the area include public, charter and private schools. This section gives you information about schools and child-care facilities on the Crystal Coast. Our Higher Education and Research chapter contains information about community colleges and research facilities in the area.

Public Schools

CARTERET COUNTY SCHOOLS

The Carteret County Public School System ranks among the top systems in the state on academic achievement. Of the 115 public school systems in the state, Carteret County ranks third in the state on the nine-subject End-of-Course scores, which are administered to students in high school and those taking Algebra I in grade 8. Carteret County ranks 12th in the state on grades 3 to 8 reading scores and 20th in the state on grades 3 to 8 math scores. The county ranks 12th in the state on grades 3 to 8 reading and math scores combined. These scores indicate the continued academic growth of students and the outstanding dedication of the school system's employees.

The Carteret County Public School System serves the students of Carteret County, a county located on the beautiful Crystal Coast of eastern North Carolina. From Cedar Point to Cedar Island there are 85 miles of beautiful coastal scenery, friendly towns, and 16 public schools that are committed to creating opportunities for all students to do their best and to succeed.

The school system employs approximately 1,200 individuals and is the largest employer in the county. The system's student enrollment for the 2005–06 school year is about 8,300.

Test results for the 2004-05 school year indicate that seven of the 16 schools were designated "Honor Schools of Excellence" by the state, meaning the school met expected academic growth, had 90 to 100 percent of the students proficient, and made Adequate Yearly Progress (AYP). Two schools were designated as "Schools of Excellence," meaning the school met expected growth and had 90 to 100 percent of the students proficient. Four schools were named "Schools of Distinction," meaning the school met expected growth and had at least 80 percent of the students proficient.

For the sixth consecutive year, the combined Scholastic Assessment Test (SAT) scores of Carteret County students both increased and remained above the North Carolina state average. As a group, the county's graduating Class of 2005 recorded a verbal score of 508 and a math score of 515, for a combined SAT score average of 1023. This combined score was only five points below the national average. The county's SAT verbal score of 508 matched the national average and was nine points above the state average. The county's SAT match score was five points below the national average and four points above the state average.

Carteret County public schools are governed by an elected seven-member board of education. Members serve four-year staggered terms and are chosen in countywide, nonpartisan elections. School board members meet in open session each month.

For information about the public school system, including information about curriculum, testing, transportation, employment and more, visit www.carteretcountyschools.org or contact the Carteret County Public School System's Central Office (Board of Education), 107 Safrit Drive, Beaufort, NC 28516, (252) 728-4583.

There are also two publicly funded charter schools in the county that offer an alternative educational approach.

ONSLOW COUNTY SCHOOLS

Onslow County is situated on the coast of North Carolina. The system opened the 2005-2006 school year with 2,099 students, up by 1,078 from the opening of the previous school year. The system includes 18 elementary schools, eight middle schools, seven high schools, one early childhood center and one alternative learning center. Five of these schools are in the Swansboro area, just west of the Carteret County line.

Onslow County is one of the largest school system in the state, and the student population is indicative of the transient nature of the military community. Onslow County is the home of Camp Lejeune, the largest amphibious Marine base in the world. Approximately one third of the students move into or out of the system or between schools within the system during the school year. Much of this movement is attributed to the percentage of students from military or military-connected families, and that number will continue to grow as more and more troops are scheduled to arrive in the area this year. Like the student population, the professional personnel of the Onslow County School System is also impacted by the military community. The system hires about 350 teachers new to the system each year. Approximately 25 percent of the classroom teachers in Onslow County Schools hold a graduate license.

For information about the Onslow County Public School System, visit http://www.onslow.k12.nc.us or call (910) 455-2211.

Charter Schools

Two charter schools offer educational alternatives to students in Carteret County. Charter schools are considered public, as they receive public funds, yet by virtue of their charters with the State Board of Education, they are free from many rules and regulations that public schools must follow. Admission is by application and lottery selection. For more information on charter schools, call the N.C. Department of Public Instruction, (919) 807-3722.

Cape Lookout Marine Science High School
1108 Bridges St., Morehead City
(252) 726-1601

This charter school for grades 9 through 12 features smaller class sizes and offers a regular high school curriculum. With a maximum number of 150 students, the school is known for providing one-on-one services to students.

The Tiller School
1950 U.S. Hwy. 70, Beaufort
(252) 728-1995
1600 Fisher St., Morehead City
(252) 726-1826

The Tiller School, a public charter school, serves students in kindergarten through 7th grade in two locations. Originally a private school founded in 1992, it was granted charter status in 1998. The school is not church affiliated. The Beaufort location offers classes for students from kindergarten through 5th grade. The Morehead City location offers classes for 6th, 7th and 8th grade students.

When you live at the beach, you get to see the ocean every day.

photo: George Mitchell

Private Schools

Several private schools offer county students an alternative to public education. The grade level served varies by organization. There is also a small group of home-school participants. For information about home schools, contact the N.C. Department of Non-Public Instruction, (919) 733-4276, or the Carteret County Schools Central Office, (252) 728-4583.

Crystal Coast School of the Arts
4907 Bridges St., Morehead City
(252) 726-5050

This school offers a variety of services, with its major focus on dance, music, arts, Kindermusik and drama. The school offers a preschool program for 3 and 4 year olds. After-school programs for older children are also offered, as well as specialized summer programs.

Gramercy Christian School
U.S. Hwy. 70, Newport
(252) 223-4384, (252) 223-5199

This school is a ministry of the Faith Evangelical Bible Church. It provides a traditional Christian educational program for a growing number of students in kindergarten (at least age 5) through 12th grade.

St. Egbert's Catholic School
1705 Evans St., Morehead City
(252) 726-3418

This school is affiliated with St. Egbert's Roman Catholic Church and provides a Catholic-based education to students in kindergarten through 5th grade.

Newport Development Center
903 Church St., Newport
(252) 223-4574

The Newport Development Center is licensed to train children from birth through 21 years of age who need help because of developmental and language disorders, mental retardation, autism, emotional handicaps or learning disabilities. The program operates during daytime hours Monday through Friday. It also provides day care for typically skilled children from 6:30 AM to 5:30 PM. The center provides transportation.

Child Care

Fees for day-care services vary and are usually based on the child's age, the number of hours the child spends at the facility and the number of children in the same family attending the facility. Many child-care centers provide transportation to and from school if needed, and most offer summer programs. Several day-care centers offer extended hours on weekends, so be sure to call for schedules.

Carteret County and the State of North Carolina regulate day-care homes and day-care centers through the issuance of registrations and licenses. Regulations call for all such facilities to meet health and safety standards. In the case of nonsectarian child-care institutions, standards for children's learning and play programs must be met. For a complete list of regulated day-care homes and licensed day-care centers, call the Carteret County Department of Social Services, (252) 728-3181.

DAY CARE

Morehead City

My School Child Care
3415 Eaton Dr., Morehead City
(252) 247-2276

My School serves youngsters from age 6 weeks through age 12, and provides a preschool program, before- and after-school care, and a summer program. Transportation to and from some public schools is available.

Colony Day Care
700 N. 35th St., Morehead City
(252) 247-4831

Colony Day Care offers care for children from 12 months through 5 years of age. The sister business, Kids Kampus, offers services for older children. Colony Day Care is open from 6:15 AM to 6 PM.

Kids Kampus
601 N. 35th St., Morehead City
(252) 247-1866

Kids Kampus is designed for children from ages 5 years through 6th grade who need before- and after-school care. Transportation is provided to and from Bogue Sound Elementary, Morehead City Elemen-

tary, Morehead City Middle, Morehead City Primary and Newport Elementary. The sister business, Colony Day Care, provides services for younger children.

First Presbyterian Church
1604 Arendell St., Morehead City
(252) 247-2202

This church program offers preschool and half-day kindergarten for children ages 3, 4 and 5. Care is offered from 8:30 AM to noon Monday through Friday from early September through early May.

Beaufort

Ann Street United Methodist Church Preschool
500 Ann St., Beaufort
(252) 728-5411

This church facility has been providing child care since 1972. Ann Street offers programs for children ages 2, 3 and 4 years from 7:30 AM to 5:30 PM. Parents can select the full-day program or the half-day program.

Beaufort Child Development Center
201 Professional Park Dr., Beaufort
(252) 728-2786

Beaufort Child Development Center serves children from 6 weeks through 5 years, with a special focus on students who qualify for the Head Start program. The center offers after-school care for children from kindergarten through age 7. Summer programs are also offered, and the center is open from 6:30 AM to 5:30 PM.

Beaufort Christian Academy
U.S. Hwy. 70 E., Beaufort
(252) 728-3165

Beaufort Christian offers day-care services during the day for children ages 2 through 5 including a pre-kindergarten and kindergarten program. After-school care is provided for students up to age 10.

Western Carteret County

The Sandbox Child Care
130 Fort Benjamin Rd., Newport
(252) 223-3432

In the heart of Newport, just off Old U.S. Highway 70 E., The Sandbox serves children from ages 2, if potty trained, to 12 with full day-care service, morning preschool and before- and after-school programs. Sandbox also offers a complete summer program. It is open from 6:30 AM until 5:30 PM weekdays.

St. James Day Care and Preschool Center
1011 Orange St., Newport
(252) 223-3191

St. James offers care for children from 6 weeks through 5th grade. A day-care program is offered during the day and before- and after-school care is provided. Open 6:30 AM to 6 PM Monday through Friday, school buses pick up and drop off children at St. James. The center also offers summer programs.

White Oak Christian Day Care
U.S. Hwy. 24, Bogue
(252) 393-7808

In Bogue near Cape Carteret, the White Oak Christian Child Care offers day care and preschool activities for children aged 12 months through 5 years old and after-school care for children. A complete summer program is also offered.

Swansboro

Swansboro United Methodist Child Care and Preschool
665 W. Corbett Ave. (N.C. Hwy. 24 W.), Swansboro
(910) 326-3711

This center accepts children from ages 6 weeks to 9 years. The younger children are offered day care services and there is an after-school program for children up to the age of 10. Swansboro Elementary School buses provide transportation for children.

BABYSITTING

Nancy's Nannies Inc.
P.O. Box 3375, Morehead City, NC 28557
(252) 726-6575

Reliable, experienced sitters are available on the Crystal Coast through this service. Nancy's Nannies is used widely and offers responsible adult babysitters for in-home child care, as well as care for visitors to the area staying in rentals and hotels. This service provides sitters for a day, night, weekend or longer. Nancy's Nannies has been in business since 1991 and provides services to the coastal area, New Bern and Raleigh.

HIGHER EDUCATION AND RESEARCH

Several higher-education institutions are accessible to Crystal Coast residents interested in pursuing additional education or seeking enrichment. The area is also home to many well-known and respected research laboratories. Many residents of the Crystal Coast commute to Greenville to earn degrees from East Carolina University. (For more information about ECU, see our New Bern Education and Child Care chapter.)

Higher Education

Carteret Community College (CCC)
3505 Arendell St., Morehead City
(252) 222-6000

Carteret Community College is located on the shore of Bogue Sound off U.S. Highway 70 in Morehead City. The college offers the latest vocational-technological training and features programs that prepare students for the skills they need in the fast-paced information age, where computers and the Internet have changed the way business is done.

Students can pursue Associate in Science, Associate in Arts and Associate in Fine Arts degrees as well as associate degrees in programs for business and computer technologies, health sciences, vocational licensure fields, and public and legal services. In addition, a variety of shorter diploma and certificate programs also enable Carteret Community College to provide students with the training needed to find employment in a changing workforce.

With programs like Aquaculture Technology, Cosmetology Technology, Internet Technologies, Paralegal Technology, Culinary Technology, Hotel and Restaurant Management, Marine Propulsion Systems, and Boat Manufacturing and related marine trades, CCC students have a wide range of options. Additionally, students can work toward careers in Interior Design and a variety of health science related fields, including the new Associate Degree in Nursing program.

As an authorized academic training partner of the Microsoft Corporation, the college has the Microsoft seal of approval to teach students how to use its software products. Students can also test for Microsoft and Cisco certifications, which tell prospective employers they have mastered their technical specialties.

In the Corporate and Community Education Division, the college provides businesses and industries with training opportunities for employees in a variety of subjects. Supervision, leadership and customer-service training can be customized to meet an organization's needs. Seminars addressing the needs of small business and entrepreneurs are available to the public.

With occupational training courses such as electrical, plumbing, HVAC and carpentry, students are taking advantage of the flexible training opportunities available at the college. Furthermore, the Basic Skills Department provides students with an opportunity to obtain their GED, attend Adult High School or improve their English if it is their second language.

The Corporate and Community Education Division also offers pre-licensing courses for insurance, real estate, general contractor and marine captain. From a public safety training standpoint, students can enter the six-month Basic Law Enforcement Training Program or participate in shorter emergency medical training and fire-fighting programs.

Construction on three new job-training facilities was recently completed, allowing expanded training opportunities in Aquaculture, Business Technologies, Health Sciences and Marine Trades.

The college's library is open to the public and has one of the fastest Internet connections in the region. CCC was the first community college in North Carolina to be connected to the University System's North Carolina

Research and Educational Network. From audio books and best sellers to an interlibrary loan program with colleges and universities throughout the state, the college's library is an excellent research facility as well as quiet place to get away.

Coastal Carolina Community College
444 Western Blvd., Jacksonville
(910) 938-6394

Coastal Carolina Community College is a fully accredited state institution with more than 50 curricular programs in college transfer, general education and vocational and technical training programs. Many of these programs are available during the daytime, evening and at specially scheduled times. While the main campus is located on Western Boulevard in Jacksonville, the college also offers classes at Camp Lejeune and New River Air Station. More than half of the college's students are enrolled in the college transfer curriculum. Business and marketing, education and engineering are just a few of the many areas of study available to transfer students. Military family members, regardless of their state of residency, receive in-state tuition rates. Active-duty military are eligible for tuition assistance from the military. Last year more than 19,500 students enrolled in the college's continuing education courses. These practical, academic and technical programs are designed to increase an individual's employment opportunities and performance.

Craven Community College
808 College Ct., New Bern
(252) 638-4131

Like Carteret and Coastal Carolina Community Colleges, Craven Community College offers a variety of two-year degrees at its New Bern and Havelock campuses. (For more information, see our New Bern Education and Child Care chapter.)

Mount Olive College
2131 S. Glenburnie Rd., Ste. 6, New Bern
(252) 633-4464, (800) 868-8479

Mount Olive offers accelerated degree completion programs in Criminal Justice Administration, Management and Organizational Development, Religion and Early Childhood Education. Adults who already have about two years of college credits can take advantage of a special time-condensed format that allows them to complete their degree in about 14 months, while continuing to work full-time. For working adults who have little or no college credit, Mount Olive College in New Bern also offers a three-semester program, called the Heritage Program, which provides students with the core courses needed for associate or bachelor degree programs. (For more information, see our New Bern Education and Child Care chapter.)

Research Facilities

The Crystal Coast is home to numerous research facilities and has one of the largest concentrations of marine scientists on the East Coast at the North Carolina State University Center of Marine Sciences and Technology. All of the research facilities discussed here have something to do with the surrounding water and water-related resources. They offer research, product development and personnel training for corporations around the world. Area laboratories have been involved in developing many products. Contract research has included work with companies such as Strohs Brewery, W. R. Grace, Hercules Chemical, Biosponge Aquaculture Products, International Paint, Allied Chemical, Sunshine Makers, Aquanautics, Mann Bait Company, 3M Corporation and General Dynamics.

North Carolina State University Center for Marine Sciences and Technology (CMAST)
303 College Cir. (off Arendell St.), Morehead City
(252) 222-6300

The Center for Marine Sciences and Technology at North Carolina State University is a consortium of research scientists, extension specialists and other marine-related experts. Established in 1999, the center supports the educational and applied research activities for faculty throughout the North Carolina state university system. Knowledge generated here is to improve the well-being and quality of lives of North Carolinians, enhance the coastal environment, and foster coastal resource management. Faculty, staff and students from N.C. State University, Carteret Community College, North Carolina Cooperative Extension Service and the North Carolina Sea Grant College Program occupy the

CMAST facility that was completed in August 2000.

North Carolina State University Seafood Laboratory
303 College Cir. (off Arendell St.), Morehead City
(252) 222-6334

Established in 1970, the N.C. State University Seafood Laboratory is an applied research and extension education unit of the Department of Food Science. Located in the Center for Marine Sciences and Technology, the Seafood Lab focuses on seafood safety and technology, seafood product development, and seafood marketing. Personnel work with seafood-related industries, public health professionals and consumer groups on seafood quality and safety issues, nutrition and utilization, innovative processing technologies, and value-added fishery products. Support is provided through the N.C. Cooperative Extension Service, N.C. Agricultural Research Service and N.C. Sea Grant Program.

Duke University Marine Laboratory
135 Duke Marine Lab Rd., Piver's Island, Beaufort
(252) 504-7503

This inter-disciplinary facility has three objectives – research, teaching and the translation of sound science into effective environmental policy. The laboratory's large resident academic staff and visiting professors and researchers from throughout the United States and abroad have contributed to its worldwide reputation. The laboratory maintains a full-service campus, two large research vessels and a fleet of smaller boats. The largest is the R/V Cape Hatteras, a 135-foot ship owned by the National Science Foundation and run by Duke on behalf of the Duke University-University of North Carolina Oceanography Consortium.

This 65-year-old lab, located adjacent to the Rachel Carson Estuarine Research Reserve and Cape Lookout National Seashore, has a long and productive relationship with the town of Beaufort and surrounding areas, and the faculty serve on many local, state and national scientific and environmental boards and commissions. Founded by zoology professor A. S. Pearse in 1937, the laboratory began with seven cottages and two six-week terms for college seniors and graduate students. Now the lab consists of 23 buildings – research facilities, dormitories, shore installations to support research vessels, a library and an auditorium with year-round classes for undergraduate, professional masters and Ph.D. students. Tele-video links connect the lab to learning centers and collaborators worldwide.

University of North Carolina Institute of Marine Sciences
3431 Arendell St., Morehead City
(252) 726-6841

The Institute of Marine Sciences (IMS) is an off-campus research, training and service unit of the University of North Carolina at Chapel Hill. Its mission is to serve the state and nation by conducting high-quality basic and applied marine sciences research, by training young scientists to continue this tradition and by providing professional expertise and leadership in marine issues ranging from local to global scale. Resident faculty are actively involved in addressing important scientific questions related to the nature, use, development, protection and enhancements of marine resources, as well as communicating research results and information about new technologies to professional and public audiences.

North Carolina Division of Marine Fisheries
3441 Arendell St., Morehead City
(252) 726-7021

This large facility is charged with stewardship of marine and estuarine resources in coastal creeks, bays, rivers, sounds and the ocean within 3 miles of land. This state agency carries out the policies set by the nine-member Marine Fisheries Commission and the Secretary of the Department of Environment and Natural Resources. The DMF has a marine patrol section that works in law enforcement districts along the North Carolina coast. Their job is to protect the state's fisheries resources and to make sure people comply with conservation regulations. Officers also inspect seafood houses, fish dealers and restaurants that buy or sell North Carolina seafood.

Artificial reefs have gained popular support in recent years -- artificial reef organizations, sportfishing clubs, local governments and civic organizations are all interested in

their construction, management and evaluation. The DMF is in charge of the state's Artificial Reef Program, which has 40 ocean sites and seven estuarine sites ranging from a half-mile to 38 miles from shore. It is one of the most active artificial reef programs in the country and receives funding from the groups noted above as well as from the state legislature. Other sections of the DMF conduct fisheries and gear research, collect and process the catch statistics of all commercial and recreational fisheries and do shellfish mapping, shellfish leasing and shellfish disease work. The DMF also administers the popular North Carolina Saltwater Tournament and the Governor's Cup Conservation Billfish Tournament series.

Rachel Carson Reserve
Beaufort
(252) 728-2170

The Rachel Carson Reserve, part of the four-component North Carolina National Estuarine Research Reserve, is just across Taylor's Creek from Beaufort. It may look like just a collection of small marshy islands - including Town Marsh, Bird Shoals, Carrot Island, Middle Marshes - but the reserve is an active field research and classroom site. The program is a joint program through the National Oceanic and Atmospheric Administration and North Carolina State Division of Coastal Management. The reserve system was created to maintain undisturbed estuaries for research on the natural and human processes that affect the coast, and the Rachel Carson site serves that purpose well. Field trips by foot and by boat are offered Memorial Day through Labor Day. Insiders recommend a visit; there are many fascinating things to be observed while touring the reserve's 2,600 acres of uplands, marshes and intertidal/subtidal flats. The site is always open to the public and is accessible only by boat. Trail brochures are available. For more information about the Rachel Carson component, call the number above and also see our Attractions chapter.

COMMERCE AND INDUSTRY

Tourism and commercial fishing are big parts of the area's economic picture, but a number of domestic and international companies call Carteret County home. The Carteret County Economic Development Council Inc., (252) 222-6120 or (800) 462-4252, and the Carteret County Chamber of Commerce, (252) 726-6350, can provide detailed information about area businesses and industries.

The North Carolina Port at Morehead City is the county's most visible industry. Situated on the east end of Morehead City, the 116-acre main facility is just 4 miles from the open sea. The port includes part of Radio Island, the body of land on the southeast side of the Morehead City–Beaufort high-rise bridge. With a 45-foot-deep entrance channel and equally deep bulk berths, the Morehead terminal can accommodate the biggest ships in the industry. Its turning basin is one of the deepest in any East Coast port. Established in 1945, the Port of Morehead offers a foreign trade zone and direct rail service through Norfolk Southern Corporation. It is one of two state-owned ports; the other is in Wilmington.

North Carolina's ports link the state's citizens, businesses and industry to world markets. From Morehead City, PCS Phosphate (Potash Corp. of Saskatchewan) exports phosphate-based materials throughout the world and utilizes the Intracoastal Waterway to barge these materials to the port from the company's mine in Aurora, North Carolina. Recycled steel for the Nucor mill in Hertford County arrives at the port via ship or ocean-going barge and is transferred to barges for transport up the Intracoastal Waterway to the mill at Tunis.

Regional tire manufacturers rely on imports of raw rubber through Morehead City from Southeast Asia and Indonesia. Much of the rubber is taken to the two North Carolina plants, one in Fayetteville and one in Reidsville. Agribusiness in the region receives fertilizers through the port. Ore used to manufacture fiberglass products is also imported through Morehead City.

Atlantic Veneer Corporation in Beaufort is the world's largest manufacturer of hardwood veneers in North America, with manufacturing facilities on three continents. It exports about half of its products. Atlantic Veneer also operates a local retail outlet, which is an important source of lumber and hardwoods for boat builders and cabinet makers. With approximately 363 area employees, this corporation is the county's largest private employer.

Veneer Technologies, employing 114 people, has operated a plant in Newport since 1993. It makes three main products: face veneers, flexible-sheet veneers and edge banding. Its products are sold throughout the United States and around the world.

SPX Air Treatment, formerly Hankinson International, is a manufacturer of compressed-air treatment products, which are used in a variety of industries, such as furniture finishing and painting. The company has substantially expanded its plant, which is located in Newport on N.C. 24. Several new positions were created in 1997 because of the success of Hankinson's new filtration and refrigerated air-dryer product lines. The company employs 150 people in Carteret County.

Bally Refrigerated Boxes Inc., located off U.S. 70 in Morehead City, manufactures walk-in refrigerated units, coolers and freezers. Bally specializes in custom cooler units ranging from 6 to 28 feet high. Its freezers are designed to be stacked to create coolers as much as 100 feet high and as long as a football field. Hospitals, restaurant chains, restaurant equipment dealers and refrigeration wholesalers make up most of Bally's customers, and about 30 percent of its business is exported. Recent developments include the addition of mortuary units to the product line and the purchase of the largest lot in the Business Park for future expansion. The company employs about 170 people.

Creative Outlet Inc., a family owned-and-operated firm in Morehead City, makes a wide variety of apparel for the healthcare industry -- hospital gowns, scrubs, bed sheets, pajamas -- that are sold throughout the nation. One of a dwindling number of apparel manufacturers in this textile state that was once home to many, this aggressive small manufacturer is growing to retrieve exported jobs still needed at home. Creative Outlet also has retail stores in Morehead, Kinston and Fayetteville and has 122 employees.

Carteret County's largest single landowner is a farming company. Of the 90,000 acres of farmland here, 44,000 acres make up Open Grounds Farm, one of the largest farms east of the Mississippi. The Italian-owned farm tills about 35,000 of these acres, producing corn and wheat for the poultry-feed and hog-feed industries, soybeans for instate processing plants and cotton for North Carolina gin mills. The farm, which stretches north from Merrimon Road outside Beaufort to U.S. 70 east near Sea Level, also raises some livestock. You can get a look at the farm by checking in at the main gate on Merrimon Road. Permission to enter is most often granted, although visits are not recommended on Sundays or during busy planting or harvesting times.

Beaufort Fisheries, at the east end of Front Street, opened in 1934 and is called the oldest existing industry in the area. Where once there were many, now there is only one menhaden plant operating in the state. It is now one of only two operating along the Atlantic seaboard. Menhaden, an oily, high-protein fish, is caught by company vessels and brought to the docks along Taylor's Creek to be processed into fish meal and oil. Fish meal is used as a protein component in many animal feeds. The fish oil is used in margarine, cosmetics and paints. The oil is also used for human consumption -- the omega-free fatty acids are said to help prevent heart disease and some cancers. During processing, a unique smell can travel through the seaside town. Locals, particularly the older folks who remember when fish plants were the biggest businesses in town, call it "the smell of money." Annual production at Beaufort Fisheries is estimated at 10,000 tons of meal and 300,000 to 450,000 gallons of oil. Today the company has about 39 employees and operates two menhaden boats.

Parker Marine Enterprises Inc. specializes in the construction of fiberglass fishing and pleasure boats. The company plant is on N.C. 101 outside Beaufort and recently underwent a significant expansion. Boats are sold through authorized dealers. Parker has about 144 employees. The company has recently expanded and anticipates further development in the near future.

Another boating enterprise is Jarrett Bay Boatworks Inc., founded in 1986, located in the heart of the 175-acre JBBW Marine Industrial Park six miles north of Beaufort on N.C. Hwy. 101 by land and ICW MM 198 by water. The JBBW Park is a public-private partner-

ship among Jarrett Bay, the town of Beaufort and the Economic Development Council of Carteret County. It is a one-of-a-kind, full-service facility specializing in the building of custom Carolina sport-fishing boats, servicing boats up to 220 tons and brokering new and pre-owned boats. The JBBW Park features on-site marine businesses such as Covington Detroit Diesel, Gregory Poole Caterpillar, Bansch American Towers, Offshore Marine Electronics, ZF Marine and the JBBW Ship Store with dockage and fuel.

Just as fishing is big business in Carteret, fishing gear grows annually as a significant part of its economy. Henry's Tackle, a division of the international Big Rock Sports company, is the 10th largest privately held company in the state. Growing also is Sea Striker, a locally owned and operated manufacturer of fishing tackle.

Quietly entering the business community here is national giant Securities Services of America, which employs over 40,000 internationally. The company set up a shop in Morehead City that is 62nd in North Carolina in annual gross sales.

The largest employers in Carteret County are the Carteret County Public School System, 1,418 employees; Carteret General Hospital, 842 employees; Wal-Mart, 563 employees; Carteret Community College, 350 employees; and Carteret County, 345 employees. New employment opportunities arrive with regularity. The stretch westward continues in Morehead City. New chains and businesses move to the area on an almost monthly basis, offering residents a variety of options when seeking employment.

As the natural westward progression into open land continues, Morehead City is working to make its downtown area more attractive. Business and property owners formed the Downtown Morehead City Revitalization Association in the late 1990s to help maintain the vitality of the downtown area. The group's goal is to improve the physical appearance of downtown, beautify Arendell Street, preserve historic buildings and provide better transportation to and around Morehead City. It also helps foster current businesses in the area and helps promote the downtown area as a great place for new business. The DMCRA promotes festivals and special events in pursuit of its goals. It is the sponsor of the annual Blackbeard Festival (see our Annual Events chapter).

To help attract new industry, Carteret County has developed the Crystal Coast Business Park, a 58-acre park located west of Morehead City on U.S. 70. The park is zoned for industrial purposes, including warehousing and distribution facilities. It offers 11 parcels ranging in size from 1.84 acres to 13.78 acres. Morehead City provides the water, sewer and utilities. With proximity to railroad service, the N.C. State Port and U.S. 70, the park promises to be an excellent location for business and light industry.

As with any seasonal community, unemployment rates peak in December and January in Carteret County. The December 2005 unemployment figure of 4.8 percent showed a slightly lower rate than the state and national average of 4.9 percent. With a growing number of the county's residents retired, the actual number in the labor force is currently a little over 33,000.

The military continues to be a major factor in the county's economic well-being (see our Military chapter) with 1,770 Carteret County residents, about 30 percent of the civilian workforce, employed at Marine Corps Air Station Cherry Point and the Naval Air Depot. Carteret County is also home to a number of the active-duty military personnel and their families. About 10 percent of the active and retired military population from Cherry Point lives in Carteret County, making up about 16 percent of its total population. In addition, the U.S. Coast Guard has a strong presence in Carteret County as it helps monitor the area's waterways and state port.

While continuing to depend on service industry jobs to support its robust tourism industry, the economic base for Carteret County continues to diversify and remain healthy. Wages do not compete with those in metropolitan areas, but compare well when held against the cost of living. Many Insiders find Carteret County and its small-town, laid-back way of doing things to be the ideal place to live, work and play.

Business Services

The UPS Store
4915 Arendell St., Morehead City
(252) 726-4433
www.theupsstore.com

The UPS Store, the world's largest pack and ship business service, has a location in Morehead City at 4915 Arendell Street, where it offers all the conveniences you would expect to receive in any major city. Services include packing and shipping, fax sending and receiving, color and black and white photocopying, as well as computer station rental. They now offer notary, laminating and blueprint copy services.

Starfish Internet Service
1500 Bridges St., Morehead City
(252) 727-0303, toll free (877) 439-7834

Starfish Internet Service started business in the county in 1997 and it continues to grow. The company now serves all of Carteret, Pitt and Craven counties. Residential customers are offered three e-mail addresses at no extra charge, technical support seven days a week and five megabytes of space for personal websites. Business plans include hosting of commercial websites, dial-in access, up to 10 e-mail addresses and 50 megabytes of space. The company's connection speeds are 56K and ISDN service, which is either 64K or 128K. T-1 and frame relay service are also available. Starfish also offers dedicated connections (24/7) and co-location of servers. DSL and wireless DSL service is now available as well.

Sailing is a popular pastime on the local waterways.

photo: NC Department of Travel and Tourism

HEALTHCARE

Routine and specialized medical care, diagnostic procedures, treatment and surgery are available along the Crystal Coast. It may be considered mostly rural and small-town, but Carteret County, with the help of nearby universities, has made a conscious effort to stay on the cutting edge of medical care. In cases requiring equipment not presently available here, referrals are usually to nearby New Bern or Greenville, which are no more than two hours away. In cases of emergency, residents and visitors receive medical attention on a walk-in basis at several locations around the county during weekday business hours. At other times Carteret General Hospital's emergency room provides excellent care.

In almost every town or community throughout the county, there are clinics or specialized practices that are willing to work in appointments for emergency care. And, of course, asking an Insider is also a great way to find a new family physician.

Various home healthcare services help to bring people home earlier from surgeries, injuries and illnesses that have traditionally required hospital recoveries. A kidney dialysis unit able to serve patients is in Morehead City, and the Raab Clinic at Carteret General Hospital allows patients in need of cancer treatment to receive their chemotherapy and radiation therapy while remaining in the county. As Carteret County's population continues to grow, the healthcare community strives to keep pace. While you can still receive a taste of small-town care, Carteret County stays current in the latest high-tech treatments and facilities.

Alternative healthcare options available on the Crystal Coast facilitate self-healing. Practitioners of a variety of holistic approaches to well-being include preventative medicine and the relief of pain in ways that include massage therapies, yoga and herbal remedies.

Hospitals

Carteret General Hospital
3500 Arendell St., Morehead City
(252) 808-6000

Carteret General Hospital in Morehead City is an acute care 117-bed hospital serving the Coastal Carteret County community and its visitors. The hospital's medical staff includes 57 active staff physicians representing most medical specialties plus 63 consulting staff physicians and over 900 employees. The facility offers 24-hour emergency services in a newly renovated emergency department and patient registration area.

Additional top-quality patient services provided include vascular surgery, cancer treatments, cardiac care that includes an outpatient rehabilitation program, home health and hospice care. The hospital's full-service laboratory and radiology services provide state-of-the-art diagnostic services including ACR Accredited MRI, nuclear medicine and 16-slice CT scans. Carteret General's Imaging Center on Arendell Street provides convenient outpatient diagnostic procedures and tests, including routine X-ray, CT scans, ultrasounds, mammograms and fluoro procedures.

The Raab Cancer Clinic provides medical oncology, chemotherapy services and other outpatient procedures. The Radiation Center is a collaboration between Carteret General Hospital and the East Carolina University School of Medicine, and provides high-quality radiation treatments for almost 200 patients a year using a state-of-the-art linear accelerator and simulator. The Brady Birthing Center offers a comfortable birthing environment for the average 570 annual births at Carteret General. Cardiac Rehabilitation offers patients with heart disease an opportunity to build strength through exercise and education.

The hospital also operates Carteret Home Health, (252) 808-6081, which provides a continuum of care for recovering and long-term care patients. Hospice of Carteret County, (252) 808-6085, formerly operated by volunteers, is now a service provided by Carteret General Hospital. It offers care and family relief for at-home patients in the end stages of life. The hospital also has a community wellness program that offers health education and intervention services to employees of participating county businesses.

Continual additions of facilities, services and equipment keep Carteret General Hospital abreast of the latest developments in medical diagnosis and treatment. The planned addition of a 32-bed private wing for surgical patients will enable the hospital to convert to mostly private rooms. Carteret General Hospital prides itself on being committed to providing excellent service, treating every individual with respect, compassion, and dignity, while constantly striving to exceed the expectations of its customers.

Craven Regional Medical Center
2000 Neuse Blvd., New Bern
(252) 633-8111

This major, 313-bed medical facility provides a full complement of inpatient services, including medical/surgical areas and units for neurosurgical, intensive and intermediate care, women's care, pediatric care and cancer care. The center has a medical staff of more than 180 board-certified/board-qualified physicians representing nearly all medical specialties. The center includes 24-hour emergency room service, outpatient surgery, diagnostic services, critical-care units, cardiac-care services offering diagnostic catheterization and open-heart surgery and radiation oncology. Magnetic resonance imaging (MRI), CT scanning, home care, long-term care for older adults, speech and language therapy, rehabilitation, adult psychiatric services and women's health services are also offered. For more information, see the New Bern Healthcare chapter.

Onslow Memorial Hospital
317 Western Blvd., Jacksonville
(910) 577-2345

Onslow Memorial Hospital is a 162-bed facility that is accredited by the Joint Commission on Accreditation of Healthcare Organizations. With more than 100 physicians on its medical staff, Onslow Memorial Hospital provides a wide range of specialties including cardiology, (Cardiac Cath Lab), ENT, family practice, general surgery, orthopedic and pediatric surgery, internal medicine, OB-GYN, neonatal intensive care, neurosurgery, pain management, urology, a heartburn center and the Women's Imaging Center.

Pitt County Memorial Hospital
200 Stantonsburg Rd., Greenville
(252) 816-4100

Pitt County Memorial Hospital provides comprehensive acute, intermediate, rehabilitation and outpatient health services to more than 1.2 million people in 29 counties. In an average year, about 33,000 inpatients and more than 266,000 outpatients are treated at Pitt Memorial. More than 3,000 babies are born in the facility in a typical year. The clinical staff includes more than 500 physicians and 1,200 nurses.

Pitt Memorial is one of four academic medical centers in North Carolina and is the flagship hospital for University Health Systems of Eastern Carolina. The hospital offers a full range of inpatient and outpatient services and serves as the teaching hospital for the Brody School of Medicine at East Carolina University. Pitt Memorial is considered a regional resource for all levels of health services and information.

Naval Hospitals

Camp Lejeune
(910) 450-4300

Cherry Point
(252) 466-0266

In- and outpatient medical services are provided for active duty and retired military and their families at the Camp Lejeune Naval Hospital and the Halyburton Naval Hospital at the U.S. Marine Corps Air Station Cherry Point in Havelock.

Home Health Care

Several home-healthcare businesses are located in Morehead City and provide services to patients in the Crystal Coast area. Each offers varying degrees of nursing, rehabilitation therapies, medical social work, in-home aides, medical equipment and supplies that allow patients the opportunity to live comfortably within their own homes. Many of the services are reimbursable through insurance, so be sure to ask. For additional providers, contact your physician.

Carteret Home Health Care
302 Medical Park, Morehead City
(252) 808-6081

As a service of Carteret General Hospital, Carteret Home Health Care provides nursing-care services for the home bound, including recovery therapies, personal care and family-aid services. Aides can assist with bathing, meal preparation and light housekeeping. Special needs such as IV therapies, colostomy care, tube feedings and diabetic instruction are also available for patients.

Liberty Home Care
3601 Bridges St., Ste. F, Morehead City
(252) 247-4748

Liberty Home Care is a private business that offers a range of homecare services aimed at speeding recoveries and shortening hospital stays. It offers skilled nursing care, physical and occupational therapies, and other services and supplies as needed. Liberty Home Care has offices throughout North and South Carolina.

Professional Care Service
212 N. 35th St., Morehead City
(252) 247-6911

Professional Care Service is a private firm that provides professional aid care. A professional will assess the needs of the individual in his or her home. Sitters and certified assistances can then, based on need, assist with bathing, transfers from bed to chair, meal preparation and light housekeeping.

Physical Therapists

Physical therapy is often just the thing individuals need to fully recover from surgery or an injury.

Beaufort Physical Therapy
106-A Professional Park Dr., Beaufort
(252) 838-0222

Wendy Jones and her staff of licensed physical and occupational therapists provide outstanding care. This group of professionals provide rehabilitation services as well as treat muscular skeletal disorders and sports-related injuries. They also provide ergonomic assessments and stroke rehabilitation services.

Carteret Physical Therapy
3700 Symi Cir., Morehead City
(252) 247-2738

This firm has provided care for area residents and visitors for years. With licensed physical therapists and assistants, this firm specializes in physical medicine, rehabilitation, work conditioning, women's health, aquatic therapy and orthopedics/sports physical therapy.

Cape Carteret Physical Therapy
300 Taylor Notion Rd., Cape Carteret
(252) 393-1001

This is a full-service physical therapy practice that is staffed by licensed physical therapists. They offer orthopedic physical therapy, treatment for sprains and strains, ergonomic assessments, and post surgical and cardiac/stroke rehabilitation. Women's health issues, workers compensation claims and injuries from auto accidents are also treated here.

Alternative Healthcare

Finding and maintaining wellness is the primary goal of alternative health care. Practitioners in the Crystal Coast community offer integrated, natural healthcare methods to relieve stress, ease pain and move patients toward self-healing. A variety of massage and movement therapies are offered for stress reduction, pain relief, better posture and flexibility, recovery from surgery and accidents, and relief of migraines, carpal tunnel and repetitive-stress syndrome. Area practitioners of varied specialties form the Whole Health Resource Network. A complete directory of these alternative services is available at the Carteret County Chamber of Commerce in Morehead City, as well as Coastal Community Market, 606 Broad Street, Beaufort, (252) 728-2844.

MASSAGE THERAPISTS

Massage therapy can provide relief and rehabilitation for physical injury as well as provide relief from day-to-day stress. Carteret Community College offers courses in massage therapy, and often students provide free or discount massages as a practicing service. There is nothing as relaxing as a complete massage from a qualified and knowledgeable therapist. Whether you select a full-body massage, a back massage or a foot and hand massage, the human touch is a powerful thing. We have listed here a few of the therapists recommended by Insiders. Day spas providing massage therapy treatments are listed in the Salon and Spas chapter.

Coastal Therapeutic Massage
#1 Medical Park, 202 Penny Ln., Morehead City
(252) 342-3876

Lynn Choate is a licensed massage and bodywork therapist and, because of her thorough knowledge of the body, she provides excellent care. Lynn offers relaxing and therapeutic massage as well as travel trigger point therapy and relief from fibromyalgia. Contact Lynn about spa packages or a gift certificate to treat a special friend to a relaxing massage.

Elizabeth Hawkes
606 Broad St., Beaufort
(252) 504-2651

Elizabeth is well-known throughout the area and specializes in therapeutic massage and reflexology. Elizabeth is a favorite of local athletes and runners. Two other licensed therapists share the salon space as well.

Coastal Acupuncture & Massage
142 Fairview Dr., Emerald Isle
(252) 354-7672

Bright Walker is a licensed professional in massage therapy and acupuncture.

ACUPUNCTURE

Acupuncture has been accepted as an important treatment for many physical conditions as well as for stress relief and improved health. However, services have been slow in coming to the Crystal Coast.

Coastal Acupuncture & Massage
142 Fairview Dr., Emerald Isle
(252) 354-7672

Bright Walker is a licensed professional in acupuncture and massage therapy.

Stephanie Kaplan
Pine Knoll Shores
(252) 727-0944

Stephanie provides quality services and she is a licensed acupuncturist.

Mental Health

Brynn Marr Behavioral Healthcare System
192 Village Dr., Jacksonville
(910) 577-1400,
(800) 822-9507 Help Line Nurse

Brynn Marr Hospital extends comprehensive services throughout eastern North Carolina in treatment of emotional and behavioral problems, mental illness and chemical dependencies for individuals of all ages through full hospitalization and residential care programs. Brynn Marr's Help Line is a free crisis and referral service that offers confidential, telephone help in identifying needs and recommending an appropriate next step toward problem solution. Individuals can receive the services of a nurse at Help Line offices in Jacksonville. Brynn Marr also offers numerous support services and free community education programs.

Urgent and General Medical Care

The Heart Center of Eastern Carolina
3332 Bridges St., Ste. 3B, Morehead City
(252) 808-0145

The Heart Center of Eastern Carolina is a full-service cardiology practice featuring the most up-to-date treatments in the diagnosis, treatment and prevention of cardiac and vascular diseases. This medical practice of eight board-certified cardiologists offers patients many kinds of non-invasive and invasive treatments: diagnostic catheterization, balloon angioplasty, nuclear cardiology, peripheral vascular disease treatments, atherectomy, stent placement, pacemaker implant and follow-up echocardiology, hypertension treatment, and lipid management. Patients are seen by referral and appointment. The Heart Center of Eastern Carolina, which is available 24 hours a day for emergency service for patients, also has offices in New Bern (see our New Bern Healthcare chapter), and at 47 Office Park Drive, Jacksonville, (910) 577-8881.

Eastern Carteret Medical Center
U.S. Hwy. 70, Sea Level
(252) 225-1134

Eastern Carteret Medical Center, a subsidiary of Carteret General Hospital, provides treatment of minor emergencies and illnesses and offers complete family care. It is open Monday, Tuesday, Wednesday and Friday from 9 AM until 4 PM.

Beaufort Care
106-D Professional Dr., Beaufort
(252) 728-5003

Beaufort Care offers urgent care and primary care. Care to patients is provided by a physician and a physician's assistant. It is open Monday through Saturday rom 9 AM until 5:30 PM.

ECIM Urgent Medical Care
906 W. B. McLean Dr., (N.C. Hwy. 24 E.), Cape Carteret
(252) 393-9007

The ECIM office in Cape Carteret provides primary care along with urgent medical care for patients in Carteret County and surrounding areas. Emergency-trained physicians and physician assistants at ECIM Urgent Medical Care, part of the ECIM network based in New Bern, provide treatment for minor emergencies and family medical needs. Hours of operation are Monday through Friday 8:30 AM to 5 PM. Appointments may be scheduled for primary care; however, no appointment is necessary for urgent medical care.

Emerald Isle Primary Care
Veranda Sq., 7901 Emerald Dr., Ste. 7, Emerald Isle
(252) 354-6500

A medical doctor, surgeon, cardiologist, pediatrician, physician's assistant and family nurse practitioner are all available in Emerald Isle six days a week for complete outpatient medical services. The physicians rotate their times and all provide quality services by appointment or on an emergency walk-in basis. The facility is open Monday through Friday 8 AM to 5 PM and Saturday 9 AM to 12:30 PM.

Med Center One
Atlantic Beach Cswy., Atlantic Beach
(252) 247-2464

This privately owned facility treats minor emergencies and offers primary general medical care. The facility offers an in-house X-ray service and a dispensing pharmacy for patients of record. Med Center One provides services on a walk-in basis. Hours are Monday through Friday 9 AM until 6 PM , Saturday 9 AM to 6 PM and Sunday noon to 5 PM.

Beach Care Urgent Medical Care Center
5059 U.S. Hwy. 70 W., Morehead City
(252) 808-3696

From colds to cardiac problems, BeachCare treats emergencies, offers primary care and performs minor surgery. The center has in-house lab and X-ray services. This privately owned center, staffed by a full-time physician and a physician's assistant, is open Monday though Saturday 9 AM to 9 PM and Sunday 9 AM to 5 PM.

Newport Family Practice Center
338 Howard Blvd., Newport
(252) 223-5054

Since the nearest emergency room and hospital facilities are in Morehead City or New Bern, Newport Family Practice Center offers a needed service in the Newport community. This privately owned clinic, which has in-house X-ray and lab facilities as well as a pharmacy next door, is open from Monday, Tuesday, Thursday and Friday 8:30 AM to 5 PM, Wednesday 10 AM to 5:15 PM and Saturday from 9 AM to noon. The center prefers seeing patients who have made appointments in advance but will accept walk-ins in an emergency.

Carteret Urgentcare Center
3104 Arendell St., Morehead City
(252) 247-0770

Vacationers and regular patients are welcome without an appointment at this privately owned practice. With a resident physician always on site, this center provides routine medical care and urgent care with on-site X-ray, lab work, EKG, pharmacy and other services. Center hours are Monday noon to 8 PM, Tuesday and Thursday 8:30 AM to 5 PM, and Wednesday and Friday 8:30 AM to 2 PM. Carteret Urgentcare Center files all types of insurance.

Support Groups and Services

In Carteret County there are a number of active support groups with concerns related to children and family difficulties, mental and physical health, lifestyle changes, challenges and substance abuse. Many support groups meet at Carteret General Hospital or at area churches, but that certainly doesn't cover all of the locations. Following are some of the groups who meet regularly in the area. If the list doesn't include a group related to your concern, contact Help Line, (252) 247-3023 or Carteret General Hospital, (252) 808-6000.

•Angels Touch Support Group for Dealing with Death, (252) 728-2841

•Better Breathers, (252) 808-6195

•Brain Injury Support Group, (252) 636-5029

•Cancer Support Group, (252) 808-6177

•Compassionate Friends, (252) 223-2391, (252) 223-5254

•Diabetes Support Group for Patients and Families, (252) 729-1476

•Fresh Start - Stop Smoking Program, (252) 808-6611

•Gastric Bypass Support Group, (252) 247-2101

•Hospice of Carteret County, (252) 808-6085

•Insulin Pumpers, (252) 729-1476

•Let's Talk - Cancer Support, (252) 808-6177

•Parkinson's Disease Support Group, (252) 808-6000

•Prostate Cancer Support, (252) 808-6177

•Meals on Wheels, (252) 728-4279

•National Alliance for the Mentally Ill, (252) 838-0017

•Tough Love Parent Support Group, (252) 504-2791

•TOPS - Taking Pounds Off Sensibly, (252) 240-3098

Emergency and Other Phone Numbers

Dial 911 from anywhere in the area for emergencies (police, sheriff, fire and rescue services).

Help Line, (252) 247-3023

Alcoholics Anonymous/AL-ANON, (252) 726-8540

American Red Cross, (252) 637-3405, (888) 446-0979

Carteret County Humane Society Animal Shelter, (252) 247-7744

Outer Banks Wildlife Shelter (OWLS), (252) 240-1200

Rape Crisis Program, (252) 504-3668

Department of Social Services, (252) 728-3181

Carteret County Domestic Violence Program, (252) 728-3788

Carteret County Health Department, (252) 728-8550

VOLUNTEER OPPORTUNITIES

Volunteers make up the core of many organizations on the Crystal Coast. These individuals of all ages to render their time, talents, experience and services. Through a variety of volunteer opportunities, residents donate their talents in gardening, narrating historical tours, helping students, directing tourists, preserving the natural environment, building houses, offering tax preparation assistance and assisting hospital patients and underprivileged families. Volunteering brings satisfaction to many people's lives and offers the chance to not only give back to the community but also meet other people with common interests.

People who enjoy studying history, meeting the public or guiding tourists through interesting historical restorations will like channeling some spare time in the direction of the aquarium, museums and historic sites. Those more fitted to physical work will be welcomed into the fold at Habitat For Humanity or Hammocks Beach State Park, where they are always glad for another helping hand. All of the public libraries rely on volunteer help in children's programs, one-on-one assistance for patrons and outreach programs. To make a lasting contribution to the community, volunteer to help with reading or other programs in one of the county's public schools.

Volunteers preferring the company of animals will be delighted with the opportunities at the Outer Banks Wildlife Shelter or the Humane Society's animal shelter in Newport. The Carteret General Hospital Auxiliary places volunteers in nearly every department. Meals on Wheels and Hospice of Carteret County both depend on volunteer kindness to deliver meals or offer relief to caregivers. The Carteret County Domestic Violence and Rape Crisis programs train volunteers who are interested in offering specific care in crisis situations. Helpline, the 24-hour crisis telephone line, is fully staffed by trained volunteers who are available to lend an ear and offer referral information. The Retired and Senior Volunteer Program (RSVP) is very active and recognized for its matchmaking of retired volunteer expertise with appropriate recipients.

For those with time to share, volunteering will open new doors through many worthwhile organizations that always welcome and train new volunteers. Volunteering offers an opportunity to learn something new or teach others, and groups such as these will welcome the call.

Public Sites and Parks

Beaufort Historical Association
138 Turner St., Beaufort
(252) 728-5225

Training sessions for volunteers at the Beaufort Historic Site occur each spring, and classes always fill up early. This large preservation organization relies heavily upon volunteers. From docents and tour guides to bus drivers and office staff, there are literally dozens of jobs for people of all ages at the BHA. The site maintains Beaufort's oldest art gallery, the Mattie King Davis Art Gallery, and the thrift shop that helps raise funds. Both are staffed by volunteers. Groups such as the Warped Weavers and the Beaufort Herb Society are always looking for new members. And, of course, folks who are good with a sewing machine are needed to help create docent costumes. Whether you want to volunteer on a regular basis or just offer your expertise during a special event, BHA is always excited to hear from potential volunteers.

Carteret County Public Library
210 Turner St., Beaufort
(252) 728-2050

Each of the four Carteret County public libraries has a Friends of the Library volunteer group that extends services in such established library programs as Storytime for Kids. The Friends also operate book sales throughout the year to keep the collections refreshed.

Contact the individual libraries in your area for details:

Beaufort -- (252) 728-2050

Bogue Banks -- (252) 247-4660

Western Carteret -- (252) 393-6500

Newport -- (252) 223-5108

Down East Library
373 U.S. Hwy. 70, Beaufort
(252) 728-5412, (252) 729-7681

This library was formed based on the need to have library services in the Down East area of Carteret County. Founded, supported and staffed by volunteers, this library is offering a wonderful service to the area. Volunteers of all types are needed -- from those interested in answering the phone or shelving books to those interested in helping with the children's reading program. Book donations are also needed.

Carteret County Public School System
107 Safrit Dr., Beaufort
(252) 728-4583

Volunteer opportunities in the public school system are many and varied. Each of the county's 17 public schools seeks individuals interested in tutoring students, helping with special projects, working with band programs or assisting in the office. Whether you are interested in listening to a first grader read, helping a fourth grader with multiplication, having lunch each week with a special student or working out chemistry problems with a tenth grader, the school system would be excited to have your help.

Core Sound Waterfowl Museum
Island Rd., Harkers Island
(252) 728-1500

Core Sound Waterfowl Museum depends on volunteer help for daily carving demonstrations and special programs year round. Demonstrations, revolving local exhibits and programs focusing on local heritage are offered year round. The museum houses the area's finest collection of carvings and waterfowl art and archives oral histories and artifacts from the Down East communities. Volunteers are needed to help with programs for school groups and bus tours, to assist staff with administrative duties and to serve on committees and boards. Construction continues at the new facility, with 8,000 square feet still to be completed. For more information at the museum, see the Attractions chapter.

Cape Lookout National Seashore
131 Charles St., Harkers Island
(252) 728-2250

Volunteers are needed for many of Cape Lookout National Seashore's programs. At the Harkers Island headquarters, volunteers can help with administrative duties, greet visitors and provide information. For those volunteers who like to be outside and active, there are many programs. Some volunteers live at the National Seashore for short periods of time to greet visitors and answer questions. Other volunteers help with the regular round-up of the ponies on Shackleford Banks. Whatever your interest, the National Seashore can help you select the volunteer position that is just right for you.

Fort Macon State Park
MM 1, N.C. Hwy. 58, Atlantic Beach
(252) 726-3775

Volunteers, working through the Friends of Fort Macon, are trained as guides at this historic site throughout the year. Training is usually conducted in February of each year. Volunteers perform re-enactments and help park rangers with special group tours and presentations. Fort Macon is one of the busiest state parks in North Carolina, and volunteers play an important role in facilitating visitation. The Friends of Fort Macon hold regular meetings and special events throughout the year.

The History Place
1008 Arendell St., Morehead City
(252) 247-7533

The History Place has become a landmark of Morehead City. It highlights all areas of Carteret County through exhibits and displays in the 12,500-square-foot facility that houses the museum, research library, museum store, classroom and auditorium/learning center. Docents, or volunteers, are the backbone of this organization. The History Place has only one paid staff member; the rest are volunteers. Docents greet visitors and answer questions, with shifts usually set at three hours either once a week or once a month, generally from 10 AM to 1 PM or 1 to 4 PM. Museum hours are 10 AM to 4 PM Tuesday through Saturday. You can assist visitors either in the gallery, museum store or in the library. Docents also assist, on occasion, with folding brochures and newsletters or helping keep the museum scrapbook up-to-date. There is always a need for volunteers to assist in preparing for events and programs. Training for volunteers is provided.

N.C. Aquarium at Pine Knoll Shores
MM 7, N.C. Hwy. 58, Pine Knoll Shores
(252) 247-4004
www.ncaquariums.com

The aquarium relies upon a large force of cheerful volunteers to help visitors enjoy the many exhibits and programs, and to assist the staff with a variety of other tasks. The aquarium recently reopened after a $25 million expansion that tripled its size, creating many new opportunities.

Volunteers interpret exhibits, discuss marine life in the touch tank, staff discovery carts, run projectors, greet school groups and help with kids' crafts, among other things. New workstations include an information desk, string ray touch pool and a sport-fishing gallery. And, volunteers with their SCUBA certification star in the popular diving demonstration programs in the 306,000-gallon Living Shipwreck exhibit, and help with cleaning and maintenance of it and other large displays.

N.C. Maritime Museum
315 Front St., Beaufort
(252) 728-7317
www.ncmm-friends.org

North Carolina Maritime Museum volunteers are renowned for their hospitality and helpfulness. They work at the museum's information desk, serve as interpreters at displays and as guides for school and other groups, do restoration and construction work in the museum's Watercraft Center and ship model shop, serve on the Board of the Friends of the Museum, assist with the Cape Lookout Studies and Junior Sailing Programs, maintain the reference library, perform clerical duties and help at special events and programs.

Animal-Care Services

Outer Banks Wildlife Shelter
100 Wildlife Way, Newport
(252) 240-1200

This shelter for injured wildlife is operated with volunteer help, including the help of licensed rehabilitators. Funding efforts include daily aluminum-can recycling, an annual benefit dinner, an art auction, and contributions of visitors and rescuers of injured animals. Feeding and animal care is volunteered. Volunteers are always needed and must must be 18 years of age or older. The Baby Bird Feeders program offers opportunities for those 13 years of age and older. On-the-job training is provided to all volunteers.

Humane Society of Carteret County
Hibbs Rd., Morehead City
(252) 247-7744

Members provide staffing for administration and animal care services, usually for dogs and cats that are in between homes. Volunteers are needed at the shelter primarily to help clean up the facilities and care for animals. Volunteers are also needed to operate the Humane Society Thrift Store, 1113 Bridges Street in Morehead City, (252) 726-1399, which is open Tuesday and Thursday 10 AM to 5 PM and Friday and Saturday 10 AM to 4 PM.

Human-Care Services

American Cancer Society
(252) 695-9028

The American Cancer Society plans an annual Relay for Life, a 24-hour, track-based fund-raising event each May in Carteret County. The event takes place on a high school track in the county, bringing groups from churches, businesses and families together in the fight against cancer. Volunteers not only participate in the relay but organize it as well. Help is always needed.

Boys & Girls Club of Coastal Carolina Inc.
P.O. Box 1514, Morehead City, NC 28557
(252) 222-3007

The Boys & Girls Club of Coastal Carolina includes clubs in Morehead City, Beaufort and Havelock. The club relies on volunteers in all aspects of its operation, including, tutoring, special skills training, fund-raising, homework help and administrative support. Best of all, they provide positive role models for kids. Programs are in place in western Carteret County at Bogue Sound and White Oak elementary schools.

Broad Street Clinic
500 N. 35th St., Morehead City
(252) 726-4562

The Broad Street Clinic offers medical treatment for chronic illnesses for the under-served and non-insured who meet the agency's income criteria. Volunteers help in administrative capacities and as receptionists, and medical professionals donate their time to offer services. There are volunteer opportunities during the day and evening, and training is provided.

Carteret County Domestic Violence Program
(252) 728-3788

Volunteers help in a variety of capacities for the Carteret County Domestic Violence Program. An upscale resale shop, Caroline's Collectables, 3716 Arendell Street in Morehead City, is completely staffed by volunteer help. Additional volunteers serve on the board, assist at the program's center for nonviolence, help in Caroline's House, and help raise funds for the deserving organization. Volunteers are also needed to provide transportation and to serve as child care sitters.

Carteret General Hospital Auxiliary
Carteret General Hospital, Morehead City
(252) 808-6046

The Carteret General Hospital volunteer program began in 1977 and today has a vital group of volunteers helping in all areas of the hospital. The auxiliary also raises funds used for equipment and renovations to enhance patient care. The largest fund-raiser is the Gift Gallery, a unique gift shop located in the Arendell Street entrance of the hospital. All fund-raisers are open to the public. For more information, please contact the hospital's Volunteer Director.

Carteret Literacy Council
Morehead City
(252) 808-2020

This program matches tutors with students, often adults, who need help with reading, writing or math. Sessions are arranged by the tutor-student team who meet once or twice a week at a location convenient to both parties. Volunteer training is coordinated by the Literacy Council every three months. In addition, the program offers tutors to the public school system.

Crystal Coast Habitat For Humanity
1412 Bridges St., Morehead City
(252) 808-2757

Habitat For Humanity provides volunteer labor to build homes for qualified families, and volunteers support the program every step of the way. Volunteers serve on the board and are involved in administrative functions, in the hands-on acts of building and in fund-raising efforts. The program's resale home store also relies on volunteer labor. Volunteer forms are available in the Habitat office or by mail.

Foster Grandparent Program
301 McQueen Ave., Newport
(252) 223-1630

The Foster Grandparents Program, administered by Coastal Community Action, serves Carteret, Craven, Pamlico and Jones counties. It provides a stipend for limited-income participants ages 60 and older who have 20 hours a week for one-on-one extra assistance of children in school, libraries or in the hospital, where they must annually meet safety training requirements of hospital employees. Volunteers must apply.

Guardian ad Litem
Courthouse Square, Beaufort
(252) 728-8574

After training, Guardian ad Litem volunteers are assigned by the juvenile court to investigate cases of child neglect or abuse and to report their findings to the court. This advocate for the child ensures that the child's interests are properly presented and represents the child's best interest to the judge.

Helpline of Carteret County, Inc.
(252) 247-6434

Helpline is the county's 24-hour information, referral and crisis-intervention line. Volunteers assist callers with varied problems and needs through their home telephone. Calls are routed from one home to another at shift changes by the Domestic Violence Program. An in-depth training program is offered to interested volunteers.

Hope Mission
1410 Bridges St., Morehead City
(252) 247-2543, (252) 240-2359

Hope Mission exists to meet the immediate needs of people requiring help. At the mission's soup kitchen, volunteers assist in serving food provided by area churches, restaurants and private donations. Lunch is served daily to people in need, and special dinners are served during the holiday season. Volunteers are also needed to assist in outreach ministries and in preparing gifts during special times.

Hospice of Carteret County
302 Medical Park Ct., Morehead City
(252) 808-6085

A division of Carteret General Hospital, the Hospice of Carteret County trains volunteers to serve patients and care-giving families. They provide relief and support for family members by keeping the patient company, running errands and serving as a vital link between the family and Hospice staff.

Martha's Mission Cupboard
901 Bay St., Morehead City
(252) 726-1717

This is an emergency food pantry for families in crisis in Carteret County. Every month, the mission provides food for 300+ families, senior citizens and mentally and physically challenged persons. Martha's Mission operates strictly on donations, and volunteers are used to sort and distribute the incoming food. The Mission Cupboard is open Monday, Wednesday and Friday from 10:30 AM to 3 PM.

Project Christmas Cheer
(252) 247-7275

Project Christmas Cheer began in 1985 when a group of people volunteered their time to assist an overflow of families seeking assistance from the Carteret County Department of Social Services. Volunteers take applications in the fall and match the applicants with donors. Before Christmas each year, the donors make arrangements to deliver Christmas gifts such as food, toys, blankets, fuel oil and things that would really help during Christmas of a difficult year. Project Christmas Cheer assists about 650 families each year. Volunteers serve on the program's board of directors and help take applications each year. The offices are open from October through December.

Retired and Senior Volunteer Program (RSVP)
301 McQueen Ave., Newport
(252) 223-1630

The mission of RSVP is to meet vital community needs by providing volunteer opportunities for seniors. Members of RSVP are age 55 and older and pledge to perform at least one hour of service each week. These active, energetic volunteers are matched with tasks that suit their abilities, interests and experience. The current focus is on providing tutors to schools from primary level to college. RSVP volunteers also help homebound seniors with meal delivery, shopping and errands.

Environmental Services

N.C. Big Sweep
N.C. Cooperative Extension Service, Morehead City
(252) 222-6359

N.C. Big Sweep is a statewide effort to clean trash out of the state's waterways. It's a one-day effort that occurs in Carteret County annually on a Saturday in late September or early October. Big Sweep is locally coordinat-

Spending time with children is a great way to volunteer.

photo: George Mitchell

ed through the N.C. Cooperative Extension Service office in Morehead City.

N.C. Coastal Federation
3609 N.C. Hwy. 24, Ocean
(252) 393-8185

This coastal environmental protection organization offers education, information and legislative accountability and is funded through membership contributions. Volunteers are needed to help with marsh-grass plantings in the late spring and to work on trail maintenance. Volunteers are also needed in the office to type, file, answer phones and more. Help with membership drives and fund-raising is always needed. Specific expertise is welcomed, as NCCF coordinates special projects and events.

Rachel Carson Reserve
135 Duke Marine Lab Rd., Pivers Island, Beaufort
(252) 728-2170

Staff members from the Education Office of the N.C. National Estuarine Research Reserve on Pivers Island train volunteers to lead field trips to the beautiful Rachel Carson Reserve in Beaufort. You will get firsthand knowledge of estuarine ecosystems and walk in the steps of famed scientist and writer Rachel Carson, who visited Beaufort in the 1930s. Trips are conducted each week during the summer; special trips are also scheduled. Volunteers lead interpretive programs on ecology and history, enjoy visits to other estuarine sites and help with periodic beach sweeps.

MEDIA

The print and electronic media in Carteret County are a strong and growing presence. Although there is no daily newspaper printed in the county, the Carteret County News-Times, a local news tri-weekly, is published here and a neighboring county daily, the Jacksonville Daily News, has a bureau in the county and circulates daily. A state daily, the Raleigh News and Observer, also circulates here, as do several local weekly papers. Several radio stations are based in the area, and the Fox Network has a local affiliate based in Morehead City. Other networks have television stations close by to cover local news. Time Warner Cable, located in Newport, offers the full spectrum of cable channels as well as digital service and Road Runner cable modem service.

Print

Carteret County News-Times
4034 Arendell St., Morehead City
(252) 726-7081
www.carteretnewstimes.com

Many of the county happenings can be found on the pages of the Carteret County News-Times, published Wednesday and Friday afternoons and Sunday morning. Produced by a staff of writers, many of whom have been at the job long enough to know the ins and outs of Carteret County, this is a good source of information for vacationers who want to know the schedules of tours, festivals, kids' programs, seminars, exhibits and events of all types within the county. The paper has an expanded area sports section and entertainment section, and a business portion is included on Wednesday. The News-Times, which has been in business for about 96 years, is available by subscription and in vending machines throughout the county. The News-Times also publishes the Tideland News based in Swansboro and the Topsail Voice in Hampstead.

The Beaufort Gam
430 W. Beaufort Rd., P.O. Box 300, Beaufort
(252) 728-2435

The Gam is a free weekly newspaper focusing on local news, including municipal and county governments, information on school and community events, and informative columns. The Gam distributes over 10,000 copies every Thursday to more than 300 distribution outlets throughout Carteret County and extending into Swansboro.

This Week Magazine
4034 Arendell St., Morehead City
(252) 726-7081
www.thisweek.mag.com

This Week Magazine (TWM) is considered the ultimate authority on entertainment for the Crystal Coast, and has been for 27 years. Locals and visitors alike turn to TWM to find out what is happening in the area and region. Each Thursday, 20,000 free copies are distributed to racks and stands throughout eastern North Carolina. TWM offers a comprehensive calendar of events, spotlighting festivals, concerts, theater, fishing, NASCAR news, book reviews, the arts and the newest dining out feature - A La Carteret. And now, TWM is the entertainment section of the Friday edition of the Carteret County News-Times.

Tideland News
774 W. Corbett Ave., Swansboro
(910) 326-5066

Tideland News is published each Wednesday from its office in Swansboro. Owned by Carteret Publishing Company of Morehead City, which also publishes the Carteret County News-Times, the paper covers news and activities in Swansboro, the eastern portion of Onslow County and western Carteret County. The communities covered by this weekly include Hubert, Bear Creek, Stella, Peletier, Cedar Point, Cape Carteret, Emerald Isle, Bogue and Ocean.

Coaster
201 N. 17th St., Morehead City
(252) 240-1811

Coaster is called the Guide to the Crystal Coast for a reason - because it provides such a great overview of area happenings and attractions. The magazine may be small in size, but it is big in content and offers needed information to residents and visitors. You'll enjoy the features, the area attraction information, and guides of all types. Maps, a calendar of events, ferry schedules and tide tables are also offered.

Arts Alive
4034 Arendell St., Morehead City
(252) 726-7081

Arts Alive is a regional magazine designed to showcase the arts of Carteret, Onslow, Craven, Pitt, Beaufort and Pamlico counties. Arts Alive is a key resource for everyone interested in enjoying, participating in and preserving the arts. Local arts councils use Arts Alive as a forum to promote coming exhibit, concerts, classes, contests and plays. Arts Alive is published monthly, except when a double issue is published for January and February. Arts Alive is distributed free through racks and stands in the six counties.

The Daily News
724 Bell Fork Rd., Jacksonville
(910) 353-1171

Many people on the Crystal Coast turn to The Daily News as a source for just that, their daily dose of news. The morning paper covers state and national events, Jacksonville, Onslow County and Marine Corps Base Camp Lejeune. The paper also has a Carteret County bureau with writers and a photographer who provide coverage of Carteret County activities and county-wide issues. One reporter also focuses on fisheries and environmental issues in eastern North Carolina. Home delivery is available to Carteret County subscribers.

Television Stations

Time Warner Cable Channel 10
U.S. Hwy. 70, Newport
(252) 223-6410

With an office and studio in Newport, Time Warner Cable Channel 10 is the area's community channel. Its programming includes a variety of topics, from schools and health issues to sports and talk shows. The station also broadcasts tapes of the meetings of County Commissioners and Boards of Education from Carteret County and neighboring Craven County. Locally produced programs focus on community events and disseminate information about community projects and community-service activities.

Headline News Local Edition
P.O. Box 2057, Beaufort
(252) 838-0006

Operated by Doug Raymond Productions, Headline News Local Edition is featured at 24 minutes after each hour and six minutes before each hour on Channel 49. Headline News offers coverage of all types of local events and of meetings of County Commissioners, Town Boards, the Board of Education and more. This newscast provides viewers a chance to see what is really happening in their community.

UNC Center for Public Television
Research Triangle Park, Raleigh
(919) 549-7000

North Carolina public television is broadcast locally on Channel 13. Viewers may choose from the public television programs to which they are accustomed along with regional features tailored to the interests of North Carolina residents.

WFXI-FOX
U.S. Hwy. 70, Morehead City
(252) 240-0888

Television Channel 8 shows the regular Fox programming and offers a local news show each night at 10 PM. With an office in Morehead City, the channel offers some local television coverage.

WCTI
225 Glenburnie Dr., New Bern
(252) 638-1212

Television Channel 12, the local ABC affiliate, provides comprehensive local coverage as well as ABC programming. The station offers local news, sports and weather each weekday at 5:30 AM, noon, and 5, 6 and 11 PM. This station has a reporter and photographer dedicated to covering events in Carteret County.

WITN
U.S. Hwy. 17 S., Washington, NC
(252) 946-3131

Television Channel 7 is the local NBC affiliate. Along with NBC programming, the station has area news coverage, including high school and college sports. News is broadcast at 5:30 AM, noon, and at 5, 6 and 11 PM.

WNCT
3221 S. Evans St., Greenville, NC
(252) 355-8500

Television Channel 9 is the regional CBS affiliate and carries all of the network's programming. Local news, sports and national news are shown at 5 and 6 AM, noon, and 6 and 11 PM.

Cable Television

Time Warner Cable
500 Vision Cable Dr., Newport
(252) 223-6400

Time Warner is a franchised cable provider for Carteret County, as well as Craven and Onslow counties. This company provides digital cable services, high-speed interact and digital phone service. For hookup service, or additional information, call the office.

Radio Stations

WTKF 107.3 FM
U.S. Hwy. 70, Morehead City
(252) 247-6343
www.wtkf107.com

North Carolina's first FM talk station, WTKF 107.3 exclusively offers "Coastal Daybreak" with Ben Ball, the area's only morning show that's all talk. Ball taps into all the area happenings, history, book reviews, hot health issues and more, keeping eastern North Carolina citizens up to date. On The Talk Station you'll also find Rush Limbaugh, Laura Ingraham, Michael Reagan and other talk-radio favorites. These include many locally produced programs like Viewpoints, Youthpoints, Positive Living and The Wine and Dine Radio Show. Sports coverage includes the Tar Heels of North Carolina, the Carolina Panthers, local high school games and Sporting News Radio. News and weather every thity minutes. Now also heard in Jacksonville on WJNC 1240 AM, The Talk Station is Smart Radio.

Public Radio East 88.1/88.5/89.3/90.3 & 91.5 FM
800 College Ct., New Bern
(252) 638-3434

With studios on the Craven Community College campus, Public Radio East offers listeners two distinct formats. The news and classical music format is heard on 89.3 and presents nearly 120 hours of classical music each week plus in-depth news weekday mornings and afternoons during NPR's "Morning Edition" and "All Things Considered." The News & Ideas Network -- heard on 88.5 in New Bern, 90.3 in Goldsboro-Kinston, 91.5 Atlantic Beach and 88.1 in Greenville -- offers those NPR signature programs and more, including "Talk of the Nation," and news from the BBC, as well as "The Sound," a weekday evening program of roots rock, Americana and contemporary folk. During weekends on all the Public Radio East frequencies, it's America's favorite mechanics Tom and Ray Magliozzi during "Car Talk" Saturday at 10 AM, music and storytelling Saturday evening at 6 during "A Prairie Home Companion" and five hours of jazz Sunday at 6 p.m. during "An Evening with the Jazzman."

HANK 94.1FM
Oriental

HANK 94 is "everything country", offering a great selection of today's country hits.

Lite 98.7FM
Jacksonville

This is the station for on-the-job easy listening.

107.9FM

Oldies 107.9FM plays old-time rock and roll. A favorite DJ is Uncle Doug and the first day of the week is Motown Monday.

WORSHIP

Whether you're a resident, visitor or newcomer, you have hundreds of worship options on the Crystal Coast. You can attend a service, admire the architecture or learn about local history by visiting the local churches. Many of the area's community activities and volunteer efforts are spearheaded by local houses of worship.

Churches are around every corner, but that's not unusual for an area many refer to as the "Southern Bible Belt." Baptist, Methodist and Pentecostal churches predominate. Episcopal, Presbyterian, Friends, Unitarian/Universalist and Catholic churches are also represented, along with many other denominations. Visitors who choose to worship at a synagogue may visit Temple B'Nai Sholem Synagogue, 505 Middle Street, New Bern.

Many of the oldest churches are in Beaufort. For the most part, these are wooden structures preserved to look just as they did hundreds of years ago. Each church is distinct -- some are modern structures, some are classic brick designs, others are weathered and vine-covered. Each has its own legends and stories held dear by its congregation.

It's not possible for us to list the hundreds of worship centers located around the Crystal Coast. We have described a few of the churches that are noted for their historic buildings, the sizes of their congregations or their convenient locations.

For more information about other churches in the area, check the Yellow Pages or the Friday evening edition of the Carteret County News-Times, where you will find a directory of local churches.

Ann Street United Methodist Church, on Ann and Craven Streets in Beaufort, (252) 728-4279, was built c. 1854. The church features curved wooden pews, beautiful stained-glass windows and hand-carved rosettes in the ceiling. The steeple, stretching high above the houses on the low coastal land, was shown on old mariners' charts as a point of reference, a beacon to aid those at sea. It is one of three churches surrounding the Old Burying Ground (see our Crystal Coast Attractions chapter). The church's modern educational building stands across the street and is used for community events.

Purvis Chapel AME Zion Church, 217 Craven Street, (252) 504-2605, is Beaufort's oldest continuously used church. Built in 1820, it stands on the same block as the Ann Street United Methodist Church. Originally built by the Methodist Episcopal Church, Purvis Chapel was later deeded to the AME Zion congregation and is still owned by that group. The church's bell was cast in Glasgow, Scotland, in 1797. The building is listed on the National Register of Historic Places, and in 1998 the Purvis Chapel was recognized with a second Kathryn Cloud Historical Preservation Award. The church you see today, though modified somewhat, closely resembles the original structure.

The area's oldest Episcopal church is St. Paul's, c. 1857, located at 209 Ann Street, (252) 728-3324, in Beaufort. Local shipbuilders built the church in two years. Visitors will notice that the interior of the sanctuary bears a striking resemblance to an upside-down ark. It is reported to be one of the ten most acoustically perfect buildings in North Carolina. Holy Eucharist is on Sunday and a midweek Eucharist is conducted each Wednesday.

St. Stephen's United Church of Christ, 500 Cedar Street, Beaufort, (252) 728-4918, was built in 1867, along with the neighboring two-story school building that housed

---

Every Easter Fort Macon State Park is the site of a Sunrise Worship Service conducted by the Carteret County Ministerial Association. For more information call the park at (252) 726-3775.

---

i

the Washburn Seminary. Records show the lot was purchased for $100 in 1867, and the seminary served as a school for many years. St. Stephen's pews are the original dark mahogany and still have the center railing that separated families and Sunday school groups. Through the years, no major modifications have been made to the church's exterior.

The First Baptist Church of Morehead City, 810 Bridges Street, (252) 726-4142, is one of the town's oldest churches. The congregation first met in July 1873 and originally shared a small building near the waterfront with the town's Methodists. After the Civil War, the congregation built the current structure. An adjacent 18,000-square-foot Family Life Center was dedicated in 1994 and is available for community activities, meetings and weddings.

Located at 900 Arendell Street in Morehead City, the First United Methodist Church, (252) 726-7102, was founded in 1879 but has roots that go back to Shepard's Point in 1800. Today's sanctuary was dedicated in 1952.

St. Egbert's Catholic Church, 1706 Evans Street, (252) 726-3559, had its start in More head City in 1929. Community service is an important part of this church, and support and Bible study groups regularly meet in church facilities. Parish services are offered Saturday and Sunday, and mass is held daily. The church also operates a private school for students from kindergarten through 5th grade.

The Unitarian Coastal Fellowship, 1300 Evans Street in Morehead City, was organized in Carteret County in 1980 and promotes religious diversity. Services are held in the fellowship hall on Sundays at 10:30 AM. Religious education and child care are available. Call the Rev. Sally White at (252) 240-2283 for more information.

Glad Tidings Pentecostal Holiness Church, 4621 Country Club Road in Morehead City, (252) 726-0160, grew from a 1930s tent revival. In 1997 the church dedicated a 20,000-square-foot worship and outreach center, which seats 1,200 and features a state-of-the-art sound and lighting system and a catwalk for theatrical and musical productions. The building also contains a main floor with a balcony, a bridal-hospitality room for weddings and welcoming first-time visitors, and a bookstore, Inspiration Station. Glad Tidings has a 10,000-square-foot family life center, with a large open area, classrooms, a kitchen and offices. The center is available for weddings, conferences and meetings.

MILITARY

Military bases and training facilities dot North Carolina's Crystal Coast, but they haven't spoiled its beauty. They have just added a few more people, a little noise, extra traffic every now and then -- and a lot of patriotism.

Occasionally, residents express concern about low-flying aircraft, the noise caused by a night-training flight or the increased traffic on the roads, but overall the military bases are excellent neighbors. They provide employment and income and contribute to the community through uncountable volunteer hours. Military personnel often volunteer to tutor students, clear and construct school athletic fields, help nonprofit groups with projects, and raise funds for holiday programs. We're glad to have them in Carteret and Craven counties.

Of the surrounding bases, the Marine Corps Air Station base at Cherry Point in Havelock has the greatest impact on the Crystal Coast. One of the most valuable assets is the base's Naval Aviation Depot (NADEP). Of about 4,000 NADEP employees, 1,329 live in Carteret County. NADEP pays more than $275 million in salaries annually, $90 million of that to Carteret County residents. See the Havelock chapter for more information on Cherry Point.

The Port of Morehead City is the port of embarkation and debarkation for the Second Division of the U.S. Marine Corps at Camp Lejeune. This base is near Jacksonville, and military troops often travel N.C. Highway 24 from Swansboro to Morehead City. Another area establishment is Seymour Johnson Air Force Base in Goldsboro, which is about a two-hour drive from the Crystal Coast.

What follows is information about some of the closest military establishments.

Marine Corps Auxiliary Landing Field
Bogue Field, off N.C. Hwy. 24

This 875-acre landing field fronts Bogue Sound. It is primarily used for field carrier landing practice, and pilots perform many of these landings at night to simulate landing on an aircraft carrier. It serves as the Marines' only East Coast site for such training and includes the maintenance and operation of an expeditionary airfield. This capability helps ensure success for the Corps. It provides the force with the means to forward deploy its aviation assets in order to have a more readily accessible aviation punch for the Marine Air Ground Task Force commander on the battlefield.

Atlantic Outlying Field and Piney Island (Marines)

These two training facilities are in the Down East area of Carteret County. Atlantic Outlying Field is a 1,514-acre facility in the community of Atlantic. Piney Island, or BT-11 as the military refers to it, is a 10,000-plus-acre electronic practice range at the eastern tip of Carteret County. As part of the Mid-Atlantic Electronic Warfare Range (MAEWR), Piney Island is used by various military groups, including active-duty personnel and reservists. While planes actually do fly over the area, bombing simulations are recorded and scored electronically via computers to lessen the environmental impact.

Coast Guard Group Fort Macon
N.C. Hwy. 58, Atlantic Beach
(252) 247-4598

Coast Guard Group Fort Macon is at the east end of Bogue Banks and is the home port of one large cutter and several smaller vessels. The base is charged with patrolling the waters from Drum Inlet on Core Banks south to the North Carolina–South Carolina border. Coast Guard missions include homeland security, search and rescue, and law enforcement.

Coast Guard Station Emerald Isle
Station St., Emerald Isle
(252) 354-2462

The vessels of this station, located at the west end of Bogue Banks in Emerald Isle, patrol about 50 nautical miles of the Atlantic Intracoastal Waterway, including Bogue Inlet, New River Inlet, White Oak River and New River all the way down to Surf City. The primary focus is on homeland security, search and rescue, and law enforcement.

NEW BERN

To really appreciate the New Bern of today, it's important to know the New Bern of yesterday. This river town maintains its heritage by standing guard over its Colonial, Georgian, Federal, Greek Revival and Victorian architectural styles, while its citizens still maintain an attitude of friendliness and Southern gentility.

New Bern was originally settled in 1710 by Swiss and German immigrants who named it after Bern, the Swiss capital. The town was officially founded by Swiss Baron Christoph deGraffenried. Just like its mother city, New Bern is distinguished by its imposing clock tower above City Hall. The city emblem, as in old Bern, is a black bear going up a golden road, and this symbol appears frequently throughout the city.

New Bern has been fought over by Native Americans, Swiss, British, Colonials, Yankees and Rebels. After each skirmish, it pulled itself up by its boot straps and plodded onward. The result is a panoply of American history along tree-lined streets - an odd mix that makes the town quite picturesque.

Historic markers point out the houses where the first elected assembly in the colonies met in defiance of the crown in 1774, where a signer of the U.S. Constitution lived, and where George Washington slept - twice. Markers also show you the office of jurist William Gaston, the first chief justice of the state Supreme Court and composer of the state song.

The second-oldest city in North Carolina, New Bern is the site of many firsts. The first state printing press was set up and the first book and newspaper were published in New Bern. The state's first public school opened here. The first official celebration of George Washington's birthday was held in New Bern, and it was here that the world's first practical torpedo was assembled and detonated. In the 1890s C. D. Bradham, a New Bern pharmacist, invented Brad's Drink, now known as Pepsi-Cola (see our Close-up on Bradham and Pepsi-Cola in our Restaurants chapter).

Without question, New Bern's centerpiece is Tryon Palace, the lavish Georgian brick mansion named after William Tryon, the British Colonial governor who had it built in 1770. After the Revolutionary War, the palace served as the home of the state capital until 1795. The original palace burned in 1798, but the current is a reproduction built in the 1950s from the original plans, which were found in England. It is a sumptuous showplace inside and out.

But even before all that, before the palace, the school and the white man's voice, this site on the Neuse and Trent rivers captured the interest of the Tuscarora Indians. It is believed the Indians may have had hunting camps and villages here for thousands of years.

Downtown New Bern (see our map of New Bern's Historic District) sits on a point of land at the confluence of the Neuse and Trent rivers. Once the main hub, the downtown area fell into great disrepair in the early 1970s due to the development of shopping malls and suburban housing outside the business district.

That all changed, however, when in 1979 local government gave Swiss Bear Inc., a nonprofit corporation of civic leaders, the authority and responsibility to revitalize the downtown area. Today, art galleries, specialty shops, antiques stores, restaurants and other businesses have resurrected downtown, turning it into a bustling hub of activity.

Progressive and exciting improvements are continuously underway. Built and dedicated in 1995, James Reed Lane is a lovely downtown mini-park and pedestrian walk-through on Pollock Street across from Christ Church. The pleasant respite amid downtown activity was planned and funded through efforts of Swiss Bear Inc., in honor of the first rector of Christ Church. New Bern's downtown blocks grow more distinctive and beautiful every day as private restoration efforts return many of the building facades to their turn-of-the-last-century elegance.

Just downstream from downtown New Bern, the Neuse River slows and quickly broadens into a mile-wide concourse. Joined by the Trent River, the Neuse takes a lumbering left turn and widens to 4 miles across, making it the widest river in the United States. The two rivers converge at downtown's Union Point Park, one of New Bern's best picnic spots.

This inviting link to the broad, shallow Pamlico Sound and the Atlantic Ocean helped shape New Bern's destiny. The town long thrived on the richness of its rivers and the fertile soil surrounding them. In Colonial times, West Indian and European vessels would dock here to trade merchandise. The river led inland to pitch, tar and tobacco and, of course, to local hospitality. Now the rivers serve as the focus of the area's recreational activities: water-skiing, sailing and fishing. Hotel-based marinas for modern-day skippers edge toward the Trent River channel from Union Point Park and also front the Neuse. New Bern's rivers are a tremendous source of area pride, and recent pollution symptoms in the Neuse have stirred tremendous state and local efforts in restoring its health.

New Bern's southeastern boundary is only a few miles from the Croatan National Forest, a 157,000-acre preserve that shelters deer, bear, alligator and the rare Venus' flytrap, a carnivorous plant. Canada geese and osprey are common sights along the rivers, as are the resident great blue herons. Given the right weather conditions and saltwater intrusion, the Neuse River has been known to hide 8- to 10-foot blacktip sharks.

New Bern has three historic districts with homes, stores and churches dating back to the early 18th century. Within easy walking distance of the waterfront are more than 150 homes and buildings listed on the National Register of Historic Places. Also nearby are several bed and breakfast inns, hotels, outstanding restaurants, banks, antiques and specialty shops, Tryon Palace, city and county government complexes and many of the town's 2,000 crape myrtles.

The crape myrtle is New Bern's official flower, and it's no wonder. On those hot summer days when you feel like drooping, the crape myrtle seems to laugh with energy as it bursts forth in a profusion of blossoms. New Bern does its gardening quietly. Led by the example of the professionally pampered Tryon Palace gardens, the town's residents have a yen to make things grow. During the spring explosion of dogwoods and azaleas, a ride through many neighborhoods can be breathtaking.

Gardens, both public and private, extend throughout the city and its suburbs. Summertime brings day lilies, dahlias, zinnias, black-eyed susans and petunias. Home gardens produce tomatoes, herbs, squash, corn and other favorites. In fall it seems everyone goes slightly crazy for chrysanthemums. (See our New Bern Annual Events chapter for information about the fall Mumfest.) Flowering cabbage and pansies brighten the winter.

Besides the downtown historic district, New Bern also has the Ghent and Riverside neighborhoods, both of which carry official historic neighborhood designations. Ghent, across Trent Road from the DeGraffenried neighborhood, was the town's first suburb, and its tree-planted median on Spencer Avenue was once the bed of a trolley. The neighborhood displays an eclectic collection of architectural styles.

Riverside, developed at the turn of the 20th century and across town from Ghent, runs between the Norfolk Southern railroad tracks and the Neuse River to Jack Smith Creek. It has a sort of baron-and-worker feel to it, with imposing mansions along National Avenue giving way to more modest residences on neighboring streets.

Tucked between New Bern and the Trent River is Trent Woods, one of the wealthiest of North Carolina's incorporated towns. Here is the New Bern Golf and Country Club, the Eastern Carolina Yacht Club and some of the area's priciest real estate. Trent Woods' costly, pine-shaded real estate is, more and more, in similar company within New Bern's housing market. About 5 miles south of town off U.S. Highway 17 is River Bend, which began as a planned development but later incorporated. Like Trent Woods, it has its own country club, golf course, tennis club, marina and waterfront acreage along the Trent River and the canals that lead to it.

Both River Bend and Fairfield Harbour, another planned community about 8 miles east of New Bern on the Neuse River, have attracted retirees primarily from the Northeast. Fairfield Harbour's amenities include a couple of golf courses, two swimming pools, tennis courts, a marina, a restaurant and lounge, horseshoes and walking and riding paths.

If all this sounds boringly nice, take heart. There are a few trouble spots. Insiders' brows furrow when they talk about the town's traffic lights and its lack of nightlife.

First, the traffic lights. New Bern has an overabundance of them on U.S. 17, which is called Broad Street downtown and Dr. M. L. King Jr. Boulevard as you head south toward Jacksonville. With the closing of the bridge at the foot of Broad Street, several traffic lights downtown were removed. But if you're headed south and don't catch the lights just right, once you hit Dr. M. L. King Jr. Boulevard expect plenty of stops along U.S. 17. And, at the peak hours of 8 AM, noon and 5 PM, you can expect bottlenecks around the road's intersections with Simmons Street, U.S. 70, McCarthy Boulevard and Glenburnie Road.

Downtown's traffic woes were eased with the opening of the high-rise Neuse River Bridge in late 1999. The bridge spans the Neuse River and goes from Bridgeton on U.S. 17 to James City on U.S. 70. The bridge replaced the John Lawson drawbridge that connected directly to Broad Street and almost always caused major traffic back-ups when opened. The old bridge was dismantled.

As for New Bern's nightlife, there are a few lounges, some live music and two movie theaters, but those with a hankering for more need to hit town at the right time. New Bern has good professional and amateur acting groups (including the annual Shakespeare festival), several subscription performance seasons, and an annual Sunday Jazz Showcase worth the wait.

The town also has wonderful festivals and shows. Mumfest, New Bern Preservation Foundation's Antique Show and Sale, the Spring Homes and Gardens Tour, Ghostwalk, and Tryon Palace Christmas Candlelight Tours are among the favorites (see our Annual Events chapter). Residents also gather for special occasions on the Trent River water-front -- on July Fourth for the fireworks and in early December for the Christmas flotilla. But, otherwise, the town's social life takes place in private homes and social clubs and at various civic and charity functions that are staged on an annual basis.

To really get to know New Bern, you have to take it as it is. Think of the river city as a slow treasure hunt where gems are revealed as you walk its streets. It's there that you will discover the real New Bern. Take time to read the historic markers and talk to the people in their gardens and on their porches.

You're likely to find a sailor from California, a cyclist from New Zealand, an urban refugee from New York or a retired shop owner from Honolulu sharing your park bench. Ask them why they chose to live here. New Bernians like to talk about their town.

New Bern is a gentle place, a place where one can really enjoy the passing scene and where people know how to appreciate a pretty day. It's just that kind of town.

GETTING HERE, GETTING AROUND

New Bern is growing in many ways. The number of retirees and new residents moving in and the number of tourists coming to explore the area's many treasures increases every year. No matter how they arrive - by land, air or sea - all routes lead to attractions that everyone will enjoy.

LAND

From the north, U.S. Highway 17 leads directly into the heart of New Bern. From the west, Interstate 95 leads to U.S. Highway 70, which continues straight into New Bern. From the north or south, U.S. 17 is the most direct route to the area. From the east, the drive here is along U.S. 70 from the Morehead City area.

The $93 million Neuse River Bridge, the costliest in North Carolina's history, opened in late 1999. The 1.9-mile, four-lane bridge spans the Neuse River from Bridgeton to James City, connecting U.S. 17 to U.S. 70. At its highest point, the bridge arches 65 feet above the Neuse River. It replaced the two-lane John Lawson drawbridge, which was dismantled shortly after the opening of the new bridge. The Neuse River Bridge allows travelers heading directly to the beaches from the south or north to bypass the heart of New Bern. Exit ramps along U.S. 70 can take you into the downtown historic district, to Trent Woods (Pembroke), to U.S. 17 N. or to Glenburnie Road.

The Alfred Cunningham Bridge, which spans the Trent River and connects the downtown historic district with the Neuse River Bridge and U.S. 70 is scheduled for replacement; construction is expected to start in 2007. During the two-year construction period, traffic to the downtown area will be routed through the Trent Woods (Pembroke) exit.

Bus Service

Carolina Trailways/New Bern Bus Terminal
504 Guion St., New Bern
(252) 633-3100

Carolina Trailways provides bus service to and from New Bern. Direct service to all points north and south depart and arrive daily. Connections to New Bern from all directions are made in Raleigh. New Bern's bus station schedule operates around departures and arrivals. Call for schedule and fare information; the terminal is open 10:30 AM to 3:30 PM and 6:30 to 8 PM daily.

Taxi and Shuttle Services

New Bern offers several professional taxi franchises that run 24 hours a day. The cars are clean, the drivers are courteous, and the fares are moderately priced. If you need a cab, try:

New Safeway Taxi Service, (252) 636-9000 or (252) 633-2828

Tryon Cab Co., (252) 638-8809 or (252) 636-9335

Carolina Limousine And Shuttle Service (CLASS)
233 Middle St., New Bern
(252) 637-RIDE (7433)

This service offers transportation services for all events and occasions, utilizing its fleet of Excursions, Hummers, Town Cars and antique wedding cars. You'll enjoy the red carpet treatment offered at reasonable rates.

Car Rental

You will need a car if you plan to see more of the area than downtown New Bern. A few car rental businesses are based at the Craven County Regional Airport, 200 Terminal Drive, New Bern.

Avis Rent A Car, (252) 637-2130

Hertz Rental Car, (252) 637-3021

National/Alamo Car Rental, (252) 637-5241

AIR

Craven Regional Airport
200 Terminal Dr., New Bern
(252) 638-8591

Arriving by plane is as easy as flying into the Craven Regional Airport, 2 miles southeast of downtown New Bern off U.S. 70. The airport offers seven daily flights on US Airways Express, (800) 428-4322, to and from the large hub airport in Charlotte. Food is available in the terminal, and airport parking is available for 50¢ an hour or $6 daily.

Michael J. Smith Airport
N.C. Hwy. 101, Beaufort
(252) 728-1928

Within an hour's drive of New Bern, this airport only offers chartered or private aircraft service. The fixed-base operator is Segrave Aviation, (252) 728-2323, which handles fueling, car rentals, flight instruction, charters, sightseeing flights, pilot supplies and charts, maintenance and more.

Albert J. Ellis Airport
264 Albert J. Ellis Airport Rd., Richlands
(910) 324-1100

Daily US Airways Express flights to and from Charlotte also are available at the Albert J. Ellis Airport, located 30 miles south of New Bern. Short-term parking prices range from free for the first 10 minutes up to $1.75 for over two hours, while long-term parking is $6 per day. Car rentals through Avis, Hertz and National, as well as a restaurant and gift shop, also are located on-site. Fixed-base services are available through Jacksonville Flying Service, (910) 324-2500.

Raleigh-Durham International Airport
Aviation Pkwy., Morrisville,
10 miles from Raleigh and Durham, right off I-40, Exits 284B-285
(919) 840-2123

Raleigh-Durham (RDU) is the major international airport serving North Carolina from the Research Triangle Park area. RDU, a two-hour drive from New Bern, is a major hub for domestic and international travelers and is served by all major domestic carriers, feeder carriers and by Air Canada. Car rental services are at the airport.

SEA

Boaters arriving on the water come up the Intracoastal Waterway and then travel the Neuse River to New Bern. The Neuse River flows into the Pamlico Sound and has well-marked channels. New Bern also fronts the Trent River, which flows into the Neuse. A complete description of the rivers, bridge and ferry schedules and marinas is offered in our New Bern On the Water chapter.

ONCE YOU'RE HERE

If you arrive by air or water and are interested in exploring all that New Bern has to offer, a rental car would be a good investment. There is no public transportation in New Bern.

Bikes are a wonderful way to get around the downtown and waterfront areas. However, because of the narrow shoulders and increasingly heavy traffic, we wouldn't recommend biking along the highways that immediately lead to and from New Bern.

Walking is the most interesting way to travel in the downtown area, so park the car in any of the well-planned downtown parking areas and see New Bern at a slower pace.

The Neuse River Basin is identified by signs at bridge crossings on highways in eastern North Carolina. These signs are reminders of the numerous sources and vast area that influences water of the Neuse River.

Tourism/Relocation Information

New Bern-Craven County Convention and Visitors Center
203 S. Front St., New Bern
(800) 437-5767

If you are a visitor, here's your first stop - the friendly staff would love to help you prepare your stay in New Bern and Havelock. Located in the New Bern Riverfront Convention Center, the New Bern-Craven County Convention and Visitors Center staff will equip you with maps, brochures and suggestions that will get your visit off to a fantastic start. You'll be warmly greeted from 8 AM to 5 PM Monday though Friday, 10 AM to 4 PM on Saturday and (between Memorial Day and Labor Day) 10 AM to 2 PM on Sunday.

New in New Bern? Call NEIGHBORS of New Bern at (252) 633-4094 or (252) 638-5799 to arrange an in-home visit from Sandie Swigart and Liza Granlund, who will welcome you to the area by providing information about local businesses, the community, civic organizations, and volunteer opportunities. They also can tell newcomers how to become a part of the Newcomers Club of New Bern. Sandie and Liza also visit engaged women, families who have changed their residence, and families with new babies.

New Bern Area Chamber of Commerce
316-B S. Front St., New Bern
(252) 637-3111

If you are exploring the possibility of opening a new business or relocating to New Bern or the surrounding area, contact the New Bern Area Chamber of Commerce for specific information to help with your considerations. Chamber hours are Monday through Thursday 9 AM to 5 PM and on Friday from 9 AM to 3 PM.

New Bern Riverfront Convention Center
203 S. Front St., New Bern
(252) 637-1551

The New Bern Riverfront Convention Center features 28,000 square feet of meeting and special event space, including a 12,000-square-foot ballroom. It is within walking distance of nearly all downtown accommodations and shopping. Businesses and groups can take advantage of the Center's many amenities to host successful meetings and conventions. The Center has a large waterfront veranda overlooking the Trent River and in-house kitchen facilities for on-site catering. Handicapped accessible and with ample parking, the Center is home to a number of great annual trade shows and special events, many of which are open free to the public. Insiders consider the New Bern Riverfront Convention Center a great asset to the downtown historic district.

NEW BERN RESTAURANTS

A delightful variety of dining options is available to New Bern residents and visitors. Restaurants feature culinary fare from around the world, and you'll find everything from traditional Southern home cooking to fine European cuisine. If you're looking for good seafood, you'll love dining out in New Bern. In fact, you would be hard-pressed to find a restaurant that does not offer some type of shellfish or other seafood.

The following guide alphabetically highlights some of the Insiders' favorite local restaurants. We did not list popular chain and fast food restaurants with which you are probably familiar. We encourage you to ask locals for other recommendations and to call ahead for hours of operation.

PRICE CODE

The price code we use in this section reflects the average price of a dinner for two. Because entrees come in a wide range of prices, our price code reflects an average cost of entrees, not the most expensive item or the least expensive item. For restaurants that do not serve dinner, the price code reflects the cost of lunch fare. Price code averages do not include appetizers, drinks, desserts, gratuity or the state's 7 percent sales tax. Prices are also subject to change. Unless otherwise noted, all of these establishments accept credit cards.

$	Less than $20
$$	$20 to $30
$$$	$31 to $40
$$$$	$41 or more

A Catered Affair Cafe **$$**
3402-B Trent Rd., New Bern
(252) 637-7331

A Catered Affair is an inviting and romantic dinner stop for New Bern Insiders and a favorite location for special-occasion dinners and private parties. Diners will enjoy the romantic atmosphere created by a combination of the beautifully decorated dining room and the appetizing smells from the kitchen. Owner Stacia Reed's culinary creations always include the freshest ingredients prepared in creative and tasty ways. A Catered Affair Cafe is open for dinner Thursday through Saturday nights. Reservations are recommended. Stacia and her crew also provide catering services. Catered lunches are available for groups of 10 or more.

The Baker's Square **$$$**
227 Middle St., New Bern
(252) 637-0304

The Baker's Square is fast becoming a favorite among Insiders for its generous portions, fantastic prices and outstanding service. Open Tuesday through Saturday, The Baker's Square serves breakfast, lunch and dinner. The Baker's Breakfast platters, featuring either pancakes, French toast, biscuits and gravy, or eggs with your choice of sausage or bacon, are on the menu. Or you can create your own combination from a list of breakfast items. For lunch, enjoy a home-cooked meal of beef, chicken, seafood or catfish, and for dinner choose from selections including prime rib, shrimp, soft-shell crabs, catfish and pork, all prepared in tantalizing dishes and served with sides of vegetables, cole slaw and Baker's Rolls. Insiders highly recommend the country fried steak. Salads and sandwiches also are offered on the lunch and dinner menus. You'll definitely want to top off your dinner with a tempting dessert of pie, cheesecake and pastries. The Baker's Square is a very popular restaurant -- Insiders recommend you time your visits to miss the crowds, particularly on Friday and Saturday nights.

BearTown French Bakery & Bistro **$**
1905 S. Glenburnie Rd., New Bern
(252) 634-BEAR
www.breadandpastries.com

Formerly in a hidden location in New Bern, BearTown French Bakery & Bistro

moved in 2004 to its new location on popular Glenburnie Road beside Cooks and Connoisseurs, and continues to expand its menu. The atmosphere is that of a European bistro, with warm yellow walls and black-and-white checkered floor, and the staff is friendly and inviting. BearTown now serves breakfast, lunch and dinner, and offers a select wine list chosen carefully for quality and value.

Lunch items include all homemade soups, salads and sandwiches. Insiders highly recommend the Tomato Basil Bisque, a year-round staple. Sandwiches – including the Trent Woods Dip, a roast beef sandwich with melted provolone, caramelized onions and au jus – are named after many of the popular neighborhoods in New Bern and towns in Craven County. Affordable lunch combinations (such as half-sandwich and cup of soup or side salad) are offered every day, and several Bistro dinner entrees are offered nightly in addition to the sandwiches, soups and salads offered all day. Sunday Brunch lasts from 8 AM to 2 PM.

BearTown, of course, still offers its tempting array of breads, pastries, cakes, croissants and more, all made from scratch. Breads are made and baked daily with all natural, fresh ingredients. Made-from-scratch croissants come in a variety of flavors, and the creamy, light and crispy pastries are full of rich flavor. Just an example of some of the other yummy treats include its very popular cranberry orange scones (and other flavors), cream puffs and eclairs filled with their own Bavarian pastry cream, and fresh fruit tarts. As the bistro continues to grow into its new location, owner Katherine Kent will be adding to the offerings, so each trip you make will offer tasty surprises

Capt. Ratty's Seafood & Steakhouse $$$
202 Middle St., New Bern
(252) 633-2088

Open daily, Capt. Ratty's menu features a variety of seafood and steaks cooked just about any way you like. Owner Tom Ballance says the restaurant serves some of the best steak in the state, due partially to Capt. Ratty's high standards in selecting steaks for its customers. You can have your NY strips, rib-eyes and filets cooked to order. Crab, shrimp and oysters come prepared in a variety of dishes sure to please even the pickiest eaters. Our seafaring Insider recommends the Peck of Oysters and Captain's Platter with its generous servings of crab legs, oysters, clams, shrimp and mussels -- but not on the same night, of course. The price of the oysters depends on whether you shuck or the Capt. Ratty's staff shucks. Bring your shucking knife, just in case. Our Insider Kid (who doesn't have his sea legs yet) highly recommends the kids' menu, which features grilled cheese and hamburgers. Clam chowder, sandwiches and salads round out the menu. Beverages include soft drinks, tea, coffee, beer and mixed drinks. Capt. Ratty's also is noted for its excellent selection of wines.

Pepsi's Beginnings in New Bern

You never know what legacy you might leave the next millennium. When New Bern's would-be pharmacist Caleb Bradham concocted what he called Brad's Drink in 1898, he couldn't possibly have guessed what impact it would have on 20th-century culture and beyond. The ultimate fate of his peppy solution, which he later named Pepsi-Cola, would have seemed as far-fetched to him as satellite TV or computers.

In 1998 Pepsi-Cola, now an international corporation, celebrated its 100th anniversary, and the local Pepsi-Cola Bottling Company of New Bern opened The Birthplace of Pepsi Cola at the corner of Middle and Pollock Streets, (252) 636-5898. This shop includes a reproduction of the soda fountain where Bradham first served his popular drink, and includes local Pepsi memorabilia. You also can purchase a variety of merchandise emblazoned with the Pepsi logo. Outside, a historical marker on Pollock Street also marks the spot where Brad's Drink was invented.

Caleb Bradham, born in 1867 in Chinquapin, North Carolina, just wanted to be a pharmacist. He graduated from the University of North Carolina and started medical school. Due to family finances, he had to leave school. Bradham then relocated to New Bern and became a high school teacher.

When Bradham learned that a drugstore was being offered for sale at the corner of Middle and Pollock streets, he bought it with the help of investment partners. Bradham worked at the drugstore and studied until he passed the Board of Pharmacy examination in 1895 with the highest score that year.

This Broad Street drugstore (now the location of The Chelsea restaurant) was the second location of Bradham's drugstore. He invented Pepsi in his original pharmacy, which was located on the corner of Middle and Pollock Street, where a reproduction of his soda fountain exists today.

Soon after purchasing the store, Bradham concocted a new drink for his soda fountain that he called Brad's Drink. His advertising described Brad's Drink as "exhilarating, invigorating and aids digestion." By 1898, young Bradham had bought the store from his partners and he named the new carbonate Pepsi-Cola.

Bradham began his cola operation on an organized basis in 1903. The company packaged the syrup for sale to other soda fountains. The bottling process was on the rise and, by 1910, had exceeded sales at soda fountains.

Business boomed until right after the World War I years, when sugar jumped

Carolina Bagel and Deli Company $
Village Square, 3601 Trent Rd., New Bern
(252) 636-0133

Carolina Bagel Company, open daily, may be one of New Bern's best-kept breakfast and lunch secrets. Tucked away in Village Square on Trent Road, Carolina Bagel offers fresh-baked bagels all day, and you can top those with your pick of Carolina Bagel's homemade cream cheese spreads. In addition, Carolina Bagel makes delicious pastries and homemade brownies from scratch daily. For lunch, choose from the salads, platters and sandwiches. A kids' menu features a PB&J, BLT and grilled cheese. Catering also is available.

Chadwick House Cafe $$
712B Pollock St., New Bern
(252) 637-2018

Insiders like the Chadwick House Cafe because of its delicious food and relaxing atmosphere. Although small in size, the cafe is big on service. Owners Amy and John Faulkenberry provide a simple but tasty menu that includes Southern staples such as chicken salad and pimiento cheese. You can have either those or your turkey, ham and roast beef sandwiches prepared on white or wheat bread or croissants. You can choose one of the salads to go along with a cup or bowl of soup, and top off your lunch with a slice of pie or cheesecake. (Insiders highly recommend the chicken salad sandwich, the from 5.5¢ a pound to 22.5¢ a pound. For Pepsi-Cola, which was retailing at 5¢ per bottle, this spelled financial disaster.

After collapsing into bankruptcy, the company changed hands four times before winding up in 1931 as a subsidiary of Loft, parent company of today's internationally known Pepsi-Cola. Bradham continued to run the Bradham Drug Company until his death in 1934, but he never saw any of the media frenzy surrounding his drink, such as Michael Jackson dancing with a Pepsi or Ray Charles crooning about the right thing.

You can see Caleb Bradham's home, which still stands on the corner of Johnson and E. Front Streets. You can also visit the building at the corner of Broad and Middle streets that was leased by the Bradham Drug Company for the second location of its state-of-the-art drugstore pharmacy. The building now houses The Chelsea restaurant, which features a wall mural depicting the Pepsi-Cola story. At Middle and Pollock, near the historical marker, you're going to find it hard to resist ordering Brad's Drink at the Pepsi store -- or anywhere else in New Bern.

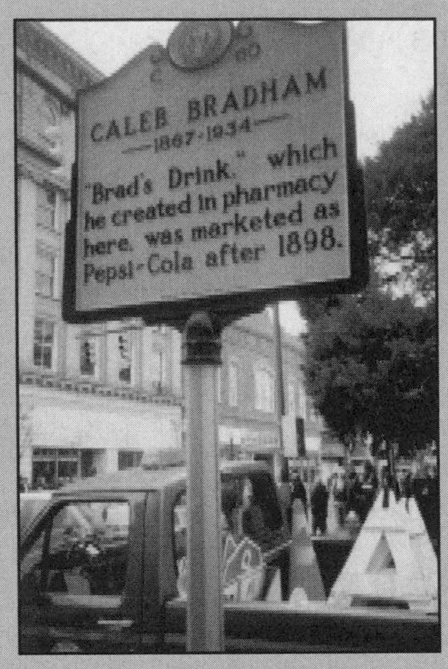

New Bern is the birthplace of Pepsi-Cola.

photo: Janis Williams

Senate bean soup and the chocolate chip cheesecake.) Open for lunch Monday through Saturday from 11 AM to 3 PM, the Chadwick House Cafe also features a daily special and a soup of the day. The cafe also sells many of its menu items by the pound or half-pound, and pies and cakes are available with advance notice; just call or stop by for details. Chadwick House Cafe does not serve alcohol nor does it accept credit cards. Off-street parking is available.

The Chelsea **$$$**
335 Middle St., New Bern
(252) 637-5469

You'll want to see the restored details of this 1912 building, which was the second drugstore of pharmacist Caleb Bradham, the inventor of Pepsi-Cola. But come to The Chelsea for the delight of good food. Fine detail is apparent in every preparation from the kitchen. Among the varied selection of appetizers try the Southwestern Egg Rolls, stuffed with a blend of chicken, cheese, black beans, corn and Southwestern spices and topped with Southwestern spiced sour cream. For an exciting blend of tastes, try the turkey pita club sandwich, combining smoked turkey, bacon, Monterey Jack cheese, lettuce and tomato in herbed pita bread and served with raspberry mayonnaise. For lunch or dinner, the Shrimp Sonoma, with shrimp and bacon over pasta with a special cream sauce, is a particular favorite of Insiders all over town. The Coastalina Shrimp and Grits, a combination of shrimp, smoked sausage, cheese and the Southern staple of grits is also pleasing fare. Surprises are mixed with traditions on the menus that are nicely varied. The Chelsea offers a wide selection of domestic or imported beers and wine and mixed drinks. This also is a popular nighttime gathering place (see our New Bern Nightlife chapter). The restaurant serves lunch and dinner daily except Sunday.

China Wok $$
3321 Dr. M. L. King Jr. Blvd., New Bern
(252) 636-5288

Insiders like China Wok because of the speed and efficiency involved in getting your food. Whether you choose to eat in or take out, your wait is never a long one. Located in McCarthy Crossing Shopping Center, China Wok does not go in for the lavish décor or fancy dinnerware, but what it lacks in atmosphere, it more than makes up for in scrumptious food and over-sized portions. Its menu features nearly 100 possibilities in pork, chicken, seafood and beef, some available in hot and spicy combinations that will make your eyes, in addition to your mouth, water. China Wok is open daily, with lunch specials available Monday through Saturday.

Clementine's American Bistro $$
3515 Trent Rd., Ste. 14, New Bern
(252) 637-2244

Located in Village Square Shopping Center, Clementine's American Bistro appeals to the diner who is in search of an experience instead of a meal, according to chef and owner Chris Izzo. The bistro features a creative and complex menu that offers a blend of traditional and nouveau cuisine. Clementine's has all ABC permits and its wine list focuses on vintage wines of California and Australia. Two private dining rooms are available for parties and other special occasions. Clementine's is open daily for dinner, Monday through Friday for lunch, and for Sunday brunch.

Country Biscuit Restaurant $
809 Broad St., New Bern
(252) 638-5151

Early birds will appreciate the Country Biscuit's opening hour of 5 AM. Eat your breakfast on a biscuit -- your choices are steak, ham, tenderloin, sausage, bacon and cheese. Breakfast plates with your choice of the above and eggs also are available. Country Biscuit also has a lunch menu, with plates and sandwiches. Insiders recommend the baked ham if you're in the mood for a plate; the cheeseburger if you want a sandwich. Breakfast choices come with a side of grits or hash browns; lunch with your choice of vegetable. No time to stop? Swing through Country Biscuit's drive-through window.

The Cow Cafe $
319 Middle St., New Bern
(252) 672-9269

The Cow Cafe is not only for the young but also the young at heart. In fall 2004, the Cow Cafe - New Bern's only "Four Hoof" restaurant - mooved to the historic downtown area. Its delicious menu features such delights as the Save-A-Cow barbecue baskets, the Grazin' Garden Salad, El Moo's Chili and other sandwiches, soups and salads. Of course, you'll want to save some room for gourmoo popcorn, ice cream and tasty milk shakes. The cow boutique features plenty of cow-inspired items, where you can find the perfect gift for all ages that says "I love moo." The Cow Cafe is open Monday through Saturday for lunch and dinner.

El Cerro Grande $$
2305 Dr. M. L. King Jr. Blvd., New Bern
(252) 638-8938

For authentic Mexican food, El Cerro Grande has an extensive Mexican menu that includes combination, vegetarian and children's dinners. The combination dinners give you not only a great bargain, but also the opportunity to sample a variety of dishes, including chalupas, chile rellenos, enchiladas, tacos and burritos, with the diner's choice of chicken or beef as filling. El Cerro Grande offers Mexican and domestic beers, wine by the glass, margaritas (also available by the pitcher) and mixed drinks. El Cerro Grande is open daily for lunch and dinner.

Flounders Seafood $$
425 Hotel Dr., New Bern
(252) 636-1200

Now located in the old Calypso Clyde's building, Flounders Seafood has built a reputation for providing excellent service and savory food. Owner Chris Tompkins utilized his 15-plus years of experience in the restaurant industry to create a family-friendly establishment that features daily specials and moderate prices. From appetizers to dinner platters, Flounders offers all of your favorites in shrimp, scallops, flounder, catfish, trout, crab, clams, oysters and more. (Steak and pork entrees are available for those in the mood for something other than seafood.) The delicious menu is rounded out with homemade desserts, and, of course, the sweet iced tea should be your beverage of choice. Although

Flounders has all ABC permits, it does not serve alcohol on Sundays. Flounders is open daily.

Fred and Claire's **$$**
247 Craven St., New Bern
(252) 638-5426

This cozy establishment in the downtown historic district is the oldest restaurant in New Bern still in operation. Many people tell stories of when it was Mike's during the 1930s but it's quite different now. Martin and Jan Czaykowski of Fred and Claire's offer a variety of delicious dishes prepared fresh daily. At lunch you will always find homemade soups and quiches; cream of tomato basil and crab bisque are among the favorites. Lunch specials may include grouper hoagies, crab cake sandwiches or Mediterranean salad with fresh North Carolina seafood along with such favorites as black angus burgers, homemade chicken salad, the leanest Reuben in town and tasty club sandwiches. For dinner, Fred and Claire's serves Southern, international and American cuisine. Favorites such as pork schnitzel and homemade potato pancakes are still a local favorite, but specials could include Grouper Napoleon stacked with crab meat or fresh North Carolina sea scallops with saffron sauce. Chicken dishes, crab cakes and seafood pasta are also on the menu. Fred and Claire's creates quite a dinner atmosphere when it turns the lights down low and plays in the background music by Dean Martin, Tony Bennett or Frankie himself. All desserts are made in house -- creme brulee, Key Lime pie, bread pudding with brandy sauce and more. Domestic and imported beer and a nice wine list complement your meal. Call for lunch and dinner hours Monday through Saturday. The staff at Fred and Claire's take Sunday off.

Gina's Pizza **$**
1904 S. Glenburnie Rd., New Bern
(252) 633-9000
1904 U.S. Hwy. 70 E., James City
(252) 672-9063

Looking for something quick but delicious? Give Gina's a call. New Bern Insiders recommend the Veggie Gourmet Pizza, The Works Gourmet Pizza (sampling of all the toppings), and the stromboli and lasagna dinners as favorites. But Gina's offers a fairly extensive menu, including salads and hot wings. Best of all, Gina's prices are a bargain, and daily specials are offered as well. Open Monday through Saturday until 10 PM, Gina's delivers with a minimum order of $7; however, Gina's no longer accepts personal checks so be prepared to pay with either cash or a debit/credit card.

Harvey Mansion
Historic Inn & Restaurant **$$$**
221 S. Front St., New Bern
(252) 635-3232
www.harveymansionhistoricinn.com

The Harvey Mansion Historic Inn & Restaurant offers three great locations in one beautiful setting: a classy restaurant, an elegant bed-and-breakfast and a fun nightclub. The 9,000-square-foot house, built from 1797 to 1804, is the last remaining structure fronting the Trent River from New Bern's time period as a thriving colonial seaport. On the first and second floors, diners will enjoy their selections of seafood, beef, poultry or lamb dishes in one of six dining rooms, including the green room which originally was the house's formal parlor and still features its ornate woodwork and molding. All dishes, from the menu created by chef Scott Weiss, come with a house salad and fresh dinner rolls. Specialties include such favorites as Beef and Brie En Croute, Lamb Osso Bucco, Asian Ahi Tuna Stack, Chicken Chesapeake, and Coastal Carolina Crab Cakes. Delicious appetizers, homemade desserts, an extensive wine list and nightly specials are also among the items

that have made the Harvey Mansion a great destination for dinner.

Latitude 35 **$$$**
Sheraton New Bern, 100 Middle St., New Bern
(252) 638-3585

Although the elegant decor and menu at this hotel restaurant suggest strictly fine dining, don't be put off if you've just jumped off your boat. You can come as you are and enjoy the cuisine and the panoramic view of the Neuse River and hotel marina. Latitude 35's weekend breakfast buffet, with its selection of egg dishes, grits, breakfast meats, French toast, waffles, muffins, wonderful biscuits, fresh fruit and cereals, is a favorite of locals and visitors. Weekday lunches offer sandwiches, soups and creative salads along with light plates featuring pasta, salad, seafood or meat. Attention turns to seafood in the evening. You'll find all types of fish and shellfish that can be broiled, baked, fried, grilled, peppered or blackened. The salad bar is included with each entree. For landlubbers Latitude 35 offers pasta, chicken and beef, and there is an extensive children's menu. The Friday night seafood buffet is elaborate, with fried, steamed, baked, broiled, Newburg and jambalaya seafood preparations. Latitude 35 is open daily for breakfast, lunch and dinner.

Marina Sweets Cafe & Deli **$**
208 Middle St., New Bern
(252) 637-9307

Enjoy "food with an attitude" at Marina Sweets Cafe & Deli. Open daily, Marina Sweets offers breakfast treats such as chocolate chip Belgian waffles, omelets made to order and croissant sandwiches featuring egg and cheese and your choice of ham or bacon. For lunch or dinner, enjoy shrimp, turkey, chicken, roast beef, ham and more, all creatively prepared and served in pitas and wraps. Insiders love the Historically BLT wrap, a delicious twist on an old favorite. Since its portions are so large, Marina Sweets offers a share plan, where for $1 extra two people can split the cost of a wrap and each receive chips and hummus. Marina Sweets also features homemade soups and fresh bread baked daily, as well as specialty coffees, cappuccinos and low-fat frappuncinos. A kids' menu features PB&J, a pita cheese melt and hot dogs, but our Insiders Kid loves Marina Sweets for its yummy offerings of ice cream, sundaes, milk shakes and cookies.

MJ's Raw Bar & Grille **$$**
216 Middle St., New Bern
(252) 635-6890

With its good prices and excellent portions, MJ's Raw Bar & Grille makes a great stop for lunch and dinner. From its early bird specials to its homemade soups and desserts to its famous Maryland crab cakes, MJ's has something to please every palate. Insiders recommend you try the scallop-stuffed mushrooms as an appetizer, but a variety of other options are available too. Enjoy shrimp, oysters, clams, crawfish, scallops and mussels from the raw bar, or feast on a blackened Angus burger, a Portobello mushroom burger or the Southern fried chicken sandwich. Homemade delicacies include the soup of the day and a yummy array of desserts. MJ's also stocks a full-service bar - stop by on Fridays from 4 to 6 PM and enjoy free hot wings - and offers a fine selection of wines with an international flair. MJ's is open daily.

Moore's Olde Tyme Barbecue **$**
3621 Dr. M. L. King Jr. Blvd., New Bern
(252) 638-3937

Since 1945 Moore's has specialized in eastern North Carolina chopped barbecued pork, but it offers more than that. Whether you eat in or take it out, the food at Moore's is good, home-style cooking. A meal of pork or chicken barbecue is served with cole slaw, french fries and hush puppies. There's also a seafood plate with shrimp, flounder and trout. And Moore's serves an honest to goodness shrimpburger. But before you decide what you want, check the specials, including the Kansas City–style ribs on Saturdays. Moore's can cater small, large or huge events or put on a North Carolina–style pig pickin'. It opens for lunch and dinner every day but Sunday.

Mustard's Last Stand **$**
E. Front St., New Bern
(252) 638-1937

Mustard's Last Stand is a movable concession stand that offers the very best in Sabrett hot dogs and Polish sausages on buns. It's the perfect place to stop while on a walking tour of downtown New Bern. Mustard's also serves foot-long hot dogs and jalapeno and cheese dogs, and you can get those served with the works -- chili, mustard, ketchup, sauerkraut and cooked onions. Mustard's also offers drinks, chips and more. The hot dogs are better than those at any ballpark, and you don't have to fight for a parking space. Mustard's two locations are open 10:30 AM until 2:30 PM Monday through Saturday, including its long-time stand on E. Front Street across the street from Union Point Park. Mustard's also operates a hot dog stand in front of Lowe's at 150 Lowe's Boulevard.

Theo's Restaurant **$$**
309 Middle St., New Bern
(252) 636-2667

Tucked away in downtown's historic Kress Building, Theo's serves up Greek and Italian specialties along with All-American favorites like rib-eye steaks and Philly cheesesteak sandwiches for lunch and dinner. Insiders appreciate the high-quality cooking offered at good prices, and the diner atmosphere allows for an casual evening out. Theo's serves mixed drinks, beer and wine along with non-alcoholic drinks like soda and tea. On Thursday, Friday and Saturday night, Theo's features live entertainment.

Trent River Coffee Company **$**
208 Craven St., New Bern
(252) 514-2030

This complete coffee bar and retail coffee shop is the social gathering place for locals on most weekday mornings for endless coffee or hot chocolate and a selection of breakfast breads and pastries. Looking for something a little cooler? Trent River Coffee Company also serves ice cream and milk shakes. On announced evenings, this is the staging place for the Down East FolkArts Society live performances and other performing musicians. Coffee and a world of other things are brewing every day.

Tryon Palace Seafood **$**
520 S. Front St., New Bern
(252) 638-2280

Open Monday through Saturday, Tryon Palace Seafood is a great stop to pick up fresh selections - shrimp, oysters, flounders, scallops and more - to prepare at home. But this South Front Street treasure also offers a small take-out counter where you can pick up tasty shrimp and oyster burgers, soft crab and crab cake sandwiches, fish and chips, and more with sides of fries, slaw and hushpuppies. Lunch and dinner plates and combination platters also are available. Wash down your tasty treat with Snapple beverages or that Carolina staple, sweet ice tea. Insiders are intrigued by the offer of the "frog leg plate," but have yet to give it a try.

NEW BERN NIGHTLIFE

Although it isn't overrun with entertainment spots -- a refreshing factor for a riverfront city -- New Bern offers a nice variety of nightlife. Nighttime entertainment here mainly revolves around smaller gathering places where friends meet to mix and mingle.

New Bern also has an active cultural arts scene. The city is home to three theater organizations. Two of these groups stage a number of performances throughout the year, and there are several performances for children, while the other offers a new Shakespeare presentation every summer. See our New Bern Arts chapter for more information.

As for the wander-in, sit-down-and-enjoy-yourself type of nightlife, New Bern has that to offer too. Not all of New Bern's nightspots are listed here for several reasons -- it may have just opened, was unintentionally overlooked or may not be a place we would recommend to a friend. So although there may be others, the nightspots that follow are among the more popular with Insiders. Some of New Bern's bars are private and require membership fees and a waiting period before the memberships become valid. We have indicated which clubs are private so be sure to call ahead for membership information.

1797 Steamer Bar
Harvey Mansion, 221 S. Front St., New Bern
(252) 635-3232
www.harveymansionhistoricinn.com

This nightclub, which Insiders love for its Cheers-type atmosphere, is located in the cellar of the Harvey Mansion. It features the house's original kitchen fireplace and andirons, as well as a copper-top bar, exposed beams and low ceiling to complete its casual and cozy environment. The bar serves wine, domestic and imported beer and mixed drinks, along with steamed seafood, nachos, chicken wings, sandwiches and other snacks. Live entertainment is offered on occasion.

Captain Ratty's Seafood & Steakhouse
202 Middle St., New Bern
(252) 633-2088

The upstairs bar of Captain Ratty's, open Thursday, Friday and Saturday evenings, is a great place to unwind after work, enjoy a drink and dinner, and listen to free live entertainment. Capt. Ratty's is well-known to Insiders for its great wine selection. On other nights of the week, the upstairs section of Captain Ratty's is available for private parties or seats overflow from the downstairs dining room.

The Chelsea
335 Middle St., New Bern
(252) 637-5469

The Chelsea is a popular downtown gathering place for those interested in min-

According to North Carolina law, a person is legally impaired with a blood-alcohol level of .08 or higher. If you've had your limit, call New Safeway Taxi Service at (252) 636-9000 for a safe ride home. Safeway operates 24 hours a day.

New Bern is known for its historic architecture.

photo: George Mitchell

gling with friends or soon-to-be friends. The bar is in the restaurant area (see our New Bern Restaurants chapter) and serves mixed drinks, beer and wine. The building and the decor are interesting in themselves, with lots of Pepsi memorabilia.

The Ice House
3709 Trent Rd., New Bern
(252) 637-3780

Celebrate with other fans as you watch seasonal sports and NASCAR racing on The Ice House's 52-inch color television. Open seven days a week year round, the club offers snacks, mixed drinks and beer. The Ice House is a private club; call for membership information. The Ice House features darts, pool tables, golf games and pinball machines. Music favorites are available on the jukebox, and Saturday night features karaoke.

MJ's Raw Bar & Grille
216 Middle St., New Bern
(252) 635-6890

Open daily, MJ's offers a full-service bar to go along with its extensive menu of seafood favorites. It also features an extensive wine list with an international flair, including wines from France, Italy, Germany and Australia, as well as several from California and North Carolina. But Insiders love the Friday night special -- free hot wings, chips, salsa and con queso dip at the bar. MJ's is a great place to unwind and relax after work or on an outing with family and friends.

Mr. Stix Billiards
2724 Neuse Blvd., New Bern
252) 638-2299

Practice your shots in a quiet, inviting place where, after warming up, you can always find a challenging game. Bring your own stick, or you can buy or borrow one. The 9-foot regulation tables in the back are rented by the hour; those in the front operate on quarters. Open daily, Mr. Stix is a beer-only club.

Sheraton New Bern
100 Middle St., New Bern
(252) 638-3585

The Sheraton features three different options for nighttime entertainment. The nightclub Grand Escape opens at 9 PM on Fridays and Saturdays. Ladies always get in for free on Friday nights until midnight, and the cover charge is waived for hotel guests. Looking for something a little more on the quiet side? The ProSail is the place to enjoy casual relaxation in a sailor's haven. The club features a long, irregular-shaped bar, comfortable seating and lots of windows overlooking the marina. Live entertainment is offered on most weekends, and there is a large-screen television. The ProSail opens daily at noon. From mid-April until mid-October, the Quarterdeck, located outside the ProSail, hosts the Cool Cabana Deck Party on Friday nights.

Theo's Restaurant
309 Middle St., New Bern
(252) 636-2667

In addition to its tasty Greek and Italian menu, Theo's serves up live entertainment along with beer, wine and mixed drinks on Thursday, Friday and Saturday nights. You'll find Theo's tucked away in the back of the historic Kress Building.

Movie Theaters

Discounts for children and matinees are available at New Bern's movie theaters. For what's showing, call the theaters or check listings in the local newspaper.

Southgate Cinema 6, 2806 Trent Road, New Bern, (252) 638-1820

Neuse Boulevard Cinema, 2500 Neuse Boulevard, New Bern, (252) 633-2438

Liquor Laws and ABC Stores

ABC stores are the only establishments in the state allowed to sell liquor by the bottle. Beer and wine are sold in grocery and convenience stores and in specialty food shops throughout the area. New Bern's two ABC stores are open Monday through Saturday, but the hours vary. No personal checks are accepted, and only those age 21 and older are allowed in the stores.

ABC Store No. 1, 318 S. Front Street, New Bern, (252) 637-3623

ABC Store No. 5, 2003 Glenburnie Road, New Bern (in the same shopping complex as Harris Teeter), (252) 638-4847

NEW BERN HOTELS AND MOTELS

Overnight lodgings in New Bern present a delightful variety of vantages from which visitors may enjoy the town. The river city has several major hotels silhouetting its skyline and a number of excellent bed and breakfast inns. One inn is said to be inhabited by a friendly ghost, but if you're seeking less spiritual digs, you may choose from a nice variety of options. Many visitors choose the advantages of packages that offer discounted rates at lodgings and golf courses or dinner plans and a therapeutic massage.

Hotels positioned along the city's picturesque waterfront offer lovely views of the Trent and Neuse rivers, and a number of economy and budget motels are near the downtown or outlying commercial areas. Cozy and architecturally interesting bed and breakfast inns are sprinkled throughout the historic district (see our New Bern Bed and Breakfast Inns chapter). The alphabetical listing of hotels, motels and condos in this section is not intended to recommend one lodging over another. We feel comfortable recommending all of the accommodations listed in this chapter.

PRICE CODE

Room prices fluctuate with the seasons, but for the purpose of reflecting rate information, we have shown high-season rates for double occupancy. Winter rates may be substantially lower. Rates are subject to change; therefore we urge you to verify rate information when making your reservations. All hotels accept most major credit cards.

$	$59 and less
$$	$60 to $79
$$$	$80 to $124
$$$$	$125 and more

BridgePointe Hotel and Marina **$$**
101 Howell Rd., New Bern
(252) 636-3637, (877) 283-7713

The 116-room BridgePointe Hotel and Marina is just across the Trent River from New Bern's historic downtown area. All guest rooms have a beautiful water view of either the Neuse River or Trent River. Coffee makers, refrigerators, microwaves, irons and ironing boards, data ports and satellite television with four HBO channels are standard in every room. Room choices include a room with one king-size bed, a room with two double beds or a room with a Jacuzzi suite. Guests of the BridgePointe Hotel are allowed to use the amenities available at Courts Plus, located off Glenburnie Road (see our New Bern Recreation and Parks chapter). In season, you also can relax at the BridgePointe Hotel's outdoor pool, and golf packages are available. A restaurant is located on-site, and the Outback Steakhouse is next door.

Comfort Suites Riverfront Park **$$$**
218 E. Front St., New Bern
(252) 636-0022, (800) 517-4000
www.comfortsuitesnewbern.com

Located in New Bern's Historic District, this newly renovated hotel, which won the Comfort Suites of the Year award in 2000, features a Colonial look and a warm, friendly atmosphere. This hotel has been a Gold Hospitality Award winner for eight consecutive years. It has 100 suites, many with waterfront balconies that offer beautiful views of the mile-wide Neuse River and others with views of Union Point Park. All suites are decorated in rich teal and burgundy with traditional-style furnishings and your choice of two double beds or a king-size bed. All are equipped with a refrigerator, microwave, coffee maker, iron and ironing board. Whirlpool suites are also available. Other amenities include free local calls and high-speed Internet access,

CLOSE UP

Historical Hotheads: The Stanly-Spaight Duel of 1802

Article Courtesy of Tryon Palace Historic Sites & Gardens

"Heated argument leads to gunfire and death" – while this information may sound ripped from today's headlines, it in fact occurred over 200 years ago when two New Bern politicians engaged in a heated exchange of letters that ultimately led to a duel. After the smoke cleared late that September afternoon in 1802, Richards Dobbs Spaight was mortally wounded and John Stanly Jr. found himself on the wrong side of the law.

Although they were nearly 20 years apart in age, Spaight and Stanly were both successful politicians who, at one time, were both members of the Federalist Party. Over the course of their political careers, they had represented New Bern in the state General Assembly and North Carolina in the U.S. Congress. Spaight also was the first native born North Carolinian to serve as governor of the state.

The cause for the disagreement started in 1798 when Spaight switched his party allegiance over his opposition to the Alien and Sedition Acts and entered Congress as a Democrat-Republican. Spaight's support of the repeal of the Acts and of Thomas Jefferson's election in 1800 no doubt earned him the enmity of staunch Federalists everywhere. Spaight, who lost his seat in Congress to Stanly in 1800, ran for the State Senate in 1802. Spaight immediately fell into disfavor with Stanly, who actively tried to foil his opponent's campaign. Stanly, known for his stinging political attacks, referred to Spaight as a renegade from the Federalist Party and made disparaging remarks about his alliance with the Republicans.

On August 8, 1802, on a New Bern street corner, Stanly started questioning Spaight's voting record and his Republican convictions. Spaight heard about these remarks and challenged Stanly to a duel. While Stanly argued his way out of the duel temporarily, what ensued was a series of written attacks in the form of let-

an outdoor pool with a waterfront courtyard, a waterfront gazebo, an outdoor heated whirlpool, a fitness center, a guest laundry room, a board room and meeting facilities. Complimentary deluxe continental breakfasts are served each morning, and a complimentary evening guest reception is held nightly Monday through Thursday. The hotel is within walking distance of New Bern's downtown area and historic sites, as well as the New Bern Riverfront Convention Center. Significant discounts on room rates are available, so be sure to ask about the options.

Hampton Inn **$$**
200 Hotel Dr., New Bern.
(252) 637-2111, (800) HAMPTON

Off N.C. Highway 17 at the U.S. Highway 70 bypass, this modern and national award-winning Circle of Excellence 101-room hotel is in a park-like setting among nearby restaurants and shopping. Tastefully furnished like other hotels in its chain, this Hampton Inn offers its guests use of an outdoor pool and whirlpool, complimentary copies of USA Today, meeting facilities, free local calls, phones with data ports, high-speed Internet access, and a choice of rooms with either one king or two double beds. Other comforts offered to Hampton Inn's guests are irons and ironing boards, hair dryers and free deluxe continental breakfasts. Seventy-five percent of the rooms are designated for nonsmoking guests.

Shuttle service to the hospital, airport and convention center is available. Twin Rivers Shopping Mall and lots of other shopping is right in the neighborhood. Golf packages and tour packages of New Bern's historic district, which is about 3 miles from the hotel, can be arranged by the hotel staff, and ters, newspaper publications and handbills circulated around town. Each vitriolic response served to escalate the situation, bringing both men closer to violence. Finally, on Sunday morning, September 5, by way of his friend, Attorney Edward Graham, Stanly issued his own challenge to Spaight for a duel.

The challenge was accepted and two men's "seconds," Edward Graham for Stanly and Dr. Edward Pasteur for Spaight, arranged the duel. It was set for the same day, September 5, 1802, at 5:30 p.m. behind the local Masonic Hall. Duels were frowned upon in 1802, but they were not yet illegal. The duel itself attracted a large number of spectators.

The two men fired a series of four shots at one another. Neither was hit on the first shot, but on the second, Stanly's coat was ripped by Spaight's bullet. Neither was hit on the third shot, but on the fourth shot, Spaight was wounded. He was shot in the side and carried off the field. He died the next day, on September 6, 1802, and was buried outside of New Bern in the family sepulcher at his Clermont estate.

Spaight's influential friends brought a homicide charge against Stanly. Stanly ultimately received a full pardon from Governor Benjamin Williams, absolving him of any responsibility. However, as a result of this public duel between two well-known officials, the North Carolina Assembly passed a law outlawing dueling just two months later on November 5, 1802.

To learn more about this famous duel, be sure to attend the Stanly-Spaight duel re-enactment, held every September on the grounds of the New Bern Academy Museum. Attendance is free. Call (252) 514-4900 for more information.

A re-enactment of the Stanly-Spaight duel is held every September at the New Bern Academy Museum.

Courtesy of Tryon Palace Historic Sites & Gardens

guests receive complimentary use of Gold's Gym and reduced rates at the nearby YMCA (see our New Bern Recreation and Parks chapter). Hampton Inn hosts a complimentary reception for guests on Tuesdays, serving pizza, subs, beer and wine. Room service is offered Tuesday through Friday nights. The hotel has a special plan in which third and fourth adults stay free in one room. Children younger than age 18 stay free with their parents.

Holiday Inn Express $$
U.S. Hwy. 17 S. at Glenburnie Rd., New Bern
(252) 638-8266

New Bern's Holiday Inn Express offers the comfortable standards of Holiday Inn at a no-frills price for the absence of such amenities as an on-site restaurant. However, the motel is in an area with bountiful restaurant options, and it offers guests a morning breakfast bar, a pool and a fitness room. All guest rooms have two double beds. The Holiday Inn Express is within easy access from U.S. 70 at the U.S. 17 S. exit, on Dr. M. L. King Jr. Boulevard, where there are also numerous shopping opportunities. Transportation is necessary to see New Bern's attractions.

Sheraton New Bern Hotel and Marina $$$
100 Middle St., New Bern
(252) 638-3585, (800) 326-3745

One of the attractions of this downtown hotel is that all 99 guest rooms overlook the Trent River and the hotel's marina. An additional inn has 72 guest rooms, suites and mini-suites in the style of grand Southern inns. The inn is attached to the hotel via a covered walkway and offers both waterfront and city-side views. The inn has an executive level made up entirely of suites. Hotel rooms have either one king-size or two double beds, and fifth-floor rooms also feature balconies. Dogs are allowed in certain rooms; be sure to call ahead for details if you are interested in bringing your "best friend" along.

To serve the hotel and inn, a restaurant and three lounges offer opportunities for dining and relaxing. Of these, Insiders recommend the inviting, quiet atmosphere of Latitude 35, which overlooks the marina and features full breakfast, lunch and dinner menus spotlighting the chef's signature entrees. A dance club features live entertainment on Friday and Saturday evenings, while The Pro Sail Lounge is a great place for a relaxed day's end. The Quarterdeck Gazebo & Bar extends the night under the stars with seasonal outdoor entertainment on Fridays.

The Sheraton has ample meeting facilities, a swimming pool and an exercise room. Golf and tennis privileges at area clubs can be included in your stay. Group rate packages and senior discounts are available.

Vacation Resorts International $$$
1141 Broad Creek Rd., New Bern
(252) 633-1151

A professional management company since 1964, Vacation Resorts International manages properties in the Fairfield Harbour community, offering fully furnished one- to three-bedroom condominiums on a daily or weekly basis. The price code shown is based on four people sharing a two-bedroom unit during the summer. All units at Fairfield Harbour will accommodate six to eight people, and guests are extended all development amenities, including the country club's three swimming pools and two golf courses. For rentals on a daily basis, a minimum of two days is required; for holiday weekends, a minimum of three days is required.

NEW BERN BED AND BREAKFAST INNS

New Bern's history as the first Colonial capital of the Carolinas is brought to life by a stay in one of the town's historic bed and breakfast inns. The knowledge and hospitality of your hosts will offer you an instant familiarization with New Bern, and the comforts and decor of each room in each house make for a relaxing getaway in the context of a very interesting town. Add to that the option of antiques shopping, mystery weekends, or fine dining and pampering, and choosing among the bed and breakfast accommodations in New Bern is an enviable task.

When you reserve, ask the innkeepers about anything that may concern you, such as smoking, handicapped accessibility or pets. Also ask about the inn's credit card, reservation and cancellation policies. The inns listed here accept credit cards unless noted otherwise.

PRICE CODE

The codes indicated here reflect an average price for a night's stay for two people. Each inn's amenities vary, depending on the rooms, suite of rooms or packages offered. Be sure to ask what your price includes.

$	Less than $85
$$	$85 to $100
$$$	$101 to $140
$$$$	More than $140

The Aerie Bed & Breakfast **$$–$$$**
509 Pollock St., New Bern
(252) 636-5553, (800) 849-5553
www.aerieinn.com

Experience the warmth and charm of historic New Bern by day and relax in comfort at night in The Aerie, an 1880s Victorian bed and breakfast located just one block from Tryon Palace. The Aerie features period furnishings in seven gracious guest rooms with private baths. All rooms feature a private bath, TV/VCR, CD player and free high-speed Internet access. A full breakfast, with your choice of three entrees, and evening refreshments are offered daily. Whether you are in New Bern on business or for pleasure, your stay at The Aerie will be one surrounded with personal attention, an experience you will want to repeat. The Aerie has a AAA 3-Diamond rating and is a Condé Nast recommended property. It also was voted "Simply the Best Bed & Breakfast" for 2004 by readers of the local newspaper. Innkeepers Michael and Marty Gunhus invite you to come home and experience the quintessence of charm that is The Aerie.

FoxBern Manor Bed & Breakfast **$$-$$$**
935 Rollover Creek Rd., New Bern
(252) 635-6697
www.foxbernmanor.com

Located in a quiet country setting, but conveniently close to downtown historic New Bern, FoxBern Manor Bed & Breakfast features two luxury suites beautifully appointed with antiques, local art, lovely linens and more. An East Wing two-bedroom suite accommodates family travelers with its dining area and center bathroom. The West Wing one-bedroom suite features a queen-size canopy bed, a sitting/dining area and a beautiful Victorian bathroom with a champagne slipper tub. Hosts Linda and Kevin McBride offer sumptuous breakfasts (served either in your suite or the Summer Room), afternoon tea and evening refreshments. Children older than 12 are welcome at the FoxBern Manor Bed & Breakfast.

Hanna House Bed & Breakfast **$**
218 Pollock St., New Bern
(252) 635-3209, (866) 830-4371
www.hannahousenc.net

Located in the Rudolph Ulrich house (c. 1896) in New Bern's historic district and listed on the state Register of Historic Places, the Hanna House's three guest rooms are tastefully furnished in period antiques and each has its own private bath, one with a Jacuzzi. Guests are given a menu with breakfast options upon checking in, and they wake up to the smell of freshly brewed coffee and baked breads and muffins. Special spa packages are available through Dun'Artie Salon & Day Spa. The Hanna House is conveniently located within walking distance of many of New Bern's attractions. Hosts Camille and Joe Klotz are dedicated to making your stay a comfortable one.

The Harmony House Inn **$$-$$$**
215 Pollock St., New Bern
(252) 636-3810, (800) 636-3113
www.harmonyhouseinn.com

The rocking chairs and swing on the long front porch and the two front doors (you'll see what we mean) distinguish this Greek Revival-style bed and breakfast in the downtown historic district. The original part of the house was built sometime before 1809, and additions and porches have been added. Around 1900, the house was sawed in half, and the west side was moved nine feet to accommodate a new hallway and staircase. The inn now has seven guest rooms and three romantic suites, all furnished with antiques and homemade crafts. Two of the suites have heart-shaped Jacuzzis, and all rooms have private baths and decorative fireplaces. A full breakfast -- which may include house specialties such as stuffed French toast with homemade blueberry maple syrup, cheese strata, potato, bacon and cheese casserole, and homemade coffeecake -- is served each morning in the dining room. Another Harmony House specialty is the Toffee Bar Coffeecake, which was featured in the December

1999 issue of Bon Appetit. Owners Ed and Sooki Kirkpatrick host a social hour each evening, offering wine and cheese or other hors d'oeuvres. Before bed, a glass of sherry or port is available.

Harvey Mansion Historic Inn **$$$**
221 S. Front St., New Bern
(252) 635-3232
www.harveymansionhistoricinn.com

The Harvey Mansion Historic Inn & Restaurant offers three great locations in one beautiful setting: a classy restaurant, an elegant bed-and-breakfast and a fun nightclub. The 9,000-square-foot house, built from 1797 to 1804, is the last remaining structure fronting the Trent River from New Bern's time period as a thriving colonial seaport. The inn features three guest rooms with king or queen accommodations available. The inn has several private bathrooms -- one includes a Jacuzzi bath and shower combination. All rooms share a common living area with a balcony that overlooks Union Point Park and the Neuse and Trent rivers. Rooms also have telephones and dataports should you wish to stay in touch with the modern world while feeling so comfortably away from it.

Howard House Victorian Bed & Breakfast **$$-$$$**
207 Pollock St., New Bern
(252) 514-6709, (800) 705-5261

Howard House, a restored Victorian in the heart of the downtown historic district, was built between 1888 and 1893 and reflects the detailed craftsmanship of the period. Owners and hosts Steven and Kimberly Wynn offer six lovely guest rooms, each with a private bath. The house features a five-sided turret that encloses an upstairs guest room with a river view and an oversized antique double bed. Other guest rooms are beautifully furnished in period antiques; one has an antique sleigh bed, another, a queen-size four-poster bed. Guests are pampered with special touches, such as desserts every evening and freshly baked cookies just about any time. Attention to special occasions like birthdays and anniversaries is easy to arrange; simply ask your hosts. Bicycles are available for seeing the town, and complimentary airport transportation is provided. A full and scrumptious breakfast served each morning may include apple-pecan pancakes, Canadian bacon, homemade breads, muffins and fresh ground coffee, teas and juice.

Meadows Inn **$-$$**
212 Pollock St., New Bern
(252) 634-1776, (877) 551-1776

The home of the Meadows Inn, the first bed and breakfast in New Bern, was a private residence until 1980. The ca. 1847 structure is named for its original owner, New Bern merchant John Alexander Meadows. Meadows Inn has seven guest rooms, each with a television, VCR, private bath and antique and reproduction furniture. The third floor, two-bedroom suite is perfect for families traveling together, as children are always welcome at Meadows Inn. Phones are available in each room, and local calls are free. WIFI Wireless Internet access also is available at no charge. A full breakfast is served every morning in the breakfast room, including hot entrees, fruits, breads and choice of coffee or tea. Complimentary soft drinks and tea are always on hand. Romantic getaways, business meetings, destination weddings, family reunions, small group retreats and conferences at the nearby New Bern Riverfront Convention Center are but a few of the ways to stay at Meadows Inn and experience hospitality with history.

New Berne House Inn **$$**
709 Broad St., New Bern
(252) 636-2250, (866) 782-8358

This Colonial Revival–style bed and breakfast, located about a block from Tryon Palace, dishes up "Sweet Revenge" several times each month with its popular mystery weekend, full of intrigue and wonderful food at one price per couple. But staying here any time can be a real treat. All seven guest rooms are air-conditioned and have private baths. Rooms accommodate two people and are furnished with twin, queen or king beds (one even features the "notorious" brass bed said to have been rescued from a burning brothel in 1897). Guests always have access to the house library. Host Barbara Pappas serves refreshments and beverages and treats her guests to full, home-cooked breakfasts served on her collection of vintage dishes, featuring many distinctive and striking patterns.

NEW BERN CAMPING

If you enjoy communing with nature, you're in for a treat when camping in the New Bern area. Nature enthusiasts can rough it at Croatan National Forest campsites that are off the beaten path. If you prefer modern camping comforts, you'll find commercial campgrounds that provide a number of services.

The Croatan National Forest allows primitive camping anywhere except picnic areas and parking lots. Reservations are not accepted for any recreation area in the Croatan. The camping facilities in the Croatan National Forest can accommodate any size recreational vehicle. The forest has several camping areas with various kinds of facilities. For detailed camping information, call the district ranger's office, (252) 638-5628, or stop in and pick up maps at the Ranger Office, 141 E. Fisher Avenue, 9 miles south of New Bern off U.S. Highway 70 E. Office hours are 8 AM to 4:30 PM Monday through Friday. A map machine is available outside the office 24 hours a day. For a complete description of this magnificent forest, see our Crystal Coast Attractions chapter.

Moonlight Lake RV Park
180 Moonlight Lake Dr., New Bern
(252) 745-9800

Located within 10 minutes of historic downtown New Bern, Moonlight Lake RV Park is one of the area's newest parks. Moonlight Lake currently has 31 lots; future plans call for it to expand to 60 lots. Amenities include lots with 50/30 amp electrical hook-ups, water and sewer service, garbage disposal, a playground, horse shoes, picnic tables and laundry facilities. Rates for sites with 30 amp electric service are $20 daily, $100 weekly and $300 monthly; 50 amp service rates are $25 daily, $125 weekly and $375 monthly. Cable TV and phone service are available at an extra charge.

New Bern KOA
1565 B St.,
5 miles north of New Bern on U.S. Hwy. 17
(252) 638-2556, (800) 562-3341
www.newbernkoa.com

Formerly known as the Neuse River Campground, the full-service, riverfront New Bern KOA has been completely remodeled and features a number of attractive amenities, particularly for those campers who are used to the high standards KOA sets for its campgrounds.

Shaded full and partial hook-ups for RVs and tents are available on the Neuse River, as are one- and two-bedroom Kamping Kabins and lodges, which take the rough out of roughing it with heat, air conditioning and beds with soft mattresses. Other amenities include clean restrooms and hot showers, a swimming pool, laundry facilities, a full-service camp store, propane, cable, a playground, a game room, storage, and broadband and wireless Internet access. Pets also are welcome at KOA and will enjoy their very own Bark Park. The campground recently added its own pier with 10 boat slips and a ramp. Fishing and crabbing from the pier while the sun sets over the river is always a nice way to end the day. KOA offers value season, adventure season and holiday rates.

i

The Croatan National Forest is home to a rare combination of five insectivorous plants: pitcher plants, sundews, butterworts, Venus flytraps, and bladderworts. These plants trap and eat insects, a source of nitrogen which in turn allows these plants to thrive in poor soils. These plants also thrive where controlled burns release nutrients, remove competition, and open their sites to sunlight. It is against the law to remove any of these plants from the Croatan National Forest.

Because fire normally plays a big role in the forest ecosystem, Forest managers use controlled burns, at the right time of the year and under certain weather conditions, to maintain a natural balance. For example, controlled burns help maintain the habitat of the endangered red-cockaded woodpecker in mature longleaf pines, and remove competing vegetation to ensure the survival of some of the forest's more unusual plants, such as the Venus flytrap.

Weekly and monthly rates also are available. Children younger than age 12 camp free when accompanied by an adult. Reservations can be made using Visa, Mastercard and American Express.

Fishers Landing
Croatan National Forest, U.S. Hwy. 70 E., Riverdale
(252) 638-5628

Perched on a bluff above the Neuse River about 8 miles south of New Bern, Fishers Landing is found by turning left across U.S. 70 E. at the Riverdale Mini-Mart. This recreation area offers only the barest of amenities, but what it lacks in creature comforts is more than compensated for by the chance to be among nature's creatures. Take an early morning walk along the crescent-shaped sandy beach, accessible by wooden stairs set into the cliff, and you'll see ospreys, egrets, sea gulls and herons. Between the small parking lot and the bluff is a wide, grassy area backed by a row of trees. You can swim in the Neuse River here, but we suggest wearing shoes for protection against the rocks and tree stumps on the river bottom. The wheelchair-accessible site offers unimproved walk-in tent camping and picnicking, non-flush toilets, grills and drinking water. Fishers Landing is open year round.

Neuse River (Flanners Beach) Recreation Area
Croatan National Forest, U.S. Hwy. 70 E., New Bern
(252) 638-5628

Locals call this area Flanners Beach. Open March through November, it is 10 miles south of New Bern off U.S. 70 along the Neuse River. The site has 45 units (14 with electrical service), flush toilets, warm showers, drinking water and a dump station. A nightly fee of $12 is charged for campsites; it's $17 for sites with electrical hook-ups. Day-trippers can enjoy the area's free public facilities, including a swimming area, toilets, cold showers and a picnic spot with 44 tables and drinking fountains. Visitors also will enjoy the 3-mile hiking/biking trail. A 1-mile loop of the trail goes around the campground and is paved for easy handicapped access. Flanners Beach is closed from December 1 through March 1.

NEW BERN SHOPPING

New Bern offers many shopping opportunities, from large department stores to specialty shops and boutiques. Scattered among the streets in New Bern's Historic Downtown, you'll discover a distinctive selection of shops that make anyone's must-shop list. For a pleasant meander, stroll along Middle, Pollock, Hancock, Craven and South Front streets. We've highlighted a few of the shops you'll find along the way and a few others around New Bern. These shops are certainly not the totality of the New Bern shopping experience, but they'll whet your spending appetite. Because shops can -- and do -- change their hours to accommodate the needs of their customers, and because many have seasonal hours, you should call ahead to check what days and hours they are open. Antiques shops are featured at the end of this chapter. And don't forget to also check out our listing of art galleries in the New Bern Arts chapter.

The Downtown New Bern map (at the front of this book) shows the four free public parking lots in historic downtown. New Bern imposes a two-hour parking limit, and public employees are always on the move checking for time-limit violators.

Downtown New Bern

Fraser's Wine, Cheese, Chocolate and More
210 Middle St., New Bern
(252) 634-2580

Fraser's is an extraordinary shop that features, much as its name implies, wine, cheese, chocolate and more, including specialty foods and imported and domestic beer. Also available are whimsical yet classy wine accessories, home decor items and Fraser's Fantasy Bags.

Art of the Wild
218 Middle St., New Bern
(252) 638-8806

Claudia Lindsey's Art of the Wild is a magical mix of local and imported art objects. The artwork is predominantly birds and animals in the wild, sculpted and carved in wood, marble resin, water buffalo horns, driftwood and tree roots. You'll find the carvings of the late Jeth Lindsey as well as the work of his sons, Arden and Vol, and other local artists. Art of the Wild sells framed and unframed prints, jewelry and decorative wall objects.

Middle Street Landing
225 Middle St., New Bern
(252) 514-0000

Middle Street Landing is a delightful mix of old and new. Antique glassware, furniture and framed art are pleasantly spread throughout this attractive shop. It features a grand selection of handbags, luggage, tabletop accessories and stationery by Vera Bradley. Insiders love the unique jewelry in sterling, gold and gemstones, including Heartstrings engraved jewelry and creations by Betsy Gay Hart. Middle Street Landing also invites shopper to pamper themselves with bath and fragrances from Crabtree & Evelyn, Lady Primrose, The Thymes and Archipelago, and Cozy Chic robes and throws by Barefoot Dreams. Other great products featured are Physician Endorsed hats and

i

If you did lots of shopping during your visit to New Bern but have little room in your suitcase or vehicle to haul home all the goodies, consider a stop by The UPS Store, 1822 S. Glenburnie Rd., (252) 637-7500. Owners Mack Paul and Pat Drake and their staff will be happy to pack and ship your items to make sure they safely reach their destination.

CLOSE UP

The Bears of Bear Plaza

The showpieces of Bear Plaza, located on Middle Street between South Front and Pollock Streets, are its towering wooden black bear sculptures. If you think the bears look a little different, you're right: They were replaced in spring 2000. Have you ever wondered how the bears got there in the first place?

The black bear is the symbol of the City of New Bern, and the bears of Bear Plaza are a nod to the city's heritage. Woodcarver Tom Penney carved the original bears for a business in Pamlico County. When that business went under before the bears were delivered, Penney offered to sell them to the city. It was the spring of 1994.

"Once we saw them, we had to have them," said Susan Moffat-Thomas, executive director of the downtown revitalization group Swiss Bear. "They were perfect for Bear Plaza, which was basically empty at the time."

A fund-raising campaign to buy the bears didn't take long. By November of that year, Swiss Bear had raised the necessary funds, even a bit extra for the plaza's lights. Local people contributed to the effort to bring the bears to Bear Plaza, the majority of them contributing in the names of their grandchildren, whose names are memorialized on a plaque located in the plaza. Since New Bern is a retirees' haven, the majority of the children listed on the plaque do not live in New Bern. It's a special treat when they come to town to visit their grandparents and see their name on the Plaza wall.

Unfortunately, it didn't take long for the bears to fall victim to termites. The late Jeth Lindsey of Art of the Wild did his best to save the bears, but despite his constant patching and valiant efforts, the bears continued to deteriorate.

By spring 1998, the truth was apparent: No amount of patching could fix the damage caused by termites, and the bears would need to be replaced. And in September 1999, one of the bears toppled, either due to gusting winds or vandalism. When a Mumfest trivia contest asked the question, "What animals live in the downtown plaza?" no one was surprised to see, and contest organizers were amused by, such answers as "wooden bears and termites."

The bear is the official mascot of New Bern

Photo: Janis Williams

By the time that bear toppled, however, Swiss Bear had received the necessary funds from the Municipal Service District Advisory Committee (a group of downtown property owners) to replace the bears. Swiss Bear tracked down Penney, now a resident of Myrtle Beach, South Carolina.

"We really like his work and wanted him to do the very same bears," Moffat-Thomas said.

In October 1999, Penney returned to New Bern and carved the biggest of the new bears during Mumfest. He later completed the other two. The new bears, carved from cypress and thoroughly pretreated to prevent termite damage, were placed on Bear Plaza in spring 2000. The new bears are so life-like, you almost expect Goldilocks to scamper through at any moment.

sunglasses; Mycra Pac coats; greeting cards, bridge sets, candles, gift wrap and napkins by Caspari; and Christmas collectibles include Christopher Radko, Old World Ornaments, Dept 56, Possible Dreams and Byers' Choice. Custom gift baskets also are available. Middle Street Landing is open Monday through Saturday.

Treasures on the Trent
250 Middle St., New Bern
(252) 637-7900

Treasures on the Trent specializes in gifts for the hard-to-please, and now it's bigger and better than ever with its recent move to the old Great Rooms location. You'll always find something unique, whether you are looking for a goodie for the golf enthusiast, a distinctive present to celebrate a wedding or housewarming, or a special gift for the new baby in the family. Decorative glass, leather jewelry cases, fine jewelry and sterling silver, artwork and more are but a few of the items you'll enjoy browsing through with a stop at Treasures on the Trent. A bridal and gift registry service also is available.

Four C's (Coastal Casual Clothing Co.)
252 Middle St., New Bern
252) 636-3285

Open seven days a week, Four C's is an adventure in itself. You'll find a mix of gifts and sportswear for men and women, plus camping gear, travel accessories and equestrian supplies. The shop carries a nice variety of active wear made by Columbia, Woolrich, Atlantis and other well-known brands. For your feet, choose trendy sandals by Teva and Naot, clogs by Dansko, athletic shoes and hiking boots. Besides all this, you can buy hats, books, toys and jewelry – great gifts for all ages. Four C's even throws in the gift wrapping for free.

The Birthplace of Pepsi Cola
256 Middle St., New Bern
(252) 636-5898

Come see where this popular soft drink got its start and enjoy an ice-cold Pepsi at the reproduction of pharmacist Caleb Bradham's soda fountain. Bradham invented what was first known as "Brad's Drink" in 1898. A gift shop offers a plethora of Pepsi merchandise, everything from bags, books and bears to shirts, toy trucks and limited-edition collectibles.

Bear Essentials
309 Middle St., New Bern
(252) 637-6663

Pamper yourself at Bear Essentials, which offers an attractive and useful array of organic and natural personal-care products including soaps, lotions, cosmetics, balms and more. This Insider was particularly drawn to apricot soap that includes honey in every bar – it not only smells good but makes skin feel silky smooth. Located in downtown's Kress Building, Bear Essentials also features a cute selection of baby clothing made from all natural cotton and a line of women's clothing made from hemp. Custom gift baskets also can be created from your selections

Fun Essentials
309 Middle St., New Bern
(252) 635-6640

Those looking for unusual items to make a one-of-a-kind statement are never disappointed at Fun Essentials, a short stroll from the waterfront in downtown New Bern's Kress Building. Shoppers will enjoy the great selection of jewelry, handbags and everything needed – from "FUNctional to FUNkadelic" – to entertain in style. Insiders particularly enjoy the selection of beaded, feathered and sequined handbags. Fun Essentials features a wide variety of distinctive and humorous items to decorate the home, and it's a great place to find just the right gift with the right dose of attitude.

Rosemary St. Clair Originals
"The Red House" at 711-B Pollock St., New Bern
(252) 636-3589

Rosemary St. Clair Originals, which offers a truly unique shopping experience, has moved to a new location – "The Red House" just down the street from Tryon Palace. Rosemary creates hand-painted, appliqued, quilted and embroidered clothing for regular and plus -size figures. Many of these Art-to-Wear clothing items and purses are one-of-a kind collectables. You've got to see A Weekend in the Sack – a mix-and-match travel set that makes up to 48 outfits, all from one little sack and each individualized to meet your travel needs. Rosemary also features hand-painted T-shirts, patchwork vests and quilted jackets, along with a wonderful line of costume and handmade jewelry. Gift certificates and free gift wrapping are available, and layaways and special orders are always welcome.

Tryon Palace Museum Store/Craft and Garden Shop
610 Pollock St., New Bern
(252) 514-4932 Museum Store,
(252) 514-4927 Garden Shop

Tryon Palace has two shops, one featuring New Bern and Colonial memorabilia and gift items, and the other devoted to garden things and local crafts. The museum shop, on the corner of Pollock and Eden streets, facing Eden, carries distinctive jewelry; fine home-decor items in glass, paper, porcelain, silver and other materials; books on the history of New Bern, Craven County, North Carolina, the South and decorative arts; and much more. The garden shop features a selection of heirloom plants, crafts, books and tasty sauces and jellies. Both shops offer a wonderful selection of souvenirs for children. If you are not buying a general admission ticket to tour Tryon Palace and its gardens, you'll need to pick up a pass at the Visitors Center or the museum shop in order to get to the garden shop because it is located inside the gate on palace grounds. Both shops are open daily.

Carolina Creations
317-A Pollock St., New Bern
(252) 633-4369
www.carolinacreations.com

Carolina Creations is an art, craft and gift gallery par excellence. Many potters, glass blowers, woodworkers and jewelers are represented, and the result is a broad selection of practical and decorative art for the home, including works by resident potter Michael Francoeur and others. Stop and see the local art – Carolina Creations features a unique collection of original art, prints and note cards by local artists, as well beautiful paintings and delightful pen-and-ink drawings by resident artist Janet Francoeur. Free gift wrapping, layaway plans and a bridal registry are offered.

Branch's
309 Pollock St., New Bern
(252) 638-5171

For more than 50 years, Branch's has offered New Bernians a unique shopping experience. A third-generation, family-owned business, Branch's now focuses on providing quality furniture for the home and office, accessories, prints, mirrors, lamps and more in over 200 product lines. Branch's features fine gift items such as Howard Miller clocks, Gibson photo albums, scrapbooks, address and guest books, Michael Healy doorbell covers and doorknockers, and Yankee candles.

Mitchell Hardware - Since 1898
215 Craven St., New Bern
(252) 638-4261

This is a place you have to experience. The window display is like a historic showing of farm and garden equipment. Step inside to find an eclectic offering of traditional hardware items in a turn-of-the-century setting. Mitchell's carries a complete line of hardware, garden and yard equipment, practical gifts, cast-iron and enamelware, and garden seeds. There is also a large country store section with everything from country hams to crockery and pottery. But Mitchell's, which has been in business for more than 100 years, is an honest-to-gosh, no-nonsense hardware store that opens at 6:30 AM Monday through Saturday. It's the place Insiders depend on to get those difficult-to-find items they remember from Grandma's kitchen and Grandpa's tool shed.

Farmer's Market
421 S. Front St., New Bern
(252) 633-0043

This terrific market, housed in a large, airy building, is the place to go for fresh vegetables and fruits, seafood, flowers and crafts. On any given weekend, you also might find jams, jellies, pickles, preserves and vinegars, along with home-baked cakes, breads and pastries. It runs March through December on Saturdays from 7 AM to 1 PM. A word to the wise: Go early when the market first opens, before all the good stuff is gone. Entertainment and demonstrations are also featured on selected weekends.

Around New Bern

Outside of the historic district, New Bern has several shopping centers and one mall. The stores we mention in this chapter are by no means all there is to New Bern shopping; we've chosen ones throughout the area to give you an idea of what's available.

As you bear west on U.S. Highway 70, the second exit after the Historic District is the U.S. Highway 17 exit. In New Bern, U.S. 17 is named Dr. M. L. King Jr. Boulevard. Many stores and shopping centers are found on King Boulevard, which runs north to south. Twin Rivers Mall is on King, at the end of the U.S. 17 exit from U.S. 70. Anchor stores Belk and JCPenney have outside entrances. Inside, shoppers have access to about 30 stores, ranging from a video arcade, electronics boutique and pizzeria to jewelry shops and shoe stores. Across King Boulevard from Twin Rivers Mall is Rivertowne Square, anchored by Books-A-Million, Goody's Family Clothing and Wal-Mart. Continue south along King Boulevard to the intersection of McCarthy Boulevard, and you'll find Staples, Target and New River Pottery.

Bill's Pet Shop
2636 Dr. M.L. King Jr. Blvd., New Bern
(252) 637-3997

Pet lovers will enjoy this shop at Berne Square Shopping Center. It's worth a stop just to see the adorable puppies and kittens on display. There are plenty of other pets available as well, including birds, ferrets, some reptiles and a wide variety of fish. This full-service, one-stop shop carries food, treats, pet-care products, toys, leashes, crates, medications and everything else you'll need to care for your best friend. Bill's features a complete tropical and saltwater aquarium section with a professional staff ready to guide you in the proper set up and care of your tanks. There are sister stores in Havelock and Morehead City.

Books-A-Million
Rivertowne Square,
Dr. M. L. King Jr. Blvd., New Bern
(252) 635-6963

Books-A-Million (a chain store with locations in the South and West) offers every genre of book you can think of (at discounted prices), a large number of magazines and newspapers and an impressive children's book section. Kids also can enjoy a free movie every Friday night as well as reading activities scheduled throughout the week for various age groups. The newly remodeled Rivertowne Square store is huge, attractive and hard to leave. Customers are encouraged to relax in the comfy chairs and linger over the books or join friends in the store's coffee shop, Joe Muggs, which features espresso, pastries and more. Members of the Millionaire's Club -- membership is open to anyone -- entitles you to a 10 percent discount on everything in the store, even sale items.

Hearne's Jewelers
Rivertowne Square,
Dr. M. L. King Jr. Blvd., New Bern
(252) 637-4590

Hearne's offers quality men's and women's jewelry and is a trusted, well-established company. Founded in 1972 by Mickey Hearne and now run by his son Mike, the business combines courtesy with integrity. Hearne's offers exquisite rings, earrings, necklaces and bracelets as well as a fine line of watches, including those made by Seiko and Citizen. This is also the place to go for jewelry and watch repair and to have stones mounted.

Party Suppliers
2025 S. Glenburnie Rd., New Bern
(252) 637-7722

Make your next occasion a memorable one with a stop at Party Suppliers. While a couple of aisles are always devoted to upcoming holidays (and you definitely won't want to miss stopping by here at Halloween and Christmas), Party Suppliers always offers the latest trends, designs and colors in invitations, decorations, table settings, party favors, banners and more. Birthday party themes range from Scooby Doo and Clifford the Big Red Dog (for the younger set) right on up to the Aged to Perfection and Over the Hill collections (for the young at heart).

Cooks & Connoisseurs
1907 S. Glenburnie Rd., New Bern
(252) 633-2665

This wonderful specialty food store carries gourmet and international foods from around the world. A variety of coffees and cheeses, necessary cooking tools and gadgets, and an extensive selection of wines are for sale. You'll also find impressive glassware and gourmet cookware. Cooks & Connoisseurs prepares gift baskets. Cooking classes are available; call for a current schedule.

Sewing Solutions
Market Place Square,
1505 S. Glenburnie Rd., New Bern
(252) 633-1799

This shop, owned by Debbie Woods-Tyer, doubles as a display room for her many projects. Decorative embroidery work, home crafts and decorations and quilt squares are among the many creations you can see. Debbie offers Pfaff sewing machines, sergers and embroidery machines, as well as a wide variety of sewing notions, patterns, quilting supplies and books on sewing and quilting. Debbie also teaches sewing classes for all levels and produces a free quarterly newsletter with new product listings, sewing tips and class schedules. Sewing Solutions also has a great selection of those hard-to-find vacuum cleaner bags and belts.

New Bern Fabric Center
1218 S. Glenburnie Rd., New Bern
(252) 633-4780

New Bern Fabric Center offers a large selection of reasonably priced fabric, notions and supplies for quilting, smocking, heirloom and embroidery projects. New Bern Fabric Center also carries a full line of Bernina machines, products and accessories. Clubs devoted to utilizing the machines to their full potential meet on a monthly basis. Classes also are offered for adults and children; call the store for a complete schedule.

Flythe's Bike Shop
2411 Trent Rd., New Bern
(252) 638-1544

Why buy a bike in a box and endure the frustration of putting it together when Flythe's can offer you a quality bike already assembled? Insiders like this place because of the selection of bikes and recumbents available for adults and kids. You'll also find scooters, baby bike seats, baby joggers and strollers, bike trailers and more. If you just need a bike while you're in town for a visit, Flythe's also has bike rentals (a credit card is required for rentals), including free pickup and delivery. Flythe's also is a complete repair shop, and you just can't beat the friendly customer service. Layaway and gift certificates are available.

Antiques

New Bern offers plenty of antiques shops to nose around in and discover lost treasures. Although for several years New Bern's wonderful antique shops tended to cluster in the downtown area, over the past few years old favorites have relocated and new ones have popped up all over town. We've included a few of our favorites to get you started. If you're interested in antiques shows, the New Bern Preservation Foundation, (252) 633-6448, hosts an antiques fair showcasing invited dealers every February.

Andrea's Attic Antiques
2104 B Trent Blvd., New Bern
(252) 63-2255

Andrea's Attic Antiques offers a fine and wide selection of antiques and collectibles, so much we'd be hard-pressed to even begin to list all the great things shoppers can find here. Insiders particularly love to browse the incredible selection of antique and vintage jewelry, although collectors who specialize in a niche will want to explore the cut glass, hats, dishes, cookie jars, books, art and prints, Pepsi and Coke items, and even more on display. Andrea's is open Monday through Saturday.

Jane Sugg Antiques
228 Middle St., New Bern
(252) 637-6985

Here you will find high-quality period and reproduction furniture, lamps, crystal and rugs. Jane Sugg also features some exquisite sterling tea sets and flatware.

Middle Street Antiques & Flea Market
221 Middle St., New Bern
(252) 633-4876

Insiders love the selection of antique and reproduction stained glass available at Middle Street Antiques. Hanging in the front window of the shop, these pieces of art frame an enticing invitation to come in and browse the antique and reproduction furniture, dishes, toys, books and more that are arrayed in ever-changing displays. Open daily, Middle Street Antiques is a must-see for those interested in old-time collectibles.

Tom's Coins and Antiques
244 Middle St., New Bern
(252) 633-0615

As the name implies, this shop sells coins and all manner of antiques. The shop has beautiful antique and reproduction furniture, estate jewelry, crystal, china, stamps and sports cards. There are lots of nostalgic items and collectibles. Owner Tom Faulkenberry is an appraiser and auctioneer.

Seaport Antiques
504 S. Front St., New Bern
(252) 637-5050

This market is a multi-dealer shop specializing in quality antiques and collectibles, including china, furniture, chandeliers, art, jewelry and more, at very reasonable prices. Insiders find Seaport Antiques is a great place to browse and look at all the treasures.

Poor Charlie's Flea Market and Antiques
208 Hancock St., across from Farmer's Market, New Bern
(252) 672-0208

Poor Charlie's dealers offer just about everything a nostalgia buff could want. The old warehouse that houses the dealers suggests long-ago places; it's complete with a dimly lit interior and that alluring smell of old, stored-in-the-attic stuff. Patrons will find antiques, collectibles, home accessories, heirloom jewelry, furniture and household items.

Habitat for Humanity Resale Store
930 Pollock St., New Bern
(252) 633-5512

While the Habitat for Humanity Resale Store is not an antiques store, it's one of those cool shops that offers a lot of "stuff" you can't find anywhere else. The store regularly features an assortment of quality furniture, tested appliances, household furnishings and fixtures, office equipment and building materials. The Resale Store is a terrific place to visit when you are remodeling, furnishing a college dorm room, or looking for that special accent piece for your home. Twice a year, the store also features fantastic Progressive Clearance Sales, where merchandise is progressively marked down 35 to 50 to 65 percent off in order to clear the floor for new items. The Resale Store supports the mission of Habitat for Humanity of Greater New Bern: to provide safe, decent housing for all families in New Bern and around the world. The store is open Monday through Saturday.

Gardeners who visit Tryon Palace during the Historic Homes and Gardens tour in the spring or MUMfest in the fall will enjoy shopping for plants and herbs sold at the Heritage Plant Sale.

J L Kirkman's Antique Flea Mall
1198 U.S. Hwy. 17 N., Bridgeton
(252) 634-2745

JL Kirkman's is located across the Neuse River Bridge just five minutes from downtown New Bern. JL Kirkman's, just right off the highway in Bridgeton in the old Eagle Supermarket building, prides itself on having the highest quality solid wood used furniture in the area at the most affordable price. With more than 48 vendors in its 10,000 square-foot showroom, JL Kirkman's has a tremendous variety of furniture, glassware and home décor items. You'll also find the best prices on new mattresses in the area. Ice cold drinks and free popcorn are always available to enjoy as you browse.

New Berne Antiques & Collectibles
1000 Greenleaf Cemetery Rd., New Bern
(252) 637-0206

New Berne Antiques & Collectibles moved in late 2004 from downtown to the old Sunshine Gardens building, and is now bigger and better than ever. (To find it, just make a left off Dr. M. L. King Jr. Boulevard one traffic light south of the turn to New Bern High School.) If you love old stuff, you'll love browsing New Berne Antiques & Collectibles' many booths. You're bound to see a "thingy" grandma used to have or a toy that brings to mind memories of your childhood. Just about everything you can imagine is for sale, including toys, Pepsi memorabilia and antique tools, in more than 12,500 square feet of space.

NEW BERN ATTRACTIONS

The importance of New Bern's history cannot be overemphasized. The city of New Bern was settled in 1710 at the confluence of the Neuse and Trent rivers and began to flourish as a farming and shipping community. The city soon became an important port, exporting naval stores and, later, tobacco and cotton. The captains of the ships that hauled these high-demand products used the spires of New Bern's churches to guide them up the Neuse River, which at the time had few navigational aids or other landmarks. Several of the older homes in New Bern have widow's walks projecting above the roofs, where wives would watch for their husbands' ships returning from long sea voyages.

Pirates also found the dark coves and creeks along the rivers ideal for subversive activities and, of course, for hiding treasures. Blackbeard supposedly stayed in a huge house by the Neuse, where he planned his raids on oceangoing ships carrying rich cargo between the American colonies, England and the West Indies.

New Bern can credit its gentility to its once-thriving plantations that produced exportable products to be shipped around the world. The plantations themselves often became small towns, but today little remains of the beautiful estates that depended on the dark waters of the Neuse and Trent rivers for livelihoods. What does remain are the moss-hung oak and cypress trees guarding the many creeks and sloughs along the winding Trent and broad Neuse.

Like other cities, New Bern endured the pangs of growth and change, eventually developing a character all its own. It did not, however, forget its past. History taught New Bern many hard lessons, one of which was to value its heritage. To that end, a great number of old homes and churches have been restored, and, in cases of potential loss, relocated, thanks to groups such as the New Bern Preservation Foundation. Salvaged structures now number more than 150, and restoration efforts are continuous. For more about the city's history, see our New Bern chapter.

While the historical sites, homes and buildings are the focal points of New Bern, the art and cultural events of the town are constant attractions. A large community of reputable visual artists grace New Bern with their work, which is often exhibited at the Bank of the Arts, the public library and commercial art galleries (see our New Bern Arts chapter). Performing arts events and festivals occur year round (see our New Bern Annual Events chapter).

Not listed in any guidebooks (except this one) but known to New Bernians are the town's churches, each distinctive and worthy of a sightseeing visit. Of the area's many historic houses of worship, it is perhaps Christ Episcopal Church on Pollock Street that has the most interesting lore. Included in the church's regalia is a silver communion service donated by King George II. The service survived two fires and reconstruction but, according to local history, was stolen in the 1960s or '70s. The thief, so goes the tale, fenced it with a man who recognized it for what it was and returned it to the church. For more information on New Bern's churches, see our New Bern Worship chapter.

In addition to the official sights of New Bern, walking tours of the historic district are very popular. Attractions open to the public primarily focus on the town's history; however, many of the historic homes are private residences and are closed to the public. Nonetheless, walking the streets and viewing the architecture and landscapes of these grand old homes will give you the feel of the city's Colonial heritage.

Most of the attractions are within walking distance of each other, and we have listed a number of the sites here. For heritage walking tour information, including maps focusing on historic homes, the Civil War, New Bern's African-American heritage, and historic churches and cemeteries, let your first stop be the New Bern-Craven County Convention and Visitors Bureau, located in the New Bern Riverfront Convention Center at the corner of East and South Front Streets, (252) 637-9400 or (800) 437-5767. Everyone there is very helpful with orienting you to the town. Hours are Monday through Friday 8 AM to 5 PM, Saturday 10 AM to 4 PM and (between Memorial Day and Labor Day) Sundays from 10 AM to 2 PM.

For those who enjoy the woodlands as well as the city, nearby Croatan National Forest provides a close-up look at coastal marshes, estuaries and forest. The 157,000-acre preserve is home to insectivorous plants, uncommon wildflowers, marsh and shore-birds, and a variety of forest animals such as black bears, alligators, deer and wild turkeys. Forest hiking trails and overnight campsites are popular with nature lovers. For a detailed description, see our Crystal Coast Attractions chapter.

Tryon Palace Historic Sites and Gardens
Pollock and George Sts., New Bern
(252) 514-4900, (800) 767-1560

Tryon Palace, built in 1770 by Royal Gov. William Tryon, was known at the time as one of the most beautiful buildings in America. The elegant, Georgian-style mansion is mostly a reconstruction of the original building that stood at the same site. After its use both as a Colonial and state capitol, the palace fell into disrepair. The main building burned in 1798 and the kitchen office was dismantled in the early 19th century. When reconstruction was undertaken in the 1950s, only one wing - the stables - remained standing. The palace now houses an outstanding collection of antiques and art, and the grounds are devoted to extensive landscaping, ranging from English formal gardens and a kitchen garden to wilderness garden areas.

Included as part of the main palace complex are the John Wright Stanly House (1783) on George Street, the George W. Dixon House (1828) on Pollock Street and the Robert Hay House (1810) on Eden Street. The Stanly home, which was originally on New Street and moved to its present location in the late 1960s, was built by a Revolutionary War patriot. George Washington stayed in this house for two nights in 1791. The Dixon House is a prominent Federal-style home noted for its rare neoclassical antiques. The restoration of the 1810 Robert Hay House on Eden Street is an accurate reflection of the lifestyle technology of its period.

Palace tours take place daily, with special tours added during the Christmas season. A self-guided interior tour of the Kitchen Office focuses on the behind-the-scenes tasks necessary to maintain the daily 18th-century operations of the palace and its occupants.

Annual events include the colorful Colonial Christmas and candlelight tours in December, the Decorative Arts Symposium in March, Gardener's Weekend during New Bern's Historic Homes and Gardens Tour in the spring, and the July Independence Day Celebration (see our New Bern Annual Events chapter for more about these events). The African-American Lecture Series and the African-American Walking Tours run monthly from spring through fall. Blacksmithing and weaving are also among regular crafts demonstrations.

The palace gift shop in the Jones House and the crafts and garden shop behind the palace west wing are open during regular palace hours. An audiovisual orientation program is shown at the visitors center for all guests.

The palace is open year round, Monday through Saturday 9 AM to 5 PM and on Sunday from 1 to 5 PM. The last tour begins at 4 PM. The palace is closed on Thanksgiving Day, December 24 through 26 and New Year's Day. A number of tour options are available, including two-day and annual passes, and group discounts are extended to pre-arranged groups of 20 or more. General admission is $15 for adults and $6 for students in grades 1 through 12. Children in kindergarten or younger get in free. For specific tour price information or group reservations, call the numbers above. The historic sites and gardens are partially equipped for disabled visitors.

John Wright Stanly House
307 George St., New Bern
(252) 514-4900, (800) 767-1560

On his Southern tour in 1791, President George Washington dined and danced at Tryon Palace, but his two nights in New Bern were spent at the nearby home of John Wright Stanly. Stanly died of yellow fever

in 1789, but New Bern residents reopened and refurnished the residence, then located on Middle Street, just for Washington's visit. Washington described his overnight accommodation as "exceeding good lodgings."

During the Revolutionary War, Stanly's merchant ships plied the waters as privateers, capturing British ships to aid the American cause. The elegance of Stanly's house, built in the early 1780s, reflects the wealth of its owner. Distinctive American furniture of the period complements the elegant interior woodwork, and the Stanly family history provides a fascinating chronicle of father and son, epidemic and duel, war and wealth. Admission is charged as part of the Tryon Palace Complex admission.

George W. Dixon House
609 Pollock St., New Bern
(252) 514-4900, (800) 767-1560

The Dixon House, built in 1828, epitomizes New Bern's lifestyle in the first half of the 19th century, when the town was a prosperous port and one of the state's largest cities. The house, built for a New Bern merchant, is a fine example of neoclassical architecture. Its furnishings, reflecting the Federal period, reveal the changing tastes of early America. The house was converted into a regimental hospital when Union troops occupied New Bern during the Civil War. Admission is charged as part of the Tryon Palace Complex admission.

Robert Hay House
Eden St., New Bern
(252) 514-4900, (800) 767-1560

The tour of the Robert Hay House provides insight into the lives and society of middle-class craftsmen and artisans essential to everyday life in the early 19th century. Scottish-born Robert Hay was a skilled craftsman of carriages and riding chairs. He purchased the house in 1816 and lived there until his death in 1850. The original structure, purchased for $1,000, was a single heated room on the first and second floors, with a cellar kitchen and large cooking fireplace. Hay enlarged the house between 1820 and 1830 with a rear addition consisting of a double porch and two small heated rooms.

The house gives visitors a firsthand experience with early 19th-century methods of climate control. Heating for winter is provided by working fireplaces in the parlor and working kitchen, and summertime cooling is provided by using the open doors and windows to harness the breeze off the nearby Trent River. In addition, louvered shutters on the sunny sides of the house are closed to block the sun's hot rays.

The Robert Hay House, which was opened to the public in late 1998, has been restored to the appearance it had between 1830 and 1850. The house is furnished with accurate reproductions made by skilled woodworkers using traditional hand methods, a move necessary because the house is not equipped with the modern climate controls needed to protect antiques. Admission to the Hay House is included as part of the Tryon Palace Complex admission.

New Bern Academy Museum
New and Hancock Sts., New Bern
(252) 514-4900, (800) 767-1560

Founded in 1764 and built in 1809, New Bern Academy is the oldest public school building in North Carolina and one of the oldest in America. It was still used as a school recently enough to have been attended by some of New Bern's current residents. After it closed, it sat vacant for several years before being purchased and renovated in the 1980s by Tryon Palace. Today, the museum houses exhibits illustrating the 300-year-old history of New Bern and eastern North Carolina, including exhibits on architecture, education and the Civil War (during which it was used as a hospital). The academy is open Monday through Saturday from 1 to 4:30 PM, with admission charged as part of the Tryon Palace Complex admission.

Walking Tour Attractions

As we mentioned in the introduction, many of New Bern's historic homes are private residences and therefore not open to the public. However, a leisurely stroll along riverwalks through the historic district will allow you to observe the landscapes, architecture and gardens of these vintage homes. Walking also will give you a real sense of the many Old World customs that characterize this Colonial town. The New Bern-Craven County Convention and Visitors Bureau, located in the New Bern Riverfront Convention Center at the corner of East and South Front Streets, has several newly developed self-guided walking tour maps covering different aspects of New Bern's long and interesting historical heritage, including the Civil War era and the town's historic churches and cemeteries.

Don't feel embarrassed to wander residential streets or stop and gaze at any of the houses in the historic district. Everyone appreciates your admiration.

New Bern Tours offers guided walking tours for 10 or more people by reservation, (252) 637-7316.

A few of the town's more notable residences and buildings are listed here. Please note that most of these homes are private residences and are not open to the public.

•The John Horner Hill House, 713 Pollock Street, is a Georgian-period dwelling built between 1770 and 1780. It is noted for its rare nine-over-nine sash at the first-floor windows.

•The Henry H. Harris House, 718 Pollock Street, was built in 1800 and is a well-preserved example of vernacular Federal-period architecture.

•The Anne Green Lane House, 804 Pollock Street, is a transitional late-Georgian-early Federal house built between 1790 and 1800. It was remodeled during the Victorian period.

•The John H. Jones House, 819 Pollock Street, is a small Federal house with an unusual central chimney. Its original separate kitchen remains at the rear.

•The White House, 422 Johnson Street, is a simple sidehall Federal house built c. 1830–40. It is noted for its two end chimneys with a small pent-roofed closet in between.

•The Cutting-Allen House, 518 New Street, is a transitional late-Georgian–early Federal sidehall house built in 1793. It is considered unusual because of its flanking wings and large rear ballroom. It was saved from demolition in 1980 and moved to its present location.

•The Hawks House at New and Metcalf Streets offers a side-by-side comparison of styles. Dating from the 1760s, the western part of the house is Georgian, and the eastern section is Federal, added by Francis Hawks, son of John Hawks, architect of Tryon Palace.

•The Clark House, 419 Metcalf Street, was built between 1795 and 1804. It is one of several gambrel-roofed houses in the historic district.

•The Attmore-Wadsworth House, 515 Broad Street, is an unusual one-story, Italianate-style house built c. 1855. Several Italianate-style homes are part of the city's historic architecture.

Area festivals draw visitors from near and far.

photo: George Mitchell

•The Thomas McLin House, 507 Middle Street, is a Federal-style cottage unique for its strict symmetry and diminutive scale.

•The W. B. Blades House, 602 Middle Street, was built in 1903 and is noted for its elaborate Queen Anne design.

•The Jerkins-Duffy House, 301 Johnson Street, was built c. 1830 and is unusual because of its exterior Federal design and interior Greek Revival elements. It is also noted for its captain's walk and exposed-face chimneys.

•The George Slover House, 209 Johnson Street, was built c. 1894 and is an eclectic combination of Queen Anne and shingle-style architecture.

•The Charles Slover House, 201 Johnson Street, is a stately brick townhouse built in 1848–49 that was selected as headquarters by Gen. Ambrose Burnside during the Civil War. C. D. Bradham, inventor of Brad's Drink (now known as Pepsi-Cola), purchased the house in 1908.

•The Eli Smallwood House, 524 E. Front Street, is one of the finest of New Bern's Federal brick sidehall houses, built c. 1810. It is noted for its handsome portico and elegant interior woodwork.

•The Federal-style Dawson-Clarke House, 519 E. Front Street, was built c. 1807–10 and enlarged in 1820. It is one of several historic homes exhibiting the use of double porches, a popular style in the coastal region.

•The Gaston House, 421 Craven Street, is a Georgian home (c. 1770) built by architect, builder and patriot-statesman James Coor. It was purchased in 1818 by Judge William Gaston and was the scene of the founding of St. Paul's Roman Catholic Church. Gaston was a brilliant orator, lawyer, member of Congress, State Justice and author of the state song. The house was enlarged c. 1850.

•The David F. Jarvis House (c. 1903), 220 Pollock Street, is a good example of neoclassical revival architecture.

•The Edward R. Stanly House and Dependency, 502 Pollock Street, was built c. 1849 in the Renaissance Revival style. The cast-iron grills over its windows are unique in New Bern.

•The Wade House, 214 S. Front Street, was built in 1843 and remodeled before 1885

On the corner of Pollock and Middle Streets is a cannon buried muzzle down. The cannon was taken from the Revolutionary British ship-of-war Lady Blessington following an engagement with a privateer owned by New Bern patriot John Wright Stanly.

in the Second Empire style. The cast-iron crest on the mansard roof and the iron fence are notable surviving features.

African-American Walking Tours

Tryon Palace Historic Sites & Gardens offers a monthly African-American walking tour spring through fall. The walking tour, which lasts about 90 minutes and covers 16 blocks, features 300 years of African-American history. There is a fee charged for this tour, and reservations are required. For information, call (252) 514-4900 or (800) 767-1560.

The Craven County Tourism Development Authority offers a series of self-guided walking tours, one of which covers New Bern's African-American history. The tour sheet is available at the Craven County Convention and Visitors Center at the corner of East and South Front Streets and it details historic sites important to local African-American heritage. These include churches, businesses, residences and social organizations, a few of which are described below.

•The George H. White House at 519 Johnson Street was the home of lawyer George H. White, who was elected to the U.S. House of Representatives in 1897. He later fled to Philadelphia and was the last African American in Congress from the South until the 1960s.

•Built in 1923, the Rhone Hotel, 512 Queen Street, was not only the first African-American owned hotel in town but also the home of Charlotte Rhone, New Bern's first black registered nurse and Craven County's first social worker. (Charlotte's sister Henrietta owned the hotel.) The Rhone Hotel was in business from the 1920s to the 1950s.

•Dr. Fisher's Office, 830 Queen Street, was the office of Dr. Hunter Fisher from 1920 to 1947. When the building was being constructed with its soaring false front, it was surrounded by other commercial buildings; now it stands alone.

•The First Baptist Church at 819 Cypress Street is the oldest African-American church building standing in New Bern. Its congregation was established in 1869, and the current building was built in 1906. Booker T. Washington lectured here in 1907. In 1922 the church's brick walls protected it from the Great Fire of that year, and it served as a shelter for victims left homeless.

Attmore-Oliver Civil War House Museum
511 Broad St.
(parking entrance at 512 Pollock St.),
New Bern
(252) 638-8558

The Attmore-Oliver Civil War House Museum was originally built in 1790 by prominent New Bernian Samuel Chapman. Today, it serves as a house museum for the New Bern Historical Society. It was enlarged to its present size in 1834 and houses 18th- and 19th-century antiques, a doll collection and Civil War memorabilia. Of particular interest are the fine Greek Revival portico and two-story porches at the rear of the house. The house is open seasonally, Tuesday, Thursday and Saturday from 1 to 4 PM and closes from mid-December through the end of March. Otherwise, it is shown by appointment. Admission is $4.00 for adults, with children being admitted for free. The house may be rented for private functions. Be aware, however, that it is not handicapped accessible.

Christ Episcopal Church
320 Pollock St., New Bern
(252) 633-2109

More than 260 years old, Christ Episcopal Church is the oldest in New Bern and one of the oldest in North Carolina. This is actually the third church building to stand in this area. The first was completed in 1750 and was later destroyed by fire. The foundation of that first church is on the current church grounds. The second church was completed in 1824 and destroyed by fire in 1871. The church you see today was completed in 1875; it is a Gothic Revival building that incorporates surviving walls of that second church. The steeple, with its four-faced clock, is one of the identifying marks of the downtown skyline. Among the treasures on display are a 1752 Book of Common Prayer, a huge 1717 Bible and a five-piece

CLOSE UP

Good-bye City Life! Stumbling Around the Corn Maze

By Vina Hutchinson Farmer

When Julia Bircher e-mailed me one fall with an invitation to A Day at the Farm's Corn Maze, I wasn't sure how to react. It sounded as though it had all the elements of a few things of which I'm not fond: being outdoors (with all the potential of getting hot and sweaty) and walking through plant life that attracts all sorts of stinging, zinging bugs.

My son Nick and I talked it over, and with his past experiences at the Corn Maze as a participant in A Day at the Farm's summer camp program, he gave it a double thumbs up. We made our reservations.

OK, I know what you're thinking: Corn? Corn! C'mon! We might as well bathe in the city water tower and declare ourselves stuck in TV Land somewhere between Petticoat Junction and Mayberry R.F.D. But I'm serious when I say it's so worth a visit and you'll have more fun than you could ever imagine. Nick and I laughed from the moment we entered the Maze until the time we left - both times, that is, but more about that in a moment.

A Day at the Farm is owned and operated by sisters Julia Bircher and Melissa Barnett, who have transformed their old family farm into a wonderful attraction that introduces children to farm life and offers a delightful setting for picnics and other gatherings.

The farm has been in the family since 1846: Julia and Melissa's father, Woodrow McCoy, converted it into a dairy farm in 1947. The farm, which was phased out in 1993, was the last milk-producing dairy farm in Craven County. Today, the sisters give children a peek at the rapidly disappearing way of life in rural America with tours of the old kitchen, the old wash house, the dairy barns and more.

Children of all ages - including this author! - enjoy seeing the animals, especially the baby animals. (We got to see a baby calf on our latest venture but I will never forgot one memorable summer a few years ago when the kids - that's baby goats to you city slickers - arrived.) And of course as always Abraham, the trick goat who has been featured on the Animal Planet channel's show, World's Funniest Animals, is still around. (And no, I'm not going to tell you what his trick is. You'll have to make a reservation and go see for yourself.)

A Day at the Farm also hosts seasonal events at Christmas and Easter, in addition to its popular summer camps. A Pack House is available for parties, family reunions, Scout campouts and more.

But back to our Corn Maze adventure: Spooked by repeated references to Stephen King's Children of the Corn, Nick and I headed off one clear Saturday night for the farm, which is located right off the Cove City exit on Highway 70. After a delightful hayride with a group from the Tanglewood Church of God in Kinston, we all divided into teams and headed off into the Corn Maze. Our mission: To find seven mailboxes and use the color markers contained within to answer questions about geometric shapes.

I'll offer a handy tip: In addition to bringing your insect repellent, make sure you have an adequate flashlight, a spare and extra batteries.

We found the first mailbox pretty quick. As we meandered our way down various paths on a moonless night, Nick made the observation that in the failing light the various leaves on the corn stalks looked like arms reaching out for us. We both laughed a bit nervously. As it got even darker, we joked with each other by making references to Samara from The Ring and Scary Hair Lady from The Grudge. And then Nick scared the bejeebees out of me by smirking, "Is that a leg sticking out the corn?"

"No!" I said. "No reference to the movie Signs! We've got enough to worry about - I think the flashlight batteries are dying!" Sure enough, the light from our mega-kilowatt handheld shop light borrowed from Dad was failing and here we were stuck without a spare. It felt exactly like one of those moments from Friday the 13th when the victim walks into the darkened basement and, even after she realizes the light won't come on, still keeps walking.

(And, to make matters even spookier, there *was* a leg sticking out of the corn. Morbid curiosity propelled us forward, when we found a scarecrow sitting on a bench.)

We wasted part of the hour we had to complete our mission in finding our way to the exit (mostly in the dark since the flashlight was dead) and sheepishly asked Julia and Melissa to loan us a flashlight. They were gracious enough to rustle up two.

We plunged back into the Corn Maze, laughing at our silliness but determined to find the other six mailboxes. We could see the lights from the other groups and hear they were having just as good a time as we were.

After walking around in circles and going down this path and the other (with Nick making the scary throat rattle from The Grudge although we did have one heart-stopping moment when he swore it wasn't him), we finally found another mailbox. I forget what the actual answer was supposed to be but given my faulty math skills - plus my totally boneheaded move of interpreting the clue of "subtract your fingers and toes" as 10 and not 20 - you might as well know we got the answer wrong on that one.

Although we eventually found a third mailbox, it was downhill after that for our expedition. We managed to walk ourselves around in a few circles (later learning that we'd missed a mailbox by "that" much) and found two of the three mailboxes we'd already located. Finally when our time was up - signified by the blast of an air horn - we couldn't even find our way back to the exit we'd found so easily before! Thank goodness for the lights around the picnic shelter. They gave us a guide to follow back to the entrance where we emerged defeated but laughing.

The Corn Maze is open during the late summer and fall months after the corn reaches its full height. The paths vary from year to year to keep the Maze a challenge to those who've visited before. Reservations are required. For pricing, times and reservations, call Miss Julia and Miss Melissa at (252) 514-9494.

silver communion service given to Christ Church by King George II. Each bears the royal coat-of-arms. Docents provide church tours Monday, Tuesday, Thursday and Friday from 10 AM to 1 PM; on Wednesday, tours take place from 1 to 4 PM.

Centenary United Methodist Church
309 New St., New Bern
(252) 637-4181

First organized as a congregation in 1772, the current Centenary United Methodist Church was designed by Herbert Woodley Simpson and completed in 1905. Its rounded walls and turrets have an almost Moorish look. Guided tours, which are available weekdays between 9 AM and 4 PM, begin with a stop by the church office.

First Presbyterian Church
418 New St., New Bern
(252) 637-3270

The oldest continually used church building in New Bern, First Presbyterian was built in 1819–22 by local architect and builder Uriah Sandy. The congregation was established in 1817. The Federal-style church is similar to many built around the same time in New

England but is unusual in North Carolina. Like that of Christ Church, the steeple on First Presbyterian is a point of reference on the skyline. The church was used as a Union hospital and lookout post during the Civil War, and the initials of soldiers on duty in the belfry can still be seen carved in the walls. Tours between 9 AM and 2 PM weekdays are self-guided, but visitors should stop by the church office first.

Craven Arts Council & Gallery
Bank of the Arts
317 Middle St., New Bern
(252) 638-2577

Built in 1911, this interesting granite structure once served as a bank but now houses the headquarters for the Craven Arts Council and Gallery. The classical facade of the building features Ionic columns leading into the open, two-story gallery. Changing exhibits of various media - painting, sculpture, photography, pottery, fiber art and other art forms -- showcase the work of local and Southeastern artists. Many special events, such as concerts, lectures and receptions, are offered here throughout the year. The Bank of the Arts does not charge an admission fee (donations are welcome), and visitors are welcome to browse. It is open Tuesday through Saturday from 10 AM to 5 PM. The building is handicapped accessible.

The Firemen's Museum
408 Hancock St., New Bern
(252) 636-4087

The New Bern Fire Department is one of the oldest in the country, still operating under its original 1845 charter as the Atlantic Hook and Ladder Company. The museum houses steam pumpers and an extensive collection of other early firefighting equipment. Also on exhibit are rare photographs, Civil War relics and even the mounted head of Fred, the faithful old fire horse who, according to legend, died in his tracks while answering what turned out to be a false alarm. The museum is open year-round Monday through Saturday from 10 AM to 4 PM. Admission is $5 for adults and $2.50 for children.

i

Plans are underway to preserve the area where the Battle of New Bern took place in March 1862 during the Civil War. (The Union forces triumphed and occupied New Bern for the rest of the war.) The New Bern Historical Society now owns 26 acres of the original battlefield, located near Taberna, and plans to preserve this acreage in its natural state. Future plans call for the addition of nature trails and interpretative markers.

Cedar Grove Cemetery
Queen and George Sts., New Bern

If you're one of those people who loves wandering through old graveyards, you'll not want to miss this one. Statuary and monuments beneath Spanish moss-draped trees mark burial traditions from the earliest days of our nation. One smallish obelisk lists the names of nine children in one family who all died within a two-year time span. The city's monument to its Confederate dead and the graves of 70 soldiers are also here. The cemetery's main gate features a shell motif, with an accompanying legend that says if water drips on you as you enter, you will be the next to arrive by hearse.

New Bern National Cemetery
1711 National Ave., New Bern

Encompassing nearly eight acres, New Bern National Cemetery was established in 1867 as a final resting place for veterans. The grounds where the cemetery was established were once the site of military drills by occupying forces during the Civil War. Once inside the gates, visitors are impressed by row after row of matching government standard-issue white marble gravestones, precisely lined. Civil War monuments dedicated during the early 20th century to the fallen of companies of New Jersey, Rhode Island, Connecticut and Massachusetts are also located on the grounds. The cemetery is the site of a moving Memorial Day service every year.

New Bern Trolley Tours
Tours depart at the corner of Pollock and George Sts., New Bern
(252) 637-7316

Touring the town by trolley is a comfortable and interesting alternative to a walking tour. Narrated 90-minute tours depart the corner of Pollock and George Streets, and tickets can be purchased either on the trolley car or at the trolley office, 333 Middle Street. During the months of January, February, March, November and December, call for tour times. April through October, tours are scheduled for 11 AM and 2 PM Monday through Saturday and 2 PM on Sunday. In July and August, tours are set for 9 AM and 11 AM Monday through Saturday and 2 PM on Sunday. Tours or charters for special groups or occasions may also be arranged. Professional guides narrate the tours with attention to historical and architectural interests and spice the narrative with folklore and local knowledge. Special 90-minute tours focusing on Civil War history and African-American history are available by charter. Trolley tours are $12 for adults and $6 for children 12 and younger. Tickets are sold on the trolley car or at the trolley office, 333 Middle Street.

New Bern River Rats
New Bern High School
(252) 670-2633

New Bern once again has its own baseball team, the Coastal Plain League's River Rats. Home games are played at New Bern High School; admission is $4. Part of the Coastal Plain League, which features 13 teams in North and South Carolina and Virginia, the River Rats fields college baseball stand-outs from all over the country.

Croatan National Forest
141 E. Fisher Ave., New Bern
(252) 638-5628

Croatan National Forest is an expansive nature preserve bordered by New Bern, Morehead City and Cape Carteret. The district ranger's office is on Fisher Avenue, which is approximately 9 miles south of New Bern just off U.S. Highway 70 East. Well-placed road signs make the office easy to find.

Due to its coastal location, the forest has many unique features. Some of the ecosystems present include pocosins, longleaf and loblolly pine, and bottomland and upland hardwoods. Sprinkled throughout the Croatan are 40 miles of streams and 4,300 acres of wild lakes. Black bears, otters, deer, raptors and many other forest creatures live in this coastal woodland. Within the forest's boundaries are insectivorous plants such as the Venus's flytrap, butterworts, pitcher plants, sundews and bladderworts, which find the forest an ideal habitat. These rare plants are protected by law. The forest is also well-known for its beautiful wildflowers. Pamphlets on the wildflowers and insectivorous plants are available at the district ranger's office.

The forest areas are excellent for hiking, swimming, boating, hunting, fishing and picnicking. Miles and miles of unpaved roads lace through the woodland, providing easy if sometimes roundabout access to its wilderness. Recreation areas are available for a day's outing or for longer visits. Camping fees vary, so call the district ranger's office for seasonal rates.

Because the Croatan is so expansive and undeveloped, it is best to stop in at the district ranger's office on Fisher Avenue and pick up a forest map before heading out. The best times for venturing into coastal woodlands are fall, winter or early spring. Summer can be very hot and buggy, so prepare yourself with insect repellent. For more information on the Croatan National Forest, see our Crystal Coast Attractions chapter.

Tradewind Aviation Scenic Rides
820 Aviation Dr., New Bern
(252) 636-0716

What could be a more interesting and unusual way to see New Bern than to see it from the air? Tradewind Aviation, based at Craven Regional Airport, offers reasonably priced 30-minute and one-hour tours for one to three passengers aboard a Cessna 172.

NEW BERN KIDSTUFF

Once upon a time, there was a beautiful place at a point where two rivers met. It was such a beautiful place that even the first person who ever saw it, a Tuscarora Indian, wanted to live there. In fact, the entire tribe decided it was the best place to live. And it was. There were lots of fish in the two rivers, and there was a big forest with many trees that the Native Americans could use to build all the things they needed, such as boats.

One day, some other people arrived in the beautiful place. Their leader was from a far-away place called Bern, Switzerland. The people saw the two rivers that came together here and admired the big forest that had what they needed to build things. They also decided that this was the best place in the New World to live. They called the place New Bern to remind them of their old city. Except for once or twice, the people of New Bern got along pretty well with the Tuscarora Indians, but that's another story.

The people of New Bern built quite a fine town with pretty houses, and their town became a capital where the king sent a governor to rule the whole land. The people built a palace in New Bern for the governor. Everyone loved the palace, and people came from all over the land to enjoy it. Even pirates came up the river from the sea to see the town with the palace. And because it was always a beautiful place to live, people kept coming to New Bern.

Over the years, the people of New Bern got together to build a fort for their children to play in and places where their children have parties, eat ice cream and purchase toys. Today, they bring wonderful performers from far away to teach and entertain the kids. They even have a variety of summer and Christmas-break camps where kids can feed farm animals, experience colonial life or just have fun being a kid.

The people of New Bern continue to live happily ever after. From near and far, visitors bring their kids to New Bern to enjoy the town with a real palace. Read on for the details. This is hardly The End.

Arts

The Accidental Artist
220 Craven St., New Bern
(252) 634-3411

You might think The Accidental Artist is a great place to spend a rainy afternoon when the kids have decided there's nothing else to do. But, heck, this is a great place to have fun no matter what the weather is like! At this studio, you can showcase your creativity by painting your own pottery, which The Accidental Artist will then fire for you to complete your one-of-a-kind masterpiece. Come relax in the informal atmosphere and give your artistic impulses free reign. You can even book studio space for birthday parties, club meetings and other special occasions. The Accidental Artist is open Tuesday through Saturday.

Art & Materials
219 Middle St., New Bern
(252) 514-2787

Art & Materials is a great place for kids (of all ages) to explore their artistic impulses, featuring a variety of workshops in painting, drawing, scrap-booking and more. Owners Chris and Shelley Mathiot bring in some of the finest local artists to teach summer camps, after school art lessons, special holiday sessions and classes for home school students.

Craven Arts Council & Gallery
Bank of the Arts, 317 Middle St., New Bern
(252) 638-2577

The Craven Arts Council & Gallery sponsors three week-long fun and educational Summer Arts Camps for children ages 4 to 13. Day campers strengthen their creativity in process-oriented activities in arts disciplines such as creative drama, music, creative movement and visual arts. Classes for particular age groups are limited, so early registration is a good idea.

Eats

Bear City Fudge Company
244 Craven St., New Bern
(252) 670-8675

What better way to treat the kids -- and yourself, too -- than with a delicious piece of homemade fudge? Bear City Fudge Company offers 25 or so flavors, sold starting at half-pound increments. Sample tastes are offered to help you decide between the classic flavors and the more exotic ones. Platters, special orders and other services also are available. While you're waiting for your order, you'll enjoy looking at the many teddy bears on display and the mural which depicts the Craven Street of days gone by. Bear City Fudge Company is open Monday through Saturday.

The Cow Cafe
319 Middle St., New Bern
(252) 672-9269

The Cow Cafe is not only for the young but also the young at heart. New Bern's only "Four Hoof" restaurant is in the historic downtown area. Its delicious menu features such delights as the Save-A-Cow barbecue baskets, the Grazin' Garden Salad, El Moo's Chili and other favorites among the sandwiches, soups and salads offered. Of course, you'll want to save some room for gourmoo popcorn, ice cream and tasty milk shakes. The cow boutique features plenty of cow-inspired items, where you can find the perfect gift for all ages that says "I love moo." The Cow Cafe is open Monday through Saturday for lunch and dinner.

The Festival of Fun, hosted every April by the New Bern Recreation and Parks Department, features amusement rides, games, clowns, hands-on education activities, exhibits, pony rides and other activities for children and families.

Marina Sweets Cafe & Deli
208 Middle St., New Bern
(252) 637-9307

Marina Sweets has long been an Insider Kid's favorite because of its chocolate chip cookies and ice cream. Milk shakes, banana splits and sundaes are cool treats during a busy expedition in New Bern. Parents will appreciate the opportunity to introduce their children to the old-fashioned atmosphere of an honest-to-goodness ice cream shop.

Farms

A Day at the Farm
183 Woodrow McCoy Rd., Cove City
(252) 514-9494, (877) 514-1251

For an "udderly" good time, visit A Day at the Farm, located 20 minutes west of New Bern off U.S. Highway 70. A Day at the Farm, a former dairy that operated from 1947 to 1993, offers kids a chance to see how an old-time dairy farm operated by exploring old barns, an old kitchen and other outbuildings dating back to 1896. Children and their families can hike a nature trail, play in the hay, see and feed traditional farm animals, and, depending on the time of year, get lost in the Corn Maze or enjoy an Easter Egg Hunt, a Live Nativity and other activities scheduled around holidays. Other group activities may include butter-making the old-fashioned way. A Day at the Farm also sponsors a week-long summer camp that gives young people (and the young at heart) an idea of the fun and chores of farm life. Prices vary depending on activity; call ahead for more information and for an appointment. Gifts and treats are available in the ice cream parlor and gift shop.

Kirkman's Farm & Petting Zoo
5255 N.C. Hwy. 55 W., Cove City
(252) 638-1847

A family-run operation located about 20 minutes west of New Bern, Kirkman's Farm is a real working farm where visitors can see many of the day-to-day activities that go along with growing crops such as corn, wheat, rye oats, hay and pumpkins. In addition to seeing the farming activities, children will enjoy the opportunity to feed and pet the farm's many barnyard buddies, including goats, potbelly pigs, rabbits, ponies, cows, a miniature donkey and more. In season, the farm offers hayrides and a pumpkin patch. At Christmas, hayrides tour the farm's lights and decorations. Anytime you plan to visit, be sure to call ahead for an appointment.

Learning

Build and Grow Program
Lowe's, 150 Lowe's Blvd., New Bern
(252) 638-6777

Build and Grow is a free program held the second Saturday of every month for children grades 2 through 5. Our Insider Kid, who declares this program "really fun," has built a variety of household or seasonal items, such as a pencil box for school, a spice rack for Mother's Day and a trivet for the kitchen. Lowe's provides all materials and supplies, and each child is given his or her own work apron and safety goggles. As children complete a project, they are awarded a certificate, as well as a patch for their apron. A parent must accompany the child throughout the activity. A word to the wise: Pre-registration is absolutely required at the Customer Service Desk as Lowe's only receives enough kits for the number of children who are pre-registered.

Carolina Coastal Railroaders
Parker Plaza, 1910B Trent Rd., New Bern
(252) 637-4026

Interested in model railroading or just want to see the developing miniature empire? Carolina Coastal Railroaders, a group devoted to miniature trains, has developed an impressive layout of tracks and tunnels that kids of all ages will enjoy seeing. You'll also see villages that include shops, restaurants, houses, a skyscraper and buildings still under construction. There's a fun scavenger hunt where you can look for things such as a lighthouse, a bathtub, a cigar store Indian -- even a man in an outhouse! Open Mondays and Thursdays from 7 until 9 PM and Saturdays from 9 AM until noon, this railroading paradise is, in the words of our Insider Kid, "the best place in the world to watch trains." There is no admission fee, but donations are always appreciated. For information, call Tommie Phelps at the number above.

i

Abraham, the talented trick goat at A Day at the Farm, has been featured on the Animal Planet show Planet's Funniest Animals.

Masterminds
2500 Trent Rd., Ste. 34, New Bern
(252) 633-4112

Masterminds is the creative place for learning that not only provides tutorial and homework help but also fun enrichment activities that explore cooking, science and art. Classes are divided according to age groups. Afternoon book clubs also meet weekly to discuss the latest children's book and take part in related activities and crafts. Call for registration information and class schedules.

New Bern-Craven County Public Library Children's Programming
400 Johnson St., New Bern
(252) 638-7815

The newly-renovated children's library at the New Bern-Craven County Public Library is well-organized for toddlers through 6th-graders to enjoy selecting from the collection of books, videotapes and audio cassettes. Stories on CD-ROM are available for use in-house on the department's computers. Help is plentiful. Weekday programs for children include Time Out For Toddlers on Friday from 9:30 AM and 10:30 AM, featuring stories, songs and finger plays for children ages 3 and younger. Preschool Storysteps for ages 3 to 5 takes place Tuesdays at 9:30 AM and 10:30 AM, offering stories, puppet plays, music and other fun. The Children's Story Hour is held Thursday at 4 PM for kids between the ages of 5 and 9, and involves storytelling, movies and creative activities, while the Story Seekers program fosters the imaginations of children ages 10 and up through puppetry and storytelling. (Pre-registration is required for Story Seekers.) The library hosts a number of other special programs throughout the year, including the Summer Reading Book Club.

New Bern Historical Society
512 Pollock St., New Bern
(252) 638-8558

Every spring, the New Bern Historical Society hosts a Civil War Adventure Day for boys and girls at the location of the Battle of New Bern, which took place in 1862. This event brings history to life in an encampment-style environment that features authentic drills, musket shooting demonstrations and more in an encampment-style atmosphere. While these programs are fee-based, members of the historical society receive a discount.

Tryon Palace Historic Sites & Gardens
Pollock and George Sts., New Bern
(252) 514-4900, (800) 767-1560

Besides the standard admission fee of $6 for children grades 1 to 12 (and free for children kindergarten-age and younger), Tryon Palace offers a number of pint-sized programs designed to foster an interest in history, among them the summer Camp Yesteryear, the Colonial Fife & Drum Corps and holiday day camps, concerts, films and more. Information on age limitations, registration and fees, where applicable, is available by calling the number above.

Parks

Creekside Park
Old Airport Rd., New Bern
(252) 636-6606

Creekside Park is located on 111 acres next to Craven Regional Airport. Developed by the Craven County Recreation and Parks Department, it features 12 athletic fields, perfect for soccer, baseball, softball and football; a large playground where children ages 5 to 12 will enjoy climbing, swinging and sliding; a sand volleyball court; and a quarter-mile paved walking trail. The latest area to be developed is the park's waterfront, which has a fishing dock, playground, nature trail and a gazebo. Restrooms and picnic shelters also are available. Reservations for these facilities can be made by calling the department at the number above; rental fees apply to the picnic shelters and athletic fields.

Fort Totten Park
Corner of Fort Totten Dr. and Trent Blvd., New Bern
(252) 639-2901

Let your kids burn some energy jumping, climbing, swinging, spinning and sliding in Fort Totten Park's fantastic playground. (Meanwhile, parents can relax on one of the many park benches located beneath shady trees.) The park, which also features a lighted baseball diamond, public restrooms and a picnic shelter with two grills, is located close to New Bern's downtown historic district.

Kidsville Playground
1225 Pine Tree Dr., New Bern
(252) 639-2912

Kidsville, a beautifully planned active and interactive fort-like play environment that captivates both children and adults, is located next to the West New Bern Recreation Center on Pine Tree Drive near the intersection of U.S. Highway 70 and N.C. Highway 17. With or without a kid, Kidsville merits a visit. Whether you choose to slide, swing, climb, clamber or scamper through its interesting twists and turns, Kidsville will wow you and is the perfect place for a sunny afternoon picnic. Groups of 15 or more must make reservations by calling ahead.

Recreation

Craven County Recreation and Parks Dept.
406 Craven St., New Bern
(252) 636-6606

The Craven County Recreation and Parks Department offers programs and classes for preschool and school-age kids throughout the school year and in summer day-camp programs. Karate is instructed year round for ages 3 and older. Tennis lessons, baton twirling, girls' softball, T-ball, coach pitch baseball and little league, soccer, Pop Warner football and basketball for girls and boys are among the sports activities organized and supervised seasonally. In addition to its regular summer day-camp program, the recreation department teams up with Tryon Palace to offer Camp Yesteryear for 4th- and 5th-grade students each summer and sponsors special programs such as the annual Easter Egg Hunt for ages 1 to 11.

Craven County 4-H
Cooperative Extension, 300 Industrial Dr., New Bern
(252) 633-1477

4-H is a volunteer-based skill-building organization for children and teens ages 5 to 18. Children participate in 4-H community clubs, after-school workshops, field trips, camp-outs and other special events and hands-on activities taking place on weekends, evenings and school holidays. There are currently six active 4-H clubs in Craven County, and approximately 450 children participate each year in 4-H sponsored educational activities. These activities focus on a wide range of interests, including camping, cooking, horses, the environment, computers, sports, recycling, wildlife and more.

New Bern Recreation and Parks
248 Craven St., New Bern
(252) 639-2901

The New Bern Recreation and Parks Department offers a number of sports programs throughout the year for children, including cheerleading, baton twirling, fencing, baseball, soccer, basketball, track and field, karate, tennis, wrestling and football. Recreation centers are located at 901 Chapman Street, (252) 639-2919, and 1225 Pine Tree Drive, (252) 639-2912. For teens the department hosts Young Adults Active in the Community (YAAC), a teen council that gives local teens a place to share ideas and bring new recreational opportunities to town. Scheduled events and clubs such as CHOICES, Saturday Night Madness and Teen Night also give local teens opportunities to socialize and share their thoughts and opinions.

In addition to its programs and clubs throughout the year, the department also offers the BEAR After School Program for ages 8 to 14 during the school year and the Bern Bear Bunch Day Camp during the summer. Offered 9 AM to 4 PM weekdays for three two-week sessions, the Bern Bear Bunch Day Camp is open to children ages 6 to 12. Residents living within the city limits are allowed to register two weeks earlier than everyone else. Campers participate in games, contests, arts and crafts, swimming, water games, movies, sports, field trips, cookouts and much more.

Courts Plus features a Sports Summer Camp for kids that's packed with fun. Weekly sessions are offered throughout the summer, with racquetball, basketball, swimming, soccer, volleyball and more. Nonmembers are welcome, and parents can either sign up their junior sportsmen for the entire summer or per week as needed. Call (252) 633-2221.

Strike Zone Family Fun Center
3550 Dr. M. L. King Jr. Blvd., New Bern
(252) 637-6033

The Strike Zone Family Fun Center offers hours of entertainment for kids and their parents too. The Strike Zone offers 24 bowling lanes, a full-service snack bar, a soft play zone for younger children and a fantastic arcade. Strike Zone offers several family fun specials. The Family Special Mondays through Wednesdays features a game of bowling, large pizza, pitcher of soft drink and 20 arcade tokens for $29.95 for up to four people. Other deals include the Monday Quarter Mania, where for $3 per person, you can bowl and play all the arcade games you want for 25 cents per game; and Two for Tuesday, with its buy-one-bowling-game, get-one-free deal.

The Strike Zone is the perfect place to host a birthday party. The price is $99 for two hours, including up to 12 people, which includes shoe rental, two hours of bowling, unlimited soft drinks and all paper products. Add $2.25 per person for birthday meals and another $1 per person for popcorn. Birthday parties are scheduled for Saturdays and Sundays.

See our New Bern Recreation and Parks chapter for more information about The Strike Zone.

Swing Zone
4605 U.S. Hwy. 70 E., New Bern
(252) 634-GAME

This new entertainment complex offers plenty of family fun for all ages. The 18-hole miniature golf course includes sand traps, rough turf and plenty of water among its many challenges that will keep your game interesting. The park also features four batting cages and the area's only paintball course. Paintball participants must buy their paintballs from Swing Zone, which offers equipment rentals. Indoors, Swing Zone boasts the largest arcade in Craven County with more than 25 action and redemption games, a snack bar featuring freshly baked Freschetta pizza and Otis Spunkmeyer cookies, plus Maola ice cream and that hometown favorite, Pepsi. Swing Zone can book parties for seven to 50 people and can customize packages to include indoor and outdoor activities. Season passes and reloadable gift cards also are available.

YMCA Youth Sports and Services
Twin Rivers YMCA, 100 YMCA Ln., New Bern
(252) 638-8799

The YMCA's new Aquatic Center features lots of room for kids to swim and play and includes water slides, a splash park and a zero-entry section. To keep all play safe, the YMCA also specializes in swimming instruction ranging from beginning lessons to Water Safety Instructor certification. With the emphasis on fair play, participation and fun, the YMCA offers year-round sports activities for all age groups in gymnastics and competitive swimming, as well as seasonal basketball, T-ball, girls softball, flag football and more. Summer day-camp programs offer a terrific range of sports activities for all age groups. The Youth Center for ages 6 to 18 years provides supervised gaming such as bumper pool and table tennis. Child care services are available for parents using the YMCA facilities.

Shopping

Snapdragon Way Cool Toys
214 Middle St., New Bern
(252) 514-6770

If you have a child with you while you're shopping the historic downtown district, reward both of you with a play break at the Snapdragon, which has the coolest in specialty toys. Little ones can play at the Thomas the Train play table while parents explore all this unique shop has to offer. Featuring toys for children ages newborn on up, Snapdragon offers an inviting selection craft, scientific and magic kits, as well as dolls, plush toys, books, Playmobil sets, action figures, and a variety of just fun stuff. (Our Insider Kid finds the Snapdragon a fascinating store to explore and a must-stop on any downtown excursion.)

NEW BERN WEDDING PLANNING

Getting married is a monumental event, and everyone involved wants to make it as special as possible. From historic churches to stately homes, lovely waterfront locales to contemporary settings, New Bern offers a number of exciting locations to make your wedding day an extraordinary one. In this chapter, we highlight just a few of the locations and services available in the New Bern area, including information on where and how to obtain the marriage license.

Wedding Show

Bridal Expo
New Bern Riverfront Convention Center, New Bern
(252) 638-8101

Those planning a wedding in the New Bern area will want to mark their calendars for this show, held annually in January. The expo highlights services available locally, including catering, photography, musicians and more. It also includes a fashion show and prize drawings. Admission is $5.

Marriage Licenses

North Carolina requires that all couples get a marriage license before the marriage takes place. Licenses are available at any Register of Deeds office in North Carolina. The Craven County Register of Deeds office is located at 226 Pollock Street, (252) 636-6617. To obtain a marriage license, those age 20 and older need to come in together and bring their driver's licenses, Social Security cards and $50 in cash; those 18 and 19 years of age also need to bring along certified copies of their birth certificates. (Those 17 and younger should call the Registrar's office for more information about other requirements they need to meet.) If you have been divorced within 30 days, bring your divorce papers. The Register of Deeds office issues marriage licenses Monday through Friday between 8 AM and 4 PM. The license is valid for 60 days in any county in North Carolina. After the wedding, certified copies of the marriage certificate are available from the Register of Deeds for $10 each.

In North Carolina, you can be married by a magistrate -- the Magistrate's Office is located in the Craven County Law Enforcement Center at 411 Craven Street, (252) 639-9015, next door to the courthouse. You'll need to bring two witnesses, your marriage license and $20 in cash for state fees; otherwise, the magistrate typically does not charge anything for performing the ceremony, although tipping is permitted. The Magistrate's Office is open 24 hours a day, seven days a week (but keep in mind that jail visitation takes place between 11 AM and 4 PM on Saturdays and Sundays, so the lobby of the office can get crowded).

The Register of Deeds office, (252) 745-4421, in neighboring Pamlico County has a few different requirements. Located on the first floor in the courthouse on N.C. Highway 55 in Bayboro, the office requires that couples who have ever been divorced at any time should bring in a copy of their divorce decrees. Marriage licenses are issued Monday through Friday from 8 AM to 4 PM; the bride and groom will both need to be present in order for the license, which costs $50 in cash, to be issued. Those 18 and over should bring along their driver's licenses and Social Security cards, although the Pamlico County office allows the use of a W-2 or tax return in lieu of a Social Security card. (Those 17 and younger should call for more information.) The license is valid for 60 days. After the marriage, the couple can pick up one free certified copy of the marriage certificate; copies after the first one are $10 each. The Magistrate's Office, (252) 745-6010, also is located in the courthouse.

Wedding and Reception Locations

New Bern has many beautiful old churches that provide exceptional locations for your wedding. A list of churches is available in our New Bern Worship chapter. You will need to call the churches for more information as each has its own policies and fees concerning weddings. Other sites are listed below.

Attmore-Oliver House
511 Broad St. (parking entrance on Pollock St.), New Bern
(252) 638-8558

Looking for a beautiful and historic location for your wedding? The 1790 Attmore-Oliver House is available for special occasions and its size allows for larger weddings and receptions (and for parties and business functions as well). Call the New Bern Historical Society at the number above for fees, which were recently reduced, and other information.

New Bern Riverfront Convention Center
Corner of East and South Front Sts., New Bern
(252) 637-1551

With its 12,000-square-feet in the Colonial Capital Ballroom downtown, along with smaller spaces upstairs in the Tryon Rooms, Berne Room and Craven Boardroom, and a beautiful waterfront veranda, the New Bern Riverfront Convention Center has the flexibility to host groups from 50 to 1,350. Its proximity to three hotels and numerous bed-and-breakfast inns downtown makes it a good location for weddings and reunions with a number of out-of-town guests. The center also maintains a preferred caterers list, making the hunt for that service a bit less stressful.

Sheraton Grand New Bern
100 Middle St., New Bern
(252) 638-3585

The Sheraton Grand has a wedding specialist on staff to assist the bride in planning her bridesmaids' brunch or luncheon, the rehearsal dinner and wedding reception. Group rates are available for accommodations for guests and members of the wedding party, and the honeymoon suite can be reserved for the bride and groom.

Inns of New Bern
Downtown New Bern

Downtown New Bern's seven bed-and-breakfast inns offer unique settings for small weddings, bridal showers, honeymoons and overnight accommodations for wedding guests. See our New Bern Bed and Breakfasts chapter.

Waterside weddings are the most memorable.

photo: Scott Taylor

Accommodations

See our New Bern Hotels and Motels and New Bern Bed and Breakfasts chapters for a listing of hotels and bed-and-breakfast inns in the area.

Event Planners

Occasions to Celebrate
2500 Trent Rd., Suite 30, New Bern
(252) 637-9100

The event planning professionals at Occasions to Celebrate can turn your vision of a beautiful wedding into a reality. With more than 20 years of experience, Occasions to Celebrate can take the stress off you and handle everything from set up to clean up. They specialize in exceptional balloon and floral arrangements and will work with your caterer, facility and entertainment to ensure that your wedding and reception run as smoothly as possible. Occasions to Celebrate also offers tuxedo and equipment rentals and carries a selection of beautiful invitations. Call for a free consultation.

Bridal-by-the-Sea
Rachel Munro
(252) 259-4992
www.bridalbythesea.com

Rachel Munro is passionate about helping brides and grooms make their wedding day an unforgettable occasion and cherished memory. Rachel uses her 10 years of experience along with full hands-on service to work with couples and wedding parties throughout the planning process to ensure that timelines and details flow smoothly. She has worked with budgets of all sizes, ranging from backyard barbecues to swanky gala affairs with celebrity guest lists, and she devotes the same amount of enthusiasm and professionalism to each and every one. Rachel offers a number of wedding packages, ranging from simple consultations and contract reviews to a complete coordination package that arranges all the details of the big day, based on the selections and wishes of the bridal couple, including the rehearsal, ceremony and reception. Rachel not only works with vendors of the wedding couple's choice but also can recommend others as needed. Certified by the Association for Certified Professional Wedding Consultants, Rachel offers a complimentary initial consultation. Insiders find her pleasant to work with as well as ardent and professional about planning the perfect wedding.

Promised Hearts Wedding Planning
Pam DuVal
(252) 637-9100

Enjoy a stress-free, beautifully memorable wedding with the assistance of wedding planner Pam DuVal and team. With years of experience planning weddings of all sizes, Pam can coordinate and direct the rehearsal, wedding ceremony and reception. Pam offers several wedding packages and she adjusts her prices accordingly to fit each wedding, number in the bridal party and guests, location and amount of time involved. And as a native of the area, she has the inside information wedding parties need about the best in local vendors. Most of her preferred vendors give her brides a discount or special gift. (All of Pam's brides also receive special gift baskets, chock full of goodies from local businesses.) Pam also offers consulting and decorating services, and invitations and favors can be ordered through her website. Pam is enthusiastic about creating memorable occasions for couples starting out on their new life together. Contact her for a free one-hour "meet and greet" session, and you'll see why Insiders rave about her knowledge, attention to detail and creative ideas.

Florists

Greenleaf Park Florist
4110 Dr. M. L. King Jr. Blvd., New Bern
(252) 638-5156

The staff at Greenleaf Park Florist is ready to sit down with everyone involved with planning the wedding to answer questions and provide other guidance on the important decisions of flowers. Greenleaf, which prefers planning to take place at least three months prior to the wedding, can deliver fresh and silk flowers in beautiful arrangements to the wedding site, as well as provide flowers for the wedding party, parents, grandparents and other important guests.

Wiley's Flowers & Gifts
2100 Trent Blvd., New Bern
(252) 637-4133

This full-service florist is well-known in New Bern for providing distinctive and beautiful floral arrangements, silk or live, for every occasion. From the wedding to the reception, Wiley's can provide flowers, bouquets, corsages and boutonnieres for the wedding party. They also provide wedding equipment such as candelabras. Delivery and set-up services are available. Wiley's prefers to have at least two months' notice, if not more, depending on the size of the wedding and the reception. Call for a free consultation.

Catering and Cakes

A Catered Affair Cafe & Catering
3402B Trent Rd., New Bern
(252) 637-7331

Owner Stacia Reed and her crew can add a special touch to your bridal shower, bridesmaids' luncheon, rehearsal dinner and reception with the same marvelous and delicious food that has made her restaurant such a favorite in New Bern. A Catered Affair is a preferred caterer for the New Bern Riverfront Convention Center, and the restaurant's beautifully decorated dining room also is available to rent for special occasions.

The Chelsea
335 Middle St., New Bern
(252) 637-5469

The Chelsea can bring the fusion cuisine that New Bernians love so much to your reception. Housed in Pepsi inventor Caleb Bradham's second pharmacy, The Chelsea also has wonderful banquet facilities located upstairs (an elevator is available) and can seat up to 120 guests. Call for more information and available booking dates. The Chelsea is a preferred caterer for the New Bern Riverfront Convention Center.

Kathy's Cakes, Candies & Supplies
1906 Dr. M. L. King Jr. Blvd., New Bern
(252) 637-5700

Kathy's Cakes is your "confection connection," featuring high quality, delicious

cakes in a variety of shapes, sizes and flavors. The area's leading wedding cake designer, Hazel's can provide custom wedding cakes starting as low as $2 per serving. Insiders love Kathy's because of its friendly staff, outstanding customer service and ability to produce distinctive personalized cakes. Candy, pies, sugar-free cakes and gift baskets also are available.

Rental Equipment

Country-Aire Rental
1253 Glenburnie Rd., New Bern
(252) 638-6000

Country-Aire Rental offers a complete line of equipment for weddings and receptions, everything from the big items such as archways and candelabras for the ceremony right down to the bud vases on reception tables. A staff wedding and event coordinator is on hand to assist in handling everything you need for the big day, including decor items, glassware, china, flatware, linens, tents, tables, chairs and more. Pickup and delivery services are available for Country-Aire's diverse rental selection of wedding items in brass, silver, white lattice, wood and wicker. Tuxedo rental also is available.

Photographers and Videographers

Dozzi Photography
244 Middle St., New Bern
(252) 636-2373, (800) 479-2373

Dozzi Photography, now located over Tom's Coins & Antiques on Middle Street, features a unique approach to wedding photography designed to capture all the intimate and wonderful moments of your special day

Weddings are such joyful times!

photo: Scott Taylor

as they happen. In addition to their documentary wedding package, traditional bridal and engagement portraits are also available. A deposit is required to hold the date and time, and owner Kevin and Renee Dozzi are very open to new ideas and encourage the bride and groom to offer their ideas and suggestions to create memorable wedding photographs. Kevin and Renee also offer a selection of other products, including holiday portrait greeting cards; family, individual, business and high school senior portraits; fun and whimsical "That's My Name" portraits of children; and commercial photography. The Dozzis can copy, restore and scan old family photographs, and they sell historic prints of New Bern from the old Benner's Studio archives.

Formal Wear

The Intimate Bridal and Formal Wear
230 Middle St., New Bern
(252) 638-1220

Now with two great locations (the other is in Morehead City), you'll see why brides-to-be consider The Intimate eastern North Carolina's premier bridal shop. The Intimate features the latest styles, accessories and shoes for brides, with gown sizes ranging from 2 to 30. Come shop the selection of exclusive brand names, including 2Be Bridal, Jasmine, Venus Bridal, Private Label by G, Maggie Sottero and others. The shop also carries a selection of fashions, dye-able shoes and accessories for the bridal party and the mother of the bride and groom, and offers tuxedo rentals and sales as well. A certified wedding planner is on staff to help you coordinate your special day. You'll also enjoy shopping The Intimate's selection of cocktail dresses and prom apparel for those other special occasions.

Goody's Family Clothing
Rivertowne Square, Dr. M.L. King Jr. Blvd., New Bern
(252) 634-9747

Book your tuxedo rentals early to ensure the best selection at Goody's, where you can rent five tuxedos and get the sixth one for free. Tuxedoes offered include those styled by Bill Blass, Ralph Lauren, Jean Yves, Perry Ellis and others. Accessories available include shoes, cummerbunds, ties and vests. If you're in the market to buy a tuxedo, Goody's also is a good stop for that.

Jewelry/Gifts/ Bridal Registry

Hearne's Jewelers
Rivertowne Square, Dr. M. L. King Jr. Blvd., New Bern
(252) 637-4590

Founded in 1972 by Mickey Hearne and now run by his son Mike, Hearne's combines courtesy with integrity. It has one of the area's largest and best selections of loose diamonds, ready to mount in exquisite rings, earrings, necklaces and bracelets. Brides and grooms also will want to check out the selection of Benchmark rings, available in gold and platinum with distinctive designs and diamonds. Another unique option are the stackable rings by Hidalgo, which offers couples the opportunity to create one-of-a-kind rings in gold and platinum with diamonds, precious stones and enamel.

Treasures on the Trent
250 Middle St., New Bern
(252) 637-7900

Treasures on the Trent may be one of Middle Street's newest gift shops but it is fast becoming one of the more popular ones. Shop here for a wonderful selection of gifts, including leather full-size and travel-size jewelry boxes, desk accessories, clocks and beautifully crafted game sets by Wolf Designs, and men's fashion products such as grooming sets, valet trays, cufflinks and more. You'll also find Peggy Karr glass, Caswell-Massey bath and body products, Baldash crystal and many other distinctive gifts for the bride, the groom and their new home. Treasures on the Trent also offers a select of wedding invitations, and the Imprintables line of invitations, which are perfect for bridal showers, bridesmaid luncheons, rehearsal dinners and other wedding occasions.

A wedding at Cape Lookout National Seashore is an unforgettable occasion for everyone.

photo: George Mitchell

Carolina Creations
317-A Pollock St., New Bern
(252) 633-4369
www.carolinacreations.com

For the bride and groom who might already have an established household, a distinctive piece of art from Carolina Creations will make a memorable and appreciated wedding gift. Whether it be a work by resident potter Michael Francoeur, a beautiful painting or pen-and-ink drawing by resident artist Janet Francoeur, or artwork by other local artists, Carolina Creations always has something new and unique to offer. Brides may indicate their preferences by using Carolina Creations' bridal registry service both in the gallery and on-line for out-of-town guests.

Invitations and Supplies

Party Suppliers
2025 S. Glenburnie Rd., New Bern
(252) 637-7722

Party Suppliers carries a full aisle of wedding supplies, including cake toppers, personalized albums and guest books, garters, printed napkins, toasting glasses, unity candles and more. Its aisle of plastic and paper table settings, napkins, serving pieces and more will ensure that you can find the wedding supplies you need in the colors of your choice. Helium tank rentals and balloons of all colors are available for those plan to use or release balloons as part of the celebration. Party Suppliers also offers custom-made banners, a complete line of printable papers (which can be customized on the spot with your message or invitation) and beautiful custom invitations discounted 30 percent off the manufacturer's list price.

tem. The salon also can wax away unwanted facial hair, and help you have your best tan ever, via the tanning bed or spray-tanning services. Coastal Cuts & Clippers even has a nurse on staff who can use micro-dermabrasion to exfoliate the dead skin cells off your face, giving your skin a healthy glow. For hair services, the salon provides service either by appointment or on a walk-in basis; tanning and micro-dermabrasion are available by appointment only. Hair-care products, including Nexxus, Redkin and the Coastal Cuts & Clippers line, also are available. This unisex salon is open Monday through Saturday.

Fantastic Sams
1505 S. Glenburnie Rd., New Bern
(252) 636-1144

Locally owned, this Fantastic Sams franchise features salon-quality cuts and styles for adults and children at affordable prices. Those opting for a new look will benefit from Fantastic Sams' texturizing, coloring and highlighting services. Hair conditioning, beard and mustache trimming, facial waxing and hair straightening are but a few of the many services available. The salon carries a great selection of hair-care products, including Nexxus, Bedhead and the Fantastic Sams brand. Walk-ins are always welcome at Fantastic Sams, which is open Monday through Saturday.

Leigh & Co. Hair Salon
1503-D Glenburnie Rd., New Bern
(252) 635-9255

Located near Market Place Shopping Center, Leigh & Co. is more than your standard beauty salon. Leigh Broome and her stylists keep up with education and training to offer women, men and children the latest in progressive cuts, styles, permanent waves, foiling techniques, hair conditioning and more. Leigh & Co. also offers its customers spa manicures and pedicures. Another great service is the Princess parties for little girls, where up to 10 divas-in-training are pampered with hair updos and manicures. In business since 2000, Leigh & Co. sees clients by appointment or on a walk-in basis Tuesday through Saturday.

Beautiful views make relaxing easy.

photo: George Mitchell

NEW BERN DAY SPAS AND SALONS

Looking your best is an important part of feeling your best. New Bern is fortunate to have some very creative talent available to help you take advantage of your best features. From the top of your head to the tip of your toes, you can maximize your looks through skin-care products, safe tanning techniques, the latest hair styles, manicures and pedicures offered at salons and spas in New Bern. And, of course, some businesses offer the ultimate in relaxation -- therapeutic massage. While New Bern has a plethora of beauty related businesses, Insiders recommend these to help you get started.

Day Spas

The Comfort Zone Massage & Day Spa
714 Pollock St., New Bern
(252) 638-1616

If you are working too hard and need some help relaxing, The Comfort Zone's therapists have appointments available six days a week. The Comfort Zone specializes in aromatherapy massages, hot stone massages, herbal detox wrap massages, paraffin wraps and massages, facial rejuvenation, and hand and feet massages. Spa products and gift certificates also are available.

Dun'Artie Salon & Day Spa
1706-C U.S. Hwy. 70 E., New Bern
(252) 637-5507

Prepare to be pampered at Dun'Artie Day Spa, where "your robe and slippers are waiting." However busy your life may be, you'll enjoy the opportunity to relax and take advantage of Dun'Artie's many services. Massage therapy and body treatments are designed to relieve muscle tension and leave you feeling refreshed and renewed. Facials and chemical facials are customized to your skin type and condition. Also available are hair-care services, including coloring and permanent wave styling, a wide range of nail services, and waxing. Dun'Artie features several special spa packages, such as the Cinderella's Ball for ages 15 and younger, Mommy & Me prenatal massage, and bridal party packages. Gentlemen's spa services include massage, body and face treatments, manicures and pedicures, and a barber is on staff to provide haircuts, beard trims, shaves and more. Although Dun'Artie accepts walk-ins, appointments are highly recommended. Dun'Artie is open Tuesday through Saturday.

Salons

Advanced Attractions Salon
204 Craven St., New Bern
(252) 638-6191

Advanced Attractions Salon, located in New Bern's historic downtown, features a full range of services. Its stylists, who train extensively each year to keep up with the latest skills, offer shampoos, cuts, styles and permanent waves, and specialize in highlighting and color services. Facials, manicures and pedicures are also available. Advanced Attractions carries a full line of Aveda and Redkin hair-care products. Services are available either by appointment or on a walk-in basis.

Coastal Cuts & Clippers
3336 Wellons Blvd., New Bern
(252) 637-9295

The stylists at Coastal Cuts & Clippers can offer you a great shampoo, cut and style, even new color or a permanent wave if you'd like to make a major change. But they also go the extra step. You can get longer or straighter hair with Great Length hair extensions and the Bio-ionic hair-straightening sys-

All kinds of treasures await shoppers in New Bern and along the Crystal Coast.

courtesy of Tryon Palace Historic Sites & Garden

Supercuts
2027 Glenburnie Rd., New Bern
(252) 672-5611

If you'd like a hip hairstyle at an affordable price, Supercuts is just the place for you. Insiders really like Supercuts because of their call-ahead service for walk-in customers. You simply call in and the staff will add your name to its waiting list and give you an idea of how long the wait will be, usually between 15 to 45 minutes. All you have to do is show up, hop in the stylist's chair and enjoy Supercuts' many services, including cutting, styling, coloring and more. Supercuts also offers a wide selection of high-quality hair products. The salon, located in the Harris Teeter shopping plaza, is open every day.

Uptown Looks
1701-B Red Robin Ln., New Bern
(252) 635-9930

Cuts, styles, permanents, straightening services, highlighting, coloring and more are available at this full-service salon. Other services include manicures, pedicures and waxing. The salon also carries a complete selection of hair-care products that include such well-known name brands as Osis, Retro, Texture and Biolage. Uptown Looks is open by appointment only on Mondays, but walk-ins are always welcome Tuesday through Saturday.

Cosmetics

Merle Norman Cosmetic & Nail Salon
3601 Trent Rd. #8, New Bern
(252) 638-3665

Discover the beauty in you with the aid of Merle Norman cosmetics and accessories. At "The Place for the Beautiful Face," you'll enjoy free makeovers, skin-care lessons, five-minute hydrating facials, manicures, pedicures and nail enhancements. You can even try out up to 24 new hairstyles via the shop's Styles on Video. Merle Norman offers the area's largest selection of magnifying mirrors, Tweezerman products and a small gift section that includes cosmetic bags and candles. Merle Norman is open every day but Sunday. It's located in the Village Square shopping complex.

Tanning

Totally Tan & More
2704 Neuse Blvd., New Bern
(252) 635-1189

In business for more than 10 years, Totally Tan & More uses Wolff Tanning Systems to help you safely achieve that summery golden glow. In addition to tanning beds, the full-service salon also features spray-on tanning via a self-contained unit. Hair, nail and massage services are available as well. The business, a state training facility for other salons, also offers tanning bed sales and service. Totally Tan & More accepts appointments Monday through Saturday during the summer season, but is closed weekends during the winter.

NEW BERN ARTS

For the first three decades of the 20th century, New Bern was known as the "Athens of North Carolina" because of its many artistic and educational endeavors. While the Great Depression put a halt to much of the activity, a rebirth occurred in the 1970s, and today locals enjoy performances and exhibits from an ever-increasing number of area and touring artists.

The Craven Arts Council and Gallery, located in the Bank of the Arts on Middle Street, supports and features all art disciplines and sponsors the popular New Bern Sunday Jazz Showcase and many other visual and performing arts events throughout the year.

The evidence that the arts are treasured in New Bern is most apparent on a walk through the city's historic downtown. Galleries are proliferating in renovated buildings, and murals on the walls of public buildings reflect the work of varied artists interpreting New Bern's history.

The New Bern-Craven County Public Library at the corner of Johnson and Middle Streets, (252) 638-7800, selects an artist of the month and displays his or her work in its attractive building.

New Bern is also home to active community theater groups, the New Bern Civic Theatre, the River Towne Repertory Players, which stage and sponsor a number of productions annually. The Carolinian Shakespeare Festival puts on impressive performances for three weekends in August, and numerous musical groups and dancers, including historical dancers, stage other performances throughout the year.

Local artist Doug Alford painted the murals in the New Bern Riverfront Convention Center. The four murals depict four essential eastern North Carolina elements: fishing, farming, forestry and faith.

In this chapter we describe our arts organizations. If a group doesn't have a street address or regular office, we have given the contact person's name and phone number.

Visual Arts

Craven Arts Council and Gallery
317 Middle St., New Bern
(252) 638-2577

Besides nurturing local artists, this organization provides exhibition space for local, regional and national artists in the Bank of the Arts, a reclaimed 1911 bank building that also houses the arts council's administrative offices.

The large, open main gallery, open Tuesday through Saturday 10 AM to 5 PM, is the staging area for 12 exhibits each year. Popular traveling exhibits are often featured, and overall works include a variety of media, ranging from traditional to contemporary. At Christmas, the gallery becomes a huge gift shop for the sale of artworks, cards, fine crafts and other original creations.

The Vault, the council's new gallery shop, features the work of Carolina artists and is open year-round.

The Craven Arts Council is a membership organization with various sponsorship levels available. Members are entitled to ticket discounts and receive a monthly newsletter, Luminary, that announces upcoming arts events.

The Accidental Artist
220 Craven St., New Bern
(252) 634-3411

At this studio, you can showcase your creativity by painting your own pottery, which The Accidental Artist will then fire for you to complete your one-of-a-kind masterpiece. Come relax in the informal atmosphere and give your artistic impulses free reign. You can even book studio space for birthday parties, club meetings and other special occasions. The Accidental Artist is open Tuesday through Saturday.

Art & Materials
219 Middle St., New Bern
(252) 514-2787

Art & Materials sells paints, brushes, how-to books and other supplies for those who work in oils, acrylics, pastels and watercolors as well as paper and sculpture clay. The business, owned by the Mathiot family, also carries a line of scrapbooking and rubber stamping materials. In addition to ifeaturing the works of local artists, Art & Materials schedules a variety of workshops and classes for adults and children who want to explore their artistic talents, and offers summer camps, after school art lessons, and special classes for home school students. The Flying Cat Bead Shop also is located inside Art & Materials for those interested in creating their own distinctive jewelry.

New Bern Camera Club
Kyle Arrowood
(252) 633-5633

The New Bern Camera Club, which meets the third Saturday of every month (except December), is open to people of all ages and skill levels who are interested in photography. In-club photo competitions, field trips, photography-related lectures and other activities provide club members with opportunities to share knowledge and learn new skills.

Crystal Coast Chapter, American Needlepoint Guild
Shirley Kulow
(252) 636-0065

The Crystal Coast Chapter of the American Needlepoint Guild is an educational, nonprofit organization dedicated to the art of needlepoint. Experienced and beginning stitchers are invited to attend the group's meetings, held at 10 AM the first Monday of each month at the West New Bern Recreation Center on Pinetree Drive. Programs consist of stitching projects, instruction and demonstrations as well as fellowship.

Theater

Carolinian Shakespeare Festival
Scottish Rite Temple, 516 Hancock St., New Bern
(252) 634-3269

Carolinian Shakespeare Festival (CSF) performances are presented the first three weekends of August at the Scottish Rite Temple in downtown New Bern. This professional theater company has staged some of the Bard's most well-known works, including Romeo and Juliet, The Winter's Tale, A Midsummer Night's Dream, Hamlet, Twelfth Night and The Comedy of Errors. CSF will present Macbeth as its 2006 production. The goal of CSF is to make the classics entertaining and accessible to everyone. Discounts are available for students and seniors. Tickets are sold at various locations around town, including the New Bern Riverfront Convention Center. Auditions usually take place in March each year for the upcoming season, with rehearsals scheduled for the month of July.

New Bern Civic Theatre
Theater and box office, 414 Pollock St., New Bern
(252) 633-0567
Theater business office, 412 Pollock St., New Bern
(252) 634-9057

A nonprofit organization, New Bern Civic Theatre was organized in 1968 to provide community theater for area adults and children. The group's theatrical productions range from serious drama to lively musicals, including original works. NBCT also offers a number of art education opportunities for children, including StageHands, a performing group of the civic theater that annually stages a special production by children for children. Its unique performances are presented simultaneously in sign and spoken language. The theater also hosts popular two-week Children's Acting and Technical Workshops in the summer.

River Towne Repertory Players
Ruth Waters
(252) 637-2662

This nonprofit community theater group, formed in 2001, is dedicated to encourag-

ing, promoting and practicing the theatrical arts in the community. The group's six annual performances take place at the Sudan Shrine Center downtown. Membership in the Players is open to anyone 16 years and older with a desire to be involved in the organization's operation, including acting, singing, directing, lighting, producing and more. Annual dues are $15 per person. Tickets are available at the Sudan Shrine Center Monday through Friday.

Dance

Atlantic Dance Theatre/Baroque Arts Project
Paige Whitley-Bauguess
(252) 636-0476

Atlantic Dance Theatre, now under the direction of Paige Whitley-Bauguess, presents a Baroque Arts Project season, combining music and dance in exciting performances. Season tickets are available. The Baroque Arts Project, which specializes in music and dance of the 17th and 18th centuries, offers many engaging educational programs in addition to its public performances and tours.

Craven Historical Dancers
Paige Whitley-Bauguess
(252) 636-0476

This unique dance troupe performs, in costume, 18th-century social dances, including reels, country dances, minuets, cotillions and jigs. They entertain through holiday performances, festivals and other events. The group meets weekly and each fall accepts new members with or without previous dance experience. Whitley-Bauguess also recently formed the New Bern Dancing Assembly, a new Baroque dance performing group for boys and girls in fourth through 12th grades. Baroque dance classes and workshops are offered at Down East Dance.

Dance Theatre Performing Arts Studios, Inc.
2107 S. Glenburnie Rd., New Bern
(252) 637-1818

Open since 1990, Dance Theatre Performing Arts Studios, under the direction of Veronica Sabiston, is a training ground for dance students of all ages and skills, from the absolute beginner to the very advanced. Dance Theatre's comprehensive program offers a diversified curriculum including classical ballet and pointe, lyrical, jazz, hip hop, video jazz, tap, creative dance and jumpstart. This dance school also features classes for boys and adults and offers multiple classrooms for personalized attention.

The award-winning Dance Theatre offers opportunities for students to participate in regional and national competitions and on the local level take part in mall shows, festivals, parades, telethons and more. The studio conducts a local school performance tour and hosts many performances throughout the year, including its annual Spring Performance in May. Excerpts are aired on local television Channel 10 each summer.

Dance Theatre prepares students for auditions each year for the North Carolina School of the Arts (NCSA), American Ballet Theatre (ABT) and Joffery Ballet. It's also proud to have directed many of its students toward roles in national television, major motion pictures and music videos as well as dance-related presentations for Walt Disney World, Kings Dominion and Busch Gardens.

Down East Dance
2500 Trent Rd., Suite 4, New Bern
(252) 633-9622

Down East Dance prides itself in educating students of all ages in the art of dance. Classes in ballet, pointe, jazz and tap are designed to create positive, joyful learning experiences, which encompass coordination-building skills, flexibility, strength, technique, correct alignment and creativity. Every other year, the Down East Dance ballet faculty and students stage an impressive performance of The Nutcracker with guest artists. Down East Dance also showcases two youth performance groups: The Contemporary Dance Exchange, a non-competitive group directed by Wendy Daw, whose primary goal is to share the art of dance; and The New Bern Dancing Assembly, which studies and performs 18th-century dance under the direction of Craven Historical Dancers founder and director Paige Whitley-Bauguess.

Rivertowne Ballroom
305 Pollock St., New Bern
(252) 637-2003

Want to learn how to swing, cha cha or tango? Maybe the fox trot and the waltz are more your speed. If you've ever had an interest in learning ballroom dancing, this is the place to go. Private and group lessons are offered, and dance students get an opportunity to practice their skills at weekly parties.

Wanda Kay's School of Dance
801 Cardinal Rd., New Bern
(252) 636-2811

Wanda Kay offers tap, jazz and ballet for ages 3 through adult in her specially designed studio. The Wanda Kay Dancers, a group of 100 advanced dance students, perform at fairs and festivals throughout the area, including MUMfest. All of Wanda Kay's dancers ages 7 and older open the New Bern Christmas Parade every year.

Music

Coastal Carolina Chamber Music Festival
Various locations, downtown New Bern
(252) 626-5419

The Coastal Carolina Chamber Music Festival, now in its third season, features two fall weekends of beautiful classical music performed by world-class musicians at a variety of locations throughout downtown New Bern. Each year's roster includes talented professionals who perform internationally as soloists and members of the country's finest ensembles, including the Boston Symphony Orchestra, the Boston Pops and the Metropolitan Opera Orchestra. Festival events include not only musical performances but also interactive and entertaining social events that combine to create an up-close and personal concert experience. Season, individual and mix-and-match ticket options are available.

Fairfield Harbour Chorus
Pat Rivett
(252) 638-8470

This chorus began with 24 enthusiastic members in 1984. Today, membership totals approximately 65 vocalists. The group performs about 15 concerts each year, featuring all types of music, including show tunes, gospel, Broadway hits, holiday arrangements, pop and contemporary. It has given numerous performances in area churches, rest homes and retirement homes and has combined talents with other choruses at Cherry Point and Craven Community College. Members must be residents of Fairfield Harbour. Rehearsals are conducted on Monday evenings at 7 PM at the Fairfield Community Center. Rehearsals begin the first Monday after Labor Day and continue until mid-May.

Craven Community Chorus
Philip Evancho
(252) 638-7357

This large choral group, formed in 1985, performs locally as well as in surrounding counties and out of state. There are no auditions, and membership is open to anyone from 18 to 80 who can carry a tune and enjoys singing. The 70-member group likes to include musicians whenever possible and usually plans its shows around a theme. Past performances have featured Dixieland standards, Old West favorites, Big Band hits and classic '50s rock 'n' roll, as well as annual spring and Christmas productions. Weekly practices take place from 6:30 to 8:30 PM Tuesdays at Craven Community College's Orringer Auditorium.

Craven Concerts Inc.
Grover C. Fields Middle School, Dr. M. L. King Jr. Blvd.
(252) 637-1119

This organization, in existence since 1927, schedules five musical concerts each year, staged at Grover C. Fields Middle School auditorium on Dr. M. L. King Jr. Boulevard. Season tickets are $50 for adults and $10 for students. Productions feature a variety of performances, including one by the North Carolina Symphony, and season ticket-holders are entitled to admission to reciprocal concerts in nearby communities. Membership forms and more information are available by calling the number above or writing P.O. Box 12213, New Bern, NC 28561-2213.

Fuller's Music
2310 Trent Rd., New Bern
(252) 638-2811

Fuller's Music carries a complete inventory of instruments, sheet music and other items for both beginning and experienced musicians. Lessons on a variety of instruments, including guitar, piano, drums, flute, clarinet, saxophone, trumpet, trombone, banjo, mandolin, fiddle, violin and dulcimer, are taught by talented instructors.

North Carolina Symphony, New Bern Series
New Bern Riverfront Convention Center
(252) 637-9400

The North Carolina Symphony comes to New Bern with an outstanding series of concerts featuring classical favorites. Several seating options and price ranges are available. Three performances take place at the New Bern Riverfront Convention Center, with a free concert scheduled during early summer at Tryon Palace Historic Sites & Gardens. Season tickets are available by calling the New Bern/Craven County Convention and Visitors Center at the number above.

Commercial Galleries

ART Gallery Ltd.
502 Pollock St., New Bern
(252) 636-2120

On the second floor of the Edward Stanly house, this gallery offers fine works in contemporary North Carolina arts, including paintings, art glass, sculpture, jewelry, stoneware, porcelain and tapestry. It's open daily by appointment.

Carolina Creations
317-A Pollock St., New Bern
(252) 633-4369
www.carolinacreations.com

An artist-owned studio and gallery open since 1990, Carolina Creations offers handcrafted American and North Carolinian fine art and contemporary craft by more than 250 professional artists, including potters, glass blowers, woodworkers and jewelers, as well as original art and prints by owner Janet Franceour and pottery by her husband Michael. Well known artists carried include

At The Accidental Artist at 220 Craven St., you are the artist. Just buy a piece of pottery, paint it any way you want, and then let The Accidental Artist fire your finished product for later pick-up. It's the perfect place for a rainy day outing with kids, or an informal gathering of friends.

CLOSE UP

New Bern's Copper Bears

New Bern has a number of distinctive bears around town, the bear being the city's symbol as homage to its Swiss roots. Three of the more unusual bears -- two of them on City Hall facing Craven and Pollock Streets, and the other on the old fire department on Broad Street -- date from 1914, when they were purchased for around $75 each.

This is one of the Copper Bears on display in New Bern

photo: Vina Hutchinson Farmer

What is not commonly known is that these three copper bears were unofficially named in tribute to three city leaders. The bear on the old fire department building is King William I and was named for William Ellis, who served as mayor from 1903-05 and alderman from 1909-17. Ellis also was a fireman with the Atlantic Fire Company. The bear facing Pollock Street is King William II, named for William Blades, who served not only as alderman from 1913-17 but also on the Building Committee when City Hall was renovated in 1913-14. (Blades resigned his position as alderman on Nov. 6, 1917.) The bear facing Craven Street is Crown Prince Albert, named for Albert Bangert. He served as the city's mayor from 1913-17 and 1925-29 and as an alderman from 1903-07, 1911-13, 1917-19 and 1921-25.

The bears were originally located on the old City Hall on Craven Street and were apparently moved to their current locations when City Hall moved to the old Federal building in 1936.

Victor Jones and John Lays provided the information for this article.

the painted furniture line Sticks as well as sculpture and prints by StoryPeople. Carolina Creations is open daily, and there is always something new to discover.

Framing Fox Art Gallery
217 Middle St., New Bern
(252) 635-6400, (800) 237-6077

Butch Miller has combined his love of fine arts and talent for framing into a successful shop that features the work of leading national artists covering a range of subjects, from the contemporary NASCAR to the beauty of limited edition Civil War collectibles and a little bit of everything else thrown in between. Many of the pieces available are numbered and signed, and of course custom framing services are available. Framing Fox is open Monday through Saturday.

Weavers Webb Gallery
602 Pollock St., New Bern
(252) 514-2681

Featuring a wide selection of hand-woven items, such as baby blankets and table linens, this gallery offers an expanded selection of knitting and needlepoint supplies, as well as crochet and cross-stitch items. Classes are available in needlepoint, weaving, crochet and knitting.

NEW BERN ANNUAL EVENTS

The town of New Bern does an incredible job of entertaining and educating throughout the year. Tryon Palace Historic Sites & Gardens hosts a variety of special events, and the Craven Arts Council and Gallery and other arts organizations sponsor art exhibitions, music and dance performances year round. Several concert series and performing artists provide musical and visual entertainment at various venues. The New Bern Civic Theatre and the River Towne Repertory Players schedule a variety of dramatic and comedic presentations, and numerous musical and art organizations annually schedule shows and perform at city functions and festivities. Current calendar information may be obtained through the New Bern Craven County Convention and Visitors Center, (252) 637-9400 or (800) 437-5767.

January

Handel's Messiah
Centenary United Methodist Church,
309 Middle St., New Bern
(252) 637-4181

A local favorite since 1981, performances of this classic around the time of "Old Christmas" in early January combine 150 community voices and North Carolina Symphony musicians with conductor James Ogle, artistic director of the Boise Philharmonic Association. Tickets are available for two afternoon and two evening performances.

Shriners' Parade
Downtown New Bern
(252) 637-5197

The Shriners host a colorful and entertaining parade in downtown New Bern, featuring clowns, horses, mini-cars, bands and more. Shriners' parades, wherever performed, are fun, funny and as festive as a fez. The parade is part of the Winter Ceremonial, which occurs annually during the fourth weekend of January, bringing in thousands of Shriners from all over North Carolina for events centered at the Sudan Shrine Center at the corner of Broad and E. Front Streets.

February

New Bern Preservation Foundation Antiques Show & Sale
New Bern Riverfront Convention Center
(252) 633-6448

Antiques take the stage in mid-February when the New Bern Preservation Foundation sponsors its annual three-day Antiques Show & Sale at the New Bern Riverfront Convention Center. The show hosts as many as 40 dealers who sell, demonstrate, instruct and exhibit 18th- and 19th-century American antiques. Experts also are on hand to identify whether your items are "antique or junque." Tickets cost $5 for all three days. Proceeds from the show benefit the Preservation Foundation's restoration projects and many other properties that are saved by the foundation's revolving fund program.

Attic, Basement, Closet Sale
Knights of Columbus Building,
1125 Pinetree Dr., New Bern
(252) 638-8558

Known as the annual ABC Sale, this event offers New Bernians a bargain opportunity each year in late February. Locals contribute a full building of sale items ranging from appliances to original art, then wait in line for the doors to open at 8 AM for the one-day sale. The event benefits programs of the New

In December, visit Santa Claus in his special Santa House on the corner of Broad and Middle Streets in downtown New Bern. He'll listen to your Christmas wishes Monday through Friday evenings, and all day on Saturday right up until Christmas Eve.

i

Bern Historical Society, which organizes the annual sale.

March

Decorative Arts Symposium
Tryon Palace Historic Sites & Gardens, Pollock and George Sts., New Bern
(252) 514-4900, (800) 767-1560

In addition to their gardens, New Bernians are proud of the authenticity of their vintage belongings. Here again, Tryon Palace Historic Sites & Gardens fills the bill with its annual Decorative Arts Symposium in March, which offers unique perspectives on decorative arts and American history. This event includes nationally recognized speakers as well as meals, social events and special tours. A registration fee is charged, and a brochure is printed each year outlining the thematic events.

Model Train Show
New Bern High School, Academic Dr., just off N.C. Hwy. 17, New Bern
(252) 637-4026

Mid-March brings the annual weekend Model Train Show of the Carolina Coastal Railroaders. The interesting collection of miniatures and model trains shown in the New Bern High School auditorium is a great stop for kids younger than 11, who are admitted free with an adult. Admission for ages 12 and older is $5.

Spring Historic Homes and Gardens Tour
New Bern Historical Society, 512 Pollock St., New Bern
(252) 638-8558

Many people enjoy visiting New Bern in late March and early April for the New Bern Spring Homes and Gardens Tour. The event is cosponsored by the New Bern Historical Society and the New Bern Preservation Foundation, and the town puts on its prettiest face to welcome visitors. The tour includes private homes, gardens and churches in the historic district, with guides and location maps provided. The tour can best be enjoyed on foot and is an ideal opportunity to explore selected homes and landmarks in this river city. During the two-day event, Tryon Palace also opens its gardens for free. Historic Homes and Gardens Tour tickets, $18 on tour days or $15 in advance, may be purchased at the New Bern Historical Society office. Tickets can also be ordered in advance by mail.

Gardeners' Weekend
Tryon Palace Historic Sites & Gardens, Pollock and George Sts., New Bern
(252) 514-4900, (800) 767-1560

The weekend of the New Bern Spring Historic Homes and Gardens Tour is the same as Gardeners' Weekend at Tryon Palace Historic Sites & Gardens. Palace gardens are open free throughout the weekend. The 14 acres of gardens are planted with more than 30,000 bulbs and spring flowers, resulting in a riot of lovely colors. Thousands of gloriously colored tulips are in bloom, along with expansive plantings of blazing daffodils and pansies. All of this is set against a luxurious background of azaleas and dogwoods. It's quite a sight. The palace also hosts a Heritage Plant Sale, which features perennials, herbs, annuals, trees and shrubs as well as a collection of rare and historic plants, all available for purchase.

April

Annual Shriners' Fish Fry
Various locations
(252) 637-5197

In 2006 this annual tradition celebrates 39 years of providing New Bernians with delicious fish plates. Proceeds from the event benefit Shriners' Hospitals for Children. Fish plates, $5 each, are served in the Furniture Fair parking lot at 2880 Neuse Boulevard and the New Bern Shrine Club on 2102 S. Glenburnie Drive, both in New Bern; the Broad Creek Service Station on N.C. Highway 55 in Bridgeton; and at the Food Lion in James City. Serving times are 11 AM to 1:30 PM and 4:30 to 7 PM. Local businesses can arrange to have plates delivered.

Festival of Fun
Union Point Park, New Bern
(252) 639-2901

This fun-filled day of entertainment for children and their families includes amusement rides, games, clowns, hands-on educational activities, exhibits, pony rides and lots of other fun activities. Organized by the New Bern Recreation and Parks Department, the

festival takes place at beautiful Union Point Park on East Front Street.

May

Strawberry Festival
Vanceboro
(252) 244-0017

Celebrating this delicious, locally grown fruit, the Strawberry Festival features food, rides, music, games and much more, all in a family atmosphere. The festival is sponsored by the Vanceboro Rescue Squad. To get to Vanceboro, located 20 miles from New Bern, cross the Neuse River Bridge and take U.S. Highway 17 north to N.C. Highway 43 and follow the signs.

Tryon Palace Concert Series
Tryon Palace's South Lawn,
Pollock and George Sts., New Bern
(252) 514-4900, (800) 767-1560

This four-concert series of free evening performances on the palace's South Lawn runs from mid-May through late June each year and includes concerts by a broad range of ensembles, including the North Carolina Symphony.

i

Eastern Neuse River Initiative for Community Health (ENRICH) presents its annual Health and Safety Expo every May. Local businesses and non-profit groups celebrate health and safety with health screenings, nutritious snacks, health and fitness demonstrations, nutrition information and more. ENRICH is a local Healthy Carolinians partnership for Craven and Pamlico counties that works to improve the health and well being in the community. For information, dates and locations, call Kari Garner at (252) 636-4920, ext. 3722.

June

Neuse River Days
Union Point Park, New Bern
(252) 637-7972

Sponsored by the Neuse River Foundation, this festival is designed for people who enjoy outdoor activities. Kayak and canoe races, including the Neuse River Classic and the River Dog Relay Race, are among the festival's most popular features for all levels of competitors. The not-so-serious are invited to race homemade rafts in the Great Twin Rivers Raft Race. Every year participants are always entertained by the unusual entries, some of which actually float. Of course Neuse River Days also offers music, crafts, games and other festival favorites.

July

Fourth of July
Various locations, New Bern
(252) 637-9400, (800) 437-5767

As one of America's first towns to have a Fourth of July celebration, New Bern still enjoys a well-turned-out celebration with traditional hot dogs and fireworks. Swiss Bear coordinates the impressive fireworks display that takes place at Union Point Park on the downtown waterfront. Bands traditionally perform patriotic music to complement the event. Additional holiday activities take place at Tryon Palace Historic Sites & Gardens, where the gardens are open for free.

August

Carolinian Shakespeare Festival
Scottish Rite Temple, 516 Hancock St.,
New Bern
(252) 634-3269

Carolinian Shakespeare Festival performs the works of the Bard in a three-week run the first three weekends of August. Discounts are available for students and seniors.

North Carolina's roadside wildflowers are a beautiful sight.

photo: George Mitchell

Greater New Bern Business Expo
New Bern Riverfront Convention Center
(252) 637-3111

The Greater New Bern Business Expo, hosted by the New Bern Riverfront Convention Center and presented by the New Bern Area Chamber of Commerce, demonstrates the diversity of the business community in the Craven County area. Businesses and non-profit organizations set up displays, offer free samples, discounts and door prizes, and share information about their products and/or services. Admission is free.

September

Coastal Carolina Chamber Music Festival
Various locations, downtown New Bern
(252) 626-5419

The Coastal Carolina Chamber Musical Festival brings some of the nation's most talented musicians to eastern North Carolina for concerts that are entertaining, educational and interactive. Taking place at various locations over two weekends, the festival includes special open rehearsals that offer behind-the-scene peeks and opportunities to meet the artists, as well as a free family concert that offers discovery and adventure for all ages. Festival packages as well as individual concert tickets are available.

Pet owners are invited to bring their pets to Christ Episcopal Church's Blessing of the Animals, held every fall in honor of St. Francis of Assisi.

DUFFEST
Henderson Park, New Bern
(252) 639-7586

This annual festival -- DUFFEST is short for Greater Duffyfield Unity Family Festival -- celebrates the heritage of this historic African-American neighborhood with a parade, live music, food and other cultural activities. Sponsored by the Greater Duffyfield Residents Council, the festival is designed to foster community pride and unity.

October

Oktoberfest
Farmer's Market, 421 S. Front St., New Bern
(252) 637-3199

Oktoberfest, a celebration that usually signals the beginning of October, is annually celebrated by members of the New Bern Alpenverein. Oktoberfest gathers New Bernians, with or without European roots, for an evening celebration at the Farmer's Market on S. Front Street. German bands and dancers are usually there to provide the music and entertainment, and a real German dinner is served. Purchase of a dinner is required for admission.

Mumfest
Downtown New Bern
(252) 638-5781

Swiss Bear Downtown Development Corp. has organized and coordinated the annual fall event now known as Mumfest for the past 25 years. In cooperation with the City of New Bern, Tryon Palace Historic Sites & Gardens, area organizations and businesses, this three-day celebration, always the second weekend in October, highlights the city's assets and attracts more than 70,000 visitors to the downtown area and its waterfront.

Mumfest, one of the top 10 festivals in the state, kicks into high gear on Saturday and Sunday, with an endless diversity of festival foods, arts and crafts, corporate exhibits, and a kids' corner with amusement rides, fun activities, puppets, rock climbing, a petting zoo and more. Those attending also can enjoy such attractions as live-stage and roving entertainment; a model railroad exhibit; military vessel tours; flower and art shows; and a boat show. Tryon Palace Historic Sites & Gardens features free admission to its gardens.

A free trolley shuttle makes parking easy – just park at Twin Rivers Mall or one of the other convenient locations and ride the trolley into the downtown area.

Coastal Carolina Fair & Expo
Craven County Fairgrounds,
U.S. Hwy. 70, 4 miles east of New Bern
(252) 636-0303

Livestock and produce events are always interesting to see at this fair, sponsored by the Craven County Jaycees, but most folks come for the midway. Admission is available at the gate and includes all rides, special events, exhibits and parking, but the midway has lots of ways to entice more money from your pockets, including food, games and concessions.

New Bern at Night Ghostwalk
New Bern Historical Society,
512 Pollock St., New Bern
(252) 638-8558

In late October, the New Bern Historical Society conducts its New Bern at Night Ghostwalk, complete with ghosts from New Bern's past. Walking tours feature historic homes, churches and the Cedar Grove Cemetery. (Insiders recommend you attend all three nights. Attend the cemetery tour the first night -- which is the only attraction open the first day of the tour -- and then divide up the rest of the attractions over the next two nights. This will give you more time to enjoy the walk.) Ghostwalks focus on historic events particular to New Bern, and ghosts from historic occasions are present in homes and historic buildings on the tour to tell how the times affected them. Tickets are available at retail locations and the historical society's headquarters, the Attmore-Oliver Civil War House Museum.

New Bern Jazz & Blues Fest
New Bern Riverfront Convention Center
(252) 634-3261

The New Bern Jazz Preservation Society hosts two nights of hot jazz and cool blues in late October. This popular two-day event features nationally known headliners.

November

Craven Arts Council Holiday Showcase and Sale
Bank of the Arts,
317 Middle St., New Bern
(252) 638-2577

The Craven Arts Council's annual Holiday Showcase and Sale kicks off the day after Thanksgiving. Shoppers will find many unique handcrafted gift items, including jewelry, pottery and stoneware, floral arrangements, birdhouses, fine knitted baby wear, stuffed animals, toys and more. Admission to the sale is free.

December

Coastal Christmas Celebration
Various locations, New Bern
(252) 637-9400, (800) 437-5767

You can easily catch the spirit of the season in New Bern. Annual events of New Bern's Coastal Christmas Celebration during the month of December include the Craven County Jaycees' festive parade the first Saturday of the month in downtown New Bern, and the Craven Regional Medical Center Foundation's Festival of Trees gala, including the popular Breakfast with Santa for children. Downtown merchants host a special First Friday event, staying open late and offering fantastic bargains. Caroling, musical performances, prize drawings and other events round out this event. The New Bern Women's Club hosts its annual "The Holly and the Ivy" Homes Tour. Santa Claus also hears the Christmas wishes of good little boys and girls in his Santa House on the corner of Broad and Middle Streets. Performers from Down East Dance offer The Nutcracker ballet every other year.

Coastal Christmas Flotilla
Union Point Park, New Bern
(252) 672-0309

Santa arrives in downtown New Bern in style abroad a Hatteras yacht as part of the Coastal Christmas Flotilla, which takes place the first Saturday of the month and is organized by New Bern Recreation and Parks. The flotilla of gaily decorated boats of all sizes proceeds down the Trent River and passes Union Point, giving spectators a long, lingering look at the boats festooned with sparkling lights, diving dolphins and red-nosed reindeer.

Tryon Palace Holiday Celebration
Tryon Palace Historic Sites & Gardens, Pollock and George Sts., New Bern
(252) 514-4900, (800) 767-1560

Staff and volunteers prepare for weeks for the Tryon Palace Holiday Celebration. By the beginning of December the palace looks much as it did during the holidays in 1770 when Governor William Tryon hosted a "very grand and noble Entertainment and Ball" to celebrate the grand opening of his sumptuous home and the Royal capital. The palace is lighted and adorned with fresh fruit and fragrant greenery. Cooks are busy in the kitchen preparing confections and delicacies, and the air is filled with holiday aromas. The tours run throughout the month of December and include all of the site's historic homes. Special events include Candlelight Tours, fireworks displays and the Jonkonnu celebration. Admission prices are $15 for adults and $6 for children.

NEW BERN ON THE WATER

With New Bern's location at the confluence of the Neuse and Trent rivers, it's not surprising that its citizens take to the water like, well, ducks. The weather is mild enough year round to entice the locals into sailing, skiing, fishing or relaxing on or around the rivers.

Waterways

Boaters, fishing enthusiasts and outdoorsy types in the New Bern area have two waterways to explore: the expansive Neuse River that flows into Pamlico Sound or the slow, meandering Trent River that flows into the Neuse.

The Neuse River is ideal for cruising by sail or power, with miles of sandy beaches, clearly marked channels, easy access via the Intracoastal Waterway (ICW) and Pamlico Sound and many marinas and protected anchorages. The Trent River is deep, has a marked channel and is navigable by small boat. Its lower reaches are fine for uncrowded water-skiing. Brices Creek, a tributary of the Trent, winds far into the Croatan National Forest and offers excellent fishing and wildlife observation.

The rotating bridge over the Trent River leading into downtown New Bern opens on request weekdays except from 6:30 to 8:30 AM and 4 to 6 PM, with openings for any waiting boats scheduled for 7:30 AM and 5 PM. On Saturdays, the bridge opens by request only. On Sundays and federal holidays between Memorial Day and Labor Day, the bridge is closed between 2 and 7 PM to accommodate vehicular traffic, with openings for accumulated boat traffic scheduled on the hour and half-hour. The remainder of the year, the daily schedule is in effect seven days a week. The bridge tender monitors channel 13 VHF, and the bridge's call sign is KA97360. The bridge phone number is (252) 514-4733. The railroad bridges upriver from New Bern are always open except when in use, usually during the very early morning hours and only occasionally during the day. National Oceanic and Atmospheric Administration (NOAA) stations in the area are New Bern and Beaufort, WX-2 (162.475 MHz) and Hatteras, WX-3 (162.40 MHZ).

Note: In 2007 the state Department of Transportation will start a two-year project to replace the Alfred Cunningham Bridge, which spans the Trent River and connects downtown New Bern to U.S. Highway 70. While the project is underway, traffic will be diverted to the Trent Woods/Pembroke exit, located just minutes from downtown. Although a definite timetable has yet to be established, the bridge is scheduled to be replaced by 2010.

A clearly marked channel up the Neuse from the Intracoastal Waterway will bring you into historic New Bern. The natural channel depths generally run between 8 and 12 feet, with little noticeable tidal effect. A strong easterly or northerly wind will raise the level, while a sustained westerly breeze, say 25 knots, can lower this level by as much as 2 feet. Also noteworthy to boaters are the sapling stakes dotting the river. The stakes are strung with nets in the early spring and late fall. The nets are usually buoyed by corks or plastic bottles or marked by white flags.

The Neuse is a wide river, which invites sailing in addition to motor-cruising and water-skiing. The many wandering tributaries promise scenic canoeing and exciting fishing. Much of the Neuse River's shoreline south

i

Croatan National Forest maintains a number of sites that offer handy access to water. Boat ramps and fishing piers at Brices Creek, Haywood Landing and Cahooque Creek are handicapped-accessible. A complete list of boat ramps and launching sites is available from the ranger's office at 141 E. Fisher Avenue, New Bern, (252) 638-5628.

of New Bern forms one of the boundaries of the vast 157,000-acre Croatan National Forest. Here, locals and visitors enjoy public recreation areas, with swimming and picnic facilities near the Minnesott ferry terminal and at Flanner's Beach south of New Bern.

Fishing

Expect to hook bass, bream, flounder and many more fish in local waters. The Neuse River is also home to many crabs, the catching of which provides tasty and profitable rewards.

Nearby Croatan National Forest permits fresh- and saltwater fishing; however, fishing in the forest's freshwater lakes is poor because of the acidity of the water. But along its river shoreline, oystering, crabbing and flounder-gigging can be worthwhile efforts. To find out about the best fishing spots, talk to a ranger at the ranger office at 141 Fisher Avenue, 9 miles south of New Bern just off U.S. Highway 70 E. The office is open weekdays from 8 AM to 4:30 PM.

If you just like to cruise backwoods waters, several forest locations have fishing piers and boat ramps, including Brices Creek, Cahooque Creek, Catfish Lake, Great Lake and Haywood Landing. Some of these sites are deep in the Croatan National Forest, so it's best to check with a ranger for specific directions. Better yet, stop by the ranger office and pick up a forest map. (For more information on places to fish in the park, see our New Bern Recreation and Parks chapter.)

Boating

MARINAS

Boats of all sizes can find berthing space in downtown New Bern and nearby marinas. Whether you're just cruising around or wish to launch your boat at one of the many local ramps, most locations have similar facilities. In the downtown area especially, it is not unusual for leisure yachters or sailors to arrive for what they thought would be a short visit only to find themselves living aboard their

There's no better place to be than by the water.

photo: George Mitchell

CLOSE UP

Good Things to Come on the New Bern Waterfront

Exciting changes are taking place along New Bern's waterfront as a variety of businesses, nonprofit organizations and public interests work together to make the area as attractive as possible for both visitors and residents. Over the next few years, the old Barbour Boat Works site on South Front Street will be transformed from an industrial site to a launching point for historical and environmental education in New Bern and eastern North Carolina.

Tryon Palace Historic Sites & Gardens broke ground in October 2002 on its wetlands restoration project, where the grounds that formerly housed the old Barbour Boat Works will be transformed into a marshy area, similar to the way the area might have look in Governor Tryon's day. Ultimately, the site, located between the palace property and the Farmer's Market on South Front Street, will house the $50 million North Carolina History Center.

TPHS&G Director Kay Williams said officials spent 15 years looking for a suitable site for the center, which will also become home to a new visitors center. The current center, a renovated 1930s gas station on the corner of Pollock and George streets, is no longer a good site because it brings pedestrian traffic and major vehicular traffic uncomfortably close. And unloading tour buses next to the visitors center is next to impossible.

Williams explained that palace officials looked at a variety of locations before settling on the site. When Barbour Boat Works closed in 1997, the state was able

vessels, staying weeks, sometimes months, even years. If you're traveling to New Bern from some distance, it is wise to call ahead to ensure docking space availability, especially during the warmer months. Here, we list the local marinas in alphabetical order.

BridgePointe Marina
101 Howell Rd., New Bern
(252) 637-7372, (877) 283-7713

BridgePointe Marina is located within walking distance of downtown New Bern's attractions, shopping and dining. BridgePointe is across the Trent River from the New Bern Riverfront Convention Center. Open year round, BridgePointe serves sail and power vessels up to 150 feet. It has 125 floating laminated cedar slips, 30 of which are transient berths, a marked entry channel with 12-foot approach depth, and a dockside depth of 8 to 16 feet. Amenities include a pump-out station, ice, electricity, showers, laundry facilities, a patio, grills, a restaurant and a lounge. Marina guests also are allowed full use of the hotel pool. Outback Steakhouse is located next door.

Duck Creek Marina
699 Galloway Rd., Bridgeton
(252) 638-1702

At the head of Duck Creek on the north side of the Neuse, this marina is open year round and serves sail and power vessels up to 46 feet. It has 55 slips, a marked entry channel with an approach depth of 6 feet, a dockside depth of 6 feet, a 35-ton lift, a storage yard for do-it-yourself repair work, marine supplies, electricity and showers. Because the marina is across the river from New Bern, you will need transportation for shopping or visiting the city's attractions.

Northwest Creek Marina
104 Marina Dr., New Bern
(252) 638-4133

Northwest Creek Marina is on the north side of the Neuse River, near the Fairfield Harbour resort development. Open year

Riverside dwellers know to plant beans and squash when the moon waxes, and that the best fishing is on a northeast wind.

to acquire the almost six-acre property for $1.75 million— $750,000 of that raised by private donations. Site preparation is currently underway to get ready for future construction work.

The overall concept of the 48,000-square-foot North Carolina History Center, according to Williams, is to provide an important introduction to the historical attractions of New Bern and Tryon Palace.

"It will be a significant history center for this area," Williams added.

Among the center's features will be a family history center, where parents and children can participate in interactive events to develop interest in history, explore issues and learn about the past. The center also will include historical exhibits that appeal to a broader general group; programming areas for lectures, films and concerts; classroom space for other programs while the orientation film is showing; exhibition space that will enable Tryon Palace to display collection objects which have been locked away in storage for many years; a refreshment area and restrooms; and space for receptions for evening tours. The outside area also will be developed with educational purposes in mind. Plans include extending the waterfront public walkway from the Sheraton to the boat works site.

Once the center is complete, TPHS&G officials anticipate attendance figures increasing from 90,000 to nearly 200,000 annually.

TPHS&G officials hope to raise the money for the center from private donations, corporate support, grants, and state and federal funding. Current plans call for the new facility to open in 2010, in time for the 300th anniversary of the founding of New Bern.

round, the marina serves sail and power vessels up to 75 feet. It has 268 slips, including transient berths, a marked entry channel with 8 feet of water depth and dockside depth of 12 feet. Amenities include gas and diesel fuel, a pump-out station, a launching ramp, electricity, showers and laundry facilities. Marina patrons can pay special rates to use the resort's amenities, including the indoor and outdoor pools and lighted tennis courts. Transportation will be needed to visit New Bern's attractions.

Tidewater Marina Co. Inc.
300 Madame Moore Ln., New Bern
(252) 637-3347

On the Trent River, Tidewater Marina Co. is open year round and serves sail and power vessels up to 40 feet. It has 30 slips, three transient slips, a marked entry channel with controlling depth of 21 feet, 15 feet at dockside, a railway and lift, a launching ramp, supplies and electricity. It also offers repairs on propellers and hulls. Because it is away from New Bern's hub, you will need transportation to see the sights.

Union Point Park
S. Front and E. Front Sts., New Bern
Lawson Creek Park
Country Club Rd. (off Hwy. 70 Pembroke Exit), New Bern
(252) 639-2900

Union Point Park and Lawson Creek Park serve as city parks and public docks. Boaters can anchor at either park to orient themselves to the area and locate more permanent moorings. The parks feature boat ramps and public facilities; however, a city ordinance prohibits overnight dockage.

NEARBY MARINAS

Nearby marinas at Clubfoot Creek and Minnesott Beach, on the Neuse River, are destinations for enjoyable day sails or cruising trips from New Bern. (See our separate chapter on Oriental for details about the marinas there.) In addition, many marinas are along the Crystal Coast, which is easily accessible from New Bern via the Neuse River and the ICW. (See our Crystal Coast Marinas chapter for listings.) For the convenience of boaters, we provide information on two marinas near New Bern that you can visit as you make your way up and down the Neuse River or toward Pamlico Sound.

Matthews Point Marina
2645 Temples Point Rd., Havelock
(252) 444-1805

Matthews Point Marina is off the beaten track on Clubfoot Creek on the south side of the Neuse River, 10 miles east of Cherry Point. Nestled comfortably in a safe harbor, the year-round marina serves sail and power vessels up to 45 feet. It has 106 slips, six of which are transient berths. It has a marked entry channel, approach depth of 7 feet and dockside depth of 6.5 feet, gas and diesel fuel, electricity, a pump-out station, laundry facilities, showers and ice. A clubhouse, cook-out area and upper-deck lounge are available to boaters. A yacht sales brokerage also is located on-site.

Wayfarers Cove Marina
1107 Bennett Rd., Arapahoe
(252) 249-1424, (800) 922-1424
www.wayfarerscove.com

This waterfront community in Minnesott Beach, on the north side of the Neuse River between New Bern and Oriental, offers a true hurricane hole in Wayfarers Cove Marina, formerly known as the Minnesott Beach Yacht Basin. Development is currently underway around this marina to add riverfront, marina-front and lakefront townhomes and single-family homes. Marina slips also are available to lot and home buyers for purchase. The year-round marina, undergoing renovations in late 2006 to a state-of-the-art Sound Marine floating dock and slip system, serves sail and power vessels up to 60 feet. It has 150 slips, with transient berths available, and a marked entry channel, approach and dockside with depths of 8 feet. Amenities include gas and diesel fuel, a 60-ton lift, dockside utilities, a pump-out station, supplies, ice, showers, laundry facilities and wireless Internet service. Full-service marine repairs are available. The marina is also contiguous to a championship golf course.

Sailing

Various sailing competitions take place throughout the year in the waters around New Bern. For more information, check the annual events calendar maintained by the Visitors Center, (252) 637-9400 or (800) 437-5767, or call Blackbeard's Sailing Club

There are many ways to get on the water in New Bern.

photo: George Mitchell

at (252) 633-3990, or On The Wind Sailing Cruises at Northwest Creek Marina at (252) 322-5804.

On The Wind Sailing Cruises
Northwest Creek Marina, Broad Creek Rd., Fairfield Harbour
(252) 322-5804

On the Wind offers a variety of charters, including day, evening, sunset and live-abroad cruises. All cruises depart from Northwest Creek Marina at Fairfield Harbour, and complimentary beer and soft drinks are served. Call for prices. Sailing instruction also is available.

Paddling

If you want to explore some interesting places by canoe, try the two open-water lakes in the Croatan National Forest. Both Great Lake, 2,809 acres, and Catfish Lake, 962 acres, are home to osprey and alligators, and black bears might be within sight. They are unusual bodies of water because they are surrounded by pocosin, the Indian name for "swamp on a hill." Pocosin is an impenetrable jungle of pond pine, titi, zenobia and greenbriers, but it supports fragile ecosystems that add to the beauty and wildness of the Croatan National Forest.

If you prefer to canoe in enclosed waters, take your canoe to the smaller creeks: Brices, Hadnot, Hancock, Cahooque, Hunters and Holston. In these waters, you can observe a rich variety of plants and wildlife. If you want to canoe in moving waters, paddle in the White Oak, Neuse and Newport rivers. Many varieties of birds show themselves in these waters, and watching them in their natural habitat is a fascinating experience.

Brices Creek Canoe Trail
S.R. 1111 to Lawson Creek Park, New Bern
(252) 636-6606

For a map of this canoeing adventure, call the Craven County Recreation and Parks Department at the number above, or pick one up at the park office, 406 Craven Street in New Bern. The trail is about 12 miles long, beginning at the bridge on State Route 1111 and ending at Lawson Creek Park on the Trent River. There are five access points, and the trail is clearly marked by directional signs. Hours of operation are dawn to dusk.

NEW BERN RECREATION AND PARKS

New Bern is surrounded by water and great open spaces, making it an unbeatable location for all kinds of recreational activities. Adults and children will find numerous places to exercise and take part in sports programs.

For those who want to sample a variety of athletic pursuits, the City of New Bern and Craven County offer year-round recreation programs and public areas for tennis, power walking, running, baseball, basketball, softball and soccer. Both the county and city maintain public boat ramps and fishing piers. Hiking trails are maintained by the Forest Service in the Croatan National Park, and the Brices Creek canoe trail is coordinated by Craven County Parks and Recreation Department (more about that in our On the Water chapter). Golfing is a favorite pastime around here; for a list of courses see the New Bern Golf chapter.

Recreation and Fitness Centers

Craven County Recreation and Parks Department
406 Craven St., New Bern
(252) 636-6606

The Craven County Recreation and Parks Department offers a variety of programs and facilities for citizens of all ages.

Activities and events vary according to age, season and interest levels. Youth programs held throughout the year feature baton twirling, karate, tennis, soccer, baseball, girls softball and youth basketball. Youth camp opportunities include summer day camps, environmental education camps and history camps. Other special events scheduled for youth involve hunting for Easter eggs, taking part in a fishing derby, and clinics to improve tennis skills. Adults will enjoy such activities as flag football, co-ed softball, road race, tennis lessons and tournaments, golf classes, dog obedience instruction, 30-and-older basketball, and senior archery. The recreation department is also a lead agency for the Neuse River Senior Games, an Olympic-style events for ages 55 and older.

The recreation department also sponsors the Craven County Special Olympics for ages 8 and up. Sports include basketball, bowling, aquatics, equestrian events, cycling, track and field, golf and bocce. More than 400 athletes compete and 500 volunteers assist in this program every year.

The department has canoes, kayaks and other sports equipment available to the general public on a rental basis. Picnic shelters and ball fields can be reserved for exclusive use through the recreation department. Rental fees and deposits are required.

Since many events and activities can vary according to season and available resources, you might want to visit the department to see what's offered when. Office hours are Monday through Friday 8 AM to 5 PM.

New Bern Recreation and Parks Department Administrative Office, 248 Craven St., New Bern
(252) 639-2901

The New Bern Recreation and Parks Department operates most of its programs from three centers: Stanley White Recreation Center at 901 Chapman Street, (252) 639-2919; West New Bern Recreation Center, 1225 Pine Tree Drive, (252) 639-2919 or (252) 639-2906; and and the Community Resource Center, 908 Bloomfield Street, (252) 636-4127. For details about seasonal programs, call the New Bern Recreation and Parks Department and ask for brochures or visit the three recreation centers. Each is staffed by a center supervisor, an athletic supervisor and program directors. They will be happy to answer your questions.

Programs include youth lessons in swimming, tennis, cheerleading, baton twirling, golf and football. Tee-ball and baseball are offered to youths between the ages of 6 and

12. Babe Ruth baseball is played by youths ages 13 through 18. Girls' softball, soccer, basketball and wrestling also are offered. Adult leagues cover softball, basketball, flag football and volleyball. For tennis lovers, the department operates eight public courts, six of which are lighted for night play.

Other classes for all ages include ceramics, creative writing, aerobics, bridge and martial arts. There are a number of clubs devoted to a number of special interests such as outdoor adventure, miniatures, model airplanes, embroidery and more. Special programs include billiards, softball, table tennis and other tournaments, as well as a ceramic and hobby show each May. The department also offers a number of programs for seniors, detailed in our New Bern Retirement chapter.

Twin Rivers YMCA
100 YMCA Ln., intersection of Fifth and Sixth Sts., New Bern
(252) 638-8799

At the Twin Rivers YMCA, you'll find a variety of programs for the entire family, including preschool swim lessons, youth progressive swim lessons, lifeguard classes, adult swim lessons, competitive swimming, aqua aerobics and arthritis aquatics. Other program offerings include preschool gymnastics, developmental gymnastics and a competitive gymnastics team.

The YMCA provides youth sports programs for basketball, soccer, tee-ball, coaches-pitch baseball and girls' softball. The YMCA directs an after-school enrichment program for children during the school year and a day camp over the summer months. Special programs for teens involve a Leaders' Club and a Youth and Government program.

Adult programs include low-impact aerobics, step aerobics, kicks and jabs aerobics, aerobics for older adults, and yoga. Other adult programs consist of volleyball, basketball and racquetball. A weight room and wellness center allow teens and adults ages 15 and older the opportunity to increase fitness through strength training and the use of a variety of cardiovascular equipment like treadmills, stair-climbers, cross-trainers and exercise bicycles. An indoor walking track allows walkers to get in their daily exercise no matter what the weather outdoors.

The YMCA's new Aquatics Center is now open, featuring water slides, a spray park, a zero-entry section, plenty of deck space, and lots of room for lap swimming, playing and fun. The outdoor pool also is available for use during cooler months, thanks to its "bubble roof."

i

Ready to hop down the bunny trail at Easter time? The Craven County Recreation and Parks Department, (252) 636-6606, and A Day at the Farm, (252) 514-9494 are among local entities hosting Easter egg hunts.

Courts Plus
2911 Brunswick Ave., New Bern
(252) 633-2221

The Broadcast Vision cardio exercise equipment at Courts Plus ensures a good workout, as do the expanded free-weight facilities and state-of-the-art weight-training equipment. A staff of five personal trainers can provide additional assistance and motivation. After your workout, you can wind down in the saunas, steam room or whirlpool. Lockers, towels and a tanning booth are also available. The pro shop offers apparel, equipment and accessories for your fitness needs. You can play racquetball on one of the four indoor courts, or go swimming and take part in aqua aerobics in the indoor and outdoor pools. You also can participate in organized karate, basketball, volleyball and aerobics, and child care and special programs for children are available. Courts Plus does not have trial memberships, but visitors may purchase a one-month, temporary membership.

Gold's Gym
3340 Dr. M. L. King Jr. Blvd., New Bern
(252) 634-9499

Located in the old Lowe's Building at the corner of McCarthy Boulevard and Dr. M. L. King Jr. Boulevard, Gold's Gym has more than 300 pieces of user-friendly exercise equipment. Cross training and bike machines, Cybex, Life Fitness and Hammer Strength machines, free weights and more are ready to help you get fit and stay fit. New members are given fitness assessments and assistance with setting realistic fitness goals by one of the gym's personal trainers, who also are available to work with members one-on-one.

Group classes are offered in Body Pump, Body Step, Body Flow, yoga, tai chi, kickboxing, floor and senior fitness, weight training and more. Other amenities include a juice bar, a nutrition center featuring vitamins and supplements, tanning beds, a stand-up, high-pressure booth for tanning, free child care and more. A variety of membership options are available at Gold's Gym, which is open daily.

Bowling

The Strike Zone
3550 Dr. M. L. King Jr. Blvd., New Bern
(252) 637-6033

This state-of-the-art smoke-free recreational facility features 24 lanes of bowling fun, with both bowling leagues and open play available. Games are $2.95 each before 5 PM ($2.75 for children younger than 12 and seniors) and $3.50 each after 5 PM. Shoe rentals are available for $2 a pair. Also scheduled for alternate Friday and Saturday nights is the spectacular, lights-out Big Bang Cosmic Bowling, complete with satellite radio, a laser show and glow-in-the-dark bowling balls and pins, for $10 per person from 9:30 PM until midnight. Reservations are recommended for this but not required. The Strike Zone also offers a snack shop, pool tables, an arcade area and a soft play zone for small children, and features a special deal for children's birthday parties (see our New Bern Kidstuff chapter for more information). The Strike Zone is open Monday through Thursday from noon to 10 PM, Friday and Saturday from noon to midnight, and Sunday from 1 to 10 PM.

Hiking

Island Creek Forest Walk
Croatan National Forest
(252) 638-5628

This half-mile trail is perfect for a morning or afternoon hike. As you traverse it, you will see a virgin-like stand of upland hardwoods, picturesque Island Creek with bottomland hardwoods and a managed stand of loblolly pines. Before setting out, stop at the district ranger's office on Fisher Avenue and pick up the Island Creek Forest Walk brochure. The brochure contains a self-guided tour that identifies trees and other trail features. It also gives a map and directions to the trail.

Neusiok Trail
Croatan National Forest
(252) 638-5628

This area is strictly for those who enjoy roughing it. No camping facilities exist along the trail, but you may primitive camp if you pack out your garbage. You'll need to bring along drinking water and wear boots to cross wet areas. The trailhead starts on the Neuse River at Pinecliff Recreation Area and ends at Oyster Point on the Newport River. It passes through a cypress-lined sandy beach, hardwood forests and thick pocosin with pond pines. The length of the trail is 21 miles, and it crosses several paved and unpaved roads. Except at Pinecliff, camping is permitted anywhere along the trail. Hikers and campers need to bring their own drinking water, and are advised to wear all-weather gear and water-repellant boots along with plenty of bug repellent. Because of summer's biting, stinging and zinging insects, fall, winter and early spring are better for camping and hiking. Catfish Lake and Great Lake also have additional primitive camping and earthen boat ramps. Boat ramps are available at Brices Creek, Cahooque Creek and Haywood Landing. Locals favor these spots for their natural beauty and handy access to water, but remember, insects can be prolific in the summer months. For directions, call or stop by the district ranger's office on Fisher Avenue.

Pinecliff Recreation Area
Croatan National Forest
(252) 638-5628

Visitors can indulge in day-use activities such as picnicking, hiking and fishing at this Neuse River–based recreation area. Chemical toilets, well water and trailhead parking for the Neusiok Trail are also provided. Pinecliff is open year round for day use only.

City Parks

The city of New Bern has lots of parks that are great places to go for outdoor enjoyment. Below we describe many of the more popular parks with playgrounds, although the recreation department also maintains a number of smaller parks that for the most

The Down East Dog Park is currently under development and will be located just inside Glenburnie Park.

part serve only their surrounding communities. For more information about reserving shelters and/or parks at no cost for birthday parties, family reunions and other gatherings, call the New Bern Recreation and Parks Department at (252) 639-2901. We have indicated below which parks and shelters are available for reservations.

Glenburnie Park
312 Glenburnie Dr., New Bern

In the Glenburnie Gardens residential area off Oaks Road, this 51-acre park is shaded by a grove of old pine trees and is considered one of New Bern's most scenic parks. It fronts the Neuse River and has a public boat ramp with paved parking, four picnic shelters with tables and grills, fishing piers, a playground, a disc golf course and public restrooms. Glenburnie Park and its shelters can be reserved.

Lawson Creek Park
Country Club Rd., New Bern

Off Pembroke Road and fronting the Trent River, this 140-acre park has two boat landings and is a major attraction for water enthusiasts. Lawson Creek Park has something for everyone -- two soccer fields, two fishing piers, a handicapped walkway and fishing pier, restroom facilities and a picnic area that includes a walkway with a gazebo, picnic tables and grills. The park and its picnic shelter are available for reservations.

Union Point Park Complex
E. Front St. and S. Front St., New Bern

This park is located downtown where the Trent River joins the Neuse. An old landfill site which was renovated in the early 1970s, Union Point Park is now a wonderful and scenic place to sit and watch the river traffic. For those who love being outdoors, Union Point offers two boat-launching ramps, a gazebo, a fishing pier, picnic tables, grills, playground equipment and public restrooms. Park-goers who want to enjoy a walk downtown can use the walkway under the Trent River Bridge to avoid vehicular traffic on E. Front Street. On the Fourth of July, Union Point Park is the perfect locale to watch the town's impres-

New Bern parks are a great place to see the indigenous plant life.

photo: George Mitchell

sive display of fireworks (just be sure to bring your own chairs and mosquito repellent). The park is included in the reservation program described above.

Fort Totten Park
Intersection of Trent Rd. and Fort Totten Dr., New Bern

This 5.4-acre park has a lighted softball field, an impressive children's playground featuring swings, slides and climbing equipment, public restrooms and a picnic shelter with two grills and two picnic tables. This is a fantastic park that is always bustling with activity. (Our Insider Kid lives close to this park and says if only he had more hands, he could give it more than a double thumbs-up.) The park and its picnic shelter can be reserved for parties and other celebrations.

Henderson Park
901 Chapman St., New Bern

This 30-acre park offers a playground and two picnic shelters with grills and picnic tables, which can be reserved for private use. The surrounding grounds have two lighted regulation-size basketball courts, two baseball fields, a half-mile walking trail, outdoor workout equipment and restroom facilities. The site adjoins the Stanley White Recreation Center.

Seth West Parrott Park
1225 Pine Tree Dr., New Bern

With 25 acres, Seth West Parrott Park is a major place for recreation and attractions for kids. The West New Bern Recreation Center is here as well as the Kidsville Playground. In addition, you'll find two lighted and two unlighted tennis courts, a lighted outdoor basketball court, two lighted baseball fields and the Heath and Cutler Babe Ruth fields, as well as restrooms and a picnic shelter. Both the park and Kidsville Playground are available for reservations.

Kidsville Playground
1225 Pine Tree Dr., next to West New Bern Recreation Center, New Bern
(252) 639-2901

Kids are enchanted with this playground, and grown-ups find it just as special, too. Constructed by volunteers in just five days in 1994, this place is the wonderful gift to the city of New Bern from the community of New Bern. Even if you're not a kid, don't miss it, especially if you still get a thrill from swinging on great swings (like the author, who also enjoys climbing in the castle and sliding down the slides. She and the Insiders Kid combine their hands to give this place the quadruple thumbs-up.) For more details, see our New Bern Kidstuff chapter.

Pierce Park
545 Neuse Ave., New Bern

Pierce Park includes two lighted Little League fields with bleachers, a playground, public restrooms and a concession stand. The fields are used for baseball and tee-ball games and practices.

OTHER PARKS

Creekside Park
Old Airport Rd., New Bern

Developed by the Craven County Recreation and Parks Department, Creekside Park is a 111-acre recreational complex located adjacent to Craven Regional Airport. The park features walking trails, a sand volleyball court, 12 athletic fields, playgrounds, restrooms and picnic shelters. The latest area to be developed is the park's waterfront, which has a fishing dock and a gazebo, as well as an area to launch canoes and kayaks. All of the public facilities may be reserved for private use. Creekside Park is located in the James City community, across the bridge from downtown New Bern.

Extension Service Gardens
300 Industrial Park, New Bern

The grounds of the Craven County Extension Service Building are dotted with a number of demonstration and community gardens, all open to the public free of charge. The Eastern North Carolina Rose Society maintains a community rose garden, with more than 70 varieties of roses ranging from climbers and shrubs to hybrid teas and miniatures. The Craven County Master Gardeners demonstrate various techniques and conduct classes utilizing their Demonstration Vegetable Garden. The food grown in the garden is donated to area programs for the needy. The Trent Woods Garden Club maintains a butterfly and bird garden, which includes structures and plants to attract butterflies and birds. To visit the gardens, take U.S. 70 west from New

Bern's Glenburnie exit about 5 miles to the Clarks exit. Take a right off the exit ramp. The immediate next right turn is Industrial Drive, and the extension service building is the third building on the left.

CLOSE UP

Beloved Landmark Focus of 'Quest'

A small but determined group of 20 downtown residents are assisting the city in its efforts to preserve and restore one of New Bern's most beloved landmarks -- the two-centuries-old Cedar Grove Cemetery.

The group -- the Earl of Craven chapter of the Questers -- is one of approximately 900 located in 43 states and two Canadian provinces. Each are part of an international organization that was founded in 1944 to foster the study of antiques and promote the preservation of historic buildings and landmarks.

Chapter president Alice Ruckart said the group chose Cedar Grove Cemetery as a focus for its restoration efforts because. "it's just such a forgotten place. We just felt there was a need that was not being addressed by anyone else."

She added, "Although the city provides grounds maintenance, it has little money in its budget to fund the extensive recommendations made by (restoration consultant) Peter Sandbeck in the1995 Condition Assessment Survey of Cedar Grove Cemetery." The survey, undertaken by Sandbeck along with architects Stephens & Francis, was funded by the Kellenberger Foundation.

"The city was delighted with our interest," she said, adding that the group enjoys a good working relationship with city public works director Danny Meadows.

The local chapter primarily raises funds through catered lunches hosted in the members' historic homes. It also has received grants from the state and international Quester organizations, and ExxonMobil.

Since its founding in 1997, the chapter has contributed to repair of the main gates, restoration of the cemetery's fountain, replacement of cedar shake roofs on two city-owned mausoleums, installation of oyster shell paths, and planting of azaleas around the Confederate Memorial. Another project completed in late 2005 is the installation of an interpretative panels that highlights the cemetery's history and directs visitors to the resting sites of New Bern notables such as Judge William Gaston and Pepsi inventor Caleb Bradham.

A memorial fund was recently established for Curtis Collison, the husband of Jeanne, an Earl of Craven Quester, with the beneficiary being the City of New Bern's Adopt-A-Tree program.

"Our efforts have been positively received," Ruckart said, "but we need for more people to participate." She encourages those who are interested in the Adopt-A-Tree program to contact Meadows at (252) 636-4025.

The overall goal of the restoration effort is to give the cemetery a more park-like appearance. "Years ago it was considered a city park," Ruckart said. "We want to re-create that park-like setting."

Husbands of the group's members also have aided tremendously in their efforts, Ruckart said, undertaking such tasks as surveying the cemetery's existing trees, creating a scale drawing of the inventory that details the location and condition of each tree, and compiling a chapter handbook.

Future projects may include replacement of deteriorating garden benches and installation of additional ones, and restoration of damaged headstones.

NEW BERN

GOLF

New Bern is well-known for its many excellent golf courses, and the area's year-round mild weather offers a perfect climate for this challenging game. Golf courses are abundant in and around the city, and many have won acclaim from professionals and amateurs alike. Resident and visiting duffers are fortunate as even the most popular courses are easily accessible.

Those who are a bit more serious about their game -- and who isn't? -- can test those skills in any number of opportunities. Every season but winter sees any number of golf tournaments sponsored by local courses and organizations. The Craven County Convention and Visitors Bureau maintains a comprehensive calendar of annual events that includes many golf tournaments, and many events are publicized in New Bern Magazine and other local publications.

What follows is a list of semi-private courses in the immediate vicinity. The fees we quote here are for 18 holes of play, unless otherwise indicated, and membership is not required for play. For information about Carteret County golf courses, see our Crystal Coast Golf chapter, which details, among others, Bogue Banks Country Club in Pine Knoll Shores; Star Hill Golf and Country Club in Cape Carteret; Brandywine Bay Golf Club near Morehead City; and Silver Creek Golf Club on N.C. Highway 58 near Cape Carteret.

Carolina Pines Golf and Country Club
390 Carolina Pines Blvd., New Bern
(252) 444-1000

On the scenic Neuse River just west of Havelock, this challenging 18-hole, par 72 course is everything the golfer could ask for. The course features elevated greens, bermudagrass fairways, abundant sand traps and ample water that rewards the accurate shotmaker. Tim Dupre, the club pro, will arrange lessons for those who are interested. Also available are a pool, a pro shop, a driving range, target greens and a clubhouse with a lounge and patio that overlooks freshwater lakes and the golf links. Fees are $28 weekdays and $33 weekends, including cart. Carolina Pines is directly off U.S. Highway 70; look for the signs.

The Emerald Golf Club
5000 Clubhouse Dr., New Bern
(252) 633-4440

Rees Jones designed The Emerald, creating the 7,000-yard course to be a challenge for golfers of all skill levels. Jones used various grasses to give each hole a different feel and appearance and sculptured the 18-hole course to create variety. Most holes have four or five pin locations. The 4th tee, for example, features four locations that hit across the water and one high land route. The fee for playing the course is $49 seven days a week year-round and includes the use of a cart. Only members are allowed to walk the course. Tee times should be reserved two weeks in advance for club members; one week for nonmembers. Anyone is eligible for membership in the club, which entitles you to the tennis, swimming pool and club facilities as well as golfing privileges. Golfers can take advantage of a fully stocked pro shop, a driving range and lessons from pros Jerry Briele, Chris Lewis and Catie Camacho.

Fairfield Harbour Golf Club
Shoreline, 1100 Pelican Dr.. New Bern
(252) 514-0050
Harbour Pointe, 1105 Barkentine Dr., New Bern
(252) 638-5338

Fairfield Harbour is a resort community with timeshare accommodations plus several large residential developments. The resort has two 18-hole championship courses, which are about 1.5 miles apart. Both the Shoreline and the Harbour Pointe have been replanted with the newly developed Tif Eagle bermudagrass greens and are open to the public seven days a week. Fees vary as Fairfield Harbour runs daily specials, so be sure to call ahead for the latest information. Walkers are allowed after 2 PM Monday through Friday at the Shoreline course and not at all at Harbour Pointe. The club has a pro shop, driving range and banquet facilities. Golf lessons are available from Fairfield's teaching pro, George Smith. To get there, cross the new Neuse River Bridge on U.S. Highway 17. Turn right on N.C. Highway 55, continue about a half-mile to the traffic light and turn right onto Broad Creek Road. Signs will direct you from there.

Minnesott Golf and Country Club
806 Country Club Dr., Minnesott Beach
(252) 249-0813

Cross the new Neuse River Bridge on U.S. Highway 17 and turn right on N.C. Highway 55 and head toward Bayboro. Right before Bayboro, take a right on Route 306 at the light and drive about 12 miles, following the road back towards the Neuse River and taking a right on Country Club Drive; at the end is the hidden treasure of Minnesott. The course, built more than 30 years ago, is an 18-hole, par 72. It offers several sand traps, eight holes with water, and a medium length of 6001 yards. Golfers can enjoy the large pines and oaks as they play the course's hybrid bermudagrass fairways. Minnesott's greens fees are 18 holes for $32 and nine holes for $16 every day; afternoon golfers can play 18 holes for $27. All fees include cart. There's a snack bar and pro shop on the premises, and PGA club pro Terry Bobbin is available for lessons.

River Bend Golf and Country Club
94 Shoreline Dr., River Bend
(252) 638-2819

River Bend Golf and Country Club is a semiprivate, 18-hole, par 71 course that accepts public play with reservations up to seven days in advance. River Bend has always had one of the area's nicest golf course layouts, and the course itself was completely rebuilt in summer 2001 to include Tif Eagle bermudagrass greens, 15 new sand bunkers, significant mounding and re-sodded 419 bermuda fairways. Lights were added to the driving range and putting green so nighttime practice is possible. Rates vary for members and nonmembers. Nonmembers can play 18 holes for $38 and nine holes for $23 weekdays and 18 holes for $40 and nine holes for $28 weekends. Junior rates are 18 holes for $20 and nine holes for $15 seven days a week. Rates include the use of a cart; only members are allowed to walk the course. Karl Thurber, the club's PGA professional, offers lessons, clinics and club repair for all levels. River Bend also offers one of the most fully stocked golf shops in the area. One special event held every summer is the junior golf camp for ages 5 to 14. The camp culminates in a mini-tournament that allows participants to test the new skills they've learned. River Bend also has two tennis courts and the area's largest outdoor swimming pool available at no charge to members and guests of members. There is also a grill room and a catering facility that will accommodate up to 120 guests.

Quaker Neck Country Club
241 Country Club Ln., Trenton
(252) 224-5736

Easily one of the area's best-kept secrets, Quaker Neck Country Club is located in neighboring Jones County, just off U.S. Highway 17 12 miles south of New Bern. This 18-hole championship golf course has a demanding layout and excellent greens that will challenge players of all skill levels. Green fees vary according to season, so golfers are advised to call ahead for information. Quaker Neck County Club offers family and individual memberships, with amenities including an Olympic-size pool, two tennis courts, a driving range, a golf shop and club repairs. Banquet facilities are available to the public for private parties and functions.

NEW BERN REAL ESTATE AND NEIGHBORHOODS

Craven County continues to grow as people from across the state and country decide to make their homes in New Bern and its environs. Many factors affect the area's growth, especially the tide of retirees flowing into the greater New Bern area and the demand for housing from nearby Cherry Point Marine Corps Air Station. New Bern's housing market has expanded substantially to meet the influx of new homeowners.

The city's vibrant community renaissance continues at a steady, yet unhurried, pace. In New Bern's three historic neighborhoods, you will still see some structures in need of repair among the beautifully restored buildings, but this is changing as Georgian, Federal and Victorian edifices are being returned to their former elegance, adding considerably to the city's charm.

Another big plus for the city is its proximity to water. Positioned where the waters of the Neuse and Trent rivers come together, New Bern is less than an hour's drive from the ocean. A moderate climate, nearby recreational waterways and challenging golf courses are added bonuses in making New Bern a popular vacation, relocation and retirement spot for people from all walks of life.

New Bern's expanding homes market offers newcomers a wide choice of neighborhoods and housing in styles and prices that are sure to appeal to any taste or income bracket. Choices include historic homes, contemporary structures, bungalows, ranch-style residences, riverfront condominiums, townhouses and building lots in ever-increasing new developments.

Because both waterfront and non-waterfront homes and lots are often within the same district, real estate values can vary widely within the same neighborhood. Prices for lots and houses quoted here are approximations and, of course, are subject to change. Our descriptions of neighborhoods will help orient you to the personality, price range and availability of New Bern housing.

If you are interested in New Bern neighborhoods, one of the most helpful guides is HOMES magazine, published by NCCoast Communications. This full-color publication contains descriptions and pictures of properties currently on the market. It's free, and you can get copies at restaurants, hotels, supermarkets, real estate firms and scores of local businesses.

Neighborhoods

DOWNTOWN HISTORIC DISTRICT

New Bern's Downtown Historic District is a very attractive 56-square-block area that for over two centuries grew along the point of land jutting into the confluence of the Neuse and Trent rivers and extending west to Queen Street. The district was officially entered into the National Register of Historic Places in 1973. The neighborhood contains the town's oldest and most distinguished homes. Its buildings and landscape elements chronicle New Bern's growth -- from its days as the Colonial capital of the Carolinas from 1766 until 1778, to its status as an important mercantile center in the mid-18th and early 19th centuries, to its time of prosperity fueled by the lumber industry in the late 19th and early 20th centuries.

The New Bern Preservation Foundation, in the years since its organization in 1972, has bought, stabilized and sold more than 60 structures of historical or architectural significance in New Bern's historic downtown. People who purchase from the NBPF must abide by restrictive covenants that protect the architectural integrity of the house. Whenever possible, the foundation provides new owners with documentary evidence of the structure's original architecture and provenance, such as photos, floor plans and old insurance maps. Once a structure is sold, the preservation foundation serves as a source of expert advice to the owners who restore the dwellings. The foundation's work has provided the impetus for many other property owners to follow suit, resulting in the restoration of more than 150 residences. A few of these date from the mid-1700s, built shortly after New Bern was founded in 1710 by Swiss colonists under Baron Christoph von deGraffenried.

The focal point of historic downtown is Tryon Palace Historic Sites & Gardens on Pollock Street. The home of William Tryon, North Carolina's colonial royal governor, the palace's gardens and buildings have been beautifully reconstructed and restored. This state historic site draws thousands of visitors each year. (For information on Tryon Palace Historic Sites & Gardens, see our New Bern Attractions chapter.) Professional offices, businesses, and bed and breakfast inns occupy tastefully renovated old homes in the surrounding neighborhood. The city has an astonishing number of landmarks listed in the National Register of Historic Places, and most of these are found in the downtown district.

Facing the Neuse River are approximately a dozen square blocks of pedigreed houses dating from the 18th, 19th and 20th centuries. Most of the elegantly restored homes have two or three stories. Fully restored historic houses are going for $250,000 and can run to more than $600,000. Smaller home restorations away from the river in this neighborhood are available starting in the $150,000 range. As you move farther away from the Neuse, blocks become more transitional and prices drop.

The cost of homes throughout the entire downtown district varies enormously, depending upon location and the degree of restoration. Sometimes homes along the fringes are offered in the $75,000 to $90,000 range, but you can bet they require a tremendous amount of work and TLC. Preservation also has stimulated demand for smaller residential spaces in New Bern's historic downtown. Townhomes and condominiums in this district range from $150,000 to $300,000.

RIVERSIDE HISTORIC DISTRICT

Riverside, also listed on the National Historic Register, consists of National Avenue and the section east of the avenue to the Neuse River. Development began in the late 1890s in response to the city's flourishing lumber industry. Riverside was originally a mixed-use community of residential buildings and commercial enterprises. People wanted to live where they worked. Regrettably, as lumber ceased to be economically important, Riverside fell into disrepair. The result is a neighborhood where beautifully refurbished homes and rundown buildings stand side-by-side. But fortunately for New Bernians, Riverside property owners are taking measures to restore this once-handsome community to its original function as home to businesses and private residences.

Many of Riverside's larger homes were built between 1896 and World War II, so there is a pleasant mix of architectural styles in the neighborhood. On National Avenue, high-peaked, two-story Victorian structures with wraparound porches and plenty of shade trees are situated well back from the road. On the cross streets perpendicular to National Avenue and the Neuse are rows of tidy bungalows.

Homes along the River Drive waterfront are of an entirely different character. You will find pretty brick ranch dwellings on small lots with plenty of trees and meticulous landscaping. Real estate values vary widely, with some of the older bungalows offered in the $70,000 to $95,000 range, and renovated historic dwellings starting at about $135,000.

GHENT HISTORIC DISTRICT

The Ghent neighborhood, which was added to the National Historic Register in 1988, contains private homes dating mostly from 1913 to World War II. The area encompasses Spencer, Rhem and parts of Park avenues. It began as a trolley-car suburb in the days when working folks wanted homes away from the hustle and bustle of downtown New Bern. Today, Spencer Avenue is considered one of the prettiest streets in New Bern, with old-fashioned street lamps along a landscaped median separating two lanes of traffic. Large flowering fruit trees throughout the neighborhood are breathtakingly beautiful in April.

Ghent is an energetic, people-oriented neighborhood where residents take to the sidewalks whenever the weather permits, which is often in the mild New Bern climate. This neighborhood has become a highly desirable section for homeowners and has

i

The Ghent neighborhood offers a holiday delight during December as many of the area's residents along Rhem, Spencer and Park Avenues lavishly decorate their home's exteriors and yards with lights and other decorations. The many trees along the median of Spencer Avenue, which now is a grassy tree-lined strip but was once the old trolley car line, also are decorated with lights for the holiday season, and, closer to Christmas, the neighborhood hosts a beautiful display of luminaria.

undergone a lot of sprucing up. Bungalows and cottage-style homes with neat lawns and open or screened porches make up a large part of the neighborhood.

The neighborhood is close to one of the area's nicest amenities, the Twin Rivers YMCA, which includes an outdoor swimming pool (covered with a "bubble" in the cooler months so the pool can used year-round), an indoor Junior Olympic–size swimming pool, a gymnasium, weight rooms and a racquetball court. The Y also offers day care and exercise classes. Ghent is also fortunate to be situated between Fort Totten Park, which has a playground, lighted baseball field, bleachers and restrooms, and the larger Lawson Creek Park, a popular fishing spot with nature trails, boat launches and picnic tables. Homes in Ghent are larger than in many of the new housing developments surrounding New Bern, but many still require remodeling and renovation. Prices range from $90,000 to $250,000. Newer homes in the neighborhood's Trolley Run area start at about $150,000.

DEGRAFFENRIED PARK

This distinguished neighborhood lies between Trent and Neuse boulevards directly north of the Ghent Historic District. Work is underway on the neighborhood's application for placement on the National Register. Homes here are generally large and well-placed on spacious, beautifully landscaped lots. Sidewalks invite neighborhood strolls, and streets carry names such as Queen Anne Lane and Lucerne Way.

Many of the neighborhood's more notable residences are stately, two-story Colonial Revival dwellings. Brick walls and wrought-iron fences embellish many of the houses in the district. You can expect to pay between $150,000 to $300,000 for these homes.

TRENT WOODS

This large, mature development lies between New Bern and the Trent River. It has been incorporated to give residents better control over their neighborhoods, and there is virtually no commercial development within its borders. Its winding lanes contain some of the most posh neighborhoods and dwellings in the area. New Bern Golf and Country Club is located in Trent Woods, and national best-selling author Nicholas Sparks is a resident of this upscale community.

Trent Woods is composed of several subdivisions, some of which are primarily waterfront property. Most of the residences tend toward conservative rather than contemporary architectural styles and are constructed of wood, brick or stucco. Homes are large, with two and three stories, and usually have attached or separate two-car garages. Lots are spacious, wooded and impeccably landscaped, often with Spanish moss draped in towering trees. If you take a drive through Trent Woods in the spring, you'll be greeted by a stunning display of flowering trees and shrubs.

In addition to the country club, the area boasts other amenities, such as the Eastern Carolina Yacht Club. The average price range for a non-waterfront home in Trent Woods is $125,000 to $600,000. Waterfront homes are quite pricey and can go up to $1.6 million.

OLDE TOWNE HARBOUR

This is one of the nicest subdivisions in New Bern, just east of Trent Woods and south of U.S. Highway 70. Though just minutes from the downtown district and the shopping malls on U.S. Highway 17, Olde Towne Harbour offers quiet seclusion in a lovely, natural setting. Here, you can find some of the most lavish, custom-built contemporary homes and condominiums in New Bern. The largest of these sprawl along the shores of the Trent River and Olde Towne

Lake (actually a river inlet). This is a strictly residential development. Homesites range from $33,000 to $229,000, depending upon location, while townhomes start at $210,000 and homes at $215,000. Waterfront homes are another story, ranging upward into the half-million-dollar category.

TABERNA

Taberna (the name translated means "place of hospitality"), about 5 miles east of downtown New Bern on U.S. 70 E, combines the best of old-fashioned Southern hospitality with new-fangled charm. Residences at this 1,100-acre golfing community include single-family homes, patio homes and townhouses. The focal point is the championship 18-hole golf course designed by Jim Lipe, a head architect for Jack Nicklaus. The community includes natural beauty such as rolling hills, dense foliage, lakes, streams and wetlands, along with man-made amenities like pedestrian trails, a canoe dock and a canoe trail system, as well as a country club.

Single-family homesites start at $40,000 and up, depending on location, while completed homes go for $225,000 and up, and townhomes begin at $140,000.

RIVER BEND

The 1,200-acre town of River Bend lies along a winding inlet on the north shore of the Trent River, about 5 miles east of New Bern. This location allows many of the homesites to have water frontage and private boat slips. The land was originally owned by the Odd Fellows, a fraternal group of black tenant farmers who raised tobacco. During the recession of 1914, they were forced to sell their land to the company store for supplies and debts. During the first half of the century, a wealthy family owned the land and continued to have it farmed for tobacco. In 1965, real estate speculator J. Frank Efird recognized the area's potential as a retirement development for people moving south from the Northeast. He organized The Efird Company to acquire and develop the old Odd Fellows farm.

True to Efird's vision, large numbers of retirees now live in River Bend, although a number of young families live there too. The

The Jones House is a noted Civil War landmark.

photo: George Mitchell

community has its own country club to service its 18-hole golf course. The club includes a well-stocked pro shop, a small sandwich shop, an outdoor swimming pool and four lighted tennis courts.

River Bend was incorporated in 1980 in order to maintain roads and provide other services. The municipal building, finished in 1986, has a 99-seat meeting hall and is adjacent to a small park with a children's play area, baseball field and small dock. The development consists mainly of single-family dwellings, all with attached or detached one- and two-car garages. In recent years, clusters of townhouses and duplexes have been added to the community. House prices begin at around $150,000 for a non-waterfront location. Townhouse prices depend on the subdivision, but the range is between $90,000 and $170,000.

FAIRFIELD HARBOUR

This well-known resort community is across the Neuse River off N.C. Highway 55 and 6 miles down Broad Creek Road. It is a 3,000-acre development that focuses on boating and golf. Homeowners can choose between the beauty of Northwest Creek and Broad Creek, with docks in deep water, or the beauty of rolling lawns near the golf course and country club, and marinas off bulk-headed waterfront property. The marinas offer unrestricted ocean access, 18 nautical miles from the Intracoastal Waterway, in sheltered waters. Fairfield Harbour is also a golfer's dream. It has two championship, 18-hole golf courses -- the Shoreline and the Harbour Pointe Golf Links -- where devotees can play practically all year round. (See our New Bern Golf chapter.)

Fairfield Harbour is a combination of mostly single-family homes, with some condominiums, townhouses and timeshare units added for good measure. The development's large canal system gives many homes water access at their back doors. In general, you can expect homes to start in the $125,000 range. There are about 900 single-family homes, 120 condominiums and 200 timeshare units.

Condominiums and townhouses at Fairfield Harbour are arranged around small artificial lakes. Winding paths and roads connect all locations, and the combination of layout and landscaping gives a feeling of privacy, even with neighbors only a few feet away. The condos were built at different times in different styles, and they have varying levels of modern amenities. Jacuzzis and Jenn-Aire ranges are common in most, as are balconies, decks and screened porches. Most have two or three bedrooms. Developers have shown careful respect for the trees that were on the lots first. It is not unusual to see decks cut to accommodate a tree. Prices for these maintenance-free homes range from the $90,000s to the mid-$150,000s.

The Harbour's combination of year-round residents and vacationers requires that a wide variety of activities be readily available. Established community activities are too numerous to list but include such interests as men's and women's golf associations, a chorus, and clubs for quilting, weaving, garden, books, bridge, RV owners, tennis and yachting. Besides the golf courses, there are three swimming pools (one is indoor); nine tennis courts, four of which are lighted; and a country cub. Boat rentals and cruises are available year round.

BRICES CREEK

The Brices Creek region lies southwest of New Bern and James City and south of the Trent River. A number of subdivisions exist in this area, including the Lake Clermont subdivision, Snug Harbor, Oakview, Deer Run, River Trace, Hunter's Ridge and The Homeplace. Many homes are on interior lots, but the more elegant residences face the waterfront and are set well away from the road on large, wooded lots. They tend to be brick or stucco in contemporary styles. Homes on the waterfront generally sell in the $200,000 to $400,000 range, depending on their water frontage. Houses away from the creek sell in the $100,000 to $300,000 range. The Craven County Airport is just east of Brices Creek.

GREENSPRINGS

Huge, contemporary dwellings on large, wooded lots grace the western banks of the Neuse River on Green Springs Road just off U.S. 70 E. between New Bern and Havelock. Waterfront homes start around $350,000, with lots in the $125,000 range. Farther east along Rivershore Drive, you can find older frame houses and large cottages tucked into the river bluffs. Prices vary greatly according to age, size and lot space. Many new neighborhoods have been developed in this area over the last few years. Prices of these homes start at about $100,000, but the value is increasing rapidly.

CAROLINA PINES

About 11 miles east of New Bern off U.S. 70 on Carolina Pines Boulevard, Carolina Pines is a large, well-established residential resort golf community along the Neuse River. It offers a blend of quiet countryside living combined with country-club flair and neighborhood charm. Housing varies and includes modest patio homes, ranch styles and elegant two-story showplaces. Houses in Carolina Pines often sell in the $120,000 to $180,000 range.

Some of the neighborhood amenities include a challenging 18-hole golf course, a golf pro, a pro shop, tennis courts, a pool, a clubhouse with a restaurant and lounge and a patio overlooking freshwater lakes and the links. An added bonus is the adjacent Croatan National Forest, where residents can enjoy camping, hiking and horseback riding.

WEST NEW BERN

This area is bounded by Neuse Boulevard on the northeast, M. L. King Jr. Boulevard on the southeast, U.S. 70 on the southwest and Glenburnie Road on the northwest. Homes in this attractive neighborhood are large, brick, ranch houses and two-story dwellings on generous lots. This part of New Bern is wooded, and there is plenty of undeveloped pine forest bordering many lots. Most of the homes have numerous large trees in the yards. Prices here begin at about $90,000 and go up to $150,000. These homes are convenient to Kidsville and the West New Bern Recreation Center, which offers tennis courts, baseball fields, a basketball court and a supervised game room with pool tables.

GREENBRIER

Greenbrier is a distinguished 700-acre subdivision right in the middle of New Bern. It is off S. Glenburnie Road and is a neighborhood well-suited for families with young children and for retirees. Lots range from an eighth of an acre to more than a full acre, and excellent architectural planning has effectively blended a variety of home styles into a delightful community. Many homes are of contemporary brick designs. All utilities are underground. Homes on spacious lots range from $150,000 to $600,000. The entire development surrounds an 18-hole championship golf course, The Emerald Golf Club, designed by Rees Jones.

The clubhouse at The Emerald Golf Club is often the chosen location for major local charity events. It contains an Olympic-size, Z-shaped pool. Four lighted tennis courts are also available. Golf club members can sharpen their skills on one of the finest new practice complexes in the state. (For more information about the golf club, see our New Bern Golf, Recreation and Parks chapter.)

From Greenbrier's front gate, you are within two minutes of major shopping, five minutes from the local schools and hospital, and adjacent to the campus of Craven Community College.

Real Estate Companies

Many reputable real estate agencies do business in New Bern. If you have questions about area real estate companies, consult the Neuse River Region Association of Realtors, (252) 636-5364. For questions about building contractors, contact the New Bern-Craven County Home Builders Association at (252) 636-3707. While many real estate companies in New Bern handle rental properties as well as sales, the New Bern Area Chamber of Commerce, (252) 637-3111, also offers a handy apartment directory.

Assist2Sell Buyers & Sellers Realty
1723 S. Glenburnie Dr., New Bern
(252) 636-5797, (800) 222-9714

"Full Service with $avings!" is Assist2Sell's motto. Those in the market to sell their home will enjoy Assist2Sell's wide range of helpful options, while those in the market to buy will find friendly and informative assistance. Assist2Sell lists existing homes, new construction, land and lots in New Bern and surrounding communities. This company also offers a free buyers' hotsheet and a relocation package, sent upon request.

Century 21 Action Associates - Jana J. Tyson
1904-C S. Glenburnie Rd., New Bern
(252) 670-1184
www.NCmove.com

The "Action Team," as they call themselves, is New Bern's original Century 21 office, now located in Blair Square. When working with sellers and buyers, the Action Team prides itself on providing quality service and personal care for all its clients. Century 21 Action Associates, (252) 633-0075, also showcases many of the New Bern's finest historic and upscale homes through its Fine Homes & Estates program. The firm also offers property management and rental services.

A resident of the New Bern area since 1994, Realtor Jana J. Tyson of Century 21 Action Associates, (252) 670-1184, is a premier agent in New Bern, with $16.6 million in transactions credited to her in 2005 alone. She works as both a buyer's and seller's agent, depending on the needs of her individual clients. For buyers, Jana J. believes in working closely with clients to learn their property needs, and tailors her search of the properties to match those needs. For sellers, Jana uses her background in business and marketing to effectively market properties both locally and beyond, using newspapers, magazines, the Internet and more.

Century 21 Zaytoun-Raines
312 S. Front St., New Bern
(252) 633-3069, (877) NEW-BERN (639-2376)

George Zaytoun began building homes in 1964, and Marvin Raines began a real estate career in 1971. In 1986 they combined their expertise to create what has become one of the area's most successful real estate companies. The firm has been awarded Century 21's most distinguished award, the Centurion Award, presented to only eight of Century 21's 176 offices throughout North and South Carolina. It's impossible to drive through New Bern and not see Zaytoun-Raines signs. Nearly 30 agents handle residential, commercial and investment properties, including those offered through the Century 21 Fine Homes & Estates program.

Coldwell Banker Willis-Smith Realty
115 Middle St., New Bern
(252) 638-3500, (800) 334-0792

This reliable firm's offices are downtown near the New Bern waterfront. The company operates as a seller's and buyer's agency, offering a full range of services that includes residential brokerage and development and referrals to and from its national network. Its well-trained and experienced agents are knowledgeable about housing in all of New Bern's long-established neighborhoods and new developments and subdivisions. Willis-Smith also handles rental properties in the New Bern area.

Fairfield Harbour Realty
750 Broad Creek Rd., New Bern
(252) 638-4411, (800) 317-3303

Fairfield Harbour Realty operates in the Fairfield Harbour planned community. Its staff handles the sales of building lots, single-family homes and condominiums.

Nancy Hollows Real Estate
624 Hancock St., New Bern
(252) 636-3177, (800) 622-3177

Nancy Hollows likes working with people who are looking for a unique property, whether that be a centuries-old home in New Bern's historic district, a waterfront property with a breathtaking view, a unique bed-and-breakfast with charm, or just an unusual house with lots of character. Hollows specializes in knowing everything there is to know about New Bern's historic homes and has a good understanding of ordinances that govern historic district properties. However, she handles sales of all types of property throughout Craven County and neighboring Carteret County. The success of her career as a real estate agent over the last 20 years is rooted in referrals from very satisfied buyers and sellers.

New Bern Real Estate
3601 Trent Rd., Ste. 5, New Bern
(252) 636-2200, (800) 636-2992

New Bern Real Estate has experienced agents ready to serve you. They pride themselves on being local, low pressure and thoroughly familiar with the entire New Bern area. They have close working relationships with all the other agents in town and can help you no matter what your real estate need.

RE/MAX By the Water
242 Middle St., New Bern
(252) 633-9300

Daynette Orr added New Bern to the RE/MAX network when she took her 15 years of real estate experience and opened her own office here in 2002. Daynette's knowledge of the local real estate market combined with her specialized marketing program allow her to provide complete customer satisfaction and positive results. Daynette specializes in properties in New Bern and throughout eastern North Carolina, and is a Certified Residential Specialist (CRS), a Graduate of the REALTORS ® Institute (GRI), and a Seniors Residential Specialist (SRES), as well as Broker/Owner of the New Bern office.

Trent River Realty, Inc. - Joan LoCascio
333 Middle St., New Bern
(252) 229-7706, (800) 663-3843
www.jlocascio-newbernnc.com

With two office locations, one in historic downtown New Bern and the other in River Bend, Trent River Realty's agents work with their customers and clients to make buying or selling a home as enjoyable as possible. Trent River Realty offers buyers and sellers not only exceptional real estate representation, but also the insight and expertise of the local real estate market that only comes with years of dedicated and outstanding customer service.

Realtor Joan LoCascio of Trent River Realty, (252) 229-7706, specializes in residential properties located in New Bern, Trent Woods, River Bend, Greenbrier, Fairfield Harbour, Taberna. the Brices Creek area, and more. A longtime resident of New Bern and a Realtor for 15 years, Joan believes in open communication, honesty and respect and remains personally involved with her clients throughout the buying and selling process. For an information packet, call Joan or email her at JLoCasioNC@aol.com.

Tyson and Hooks Realty
2402 Dr. M. L. King Jr. Blvd., New Bern
(252) 633-5766, (800) 284-6844

This firm has been serving Craven County and the New Bern area since 1972. Eight agents provide general real estate services, including the sale of commercial and residential lots, while Tyson Management Company handles property management and rentals of houses, apartments, townhouses and commercial space throughout the New Bern area.

Service Directory

TAX RATES

The Craven County property tax rate is 61¢ per $100 of assessed value (Craven

Live Oak trees dot the Carolina Coast.

photo: Scott Taylor

County budget for 2005–06). City property is taxed at both the city and county rates. New Bern's tax rate is 47¢ per $100 valuation, with an additional 18¢ per $100 assessed valuation in the downtown municipal services district. These rates are subject to change each fiscal year.

City of New Bern
606 Fort Totten Dr., New Bern
(252) 639-2750

Electric, water, sewer and garbage disposal services within New Bern and Trent Woods are provided by the City of New Bern. You are required to appear in person to establish service and pay a deposit, and you must bring a picture ID card and your rental lease or proof of property ownership. Deposits are based on the previous tenants' average usage, so this figure can vary. Deposits are refunded after a year if your bill has been paid in full and on time every month during your first year of service. Deposits can possibly be waived if you provide a letter of credit from your previous utility provider and pass a credit check, or if a current customer with a excellent credit rating agrees to co-sign for you. Office hours are Monday through Friday 8 AM to 5 PM . For same-day service, you must be in the office no later than 2 PM. The utility office is in the old Fort Totten branch of First Citizens Bank, and there is a First Citizens ATM machine available on site.

OTHER UTILITY SERVICES

If your home has natural gas cooking and heating appliances, service in New Bern and Craven County is available through Piedmont Natural Gas, (800) 752-7504. Electrical service in the areas surrounding New Bern is provided by Progress Energy Carolinas, Inc. (formerly CP&L), (800) 452-2777. Water and sewer services outside of New Bern are provided by Craven County Water and Sewer, 2830 Neuse Boulevard, (252) 636-6615. A list of private companies providing garbage disposal services in Craven County is available from the Craven County Solid Waste office, (252) 636-6659. Requirements and deposits for establishing services vary, so be sure to call for more information.

Sprint
(252) 633-9011

Phone service to the New Bern area is provided by Sprint. Based on your previous record, you may be asked to pay a deposit to establish phone service. This deposit is normally refunded after a year. Service connections can take up to four days.

Apartments

Renting an apartment in New Bern can be an interesting adventure. As in the case in many towns, location is important. Insiders advise if you are interested in an apartment that you drive through the neighborhood at different times of the day and night so you understand where you are moving. Rates can vary depending on the neighborhood -- apartments in the historic district as well as newer apartment complexes will go for much higher than those on the outskirts of town. Most of the condominiums under development downtown are for sale rather than rent. Most apartment rentals in the area are handled by real estate firms or management companies. However, there are also a number of apartment complexes that Insiders feel comfortable recommending.

Carolina Club Apartments
1350 Trent Blvd., New Bern
Office, 307 Simmons St., New Bern
(252) 633-3357

Carolina Club Apartments is located next to Fort Totten Park and very near to the historic Ghent and DeGraffenried neighborhoods. This well-maintained complex features one and two bedroom apartments. Each apartment includes central heat and air, a range, refrigerator and mini-blinds, and the monthly rental fee covers city water and sewer services. Residents have access to onsite laundry facilities. Up to two pets 25 pounds and under are permitted; however, a non-refundable pet deposit and an additional monthly rental fee are charged. A security deposit and a yearly lease are required.

Tryon Estates Apartments
307 Simmons St., New Bern
(252) 633-3357

Tryon Estates Apartments is one of New Bern's nicest apartment complexes. It features one-bedroom, one-bath units and two-bedroom, one-and-a-half bath townhouse garden and townhouse apartments in a beautifully landscaped area right off Simmons Street. The apartments feature either a private patio or balcony, and townhouses have private patios and outside storage areas. All have central air and heat and include a range, refrigerator with ice-maker, dishwasher and mini-blinds, and some townhouses are available with washer and dryer hook-ups. Other amenities include off-street parking, laundry facilities and a private swimming pool. Tenants are required to pay a security deposit and sign a one-year lease. The monthly rent includes city water and sewer services, cable and 24-hour emergency maintenance. Up to two pets 25 pounds and under are permitted; however, a non-refundable pet deposit and an additional monthly rental fee are charged. Insiders are glad to recommend Tryon Estates Apartments; it is within minutes of both downtown and the Dr. M. L. King Jr. Boulevard shopping corridor.

Woodland Crossing Apartments
2590 Woodland Ave., New Bern
(252) 633-5151

Located behind Berne Square Shopping Center, Woodland Crossing Apartments not only is located close to some of New Bern's finest shopping and restaurants but also the complex offers a secluded setting that gives residents the quiet and privacy they deserve and expect. Floor plans feature one-bedroom one-bath units, and two and three bedroom two-bath apartments, which include refrigerators, ranges, microwaves, dishwashers and garbage disposals. Amenities include a tennis court, pool, business center, fitness center, playground, and garage and storage units. Woodland Crossing is pet-friendly; however, requirements include an interview, a partially refundable pet deposit and more; call for details. The office is open Monday through Saturday.

NEW BERN EDUCATION AND CHILD CARE

New Bern residents have excellent educational opportunities. Adults have access to a state-supported university, college-level classes and a first-rate community college. Parents have the option of sending their children to the Craven County public schools or one of the private schools in New Bern. Several trustworthy child-care options are available for children who are too young for school.

Colleges and Universities

Those interested in furthering their education may choose from two-year associate's degrees, bachelor's degrees in partnership with East Carolina University, accelerated four-year degree programs and continuing education classes.

Craven Community College
800 College Ct., New Bern
(252) 638-4131

Craven Community College offers two-year degrees and adult continuing education at its New Bern and Havelock campuses. Two-year associate's degree programs in the arts and sciences and more than 30 technical and vocational programs are available. Two recently added programs cover aviation systems technology and information systems security. The college offers basic adult education programs, two-year technical and transfer programs, one-year vocational programs and extension programs in occupational, practical and vocational courses of study. Craven Community College is part of North Carolina's 58-campus community college system.

The New Bern-Craven County Public Library, 400 Johnson Street, offers weekly story times for toddlers, preschoolers and school children up to 12 years old. The newly renovated Children's Department offers special programs throughout the year, including the Story Seekers program, which fosters the imaginations of children ages 10 and up through puppetry and storytelling, and the Summer Reading Book Club. The library has a CD-ROM storybook collection for in-house use on the library's computers. Call (252) 638-7815 for more information.

East Carolina University
Office of Undergraduate Admissions, Greenville
(252) 328-6640

A little more than an hour's drive from New Bern, East Carolina University in Greenville is a state-supported university that offers a wide range of study areas for bachelor's, master's and doctoral degrees. The university has an enrollment of about 19,000 students. Two popular curriculum areas are education and health sciences. Many working adults pursue degrees by commuting to the Greenville campus. Craven Regional Medical Center in New Bern is a clinical site for students enrolled in the ECU School of Nursing.

Mount Olive College at New Bern
2131 S. Glenburnie Rd., Ste. 6, New Bern
(252) 633-4464, (800) 868-8479

Mount Olive College at New Bern provides accredited academic programs designed for working adults at an affordable price. The accelerated degree completion programs are the perfect solution for working adults who want to start or complete their college degree. Responding to the increasing demand of adults seeking to complete a four-year degree, Mount Olive College opened its New Bern location in 1993. The nontraditional programs at MOC are an innovative approach to education that gives working adults with about two years of college credits the opportunity to complete their degree while continuing their employment. Students enter as a class (called a cohort), meet four hours once a week for a specified number of weeks, and complete a sequence of courses toward a bachelor's degree in Criminal Justice Administration, Management and Organizational Development, Early Childhood Education or Religion. The time-condensed format of the nontraditional programs allows students to finish what they started.

For working adults who have little or no college credit, Mount Olive College in New Bern also offers a four-semester program, called the Heritage Plus Program, that provides students with the core courses needed for an associate's degree. Working adults interested in finding out more can contact Vaughn Purnell at the number above.

Public Schools

Craven County Schools
3600 Trent Rd., New Bern
(252) 514-6300

The Craven County School System, which serves more than 14,500 city and county students, provides a free and appropriate public education to all students within its jurisdiction. The schools are fully accredited by the Southern Association of Colleges and Schools and the N.C. Department of Public Instruction. The system employs about 1,150 teaching professionals, 5 percent of whom are National Board Certified (and the number grows each year) and about 750 support personnel to staff the county's 14 elementary schools (kindergarten through 5th), five middle schools (6th through 8th) and three high schools. Three of these schools operate on a year-round schedule, while the others follow the traditional August-to-May calendar.

The vision of the school system is that Craven County Schools will be the highest performing system of public education in North Carolina, and its mission statement reflects this -- "Craven County Schools, united with families and communities, will continuously improve student learning and educational services through a focus on expectations and values which support performance excellence." The school system has adopted the Baldrige Approach for continuous improvement, not just on the students'

The Craven County Board of Education recently adopted a 100 percent tobacco free policy that prohibits the use of tobacco products on all school property by everyone at all times.

parts but also the system and schools themselves, leading to performance excellence. All schools will be Baldrige-based by 2005.

The system's average teacher-student ratio is 1-to-26. The school system offers a comprehensive curriculum based on the North Carolina Standard Course of Study. In addition to the traditional academic courses, the education program includes music, foreign language, art, dance, theater, athletics, computer classes and advanced placement courses.

Optimum Student Achievement is the major strategic direction for the school system. Craven County students perform in the top 10 percent of school districts across the state. Student performance trend data indicates that the school system has moved from 65.8 proficiency in Reading (grades 3 to 8) in 1993 to 88.6 in 2004. Math proficiency has moved from approximately 62 to 90 percent in 2004. According to the most recent accountability report, nine schools in the system are Schools of Excellence, the highest awards given to schools in the state, and 10 schools are Schools of Distinction. Twenty of the 22 schools met or exceeded their school growth goals. Craven County Schools is also a leader in the state in efforts to close the achievement gap among all students.

Elementary education in Craven County encourages kids to meet academic objectives through developmentally appropriate activities. Hands-on experiences and problem-solving strategies are designed to harmonize with the natural characteristics of children's developmental stages. Besides the core curriculum of communication skills, science, math and social studies, students and teachers are involved in enrichment programs such as art, physical education, computers, music and drama.

Middle schools emphasize educational experiences that bridge learning between elementary school and high school. All five

Board of Education Committee meetings are held the Monday before the third Thursday beginning at 8:30 a.m. The meetings are open to the public.

middle schools operate on a team concept. Two to five teachers collaborate to develop plans and strategies to deal with the instructional, social and emotional needs and interests of students. Along with the core curriculum, students are exposed to critical thinking and problem solving, health and fitness, cooperative learning, and exploratory courses such as foreign languages, vocational education and visual arts.

The high schools focus on the creation of a positive school climate and the identification and prevention of problems that may lead to an unsuccessful high school career. All high schools are on block scheduling, which allows students to take four courses each semester in 90-minute class periods versus the traditional 55-minute classes. Instead of the maximum six courses per year, students are able to take as many as eight courses -- four per semester. Among several advantages, block scheduling gives students the flexibility of enrolling in more electives without giving up required academic classes.

To prepare students for the workplace, the Craven County School System has implemented a developmental program that helps students entering high school to choose and focus on a career path. Students may select from four career pathways: engineering, industrial and manufacturing technology; business and marketing; health and human services; and liberal and fine arts. A student's choice of career path is aided by the development of a four-year educational plan and supplemented by career guidance that helps the student make a smooth transition into the work force, or into an associate or bachelor's degree program. ROTC programs also are offered in all three high schools.

The Craven County School System offers many support services: comprehensive testing, programs for exceptional and academically gifted students, dropout prevention and drug education programs, library/media skills programs and the services of school psychologists, social workers and nurses. In addition, numerous services are available for students with visual, hearing, speech, orthopedic and other health impairments as well as for the mentally handicapped, learning disabled and homebound. Contact Exceptional Children's Programs, (252) 514-6355, for more information.

School safety is a major consideration to the school community, as is facility improvement. Each school system operation has a threat condition process, a safe schools plan and a critical incident response plan. The Craven County Board of Education has a long-range facility plan and recently passed a $28 million bond referendum. The construction of two elementary schools and two performing arts centers, major renovations to an existing middle school, plus new roofs for several schools, were recently completed.

The Craven County School System has a free information portfolio that includes a countywide activities calendar, descriptions of and directions to all 22 schools, a discussion of the system's educational curriculums, and a central services directory with the names and phone numbers of all support staff. The school system encourages requests for information; write or call the Craven County Board of Education, Director of Public Relations, 3600 Trent Road, New Bern, NC 28562; (252) 514-6333.

Other Facilities

Some children fall behind in school and need a little help to catch up, while others need an accelerated program to offer them challenges. Private learning centers can provide such assistance. Other educational facilities in New Bern include a driving school to assist teens with earning their driving privileges.

Sylvan Learning Center
1314 B Commerce Dr., New Bern
(252) 633-6380

Sylvan Learning Center offers a variety of educational programs and services for students of all ages and specializes in helping students master basic learning skills, achieve potential and gain confidence. The New Bern center offers programs in reading, math, writing, study skills and Scholastic Aptitude Test preparation.

The Driving School
2503-F Neuse Blvd., New Bern
(252) 637-0200

Teens who don't want to wait for their high school driver's education class can sign up for monthly classes at The Driving School, located in Town Park Plaza on Neuse Boulevard. The driver's education class incorporates 30 classroom hours with six hours of driving time, where students learn defensive driving techniques, safe passing skills, and how to avoid traffic hazards. The Driving School also offers adult refresher courses and driver improvement classes.

Masterminds
2500 Trent Rd., Suite 34, New Bern
(252) 633-4112

Masterminds is the creative place for learning that not only provides tutorial and homework help but also fun enrichment activities. Certified teachers provide personalized tutoring for children kindergarten through 5th grade, while the drop-in Homework Helper lab is open Monday through Thursday from 3 to 5 PM to offer that extra assistance sometimes needed, either due to confusing content and/or harried schedules. Masterminds also offers several great enrichment opportunities. Cooking, art and science exploration activities are set up according to age groups: grades 2 and 3, 4 and 5 and 6 to 8 for cooking; grades K and 1, 2and 3 and 4 and 5 for science exploration; and K and 1, 2and 3, 4 and 5 and 6 and 8 for art classes. Afternoon book clubs meet weekly to discuss the latest children's book and take part in related activities and crafts. Call for registration information and class schedules.

Oaks Road Elementary School and J. T. Barber Elementary School in New Bern, and Havelock Elementary School and James W. Smith Elementary in Havelock all require students to wear uniforms. For all other Craven County schools, the Board of Education recently adopted a strict dress code. For more information concerning Board of Education policies, contact Mary Alice Swindell, (252) 514-6346.

Private Schools

New Bern offers several private schools and another is about 40 miles west in Kinston. Additionally, many day-care and camp facilities offer private kindergartens for young children and summer programs for school children.

Calvary Baptist Church School
1821 Rhem Ave., New Bern
(252) 633-5410

A ministry of Calvary Baptist Church, this private school serves approximately 90 students in pre-kindergarten through grade 12. The school's uniforms consist of green shirts with the school logo, combined with khaki pants for boys and khaki skirts and jumpers for girls. Basketball and cheerleading are available for high school students.

Ruth's Chapel Christian School
2709 Oaks Rd., New Bern
(252) 638-1297

This school serves about 200 students in kindergarten through 12th grade and an additional 40 students in day-care and before- and after-school programs. Students are required to wear uniforms. A structured program is offered for 3- and 4-year-olds, while older children study the Abeka and Bob Jones University curricula. Volleyball, cheerleading and basketball programs are available for older students.

St. Paul's Education Center
3007 Country Club Rd., New Bern
(252) 633-0100

Serving about 300 students from pre-K (age 4) through 8th grade, this private school is affiliated with St. Paul's Catholic Church.

Arendell Parrott Academy
1901 Dobbs Farm Rd., Kinston
(252) 522-4222

Arendell Parrott offers nonsectarian instruction for students in pre-kindergarten through 12th grade and has a total enrollment of 700 students. Sports teams, musical ensembles and special interest clubs are available for older students. The school offers transportation for out-of-town students, including those from the New Bern area. The YMCA parking lot serves as the drop-off and pick-up point for local students.

Child Care

As is the case across the nation, the need for quality day care continues to grow in New Bern. We have listed here, in alphabetical order, a few of the day-care facilities in and around New Bern. Craven County and the State of North Carolina regulate day-care homes and centers through the issuance of registrations and licenses. Regulations call for all such facilities to meet health and safety standards. In the case of nonsectarian child-care institutions, standards for children's learning and play programs must be met. For a complete list of regulated day-care homes and licensed day-care centers, call the Craven County Child Care Resource and Referral, (252) 672-5921.

All About Children Preschool and Day Camp
2610 Neuse Blvd., New Bern
(252) 633-2505

This day-care center offers a variety of programs for infants, toddlers and schoolchildren. The day care accepts children ages 6 weeks to 5 years old and offers preschool classes for ages 2 and older in separated age groups. The day camp offers before- and after-school care for children up to age 12. Transportation to all city schools and James W. Smith Elementary is provided. Summer programs and swimming lessons are also available.

Childcare Network
3705 Old Cherry Point Rd., New Bern
(252) 636-3791
301 Ninth St., New Bern
(252) 638-2957
204 N. Shepard St., Havelock
(252)447-1802
Westbrooke Shopping Center, U.S. Hwy. 70 W., Havelock
(252) 444-1809
610 Fontana Blvd., Havelock
(252) 447-5437

Open Monday through Friday, Childcare Network offers day-care services and before- and after-school programs for children ages 6 weeks to 12 years (except for the Childcare Network facility at 301 Ninth Street in New Bern, which accepts children 12 months through 12 years). Star-licensed by the state of North Carolina, Childcare Network features such amenities as transportation to and from public schools, nutritious meals and snacks,

Waterfowl, such as these Canada geese, are abundant in New Bern's wetlands.

photo: George Mitchell

summer camp activities for older children, and computers for children. The Childcare Network staff prepares younger children for school by utilizing the Active Learning Series for infants and toddlers and the HighReach Curriculum for 2 to 5 year-olds. Hours vary per location. Call ahead to confirm hours and availability.

First Steps Infant and Toddler Center
403 Ninth St., New Bern
(252) 638-3245

This full-service child-care facility -- the only one in New Bern designed exclusively for infants and toddlers -- accepts children ages 6 weeks through 36 months. With a staff trained in CPR, first aid and early childhood education, the center believes children learn best through play -- so children not only gain valuable skills but have a delightful time doing so. First Steps is open Monday through Friday.

Horizons Academy Day School
704 Newman Rd., New Bern
(252) 633-1050

Open 6 AM until 6 PM Monday through Friday, this nonsectarian school currently has an enrollment of approximately 125 children. It accepts 3- and 4-year olds for the pre-kindergarten program and offers before- and after-school care for its students and for children enrolled in public schools.

Little Hands Preschool & Day Care
2314 Elizabeth Ave., New Bern
(252) 638-1434

Preschool classes are available for toddlers age 2 and older, who also enjoy playing in Little Hands' large and shady playground. For students through age 12, Little Hands offers before- and after-school care, including transportation to and from local schools during the school year, and a summer camp from May to August.

Private In-Home Care

Many parents prefer to find qualified personnel to care for their children in their own homes, while others face the need of finding occasional care for their children due to travel demands and family emergencies.

Nancy's Nannies
P.O. Box 3375, Morehead City
(252) 726-6575

Nancy's Nannies has been offering nanny placement services and professional in-home child care since 1991. Nannies and sitters provided by Nancy's Nannies are thoroughly screened, experienced and CPR-certified.

NEW BERN
HEALTHCARE

The availability of quality healthcare is a primary consideration for newcomers and residents of any area, and New Bern is particularly fortunate to have a wide range of top-notch professional healthcare services. The quality of life and the presence of an excellent medical center have attracted many physicians and specialized health professionals to the area.

With retirees continuously relocating to the New Bern area, additional healthcare services, such as home-care professionals, cardiac rehabilitation services and geriatric care, are expanding in New Bern. These services are not often available in towns of similar size. The Craven Regional Medical Center has an open-heart surgery unit that makes it the nearest hospital in North Carolina's central coastal region to offer the procedure. In addition, the medical center offers state-of-the-art diagnostic equipment and services at its New Bern Diagnostic Center, same-day surgery at New Bern Outpatient Surgery Center, a comprehensive medical rehabilitation center and a mental health unit.

Alternative healthcare practitioners play an important role for many in the treatment of ailments and in maintenance of good health. Holistic practitioners and massage therapists of varied philosophical orientations adjust mind and body.

Hospital

Craven Regional Medical Center
2000 Neuse Blvd., New Bern
(252) 633-8111

Craven Regional Medical Center is widely recognized as a leading medical facility serving eastern North Carolina and was the first in this part of the state to perform radiation therapy. Opened in 1962, the center is acutely attuned to quality medical care and implements a total quality management program.

The 313-bed facility offers a comprehensive range of services not often found outside larger urban areas. At least partly because of that, it has been named a primary health provider for a number of area counties and, most recently, for Defense Department beneficiaries in eastern North Carolina. An outstanding medical staff of more than 200 physicians, a dedicated professional and support staff of more than 1,500 and a progressive administration and board strive to combine the best of medical care with empathy for patients.

All the major specialties are represented by the medical center's physicians and staff. Cardiac care is a focal point, with the area's most advanced services for diagnosing and treating heart disease, including interventional cardiology and cardiac surgery. It was the first eastern North Carolina hospital to offer cardiac rehabilitation on an outpatient basis. Its modern cardiac surgery suite includes surgical, recovery and intensive care rooms. Likewise, the medical center's oncology services lead the area in chemotherapy and radiation therapy on an inpatient or outpatient basis, including support services.

The medical center's outpatient services include the Craven Diagnostic Center, offering state-of-the-art diagnostic imaging equipment, mammography, ultrasound, nuclear medicine, X-ray and EKGs in a comfortable private setting. Pet-CT imaging provides cancer and Alzheimer's patients with the most sophisticated diagnostic and cancer staging capabilities. Craven Regional Medical Center is the only hospital in the coastal region offering this advanced technology. You can arrange same-day surgery at the Craven Surgery Center, which includes procedures for cataracts, hernias and an ever-expanding list of surgical treatments. The Women's Center offers comprehensive gynecological care, including outpatient procedures and laser surgical techniques, and the Family Birth Place stresses family involvement in childbirth.

Specialty units include Crossroads, a 24-bed facility specializing in group-based

The Morehead City VA Outpatient Clinic is located at 5420 U.S. 70 W. and is operated by the Durham VA Medical Center. The clinic, which is open Monday through Friday, provides primary care, mental health, immunization and blood-drawing services by appointment to VA-enrolled patients in Carteret, Craven, Jones and Pamlico counties. Walk-in and emergency services are not available. For more information or an appointment, call (252) 240-2349.

care of adult mental-health disorders, and the Coastal Rehabilitation Center, a 20-bed unit designed to help victims of stroke, orthopedic and neurological disorders return to independent living and health as soon as possible.

Extended patient support services of Craven Regional Medical Center include home-care and referral services, assuring that medical needs are met and services are provided.

Health Department

Craven County Health Department
2818 Neuse Blvd., New Bern
(252) 636-4920

Located in the Craven County Human Services Complex, the public heath department offers many adult health services, including chronic disease detection, family planning and maternal healthcare, adult immunizations and a sexually transmitted disease clinic. Child health services include well child care, illness and injury care, free immunizations and cardiac and neurology clinics through physician referrals. Other services provided by the health department include the Women, Infants and Children (WIC) Supplemental Foods Program for children age 5 and younger and pregnant women; nutritional counseling for special diets or weight loss; a mobile dental care unit that provides screenings, dental services and dental health education; and educational programs for the public.

In addition, the Division of Environmental Health, (252) 636-4936, provides food, lodging and sanitation inspections, on-site wastewater inspections, lead poisoning investigations, indoor air quality and pediatric asthma management, rabies control and more.

Emergency and Important Numbers

Dial 911 from anywhere in the area for emergencies (police, sheriff, fire and rescue service).

AL-ANON, (800) 344-2666

Alcoholics Anonymous, (252) 633-3716

American Red Cross, (252) 637-3405, (888) 446-0979

Craven County Coalition Against Family Violence, (252) 636-3381,
(800) 656-HOPE

Craven County Health Department,
(252) 636-4920

Craven County Department of Social Services/Child Protective Services,
(252) 636-4948

Craven-Pamlico Animal Services Center, (252) 637-4606

Craven Regional Medical Center,
(252) 633-8111

Crisis Line, (252) 638-5995 (available 24 hours all day every day)

Drug and Alcohol Dependency Problem Hotline, (252) 637-7000

Urgent Care and Private Practices

Coastal Carolina Health Care, P.A.

Atlantic Internal Medicine
730 Newman Rd., New Bern
(252) 634-9090

Coastal Internal Medicine and Cardiology
670 Cardinal Rd., New Bern
(252) 636-6222

New Bern Family Practice and Urgent Care Center
810 Kennedy Ave., New Bern
(252) 633-1678

New Bern Internal Medicine and Cardiology
702 Newman Rd., New Bern
(252) 633-5333

Twin Rivers Family Practice
3252 Wellons Blvd., New Bern
(252) 636-2664

New Bern Cancer Care
1915 Trent Blvd., New Bern
(252) 636-5135

Coastal Carolina Imaging
3252 Wellons Blvd., New Bern
(252) 637-5480

Coastal Carolina Hospitalists
2000 Neuse Blvd., New Bern
(252) 514-2061

Coastal Carolina Sleep Medicine
3650 Neuse Blvd., New Bern
(252) 634-2240

Southern Gastroenterology Associates
3100 Wellons Blvd., New Bern
(252) 636-9000
www.cchealthcare.com

Coastal Carolina Health Care (CCHC) is a medical group practice with 10 offices in New Bern. The physicians of CCHC specialize in general internal medicine, family practice, cardiology and pulmonary medicine, respiratory allergies, digestive disorders, hematology and oncology. CCHC also offers state-of-the-art diagnostic services, including mammography, bone-mineral density testing, nuclear medicine, ultrasound, computerized tomography (CT), and magnetic resonance imaging (MRI). The practice also has 10 physicians and two ancillary providers based 24 hours a day at Craven Regional Medical Center to provide timely and dedicated service to patients.

The group's urgent-care center at 810 Kennedy Avenue, (252) 633-1678, is open Monday through Friday 8:30 AM to 8 PM, Saturday and holidays (but is closed on Thanksgiving and Christmas Day) 9 AM to 4 PM and Sunday 2 to 6 PM. During the center's normal business hours, no appointment is necessary.

Craven Regional Medical Center operates a Physician Finder Line, (252) 633-8102, to assist residents and newcomers with finding a physician.

Coastal Children's Clinic
703 Newman Rd., New Bern
(252) 633-2900
218 Stonebridge Sq., Havelock
(252) 447-8100
1004 Jenkins Ave., Maysville
(910) 743-2022

Coastal Children's Clinic is proud to have offered the most comprehensive pediatric care in the area for nearly 50 years. The practice specializes in pediatric medicine for children from birth through age 18. Coastal Children's Clinic is well known for providing excellence in pediatrics to the children of eastern North Carolina. The practice's eight physicians, pediatric physician's assistant and pediatric nurse practitioner are committed to providing the highest quality pediatric care possible in an atmosphere that is both nurturing and friendly to children. They have had office hours seven days a week for more than 30 years, which is unique for this area. All three offices are open Monday to Friday 8 AM to 5 PM, and the New Bern office is open Saturday mornings 8 AM to noon and Sunday afternoons noon to 4 PM. A physician is always on call for emergencies at (252) 633-2269 or by beeper at (252) 633-8817. Same-day appointments are available.

ECIM Urgent Medical Care
South Market Square, 2117 S. Glenburnie Rd., New Bern
(252) 636-1001

This urgent-care center provides treatment for minor emergencies and family medical needs and "after office" and weekend hours. Hours of operation are Monday through Friday 9 AM to 8 PM, Saturday 9 AM to 6 PM and Sunday 1 to 6 PM. No appointment is necessary. (ECIM Urgent Medical Care also has an office in Cape Carteret at 906 W. B. McLean Drive, (252) 393-9007, which is open Monday through Friday 8:30 AM to 5 PM.) Both centers have X-ray and laboratory services as well as emergency-trained physicians and physician extenders.

ECIM Eastern Carolina Internal Medicine
100 Berne Square, New Bern
(252) 638-4023
532 Webb Blvd., Havelock
(252) 447-7088
U.S. Hwy. 17 S., Pollocksville
(252) 633-1010

ECIM is a large medical group practice with offices in New Bern, Havelock and Pollocksville. A team of more than 40 physicians and medical providers specializes in internal medicine, family practice, pediatrics and emergency medicine. Subspecialists provide treatment in gastroenterology, hematology, neurology, nuclear medicine, infectious and pulmonary diseases, digestive disorders, arthritis, and cancer diagnosis and treatment. The practice offers full-time hospitalist service at Craven Regional Medical Center. Diagnostic services include radiology, nuclear medicine, laboratory work, CT scanning and ultrasound.

The ECIM New Bern in Berne Square, (252) 638-4023, is a full-service medical office featuring laboratory services, X-ray capability (including mammography), and a state-of-the-art endoscopy suite. Relocated at the same site, but with a separate entrance, is ECIM Pediatrics, (252) 636-1919, which serves children from birth through age 18. Another recent addition to the vast array of services offered by ECIM is an Oncology Treatment Center at its Pollocksville location.

The Heart Center of Eastern Carolina
1001 Newman Rd., New Bern
(252) 635-6777

The Heart Center of Eastern Carolina is a full-service cardiology practice featuring the most up-to-date treatments in the diagnosis, treatment and prevention of cardiac and vascular diseases. This medical practice of eight board-certified cardiologists offers patients many kinds of non-invasive and invasive treatments: diagnostic catheterization, electrophysiology, balloon angioplasty, nuclear cardiology, peripheral vascular disease treatments, atherectomy, stent placement, pacemaker implant and follow-up, echocardiology, hypertension treatment and lipid management. Patients are seen by referral and appointment. The Heart Center of Eastern Carolina, which is available 24 hours a day for emergency services for patients, also has offices in Morehead City and in Jacksonville.

New Bern Surgical Associates
701 Newman Rd., New Bern
(252) 633-2081, (800) 682-0276 Ext. 8419
www.newbernsurgical.com

The board-certified surgeons of New Bern Surgical Associates specialize in general, oncologic, vascular and advanced laparoscopic surgeries, as well as skin cancer screenings. Patients are seen by appointment or upon referral from their primary physician. For appointments, call (252) 633-2081. Patients with after-hours emergencies can call (252) 633-3557.

Home Healthcare

Many patient services provided by hospitals during long-term recoveries and illnesses are available at home with the assistance of monitoring and therapies of home-health services. Home healthcare is an alternative to institutional or hospital care that fosters patient independence and family care. All services offer nursing, rehabilitation therapies, medical social work, in-home aides, medical equipment and supplies.

Craven Regional Medical Center Home Care Services
1300 Helen Ave., New Bern
(252) 633-8182, (252) 633-8817

Craven Regional Medical Center provides continued recovery services at home for departing hospital patients as authorized by their physicians. Skilled nursing care is offered 24 hours a day, seven days a week. Other services include physical, speech and nutritional therapies and home-health aides. Home Care Services is certified for Medicare.

Home Health-Hospice Services of Craven County Health Dept.
2818 Neuse Blvd., New Bern
(252) 636-4930

The county health department provides home health and hospice services to homebound clients and those authorized for care by physicians. It provides in-home nursing services, 24-hour on-call care, home-health aid, nutritional counseling, and physical, oc-

cupational and speech therapy. It also offers hospice care for the terminally ill and their families.

Professional Nursing Service
1425 S. Glenburnie Rd., New Bern
(252) 636-2388

This service has licensed LPNs and RNs to assist with healthcare. It can provide sitter companions, certified nursing assistants, private-duty nurses and supplementary staffing.

Tarheel Home Healthcare
130 U.S. Hwy. 17 S., Pollocksville
(252) 224-1012, (800) 685-4539

Tarheel Home Healthcare is a private business that offers a full range of healthcare services for recoveries and care at home. Complete nursing services are offered in all infusion drug therapies, HIV/AIDS case management, and physical, occupational and speech therapy.

Alternative Healthcare

The encouragement of wellness and methods of coping with recurrent pain and disease are taught and practiced in New Bern through various alternative therapies and philosophical approaches. Chiropractic services are available, as are massage therapy, acupressure, acupuncture and other approaches to pain management. A Whole Health Resource Network directory to these types of services is available by calling (252) 637-4140 or by stopping in at Sunnyside Health Foods, 2500 Trent Road, Suite 2, New Bern.

Flemming Chiropractic Health & Wellness Center
3601 Trent Rd., #3 Village Square, New Bern
(252) 638-6062

Dr. Lois Flemming and her staff vow to "get you well and keep you well" through chiropractic care, acupuncture, nutritional assistance, personalized exercise programs and more.

Nova Pain Management
1813 S. Glenburnie Rd., New Bern
(252) 672-0095

Chiropractor David Donnelly and licensed acupuncturist Toni Rittenberg offer a full-service alternative healthcare center that specializes in pain management. In addition to the services of a medical physician and X-ray and lab facilities, the center also features chiropractic care, acupuncture, physical therapy and massage therapy. A full Chinese herbal pharmacy is also located on-site. Most services available at Nova Pain Management are covered by insurance.

Golf anyone?

photo: Jay Tervo

NEW BERN RETIREMENT

New Bern's popularity as a delightful retirement location is evident in its relocation statistics. Nearly 2,000 retired people move to New Bern each year, an average of about six per day. It's too hard to pass up New Bern's combination of mild climate, relatively low cost of living, beautiful surroundings and friendly people. Active retired citizens enjoy fishing, golfing, sailing, hiking and boating within a stone's throw of anywhere in the river city. Gardeners appreciate the year-round growing season. The colonial setting of the city and the wide range of social, cultural and recreational activities makes retirement in New Bern very attractive.

New residents find the city's regional hospital, doctors' offices, shopping centers, sports facilities, quality restaurants and numerous religious organizations important factors in making the decision to relocate for retirement. Those who decide to take the plunge and move to New Bern are seldom disappointed.

As more retirees settle in the area, a growing number of services and programs are created and tailored to meet their needs and interests. Several agencies and public service organizations offer an ever-expanding variety of services aimed at greeting, involving and assisting new and retired residents.

For retirees who need extra care in day-to-day living, retirement communities in New Bern are designed to create interesting, carefree and caring environments. The housing options available vary according to the needs of individuals and include assisted living, respite care, nursing and adult day-care services plus independent and assisted-living facilities and programs for memory-impaired residents. The Craven County Department of Social Services (see our listing in this chapter) is a clearinghouse for information on the various options in specialized care facilities.

Services and Organizations

A number of service agencies and organizations in New Bern are equipped to deal with the needs or problems that may confront the older population.

Area Agency on Aging (AAA) Eastern Carolina Council
233 Middle St., New Bern
(252) 638-3185

The State of North Carolina designated this agency, located in the O. Marks Building, to address the concerns and needs of the elder segment of the local population (estimated at 15 percent) as mandated through the Older Americans Act. Local citizens make up the regional council policy board. The agency is responsible for direct contracting with local providers in a nine-county area for priority services such as transportation, nutrition, in-home care, case management, housing and home improvement, legal and other services. It also provides technical assistance involving training, grant preparation, community coordination efforts, needs assessments and resource inventories. It carries out regional ombudsman assistance to county-appointed nursing home and adult care community advisory committees. The agency oversees development and implementation of aging programs, assists in the development of multipurpose senior centers and designates community focal point facilities for delivering services to the older population. The Area Agency on Aging is also responsible for the Family Caregiver program that assists and supports caregivers with their day-to-day care-giving responsibilities. New programs are always in development; call for more information.

Craven County Department of Social Services
2818 Neuse Blvd., New Bern
(252) 636-4900

The Department of Social Services offers information and assistance to seniors concerning health, Medicare and rest-home and nursing-home facilities. The department operates an in-home aide program, a Medicaid transportation program and an Adult Home Specialist Service that monitors nursing homes. It also refers clients to other agencies and organizations for help with special situations.

Craven County Senior Services
811 George St., New Bern
(252) 638-1790

Handling services geared toward senior citizens of Craven County, this agency offers a variety of programs and activities at its four senior centers for residents ages 60 and older. Popular center pastimes include quilting, crafts, exercise programs, self-help and supportive services, health screenings and various enrichment classes in cooperation with Craven Community College. Lunch is provided five days a week, except on designated holidays. The agency also operates the county's Meals on Wheels program.

Craven County Veterans Service Office
2818 Neuse Blvd., Ste. 15, New Bern
(252) 636-6611

The veterans service office provides veterans and qualified dependents with information, assistance and problem-solving services regarding veterans' programs and benefits. The office also works to promote issues of relevance to veterans.

The Craven County Chapter 2863 of the AARP meets the second Wednesday of every month at the Courtyards of Berne Village. Lunch is available for $7 and reservations are required by calling chapter president Margie Gilbert at (252) 514-3704. Feature speakers are scheduled for each meeting. Chapter memberships are available for $5 per person.

Gold Care
Craven Regional Medical Ctr., 2000 Neuse Blvd., New Bern
(252) 633-8154

This wellness program, developed by Craven Regional Medical Center, is for adults age 55 and older. Membership offers monthly education seminars, a physician-referral service, access to support groups, a quarterly newsletter, social opportunities and other activities. Annual membership is $15 for a couple or $10 for singles.

Help-At-Home
1202 S. Glenburnie Rd., New Bern
(252) 672-9300, (866) 672-3100

Help-At-Home allows seniors in Craven, Pamlico, Carteret and Onslow counties who need just a little bit of help at home to stay in their homes and enjoy their independence. This service matches caregivers to senior clients and provides services such as meal planning and preparation, light housekeeping, medication reminders and bill paying assistance, bathing safety monitoring, errand running, and local transportation. Help-At-Home is available 24 hours a day, seven days a week.

Neuse River Senior Games and Silver Arts Competition
New Bern Recreation & Parks Department
(252) 636-4061
Craven County Recreation & Parks Department
(252) 636-6606

Senior Games is an exciting health promotion program for adults 55 years of age and older. It includes events such as swimming, badminton, horseshoes, shuffleboard, cycling events, shotput, discus, bowling, table tennis, basketball, race walk and more, with gold, silver and bronze medals being awarded to the winners in each event. Medal winners also qualify for the North Carolina State Games in Raleigh. Silver Arts events include Heritage Arts, Literary Arts, Performing Arts and Visual Arts.

New Bern Recreation & Parks Department
Administrative Office, 248 Craven St., New Bern
(252) 636-4061, (252) 636-4062

In addition to its regular programs (see our New Bern Recreation and Parks chapter for more information), the New Bern Recre-

ation & Parks Department offers a number of special programs for seniors only, including dancing and exercise classes and a softball team. The department also hosts clubs devoted to special interests such as model airplanes, miniatures, stamps and coins, needlepoint, ceramics and more.

In addition to clubs and classes, the department also hosts special events for seniors only. Senior Activity Days are scheduled for Mondays and Fridays for adults age 55 and older at the West New Bern Recreation Center. Activities include table tennis, billiards, shuffleboard, basketball, badminton and more, while those who wish to pursue less-active pursuits can enjoy chess, checkers or just walking around the gym. The department also sponsors the Golden Age Club for seniors age 55 and older. The club meets on the second and fourth Thursday of each month at the West New Bern Recreation Center for fun and fellowship, with special trips planned throughout the year. For more information about Senior Activity Days or the Golden Age Club, call (252) 636-4061. The Henderson Park Senior Citizens Club, the oldest club of its kind in North Carolina, meets on the second and fourth Tuesday of every month at the Stanley White Recreation Center; for information call (252) 636-4062.

Senior Pharmacy Program
502 Middle St., New Bern
(252) 638-3657

The Senior Pharmacy Program assists eligible seniors, ages 60 and over in Craven, Jones, Pamlico and Carteret counties, with costs for prescription medications. An outreach of Catholic Social Ministries, it helps pay for prescriptions that treat chronic diseases such as cancer, high blood pressure, heart disease, diabetes, glaucoma, acid reflux, arthritis and clinical depression. Post-hospitalization medications may be covered on a limited basis. Sites for the monthly distribution of vouchers, to be used toward the prescription costs, are generally at area senior centers. Call ahead for an appointment. The program's mailing address is P.O. Box 826, New Bern, NC 28563.

In March 2005, New Bern was touted on the Today show as the great "undiscovered" place to retire, praised for its mild winter weather, great golf courses, and of course, its proximity to water which allows for sailing, boating and fishing.

Social Security Office
2822 Neuse Blvd., New Bern
(252) 637-1703, (800) 772-1213

Administering the Social Security and Supplemental Security Income programs, this office is open weekdays to provide information concerning Social Security guidelines and requirements and to answer other consumer questions. Clients are seen on a walk-in, first-come, first-served basis. Insiders recommend you either arrive early or come prepared for a wait.

Retirement Housing

The Courtyards at Berne Village
2701 Amhurst Blvd., New Bern
(252) 633-1779

The Courtyards at Berne Village, the only full-service retirement community in New Bern, is conveniently located in a residential neighborhood with shopping, entertainment and medical services just minutes away. Built in 1986 and totally renovated in 2004, the community provides a range of services that residents want and need to live as independently and as actively as possible. Residents enjoy a variety of social gatherings and planned activities. Three meals are served daily in the private restaurant, and special diet plans are available if needed or requested. The Courtyards at Berne Village also offers scheduled transportation, housekeeping and 24-hour campus and emergency care system monitoring. Amenities include a private clubhouse for meetings and parties, a library, a chapel for meditation and religious services, a cafe with patio seating, a state-of-the-art fitness center, and a barber and beauty shop.

At more than 18 acres, the park-like campus provides plenty of space for outside recreational activities such as walking, gardening and bird-watching. On-site amenities include horseshoes, shuffleboard, a putting green, croquet and bocce ball. The Courtyards at Berne Village features one- and two-bedroom apartments with full-size kitchens, private baths and individual heat and air control, all on the ground floor.

For those who need more service or need help with the activities of daily living, assisted-living apartments are available in the main building. A Special Memory Care Program is designed for those with Alzheimer's or other memory impairments. Respite care and short-term rental accommodations are also available. The Courtyards at Berne Village offers a tour and complimentary lunch for prospective residents and clients.

Homeplace of New Bern
1309 McCarthy Blvd., New Bern
(252) 637-7332

Homeplace of New Bern can accommodate up to 44 residents, who can rent suites on a month-to-month basis with the security of 24-hour help on hand. Independence is encouraged, yet assistance is available for whatever the resident needs. Kitchenettes, private baths with walk-in showers to optimize safety, independent temperature controls and attractive furniture are some of the many amenities featured in individual suites. The healthcare coordinator, who also is a registered nurse, coordinates the care and services provided by certified nursing assistance around the clock. Three delicious meals are served daily, and laundry, housekeeping and transportation services are available. An enriching activities program and its caring staff give Homeplace a distinctive and friendly reputation. The activities are varied and unique, ranging from crafts, exercise and religious activities to musical performances and excursions out on the town.

An additional 16 residents can be accommodated in a special Alzheimer's and related dementia program. The special program for individuals with Alzheimer's and related dementias is designed to provide assistance to residents while maintaining a safe environment.

Respite care and short-term stays are welcome. Prospective customers are encouraged to stop by to tour and experience the warmth and focus on customer service at Homeplace of New Bern.

In 2005 Homeplace of New Bern completed its second phase, the McCarthy Court Independent Living apartments. McCarthy Court offers 55 luxurious apartments with all of the conveniences for senior adults to be comfortable while maintaining an active lifestyle. The one- and two-bedroom apartments range in size from 753 to 1,436 square feet and feature patios or balconies, washer/dryer hookups, computer hookups and full kitchens. Month-to-month rentals include all utilities except phone and cable, a full-service evening meal, weekly housekeeping, maintenance, scheduled transportation, recreational activities and access to common areas. The staff checks in daily with residents, who also have an emergency pull-cord to summon help if needed.

Two Rivers Trent Campus
836 Hospital Dr., New Bern
(252) 638-6001

Two Rivers Neuse Campus
1303 Health Dr., New Bern
(252) 634-2560

These two residential facilities, owned and operated by UHS Pruitt Corporation, are located on either side of Craven Regional Medical Center. Two Rivers Trent Campus offers 113 beds in its newly renovated facility, which includes a large outdoor covered patio, indoor sun room and a large rehabilitation room. Two Rivers Neuse Campus has 110 beds available in private and semi-private rooms, a safe outdoor courtyard and a comfortable living room space for visitations. Both facilities feature spacious and bright dining rooms, activity rooms, wide hallways that offer easy wheelchair access, and the Wander Guard Security System for keeping residents with a tendency to wander safe and secure. The centers provide skilled nursing care, rehabilitative programs and a variety of therapies and recreational opportunities designed to keep residents healthy, alert and active. The centers also offer short-term care options for those unable to return home immediately after surgery or other treatments.

NEW BERN VOLUNTEER OPPORTUNITIES

Many of New Bern's public service agencies and nonprofit organizations rely on the services and talents of volunteers. Some simply could not operate without the assistance of their reliable volunteers. New Bern has a number of spare-time opportunities, and new ones are popping up all the time. While we've included several here, the New Bern Area Chamber of Commerce at 316-B S. Front Street, (252) 637-3111, maintains a comprehensive list of contact names and phone numbers for nonprofit and civic organizations in the area. Volunteers often find that helping out with one organization often leads to developing interests in others. The organizations and agencies listed usually provide any necessary training for volunteers.

American Red Cross
Coastal Carolina Chapter
1916 S. Glenburnie Rd., Ste. 12, New Bern
(252) 637-3405, (888) 446-0979

Serving Carteret, Craven, Jones and Pamlico counties, this well-known nonprofit organization uses volunteers to assist with blood mobiles and to serve as instructors for classes in first aid, CPR, Learn to Swim, life-guarding, babysitting and more. It also needs volunteers to aid in local and national disaster situations. Volunteers are needed to represent the chapter at fairs, parades, public informational booths and fund-raising events; perform reception, data entry, clerical and organizational assistance in the office; and serve on committees involving special projects, fund-raising, grant-writing, budgeting, auditing and financial development.

Craven County Arts Council and Gallery
317 Middle St., New Bern
(252) 638-2577

Like any county-based arts organization, the Craven County Arts Council relies on volunteers to keep its wheels moving. Council volunteers serve as hosts in the main gallery; help in the office; assist with mass mailings; conduct programs such as the popular Sunday Jazz Showcase in February and arts camps in summer; work on a variety of committees; and assist with city-wide art projects, programs and fund-raising events throughout the year. If you have an affinity for art and organization, this is your kind of place.

Craven County School System
3600 Trent Rd., New Bern
(252) 514-6333

The school system welcomes volunteers to aid teachers and students in a variety of ways and has an active community volunteer program in every school. Call the school of your choice directly or the central office at the number above if you are interested in volunteering in the schools.

Perhaps most in demand is assistance for children having problems in particular subjects, such as reading, English or math. The school system also is looking for volunteer tutors who speak a foreign language. Volunteers are needed on school field trips and in school libraries. Parent-teacher organizations and volunteer coordinators at individual schools are pleased to have help with special programs and projects to benefit the schools and students.

Craven Literacy Council
202 S. Glenburnie Rd., Suite 8A, New Bern
(252) 637-8079

The Craven Literacy Council trains volunteers to work as tutors with anyone who requests services to improve reading skills or to learn English as a second language. Volunteer tutors are trained to work one-on-one with students, and together they decide on a convenient time to meet for reading sessions. Tutor training sessions are held several times a year; call for a schedule.

Craven Regional Medical Center
2000 Neuse Blvd., New Bern
(252) 633-8127

Officials here will tell you that the hospital would not run as well or as smoothly without its faithful volunteers. The center uses its nearly 500-strong volunteer corps for everything from delivering mail and running the gift shop to manning the Healthwatch personal emergency response system. There is a youth volunteer group especially for 14- to 18-year-olds and a volunteer chaplaincy program for ordained ministers. Volunteers also help in the library, newborn nursery, emergency department and critical-care waiting areas. They operate the book cart and humor cart in the hospital, work in offices and handcraft comfort items for patients. The Gray Ladies and Gray Lads are perhaps the most active group, assisting with a variety of hospital-related duties. There's also an auxiliary group that coordinates activities in 25 different areas. If you have time and energy to spare, the center can put them to good use.

Extension And Community Association, North Carolina Cooperative Extension, Craven County Center
300 Industrial Dr., New Bern
(252) 633-1477

Formerly the Extension Homemaker Organization, this group of individuals provide valuable services to the community through collaboration with agencies such as Craven Regional Medical Center, The River Club and Coastal Women's Shelter, to name a few. Its mission is to strengthen families through leadership development, volunteer work, educational opportunities, and sharing research-based educational information generated from N.C. State and N.C. A&T universities. Membership is open to anyone who is a resident of Craven County. Residents of the county are invited to join an existing club or organize their own community club.

The Firemen's Museum
408 Hancock St., New Bern
(252) 636-4087

The Firemen's Museum is looking for volunteers who are willing to be trained to serve as museum guides. The museum is open Monday through Saturday, and scheduling for volunteers can be part-time and flexible.

Habitat for Humanity of Greater New Bern
930 Pollock St., New Bern
(252) 633-9599

Through donations of money, materials and volunteer labor, Habitat for Humanity builds modest homes in partnership with qualified families who meet Habitat's selection criteria and contribute 350 sweat-equity hours. Houses are sold to families on a no-profit, no-interest basis. To date, the New Bern affiliate has completed nearly 40 houses toward its goal of eliminating poverty housing in the area. Construction work takes place each Tuesday, Thursday and Saturday morning starting at 8 AM. Volunteers, both groups and individuals, are always needed. Habitat also operates a re-sale shop, (252) 633-5512, and volunteers are needed to help with merchandise pick-up and delivery.

Master Gardener Program
N.C. Cooperative Extension Service,
300 Industrial Dr., New Bern
(252) 633-1477

The Master Gardener Program is open to anyone who would like to learn more about gardening and at the same time assist the extension service in its horticulture education efforts. Prospective Master Gardeners are provided with 40 hours of training in return for 40 hours of volunteer service during the first year; in subsequent years, volunteers donate 20 hours to stay active in the program. Activities include presentations of Saturday morning programs, speaking to garden clubs, answering phone calls from the gardening public, meeting walk-in visitors at the extension office, planting and maintaining demonstration gardens, working with schools, and assisting with a variety of one-time educational events. Numerous continuing educational opportunities are provided to make this an ongoing learning experience for the Master Gardeners.

New Bern Historical Society
512 Pollock St., New Bern
(252) 638-8558

The historical society relies on volunteers for most of its vital functions. Volunteers make up the society's membership, education, marketing and program committees. They serve as tour guides, fund-raiser staff and help produce the Historical Society Journal. They coordinate special projects and help

New Bernians are proud of their many beautiful gardens.

photo: George Mitchell

maintain historical buildings and grounds. Volunteers are in great demand during the Spring Homes and Gardens Tour and the New Bern at Night Ghost Walk, and to assist with the Battle of New Bern Preservation project. If you enjoy history and its preservation, you will find a niche here.

New Bern Police Department
601 George St., New Bern
(252) 672-4216

The local police department is always on the lookout for good volunteers to help fill behind-the-scenes positions. Volunteers work in clerical and court liaison positions or with programs such as the Explorers Program and the Pawn Shop Reporting Program. Volunteers get started by filling out a two-page application and undergoing a background screening and reference check. After the screening is completed, volunteers are matched to available positions that take into consideration the time constraints and interests of the volunteers. Monthly meetings also are scheduled to provide training and networking opportunities.

New Bern Preservation Foundation
510 Pollock St., New Bern
(252) 633-6448

Like the historical society, the preservation foundation counts on volunteers and uses their skills to operate its organization. Most volunteers are young retirees, and the foundation could not function without them. Docents serve as hosts or hostesses for home tours; help in the office; work to produce the newsletter; help with the annual Antique Show and Sale in February and Homes Tour in the spring; cater meals; and assist with property cleanup and maintenance of historical buildings and grounds.

Public Radio East
800 College Ct., New Bern
(252) 638-3434

Volunteers interested in sharing their time with Public Radio East are welcome year-round to assist with clerical tasks and to answer telephones during fund drives. Training is provided when necessary.

Swiss Bear Inc. Downtown Development Corp.
316-A South Front St., New Bern
(252) 638-5781

Swiss Bear Inc. Downtown Development Corp. is a nonprofit organization that was established in 1979 to coordinate the revitalization of the downtown area. It organizes and coordinates the annual three-day Mumfest, held the second full weekend in October. Volunteers are needed for a variety of duties during Mumfest and for New Bern's upcoming 300th Anniversary Celebration.

Tryon Palace Historic Sites & Gardens
610 Pollock St., New Bern
(252) 514-4951

Tryon Palace Historic Sites & Garden's volunteer program offers a bounty of opportunities throughout the year. Assistance in the gardens at Tryon Palace is needed during every season but especially in the spring. Spring also brings about Young Sprouts, a elementary garden program for second grade students; volunteers who enjoy working with children will welcome the opportunities available to lead that program. In addition, drama enthusiasts interested in portraying historical characters, group leaders for school tours, guides for the New Bern Academy Museum, gate clickers and concert ushers are always needed. Prior to the holidays, hundreds of volunteers are needed to lend their talented hands with the holiday decorations for the entire site. If you have the time and interest in being a volunteer, contact the volunteer coordinator for an application.

NEW BERN MEDIA

Although New Bern's media scene is small, visitors and residents can find most of what they want to know from the news sources we describe here. The Raleigh-based News & Observer, which covers issues of statewide importance, also offers home delivery in this area. Cox Communications offers the full panoply of cable channels.

Print

New Bern Magazine
201-3 N. 17th St., Morehead City
(252) 240-1811

New Bern Magazine is published monthly and features information on events and attractions in Craven and Pamlico counties. It's distributed free at various locations, including the Craven County Convention and Visitors Bureau in the New Bern Riverfront Convention Center at the corner of East and South Front streets, and the New Bern Area Chamber of Commerce at 316 South Front Street. New Bern Magazine also is available by mail subscription for $15 per year.

The Shopper/Community Newspapers
3200 Wellons Blvd., New Bern
(252) 633-1153

The Shopper, published weekly, features advertisements, specials and coupons offered by local businesses in New Bern and Havelock. The Shopper also prints special sections dedicated to home improvement, back-to-school, holiday gift giving and other topics, as well as annual medical and hospitality guides. This 25-year-plus publication is delivered free of charge on Wednesdays to more than 34,000 households in Craven County. Classifieds ads may be placed by calling (888) 328-4802. The Shopper also publishes several monthly community newspapers, which are delivered free of charge to the residents they serve. These include the Taberna Tribune, Historic New Bern Herald, Greenbrier Gazette, The Fairfield Harbour Beacon, Trent Woods Times, River Bender, The Pines' Perspective (Carolina Pines), Sound Waves (Brandywine Bay) and The Shoreline (Pine Knoll Shores).

Sun Journal
3200 Wellons Blvd., New Bern
(252) 638-8101

This daily morning newspaper, owned by California-based Freedom Communications, provides regional coverage of Craven, Pamlico, Jones, Onslow and Lenoir counties and reports on state and national events and sports. The Sun Journal is available by home delivery or from vending machines.

Television Stations

WCTI - TV 12, ABC, 225 Glenburnie Drive, New Bern, (252) 638-1212, www.wcti12.com

WNCT - TV 9, CBS, 3221 S. Evans Street, Greenville, (252) 355-8500

WFXI - FOX 8/14, 5441 U.S. Highway 70 E., Morehead City, (252) 240-0888

C-TV 10, Cox Communications Access, New Bern, (252) 638-3121

Cable Television

Cox Communications
2907 Brunswick Ave., New Bern
(252) 638-3121

Cox Communications is the sole provider of analog, digital and high-definition cable service in the New Bern area. Featuring a variety of cable packages, Cox Communications offers such popular channels as A&E, The History Channel, Turner Classic Movies, SciFi, Lifetime, The Discovery Channel, HBO, Cinemax, Showtime Starz, pay-per-view movies and sports events, and more. Cox High Speed Internet features unlimited access, up to seven e-mail addresses and other benefits.

GREAT REASONS TO
LISTEN TO AM RADIO

Radio

Public Radio East 89.3 FM/90.3 FM/91.5 FM/88.1 FM/88.5 FM, 800 College Court, New Bern, (252) 638-3434 -- public radio

WERO BOB 93.3 FM, 1361 Colony Drive, New Bern, (800) 260-0933, (252) 639-7900 -- Top 40

WRHT Hot 96.3 and 103.7 FM, 1307 S. Glenburnie Road, New Bern, (800) 849-4688 (request line), (252) 672-5900 -- Top 40

WMGV V103.3 FM & KISS 101.9, 207 Glenburnie Drive, New Bern, (252) 633-1500 -- soft rock, R&B and contemporary

WSFL 106.5 FM, 207 Glenburnie Drive, New Bern, (252) 633-1500 -- classic rock

WXNR 99.5 FM (99X), 207 Glenburnie Drive, New Bern, (252) 633-1500 -- modern rock

WNCT Oldies 107.9 FM, 207 Glenburnie Drive, New Bern, (252) 633-1500 -- hits from the 1950s, 1960s and 1970s

WNBB/WNBR The Bear 97.9/98.9 FM, 233 Middle Street, Suite 107-B, New Bern, (252) 638-8500 -- classic country

WNOS 1450 AM, 116 S. Business Plaza, New Bern, (252) 633-1490 -- standards

WWNB 1490 AM, 114 S. Business Plaza, New Bern, (252) 635-1494 -- inspirational and gospel

Mother Nature's artistry is ever-present.

photo: George Mitchell

NEW BERN COMMERCE AND INDUSTRY

Commerce and industry in New Bern are broad-based and receive strong support from the presence of Marine Corps Air Station Cherry Point and its affiliated Naval Aviation Depot (NADEP) in Havelock. NADEP is one of the largest aeronautical maintenance, engineering and logistics support facilities in the Navy and is one of the largest civilian employers in eastern North Carolina. Managed by Marine officers, the facility has a work force of about 4,000 employees, most of whom are civilian. That number continues to grow.

The depot refurbishes a variety of military aircraft and provides emergency repair and field modification teams to do repair work on aircraft unable to return to the depot. For more information about NADEP, see the Havelock chapter of this book.

Industries with large work forces in New Bern include Weyerhaeuser, Hatteras Yachts, BSH Home Appliances Corporation, Moen, Amital Spinning Corporation, and Maola Milk and Ice Cream.

Weyerhaeuser grows and harvests timber and processes it in a huge pulp mill just outside New Bern. The company employs more than 500 people and owns more than 500,000 acres in eastern North Carolina. Hatteras Yachts builds luxury watercraft in its New Bern plant and employs about 925 people. BSH has about 400 workers, with plans to add 1,400 more. A producer of plumbing fixtures, Moen has about 1,000 employees. Maola Milk and Ice Cream has about 480 workers, and Amital Spinning employs about 325 people.

Large non-industry employers include New Bern-Craven County Schools, Craven County government, Craven Regional Medical Center and the City of New Bern.

Several New Bern groups are organized to encourage new businesses to locate here and to facilitate economic growth in the area.

The New Bern Area Chamber of Commerce, 316-B S. Front Street, (252) 637-3111, represents the interests of the local business community in the regional, state and national government arenas. It also offers networking and professional opportunities, as well as numerous programs and events designed to promote the businesses of its members.

Swiss Bear Inc. Downtown Development, 316-A S. Front Street, (252) 638-5781, is a private nonprofit group organized in 1979 to spearhead and coordinate the revitalization and redevelopment of the downtown and its waterfront. An aggressive effort based in building public-private partnerships, creative fund-raising strategies and long-range plans has led to the investment of more than $70 million for the rehabilitation and construction of new commercial buildings and major public improvements, plus the creation of hundreds of jobs. As a result, tourism is now a major industry in New Bern.

The Craven County Economic Development Commission is responsible for encouraging manufacturing and development, especially to the county-owned 519-acre Craven County Industrial Park that straddles U.S. Highway 70 about 5 miles west of New Bern. The park features an incubator facility that offers office and manufacturing space to new manufacturers. Industrial sites vary in acreage. The Economic Development Commission is constantly looking for existing businesses to expand or new businesses to move into the industrial park or into the county. Contact the Craven County Economic Development Commission, 100 Industrial Drive, New Bern, NC 28562, (252) 633-5300.

The Small Business Center at Craven Community College offers workshops, seminars and group study sessions addressing the needs of small business owners. Also provided is one-on-one counseling and specialized employee training. Resource centers also are available at both the New Bern and Havelock campuses that feature free computer and Internet access, specialized software, multimedia tools, books, magazines and other business-related materials. For more information, contact the Small Business Center Director, Craven Community College, 800 College Court, New Bern, NC 28562; (252) 638-7353.

Volunteers with the SCORE Down East Chapter 577 of the Service Corps of Retired Executives Association are available 9 AM to noon Monday and Friday and 2 to 5 PM Wednesday, at 233 Middle Street, Suite 206, (252) 633-6688, and at other times by appointment. SCORE provides free counseling and low-cost workshops to promote the formation, growth and success of small businesses in Craven, Beaufort, Lenoir, Jones, Pamlico, Pitt and Greene counties.

CLOSE UP

Hatteras Yachts

One of the best known names in the yachting world is located in New Bern, North Carolina -- Hatteras Yachts. Lauded the world over for its distinctive designs and high quality, Hatteras Yachts has sparked a revolution in boat design and elevated the expectations of boat owners worldwide since its inception in the 1950s.

The story of Hatteras Yachts started in 1959 when Willis Slane, unable to go fishing because of treacherous seas, decided to build a better boat. The result? The sleek, 41-foot Knit Wits, capable of taking on the fierce waters off Cape Hatteras. Knit Wits was one of the first boats of its size to be constructed from fiberglass. And the rest is, as they say, history.

Hatteras Yachts, which celebrated its 40th anniversary in 2000, was originally based in High Point, North Carolina. Its first manufacturing facility was located in an old Pontiac dealership on Wrenn Street. Building boats in High Point had its drawbacks -- one of those being its location 200 miles from the ocean -- and the decision was made to move the "launch and make ready" operations to New Bern in 1969. By 1997, the entire Hatteras Yachts manufacturing operation had relocated to New Bern.

Its 95-acre, state-of-the-art production and in-water facility is located on N. Glenburnie Drive on the banks of the Neuse River. The impact on the New Bern economy is immeasurable -- Hatteras Yachts employs over 920 local residents at an annual payroll of $28 million. Hatteras Yachts, best known for its distinctive modified V-hull, produces 20 different models, ranging from 50-foot fishing convertibles to cruising yachts in excess of 100 feet. Annual sales of watercraft made by Hatteras Yachts averages $97 million.

Plant tours can be arranged by calling (252) 633-3101, ext. 459.

NEW BERN WORSHIP

New Bern has a number of historic churches that are open to residents and visitors who would like to tour or attend services. In addition to the distinctive architectural styles seen in many of the downtown churches, several have features that stand out above the rest, such as the pipe organ at First Presbyterian Church on New Street; the stained-glass windows in Centenary United Methodist Church at Middle and New Streets; the gifts from King George II displayed at Christ Episcopal Church on Pollock Street; and the graceful white arches in First Baptist Church on Middle Street. All these churches are within three blocks of one another. New Bern's oldest churches are wonderful places to learn about the area's history, and you can explore most of them while walking in the downtown area. (See our New Bern Attractions chapter for more details.)

In New Bern, church-sponsored events attract community-wide interest. During the holidays, many churches conduct special concerts, plays and bazaars. Another staple of the town's holiday celebration is a full performance of Handel's Messiah by a community choir of hundreds of voices and soloists at Centenary United Methodist Church, usually around the time of Old Christmas in January. Musicians for the performance are members of the North Carolina Symphony.

All major Protestant religions as well as the Catholic and Jewish faiths have long-established churches in New Bern. Check the Sprint Yellow Pages or the church directory in the Saturday edition of the Sun Journal for a list of local options.

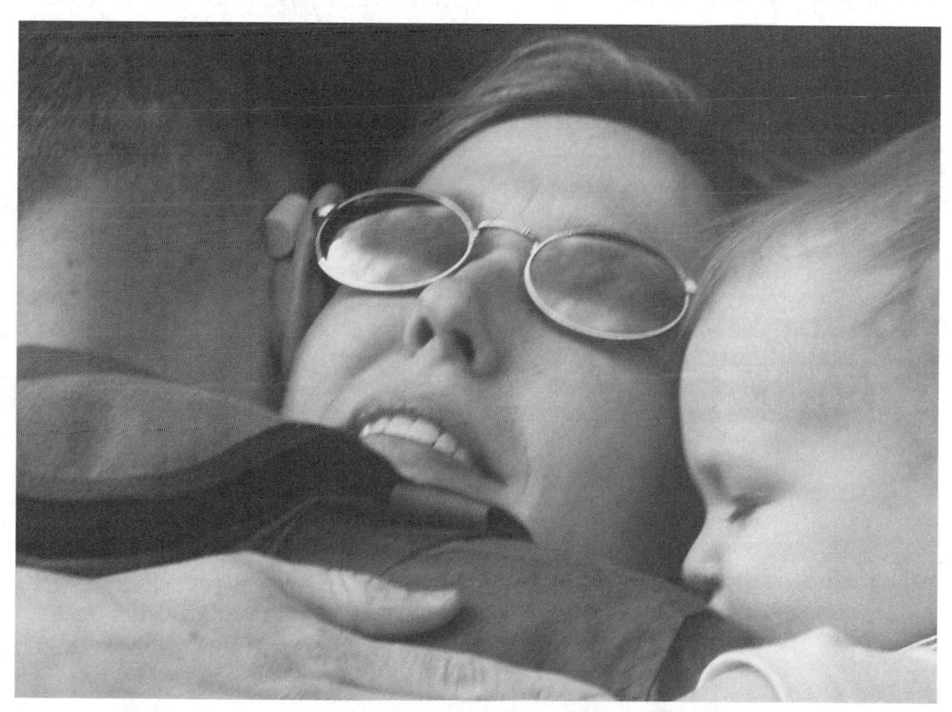

Happy homecomings and joyful reunions occur frequently in military towns.

courtesy of: NC Department of Travel and Tourism

Celebrating its 265th anniversary in 2006, the parish of Christ Episcopal Church is the oldest in New Bern and one of the oldest in North Carolina. The church, (252) 633-2109, is located at 320 Pollock Street. The current church building was rebuilt in 1871–1885 after a fire gutted the c. 1821–1824 church. The church is noted not only for its Gothic Revival details but also its graveyard that still contains a number of 18th-century stone markers.

First organized as a congregation in 1772, the current Centenary United Methodist Church, (252) 637-4181, was designed by Herbert Woodley Simpson and completed in 1905. Standing at the corner of New and Middle streets, Centenary features rounded walls and turrets that give it an almost Moorish look.

The narrow Gothic Revival First Baptist Church, (252) 638-5691, was built in 1847, though its congregation was organized in 1809. The main entrance of the church is located at 239 Middle Street, next to the O. Marks building. The main sanctuary is strikingly simple and peaceful in its design. The Sunday service is televised by WCTI-TV 12.

The oldest continually used church building in New Bern, First Presbyterian Church, (252) 637-3270, was built in 1819–22 by local architect and builder Uriah Sandy. The congregation was established in 1817. Located at 412 New Street, the church is surrounded by a cast-iron fence that dates from 1903.

Although St. Paul's Catholic Church, (252) 638-1984, is the oldest Catholic parish in North Carolina, its current home on Country Club Road was constructed about 21 years ago. The church, which was expanded in 2004, features strikingly modern architecture and is in a large, park-like setting. Sharing the land is St. Paul's Education Center, a private school. St. Paul's first church was built on Middle Street in 1840. That building is open to the public during daylight hours.

The stucco, neoclassical Temple B'Nai Sholem Synagogue, (252) 638-4545, is a beautiful, uncommon specimen of architecture in the area. A Herbert Woodley Simpson–designed structure, the synagogue was built on Middle Street in 1908 by the congregation, which was originally organized about 1824.

Six historic black churches in the New Bern area are listed on the National Register of Historic Places: St. Peter's A.M.E. Zion, St. Cyprian's Episcopal Church, Ebenezer Presbyterian Church, Rue Chapel A.M.E. Church, St. John's Missionary Baptist Church and First Missionary Baptist Church.

HAVELOCK

Welcome to the city of Havelock. Best known as the home to Marine Corps Air Station Cherry Point, the largest Marine Corps Air Station in the world, Havelock is a diverse city with much to offer visitors and residents.

The city and the military base have a population of about 22,650, making Havelock the second largest city in Craven County. This is a far cry from the 100 residents recorded in 1950. Admittedly, Havelock gained a few residents when the base was annexed, but it is still one of the fastest-growing urban areas in the state. More and more people are choosing to move here because of its proximity to the coast.

History

Havelock was named for Gen. Henry Havelock, a British general best remembered for his courageous rescue of hostages during a bloody uprising in India in the mid-1800s. A marble bust of Gen. Havelock stands in the Havelock City Hall.

First called Havelock Station, the community saw action during the Civil War when troops from the Rhode Island Heavy Artillery came ashore in 1862 near what is now the base Officer's Club. From that point, Union troops captured New Bern and Fort Macon on Bogue Banks.

At one time, the production of tar and turpentine had a large economic impact on Havelock, but once steam engines began replacing wooden ships as transporters of goods, the market for tar and turpentine fell.

Because of its proximity to waters and forests, Havelock gained notoriety in the late 1800s and early 1930s for its fishing and hunting opportunities. Area historians and artifact collectors value pictures of baseball great Babe Ruth, who often spent time in the area pursuing outdoor sports.

Today's residents and visitors to the Havelock area can enjoy being outdoors in the Croatan National Forest. This 157,000-acre forest spreads in a triangle between Morehead City, Cape Carteret and New Bern, and it borders Havelock on three sides. The forest features many ecosystems, endangered animals, plant species and wildflowers. (You can find information about the Croatan National Forest in our Crystal Coast Attractions chapter.)

U.S. Highway 70 runs through the middle of Havelock. The growth of businesses along the highway -- and the plethora of traffic lights that has resulted -- has led to traffic delays and backups, particularly at rush hours and during the busy summer seasons. The Department of Transportation is planning to construct a bypass to guide traffic off the existing U.S. Highway 70 just west of Havelock to take that traffic south of Havelock and reconnect it to U.S. 70 at the Craven County-Carteret County line on the east side of Havelock. This bypass will be connected to the city in several areas as it loops the city. Funds for construction of the bypass were recently diverted to another highway project; the start date at this point is unknown.

Havelock has a lot to offer, but don't just view the city from U.S. Highway 70. Take a turn here or there. Stop at a few businesses -- you might be surprised at what you find.

In this chapter we offer a quick look at the city of Havelock. We have given some general information about Havelock businesses, events and services. You'll find listings for restaurants, accommodations, shopping, attractions, annual events, golf courses and real estate agencies. These sections are by no

Havelock's official historian, Edward Barnes Ellis Jr., has written a delightful account of the city's colorful history, In This Small Place: Amazing Tales of the First 300 Years of Havelock and Craven County, North Carolina.

i

means comprehensive, but just a sampling of what you'll find. Information about area industry and military services is at the end of the chapter.

Cherry Point

Havelock is often referred to as the "Gateway to Cherry Point." With more than 14,500 sailors, Marines and civilians working there, Marine Corps Air Station Cherry Point is home to the largest Marine Aircraft Wing in the Corps, and it ranks as the number one single-site industrial employer east of Interstate 95.

The air station was first authorized by Congress in 1941. The arduous task of clearing the original 8,000 acres of swamp, farm and timberland began in August 1941, with actual construction beginning 17 days before the attack on Pearl Harbor.

The air station was commissioned on May 20, 1942, as Cunningham Field, in honor of the Marine Corps' first aviator, Lt. Alfred A. Cunningham. In August 1942 the first troops arrived at the air station, and the 2nd Marine Aircraft Wing officially made Cherry Point its home in November 1942.

Although stories abound on how the base took the name Cherry Point, it is believed to have been adopted from an old post office established in the area years before. The post office, used by the Blades Lumber workers, was closed in 1935. The original "point" was just east of Hancock Creek, and "cherry" came from the cherry trees that once grew there. The airfield itself, consisting of the runways and tower, is still technically named Cunningham Field.

From 1946 until the present day, the 2nd Marine Aircraft Wing has been integral in training thousands of Marines for the Korean Conflict, the Vietnam War and the Persian Gulf War. Now the 2nd Marine Aircraft Wing has elements permanently stationed at MCAS Cherry Point, MCAS New River, North Carolina, and MCAS Beaufort, South Carolina. It is equipped with helicopters, fighters, and attack and refueler/transport aircraft.

Over the years, Cherry Point has grown from a small airfield to one of the Marine Corps' most important air stations. The original 8,000-acre area has been expanded continuously and now encompasses 13,169 acres at Cherry Point and an additional 15,973 acres in assorted support locations. Built in 1941 at a cost of $14.9 million, the value of the base is now more than $1.6 billion.

Approximately 9,000 Marines and sailors stationed at Cherry Point earn an annual payroll of about $472 million. Combined with the station's nearly 6,000 civilian employees and 6,700 retired military personnel living in the area, more than $917 million is pumped into the local economy every year from Cherry Point. These salaries, plus local expenditures for supplies and capital improvements, have an economic impact of more than $1.1 billion annually on the state of North Carolina.

Visitor Information

The City of Havelock's Visitor Information Center is operated by the Havelock Chamber of Commerce, (252) 447-0014. The friendly staff helps visitors and new residents by providing maps and local information. The Visitor Information Center and the chamber are in the city's Tourist Center, located next to Hampton Inn Havelock. The 16,000-square-foot facility, built in 2003, includes an impressive aviation exhibit and is the site of many social and business meetings and community events. For information, call (252) 444-6402.

Restaurants

From fast food to family dining, Havelock eateries are sure to satisfy whatever craving you may experience. Our listings represent only a small portion of what is available. Ask locals for other recommendations or stop by the Havelock Chamber of Commerce.

PRICE CODE

The price code noted below the restaurant name will give you a general idea of the cost of dinner for two, excluding alcoholic beverages, tax and tip. Because entrees generally come in a wide range of prices, the code reflects an average meal -- not the most or least expensive items. Of course, lunch would cost less. The price code used is as follows:

$	Less than $20
$$	$20 to $35

Andy's Cheesesteaks and Cheeseburgers **$**
609 E. Main St., Havelock
(252) 444-0889

Looking for a quick and delicious lunch? Andy's is well-known throughout eastern North Carolina for its wonderful cheesesteaks, and the Havelock restaurant is no exception. Also try an Andy's cheeseburger or one of the other sandwich offerings. Andy's is open daily.

Costello's Italian Restaurant **$$**
328 E. Main St., Havelock
(252) 444-6110

Costello's is the perfect place for a romantic dinner with that special someone. Offering new variations on pasta favorites like fettuccini, linguini, spaghetti and more, Costello's offers appetizers and main dishes featuring seafood, beef, chicken, pork and veal. Diners can enjoy mixed drinks, beer and wine with their meals. Reservations are recommended at Costello's, which is open Monday through Friday for lunch, and every night for dinner.

El Cerro Grande **$$**
498 W. Main St., Havelock
(252) 444-5777

Located in front of Westbrooke Shopping Center, El Cerro Grande offers Mexican food at its best and is a popular lunch and dinner spot. Appetizers include guacamole salad and dip, chili with cheese, and chicken nachos. Entrees vary from combination plates with a choice of chicken, cheese, beef, potato or spinach fillings to special dinner platters that offer tostadas, burritos, steak ranchero and fajitas. Desserts turn to such favorites as sopaipillas and fried ice cream. The restaurant, which is open daily for lunch and dinner, serves several Mexican beers, wine and mixed drinks, including fabulous margaritas.

Uncommon Grounds **$**
600 Fontana Blvd., Havelock
(252) 444-5592

Those who love their cappuccinos and lattes need look no further than Uncommon Grounds, Havelock's only coffee shop. Although items vary due to availability, Uncommon Grounds serves hot and cold beverages, including coffees, teas, cocoa, fruit smoothies, Italian soda, Italian cream soda and more. If you're looking for something a little more substantial to go along with your beverage of choice, you can choose from muffins, bagels, pastries, cinnamon rolls, scones and more, or enjoy one of the ham, turkey or veggie wraps.

Accommodations

Visitors to Havelock will be pleasantly surprised by the diverse accommodations available. For years, only two motels served the city, with the majority of their clientele limited to traveling members of the armed services. With the increased popularity of nearby beaches and a local effort to attract industry to the area, new accommodations establishments have sprung up in recent years. We have only described a few to give you an idea of what's available.

PRICE CODE

For the purpose of comparing prices, we have placed each accommodation in a price category based on the summer rate for a double occupancy room. Our code does not include taxes, which are 12 percent (Havelock has a 6 percent occupancy tax). Please note that amenities and rates are subject to change, so it is best to verify the information when making inquiries. The code is as follows:

$	Less than $50
$$	More than $50

Comfort Inn **$$**
1013 E. Main St, Havelock
(252) 444-8444, (800) 228-5150

Comfort Inn offers a total of 58 rooms in various configurations, including standard king- and double-bed rooms and presidential and executive suites. All suites offer microwaves, refrigerators, irons and ironing boards, whirlpool tubs, hair dryers and coffeepots. Guests can enjoy an outdoor pool during the summer and an indoor exercise room year round. A free deluxe continental breakfast is

The Havelock branch of the New Bern-Craven County Library is located at 301 Cunningham Blvd. Call (252) 447-7509 for hours and other information.

served, and the inn is within walking distance of restaurants. A conference room that seats 40 is available.

Days Inn **$**
1220 E. Main St., Havelock
(252) 447-1122

Days Inn has 73 rooms that open to an interior hallway. The hotel offers the comfortable and clean rooms people have come to expect from the Days Inn chain. Each room is equipped with a microwave and refrigerator. The inn also has an outdoor swimming pool. Special rooms are available for those traveling with pets (an extra charge applies); these rooms also are Days Inn's only smoking rooms.

Hampton Inn Havelock **$$**
105 Tourist Center Dr., Havelock
(252) 447-9400, (800) 426-7866

Newly built in 2001, Hampton Inn Havelock features amenities such as in-room movies, a free newspaper, an exercise room and laundry services. An outside pool provides for relaxing fun during the warmer months. Meeting and banquet facilities, computer dataports in every room and fax services also are available. Children younger than 18 stay free with their parents.

Holiday Inn **$$**
400 W. Main St., Havelock
(252) 444-1111, (800) HOLIDAY (465-4329)

This 103-room establishment offers room service during restaurant hours. Rooms vary in size and furnishings, from a standard room to the executive suite, which features a small conference room and two adjacent bedrooms. King rooms include a microwave and refrigerator. Conference and banquet facilities for as many as 350 people are available. A restaurant and lounge are accessible from the inn's main lobby, and an outside pool is open during the summer months.

Sherwood Motel **$**
318 W. Main St., Havelock
(252) 447-3184

The Sherwood Motel is well-established, having been in business for many years. Guests will find a clean, quiet motel offering 87 rooms complete with cable TV, HBO and all the expected comforts. Refrigerators and microwaves are available, and an outdoor swimming pool is open in the summer.

Journey's End Havelock Inn **$**
310 E. Main St., Havelock
(252) 444-1414

Journey's End has 46 rooms offering a selection of sleeping arrangements. From a standard double to the presidential and honeymoon suites, there is a size and style to fit any traveler. The inn offers rooms with televisions, kitchenettes, balconies and Jacuzzis. A restaurant, a lounge and an outdoor pool are on site.

Shopping

While Havelock may not have any big shopping malls, it does have plenty of variety. Although many of the shops are service oriented -- video outlets, hairstyling salons and laundry facilities -- you'll also find a number of furniture stores, pawn shops and military surplus outlets. Below, we highlight a few of our favorite places.

Bike Depot
Century Plaza, 412 W. Main St., Havelock
(252) 447-0834

The Bike Depot offers Cannondale and Trek bicycles and makes repairs on all types. The store carries clothing, accessories, helmets and used bicycles. It's in the Century Plaza; turn into the shopping plaza when you see the big Rose Brothers Furniture sign. The Bike Depot is closed Sunday and Monday.

Bill's Pet Shop
491 U.S. Hwy. 70 W., Havelock
(252) 447-2750

Insiders love Bill's Pet Shop because it's a full-service store with everything you need to care for your pet - be it a dog, cat, bird, ferret, fish or reptile. They also have a knowledgeable staff that provides outstanding customer service. Bill's offers all types of pets for sale along with all the supplies and products needed to care for them. Bill's also features a complete tropical and saltwater aquarium section and is willing to guide you in the proper set up and care of your tanks. There are sister stores in New Bern and Morehead City.

E. T.'s Military Surplus, Inc.
347 W. Main St., Havelock
(252) 444-1977

In business for more than 25 years, E. T.'s Military Surplus offers military wear, hats, leather and dog tags, boots, patches, medals, survival gear and more in its 6,000-square-foot showroom. E. T.'s is open daily.

Palate Pleasers at Earthworks Garden & Gift Center
109 U.S. Hwy. 70 W., Havelock
(252) 447-2577

This gourmet shop is a tempting place to browse. There's an excellent selection of gourmet foods, wines, cheeses, coffees and teas, as well as many wonderful gift items. Palate Pleasers' garden center always has something new and wonderful to offer, from hanging indoor and outdoor plants, Mom's Garden (featuring seasonal plants) and gardening supplies to stepping stones, flags and distinctive yard art. Palate Pleasers is open Monday through Saturday.

Picture Perfect
600-C Fontana Blvd., Havelock
(252) 447-7654

Picture Perfect frames everything from military medals and diplomas to items such as golf clubs and christening gowns. Owners Don and Nancy Murdoch have been in business for nearly 20 years -- Nancy does the custom design work and Don does the cutting and assembling on-site. Picture Perfect offers a variety of moldings, from the traditional wood to hand-finished water-gilded gold. The shop, open Tuesday through Saturday, also carries prints by local artists, including Lisa Venema, Alan Cheek and Donna Graff.

Plaza Trade Center
Cherry Plaza, 1317 E. Main St., Havelock
(252) 447-0314

Plaza Trade Center used to be a flea market but now sells new furniture, appliances and household items. With many new items received on a regular basis, shoppers are sure to find something they both want and need for their homes. Plaza Trade Center is open nearly every day, year round (closing only for Thanksgiving and Christmas).

Swiss Chalet Bakery and Cafe
Westbrooke Shopping Center,
492 W. Main St., Havelock
(252) 447-3980

Insiders from Carteret and Craven counties often stop at this bakery to pick up loaves of European-style breads made from scratch by owners Tom and Lisa Buehler. Mouth-watering pastries, pies and cakes are for sale too. Should you care to linger (and who wouldn't?), sit at one of the tables, munch a luscious pastry and drink a cup of freshly brewed coffee. The Buehlers make wedding cakes to order and provide catering service, including box lunches and meat platters, for business meetings and other gatherings. The bakery is open Monday through Saturday year round.

Whiteman's Engraving
4 Jaycee St., Havelock
(252) 447-9793, (252) 447-8508

Whiteman's Engraving, which has proudly served the award needs of MCAS Cherry Point for more than 30 years, has shipped its award plaques to more than 100 embassies throughout the world. But this business has so much more to offer, including custom engraving on plaques (including plaques featuring clocks, a perfect gift for a special birthday, anniversary or graduation), silver, crystal, glass, trophies and other items. Whiteman's prides itself on its flexibility and fast and courteous service, so step right up with any special requests. Whiteman's is open Monday through Friday.

Annual Events

Havelock hosts a number of events each year that both residents and visitors look forward to. We have listed a few of the larger and most popular events.

MARCH-APRIL

Cherry Point Air Show
MCAS Cherry Point, Havelock
(252) 466-4241

This is one of the largest events in the area, with more than 100,000 people attending when the air station opens its gates to the public. The free air show features a variety of aerial displays of military and civilian aircraft. The numerous static displays allow visitors to get a close look at many of the military's high-tech aircraft. Wear comfortable shoes, as you may have to walk a ways. The show is conducted on a weekend in the spring and alternates between Cherry Point and New River Air Station in Jacksonville. The 2007 event will be at Cherry Point; the 2008 at New River.

Easter Egg Hunt
Havelock City Park, U.S. Hwy. 70 E., Havelock
(252) 444-6429

All children younger than age 9 are invited to the park to hunt for eggs stuffed with gift certificates, money and toys. The hunt usually takes place the Saturday before Easter morning, but to confirm the date, be sure to call ahead. Children need to bring a basket.

JUNE

Flounder Jubilee Golf Tournament
Carolina Pines Golf and Country Club, Carolina Pines Blvd., Havelock
(252) 444-1000

The competition is sponsored by the Men's Golf Association of Carolina Pines each June. There is no deadline for entering, but early entrants are given first consideration. The event is a two-person Superball competition.

JULY

Old Fashioned Fourth of July
Walter B. Jones Park, U.S. Hwy. 70 E., Havelock
(252) 444-6429

As the name says, this is the city's Independence Day celebration. It is the prelude to a grand fireworks display in the evening. For years, crowds have enjoyed a variety of entertainment, including musical groups, clowns and games. Food is available.

Havelock Two-Person Golf Tournament
Havelock-area courses
(252) 447-1101

The Two-Person Golf Tournament, sponsored by the Havelock Chamber of Commerce, draws a field of about 300 players. Held in mid-July, tournament play takes place at Carolina Pines Golf & Country Club.

SEPTEMBER

U.S. Marine Corps Battle Color Ceremony
MCAS Cherry Point, Havelock
(252) 466-4241

This ceremony is held every year in the evening at Havelock High School, usually right around Labor Day. The whole family -- from little kids to grandfolks -- will enjoy this inspiring event. The ceremony aims to demonstrate the qualities the title "Marine" embodies: pride, discipline, esprit de corps, teamwork. Featured are the Battle Colors, containing 51 streamers and silver bands representing every battle and campaign in which the Corps has participated; the U.S. Marine Drum and Bugle Corps, known as the Commandant's Own, a superbly disciplined marching band; and the Silent Drill Platoon, which performs an inspiring exhibition of precision drill without any verbal command. This is an event you will remember.

OCTOBER

Havelock Chili Festival
Walter B. Jones Park, U.S. Hwy. 70 E., Havelock
(252) 447-1101

Havelock hosts North Carolina's Chili Cook-Off Championship, and it really is a big deal. If you're a chili lover, Havelock is where you need to be on the third Saturday in October. You'll get a chance to sample some of the best chili there is. Premier chili chefs come from all over to vie for the title of state champion and the right to compete in the national cook-off contest later in the year. Contestants must follow the International Chili Society's rule: no beans of any kind. Chili without beans allows the judges to better detect the interplay of spices and assess the consistency of the chili. However, after submitting chili samples for judging, the forbidden beans are often added back to the pots, and festival-goers can pay a nominal amount at contestants' booths to taste the chili and cast a vote for the People's Choice Award. This is one event not to be missed, whether you like chili hot, mild or not at all. In addition to chili, a salsa contest, music, crafts and other displays keep everyone happy. Many local charities benefit from the profits.

DECEMBER

Christmas Parade
U.S. Hwy. 70, Havelock
(252) 447-1101

Havelock hosts a Christmas parade the second Saturday in December. Decorated floats and a visit from Santa Claus are part of the events. Holiday music is provided by the members of the Marine Corps 2nd Marine Air Wing Band as well as other area bands.

Christmas In The Park
Havelock City Park, U.S. Hwy. 70 E., Havelock
(252) 444-6429

This is one of the area's favorite Christmas celebrations. It is usually held on a Thursday before Christmas. The event consists of a Christmas carol sing-along and a live nativity scene.

Attractions

Although there are few bona fide attractions in and around Havelock, other than Croatan National Forest, the ones listed here are must-sees for anyone traveling in the area.

Harrier Monument
U.S. Hwy. 70 and Cunningham Blvd., Havelock

An AV-8A Harrier jump jet looms at the intersection of U.S. 70 and Cunningham Boulevard. Mounted on a pedestal and encircled by flags, the AV-8A is a symbol of the past. Although Cherry Point is home to the largest number of Harriers in the world, the jet was taken out of service during the mid-1980s and replaced by the new AV-8B. The most noticeable difference between the two jets is that the landing gear on the A was on the wing tips, while the B landing gear is closer to the center of the wings. This mounted jet was the second AV-8A military officials gave to civilians for display purposes (the first is on display at the Smithsonian in Washington, D.C.). In spring 2005 this aircraft was given a fresh coat of paint by the Marines of Marine Aircraft Group 14.

Aircraft Viewing

The sound and sight of aircraft in flight is a regular occurrence for locals, and it is often the very thing a visitor wants to experience.

Did you know that because of the length of Marine Corps Air Station Cherry Point's runway system (approximately 16,500 feet) it is an alternative landing site for the Space Shuttle? Cherry Point is the primary alternate landing site during the first 14 to 27 minutes of a shuttle launch. NASA's Mission Control releases all East Coast facilities once the shuttle clears Maine. Specially trained teams of Marines are on standby during launches to recover the shuttle and the astronauts.

Although there is no designated or best spot for prime viewing, a good vantage point is along N.C. 101 near the main gate. Runway 5 ends here and, if the winds are right, it is often used by Harriers, Intruders and C-130 cargo planes. The sound can be deafening, so a few words of caution: Brace yourself, warn your children and protect infants' ears from the noise.

Croatan National Forest
Ranger's Office, 141 E. Fisher Ave., New Bern
(252) 638-5628

This 157,000-acre national forest borders Havelock on three sides and offers visitors and residents a wide range of activities. Outdoor recreational activities include camping, picnicking, boating, hiking, hunting and salt- or freshwater fishing. For more information about the Croatan National Forest, see our Crystal Coast Attractions chapter.

The Trader Store
Miller Blvd., Havelock
(252) 447-5043

The Havelock Historical Preservation Society formed in late 1998, growing out of an ongoing effort to restore the landmark Trader Store on Miller Boulevard. The Trader Store, originally owned by Hugh and Elsie Trader and donated to the society by Ernest and Frances Trader, was once the center of commerce between New Bern and the coast, where families used the barter system to purchase everything from aspirin to plows. In the early 1900s, the store had the only telephone in the area. The restored store features early

20th-century artifacts, including the store's original ledger. The Trader Store is open to the public Tuesdays and Saturdays from 10 AM to 5 PM.

Golf and Recreation

The two courses closest to Havelock are the Links at Plantation Harbour, a brand-new club on Adams Creek Road at the Carteret-Craven county line, and Carolina Pines Golf and Country Club, between Havelock and New Bern. Golfers staying in Havelock can catch the free Havelock-Minnesott ferry, cross the Neuse River and play golf at the Minnesott Golf and Country Club. You can find more information about these courses in our Crystal Coast Golf chapter and the New Bern Golf chapter.

Friends Billiards & Pub
571 U.S. Hwy. 70, Havelock
(252) 444-2076

Friends Billiards & Pub offers a casual atmosphere with cold drinks, pool, darts and video games. There is no cover charge to get in. From 10 AM until 8 PM, the under-21 crowd can enjoy soft drinks, video games and billiards. Those 21 and over can take advantage of drink specials. Friends also sponsors pool, darts and horseshoes tournaments where you can test your skills against the area's best.

Marinas

Those boaters with access to the air station also have access to a number of launching facilities. Two boat ramps will get you into either Slocum or Hancock creeks. Two other marinas, one on the Neuse River and the other on Slocum Creek, provide boat rentals and docking facilities. Without base access, your choices of marinas and ramps near Havelock are limited. Check the marina listings in the Crystal Coast and New Bern sections for nearby facilities. Below are a few of the closest choices.

Matthews Point Marina
Temples Point Rd., Havelock
(252) 444-1805

At the mouth of Clubfoot Creek, this membership marina often allows transient boaters to use an available wet slip overnight. A clearly marked entry channel is provided along with facilities to accommodate both sail and power boats up to 45 feet. The approach depth is 7 feet, with a dockside depth of 6.5 feet. Open year round, the marina has gas and diesel fuel, electricity, a pump-out station, laundry facilities, showers and ice. A clubhouse, cookout area and upper-deck lounge are available to boaters. Finding the marina by land is more difficult than by water. Land seekers should follow N.C. Highway 101 toward Beaufort. Just a few miles out of Havelock, a church marks the corner of the highway and Temples Point Road. The marina is at the very end of Temples Point Road.

Cahoogue Creek
Cahoogue Creek Rd., off N.C. Hwy. 101

The National Forest Service offers a boat ramp at Cahoogue Creek, which allows boats to access Hancock Creek and the Neuse River. In addition to the ramp, the facility provides a grill, picnic table and small dock designed primarily to aid boarding. There are no restroom facilities. When driving on N.C. 101, there aren't really any landmarks to look for, so slow down and look for the road sign.

Real Estate

Residential housing is abundant in Havelock, with prices ranging from around $50,000 to $260,000. The majority of homes in Havelock and surrounding areas are less than 15 years old. Many planned communities have popped up in the neighboring areas and appeal to a wide range of individuals. Lured by the mild climate, low tax rate and relatively low cost of living, many retirees, both military and civilian, are finding a home in the Havelock area. Some of today's primary growth areas are the waterfront developments along the Neuse River and large creeks.

To get a good overview of the properties in Havelock and the services offered by the town's real estate agents, pick up free copies of Homes Magazine and other real estate publications at the Havelock Chamber of Commerce.

Because of the number of military entering and exiting the Havelock area, renting is a lot easier than in most areas. Rentals are abundant and come in many forms, including

Preserving Havelock's Past: The Trader Store

Sitting alongside a quiet stretch of road in Havelock sits a memorial to the past, to a time before the large supermarket chains came in and when the roadside grocery/gas station combination were mom-and-pop operations that also served as the center of the community.

Restored by the Havelock Historical Preservation Foundation, the Hugh Trader Store on Miller Boulevard is open 10 AM to 5 PM Tuesdays and Saturdays for tours. Dating back to the early 1900s, the store has retained many of its original features, including the wide-planked wooden floor, equipment including the meat and cheese slicers and the sausage grinder, the safe and the cash register. In its heyday, the store, operated by Hugh and his wife Elsie, offered everything from aspirin to plows. Merchandise currently on display includes old-fashioned hats and shoes, pots and pans, a Mobile Oil can display rack, and soda and beer bottles -- and the preservation society is on the lookout for donations of other merchandise, particularly from the 1940s and 1950s, to add to the display.

Pictures hanging around the room depict the Trader Store at various times between the 1920s and the 1980s. Outside, two old-fashioned gas pumps recall the heyday of the 1950s roadside station. The store, which was a stopping point not only for such famous customers as baseball legend Babe Ruth but also to thousands of Marines posted to Cherry Point during World War II, whose arrival in Havelock took place at the old train station, just down the road. Hugh Trader died in 1961; the Trader Store, which often served as a gathering place for hosting oyster roasts and pig-pickings, closed its doors in 1977.

In order to fund its restoration projects, the Havelock Historical Preservation Society offers engraved bricks for sale along its Walk of Honor. Bricks can be engraved as a memorial to a loved one, in honor of a special birthday or anniversary, or as a family or business' show of support to the society's efforts to preserve Havelock's history. Future projects include the acquisition, relocation and restoration of the Havelock Railroad Station and the African-American School House.

For more information, call (252) 447-5043.

houses, apartments or mobile homes. Rental prices vary according to the type of accommodation and could range from $425 to $750 per month. Many storage units are also available and vary in size.

1st in Flight Properties
249 U.S. Hwy. 70 W., Havelock
(252) 444-1904, (866) 425-1904

Let broker/owner Lana Cieszko put her 20 years of real estate experience to work for you. Serving all of Craven County, 1st in Flight handles residential and commercial sales, as well as offers property management services.

Century 21 Town & Country
406 W. Main St., Havelock
(252) 447-8188, (800) 334-0320

The oldest franchise real estate company in Havelock, Town & Country has been, for more than 25 years, a great place to start looking for a home in or around Havelock. An independently owned, full-service agency, Town & Country's agents handle sales of new and existing homes and investment properties. Also available are property management services and residential and commercial rentals.

Yes, you can go to the movies in Havelock. Call Carmike Cinema 6, (252) 447-1116, for a recorded message that gives you the lowdown on what's playing when; or drive over to 500 McCotter Boulevard (off U.S. 70 E.) and look at the marquee. On weekends, matinee prices are in effect until 5:30 PM.

Coldwell Banker First Realty
102 Roosevelt Blvd., Havelock
(252) 444-3333, (800) 396-7772

Owner-broker Gwen Schultz and her staff can show you excellent properties and lots available in Craven and Carteret counties. You can get assistance finding either commercial or residential property, including new construction. The staff members double as relocation specialists and are dedicated to making your next move a smooth one.

First Carolina Realtors
496-A U.S. Hwy. 70 W., Havelock
(252) 447-7900, (800) 336-5610

Located in the Westbrooke Shopping Center next door to the License Plate agency, First Carolina Realtors features listings for residential property, new construction, investment property, lots and land. Relocation services also are available.

Real Estate Management, Inc.
104 Roosevelt Blvd., Havelock
(252) 447-RENT (7368)

This management company, located across from the main entrance to Cherry Point, offers property management and rental services in the Havelock community. Residential rentals are available with either six or 12-month leases, depending on the property owners' listed preferences.

John Vesco Real Estate
326 E. Main St., Havelock
(252) 444-3790, (888) 920-3756

John Vesco Real Estate is highly recommended by Insiders who are impressed with the efficient and courteous service offered by retired Marine John Vesco and his staff of seven agents. Working with buyers and sellers throughout eastern North Carolina, primarily in Carteret, Craven, Pamlico and Onslow counties, John Vesco features competitive rates for buyers and sellers.

Media

Havelock News
228 Stonebridge Sq., Havelock
(252) 444-1999

This newspaper is distributed every Wednesday, with a readership that includes both military and civilian. Havelock News covers city schools, government and other news of interest for Havelock residents.

The Windsock
MCAS Cherry Point, Havelock
(252) 466-4241

The Windsock is published weekly and distributed on Marine Corps Air Station Cherry Point, to the Morehead City and New Bern Wal-Marts and other designated locations. The newspaper features messages from the Commanding General, Marine Corps News, Squadron spotlights and information from the Naval Air Depot (NADEP) Cherry Point. The paper also includes a sports section, recreation listings and classifieds. If you are interested in a subscription, call (252) 444-1999.

Commerce and Industry

The number of manufacturing companies in Havelock continues to grow. Through the years, several private firms have been established and are helping to diversify the economic base of the city. This growth is in part thanks to the efforts of the Craven County Economic Development Commission (EDC) and Craven County's Committee of 100. (See our New Bern Commerce and Industry chapter.) We have highlighted a few of the largest industrial and manufacturing influences on Havelock's economy. Although it is not a private company, we have listed first the Naval Air Depot (NADEP) Cherry Point because of its tremendous economic impact on the area. Wal-Mart recently announced it would build a 184,000-sqaure-foot Supercenter in Havelock, which is expected to employ about 400 people.

Naval Air Depot (NADEP) Cherry Point
MCAS Cherry Point, Havelock
(252) 464-7999

Naval Air Depot (NADEP) Cherry Point is one of eight such command sites that provide the highest standard in warfare technology through supremacy in naval aviation technologies. The depot is North Carolina's largest industrial employer east of Interstate 95 and employs more than 4,000 mostly civilian personnel. Established in 1943 as the Assembly and Repair Department, the facility has gone through several name changes over the years as well as extensive modernization and expansion. Today it is one of the Navy's finest aeronautical maintenance, engineering and logistics support facilities. Naval Air Depot (NADEP) Cherry Point is known as the Navy's center of excellence for vertical lift aircraft. The depot refurbishes helicopters such as the H-46 Sea Knight, H-53 (Super Stallion/Sea Dragon/Pave Low), AH-1 Cobra and UH-1 Huey. It is also the only depot repair point for the Marine Corps' unique vertical/short take-off and landing (V/STOL) AV-8B Harrier. The depot has extensive facilities to test and repair a number of different engine types, including the T58-400, which is used in the VH-3 presidential-executive helicopters. Naval Air Depot (NADEP) Cherry Point provides worldwide emergency repair and field modification teams to do repair work on aircraft unable to return to the depot. At a moment's notice, these field teams can be sent to any location around the world during times of war and peace.

United Parcel Service
201 Belltown Rd., Havelock
(800) 742-5877

UPS offers express letter and parcel delivery, and the Havelock facility is a regional terminal. Opened in 1986, this facility currently employs about 50 people.

Military

The military plays a large part in the lives of Havelock residents. Nearly 14,000 Marines, sailors and civilians work at the air station. And many other Havelock businesses count on the air station for patronage.

MILITARY ORGANIZATIONS

Marine Corps Air Station Cherry Point includes 13,164 acres on the air station proper, with an additional 15,973 acres of auxiliary activities, including Marine Corps Auxiliary Landing Field Bogue, along Bogue Sound in Carteret County, and Marine Corps Outlying Field (MCOLF) Atlantic in Pamlico County.

The largest commands at Cherry Point are the 2nd Marine Aircraft Wing, Marine Aircraft Group 14, Marine Wing Support Group 27 and Marine Air Control Group 28. Other 2nd MAW units include helicopter squadrons MCAS New River, North Carolina, and F/A-18 Hornet squadrons at MCAS Beaufort, South Carolina.

Marine Aircraft Group 14's flying squadrons include three AV-8B Harrier squadrons, four EA-6B Prowler squadrons and one KC-130 Hercules refueling squadron. The Marine Corps' only Harrier training squadron and Hercules training squadron are also at the air station. Those two training squadrons make 2d MAW the largest MAW in the Marine Corps.

Marine Wing Support Group 27 provides logistical support for the Wing with Marine Wing Support Squadron 274 at the air station and Marine Wing Support Squadron 271 providing support for the Bogue landing field.

Marine Air Control Group 28 employs some of the most advanced equipment for command of tactical air operations. The Marines who control the air war are defended by a battalion of Marines who employ the Stinger antiaircraft missile system to control the skies overhead.

SERVICES

A number of services are available to the military and their dependents, ranging from housing to recreational facilities. Military family housing is available for all ranks, although there is usually a short waiting period. Cherry Point is currently constructing new modern homes for ranks E-1 through E-5 families in the Slocum Village and Lanham housing areas. At the completion of these projects, more than 2,200 housing units ranging from apartments to houses will be available. Over 3,800 barracks rooms are available for single personnel.

Accredited by the Joint Commission of Accreditation of Health Care Organizations, the Naval Hospital Cherry Point provides the primary medical needs for the local area's active duty and retired military community, which is estimated to be more than 30,000. The three-story facility was dedicated in memory of Pharmacist Mate Second Class William D. Halyburton, a North Carolina native. The $34 million, 201,806-square-foot hospital houses the most modern technology to support its 23 medical/surgery beds, two operating rooms, three birthing rooms and two labor and delivery rooms.

Other facilities on the base are designed to afford military personnel a wide variety of conveniences and recreation. The Marine Corps Exchange offers a department store, grocery store, flower shop, liquor store and a number of small shops. There are also dry-cleaning and laundry facilities, a child-development center, a bank, a credit union and a service center with a convenience store.

Recreational activities are geared to Marines and their dependents. These include a large gymnasium, fitness center, three pools, an 18-hole golf course, a bowling center, a number of marinas and the base stables.

Although the base offers many services for convenience and fun, the Marine Corps stresses the importance of improving one's education. The Marvel Training and Education Center provides a wide range of educational services. Offices are operated by Craven Community College, Southern Illinois University, Boston University and Park College. The center provides services such as admissions testing, independent study course catalogs, counseling and a basic skills education program. The base has one of the most comprehensive libraries in the area with everything from reference materials to children's books.

Many more services and facilities are on base. MCAS Cherry Point is a community in itself. For more information, call Station Information, (252) 466-2811, or the Joint Public Affairs Office, (252) 466-4261.

Service Directory

TAX RATES

The Craven County and municipal tax rates are based per $100 valuation and are subject to change every fiscal year. Craven County's current rate is 61 cents (2005-2006 county budget) and Havelock's is 45 cents.

UTILITIES

Utility services are provided by a number of companies. We have listed a few of the larger providers.

Cable Television

Time Warner Cable (for MCAS Cherry Point), (252) 223-5011

Time Warner Cable (for service in Havelock), (252) 447-7902

Electric

Carteret-Craven Electric Membership Cooperative, (252) 247-3107, (800) 682-2217

Progress Energy Carolinas, (800) 452-2777

Telephone

Sprint Telephone, (252) 633-9011

Water

Havelock City Water and Sewer, (252) 444-6404

ORIENTAL

On the banks of the Neuse River, Oriental is a tucked-away sort of place. Quiet, pretty and filled with genuinely friendly people, this small village is a haven for those needing a bit of tranquility in their lives. You can get to nearly every place in Oriental by foot or bicycle. But while not fast-paced, this riverside town is certainly not boring. There's plenty to do – should you care to do anything at all.

Oriental is in Pamlico County, on the northern banks of the Neuse River directly across from Carteret County. It is only a 20-minute ferry ride from the Crystal Coast (or a short drive from New Bern). The free Cherry Branch–Minnesott Beach Ferry leaves from outside Havelock (see our Getting Around chapter in the Central Coast section), crosses the Neuse River and docks in Minnesott Beach. From there, Oriental is a short 10 miles away – just follow the road signs.

The town is situated amid six creeks: Smith Creek, Camp Creek, Raccoon Creek, Green Creek, Whittaker Creek and Pierce Creek. A 10-foot channel connects Oriental with the Intracoastal Waterway. Boat people are crazy about Oriental, which is known as the "Sailing Capital of North Carolina." Because it's on the Intracoastal Waterway, Oriental is a convenient and popular year-round port for sailing vessels. In winter, when yachts from the north are southbound, they stop in Oriental for a couple of days; in spring, headed back north again, they linger longer. An estimated 5,000 to 6,000 ICW travelers visit every year.

Unlike many other coastal communities that are experiencing newfound popularity and increased demands for housing and services, Oriental is enjoying a relaxed time. In 1910 the town's population was 2,500. Today, year-round residents number about 900. In recent years, some new neighborhoods and marinas have sprung up around the town, offering waterfront lots, boat ramps and recreational areas.

Oriental is named after the USS Oriental, a Yankee cargo ship that sank in stormy seas off the Outer Banks in 1862. Some years later, Rebecca Midyette, wife of the town's founder Louis Midyette, came across the ship's name board hanging on the wall of a private residence in Manteo, North Carolina. Mrs. Midyette liked the name, and after talking it over, the residents of Smith's Creek (the original name of the town) renamed their village Oriental. In 1899 Oriental was incorporated and the first post office was established with Louis Midyette as the first postmaster.

Oriental is a sailor's haven. That fact is apparent by the number of sail makers and chandleries offering marine supplies, equipment and repairs. In the last few years several art studios and crafts shops have opened. In our view, Oriental is the perfect getaway for relaxing, browsing, dining and enjoying the water.

On your way into town, you'll pass through the small towns of Grantsboro, Alliance and Bayboro. Bayboro is not only the county seat of Pamlico County, but also its oldest incorporated town (1881). In Grantsboro, you'll find the Pamlico County Chamber of Commerce Visitors Center, located on N.C. Highway 55. The center, also the home of the Pamlico County Historical Society, is open Monday through Friday 10 AM to 4 PM. Because it's staffed by volunteers whose availability sometimes varies, Insiders recommend you call first, (252) 745-3008, before stopping by.

It's a good idea, but not essential, to get a town map before you start to explore Oriental. Free street maps and other information are available at most of the real estate companies in Oriental, and the helpful staff at Oriental Town Hall, 507 Church Street, (252) 249-0555, will also supply you with free information. (Town Hall's mailing address is P.O. Box 472, Oriental, NC 28571.)

Oriental is also home to the Pamlico News, 406 Broad Street, (252) 249-1555, a weekly newspaper that comes out every Wednesday. The News is available by subscription or at stands throughout Pamlico County. The paper covers Pamlico, Hyde and East Beaufort counties as well as Aurora and Richland townships.

Things to Do and See in Oriental

SAILING CHARTERS AND SCHOOLS

For those who want the true Oriental experience, learning to sail or chartering a sailboat is the thing to do. Oriental's School of Sailing, located at 518 Water Street in the Oriental Harbor Village and Marina, (252) 249-0960, offers its program two ways: four consecutive days, with a new class beginning every Monday, or Saturday and Sunday over two consecutive weekends. Sailing school alumni can sign up for advanced classes. Lessons begin the first week of March and go through the last week of October. Instructors emphasize safety and hands-on experience. The school's programs are designed to introduce the novice sailor to sailing theory in the classroom as well as the basics of chartering and boat ownership. Oriental's School of Sailing also is a U.S. Sailing Certified School offering certifications in Basic Keelboat.

Another option for learning how to sail is Carolina Sailing Unlimited, P.O. Box 129, Oriental, NC 28571, (252) 249-0850, (800) 372-WIND. Or you can visit owner and Capt. Reginald Fidoe, who is from London by way of Detroit. He's at 502 Church Street. For the past 12 years, the school, stressing safety above all, tailors lessons to individual needs and interests. Capt. Reg offers personalized instruction abroad your own boat. Charter cruises for up to six passengers are offered aboard the 33-foot ketch, Puffin, for a half-day, a full day or evening sails.

PADDLING

Pirate Queen Paddling
310 Hodges St., Oriental
(252) 670-8465, (252) 249-1421

Hit the high seas with Pirate Queens Dawn Keller and Valerie Jones, who can help

A small skiff is the best vessel for navigating narrow inland creeks.

photo: George Mitchell

you select the perfect kayak and accessories and then lead you on half-day and multi-day explorations, sunset and full moon tours, and other escape expeditions on local waterways. Selected trips are offered to points beyond -- the 2005 schedule included Cumberland Island and the Okefenokee Swamp in Georgia, the Gulf of Mexico, Alaska, Cape Lookout National Seashore and other locations throughout eastern North Carolina and the southern United States. You'll be amazed by the Pirate Queens' energy and enthusiasm in promoting their sport. Kayaks and canoe rentals are available; the shop also features an eclectic selection of merchandise, such as "pirate snacks" and other touches of whimsy.

PERFORMING AND CREATIVE ARTS

Pelican Players is the community's performance company. Organized in 1983, this nonprofit volunteer organization is affiliated with both the Pamlico and the North Carolina Arts Councils. The group stages three productions a year, with performances at the Old Theater (also known as the Pamlico County Civic and Culture Center) at 609 Broad Street (across from the Town Hall). Dramas, Broadway hits and original productions make up their repertoire. Tickets are for sale at the theater door. For more information, call (252) 249-0477.

The Pamlico Musical Society presents seven to nine concerts a year by professional musicians performing everything from chamber music to down-home bluegrass. Season and individual concert tickets are available for sale at Croakertown in Oriental, Buckhorn Books in Bayboro and the Bank of the Arts in New Bern. Most performances take place at the Pamlico County Civic and Cultural Center. For more information, call (252) 745-8186 or write Pamlico Musical Society, P.O. Box 805, Oriental, NC 28571.

At 1103 Broad Street is Circle 10 Art Gallery, operated by Oriental's artists' cooperative. Art lovers can admire and purchase original creations in a variety of media: acrylics, oils, watercolors, pastels, glasswork, fiber art, jewelry and more. The gallery hosts a public reception on the first Friday of each month. In addition, four two-month-long shows are held to exhibit members' new artwork; these shows begin on the first Fridays of April, June, August and October. Workshops are offered throughout the year by local artists. Circle 10 is open 10 AM to 4 PM Thursday through Saturday and 1 to 4 PM Sunday from April to December. During the winter, it's open on weekends or by appointment. For more information about what's being scheduled, call (252) 249-0298.

Enjoy the sights and sounds of Pamlico County's waterways by joining the annual Pamlico Paddle, which combines friends and fun on the water with explorations of local waterways by canoe and kayak. Paddlers of all experience levels are welcome to take part; call (252) 670-8465 or (252) 249-3570 for more information.

EVENTS

Oriental's popularity soars on the Fourth of July weekend when thousands of visitors arrive for the annual Croaker Festival. The event honors the croaker, a very vocal, tasty fish found only in Southern waters. (If you've never heard a croaker's croak, you need to spend more time on the water.) The festival includes entertainment, the Croakette and Croaker Queen pageants, lots of good food, a baking contest, boat races, a street dance and more. But the more customary traditions of the Fourth are not neglected. The festival weekend concludes with a patriotic fireworks display that inevitably draws oohs and aahs from the holiday crowd. For information, call (252) 249-0555.

The Spirit of Christmas in Oriental is a holiday gift to the people of Oriental from the town's merchants, churches and civic groups. For well over a decade, on the second weekend in December (rain or shine), Oriental dresses up in resplendent holiday finery. Businesses and churches open their doors for fellowship and yuletide refreshments, and everyone is invited to stroll the candle-lit streets and enjoy the festivities, which start in the afternoon and continue throughout the evening. Townsfolk and visitors are entertained by local choral groups, musicians, Christmas puppets, decorated boats lining Oriental harbor, a Christmas parade and the ceremonious lighting of the Tree of Lights. This beautiful, free event is the work of nearly everyone in Oriental and is guaranteed to put you in a holiday mood. For information, call (252) 249-0555.

For more than 30 years, Oriental has commemorated New Year's Eve in its own special way. Every December 31, the community stages its annual Running of the Dragon. A huge golden Chinese dragon, with about 40 or 50 pairs of feet, appears twice during the evening beside the harbor. When it shows itself, New Year's Eve revelers pursue the dragon as it winds in and out of the town's streets. How many feet propel the dragon body depends on how many folks don't mind running around in the dark under a blanket. Needless to say, Oriental's Dragon Run attracts lots of visitors. Kids can see the dragon at 8 PM, and grown-ups can stay up for the 11 PM run. For information, call (252) 249-0555.

The Annual Oriental Rotary Tarpon Tournament is held every year around the last weekend in July. In case you didn't know, a tarpon is a big bony, silvery sport fish that averages 80 pounds and some 6 feet in length. (Tarpons have been known to weigh in at 200 pounds.) The fish winter in Florida's coastal waters and in the summer swim up the Atlantic, right into Pamlico Sound and the Neuse River. During July and August, tarpon abound in Oriental's waters. They are an excellent sporting fish, often fighting for 10 minutes to as long as an hour. The tournament, sponsored by the Oriental Rotary Club as a fund-raiser for the club's scholarship program, is a catch-and-release affair. Volunteer observers accompany the fishing boats to record official scores. The winning vessel is the one that catches and releases the most tarpon. Prizes are cash, and typically about 75 boats enter the tournament for a fee of $200. This three-day event includes a Saturday night barbecue and a Sunday afternoon awards ceremony. For more information, call Allen Propst at Mariner's Realty, (252) 249-1014.

Construction has started on widening a 14-mile stretch of Highway 55 in Craven and Pamlico counties from two to four lanes, with a center turn lane. The road will be widened between just past Bridgeton and the bridge exits all the way to Bayboro.

In mid-September don't miss the annual Oriental Cup Regatta and Boat Show - a good-time, three-day weekend party with a sailboat race in the middle. The race is geared to cruisers as well as racers, so all types of sailors, weekenders and competitors are encouraged to join the fun. Festivities start with a Friday night party with good food and live entertainment. Also on Friday evening is the start of the silent auction, featuring items donated by the Oriental business community. Saturday, rain or shine, sailboats race a triangular course on the Neuse River, the silent auction tent remains open while the race is going on, and, after the race -- guess what? -- there's another party. Sunday finds folks at the last event, the awards brunch. All monies raised by the regatta and the silent auction go to the Bill Harris Memorial Scholarship Fund (scholarships are awarded annually to Pamlico County students who letter in at least one sport and are of good character). The entry fee is $80 and covers the race and all the events. "Land" tickets are available for $25. For registration forms and tickets, write to Joe Wakeford, Box 1064, Oriental, NC 28571, or call him at (252) 249-0901.

Shopping

Many businesses in Oriental close or shorten their hours during the winter. If you want information or plan to visit when it's cold, be sure to call first

Croakertown Shop
807 Broad St., Oriental
(252) 249-0990

Croakertown Shop offers an extensive selection of cards and gifts, including nautical books, prints and photographs of local scenes by local artists. Insiders really like Croakertown for its beautiful American-made jewelry, particularly the silver and the variety of gemstones available. For the gourmet, Croakertown features a delicious array of mustards, sauces, marinades, jams and jellies. Croakertown is open daily year round.

The Bean on the Harbor
304 Hodges St., Oriental
(252) 249-4918

Insiders tell us that on your first visit to The Bean, you'll be treated like long-lost family. The Bean is your one-stop shop for coffee, tea, espresso and smoothies. If you need something more substantial, owners Rex and Patty Bragaw also offer bagels, muffins and sausage biscuits as well as ice cream and delicious desserts. This is also the place for coffee connoisseurs to pick up whole coffee beans. As for entertainment, something's always going on at The Bean, which is also available to host meetings or parties.

Hodge Podge
602 Hodges St., Oriental
(252) 249-3670

Hodge Podge carries "gently used books" for the general reader. Paperback and hardback fiction, nonfiction, classics, cookbooks, children's, craft and reference books can be found in this shop three blocks from the harbor. The store has a trade/credit policy on paperbacks and will do book searches for a small service charge. Also featured are hand-crafted and vintage jewelry, one-of-a kind vintage treasures, cards and the who-knows-what that keep the store living up to its name. May through September, the store is open every day but Tuesday; otherwise, it is open Wednesday through Saturday.

Inland Waterway Provision Company
305 Hodges St., Oriental
(252) 249-1797

From ship to shore, Inland Waterway Provision Company offers discount pricing on everything you need to float your boat under one roof. Inland Waterway carries fishing, biking and kayak gear at discount prices. Beautiful nautical-themed treasures abound, ranging from brass lanterns and sextants, to jewelry, wind chimes and flags. Inland Waterway features quality sportswear, footwear and foul-weather gear and offers a great selection of T-shirts for the whole family. Deck and casual shoes are always discounted 20 percent off retail price. Inland Waterway is open seven days a week year-round.

Marsha's Cottage
204 Wall St., Oriental
(252) 249-0334

Marsha's Cottage, located in a beautiful 1930s Sears-Roebuck bungalow, features distinctive, casually elegant sportswear and accessories for all seasons. Owner Marsha Paplham carries only those name brands known for outstanding quality and visual impact, and invites shoppers to stop by to experience the difference. Marsha's Cottage also features a wonderful selection of candles and novelty gift items. Hours are seasonal, so be sure to call ahead.

Priscilla's Too/General Store
516 S. Water St., Oriental
(252) 249-3783

Priscilla's Too is located inside the General Store in the Oriental Harbor Village Center development. The General Store carries domestic and imported beer, basic groceries and snacks for those headed out on the water or elsewhere. Priscilla's Too, tucked away in a small alcove, features more than 100 labels of world class wines. It's kept stocked by Priscilla Livingston, the owner of Priscilla's Crystal Coast Wine Store in Morehead City. Come in and enjoy weekly specials and discount on cases. Both Pricilla's Too and the General Store are open daily.

Quarterdeck Marine Store
Whittaker Creek Yacht Harbor, Whittaker Point Rd., Oriental
(252) 249-1020

This is a complete ship's chandlery, offering all the marine hardware and supplies sailors and power boaters need. There are T-shirts, foul-weather gear, shoes and shorts for adults and children. Patrons will also find

In his latest book Living Waters, Oriental resident and photographer Ben Casey tracks the Trent River from its beginning as a small stream in Lenoir County to where it empties into the Neuse River at New Bern. Casey's first book, All in One River, follows the Neuse River from Falls Dam to the Pamlico Sound. Both books are available at local bookstores and gift shops.

nautical books and charts, binoculars, sunglasses and beer and wine. Quarterdeck offers discounts to BOAT/US card holders and is open seven days a week all year. Sailboat charters, marine services and a boat brokerage also are available.

Restaurants

PRICE CODE

The price code for Oriental restaurants reflect the average price of a dinner for two that includes entrees, dessert and nonalcoholic beverages. Obviously, lunch would be less expensive. Prices are subject to change. Unless otherwise noted, all of these establishments accept credit cards.

$	Less than $20
$$	$20 to $35
$$$	$36 to $50
$$$$	More than $50

M&M's Cafe **$$$**
205 S. Water St., Oriental
(252) 249-2000

Owners Marsha and Dave Shirk have created a restaurant with the ambiance of a warm and friendly old inn. The food is delicious and imaginative, and the service is excellent. At breakfast, you can create your own omelet or choose a Red Wrapper, a sun-dried tomato tortilla with eggs, cheese, sausage and salsa. For lunch, don't pass up fresh seafood, grilled Portobello mushrooms, homemade soups, or a variety of daily pasta specials. M&M's offers several vegetarian dishes, and the specials change daily, so be sure to ask what the kitchen staff has in store on the day you dine at M&M's. For dinner the cafe serves pasta dishes, hand-cut sirloin steaks, lamb, veal, fish and homemade desserts (let the Key lime pie or pecan cheese pie tempt you).

In cold weather, M&M's patrons can dine on the glassed-in porch and enjoy the comfort of a gas-log fire while admiring the views of the water. In summer and autumn, screens replace the glass for enjoyment of the river breezes. M&M's Cafe has full ABC permits and is open every day for breakfast, lunch and dinner.

Toucan Grill & Fresh Bar **$$$**
Hodges St., Oriental
(252) 249-1818

The latest addition to the Oriental Marina & Inn complex, Toucan Grill & Fresh Bar gives diners the option to eat indoors in the spacious and attractively decorated dining room or outside on the deck enjoying cooling breezes and views of the water. The menu is appropriate for a restaurant located in a fishing village. Seafood dishes offered as either appetizers or entrees include clam chowder, cold shrimp cocktail, crab cakes, fish & chips, the House of Toucan seafood salad, fried shrimp or oyster baskets and more. Those with a yearning for something other than seafood should consider the hot buffalo wings or Oriental Dragon Scales (an appetizer of deep-fried, breaded banana pepper rings served with ranch dressing) and either rib-eye steaks, chicken kabobs, and full and half racks of barbecue ribs for dinner. If you've got room after eating the restaurant's generous portions, consider the cheesecake, peach cobbler, Irish Bash Pie or one of the other delicacies for dessert. Toucan Grill & Fresh Bar has full ABC permits and features special nights such as men's night and ladies' night that offer complimentary hors d'oeuvres. Toucan Grill is open daily; call for seasonal hours.

Accommodations

PRICE CODE

For the purpose of comparing prices, we have placed each accommodation in a price category based on the summer rate for a double-occupancy room. Our code does not include taxes. As always, call ahead to verify information.

$	Less than $50
$$	$50 to $85
$$$	More than $85

The Inn at Oriental **$$-$$$**
508 Church St., Oriental
(252) 249-1078, (800) 485-7174

Early in its history, this inn was a rooming house for teachers who taught school in the old brick buildings that still stand across the street (they're now condominiums). Marie and Hugh Grady have refurbished and added to this wonderful 1850s building, and guests will be delighted with the results -- 12 bright rooms, all of which have private baths, cable televisions, Internet access, and either queen- or king-size beds. One room has an in-room kitchenette, and an "artist's loft" is furnished with one queen, one double and a twin-size bed. Furnishings are comfortable pieces of everything -- antiques, reproductions, one-of-a-kind wall hangings and bed coverings. Colorful, imaginative motifs vary from room to room.

Come morning, guests are served at individual tables in the large dining room. The Gradys offer a full American breakfast, allowing guests to choose from many favorite breakfast items. Fresh fruit juice, freshly ground coffee, tea, hot chocolate, milk and cereal are always available, as are pancakes with seasonal fruit and walnuts and pecans. You may also order eggs cooked any way you like, Canadian bacon, French toast made with English muffins, or Belgian waffles. Hugh and Marie are always prepared to handle any guest's special dietary needs. Guests who prefer the outdoors may dine (or smoke) in the pretty garden enclosure right outside the dining room.

Two large porch decks have been added to the inn (as has expanded off-street parking). The decks are outfitted with tables, chairs and lounge chairs for visitors to stretch out and snooze or take in the quiet beauty of Oriental. In the back yard are big, fruit-bearing trees -- pecan, fig, apple and peach -- as well as specimen evergreens, azaleas and flowering bulbs. When your day is done, the Gradys make sure refreshments are right at hand. The Inn at Oriental is open year round.

Oriental Marina & Inn **$-$$**
Hodges St., Oriental
(252) 249-1818

Guests of this harbor inn are privy to beautiful views of Raccoon Creek and Old Town Harbor. The Oriental features one and two-bedroom units with efficiency kitchens. Each unit has a private bath and cable TV. A large deck and swimming pool, complete with a tiki bar, are in the back. Guests also will enjoy the Toucan Grill & Fresh Bar, open for lunch and dinner in season. The marina accommodates 13 deep-water rental slips with 30- and 50-amp electrical hookups, cable and water in-season. The inn, which is open year round, is handicapped accessible and accepts major credit cards. Kids are welcome, but pets are not allowed.

River Neuse Motel **$-$$**
Corner of South and Mildred Sts., Oriental
(252) 249-1404

This attractive two-story motel, located in a quiet residential spot right beside the Neuse River, affords visitors a spectacular view of the river. The motel offers 16 rooms with private baths, cable TV and in-room telephones. It is within walking distance of just about everything in Oriental, and its rates are very affordable. The River Neuse is open all year.

Marinas

Oriental Harbor Village Center & Marina
518 Water St., Oriental
(252) 249-3783

Oriental Harbor Village Center & Marina bills itself as the place "where the old and the new live quite comfortably, side by side" -- and it's easy to see why recreational boaters will enjoy an opportunity to stop by one of Oriental's newest developments.

Located at the mouth of the Neuse River, the complex's marina includes 120 deep-water slips, serving both permanent and transient boaters. Slips are available for sale or for rent on a monthly or nightly basis. Amenities include power and water services, a pump-out station, shower and laundry facilities, concierge services, use of bicycles, kayaks and small boats, and more. The private Harbor Club is open only to members and their guests.

The historic Delmar Hardware building and old Oriental Train Station have been meticulously restored to house the development's General Store, where boaters will find a little bit of everything, as well as the St. Bart's Yachts, Oriental Harbor Deli & Bistro, Priscilla's Too and Oriental's School of Sailing.

Phase One of the development's townhouses has been completed, and construction on Phase Two is underway. Townhouses, which include three bedrooms and two baths, also are available for rent.

Oriental Marina
Hodges St., Oriental
(252) 249-1818

This marina, just off the ICW, is open year round and serves sail and power vessels up to 70 feet. It has 13 transient slips, an 8-foot entry channel, dockside depth of 5 to 6 feet, gas and diesel fuel, electricity, cable TV hookups, ice, showers and laundry facilities. The Toucan Grill & Fresh Bar and the Oriental Inn are located adjacent to the marina.

Sea Harbour Yacht Club
Harbour Way, Oriental
(252) 249-0808

Sea Harbour Yacht Club is on Pierce Creek about a mile from town. It is open year round, has 90 slips, serves sail and power vessels up to 45 feet, and has gas and diesel fuel, a pump-out station, electricity, water hookups, a pool and restrooms.

Whittaker Creek Yacht Harbor
Whittaker Point Rd., Oriental
(252) 249-0666, (252) 249-1020

Whittaker Creek Yacht Harbor is open year round, has 160 slips including 20 transient slips, serves power and sailing vessels of up to 120 feet and has a marked entry channel with 8 feet of water on approach and at dockside. Gas and diesel fuel are available, as are a pump-out station, electricity, free high-speed wireless Internet access, supplies, a ship's store, ice, laundry facilities and restrooms. The marina offers repairs and a courtesy car.

Real Estate Companies

If you are interested in property or housing in Oriental, either to buy or rent, several firms can help you.

Century 21 Sail/Loft Realty Inc.
1000 Broad St., Oriental
(252) 249-1787, (800) 327-4189

Sail/Loft is Oriental's oldest real estate agency. It handles sales of residential and commercial property, vacation and long-term rentals along with property management services and appraisals. Sail/Loft also rents storage for boats, RVs and household dry goods.

Coldwell Banker Willis-Smith Realty
401 Hodges St., Oriental
(252) 249-1000, (800) 326-3748

Whether you are looking for land or lots, waterfront or golf course property, or a commercial establishment, this firm can find a property to suit your needs. It also offers a limited number of rentals.

Mariner Realty Inc.
704 Broad St., Oriental
(252) 249-1014, (800) 347-8246

Mariner handles residential and commercial property sales and vacation and long-term rentals. Mariner also appraises and manages property.

Tidewater Real Estate
22826 N.C. Hwy. 55, Oriental
(252) 249-9800, (866) 249-9800

Tidewater Real Estate handles listings for the Cabin Creek and Tidewater Ridge subdivisions, as well as offers an extensive selection of land and lots; residential golf course, waterfront, water- view and water-access properties; and business properties. Tidewater also handles residential and commercial rentals.

DAYTRIPS

Daytrips are the ideal way to see and enjoy more of North Carolina's coast, so we've provided this quick guide to some of our favorite getaway spots. These places are close by and are Insiders' favorites for various reasons -- the relaxed pace, scenic beauty, rich history, delicious restaurant fare or quiet evenings. After learning more about these places, you might want to plan a longer visit.

The North Carolina Travel and Tourism Division of the Department of Commerce, (919) 733-4171 or (800) VISIT-NC, offers information on sights throughout the state. Also check out other books in The Insiders' Guide® series, such as The Insiders' Guide to North Carolina's Outer Banks and The Insiders' Guide to North Carolina's Southern Coast and Wilmington. To order books, call (800) 955-1860 or go to our online order form.

Ocracoke Island

Visitors to Ocracoke love the leisurely, easy pace of this small island. From the time you arrive until the time you leave, you will be on Ocracoke Time -- so slow down and enjoy the relaxed life.

The fact that you can get to Ocracoke only by water or air has something to do with the carefree pace. Most visitors and residents travel to and from the island via state-operated ferries, so there is no need to hurry -- you can only come and go when the ferry does. The island's airstrip is about 1 mile from the village.

From the Crystal Coast, daytrippers take the Cedar Island-Ocracoke Ferry (see our Crystal Coast Getting Here, Getting Around chapter). This 2-hour ride ends in the heart of Ocracoke Village. Many people bring their cars to the island, but some passengers prefer to leave their cars on Cedar Island and walk or bike onto the ferry since there is no parking fee at the ferry terminal. Once in Ocracoke, visitors can walk or bike to just about anywhere on the island. Bikes are available for rent, as are fishing supplies, sailboats and boards, beach umbrellas and chairs, and camping and hunting supplies.

Ocracoke was established as a port by the colony of North Carolina in 1715. Early maps refer to the settlement as Pilot Town, because it was home to the men who were responsible for piloting ships safely into the harbor. About that same time, Edward "Blackbeard" Teach discovered the Outer Banks. The pirate and his crew robbed ships and terrorized island residents until 1718, when Lt. Robert Maynard of the Royal Navy and his crew ended Blackbeard's reign. Blackbeard was beheaded at a spot off Ocracoke now known as Teach's Hole. The pirate's head was mounted on the bowsprit of Maynard's ship, and Blackbeard's body was thrown overboard where, legend says, it swam around the ship seven times before it sank. (See our Close-up on Blackbeard's ship Queen Anne's Revenge in the Attractions chapter.)

The island's solid white lighthouse was built in 1823 to replace the 1798 lighthouse and remained in operation until 1818, when it was damaged in a storm. Ocracoke Lighthouse is the oldest and shortest of the Outer Banks' lighthouses, measuring only 65 feet high, or 75 feet including the lantern. A keeper manned the light until 1929, when it was converted to electrical power. It is now operated by the Coast Guard. The lighthouse isn't open for tours or climbing, but sometimes volunteers offer historical talks and answer questions.

Ocracoke Village is nestled on the edge of Silver Lake on the southern end and the broadest part of the small island. There are docks for pleasure and commercial fishing boats, inns, gift shops, private homes, historic cemeteries, seafood wholesale and retail businesses, restaurants and marshlands surrounding the water. Some homes date to the late 1800s. As more visitors discover the

island hideaway and build more homes and lodgings, the face of the village is changing.

N.C. Highway 12, the island's main road, stretches the entire 16 miles of the island, from the Hatteras-Ocracoke ferry terminal on one end to the Cedar Island-Ocracoke ferry terminal at the other end. But much of the beauty of Ocracoke lies on the side streets, of which Howard Street is the most notable. It was named for William Howard, who supposedly purchased Ocracoke Island in 1759 and is said to have served as Blackbeard's quartermaster.

Thirteen miles of undisturbed area stretch between Ocracoke Village and the Hatteras-Ocracoke Ferry terminal. On one side of the road is marsh leading to the sound and on the other is the Atlantic Ocean. This is the southern tip of Cape Hatteras National Seashore, and it is the perfect spot for shelling, fishing, sunbathing and water sports.

Because of the town's small size, many of Ocracoke's businesses do double duty. Restaurants are also nightspots, inns feature restaurants, and restaurants offer gifts. Ocracoke has a surprising number of businesses. The more you explore the village, the more places you will find tucked away.

There are all types of accommodation choices on the island, including inns, motels, bed and breakfasts, and rental cottages. While not all the places remain open year round, those that do offer some inviting winter rates. Here is a small sampling of the shops, restaurants and accommodations you will find on Ocracoke.

The village is dotted with arts, crafts, gift and apparel shops. On the Silver Lake harbor front, the Olde Ocracoke Gathering Place, (252) 928-7180, features a selection of English stained glass, nautical gifts, local and coastal art and island souvenirs. Harborside Motel & Shop, (252) 928-3111, billed as a family tradition open daily, has long been known for quality gifts and clothing, including sportswear, batik dresses, jewelry, saltwater taffy, stuffed animals and more, in addition to offering lodgings. On School Road, visit a gift shop with handmade stoneware, island-made candles, children's gifts and toys, bath products and more for both home and garden at Deep Water Pottery, (252) 928-7472.

Those wishing for a unique dining experience have several excellent options available to them. The Back Porch, 1324 Back Road, (252) 928-6401, offers relaxed dining seven nights a week on its shaded and sultry screened porch or in its air-conditioned dining room. The restaurant is an island favorite and is singularly a reason for a daytrip from the Crystal Coast, for its signature crab beignets, crab cakes, pastas, salads and creative seafood preparations, prime meats, house-secret sauces, and extensive wine list.

Howard's Pub & Raw Bar Restaurant, N.C. 12, (252) 928-4441, www.howardspub.com, is the home of the Ocracoke Oyster Shooter – a raw oyster covered with Texas Pete or

Tabasco, a shot of beer and black pepper. Try it! Howard's is a great place to go for good food and a good time. Enjoy local seafood, live Maine lobsters, burgers, subs, salads, soup or any of the many menu choices and appetizers inside, on the large screened porch, or on the roof-top deck with its view from ocean to sound. In season, Howard's features live entertainment; other times, enjoy watching major sporting events on Howard's big-screen TVs. Howard's doesn't close for hurricanes, holidays or winter, so you'll find the place open from 11 AM until 2 AM every day of the year.

To book a room at the Island Inn, N.C. 12, call (877) 456-3466 or (252) 928-4351. Guests are offered traditional rooms in the 1901 country inn or accommodations in the newly renovated villas fronting the island's only heated pool.

Bluff Shoal Motel, N.C. 12, (252) 928-4301, features large, comfortable rooms with double beds, private baths, small refrigerators, cable TV and telephones. Open all year, Bluff Shoal Motel has a harbor-view deck that overlooks Silver Lake.

Anchorage Inn and Marina, N.C. 12, (252) 928-1101, offers accommodations fronting Silver Lake Harbor and boasts of having the ultimate waterfront views. The five-story inn stands high above the traditional island structures, and its brick exterior is atypical of the local architecture. The inn features a pool, a full-service marina and dockside cafe, along with grills and picnic tables. Anchorage Inn can put together fishing packages, including the charter, lodging and food for four to six people on its boats from May to September.

Pony Island Motel & Restaurant, N.C. 12, (252) 928-4411, offers rooms, efficiency units and cottages. This reasonably priced motel has offered accommodations for more than 25 years. Amenities include grills, a heated pool, bike rentals and more. The adjoining restaurant serves breakfast, lunch and dinner.

For more information about Ocracoke, stop by the Ocracoke Visitors Center, which is in the two-story yellow house across from the ferry terminal, (252) 928-4531, or visit the Ocracoke Preservation Society Museum, open April through November, (252) 928-7375.

If you venture a little farther north than Ocracoke, you will discover all of North Carolina's Outer Banks. Of course, once you leave Ocracoke on the Ocracoke-Hatteras Inlet Ferry, you really aren't daytripping anymore -- you're traveling. The Hatteras Inlet Ferry, a 30-minute trip, puts passengers off at Hatteras Village. From there, N.C. 12 strings along the narrow islands all the way up to Corolla at the northern tip of North Carolina's Outer Banks.

For information about Ocracoke, contact the Greater Hyde County Chamber of Commerce, (252) 926-9171 or (888) 493-3826.

Bath

The small, historic hamlet of Bath is North Carolina's oldest town. Located in Beaufort County, this coastal village is about two hours by car from the Crystal Coast. It can be reached by taking U.S. Highway 70 to New Bern to U.S. Highway 17, which will lead you to Washington, where you take N.C. Highway 264, then N.C. Highway 92 to Bath. Another option is to take the more leisurely and scenic ferry route. Board the Cherry Branch-Minnesott Beach Ferry outside Havelock (see our Getting Here, Getting Around chapter), which will take you to the north side of the Neuse River on N.C. Highway 306. Drive along N.C. 306 to the Aurora-Bayview Ferry, which will deposit you on the north side of the Pamlico River. You will soon reach N.C. 92, which you follow for a few short miles into Bath. If you time the trip so you don't have to wait for ferries it can be a half-hour shorter. However, given the Aurora-Bayview schedule, that's almost impossible. Only take the ferry if you're not in a hurry.

Incorporated in 1705, Bath remains almost entirely within the boundaries of the original town plan designed by John Lawson, surveyor general to the crown of England. Today's residents are proud of their heritage and the town's significant 18th- and early 19th-century restorations. Historical markers throughout the town denote many "firsts" -- Christopher Gale, first Chief Justice of North Carolina, lived here, and the first public library and the first post road for mail delivery in the state were established here. Edward Teach, better known as Blackbeard, spent several months in Bath before his death, most likely living at Plum Point just across the creek from the colonial governor, Charles Eden.

Blackbeard moved about the town quite freely and was probably the guest of many distinguished citizens. Local legend states that Blackbeard's 14th wife was a Bath girl.

The Historic Bath Visitor Center, located on Carteret Street (N.C. Hwy. 42), offers a map noting the sites of interest in the town. You can take a walking tour on your own, or tour one or both of the period-furnished houses with a guide. Guided tours of the homes are $1 for adults and 50 cents for children. At the Visitor Center, you also can watch a free 15-minute orientation film Bath: The First Town as background for your walking tour. For seasonal hours and other information, call the Visitor Center at (252) 923-3971.

Out the back door of the Visitor Center is an oyster-shell path leading to the Van Der Veer House (c. 1790), which serves as a small museum for the town. Also along the path is the Palmer-Marsh House (c. 1751), for which there is an excellent guided tour that points out, among other things, a large double chimney and basement kitchen. The building is an excellent example of a large house from the Colonial period, and its architecture and history were the basis for its designation as a National Historic Landmark.

Crossing Main Street to Harding's Landing you will find the State Dock offering free public docking as well as a picturesque view of the town shoreline. A few early 20th century commercial structures remain on Main Street but there is no longer a business district. One of the largest buildings is Swindell's Store, built in 1905, which closed forever at the end of a business day in 1982, leaving merchandise on the shelves.

Heading south on Main Street will take you by private homes, many of which date to the late 19th and early 20th centuries. You may also notice ballast stone used for walls and building foundations of many of the town's structures -- reminders of Bath's rich maritime heritage. On the corner of Main and Craven Streets is the Williams House, often referred to as the Glebe House. Now owned by the Episcopal Diocese of East Carolina, this restored home is a private residence and not open to the public. Built around 1830, it has been the residence of several notable 19th-century Bath citizens.

Behind the Williams House on Craven Street is probably the town's greatest landmark, the St. Thomas Church. The oldest church in North Carolina, the church was built in 1734 but not fully completed until 1762. The church still operates on a daily basis and is always open to the public for a self-guided tour.

At the end of Main Street is the Bonner House (c. 1830). Built by Joseph Bonner, it was the home of the Bonner family, one of the distinguished families in Beaufort County history, for over 100 years. It is an excellent example of North Carolina coastal architecture, characterized by large porches at the front and rear.

Belhaven

If you've ventured as far as Bath, you'll be doing yourself a great disservice if you don't drive the few extra miles to scenic Belhaven. The quaint village is located on the waterfront of Pantego Creek and has a population of about 1,900. Local waterways provide a variety of outdoor activities such as: swimming, sailing and water-skiing. Fishing for crab and a wide variety of fish is an important sport, as well as hunting of white-tailed deer, geese and ducks.

Located on the Intracoastal Waterway, the town is accessible by boat or car. From the Crystal Coast, you can get to Belhaven on four wheels by taking the Cherry Branch-Minnesott Beach Ferry and the Aurora-Bayview Ferry. By boat, simply follow the Intracoastal Waterway north.

The main industries in Belhaven are fishing, boat works, farming, phosphates and forestry. The county is the state's largest soybean and pulpwood producer and is one of the largest crabmeat processing centers in the state.

The Town of Belhaven offers shopping and services with small-town Southern flair. There are three beautiful bed and breakfast inns within walking distance of local shops. There are a variety of restaurants serving anything from cheeseburgers to seafood. Shopping opportunities include bookstores, jewelry shops, clothing, hardware, drug stores and car sales. A multitude of banking services, marinas, auto repair, legal services, hairstyling and real estate surround the area.

Belhaven is fortunate to have excellent health care with the Pungo District Hospital located near the waterfront with a heli-pad and water access. Several local physicians provide primary care. Pungo Wellness & Fitness Center is open seven days a week, located in one end of the John A. Wilkinson Center.

Spectacular water views are the hallmark of the central North Carolina coastal regions.

photo: George Mitchell

Take your pick of great surf breaks along North Carolina's coast.

photo: George Mitchell

The John A. Wilkinson Center, (252) 944-4JAW, serves the area by hosting community concerts sponsored by the Beaufort County Arts Council and continuing education and G.E.D. classes sponsored by Beaufort County Community College. An art and music room is available to local artists who wish to hold workshops or classes, and the auditorium and other rooms are also available for rental to the public, businesses and local non-profits to hold events such as weddings, receptions, dinner/dances, meetings, company parties, holiday events and other gatherings.

Every year Belhaven hosts its Independence Day Celebration with craft and food vendors, a parade, military demonstrations, a fish fry, water ski shows, art exhibitions, dances, pageants and concerts. The day of excitement ends with a fireworks display over Pantego Creek. This celebration has been occurring since the 1950s and attracts over 20,000 people every year.

Belhaven's Memorial Museum is one of the 14 sites on the Historic Albemarle Tour. The City Hall, which houses the museum, is included in the National Register of Historic Places. The museum, open from 1 to 5 PM every day of the week except Wednesday, has a unique collection of items depicting the area's cultural and natural history. There is no charge for admission. Call (252) 943-3055 for information. While the museum is open year-round, many visitors also enjoy Belhaven in mid-April when the Dutch Festival in nearby Terra Ceia celebrates the riot of color provided by fields of tulips and gladiolas grown there.

Thistle Dew Bed & Breakfast at 443 Water Street in Belhaven is a Queen Anne Victorian that has been lovingly restored. The Thistle Dew features three guest bedrooms, each with private bath, that overlook the water. A full breakfast is served each morning in the dining room, and a butler's pantry, always open to guests, is fully stocked with spring water, sodas and wines. In season, guests are encouraged to relax in front of the fireplace in the large parlor or outdoors on the wicker and swing furniture on the full front porch. The bed and breakfast is centrally heated and air conditioned for guests' comfort in all seasons. Call innkeepers Pat and Bob Holz at (252) 943-6900 or (888) 822-4409 for reservations and more information.

The A-Bell Gallery features the works of Ann Bell, folk artist, author and writer of her own line of limited-edition prints, note cards and books. A sharecropper's daughter, Ann uses her artistic talent to preserve the history of eastern North Carolina during the Great Depression. While the gallery is open free to the public, it is generally open by chance or by appointment only. For information, call (252) 943-2059.

For more information about Belhaven, contact the Belhaven Community Chamber of Commerce, P.O. Box 147, Belhaven, NC 27810, (252) 943-3770, or stop by the chamber office in the renovated railroad depot at 125 W. Main Street during its new office hours of Monday through Friday from 9 AM to 1 PM.

Lake Mattamuskeet National Wildlife Refuge

OK, so a trip to Lake Mattamuskeet might require a bit more than a day. We have included it in the Daytrips chapter because it seems like an appropriate side journey if you make the jaunt to Oriental, Bath or Belhaven. The expansive wildlife refuge is on U.S. Highway 264, and well-placed road signs make it easy to find.

Lake Mattamuskeet National Wildlife Refuge stretches from Englehard on the east to Swan Quarter on the west. The refuge's 50,180 acres of water, marsh, timber and croplands are managed by the U.S. Fish and Wildlife Service. This beautiful area lies in the middle of the Atlantic Flyway. From October to March, the shallow 40,000-acre lake, which is said to be no deeper than a swan's neck, is a winter refuge for many migrating birds.

Waterfowl populations are at their peak from December through February, and so are bird-watchers. According to refuge information, 35,000 tundra swans winter at Mattamuskeet, and more than 150,000 birds gather at the lake between October and March. Thousands of snow and Canada geese and 22 species of ducks are seasonal inhabitants. The refuge provides habitat for osprey, red-tailed hawks, coots, blue herons, green-winged teals, black and ruddy ducks, cormorants, widgeons, mergansers, loons and many other birds. The refuge is also home to otters, bobcats, deer and black bears. Several endangered bird species, such as the peregrine falcon and the bald eagle, seek refuge around the lake. The refuge provides public hunting of swans, ducks and coots in season. For information on hunting, contact the refuge manager at (252) 926-4021.

The 18-mile-long and 5- to 6-mile-wide lake is the state's largest natural lake, making it and its adjacent canals a popular spot for boating and sport fishing. Largemouth bass, striped bass, catfish, bream and other species can be taken from March 1 to November 1. Fishing is excellent in the canals and along the lake shore in spring and fall.

Catching blue crabs is a very popular sport enjoyed by all ages and is permitted year round from the water control structures. All fishing activities must be conducted in accordance with state regulations. Bow-fishing for carp and other rough fish is permitted during the fishing season.

Prohibited activities in the refuge include herring dipping, camping, littering, swimming, molesting wildlife and collecting plants, flowers, nuts or berries. Fires and firearms are also prohibited without special authorization. The speed limit on refuge roads is 25 miles per hour, and no vehicles, such as overland vehicles or trail bikes, are allowed outside regularly used roads and trails. Boats may not be left on the refuge overnight without a special-use permit.

The Lake Mattamuskeet Lodge is the former pumping plant constructed in the early 1900s in an investment effort to convert the lake bottom to agricultural land and model community patterned after similar projects in Holland. The bankruptcy of one company after another in this effort led to its eventual abandonment, and the land was acquired by the U.S. Government in 1934 for the establishment of a waterfowl sanctuary. The pumping station was converted to a lodge for visitors and hunters and operated until 1974. It is now a National Historic Site of architectural and historic interest.

Plans to renovate the lodge as an environmental education center are in motion as a coordinated effort of the Partnership for the Sounds, a nonprofit organization for public environmental education, and the U.S. Fish and Wildlife Service. The building is currently closed due to structural problems from extensive corrosion. Funding has been

Batter up! A favorite summertime activity is a visit to Grainger Stadium in Kinston to watch minor-league baseball's Kinston Indians play nine innings. For a schedule and directions, call (800) 334-5467.

appropriated by Congress to correct these problems, and the U.S. Fish and Wildlife Service is currently developing plans to stabilize the building.

During the fall migration, a couple of weekend events make Lake Mattamuskeet an exciting destination. In early November, an annual Mattamuskeet Fun Ride is organized by the Hyde County Chamber of Commerce. Bicyclists may choose to take a 35-, 45- or 70-mile course around and across the lake. The courses begin and end at the lodge and offer lots of waterfowl viewing opportunities. The first weekend of December, Swan Days celebrate the annual return of tundra swan and other waterfowl for the winter. At the refuge, visitors may enjoy the exhibition and sale of native crafts, decoys and local food, and participate in educational programs and tours of the refuge.

For information about Mattamuskeet National Wildlife Refuge, contact the refuge headquarters, 38 Mattamuskeet Road, Swan Quarter, NC 27885, (252) 926-4021.

Nearby accommodations can be found in Engelhard, Fairfield, Swan Quarter and Belhaven. For additional information about area accommodations, restaurants and events, write or call Greater Hyde County Chamber of Commerce, P.O. Box 178, Swan Quarter, NC 27885, (252) 926-9171, (888) 493-3826.

Kinston

Although not normally considered a tourism destination, Kinston has a number of features that make a daytrip there a pleasant outing. Located on U.S. Highway 70 about two hours east of the Crystal Coast, Kinston has a year-round population of around 25,000.

Incorporated in 1826, Kinston is home to the CSS Neuse State Historic Site and Gov. Richard Caswell Memorial, located at 2612 W. Vernon Avenue (U.S. 70 Business). This historic site was recently designated as an official project of Save America's Treasures. The CSS Neuse is only one of three Civil War ironclad gunboats that have been recovered and the only commissioned Confederate ironclad on display in the world. In addition, the site celebrates the life of Gov. Richard Caswell, the first governor of the independent state of North Carolina. April through October, the site is open seven days a week; November through March it's open Tuesday through Sunday. For hours and more information, call (252) 522-2091.

Built in 1772, Harmony Hall, located at 109 E. King Street, was the home of Richard Caswell, North Carolina's first constitutional governor. Open for tours, it has been tastefully restored with 18th-century furnishings. For hours and tour information, call (252) 522-0421.

The Community Council for the Arts, 400 N. Queen Street, is housed in a three-story, 30,000-square-foot historical building that features six galleries with changing exhibits. The center is also home to a large permanent model train exhibit. Numerous classes and workshops are available for adults and children at a nominal charge. The gift shop offers many unique handcrafted items for sale. Admission is free; for more information call (252) 527-2517.

The Caswell No. 1 Fire Station Museum, 118 S. Queen Street, showcases the world of the late 1800s firefighter. This station was built in 1895 after a disastrous fire destroyed much of downtown Kinston. A 1922 American LaFrance Pumper is the focus of the museum, along with a collection of helmets, nozzles, ladders, fire extinguishers and other memorabilia that span a 100-year period. Admission is free; call (252) 522-4676 for seasonal hours.

And, of course, what summertime trip to Kinston would be complete without seeing a Kinston Indians baseball game? A North Carolina minor league baseball team affiliated with the Cleveland Indians, the K-tribe plays at historic Grainger Stadium from April through September. Reserved seats cost $5, while general admission is $4 for adults, $2 for senior citizens, military and students, and free for children age five and younger. Concessions and souvenirs are available. Discounted rates apply for groups of 15 or more.

For more information call (252) 527-9111 or (800) 334-5467, write P.O. Box 3542, Kinston, N.C. 28502, or stop by 400 E. Grainger Avenue in Kinston.

Race fans will enjoy watching IHRA-sanctioned racing at its finest every weekend at the Kinston Drag Strip, N.C. Highway 11 South. Call (252) 527-4337 or (252) 522-5403 for a schedule and admission fees.

For information about attractions, accommodations, restaurants and more, contact the Kinston Convention & Visitors Bureau at (252) 523-2500 or (800) 869-0032, or stop by the Visitors Bureau offices at 301 N. Queen Street.

Wilmington

A visit to Wilmington will probably require more than a day if you want to do more than drive into town, walk the waterfront and return to the Crystal Coast. This upscale but laid-back river city is about 45 miles south of Jacksonville on U.S. Highway 17, about a two-hour drive from the Crystal Coast area. It's a good jumping-off point to explore several nearby beaches and attractions.

There is much to discover about this delightful city and its nearby attractions. For a complete guide to accommodations, restaurants, shopping, sightseeing and beaches, pick up a copy of The Insiders' Guide to North Carolina's Southern Coast and Wilmington, or call (800) 955-1860 to order a copy.

There are two plantations that make for interesting sidetrips while in the Wilmington area. Poplar Grove Historic Plantation, (910) 686-9518, is an estate at Scotts Hill, 9 miles north of Wilmington at the Pender County line on U.S. 17. The 628-acre plantation and country store are open to the public year-round, but call ahead for seasonal hours. Admission to the grounds and outbuildings is free; tickets for the guided house tours are $7 adults, $6 seniors, $3 for students age 6 to 15, and free for children age 5 and younger. Poplar Grove also hosts special programs and events throughout the year, such as the Down Home Antique Fair and the Medieval Festival. Poplar Grove Plantation is listed on the National Register of Historic Places.

Orton Plantation Gardens, just south of the city and a few miles off U.S. 17, features a tour of outbuildings, gardens of brilliant azaleas, Luola's Chapel (built in 1915) and an exterior view of Orton House, built in 1725. The house is one of the region's oldest historically significant residences in continuous use. The plantation gardens and outbuildings are open March through November. Admission is $9 adults, $8 for ages 60 and older, $3 ages 6 to 16, and free for children younger than 6. For information, call (910) 371-6851.

Several beaches and attractions are a few minutes drive from downtown Wilmington. Fifteen minutes from the town hub lies Wrightsville Beach, which is primarily a family beach and small island community that features a number of quality hotels, motels, apartments, cottages, condominium developments and many marvelous seafood restaurants.

Down U.S. Highway 421 is Carolina Beach, best known for its wide, uncrowded shore, swimming, surfing, pier fishing and deep-water charter-boat fishing. Its shops, water slides, boardwalk and family amusement park offer something for everyone. Carolina Beach State Park, on the Intracoastal Waterway at Carolina Beach, is known for its collection of diverse plants, including the endangered Venus's flytrap. The state park has 761 acres with a marina, picnicking spots, hiking trails and a camping area. Call (910) 458-8206 for general information or (910) 458-7770 for the marina.

Continuing down U.S. 421 is Kure Beach, a site convenient to several attractions. It is adjacent to Historic Fort Fisher and is less than 2 miles from the N.C. Aquarium at Fort Fisher. The Fort Fisher State Historic Site on U.S. 421, (910) 458-5538, is near the mouth of the Cape Fear River and includes the remains of the old fort, a visitors center and gift shop, a museum with items salvaged from blockade runners and a reconstructed gun battery.

Only the main deck of the Battleship NORTH CAROLINA in Wilmington is handicapped accessible. If you want to explore below decks, wear good walking shoes and remember that the ladderways are steep. Be prepared to do some climbing.

With its many attractions, shops and restaurants, downtown Wilmington is daytripper heaven.

photo: George Mitchell

It's a must-see for the Civil War and history buffs of the family.

Nearby, N.C. Aquarium at Fort Fisher, which recently underwent a major renovation, highlights the theme "Waters of the Cape Fear." Highlights include a half-acre conservatory, the Coquina Outcrop touch pool and a 250,000-gallon ocean aquarium, with two-story, multi-level views of sharks, stingrays, eels and more. The aquarium offers a complete schedule of educational programs, including two daily dive presentations. Call (910) 458-8257 for more information about topics and schedules.

Back to the river city of Wilmington. This historic town is home to one of North Carolina's two deep-water ports. During the Revolutionary War, Wilmington gained importance as a point of entry, and its port was the last one on the Atlantic coast open to blockade runners during the Civil War. Continuous restoration and preservation make the town a history-buff's delight. Its fast-growing population includes many students who attend the state university, UNC-Wilmington.

Almost everyone who visits Wilmington includes a tour of the Battleship NORTH CAROLINA, (910) 251-5797, www.battleshipnc.com, located on the Cape Fear waterfront across from historic downtown Wilmington. Commissioned in 1941, the 44,800-ton, 728-foot warship wielded nine 16-inch turreted guns among its arsenal and carries nickel steel hull armor 16 to 18 inches thick. It was this platform that helped her survive at least one direct torpedo hit in 1942. The battleship, which came to its present home across the river from the downtown area in 1961, stands as a reminder of history and of the 10,000 plus North Carolinians who lost their lives in World War II.

The Battleship is open for tours 365 days a year. From Memorial Day weekend through Labor Day, it's open from 8 AM to 8 PM; from Labor Day through Memorial Day it's open 8 AM to 5 PM. The self-guided tour begins with a 10-minute orientation film. The entire experience will give you a true feel for what life was like aboard this vessel. You can visit the bridge, the Admiral's cabin, the crew's quarters, the galley and sick bay, the engine room and the radio central area. Tours cost $9 for adults and children 12 and older, $8 for seniors, active and retired military, and $4.50 for children ages 6 to 11. Children 5 and younger get in free. Ticket sales end one hour prior to closing. Keep a lookout for old Charlie, the alligator who makes his home beside the ship in the marsh. The Battleship NORTH CAROLINA Visitors Center has exhibits of the crew's recollections and WWII artifacts as well as a great gift shop.

Serving southeastern North Carolina since 1962, the Cameron Art Museum has assembled an important collection of North Carolina art and become a showcase for national and international exhibits. This 42,000-square-foot facility is located at the intersection of Independence Boulevard and 17th Street Extension, (910) 395-5999. Designed by architect Charles Gwathmey, the museum offers galleries complete with paintings, ceramics and sculptures ranging from the 18th century to the present. Cameron Art Museum also offers a number of cultural programs and has become a center of learning for both adults and children in the area. After touring the expansive permanent collections and intriguing featured exhibitions, stop by the Museum Shop for a keepsake and then have lunch at The Forks restaurant. Museum admission is $7 for adults, $15 for families, $2 for ages 6 to 18, and free for children younger than 5, museum members and active military. The first Sunday of each month is "pay what you can." The museum is open Tuesday through Sunday; call for hours.

The Bellamy Mansion Museum of History & Design Arts, 503 Market Street, (910) 251-3700, is a classic Victorian example of Greek Revival and Italianate architecture. The mansion, a stewardship property of Preservation North Carolina, currently houses a museum of the design arts, embracing regional architecture, landscape architecture, preservation and decorative arts. It's open Tuesday through Sunday, and admission is $7 for adults and $3 for children ages 5 to 12.

Cape Fear Museum, 814 Market Street, (910) 341-4350, is a must for history buffs. The long-term exhibition Waves and Currents: The Lower Cape Fear Story follows the progress of the Lower Cape Fear from settlement to the 20th century and presents an expansive picture of southeastern North Carolina's heritage. Scenes come alive with life-size figures and miniature re-creations of Wilmington's waterfront c. 1863, and the Fort Fisher Battle paints a picture of antebellum and Civil War times. (The Insider Kid was wowed more by the 15-foot-tall reproduction skeleton of a giant ground sloth, which lived in the area 1.5 million years ago.) Interactive children's activities, videos, changing exhibitions and special events add vitality to this learning experience. Personal items belonging to retired basketball great Michael Jordan are on display in the Michael Jordan Discovery Gallery, which also features an interactive natural history exhibit for the entire family. Special science programs for the entire family also are scheduled throughout the year. Admission is $5 for adults, $4 for seniors and $1 for children ages 3 to 17.

Built in 1855-1858, the Thalian Hall Center for the Performing Arts, (910) 343-3660 or (800) 523-2820, is the only surviving theatre designed by John Montague Trimble, one of America's foremost 19th-century theatre architects. Located at 310 Chestnut Street, the City Hall/ Thalian Hall building has had the unusual distinction of serving as both the area's political and cultural center. Listed with the National Register for Historic Places and with the North Carolina Division of Archives and History, historic Thalian Hall has, since its 1990 renovation, become the centerpiece of the city's thriving civic and arts community. The renovated and expanded complex, housing both the restored opera house theatre and City Hall, provides three excellent performance spaces: the Main Stage Theatre, with reserved seating for 575 and additional gallery seating for 100; the 225-seat Council Chambers Ballroom and the versatile 100-seat Studio Theatre. The lobby and technical support areas combine state-of-the-art technical facilities within the beauty and grandeur of an exceptional historic theatre. Each year, Thalian Hall hosts over 475 performances and events, with more than one of the three facilities frequently in use simultaneously.

For shopping, Wilmington's downtown streets are lined with unique stores and restaurants. Be sure to check out the Cotton Exchange, 321 N. Front Street, (910) 343-9896. Housed in eight restored 19th-century buildings on the waterfront, it features distinctive shops and several good restaurants. Also worth noting are the Chandler's Wharf Shops at 2 Ann Street and 225 S. Water Street, which feature garden ornaments, jewelry, candles, gifts and more. Westfield Shoppingtown at Oleander Drive and Independence Boulevard, (910) 392-1776, is home to more than 150 stores and boasts a 400-seat food court.

For an overnight stay, Wilmington has a number of fine chain hotels, and delightful bed and breakfasts are bountiful in the downtown historic district. A few noteworthy examples are the Dragonfly Inn, www.dragonflyinn.com, 1914 Market Street, (910) 762-7025, (866) 762-7025; the Graystone Inn, www.graystoneinn.com, 100 S. Third Street, (910) 763-2000, (888) 763-4773; C. W. Worth House, www.worthhouse.com, 412 S. Third Street, (910) 762-8562, (800) 340-8559; Rosehill Inn Bed and Breakfast, 114 S. Third Street, (910) 815-0250, (800) 815-0250; and Hoge-Wood House Bed and Breakfast, 407 S. Third Street, (910) 762-5299.

The river city abounds with fine restaurants offering delectable food. Some that come highly recommended are Elijah's, www.elijahs.com, in Chandler's Wharf, (910) 343-1448; The Pilot House, overlooking the river at Chandler's Wharf, (910) 343-0200; and the Underground Sandwich Shoppe, 103 Market Street, (910) 763-9686. But these are only a few of the many wonderful eateries available.

In early April, Wilmington's annual Azalea Festival draws visitors from miles around. Hundreds of lovely, old Southern homes are surrounded by blooming azaleas and huge trees draped with Spanish moss. The entire community gets in on the act, with home tours, parades, contests and citywide celebrations. For information, call (910) 794-4650.

When you're downtown, stop at the Cape Fear Coast Convention & Visitors Bureau, 24 N. Third Street, (910) 341-4030 or (800) 222-4757, for answers to specific questions while you're in the Cape Fear area.

Complete area information is available at www.insiders.com/wilmington.

Index

Symbols

A

B

C

D

G

H

I

J

K

L

M

N

P

T

U

V

W

Y

Z